ETHNIC CONFLICTS AND POWER:
A CROSS-NATIONAL PERSPECTIVE

ETHNIC CONFLICTS AND POWER:
A CROSS-NATIONAL PERSPECTIVE

Donald E. Gelfand
Department of Sociology
Boston University

Russell D. Lee
Department of Sociology
Harvard University

JOHN WILEY & SONS   New York ● London ● Sydney ● Toronto

Library of Congress Cataloging in Publication Data

Gelfand, Donald E   comp.
  Ethnic conflicts and power.

  1. Race problems -- Addresses, essays, lectures.
2. Social conflict -- Addresses, essays, lectures.
I. Lee, Russell D., joint author. II. Title.
HT1521.G4   301.45'1'042   72-11765
ISBN 0-471-29603-1
ISBN 0-471-29602-3 (pbk)

Printed in the United States of America

10-9 8 7 6 5 4 3 2 1

CONTENTS

INTRODUCTION

v

IV.   THE SHAPE OF INTERGROUP CONFLICT

Introduction

V.   CONFLICTS AND ALLIANCES

Introduction

VI.   CONFLICTS AND SOCIAL CHANGE

Introduction

ETHNIC CONFLICTS AND POWER:
A CROSS-NATIONAL PERSPECTIVE

INTRODUCTION

This book is the result of our experience in teaching courses on "minority groups." This kind of course often frustrates instructors because of the diverse backgrounds of the students enrolled. Students often characterize the course as being too statistical and as lacking a theoretical focus. This complaint is valid. As the first selection points out, the lack of a theoretical focus has prevented the entire area of racial and ethnic relations from achieving the academic respectability it deserves. There have been several attempts to bring a theoretical focus to the many empirical studies in this field. One admirable but limited attempt is Hubert Blalock's *Towards a Theory of Minority Group Relations.*

This volume is based on two premises: (1) that theory and racial and ethnic relations can be combined to make theoretical perspective relevant to racial and ethnic relations in many areas of the world; and (2) that students will find the book both a challenge and an introduction to sociological analysis.

We have utilized the basic theoretical framework of conflict theory. We believe that the study of racial and ethnic relations has been dominated too long by concepts such as "minority" and "majority"; there has been a lack of emphasis on the degree to which ethnic relations involve questions of economic and political power and the distribution of this power. The black-white conflicts in the United States during the past ten years have brought to light some of these questions, as have the ethnic conflicts that are constantly being reported from other parts of the world including those in Malaysia, Britain, and Canada. This book of readings details the dynamics of some of these conflicts by using as its basis the theoretical work of Lewis Coser (1956) in *The Functions of Social Conflict* and the expanded analysis of Ralf Dahrendorf's (1959) *Class and Class Conflict in Industrial Society.*

In strict scientific terms, sociology has little that can be labeled as a "theory" with the developed sets of propositions that this term implies. In this sense we can more accurately discuss a "conflict perspective." The conflict perspective stresses the competing interests of groups within a society. As Boulding (1962:5) argues, "Conflict may be defined as a situation of competition in which the parties are *aware* of the incompatibility of potential future positions and in which each party *wishes* to occupy a position that is incompatible with the wishes of the other." The conflict perspective thus devotes its attention to the ability of groups to secure and maintain their relative position of dominance vis-á-vis other groups within the society. At its most extreme position, this perspective views society as being held together not by shared norms and values that form a basis for consensus, but by coercion.

Coser's work is based on the pioneering efforts of Georg Simmel. Although Coser recognizes stable elements within society, his aim is to show that social conflict can produce positive effects. These positive functions are numerous. By bringing groups into contact and establishing their relative strengths, conflict helps to establish boundaries between these groups. Only by coming into actual conflict can groups really gauge their power. As Coser points out, however, the development of a conflict situation may reduce the need for further and more heightened conflict. The initial contact produced by the conflict may make these groups aware of mutual grievances. This can produce attempts to develop new relationships between these groups and a shift in the balance of power.

The ability to release hostility is as important for groups as it is for individuals. Groups that are incapable of developing an enemy outside of their own circle may react by developing enmity toward individuals within the group. Conflicts with outside groups thus promote internal cohesion inside the group. As they gain in intensity, this cohesion may decrease the groups' tolerance for a diversity of opinion from within. Deviating opinions may now be branded as "treasonous" or as "aiding and abetting the enemy."

Whatever their intensity, conflicts with outside groups may be either "realistic" or "unrealistic." Unrealistic conflicts are not produced by distressing conditions; they are produced by the need to displace hostilities and perhaps to draw attention away from internal problems. The cessation of conflict with outside groups will focus greater attention on internal problems that may have smoldered within the society for a long period of time. Some ethnic situations discussed here illustrate this pattern.

Our above comment on the conflict perspective has stressed conflicts between groups. Coser also devotes attention to the less visible and perhaps more subtle conflicts that occur within groups. Close relationships that require frequent contacts may promote conflicts. If these conflicts do not occur over basic norms of the relationship (such as the decision of a couple about whether to have children), they can serve as a renewing and stabilizing force within that relationship. Many of the situation comedies on American television are based on these conflicts.

Finally, conflict can result in major social changes. Few social groups can produce major social change without securing allies who provide them with both ideological and substantive resources. Conflict thus tends to ally ideologically similar groups. This is especially true of the major, intensive conflicts that are the subject of this volume.

Although Coser's work admirably details the functions of social conflict, it is less adequate in discussing the dynamics of these conflicts. Dahrendorf's book attempts to evaluate Marxian sociology by emphasizing social class and conflict. Dahrendorf's position is that conflict arises as a result of the distribution of authority in associations. The legitimate power held by civil servants, bureaucrats, and military officers is an example of a conflict-invoking situation. "Authority," Dahrendorf (1959:168) notes, "is a universal element of social structure" and conflict is thus inherent in any society. Having presented his main premises, Dahrendorf analysizes the conflicts over power and authority that occur in associations. In the same sense as Coser, Dahrendorf recognizes that there are stable elements that hold society together. Despite this, he maintains that conflict is a constant possibility.

In terms of the study of racial and ethnic relations, Dahrendorf's major contribution is his attempt to understand the differences between conflict situations. More successfully than any other sociologist, he investigates the variables that affect the shape of social conflicts. Many of these variables (examined more closely in Section IV) have a strong bearing on present and past ethnic situations. Dahrendorf's work also becomes more important in view of recent attempts by sociologists to ascertain whether racial or ethnic groups in many countries can be considered as class groupings.

Both Coser's and Dahrendorf's work have a direct relevance for the study of ethnic and racial relations. Utilizing a conflict perspective, we can study the positions of dominance and subordination that typify relationships between ethnic groups in various societies. We can also analyze the degree to which these conflicts have produced the cohesion, boundaries, release of hostilities and tensions, alliances, and social changes that Coser describes. Dahrendorf's discussion may enable us to place ethnic conflicts into a perspective that indicates that, despite their unique circumstances, ethnic conflicts have generalizable features. Of added importance to their generalizability is the predictive ability that a developed theoretical perspective should provide. Armed with this predictive ability and the energy to work for change, we hope to produce the type of conflict resolution that occurs not through the destruction of ethnic groups but through the acceptance of ethnic pluralism within society.

To summarize: while we recognize that there are instances of harmonious relationships between ethnic groups throughout the world, major ethnic conflicts continue to occur; we need a greater understanding of the positive and negative features of these conflicts as well as their dynamics to help bring about their diminution, if not their disappearance.

Adopting much of Coser's basic outline we have focused on six major aspects of social conflict. Section I examines previous research in ethnic relations. This section also emphasizes the relationship between caste, class, and ethnic conflict. Although the literature remains confusing because of the varied ways in which these terms have been defined, this volume hopefully clarifies these concepts. In Section II, the articles illustrate the value of conflict in releasing ethnic animosities and thus preventing the development of even more intense conflicts.

Conflicts between ethnic groups help to shape and maintain distinct social boundaries between ethnic groups. They also foster cohesion among various groups. The selections in Section III draw from a wide variety of interethnic situations to illustrate this pattern. Dahrendorf's attempt to distinguish the variables that effect the pattern of interethnic conflicts is the core of Section IV. Again, the readings are from a wide range of cross-cultural ethnic situations.

Section V contains articles that deal with the issue of alliances between ethnic groups attempting to produce social change. This issue has been of great concern to blacks and whites in the United States, but also applies in countries such as South Africa and Rhodesia. Finally, Section VI focuses on what may be the crux of the whole discussion: the ability to achieve social change through social conflict.

Many of the articles could have been placed in more than one section. We have included them where they are because they best illustrate a particular section's focus. Moreover, in view of the confusion about the terms race and ethnicity, some readers might argue that some articles deal with religious or racial rather than ethnic groups. We use the term "ethnic groups" to refer to groups characterized by a sense of identity and by features noted by Wagley and Harris (1958) in their discussion of "minorities," referred to in the first article of Section I. Thus we have included articles that cut across religious, racial, and so-called "ethnic" lines.

The list of ethnic conflicts can be extended far beyond the conflicts covered in this volume; therefore we make no claims to completeness. Analysis of many of these situations is an important area for future sociological research. There is little doubt in our minds, however, that the

revival of ethnic identity, not only in the United States, but in other parts
of the world, will reinforce the importance of our approach.

REFERENCES

BOULDING, KENNETH E.
   1962 *Conflict and defense: A general theory.* New York: Harper
        and Row.
COSER, LEWIS
   1956 *The functions of social conflict.* New York: Free Press
DAHRENDORF, RALF
   1959 *Class and class conflict in industrial society.* Stanford: Stanford
        University Press
WAGLEY, CHARLES and MARVIN HARRIS
   1958 *Minorities in the new world.* New York: Columbia University
        Press.

I. CLASS AND ETHNIC CONFLICTS

Sociologists in the field of race and ethnic relations have in the past dwelled on studies of the attitudes of both "minority" and "majority" group members within a society. The assumption of most academic liberals was that discrimination is really a result of miseducation. Exposing the "irrationality" of prejudice and racial stereotyping would ultimately reduce, if not eradicate, bigotry in sensible people. Thus, for nearly twenty years sociologists and psychologists were occupied with such themes as Negro attitudes towards whites, white attitudes towards Negroes, Negro self-conceptions, prejudice as correlated with measures of authoritarianism, and so forth.

   The bankruptcy of these hundreds of studies and millions of dollars in research ·funds is obvious. Racial discrimination still exists, although sometimes in less overt forms than it once did. Indeed, the overemphasis on the social psychology of ethnic relations has obscured the economic underpinnings of intergroup conflict. Conflict is generally not irrational but is tied intimately to economic and political interests.

   The basic theoretical framework developed throughout this book, and especially in this section, is that society is composed of various interest groups vying for economic, political, and social power. Ethnic groups become salient interest groups if their social position is based on their ethnicity. As will become apparent, defining the relationships among such concepts as caste, class, and ethnicity is complex.

   The article by Donald E. Gelfand is an overview of the major changes in research and theory in the field of race and ethnic relations. The general discussion of conflict theory as an alternative perspective will provide the reader with our fundamental approach. Donald L. Noel offers an interesting model for explaining a stratification system based on ethnicity. An elaboration of the interplay between ethnicity and socioeconomic class interests will demonstrate the difficulties of building a conceptual model of intergroup conflict.

In our third selection, Gerald D. Berreman argues for the reexamination of the Indian caste system as a social process. A modification of the usual approaches to the study of the caste system will enhance the applicability of this model to race and ethnic relations. Basically, Berreman proposes that the various segments of a caste system are interest groups in competition for scarce economic, political, and social resources. Such an approach, we feel, presents a dynamic model of intergroup conflict.

From a comparative perspective, Leo Kuper argues that in some societies ethnicity supersedes class affiliations during intergroup conflict. An excerpt from the writings of W.E.B. Dubois suggests that this superimposition of race and the ethnicity upon class is also true of black-white conflicts within the United States. The selection of articles in this first section thus indicates that the concepts of class and caste are having increasing relevance for the study of interethnic conflicts throughout the world.

1.   ETHNIC RELATIONS AND SOCIAL RESEARCH:
                                               A REEVALUATION

Donald E. Gelfand

This article focuses on the development of the field of ethnic relations and its current position in sociology. The author discusses alternative theoretical approaches to the field, the adequacy of conflict or functionalist models, and some of the issues examined in detail by other authors in this volume. Gelfand's major position is that the lack of a theoretical perspective in this field has hampered its development, and he argues for the relevance of a conflict theory approach.

THE SCOPE OF THE FIELD

Herbert Blumer warned in 1958 that sociologists were focusing too extensively on what he termed the "axes of prejudice." Concentrating on the presence or absence of prejudice among various ethnic groups, sociologists were finding it increasingly difficult to predict or explain behavior. Fulton's (1959) study of a racially integrated suburb is a notable case in point. Six months after its completion he found that those families whom he expected to stay in the neighborhood because of their favorable attitudes towards racial integration were planning to leave, while those he was sure would leave were doing the opposite. The results naturally raised major questions about his explanatory model. By focusing too heavily on the attitudes of whites towards blacks, Fulton neglected the importance of peer groups and institutions on ethnic relations. Equally as important as the attitudes of a white homeowner towards blacks moving into a neighborhood are the attitudes and policies of lending institutions. These policies determine whether substantial numbers of black families can purchase a home in a certain area, or whether whites, angry about integration, will be able to sell their present homes and purchase a new one in an outlying area. The discriminatory policies of banks, corporations, medical services, unions, federal agencies, and the "snob zoning" of white suburban areas are all components of ethnic segregation.

There has been a long delay in the development of an approach to ethnic relations focusing on the importance of these institutions. The reason can be traced in part to the character of social science in the United States. This is especially true for the "minority-majority" concept. Louis Wirth (1945) defined a minority group as a group

SOURCE
Original article prepared for this volume.

of people who are discriminated against and who regard themselves as objects of discrimination. Wagley and Harris (1958), attempting a complex cross-cultural analysis, provide a more detailed definition of a "minority group." The elements they stress include: (1) the relationship between the group and the state; (2) its physical and cultural characteristics; (3) the ties that develop between the group members because of these characteristics; (4) the transmission of membership in the group; (5) the group's marriage patterns; and (6) the life styles that distinguish a minority group in a society from other groups within the society. A minority group may be an ethnic group that is distinct because of culturally identifiable patterns, a racial group that has distinct physical characteristics, or a restricted membership religious group.

Both of the above definitions contain some important elements, including Wirth's emphasis on the self-appraisal by ethnic groups of their situation. Neither of these commonly cited definitions deal with the question of numbers, although this is certainly implied in the terms "minority-majority." In his recent attempt to develop a comparative approach to ethnic relations Schermerhorn (1970) perceives the dilemma that ensues from the use of this terminology. His solution is to restrict the usage of the term "minority" to groups that are small in size and lacking power, while utilizing the term "majority" to refer to large groups that are dominant in the society. He proposes the term "mass subjects" to refer to groups that are lacking either in size or power. This unsatisfactory and unnecessary solution envelops the reader in associations with "mass society" that are outside the purview of the field.

Empirically oriented sociologists have attempted to study phenomena that fit their methodology most comfortably. The scope of sociological endeavors has been restricted by the domination of survey questionnaires and attitude scales. Developing as a discipline in the 1900s, sociologists tapped the rapidly increasing number of local and federal agencies to obtain support for their efforts at gaining recognition. Attempting to gain widespread legitimation for its activities, the discipline shied away from questioning the agencies and institutions who were implicated both in discrimination against ethnic groups and the source of sociological funding. American sociology has thus developed as a conservative, apolitical field attempting to remain aloof from the strong demands for change and a critical analysis of society made by subordinate ethnic groups.

"MINORITY-MAJORITY"

The conservatism that has characterized sociology can be seen in the anachronistic terminology of ethnic relations. Wirth and Schermerhorn both acknowledge the importance of power in their definitions. It is this theme rather than one based on the "minority-majority" concept that could be developed into a comprehensive cross-culturally valid approach to the field. If, as Berry (1965) implies, "minority" was adopted by sociologists as preferable to the term "race," and has now been "divested . . . of all statistical meaning," then it is appropriate for sociologists to abandon this terminology and develop a framework built around "subordination-domination." Many sociologists already refer to "dominant" rather than "majority" groups.

THEORY AND ETHNIC RELATIONS

A solid theoretical focus is a necessity for developing this framework. Numerous discrete studies and volumes of analysis of ethnic relations have failed to approach a comprehensive macroscopic viewpoint and theoretical framework. Any theoretical perspective proposed for this field must deal with the effects of large scale institutions and bureaucracies on ethnic relations. Although the social-psychological approaches that have been extensively applied are certainly relevant, the ethnic problems facing the United States, Britain, and Malaysia are large scale conflicts that involve major societal institutions. An adequate analysis of these situations can only be accomplished through the utilization of macrosociological theory.

Conflict theory and functional theory offer possible theoretical perspectives. Although the future may prove it inadequate as a perspective from which to view developments in this field, many of the people involved in the strife-torn events of the present see conflict theory as more accurately reflecting the reality of ethnic situations than a more placid functionalist model.

Although these two schools of thought are often regarded as diametrically opposed, conflict theory and functional theory are clearly complementary perspectives. For critics such as Van den Berghe (1963), functionalism and conflict theory, exemplified by Marx's "dialectical" model rest on a model of equilibrium. Although the foundation of this equilibrium in both theories is consensus, there are differences in the manner in which this equilibrium is viewed. For functional theorists, equilibrium is a goal that arises from societal consensus based on institutionalized values. To conflict theorists equilibrium and consensus are imposed on society, and enforced by coercion and means of social control.

The equilibrium that the functionalist sees as a goal, the conflict theorist views as a temporary state that will be disrupted by major internal disputes. Thus, although both approaches view society as a "system," each views differently the mechanisms that bind the systemic parts together.

Van den Berghe (1963) correctly notes that neither of these two contrasting approaches have dealt successfully with change. Functionalists have focused their major attention on change stemming from forces outside the society. In *The Social System* Parsons (1951) devotes a great deal of attention to the impact of technology on society. Conflict theorists tend to ignore this form of change. Instead, they have discussed society as a closed system with change coming from the disputes and disagreements inside that society. There are thus important common points and differences in these two perspectives.

Coser's (1956) work on conflict was an important reaction to the criticism that the functionalist outlook is conservative (Dahrendorf, 1958), and ignores evident internal conflict. It was an attempt to widen the scope of functionalism and bring conflict back into the mainstream of sociological theory. Coser attempted to show that conflict is functional and thus fits into the patterns of binding forces that shape and maintain a social system. Reformulating Simmel, his book made a strong impact on academic sociologists who had moved away from the Marxian emphasis on conflict, apparently so unrelated to the complacent society to which they belonged. It promised to integrate conflict into functionalist theory in a manner that would not damage the existing foundations of this theoretical focus. In this sense, conflict theory as revitalized by Coser was not a new breakthrough but an important attempt to provide conflict theory with new respectability for functionalists.

THE REVIVAL OF CONFLICT THEORY

Many Americans have begun to view ethnic conflict as an intrinsic part of the society. While accepting conflicts as inevitable, especially during the "long hot summers,"

American society has attempted to place limitations on their intensity. Although intermittent personalized conflicts between racial and ethnic groups continue and will be allowed to continue for many years, groups engaged in conflicts that appear to be potentially disruptive of the American social structure, for example, the Black Panthers, have been repressed. Physically violent conflict in the United States, Britain, and Malaysia have also indicated to sociologists that ethnic conflicts are not uniquely American.

The persistence of these ethnic conflicts has resulted in a revitalization of conflict theory during the past ten years. This revitalization reflects not only the theoretical development but the politicalization of sociologists. Dahrendorf warned in 1958 that sociological analysis that stressed the concept of system was in danger of becoming a justification of the status quo. Much of the sociological thought of the 1959s reflects the static quiescence of a period when, as one noted professor has remarked, "the classrooms were like tombs" (Cloward, 1971). The revival of conflict theory in the mid-1950s and the 1960s must be linked with political developments in the United States, especially the rise of the civil rights movement. Coser's book on conflict, along with numerous studies of protest movements, and Southern sit-in tactics, appeared during this time (Oppenheimer, 1966; Frazier, 1968).

These intense ethnic conflicts have been aimed at changing "dominant-subordinate" relationships and the distribution of power within society. While it is impossible here to deal adequately with the complexities of these relationships, we can examine the mechanisms available to ethnic groups engaged in these conflicts over power, and the types of conflict that have developed between ethnic groups, and engage in some speculation on the development of racial and interethnic conflicts in the next decade.

POWER AND ETHNIC CONFLICT

The bases of power[1]

There have been numerous attempts to distinguish the bases of power. French and Raven (1959) focusing on this issue provide a classification useful for the examination of interethnic relations. They distinguish between five bases of power: (1) "Attraction power"; (2) "expert power"; (3) "reward power"; (4) "coercive power"; (5) "legitimate power." "Attraction power" is power based on a group's liking for another group. This closely parallels Merton's (1957) and Hymans's (1942) interest in reference groups. Whites may thus be able to exert power over blacks because their appearance and life style appear rewarding and valuable. This form of power has been apparent not only in the United States but in African countries where colonial rulers destroyed the traditional culture. In South Africa, this destruction of traditional culture has backfired against the colonialists. Blacks are now demanding equality and democracy instead of giving respect to the traditional chiefs who have been appointed by the nationalists authorities. This shift in values threatens the stability of the apartheid structure that the Afrikaners have attempted to impose (Van den Berghe, 1965).

The roots of "expert power" lie in the ability of one group to provide specialized knowledge and information for another. In traditional societies, priests were in a position to provide this assistance. In modern societies specialists in such occupations as psychiatry, law, and medicine have

assumed this role. Dominant ethnic groups have been able to maintain this power by controlling admissions into these occupations.

"Reward power" refers to a group's ability to provide another group with gains either of a material or spiritual nature. Control of the economic structure has provided whites in South Africa and the United States with enormous ability to dispense rewards to blacks and other subordinate ethnic groups. By developing new religious identities, groups such as the Black Muslims have attempted to destroy the control dominant groups have had over spiritual rewards.

The opposite, "coercive power," refers to the ability of a group to mediate punishment for another group. Blacks in ghetto areas of central cities of the United States possess coercive power over whites working or traveling through these areas. This power continues to increase as blacks become numerically dominant in these central cities. The full potential of this coercive power is being counteracted by metropolitan planning, which forces the central cities to be merely a component part of larger units controlled by numerically superior suburban areas. Whites also possess coercive control by virtue of their domination of the judicial, police, and military systems. Finally, legitimate power is based on the acceptance of a group's rights to prescribe opinions and behavior. This legitimacy may be obtained by elected officials in the United States, tribal leaders in African societies, or heads of families in societies where the extended family is the primary unit of social organization.

These forms of power are obviously not mutually exclusive. As the examples cited above indicate, control over different components of the social structure may provide groups with access to more than one base of power. Thus, control over mass media that Rossi cites (1960) as a power base may provide whites in the United States with

---

[1]The literature dealing with the concept of power is vast and controversial. For the purpose of this discussion power is defined as "the capacity to mobilize resources for the accomplishment of intended effects with recourse to some type of sanction(s) to encourage compliance" (Walton, 1968: 449).

both reward power and coercive power. This is even more true for "control over solidary groups" in a community. These solidary groups may be able to induce individuals and groups to move into a community or prevent unwanted ethnic groups from doing so. Finally, groups and individuals who possess one structural base of power may eventually attempt to extend the scope of their power. Indians concentrated in western states possess "coercive power" because of their control of reservation land. They are now attempting to gain "reward power" over congressional delegates by voting as an organized bloc for candidates who advance programs beneficial to their interests.

There are obvious differences in the resources of various ethnic groups. These differences are crucial in determining which of these various bases of power can be most effectively utilized by a particular group. As Bierstedt (1950) and Blalock (1967) note, primary resources include money, property, prestige, authority, control of resources, access to supernatural powers, physical strength, voting rights, and "various rights achieved by formal education apprenticeship or membership in certain organizations" (Blalock, 1967:113). Blalock (1967) in his thorough review of power does not list numbers as a primary resource although he recognizes its prime importance.

Possession of any of these resources may be countered by the resources that others possess. Groups, such as blacks in South Africa, who possess few resources find it difficult to wrest power away from whites who possess superior organization, money, property, and a host of privileges legally available only to whites. The superior organization of the Chinese in Malaysia has enabled them to move into a strong position in a traditional, agricultural, Malayan society. For many subordinate groups lacking major resources, the only power utilizable is coercive power that stems from either their superior numbers, control of an important

ecological area of the country or, in some cases, the dependence of the economy on their exploited labor. Dominant groups that are able to legitimize their power possess the possibility of implementing both reward power and coercive power. Faced with this strong pattern of control, subordinate groups may begin either to develop fawning behavior and covert means of expressing their hostility or engage in extremely intense violent conflict with dominant groups.

Violence and Intensity

There are, however, many other degrees and types of conflict. Dahrendorf has attempted to place these into perspective by distinguishing between intensity and violence. Intensity refers to the amount of energy a group invests in a conflict situation. Violence refers to the weapons chosen for this conflict. Conflicts vary with an extreme point occurring when a group attempts to overthrow another group's position by force. At less extreme levels, violence is commonly practiced on individuals in organizations by exerting authority or by verbal assaults. Although Mills (1951) contends that manipulation has replaced coercion in organizations, there are times in all organizations when coercion by threats of loss of job or pay and mild forms of violence are used.

The intensity of conflict and violence is characteristically higher when engaged in by subordinate groups than by superordinate groups. As Dahrendorf points out, it is the dominant group that is usually concerned about violence since they have been able to control subordinate groups by means that exclude physical violence. Since they control housing and jobs, dominant groups have restricted the ability of subordinate ethnic groups to purchase homes or even attain the economic means required. Subordinate ethnic groups have thus been forced to live in inferior segregated housing, where only minimal services are provided. The avoidance of physical violence allows dominant groups to exert power while maintaining the facade of an open, democratic, equalitarian society. Subordinate groups must often resort to physical violence to a degree not required by groups with greater resources. Black groups in the United States have thus continually argued that white "backlash" and concern over violence is an illegitimate reaction to their efforts since whites have practiced violence on them for many years by discriminating against them in housing, jobs, and every other facet of American life.

As intrinsic as social conflict may now appear to many Americans, it is necessary to note that many expected conflicts do not develop. Ethnocentrism may lead to hostility, but not to actual engagement in conflict between groups. There are many factors intervening between the development of hostility among ethnic groups and the occurrence of actual conflict. In many instances, power differentials may enable dominant groups to carry out their activities without engaging in conflicts with subordinate groups. Urban renewal programs in the United States have been a good example of this. In major American cities, large numbers of poor ethnic group members, especially blacks, have been forced to move from their homes. In many cases, their homes have been replaced by office buildings or luxury apartments. The decision to redevelop these areas has usually been made without consulting these ethnic groups or even considering their needs.

Differentials in power may also cause subordinate groups to mute their hostility because of fears of reprisal. Instead, this hostility may be directed at members of the same group rather than at members of other groups. Members of subordinate groups may also accept the arguments of dominant group members that their failure to achieve social mobility is related to their own inadequacies. The controversial "Moynihan

report" of 1965 stressed the breakdown of the black family as a primary cause of the retarded development of the black community. This report was regarded by black leaders as a blatant attempt to turn the attention of American whites and blacks away from patterns of discrimination and toward the personal behavior of blacks. Finally, subordinate groups may project their hostility and aggression onto other groups that have even less power to commit reprisals. This displacement of their hostility may be endorsed by dominant groups as was the case in the traditional "pograms" against Jews in czarist Russia.

Social conflicts may continue to be largely drawn along ethnic lines, for example, Chinese versus Malays, whites versus blacks, or may develop in the direction of large scale class conflicts. The extent to which conflicts develop along either of these two dimensions has major implications for their intensity and scope. Given these alternative patterns, we can examine the pattern of ethnic conflicts prevalent today and their probable future development.

Class and ethnic conflict

Many ethnic conflicts in major countries through the world occur over what Gordon (1964) has termed "civic assimilation." These are value conflicts that develop between groups in the final stages of assimilating into a society. They thus occur where ethnic groups have already achieved considerable success in gaining access to the organization and primary groups of the society. This success mutes the intensity and violence of these conflicts, which are usually carried out in electoral and judicial areas. Conflicts over birth control and abortion that divided Catholics from the rest of the population are characteristic of this pattern of conflict.

The conflicts that occupy the majority of attention today are not these muted conflicts but the intense, physically violent conflicts that arise from the inability of religious and racial groups to attain social mobility within their societies. In terms of the Marxian definitions of class these groups occupy the position of the "lumpenproletariat" (Bottomore, 1966). Chicano, Indians, Pakistanis in Britain, and blacks in South Africa typify this position. There are, however, major difficulties in applying a strict Marxian model of class to ethnic relations and ethnic conflicts. These can be articulated by examining the class position of the professional athlete in the United States, an increasing percentage of whom are black.

While in Marxian terms, these athletes do not form a subordinate class, Dahrendorf's reformulation of Marx places them in this category. As Bottomore (1966) notes, Marx's analysis of class with its emphasis on the relationship of the individual to the means of production did not adequately predict changes that began to occur as capitalism became more entrenched. These changes have resulted in the growth of an enlarged middle class, and enlarged governmental and corporate bureaucracies. Noting these changes, Dahrendorf (1959:138) rejects the traditional Marxian concept of class, preferring to substitute a definition of class that stresses the relationship of the group to authority in "imperatively coordinated associations." Groups lacking in authority are thus subordinate class and inherent conflict groups.

In terms of their relationship to their work, professional athletes occupy positions of very limited authority. They have little control over their working conditions, or even their employer from one year to the next. In compensation they are paid large sums of money and occupy positions of "influence" which could serve as bases of power (Gamson, 1968).

Many ethnic groups are attempting to utilize the influence and power of individuals who have overcome obstacles facing them and achieved rapid social mobility. For many years, blacks lost this important source of leadership to what Frazier (1957) has termed the "black bourgeoisie." Many of these same individuals have begun to look back and identify with their roots. Thus, the black or Puerto Rican athlete is not forgetting his ethnic and racial identity but rather asserting it both on and off the field. This identity, however, is not based on class consciousness but on racial and ethnic characteristics. It may be a recognition of the degree to which whites in the United States subjectively define black as lower class, despite their objective status attributes. However, this increased awareness has its foundations in racial identity. As ethnic characteristics become a rallying point for various groups, these produce an ethnocentrism that inhibits the development of ethnic coalitions. Ethnic alliances based on common class identity may develop only after the solidarity of individual ethnic and racial groups is achieved. The attainment of these alliances may escalate ethnic conflicts to a new level of intensity. It may also provide resources not available to independent ethnic groups.

We can speculate that Martin Luther King recognized the common class position of many ethnic groups in the United States. The Poor People's March he organized before his death was a first attempt to direct the civil rights movement along broadened class lines. These efforts were not as successful as he would have wished. The different backgrounds and orientations of various groups made sharing the organization difficult. What was to have been a unified march disintegrated into differential demands by separate ethnic groups.

Right now, there is no certainty about what pattern will develop, since participants in social conflicts obviously do not respond to their own needs but also to the tactics of opposing groups that may limit their actions.

These tactics may include meeting the demands of subordinate ethnic groups through specific actions, that is, by building new housing or developing new employment programs, rather than by changing the structural relationships between subordinate and dominant groups. The federal programs embodied by OEO and Model Cities may have forestalled the danger of riots and eruptions by co-opting activist leaders and removing them from positions of influence in the community (Bensman and Vidich, 1971). Employed by federal and local agencies the efforts of these leaders became directed towards administration of programs rather than political organization within their community. While these responses may prevent the development of a pattern of confrontation between ethnic groups for a period of time, they are as a whole minimal and inadequate. It is thus safe to predict that ethnic conflict will continue for a long period of time in many countries, including the United States.

CONCLUSION

Despite its long history, the field of ethnic relations has failed to provide a framework that could consistently and adequately explain the patterns discussed above. While political controversies in this area have perhaps stymied its development, Van den Berghe (1967) is probably correct in attributing many of the inadequacies of ethnic relations to the failures of sociologists themselves. These failures include: the unwillingness of sociologists to undertake cross-cultural analyses of ethnic relations, (2) their refusal to acknowledge a wealth of information because of their lack of historical perspective, and (3) a lack of any theoretical focus for the field.

The adoption of a conflict theory approach provides guidelines for future research that can make a substantial contribution to the field. It may require major shifts in the ideologies of sociologists who have shied away from what they consider the political

implications of the approach and who have refused to recognize the institutionalization of ethnic discrimination in society.

Sociological research must develop a clear delineation of the relative position of ethnic groups in various societies, the factors that explain their subordinate or dominant position, the means of control that are utilized to maintain boundaries between ethnic groups, and the extent to which ethnic distinctions are related to class distinctions within the society. Finally, conflict theorists must focus on the strategies of change utilized by various ethnic groups and the effects these conflicts have both on the internal structure of the society and the groups engaged in these social conflicts. "The analysis of power, stratification and conflict has formed the core of the discipline of sociology; continuing and more intensive attention to power, stratification and conflict will surely advance the science and our ability to make use of it" (Mack, 1965: 397). Applied to ethnic relations this approach may enable sociologists to begin the development of a model of ethnic relations that will advance this field to the position of academic importance it should, but has failed to, occupy.

REFERENCES

BENSMAN, JOSEPH and ARTHUR VIDICH
    1971 *The new American society.* New York: Quadrangle.
BERRY, BRENTON
    1965 *Race and ethnic relations.* Boston: Houghton Mifflin.
BIERSTEDT, ROBERT
    1950 "An analysis of social power." *American Sociological Review,* **15**, (December) 730-38.
BLALOCK, HUBERT
    1967 *Toward a theory of minority-group relations.* New York: John Wiley.

BLUMER, HERBERT
  1958 Race relations research: United States of America. *International Social Science Bulletin*, X, no. 3:403-43.

BOTTOMORE, T. B.
  1966 *Classes in modern society.* New York: Random House.

CLOWARD, RICHARD
  1971 "The welfare crisis: What caused it?" Boston University, Department of Sociology, Colloquim.

COSER, LEWIS
  1956 *The functions of social conflict.* New York: Free Press.

DAHRENDORF, RALF
  1958 "Out of utopia: Toward a reorientation of sociological analysis." *American Journal of Sociology,* (September): 115-27.

  1959 *Class and class conflict in industrial society.* Stanford: Stanford University Press.

FRAZIER, E. FRANKLIN
  1957 *Black bourgeoisie.* New York: Free Press.

FRAZIER, THOMAS R.
  1968 "An analysis of non-violent coercion as used by the sit-in movement." *Phylon,* 29 (Spring): 27-40.

FRENCH, JOHN R. and B. RAVEN
  1959 "The bases of social power." Pp. 118-49 in Cartwright, D. (ed). *Studies in Social Power.* Ann Arbor: University of Michigan Press.

FULTON, ROBERT
  1959 Russel Woods: A study of a neighborhood's initial response to Negro invasion. Unpublished Ph. D. dissertation: Wayne State University.

GAMSON, WILLIAM
  1968 *Power and discontent.* Homewood, Illinois: Dorsey Press.

GORDON, MILTON
  1964 *Assimilation in American life.* New York: Oxford.

HYMAN, HERBERT H.
  1942 "The psychology of status." *Archives of Psychology,* no. 269.

MACK, RAYMOND
  1965 "The components of social conflict." *Social Problems,* 12 (Spring): 388-97.

MERTON, ROBERT K.
  1957 *Social theory and social structure.* New York: Free Press.

MILLS, C. W.
  1951 *White collar.* New York: Oxford.

MOYNIHAN, DANIEL
  1965 *The Negro family: The case for national action.* Washington: U.S. Department of Labor.

OPPENHEIMER, MARTIN
  1966 "The Southern sit-ins: Intra-group relations and community conflict." *Phylon,* 27, no. 1, (Spring): 20-26.

PARSONS, TALCOTT
  1951 *The social system.* New York: Free Press.

ROSSI, PETER
  1969 Theory, research and practice in community organization, Pp. 49-61 in Ralph Kramer and Harry Specht, (eds). *Readings in community organization practice.* Englewood Cliffs: Prentice-Hall.

SCHERMERHORN, R. A.
  1970 *Comparative ethnic relations: A framework for theory and research.* New York: Random House.

VAN DEN BERGHE, PIERRE
  1963 "Dialetic functionalism: Toward a theoretical synthesis." *American Sociological Review,* 28 (October): 695-705.

  1965 *South Africa: A study in conflict.* Berkeley: University of California Press.

  1967 *Race and racism.* New York: John Wiley.

WAGLEY, CHARLES and MARVIN HARRIS
  1958   *Minorities in the new world.*
      New York:
      Columbia University Press.

WALTON, JOHN
  1968   "Differential patterns of community
      power structure: An explanation based
      on interdependence." Pp. 441-459 in

Terry Clark, (ed.), *Community Structure
and decision-making: Comparitive analyses.* Scranton, Penn: Chandler

WIRTH, LOUIS
  1945   "The problem of minority groups."
      Pp. 347-372 in Ralph Linton, (ed.)
      The science of man in the world crisis.
      New York: Columbia University Press.

2.

A THEORY OF THE ORIGIN OF ETHNIC STRATIFICATION*

Donald L. Noel

Ethnocentrism, competition, and differential power provide the necessary and
sufficient bases for constructing a theory of the *origin* of ethnic stratification.
The essence of the theory is that ethnic stratification will emerge when
distinct ethnic groups are brought into sustained contact *only* if the groups
are characterized by a high degree of ethnocentrism, competition, *and* differential power. Competition provides the motivation for stratification;
ethnocentrism channels the competition along ethnic lines; and the power
differential determines whether either group will be able to subordinate the
other. The theory is initially tested via application to the emergence of
slavery in seventeenth century America. The outcome encourages further
testing of the theory.

While a great deal has been written about
the nature and consequences of ethnic stratification, there have been few theoretical or
empirical contributions regarding the causes

SOURCE
From *Social Problems*, Vol. 16, no. 2, Fall 1968.
Reprinted by permission of the author and the
Society for the Study of Social Problems.

*It should be emphasized that the present
paper attempts only to explain the *origin* of ethnic
stratification. The author and Ernest Barth are
currently engaged in an effort to construct a general
theory of ethnic stratification which answers a
number of sociological questions in addition to
that of origin.

of ethnic stratification.[1] It is the purpose of
this paper to state a theory of the origin of
ethnic stratification and then test it by applying the theory to an analysis of the origin of
slavery in the United States. A number of
recent contributions have clarified our knowledge of early Negro-white stratification[2] but

[1] The same observation regarding social stratification in general has recently been made by
Gerhard Lenski, *Power and Privilege,* New York:
McGraw-Hill, 1966, p. ix.
[2] See Joseph Boskin, "Race Relations in Seventeenth Century America: The Problem of the Origins
of Negro Slavery," *Sociology and Social Research,*
49 (July, 1965), pp. 446-455, including references
cited therein; and David B. Davis. *The Problem of
Slavery in Western Culture,* Ithaca; Cornell U., 1966.

there has been no attempt to analyze slavery's origin from the standpoint of a general theoretical framework. The present attempt focuses upon ethnocentrism, competition, and differential power as the key variables which together constitute the necessary and sufficient basis for the emergence and initial stabilization of ethnic stratification.

Ethnic stratification is, of course, only one type of stratification. Social stratification as a generic form of social organization is a structure of social inequality manifested via differences in prestige, power, and/or economic rewards. Ethnic stratification is a system of stratification wherein some relatively fixed group membership (e.g., race, religion, or nationality) is utilized as a major criterion for assigning social positions with their attendant differential rewards.

Prior to the emergence of ethnic stratification there must be a period of recurrent or continuous contact between the members of two or more distinct ethnic groups. This contact is an obvious requisite of ethnic stratification, but it is equally a requisite of equalitarian intergroup relations. Hence, intergroup contact is assumed as given and not treated as a theoretical element because in itself it does not provide a basis for predicting whether ethnic relations will be equalitarian or inequalitarian (i.e., stratified). Distinct ethnic groups can interact and form a stable pattern of relations without super-subordination.[3] Factors such as the nature of the groups prior to contact, the agents of contact, and the objectives of the contacting parties affect the likelihood of an equalitarian or inequalitarian outcome but only as they are expressed through the necessary and sufficient variables.[4]

THE THEORY AND ITS ELEMENTS

In contrast to intergroup contact *per se*, the presence of ethnocentrism, competition, and differential power provides a firm basis for predicting the emergence of ethnic stratification. Conversely, the absence of any one or more of these three elements means that ethnic stratification will not emerge. This is the essence of our theory. Each of the three elements is a variable but for present purposes they will be treated as attributes because our knowledge is not sufficiently precise to allow us to say what degrees of ethnocentrism, competition, and differential power are necessary to generate ethnic stratification. Recognition of the crucial importance of the three may stimulate greater efforts to precisely measure each of them. We shall examine each in turn.

Ethnocentrism is a universal characteristic of autonomous societies or ethnic groups. As introduced by Sumner the concept refers to that ". . . view of things in which one's own group is the center of everything, and all others are scaled and rated with reference to it."[5] From this perspective the values of

---

[3]A classic example is provided by Ethel John Lindgren, "An Example of Culture Contact Without Conflict: Reindeer Tungus and Cossacks of Northwest Manchuria," *American Anthropologist*, 40 (October-December, 1938), pp. 605-621.

---

[4]The relevance of precontact and of the nature and objectives of the contacting agents for the course of intergroup relations has been discussed by various scholars including Edward B. Reuter in his editor's "Introduction" to *Race and Culture Contacts*, New York: McGraw-Hill, 1934, pp. 1-18; and Clarence E. Glick, "Social Roles and Types in Race Relations," in Andrew W. Lind, editor, *Race Relations in World Perspective*, Honolulu: U. of Hawaii, 1955, pp. 239-262.

[5]William G. Sumner, *Folkways*, Boston: Ginn, 1940, p. 13. The essence of ethnocentrism is well conveyed by Catton's observation that "Ethnocentrism makes us see out-group behavior as deviation from in-group mores rather than as adherence to out-group mores." William R. Catton, Jr., "The Development of Sociological Thought" in Robert E. L. Faris, editor, *Handbook of Modern Sociology*, Chicago: Rand McNally, 1964, p. 930.

the in-group are equated with abstract, universal standards of morality and the practices of the in-group are exalted as better or more "natural" than those of any out-group. Such an orientation is essentially a matter of in-group glorification and not of hostility toward any specific out-group. Nevertheless, an inevitable consequence of ethnocentrism is the rejection or downgrading of all out-groups to a greater or lesser degree as a function of the extent to which they differ from the in-group. The greater the difference the lower will be the relative rank of any given out-group, but any difference at all is grounds for negative evaluation.[6] Hence, English and Canadian immigrants rank very high relative to other out-groups in American society *but* they still rank below old American WASPs.[7]

Ethnocentrism is expressed in a variety of ways including mythology, condescension, and a double standard of morality in social relations. Becker has labeled this double standard a "dual ethic" in which in-group standards apply only to transactions with members of the in-group.[8] The outsider is viewed as fair game. Hence, inter-group economic relations are characterized by

exploitation. Similarly, sexual relations between members of different groups are commonplace even when intermarriage is rare or prohibited entirely. The practice of endogamy is itself a manifestation of and, simultaneously, a means of reinforcing ethnocentrism. Endogamy is, indeed, an indication that ethnocentrism is present in sufficient degree for ethnic stratification to emerge.[9]

Insofar as distinct ethnic groups maintain their autonomy, mutual ethnocentrism will be preserved. Thus Indians in the Americas did not automatically surrender their ethnocentrism in the face of European technological and scientific superiority. Indeed, if the cultural strengths (including technology) of the out-group are not relevant to the values and goals of the in-group they will, by the very nature of ethnocentrism, be negatively defined. This is well illustrated in the reply (allegedly) addressed to the Virginia Commission in 1774 when it offered to educate six Indian youths at William and Mary:

"Several of our young people were formerly brought up at Colleges of the Northern Provinces; they were instructed in all your sciences; but when they came back to us, they were bad runners, ignorant of every means of living in the woods, unable to bear either cold or hunger, knew neither how to build a cabin, take a deer, or kill an enemy, spoke our language imperfectly,

---

[6]Williams observes that "in various *particular* ways an out-group may be seen as superior" insofar as its members excel in performance vis-a-vis certain norms that the two groups hold in common (e.g., sobriety or craftsmanship is the production of a particular commodity). Robin M. Williams, Jr., *Strangers Next Door,* Englewood Cliffs, N.J.: Prentice-Hall, 1964, p. 22 (emphasis added). A similar point is made by Marc J. Swartz, "Negative Ethnocentrism," *Journal of Conflict Resolution,* 5 (March, 1961), pp. 75-81. It is highly unlikely, however that the out-group will be so consistently objectively superior in the realm of shared values as to be seen as generally superior to the in-group unless the in-group is subordinate to or highly dependent upon the out-group.

[7]Emory S. Bogardus, *Social Distance,* Yellow Springs: Antioch, 1959.

[8]Howard P. Becker, *Man in Reciprocity,* New York: Praeger, 1956, Ch. 15.

[9]Endogamy is an overly stringent index of the degree of ethnocentrism essential to ethnic stratification and is not itself a prerequisite of the emergence of ethnic stratification. However, where endogamy does not precede ethnic stratification, it is a seemingly invariable consequence. Compare this position with that of Charles Wagley and Marvin Harris who treat ethnocentrism, and endogamy as independent structural requisites of intergroup hostility and conflict. See *Minorities in the New World,* New York: Columbia, 1958, pp. 256-263.

were therefore neither fit for hunters, warriors, or counsellors; they were totally good for nothing. We are, however, not the less obliged by your kind offer, though we decline accepting it; and to show our grateful Sense of it, if the Gentlemen of Virginia will send us a Dozen of their Sons we will take great care of their education, instruct them in all we know, and make Men of them. [10]

Ethnocentrism in itself need not lead to either interethnic conflict or ethnic stratification, however. The Tungus and Cossacks have lived in peace as politically independent but economically interdependent societies for several centuries. The groups remain racially and culturally dissimilar and each is characterized by a general ethnocentric preference for the in-group. This conflict potential is neutralized by mutal respect and admission by each that the other is superior in certain specific respects, by the existence of some shared values and interests, and by the absence of competition due to economic complementarity and low population density.[11]

The presence of competition, structured along ethnic lines, is an additional prerequisite for the emergence of ethnic stratification. Antonovsky has suggested that a discriminatory system of social relations requires both shared goals and scarcity of rewards,[12] and competition here refers to the interaction between two or more social units striving to achieve *the same scarce goal* (e.g., land or prestige). In the absence of shared goals members of the various ethnic groups involved in the contact

situation would have, in the extreme case, mutually exclusive or nonoverlapping value hierarchies. If one group is not striving for a given goal, this reduces the likelihood of discrimination partly because members of that group are unlikely to be perceived as competitors for the goal. In addition, the indifference of one group toward the goal in effect reduces scarcity—i.e., fewer seekers enhance the probability of goal attainment by any one seeker. However, if the goal is still defined as scarce by members of one group they may seek to establish ethnic stratification in order to effectively exploit the labor of the indifferent group and thereby maximize goal attainment. In such a situation the labor (or other utility) of the indifferent group may be said to be the real object of competition. In any event the perceived scarcity of a socially valued goal is crucial and will stimulate the emergence of ethnic stratification *unless* each group perceives the other as: 1) disinterested in the relevant goal, *and* 2) nonutilitarian with respect to its own attainment of the goal.

In actuality the various goals of two groups involved in stable, complex interaction will invariably overlap to some degree and hence the likelihood of ethnic stratification is a function of the arena of competition. The arena includes the shared object(s) sought, the terms of the competition, and the relative adaptability of the groups involved.[13] Regarding the objects (or goals) of competition the greater the number of objects subject to competition,

[10]Quoted in T. Walter Wallbank and Alastair M. Taylor, *Civilization: Past and Present,* Chicago: Scott, Foresman, 1949, rev. ed., Vol. 1, pp. 559-560. The offer and counter-offer also provide an excellent illustration of mutual ethnocentrism.

[11]Lindgren, *op. cit.*

[12]Aaron Antonovsky, "The Social Meaning of Discrimination," *Phylon,* 21 (Spring, 1960), pp. 81-95.

[13]This analysis of the arena of competition is a modification of the analysis by Wagley and Harris, *op. cit.,* esp. pp. 263-264. These authors limit the concept "arena" to the objects sought *and* the regulative values which determine opportunity to compete and then partly confound their components by including the regulative values, along with adaptive capacity and the instruments necessary to compete, as part of the "terms" of competition.

the more intense the competition. Moreover, as Wagely and Harris observe, "It is important to know the objects of competition, for it would seen that the more vital or valuable the resource over which there is competition, the more intense is the conflict between the groups."[14] Barring total annihilation of one of the groups, these points can be extended to state that the more intense the competition or conflict the greater the likelihood—other things being equal—that it will culminate in a system of ethnic stratification.   In other words, the number and significance of the scarce, common goals sought determine the degree of competition which in turn significantly affects the probability that ethnic stratification will emerge.

The terms of the competition may greatly alter the probability of ethnic stratification, however, regardless of the intensity of the competition. The retention of a set of values or rules which effectively regulates—or moderates—ethnic interrelations is of particularly crucial significance. If a framework of regulative values fails to emerge, or breaks down, each group may seek to deny the other(s) the right to compete with the result that overt conflict emerges and culminates in annihilation, expulsion, or total subjugation of the less powerful group. If, in contrast, regulative values develop and are retained, competition even for vital goals need not result in ethnic stratification— or at least the span of stratification may be considerably constricted.[15]

Even where the groups involved are quite dissimilar culturally, the sharing of certain crucial values (e.g., religion or freedom, individualism, and equality) may be significant in preventing ethnic stratification. This appears to have been one factor in the enduring harmonious relations between the Cossacks and the Tungus. The influence of the regulative values upon the span of ethnic stratification is well illustrated by Tannenbaum's thesis regarding the differences between North American and Latin American slavery.[16]   In the absence of a tradition of slavery the English had no established code prescribing the rights and duties of slaves and the racist ideology which evolved achieved its ultimate expression in the Dred Scott decision of 1857. This decision was highly consistent with the then widely held belief that the Negro "had no rights which the white man was bound to respect . . . ." By contract the Iberian code accorded certain rights to the Latin American slave (including the right to own property and to purchase his freedom) which greatly restricted the extent of inequality between free man slave.[17]

In addition to the regulative values, the structural opportunities for or barriers to upward mobility which are present in the society may affect the emergence and span of ethnic stratification.   Social structural barriers such as a static, nonexpanding

---

[14]*Ibid.*, p. 263. They suggest that competition for scarce subsistence goals will produce more intense conflict than competition for prestige symbols or other culturally defined goals.

[15]Discussing the ideological aspect of intergroup relations, Wagley and Harris note that equalitarian creeds have generally not been effective in *preventing* ethnic stratification. *Ibid.*, pp. 280 ff. The operation of ethnocentrism makes it very easy for the boundaries of the in-group to become the boundaries of adherence to group values.

[16]Frank Tannenbaum, *Slave and Citizen: The Negro in the Americas,* New York: Random House, 1963.

[17]*Ibid.*, esp. pp. 49 ff.   Marvin Harris has criticized Tannenbaum's thesis arguing that the rights prescribed by the Iberian code were largely illusory and that there is no certainty that *slaves* were treated better in Latin America.   Harris in turn provides a functional (economic necessity) explanation for the historical difference in treatment of *free* Negroes in the two continents.   See Marvin Harris, *Patterns of Race in the Americas,* New York: Walker, 1964, esp. Chs. 6 and 7.

economy are a significant part of the terms of competition and they may be more decisive than the regulative values as regards the duration of the system. Finally, along with the goals and the terms of competition, the relative adaptive capacity of the groups involved is an aspect of competition which significantly affects the emergence of ethnic stratification.

Wagley and Harris assume that ethnic stratification is given and focus their analysis on the adaptive capacity of *the minority group* in terms of its effect upon the span and the duration of ethnic stratification. Thus they view adaptive capacity as:

"those elements of a minority's cultural heritage which provide it with a basis for competing more or less effectively with the dominant group, which afford protection against exploitation, which stimulate or retard its adaptation to the total social environment, and which facilitate or hinder its upward advance through the socioeconomic hierarchy.[18]

We shall apply the concept to an earlier point in the intergroup process—i.e., prior to the emergence of ethnic stratification—by broadening it to refer to those aspects of any ethnic group's sociocultural heritage which affect its adjustment to a given social and physical environment. The group with the greater adaptive capacity is apt to emerge as the dominant group[19] while the other groups are subordinated to a greater or lesser degree—i.e., the span of the stratification system will be great or slight—dependent upon the extent of their adaptive capacity relative to that of the emergent dominant group.

The duration, as well as the origin and span, of ethnic stratification will be markedly influenced by adaptive capacity. Once a people have become a minority, flexibility on their part is essential if they are to efficiently adjust and effectively compete within the established system of ethnic stratification and thereby facilitate achievement of equality. Sociocultural patterns are invariably altered by changing life conditions. However, groups vary in the alacrity with which they respond to changing conditions. A flexible minority group may facilitate the achievement of equality or even dominance by readily accepting modifications of their heritage which will promote efficient adaptation to their subordination *and* to subsequent changes in life conditions.

Competition and ethnocentrism do not provide a sufficient explanation for the emergence of ethnic stratification. Highly ethnocentric groups involved in competition for vital objects will not generate ethnic stratification *unless* they are of such unequal power that one is able to impose its will upon the other.[20] Inequality of power is the defining characteristic of dominant and minority groups, and Lenski maintains that differential power is the foundation element in the genesis of any stratification system.[21] In any event differential power is absolutely essential to the emergence of ethnic stratification and the greater the differential the greater the span and durability of the system, other things being equal.

---

[18]Wagley and Harris, *op. cit.,* p. 264.

[19]This point is explicitly made by Tamotsu Shibutani and Kian M. Kwan, *Ethnic Stratification: A Comparative Approach,* New York: Macmillan, 1965, p. 147; see also Ch. 9.

[20]This point is made by Antonovsky, *op. cit.,* esp. p. 82, and implied by Wagley and Harris in their discussion of the role of the state in the formation of minority groups, *op. cit.,* esp. pp. 240-244. Stanley Lieberson's recent modification of Park's cycle theory of race relations also emphasizes the importance of differential power as a determinant of the outcome of intergroup contacts. See "A Societal Theory of Race and Ethnic Relations," *American Sociological Review,* 26 (December, 1961), pp. 902-910.

[21]Lenski, *op. cit.,* esp. Ch. 3.

Technically, power is a component of adaptive capacity as Wagley and Harris imply in their definition by referring to "protection against exploitation." Nevertheless, differential power exerts an effect independent of adaptive capacity in general and is of such crucial relevance for ethnic stratification as to warrant its being singled out as a third major causal variable. The necessity of treating it as a distinct variable is amply demonstrated by consideration of those historical cases where one group has the greater adaptive capacity in general but is subordinated because another group has greater (military) power. The Dravidians overrun by the Aryans in ancient India and the Manchu conquest of China are illustrative cases.[22]

Unless the ethnic groups involved are unequal in power, intergroup relations will be characterized by conflict, symbiosis, or a pluralist equilibrium. Given intergroup competition, however, symbiosis is unlikely and conflict and pluralism are inevitably unstable. Any slight change in the existing balance of power may be sufficient to establish the temporary dominance of one group and this can be utilized to allow the emerging dominant group to perpetuate and enhance its position.[23] Once dominance is established the group in power takes all necessary steps to restrict the now subordinated groups, thereby hampering their effectiveness as competitors,[24] and to institutionalize the emerging distribution of rewards and opportunities. Hence, since power tends to beget power, a slight initial alteration in the distribution of power can become the basis of a stable inequalitarian system.

We have now elaborated the central concepts and propositions of a theory of the emergence and initial stabilization of ethnic stratification. The theory can be summarized as follows. When distinct ethnic groups are brought into sustained contact (via migration, the emergence and expansion of the state, or internal differentiation of a previously homogeneous group), ethnic stratification will invariably follow if—and only if—the groups are characterized by a significant degree of ethnocentrism, competition, *and* differential power. Without ethnocentrism the groups would quickly merge and competition would not be structured along ethnic lines. Without competition there would be no motivation or rationale for instituting stratification along ethnic lines. Without differential power it would simply be impossible for one group to achieve dominance and impose subordination to its will and ideals upon the other(s).

The necessity of differential power is incontestable but it could be argued that either competition or ethnocentrism is dispensable. For example, perhaps extreme ethnocentrism independent of competition is sufficient motive for seeking to impose ethnic stratification. Certainly ethnocentrism could encourage efforts to promote continued sharp differentiation, but it would not by itself motivate stratification unless we assume the existence of a *need* for dominance or aggression. Conversely, given sociocultural differences, one group may be better prepared for and therefore able to more effectively exploit a given environment. Hence, this group would become economically dominant and might then

---

[22]See Wallbank and Taylor, *op. cit.,* p. 95; and Shibutani and Kwan, *op. cit.,* pp. 129-130.

[23]See *Ibid.,* esp. Chs. 6, 9, and 12; and Richard A. Schermerhorn, *Society and Power,* New York; Random House, 1961, pp. 18-26.

[24]Shibutani and Kwan observe that dominance rests upon victory in the competitive process and that competition between groups is eliminated or greatly reduced once a system of ethnic stratification is stabilized, *op. cit.,* pp. 146 and 235, and Ch. 12. The extent to which competition is actually stifled is highly variable, however, as Wagley and Harris note in their discussion of

---

minority adaptive capacity and the terms of competition, *op. cit.,* pp. 263 ff.

perceive and pursue the advantages (especially economic) of ethnic stratification quite independent of ethnocentrism. On the other hand, while differential power and competition alone are clearly sufficient to generate stratification, a low degree of ethnocentrism could readily forestall *ethnic* stratification by permitting assimilation and thereby eliminating differential adaptive capacity. Ethnocentrism undeniably heightens awareness of ethnicity and thereby promotes the formation and retention of ethnic competition, but the crucial question is whether or not some specified degree of ethnocentrism is *essential* to the emergence of ethnic stratification. Since autonomous ethnic groups are invariably ethnocentric, the answer awaits more precise measures of ethnocentrism which will allow us to test hypotheses specifying the necessary degree of ethnocentrism.[25]

Given the present state of knowledge it seems advisable to retain both competition and ethnocentrism, as well as differential power, as integral elements of the theory. Our next objective, then, is to provide an initial test of the theory by applying it to an analysis of the genesis of slavery in the seventeenth century mainland North American colonies.

THE ORIGIN OF AMERICAN SLAVERY

There is a growing consensus among historians of slavery in the United States that Negroes were not initially slaves but that they are gradually reduced to a position of chattel slavery over several decades.[26] The

historical record regarding their initial status is so vague and incomplete, however, that it is impossible to assert with finality that their status was initially no different from that of non-Negro indentured servants.[27] Moreover, while there is agreement that the statutory establishment of slavery was not widespread until the 1660's, there is disagreement regarding slavery's emergence in actual practice. The Handlins maintain that "The status of Negroes was that of servants; and so they were identified and treated down to the 1660's."[28] Degler and Jordan argue that this conclusion is not adequately documented and cite evidence indicating that some Negroes were slaves as early as 1640.[29]

Our central concern is to relate existing historical research to the theory elaborated above, *not* to attempt original historical research intended to resolve the controversy regarding the nature and extent of the initial status differences (if any) between white and Negro bondsmen. However, two findings emerging from the controversy are basic to our concern: 1) although the

---

Comparative Studies in Society and History, 2 (October, 1959), pp. 49-66; Stanley M. Elkins, *Slavery: A Problem in American Institutional and Intellectual Life*, Chicago: U. of Chicago, 1959; Oscar and Mary F. Handlin, "Origins of the Southern Labor System," *William and Mary Quarterly*, 3rd Series, 7 (April, 1950), pp. 199-222; and Winthrop D. Jordan, "Modern Tensions and the Origins of American Slavery," *The Journal of Southern History*, 28 (February, 1962), pp. 18-30. and *White over Black*, Chapel-Hill: U. of North Carolina, 1968. See also Boskin, *op. cit.,* and "Comment" and "Reply" by the Handlins and Degler in the cited volume of *Comparative Studies* . . ., pp. 488-495.

[27]Jordan, *The Journal* . . ., p. 22.

[28]Handlin and Handlin, *op. cit.,* p. 203.

[29]Degler, *Comparative studies* . . . , pp. 52-56 and Jordan, *The Journal* . . . , pp. 23-27 and *White over Black*, pp. 73-74. Also see Elkins, *op. cit.,* pp. 38-42 (esp. fns. 16 and 19).

---

[25]The issue is further complicated by the fact that the necessary degree of any one of the three elements may vary as a function of the other two.

[26]The main relevant references in the recent literature include Carl N. Degler, *Out of Our Past*, New York: Harper and Row, 1959 and "Slavery and the Genesis of American Race Prejudice,"

terms servant and slave were frequently used interchangeably, whites were never slaves in the sense of serving for life and conveying a like obligation to their offspring; and 2) many Negroes were not slaves in this sense at least as late as the 1660's. Concomitantly with the Negroes' descent to slavery, white servants gained increasingly liberal terms of indenture and, ultimately, freedom. The origin of slavery for the one group and the growth of freedom for the other are explicable in terms of our theory as a function of differences in ethnocentrism, the arena of competition, and power vis-à-vis the dominant group or class.[30]

Degler argues that the status of the Negro evolved in a framework of discrimination and, therefore, "The important point is not the evolution of the legal status of the slave, but the fact that discriminatory legislation regarding the Negro long preceded any legal definition of slavery."[31] The first question then becomes one of explaining this differential treatment which foreshadowed the descent to slavery. A major element in the answer is implied by the Handlins' observation that "The rudeness of the Negroes' manners, the strangeness of their languages, the difficulty of communicating to them English notions of morality and proper behavior occasioned sporadic laws to regulate their conduct."[32] By itself this implies a contradiction of their basic thesis that Negro and white indentured servants were treated similarly prior to 1660. They maintain, however, that there was nothing unique nor

decisive in this differential treatment of Negroes, for such was also accorded various Caucasian out-groups in this period.[33] While Jordan dismisses the Handlins' evidence as largely irrelevant to the point and Degler feels that it is insufficient, Degler acknowledges that "Even Irishmen, who were white, Christian, and European, were held to be literally 'beyond the Pale,' and some were even referred to as 'slaves'."[34] Nevertheless, Degler contends that the overall evidence justifies his conclusion that Negroes were generally accorded a lower position than any white, bound or free.

That the English made status distinctions between various out-groups is precisely what one would expect, however, given the nature of ethnocentrism. The degree of ethnocentric rejection is primarily a function of the degree of difference, and Negroes were markedly different from the dominant English in color, nationality, language, religion, and other aspects of culture.[35] The differential treatment of Negroes was by no means entirely due to a specifically anti-Negro *color* prejudice. Indeed, color was not initially the most important factor in determining the relative status of Negroes; rather, the fact that they were non-Christian was of major significance.[36] Although

---

[30]Our primary concern is with the emergence of Negro slavery but the theory also explains how white bondsmen avoided slavery. Their position vis-à-vis the dominant English was characterized by a different "value" of at least two of the key variables.

[31]Degler, *Out of Our Past*, p. 35. Bear in mind, however, that slavery was not initially institutionalized in law or in the mores.

[32]Handlin and Handlin, *op. cit.*, pp. 208-209.

[33]*Ibid.* They note that "It is not necessary to resort to racialist assumptions to account for such measures; . . . [for immigrants in a strange environment] longed . . . for the company of familiar men and singled out to be welcomed those who were most like themselves." See pp. 207-211 and 214.

[34]Jordan, *The Journal* . . . , esp. pp. 27 (fn. 29) and 29 (fn. 34); and Degler, *Out of Our Past*, p. 30.

[35]Only the aboriginal Indians were different from the English colonists to a comparable degree and they were likewise severely dealt with via a policy of exclusion and annihilation after attempts at enslavement failed. See Boskin, *op. cit.*, p. 453; and Jordan, *White over Black*, pp. 85-92.

[36]The priority of religious over racial prejudice and discrimination in the early seventeenth century

beginning to lose its preeminence, religion was still the central institution of society in the seventeenth century and religious prejudice toward non-Christians or heathens was widespread. The priority of religious over color prejudice is amply demonstrated by analysis of the early laws and court decisions pertaining to Negro-white sexual relations. These sources explicitly reveal greater concern with Christian-non-Christian than with white-Negro unions.[37] During and after the 1660's laws regulating racial intermarriage arose but for some time their emphasis was generally, if not invariably, upon religion, nationality, or some basis of differentiation other than race *per se*. For example, a Maryland law of 1681 described marriages of white women with Negroes as lascivious and "to the disgrace not only of the English butt allso [sic] of many *other Christian Nations*."[38]   Moreover, the laws against Negro-white marriage seem to have been rooted much more in economic considerations than they were in any concern for white racial purity.[39] In short, it was not a simple color prejudice but a marked degree of ethnocentrism, rooted in a multitude of salient differences, which combined with competition and differential power to reduce Negroes to the status of slaves.[40]

Degler has noted that Negroes initially lacked a status in North America and thus almost any kind of status could have been worked out.[41]   Given a different competitive arena, a more favorable status blurring the sharp ethnic distinctions could have evolved. However, as the demand for labor in an expanding economy began to exceed the supply, interest in lengthening the term of indenture arose.[42] This narrow economic explanation of the origin of slavery has been challenged on the grounds that slavery appeared equally early in the Northern colonies although there were too few Negroes there to be of economic significance.[43] This seemingly decisive point is largely mitigated by two considerations.

First, in the other colonies it was precisely *the few* who did own slaves who

---

is noted in *ibid.,* pp. 97-98 and by Edgar J. McManus, *A History of Negro Slavery in New York,* Syracuse: Syracus U., 1966, esp. pp. 11-12.

[37]Jordan, *The Journal* . . . , p. 28 and *White Over Black,* pp. 78-80.

[38]Quoted in *ibid.,* pp. 79-80 (emphasis added). Also see pp. 93-97, however, where Jordan stresses the necessity of carefully interpreting the label "Christian."

[39]See Handlin and Handlin, *op. cit.,* pp. 213-216; and W. D. Zabel, "Interracial Marriage and the Law," *The Atlantic* (October, 1965), pp. 75-79.

[40]The distinction between ethnocentrism (the rejection of out-groups *in general* as a function of in-group glorification) and prejudice (hostility toward the members of a *specific* group because they are members of that group) is crucial to the con-

troversy regarding the direction of causality between discrimination, slavery, and prejudice. Undoubtedly these variables are mutually causal to some extent but Harris, *op. cit.,* esp. pp. 67-70, presents evidence that prejudice is primarily a consequence and is of minor importance as a cause of slavery.

[41]Degler, *Comparative Studies* . . . , p. 51. See also Boskin, *op. cit.,* pp. 449 and 454 (esp. fn. 14); Elkins, *op. cit.,* pp. 39-42 (esp. fn. 16); and Kenneth M. Stampp, *The Peculiar Institution,* New York: Knopf, 1956, p. 21. The original indeterminacy of the Negroes' status is reminiscent of Blumer's "sense of group position" theory of prejudice and, in light of Blumer's theory, is consistent with the belief that there was no widespread prejudice toward Negroes prior to the institutionalization of slavery. See Herbert Blumer, "Race Prejudice as a Group Position," *Pacific Sociological Review,* 1 (Spring, 1958), pp. 3-7.

[42]Handlin and Handlin, *op. cit.,* p. 210.

[43]Degler acknowledges that the importance of perpetuating a labor force indispensable to the economy later became a crucial support of slavery but he denies that the need for labor explains the origin of slavery. His explanation stresses prior discrimination which, in the terms of the present theory, was rooted in ethnocentrism and differential power. See *Comparative Studies* . . . ,

were not only motivated by vested interests but were also the men of means and local power most able to secure a firm legal basis for slavery.[44] The distribution of power and motivation was undoubtedly similar and led to the same consequences in New England. For the individual retainer of Negro servants the factual and legal redefinition of Negroes as chattel constitutes a vital economic interest whether or not the number of slaves is sufficient to vitally affect the economy of the colony. Our knowledge of the role of the elite in the establishment of community mores suggests that this constitutes at least a partial explanation of the Northern laws.[45] In addition, the markedly smaller number of Negroes in the North might account for the fact that "although enactments in the Northern colonies recognized the legality of lifetime servitude, no effort was made to require all Negroes to be placed in that condition."[46]   We surmise that the laws were passed at the behest of a few powerful individuals who had relatively many Negro servants and were indifferent to the status of Negroes in general so long as their own vested interests were protected.

The explanation for the more all-encompassing laws of the Southern colonies is rooted in the greater homogeneity of interests of the Southern elite. In contrast to the Northern situation, the men of power in the Southern colonies were predominantly planters who were unified in their need for large numbers of slaves. The margin of profit in agricultural production for the commercial market was such that the small landholder could not compete and the costs of training and the limitations on control (by the planter) which were associated with indentured labor made profitable exploitation of such labor increasingly difficult.[47]   Hence, it was not the need for labor *per se* which was critical for the establishment of the comprehensive Southern slave system but rather the requirements of the emerging economic system for a particular kind of labor. In short, the Southern power elite uniformly needed slave labor while only certain men of power shared this need in the North and hence the latter advocated slave laws but lacked the power (or did not feel the need) to secure the all-encompassing laws characteristic of the Southern colonies.

There is a second major consideration in explaining the existence of Northern slavery. Men do not compete only for economic ends. They also compete for prestige and many lesser objects, and there is ample basis for suggesting that prestige competition was a significant factor in the institutionalization of slavery, North and South. Degler calls attention to the prestige motive when he discusses the efforts to establish a feudal aristocracy in seventeenth century New York, Maryland, and the Carolinas. He concludes that these efforts failed because the manor was "dependent upon the scarcity of land."[48] The failure of feudal aristocracy in no way denies the fundamental human desire for success or prestige.   Indeed, this failure

including the "Reply" to the Handlins' "Comment;" and *Out of Our Past,* pp. 35-38 and 162-168.

[44]Elkins, *op. cit.,* pp. 45 (esp. fn. 26) and 48.

[45]Historical precedent is provided by the finding that "The vagrancy laws emerged in order to provide the powerful landowners with a ready supply of cheap labor." See William J. Chambliss, "A Sociological Analysis of the Law of Vagrancy," *Social Problems,* 12 (Summer, 1964), pp. 67-77. Jordan, *White over Black,* pp. 67 and 69, provides evidence that the economic advantages of slavery were clearly perceived in the Northern colonies.

[46]Elkins, *op. cit.,* p. 41 (fn. 19).

[47]By the 1680's "The point had clearly passed when white servants could realistically, on any long-term appraisal, be considered preferrable to Negro slaves." *Ibid.,* p. 48.

[48]Degler, *Out of Our Past,* p. 3.   Also see Hubert M. Blalock, Jr., *Toward a Theory of Minority Group Relations,* New York: Wiley, 1967, pp. 44-48.

opened the society. It emphasized success and mobility for "it meant that wealth, rather than family or tradition, would be the primary determinant of social stratification."[49]   Although the stress was on economic success, there were other gains associated with slavery to console those who did not achieve wealth. The desire for social prestige derivable from "membership in a superior caste" undoubtedly provided motivation and support for slavery among both Northern and Southern white, slaveholders and nonslaveholders.[50]

The prestige advantage of slavery would have been partially undercut, especially for nonslaveholders, by enslavement of white bondsmen, but it is doubtful that this was a significant factor in their successfully eluding hereditary bondage. Rather the differential treatment of white and Negro bondsmen, ultimately indisputable and probably present from the very beginning, is largely attributable to differences in ethnocentrism and relative power. There was little or no ethnocentric rejection of the majority of white bondsmen during the seventeenth century because most of them were English.[51] Moreover, even the detested Irish and other non-English white servants were culturally and physically much more similar to the English planters than were the Africans. Hence, the planters clearly preferred white bondsmen until the advantages of slavery became increasingly apparent in the latter half of the seventeenth century.[52]

The increasing demand for labor after the mid-seventeenth century had divergent consequences for whites and blacks.   The colonists became increasingly concerned to encourage immigration by counteracting "the widespread reports in England and Scotland that servants were harshly treated and bound in perpetual slavery" and by enacting "legislation designed to improve servants' conditions and to enlarge the prospect of a meaningful release, a release that was not the start of a new period of servitude, but of life as a freeman and landowner."[53]   These improvements curtailed the exploitation of white servants without directly affecting the status of the Africans.

"Farthest removed from the English, least desired, [the Negro] communicated with no friends who might be deterred from following.   Since his coming was involuntary, nothing that happened to him would increase or decrease his numbers. To raise the status of Europeans by shortening their terms would ultimately increase the available hands by inducing their compatriots to emigrate; to reduce the Negro's term would produce an immediate loss and no ultimate gain.   By mid-century the servitude of Negroes seems generally lengthier than that of whites; and thereafter, the consciousness dawns that the blacks will toil for the whole of their lives . . . "[54]

---

[49]Degler, *Out of Our Past,* p. 5; see also pp. 45-50. Elkins, *op. cit.,* esp. pp. 43-44, also notes the early emphasis on personal success and mobility.

[50]Stampp, *op. cit.,* pp. 29-33, esp. 32-33. Also see J. D. B. DeBow, "The Interest in Slavery of the Southern Non-Salveholder," reprinted in Eric L. McKitrick, editor, *Slavery Defended: The Views of the Old South,* Englewood Cliffs, N.J.: Prentice-Hall, 1963, pp. 169-177.

[51]Stampp, *op. cit.,* p. 16; and Degler, *Out of Our Past,* pp. 50-51. Consistent with the nature of ethnocentrism, "The Irish and other aliens, less desirable, at first received longer terms. But the realization that such discrimination retarded 'the peopling of the country' led to an extension of the identical privilege to all Christians." Handlin and Handlin, *op. cit.,* pp. 210-211.

[52]Elkins, *op. cit.,* pp. 40 and 48; and Handlin and Handlin, *op. cit.,* pp. 207-208.

[53]*Ibid.,* p. 210.

[54]*Ibid.,* p. 211 (emphasis added).   That the need for labor led to improvements in the status of white servants seems very likely but Degler in *Comparative Studies* . . . effectively challenges some of the variety of evidence presented by the Handlins, *op. cit.,* pp. 210 and 213-214 and "Comment."

The planters and emerging agrarian capitalism were unconstrained in a planter-dominated society with no traditional institutions to exert limits. In this context even the common law tradition helped promote slavery.[55]

Ethnocentrism set the Negroes apart but their almost total lack of power and effective spokesmen, in contrast to white indentured servants, was decisive in their enslavement. Harris speaks directly to the issue and underscores the significance of (organized) power for the emergence of slavery:

"The facts of life in the New World were such . . . that Negroes, being the most defenseless of all the immigrant groups, were discriminated against and exploited more than any others. . . . Judging from the very nasty treatment suffered by white indentured servants, it was obviously not sentiment which prevented the Virginia planters from enslaving their fellow Englishmen. They undoubtedly would have done so had they been able to get away with it. But such a policy was out of the question as long as there was a King and a Parliament in England."[56]

The Negroes, in short, did not have any organized external government capable of influencing the situation in their favor.[57] Moreover, "there was no one in England or in the colonies to pressure for the curtailment of the Negro's servitude or to fight for his future."[58]

The Negroes' capacity to adapt to the situation and effectively protest in their own behalf was greatly hampered by their cultural diversity and lack of unification. They did not think of themselves as "a kind." They did not subjectively share a common identity and thus they lacked the group solidarity necessary to effectively "act as a unit in competition with other groups."[59] Consciousness of shared fate is essential to effective unified action but it generally develops only gradually as the members of a particular social category realize that they are being treated alike despite their differences. "People who find themselves set apart eventually come to recognize their common interests," but for those who share a subordinate position common identification usually emerges only after "repeated experiences of denial and humiliation."[60] The absence of a shared identification among seventeenth century Negroes reflected the absence of a shared heritage from which to construct identity, draw strength, and organize protest. Hence, Negroes were easily enslaved and reduced to the status of chattel. The point merits elaboration.

We have defined adaptive capacity in terms of a group's sociocultural heritage as it affects adjustment to the environment. Efficient adaptation may require the members of a group to modify or discard a great deal of their heritage. A number of factors, including ethnocentrism and the centrality of the values and social structures requiring modification, affect willingness to alter an

---

[55]Elkins, *op. cit.*, pp. 38 (fn. 14), 42 (fn. 22), 43 and 49-52; and Jordan, *White over Black*, pp. 49-51.

[56]Harnes, *op. cit.*, pp. 69-70.

[57]The effectiveness of intervention by an external government is illustrated by the halting of Indian emigration to South Africa in the 1860's as a means of protesting "the indignities to which indentured 'coolies' were subjected in Natal, . . ." See Pierre L. van den Berghe, *Souith Africa, A Study in Conflict*, Middletown: Wesleyan U., 1965, p. 250.

[58]Boskin, *op. cit.*, p. 448. Also see Stampp, *op. cit.*, p. 22; and Elkins, *op. cit.*, pp. 49-52.

[59]Shibutani and Kwan, *op. cit.*, p. 42. See also William O. Brown, "Race Consciousness Among South African Natives," *American Journal of Sociology*, 40 (March, 1935), pp. 569-581.

[60]Shibutani and Kwan, *op. cit.*, Ch. 8, esp. pp. 202 and 212.

established way of life.[61] Even given a high degree of willingness, however, many groups simply have not possessed the cultural complexity or social structural similarity to the dominant group necessary to efficient adaptation. Many Brazilian and United States Indian tribes, for example, have not had the knowledge (e.g., of writing, money, markets, etc.) or the structural similarity to their conquerors (e.g., as regards the division of labor) necessary to protect themselves from exploitation and to achieve a viable status in an emerging multi-ethnic society.[62]

By comparison with most New World Indians the sociocultural heritage of the Africans was remarkably favorable to efficient adaptation.[63] However, the discriminatory framework within which white-Negro relations developed in the seventeenth century ultimately far outweighed the cultural advantages of the Negroes vis-a-vis the Indians in the race for status.[64] The Negroes from any given culture were widely dispersed and their capacity to adapt *as a group* was thereby shattered. Like the Negroes, the Indians were diverse culturally but they retained their cultural heritage and social solidarity, and they were more likely to resist slavery because of the much greater probability of reunion with their people following escape. Hence, Negroes were preferred over Indians as slaves both because their cultural background had better prepared them for the slave's role in the plantation system (thus

enhancing the profits of the planters) and because they lacked the continuing cultural and group support which enabled the Indians to effectively resist slavery.[65] By the time the Africans acquired the dominant English culture and social patterns *and* a sense of shared fate, their inability to work out a more favorable adaptation was assured by the now established distribution of power and by the socialization processes facilitating acceptance of the role of slave.[66]

CONCLUSION

We conclude that ethnocentrism, competition, and differential power provide a comprehensive explanation of the origin of slavery in the seventeenth century English colonies. The Negroes were clearly more different from the English colonists than any other group (*except* the Indians) by almost any criterion, physical or cultural, that might be selected as a basis of social differentiation. Hence, the Negroes were the object of a relatively intense ethnocentric

---

[61]See the discussions in Brewton Berry, *Race and Ethnic Relations,* Boston: Houghton-Mifflin, 1965, 3rd ed., esp. pp. 147-149; Shibutani and Kwan, *op. cit.,* esp. pp. 217f; and Wagley and Harris, *op. cit.,* pp. 40-44.

[62]*Ibid.,* pp. 15-86 and 265-268.

[63]*Ibid.,* p. 269; Harris, *op. cit.,* p. 14; and Stampp, *op. cit.,* pp. 13 and 23.

[64]The Indians were also discriminated against but to a much lesser extent. The reasons for this differential are discussed by Jordan, *White over Black,* pp. 89-90; and Stampp, *op. cit., pp. 23-24.*

[65]Harris, *op. cit.,* pp. 14-16, an otherwise excellent summary of the factors favoring the enslavement of Negroes rather than Indians, overlooks the role of sociocultural support. The importance of this support is clearly illustrated by South African policy of importing Asians in preference to the native Africans who strenuously resisted enslavement and forced labor. Shibutani and Kwan, *op. cit.,* p. 126. Sociocultural unity was also a significant factor in the greater threat of revolt posed by the Helots in Sparta as compared to the heterogeneous slaves in Athens. Alvin W. Souldner, *Enter Plato,* New York: Basic Books, 1965, p. 32.

[66]Shibutani and Kwan, *op. cit.,* esp. Chs. 10-12. Stampp observes that the plantation trained Negroes to be slaves, not free men, *op. cit.,* p. 12. Similarly, Wagley and Harris note that the Negroes were poorly prepared for survival in a free-market economic system even when they were emancipated, *op. cit.,* p. 269.

rejection from the beginning. The opportunity for great mobility characteristic of a frontier society created an arena of competition which dovetailed with the ethnocentrism. Labor, utilized to achieve wealth, and prestige were the primary objects of this competition. These goals were particularly manifest in the Southern colonies, but our analysis provides a rationale for the operation of the same goals as sources of motivation to institutionalize slavery in the Northern colonies also.

The terms of the competition for the Negro's labor are implicit in the evolving pattern of differential treatment of white and Negro bondsmen prior to slavery and in the precarious position of free Negroes. As slavery became institutionalized the moral, religious, and legal values of the society were increasingly integrated to form a highly consistent complex which acknowledged no evil in "the peculiar institution."[67] Simultaneously, Negroes were denied any opportunity to escape their position of lifetime, inheritable servitude. Only by the grace of a generous master, not by any act of his own, could a slave achieve freedom and, moreover, there were "various legal strictures aimed at impeding or discouraging the process of private manumission."[68] The rigidity of "the peculiar institution" was fixed before the Negroes acquired sufficient common culture, sense of shared fate, and

identity to be able to effectively challenge the system. This lack of unity was a major determinant of the African's poor adaptive capacity as a group. They lacked the social solidarity and common cultural resources essential to organized resistance and thus in the absence of intervention by a powerful external ally they were highly vulnerable to exploitation.

The operation of the three key factors is well summarized by Stampp:

"Neither the provisions of their charters nor the policy of the English government limited the power of colonial legislatures to control Negro labor as they saw fit. . . . Their unprotected condition encouraged the trend toward special treatment, and their physical and cultural differences provided handy excuses to justify it . . . . [t] he landholders' growing appreciation of the advantages of slavery over the older forms of servitude gave a powerful impetus to the growth of the new labor system."[69]

In short, the present theory stresses that *given* ethnocentrism, the Negroes' lack of power, and the dynamic arena of competition in which they were located, their ultimate enslavement was inevitable. The next task is to test the theory further, incorporating modifications as necessary, by analyzing subsequent accommodations in the pattern of race relations in the United States and by analyzing the emergence of various patterns of ethnic stratification in other places and eras.

---

[67]Davis asserts that while slavery has always been a source of tension, "in Western culture it was associated with certain religious and philosophical doctrines that gave it the highest sanction." *Op. cit.,* p. ix.

[68]Wagley and Harris, *op. cit.,* p. 124.

---

[69]Stampp, op. cit., p. 22.

3.   CASTE AS SOCIAL PROCESS[1]

Gerald D. Berreman

This article is a continuation of the author's well-known investigations of the caste system. In a previous article, Berreman noted the often neglected conflicts between castes that contradict the common view that subordinate caste members passively accept their position. In this article he concludes that "caste is thus a means of ordering the relations among disparate groups." Berreman thus sees the caste system as an alternative to the "assimilation" models developed by sociologists.

INTRODUCTION: CASTE DEFINED

Caste is a peculiar institution with peculiar consequences. In order to investigate its implications for a broader understanding of social organization, I have previously developed a concept of caste organization which is intended to be cross-culturally applicable (Berreman 1960a, 1962, 1966, 1967a, 1967b). I have assumed that scientific endeavor requires comparison and that comparison requires careful definition of the phenomena to be studied. Caste systems were defined in terms of three dimensions: stratification, pluralism, and interaction. "A caste system occurs where a society is made up of birth-ascribed groups which are hier-

SOURCE
From the *Southwest Journal of Anthropology* Vol. 23, (1967). **Reprinted by permission of the author and publisher.**

[1]This paper was presented, in abbreviated form, at the 65th Annual Meeting of the American Anthropological Association, in Pittsburgh, November 18, 1966.

archically ordered and culturally distinct. The hierarchy entails differential evaluation, rewards and association" (Berreman 1967a: 48, cf. Berreman 1965). In its interactional sense—the sense of differential association—a caste system is "a system of birth-ascribed groups each of which comprises for its members the maximum limit of status-equal interaction between all of which interaction is consistently hierarchial" (Berreman 1967a: 51). By reference to these definitions and their implications, castes can be distinguished from, and compared to, other types of social aggregates (e.g., kin groups, classes, local communities), and caste systems can be distinguished from and compared to other systems of organizing people in societies (e.g., pluralism, class and homogeneity of culture and rank) (Berreman 1967a, 1967b). The types of aggregates and the systems of organization are not mutually exclusive. All of the dimensions vary along continua, and each of the definitions is of the "ideal-type" variety.

In conjunction with the definitional discussions, I indicated social and psychological concomitants of caste systems—ways in which the recurrent fact of caste organization affects those who live it. I suggested that there are common consequences of caste systems for the personalities as well as the social relations of members (Berreman 1960a, 1966, 1967a; cf. DeVos 1966). I sought to identify common behaviors and attitudes associated with caste systems and in fact proposed the utility of a concept of "cultures of caste organization," analogous to Lewis' concept of the culture of poverty (Berreman 1967a, Lewis 1959). These cultures share the distinctive combination of features common to people who live in caste systems.

Now I wish to move beyond that formulation of caste systems and, in response to the spirit of Levi-Strauss' recent critique of those who study kinship systems simply to classify into types and subtypes, "try to find out how they work, that is, what kind of solidarity they help to establish within the group. . . . " (Levi-Strauss 1966:8). I shall not dwell speculatively on origins, although statements pertaining to origins will necessarily appear. My focus will be on the functioning of caste systems in society— on how caste organization affects society. I will suggest that, among other things, caste systems (1) perpetuate and enforce social and cultural diversity, (2) articulate that diversity, and (3) protect privilege through the exercise of power.

ORIGINS

To discuss social functions of caste is not an entirely novel undertaking. Many Indianists and historians have speculated on the origins of Indian caste and in the course of their speculations have implied or hypothesized functions which it serves. Anthropologists and sociologists have occasionally discussed origins or predisposing circumstances for caste in India and elsewhere. Sociologists have debated the func-

tional implications of social stratification in discussions which have obvious, and sometimes explicit, relevance to caste stratification.

As Pieris (1952) has noted, Toynbee postulated that caste systems are one of "the three possible alternative outcomes of the impact of one society upon another—that is, extermination, assimilation, and caste . . ." (Toynbee 1934:217). In the genesis of caste, either "an indigenous population may admit peaceful immigrants to live on sufferance in its midst . . . ," or a population may be conquered by powerful invaders "who forbear to exterminate it and disdain to coalesce with it, and are constrained to tolerate it . . ." *(Ibid).*[2] In both cases the less powerful group is assigned low rank. Watson (1963) refers to a broad range of societies in which he believes caste organization occurs, and attributes its origin to intensified interdependence among formerly more autonomous social aggregates. Caste systems result from contact between social systems, and therefore he refers to them as a form of acculturation.

Nadel (1954) cites evidence, from Nupe in West Africa and Beni Amer in East Africa, of caste systems which have arisen as a result of ethnic heterogeneity and conquest. He raises the question: "Is this the only way in which castes arise, viz., as a side issue of government by conquest?" (1954:15). He concludes that while some caste systems arise in this fashion, others "arise from internal differentiation of societies, in the absence of any ethnic heterogeneity or any 'struggle of races' " (1954: 21). The conditions comprising the latter

---

[2] I would suggest that pluralism, rather than caste, is the third alternative, and that caste is a common (perhaps the most common) means of organizing pluralism—it articulates the distinct sections of society in a hierarchy and defines their membership by birth. This view and its implications are elaborated below.

route to caste organization include (1) a rigid division of labor, (2) a religious sanction for that division, (3) the fact that the tasks are vital in the society and inspire some feeling of awe (1954:22). Watson rejects this explanation of the origin of caste systems, partly because "substantial cultural differences are initially necessary to permit and maintain a division on a wholly ascriptive basis between . . . segments of a composite community" (Watson, 1963:368), and he holds that such differences do not occur within a single society.

Karve (1961:12ff.), addressing the same question, points out that anthropologists dealing with the origins of caste in India have been aware that some castes have long histories as castes, others are identified as immigrant groups, and some are recognized to have emerged as castes from tribal status. Yet, she points out, a dominant belief among students of the Indian caste system, exemplified in the work of Ghurye (1952), is that the caste system in its contemporary complexity arose out of the repeated fragmentation of previously unitary social groupings (probably beginning with the three, and later four, Aryan *varnas* of the Vedic period, and culminating in the thousands of *jatis* of today). The mythical Hindu "lawgiver," Manu, set the precedent for this view when, 2000 years ago, in the first recorded description of castes in India, he ascribed their origin to the progeny of inter-*varna* unions, the number of castes growing as the mixtures and permutations thereon increased in variety (cf. Karve 1961: 53-57). Karve, in offering an alternative explanation, emphasizes the social and cultural distinctiveness of castes today (1961: 28, 31 ff.), and their mutual interdependence. She postulates that while Aryans did not have caste *(jati)*, there nevertheless may have been castes in India prior to the Aryan period, and that the invading Aryans superimposed their *varnas* at the top of the

hierarchy. In the process, some indigenous caste groups were incorporated into the *varnas*, but the majority of them were added at the bottom of the hierarchy to comprise a new, lower category—presumably the fourth *varna*. The "untouchable" category, sometimes regarded as a fifth *varna*, is often described as having a similar origin. Karve notes that "the processes of caste-making were going on throughout history and are happening even at present" (1961:58). She speculates that pre-Aryan castes arose as a result of "tribe-like separateness"—of the cultural and social distinctiveness of groups which came together at various times and under various circumstances into a single society. She cites evidence wherein the same group has been incorporated into the society of different regions of India at different levels of rank (1961:58-69). She thus sees fragmentation as a minor source of caste organization at most, and she, along with Watson (1963), sees the primary source to be in the coming together of disparate groups which remain distinct but which interact as components of a single hierarchy. From Ceylon, Pieris (1952) has provided evidence of such incorporation of disparate immigrant groups into a caste hierarchy. He concludes: "It seems, therefore, that the dominant caste is originally a powerful invading group, and, once established as the governing caste, relegates all future immigrant groups to the ranks of the aboriginal inferior castes . . . ." (Pieris 1952:414).

Speculations and inferences about the origins and development of caste systems in India and elsewhere are apparently immune to empirical verification, but the origins of particular castes, the conditions attending their origin, and the consequences of the occurrence of caste systems are not. Certainly the social functions of caste organization, once it has been established, are subject to analysis based on documentable instances. The accounts of origins cited above are relevant to such analysis insofar as they state or imply the functions served by caste organization. The following discussion is intended to be a more systematic, comprehensive, and explicit, but still preliminary, contribution.

FUNCTIONS AND PROCESSES

Every system of social stratification allocates power and privilege in the society in which it occurs (Lenski 1966, cf. Mills 1963:305-323), and most if not all such systems are associated with some ranked division of labor (cf. Davis and Moore 1945, Tumin 1953). Caste systems are systems of social stratification which, although unique in that they are based on birth-ascription, share the general attributes of such systems. Like other stratification systems, they rank people, allocate power and privilege, divide labor, and promote interdependence. But an important point that has been largely overlooked by analysts is that caste systems are more than simply unusually rigid systems of stratification. They are also systems of cultural pluralism, maintained by enforced differential association among culturally distinctive groups (Berreman 1967a, 1967b; Watson 1963; cf. Smith 1960; Benedict 1962). Consequently, they have distinct and common attributes not shared by non-caste systems of stratification. The most important of these is that they serve to separate and coordinate culturally differentiated groups of people with the result that power and privilege are rigidly controlled.

Separation and Diversity
By restricting interaction between groups, a caste system insures that the constituent groups will remain culturally distinct and may even become increasingly distinct (cf. Berreman 1960b). This results from the fact that common culture depends upon learning

via interaction. Caste systems inhibit the opportunity for shared culture by restricting interaction. They also inhibit the expression of common culture, even where the opportunity for it exists, through sanctions enforcing caste-specific behavior and attributes. One is not allowed to emulate his superiors, and one does not deign to emulate his inferiors in caste-relevant ways. When a caste attempts to emulate its superiors it must be either prevented, punished, or promoted. That is, it must be made to desist or must be acknowledged to be of a rank appropriate to the behavior and attributes of its members. Only thus can the system remain intact.

Each caste is a social and cultural entity and is expected to remain so and to occupy a rank position commensurate with the culturally prescribed evaluation of its distinctive attributes. Assimilation and acculturation are inhibited or prohibited.

Articulation (Coordination)
A plural society functions despite subcultural differences and social separation of its constituent sections because rules and mechanisms exist which facilitate interaction. Caste systems provide the epitome in rigorous definition of behavioral rules, interactional mechanisms, and the contexts in which they apply. They permit, and in fact require, some kinds of interaction among groups while inhibiting the probable consequence of unrestricted interaction: cultural homogeneity and obliteration of cultural or caste boundaries. They thus articulate the activities of socially and culturally diverse sections of society without jeopardizing their diversity. They do so by providing, enforcing, and rationalizing precise rules of interaction, interdependence, hierarchy, and the allocation of power and privilege.

To do this a minimal consensus is of course necessary. As I have suggested elsewhere, members of different castes "agree on the objective facts of . . . who has the power, and how, under what circumstances and for what purposes it is likely to be exercised. They cease to get along when *this* crucial agreement changes or is challenged" (Berreman 1967a:55, cf. Berreman 1964b). But caste systems seems to depend far less on general consensus than do other systems of stratification and to rely more heavily on behavioral conformity achieved through the threat or exercise of power in the context of socio-cultural diversity and minimal consensus. Caste systems are in this regard like other plural systems, and they contrast in this regard with other systems of stratification to the degree that those systems are non-plural (cf. Berreman 1967a, Smith 1960). The emergence of broad consensus is inimical to caste organizations, for its leads to common behavior, common attributes, and common aspirations which threaten to blue or eliminate caste boundaries, caste prerogatives, and other distinctions crucial to the system. At the same time there is a constant possibility that consensus will emerge because of the juxtaposition and potential interaction of castes. In fact, Watson (1963:375) suggests that caste systems are for these reasons "inherently transitory."[3] These facts contribute to the heavy emphasis that is placed in caste systems upon social separation between castes and the readiness of those with power to exercise it, in order to maintain that

---

[3]"Having argued the very profundity of intergroup differences when a caste system is at full tide, we may not seem consistent in asserting that caste systems are inherently transitory. Nevertheless there is both theory and fact in support of this view. If stratified differences of a caste order cannot arise solely from within one sociocultural continuum, it is reasonable that, except under most favorable (and therefore infrequent) circumstances, such differences would be too great to endure for very long periods within a single continuum" (Watson 1963:374-375).

separation and to enforce status-maintaining differential power.

Protection of Power and Privilege

The caste or castes with dominant power correctly see social separation and differential behavior among castes as necessary to perpetuation of the system and of their privileged position within it, for these features militate against combined action to challenge either the system or the position of those at the top of the hierarchy.

Distinct statuses and roles and attendant privileges are assigned to each group in a caste system according to the power it actually or potentially wields in the society. Once the group has been placed in the hierarchy, stability is sought through limiting the group's power to that which is regarded as consistent with its status.

CONTINUITY: POWER AND INTERDEPENDENCE

Economic interdependence and relative economic non-competition among castes are aspects of the fact that caste systems are systems of sharply defined differential power. Goods, services, rewards, and obligations are distributed in large measure according to caste membership. Ideally every group is socially insulated, yet every group is dependent upon the other groups in society, and decisive power is firmly in the hands of those at the top. Caste is thus a conservative system whereby a status quo of rank can be maintained so long as the system is operational.

Caste organization not only protects the distribution of power; it is also dependent upon power. Sanctions are necessary to enforce adherence to the system (Berreman 1960a). Any change in the distribution of power leads to a shake-up in the hierarchy, if not in the very system itself. If any caste threatens to assume unwonted power, sanctions are at hand to reestablish the status quo. If these prove ineffective, then alternative mechanisms must be available by which the caste's position (and hence the degree and nature of its legitimate claim to power) can be altered. If not, then the system is jeopardized, for power will not be denied—it leads to rank (cf. Lenski 1966). A powerful low caste or a relatively weak high caste is an anomaly, a dissonant element which normally leads to adjustments eliminating the dissonance (cf. Festinger 1957). Changes in power relations are undoubtedly the primary mechanism for change in caste systems.

In addition to conserving the allocation of power and privilege among groups, caste promotes the immediate self-interest of each group by providing a community of co-equals whose interests are defined by the system as shared and unique. The caste, therefore, is self-regulatory and self-promoting to a degree. Given the system, it is essential that it be so; and it is perhaps inevitable that its members will define it as their refuge in a threatening world, their haven of equality in an environment of inequality.

The specialization and interdependence of castes has the effect of assuring that the jobs in society get done, just as it assures that no caste will be able to escape the system. Davis and Moore (1945, cf. Davis 1949:364-391) note that systems of stratification function to induce the members of a society to perform the various tasks required in that society. They maintain that this is done by means of differential rewards. "Social inequality is thus an unconsciously evolved device by which societies insure that the most important positions are conscientiously filled by the most qualified persons" (Davis and Moore 1945:243).

This view has evoked a storm of criticism and defense (Buckley 1958, 1959; Davis 1953, 1959; Levy 1959; Moore 1953; Tumin 1953; Wrong 1959). I would say that power is the factor most important in determining and maintaining any system of stratification—that sanctions are more important then rewards. The most common reward for people toward the lower end of a hierarchy is absence of painful consequences. The problem is not how to get people into positions of power and privilege, but how to keep them out—how to reserve such positions for the incumbents and their progeny, relatives, friends, or allies, and how to, assure that someone will do those tasks that are necessary but undesirable, being dangerous, dirty, poorly rewarded, and even defiling. Thus stratification is primarily a system for maintaining power relations and the status quo of privilege allotment rather than one primarily for insuring recruitment of the most qualified people for the most important jobs (cf. Tumin 1953, Buckley 1959).

A caste system assigns each group of people a particular amount of power and privilege and requires them to remain exactly where they are in the system of ranked groups. In the traditional context they must fill the roles they have always filled, acquire their accustomed rewards and no others, interact outside the group only in prescribed ways symbolic of their status, and be punished if they deviate from these patterns. The caste is organized, almost by definition, for promotion of its self-interest, for self-defense and for self-regulation. It is held responsible for the behavior of all of its members and any sanction affecting one member may be extended so that it affects all. But the caste is not organized for achieving the broader interests of groups of castes or of the society at large except insofar as fulfilling its ascribed role may be assumed to benefit others.

As a self-interest group the caste is an effective kind of organization, functioning like a guild or union in many instances.

But it does so within the confines of its intrinsic power relative to other castes.[4] This power is, for most groups other than the dominant one(s), quite weak. By fractionating society, a caste system makes each group dependent upon its own resources for its overall power in the society. Because caste members regard their own caste as having common and unique interests and a distinct culture, they are unlikely to identify their interests with the interests of others, and especially not with those who are closest to them in the hierarchy and who might be the most effective allies, for those are the very castes with which they are competing most avidly for status and other advantages. Each caste is too small, too isolated, too weak, and too preoccupied with its own position, and with jockeying for position and advantage with castes near it in rank, to engineer major changes. Those groups which are powerful remain so; groups which are weak are unlikely to combine forces to confront the powerful ones, so they remain weak. Power relations become solidified and are perpetuated.

If change occurs, it must be either through a major change in the power of a single caste (e.g., loss or gain of land or clientele, access to office or to education) or through a change of the total socio-cultural environment (as in modernization and Westernization, when new avenues to power and prestige arise—avenues such as the vote—and when the old constraints decrease—constraints such as the importance attached to ritual status or traditional symbols of rank). Then people may be able to combine forces across the traditional caste lines or to

mobilize themselves for certain purposes without regard to caste at all. Many of the currents of change in caste systems are of this nature. Within a caste system, it is true that the interests of each group are best served by remaining separate. If the system were to be challenged or altered, however, it would be likely to become advantageous or even necessary for some groups to join forces. A caste system imposes structural, cultural, and psychological impediments to this. The caste system therefore comprises its own barrier against threats to privilege and power, as well as being a mechanism for perpetuating the status quo of rank. Caste organization keeps power from those without privilege and privilege from those without power. It is not a benevolent system—at best it may be paternalistic—but it is in theory, and more rarely in practice, an efficient one.

INTRINSIC CHANGE

All social systems undergo continual restructuring and redefinition as a consequence of the fact that their definition and structuring are the products of human interaction; in fact, a social system is an abstract description of interaction.

While interaction takes place within the cultural and social framework of its participants, it concurrently conditions or influences that framework. This fact has been analyzed for social rules, for definition of the self, and for small-scale, face-to-face situations by those sociologists and social psychologists who are often collectively termed "interactionists" (e.g., Harold Garfinkel, Erving Goffman, Tamotsu Shibutani), whose orientations derive from such men as George Herbert Mead, William I. Thomas, and especially Alfred Schutz. The same general fact has been analyzed for social structure on a broader scale by

---

[4]Lynch (1966:3), in his study of an untouchable caste of Agra, notes that "Caste is an adaptive structure through which its members can relate and re-relate themselves to members of other castes in terms of the potentialities provided to them by the socio-political environment in which they interact."

Edmund Leach, Fredrik Barth, and others. What this rather diverse collectivity of scholars share in their approach is a dynamic model of society emphasizing interaction and choice-making (what Firth-terms "social organization" [Firth 1956: 28ff., 40]) as crucial to that model.

Caste systems, as aspects of social structure, can be usefully analyzed from this perspective (cf. Marriott 1959). Interpersonal interaction is perhaps an even more conspicuous feature of social stratification, and hence caste, than of many other aspects of social structure. To describe a system of stratification, one abstracts from observations of interaction, from statements about interaction, and from statements or other evidence about the ideas and attitudes which condition interaction. A social hierarchy is continually redefined, affirmed, challenged, and validated by interaction even as interaction is continually constrained by the hierarchy.

Continual adjustment is inevitable because the context as well as the precise nature of interaction continually changes. Power relations change as technology, demography, economy, politics, law, religion, family, and other features of the overall situation alter. Moreover, individuals and groups do not define the hierarchical situation in identical ways. Hyman (1942) points out that subjective status may be quite different from accorded status, and either or both may be quite different from the status which would be assigned by objective application of status criteria. Also, the subjective view of status may be different depending upon whether the view is of "where I am in the hierarchy" or "where I deserve to be in the hierarchy," while accorded status may vary by the relative locations in the hierarchy of the ones judging and the ones being judged. These differential definitions of the hierarchical situation create what Festinger (1957) calls situations of cognitive dissonance, wherein there is a tendency to resolve the dissonance by bringing the various definitions into accord. The attempt to bring them into accord generates strain, resistance, and striving characteristic of caste systems.

Mobility movements of various sorts are the most dramatic of the many manifestations of change in caste systems because they are intentional and are recognized as such both by those who stand to gain and by those who stand to lose. But every caste every day is engaged in validating claims and parrying threats, enforcing conformity within the managing impressions without. Even in the absence of mobility movements—in the absence of overt striving— adjustments routinely occur which result in change in the caste hierarchy, through change in the idioms in which it is expressed, in the criteria by which it is defined, and in the order in which its constituent groups are ranked.

If one were to indulge in the perilous pastime of drawing physical analogies, the caste system might be compared to a liquid whose constituent molecules are continually moving, testing the limits of their environment (the container, the pressures of air and gravity, the temperature), taking advantage of every fissure, responding to every change, and consequently reshaping the mass in response to the changing environment. Where the analogy breaks down conspicuously is in the crucial sphere of purposive action—of meaning, choice, and the reflexive character of human interaction. Each human choice affects the conditions, the premises, for future choices, and in this manner the basic structure changes over time just as it varies in response to differing circumstances.

To study caste as social structure and to study its social functions, therefore, it is crucial that it be understood as a manifestation of interaction, of choices and decisions by people in situations defined by themselves in terms of their experience, their culture and society. That is, caste systems must be studied as social process (cf. Firth 1956:28).

ASSIMILATION VERSUS EXCLUSION

When some sections of a plural society enjoy conspicuous privileges denied to others, those others seem inevitably to wish to overcome that denial and will seek to do so if opportunity, as they define it, permits (cf. Berreman 1960a). If, as is the case in caste systems, assimilation to the high status groups and withdrawal from the system which accords them low status are both impossible, two means remain for acquisition of privilege by a low caste: (1) by emulation of high status groups, i.e., validating a claim to privilege through display of suitable attributes and (2) by organized power, i.e., validating a claim to privilege through exercise of political, economic, physical, or other power.

Orans (1959, 1965) has described as "the emulation-solidarity conflict," the dilemma of a tribal group in India faced with the choice of either emulating the dominant society in the expectation of achieving success on its terms (at the cost of loss of cohesion and distinctive group identity) or alternatively, maintaining the distinctiveness and identity of the group in order to achieve the power and intrinsic rewards which result from group cohesion (at the probable cost, in the short run at least, of losing out or being accorded low status in the dominant society). This is the common dilemma of the socially mobile or acculturating group in any society (cf. Berreman 1965a). The dilemma is especially acute in a caste situation when, as in the case of Negroes in American society, emulation of some aspects of the dominant culture is encouraged but

fails to accomplish assimilation and when, on the other hand, solidarity is discouraged as a means to bring changes in the hierarchy of power and privilege.

The contemporary plea for "black power" represents an awareness of this dilemma by Negroes—the recognition that without power, their struggle for privilege (even the privilege of equal treatment) is doomed. It includes the plea to members of the group that group interest be recognized as the way to achieve the power or influence which will serve that interest. This grows out of the awareness that the dominant group has long equated its group interest with self-interest and has long used power to serve those interests, and that it has equally long encouraged emulation rather than solidarity as the road to salvation for the very groups to which it has denied the reward which emulation is designed to achieve, namely, assimilation. That is, whites have used power to achieve their own ends but have discouraged or prevented its acquisition or use among Negroes, i.e., among those whose disadvantage they have defined as advantageous to themselves. The drive toward black power thus grows out of the experience that where assimilation is effectively denied, emulation in the absence of power simply leads to perpetuation of subordinate status and precludes the kinds of changes which would change that status or would challenge the system upon which it is based.

Here there is an important difference between caste systems and other systems of stratification. In a non-caste system, where power and privilege accompany achievable status, emulation is at least potentially effective and assimilation is a realistic goal, as most ethnic groups in America, for example, have found out. But in a caste situation, where these rewards are ascribed by birth, emulation is ineffective as long as the system persists and assimilation is impossible, as Negroes in America, for example, have found out (unless, of course, one can successfully conceal his identity and "pass" as a member of a high status group).

The only hope that a minority has of moving up in a caste hierarchy or of challenging the system is in the acquisition and exercise of power relative to other groups or relative to the society at large. This is true of castes in India just as it is of Negroes in America. In India upward mobility of castes is sought, validated, and rationalized through emulation but is achieved only in combination with power (cf. Bailey 1957:200-226; Cohn 1964: Lynch 1966:103ff.; Rowe 1960:56ff., 299ff., 1963; Sinha 1959, 1962; Srinivas 1956, 1966: 1-45, 89-117).

The current split in tactics advocated by different segments of the civil rights (or black liberation) movement in America, exemplified in the contrasting approaches of the National Association for the Advancement of Colored People and the Student Non-violent Coordinating Committee, represents primary reliance upon emulation and upon acquisition of power, respectively. It is not surprising that the latter choice has become widespread more recently than the former, for it is an outgrowth of frustration encountered in following the first choice. It is also not surprising that the second choice is more feared than the first—that it generates expression of a "white backlash"—for it has the potentiality of effectively challenging the hierarchical status quo which emulation did not. Precisely the same principles have been manifest in South Africa, in India, and other regions where the caste has confronted alternative values.

A mobile group's dilemma of emulation versus solidarity might be described, from the point of view of the dominant elements in society, as the "assimilation-exclusion conflict." Caste organization is a recurrent

means through which that conflict is resolved by the dominant group. A group which is new on the scene need not be assimilated into an existing group nor be excluded from participating in the society; it can be incorporated as a socially and culturally distinct entity, interacting with other groups in the society in ways which are rigorously defined by its assigned place in the hierarchy. The ways in which interaction is permitted are so defined as to keep the caste unassimilated (and unassimilable) into other groups as well as unexcluded (and unexcludable) from society.

The caste mechanism thus contrasts sharply with the method of enforced conversion, assimilation, or acculturation characteristic, for example, of Christianity and Islam, of Western imperialism, and of the Inca state. The ideology of caste is antithetical to the ideology of assimilation although it is perfectly possible for both ideologies to be expressed in one society with reference to different groups. It is precisely because they were regarded as unassimilable that Negroes in America have remained a caste while other ethnic groups, those regarded as assimilable, have disappeared into the "melting pot."

In a caste system, groups are incorporated essentially by being quarantined, each being assigned a private and exclusive cell in the established hierarchy, there to perform their role of interdependence with the larger society without contaminating or infringing on the social space of others, there to elaborate their own distinct culture and to accommodate to the cultures of others.

REDEFINITION

Wherever caste organization occurs, it is acutely jeopardized by modernization and nationalism. The reason for this is that under the impetus of these processes there is unprecedented pressure for, and the means to, cultural homogeneity: the direction is toward conformity, consensus, and the "replication of uniformity" in place of the traditional pluralism or cultural diversity (cf. Wallace 1962:26-29). Through such mechanisms as mass media and universal education, this pressure achieves results. McLuhan (1965:5) has noted that in America today the Negro, the teenager, and some other groups "can no longer be *contained,* in the political sense of limited association. They are now *involved* in our lives as we in theirs thanks to the electric media." This becomes increasingly the case with reference to caste groups in most societies today as modernization, accompanied by universal education and exposure to mass media, occurs. Cultural diversity diminishes; pluralism is undermined.

Common sources of information, common role-models, and common opportunities lead to common aspirations and expectations, common reference groups, common values, common attitudes and behavior. The diversity and dissensus requisite for caste systems are replaced by the homogeneity and consensus which are their nemeses. The threat of increased homogeneity in a caste system is likely to be resisted both from within and without particular castes. From without, it is resisted by the society at large (on behalf of the privileged castes who dominate it) as a threat to the system—to the hierarchical status quo. It is resisted from within particular castes as a threat to the organized efforts of the caste to promote its self-interest, e.g., to be accorded higher rank.

Under conditions of increasing cultural and social homogeneity, caste, as traditionally defined, becomes decreasingly relevant, appropriate, and effective as a mechanism for protecting self-interest, because the society and ideology within which it arose

and to which it was adapted are redefined. Individual mobility becomes possible and desirable, and the inertia of the caste group becomes a handicap. Individuals demand and achieve the means to acquire power and privilege by routes independent of caste organization, whether these be individual routes or routes involving groups other than castes. This subverts the basic principle of caste, that of birth-ascribed hierarchy. Caste becomes defined as an impediment to aspirations which can be realized if it is ignored or destroyed. The sanctions which functioned to maintain it weaken as the circumstance which supported them disappear. The recent history of the American Negro is a case in point. Attempts to change or eliminate caste systems bring conflict; this does not mean that the former system was eufunctional, but only that it protected major vested interests and that their beneficiaries are loath to relinquish them. One man's (or caste's) eufunction is another man's dysfunction.

These facts do not mean that castes simply disappear when the cultural and social environment changes, but that under these conditions castes inevitably alter their structures and functions. Whether or not they remain castes is a matter of definition and of time, for caste organization is an ideal type at one end of a continuum along which any particular group or society may move through time. "Like other structures," Watson suggests (1963:374), "they change, waxing, waning." Accordingly, we see that in India today, castes *(jatis)* join together, particularly in cities and in the context of contemporary electoral politics, to form associations with political, economic, and social power beyond the capability of any single caste (cf. Lynch 1966, Rudolph and Rudolph 1960). This is an effort toward the exercise of power by increasing the size and solidarity of the contending groups. In some instances in India the traditional *jatis* remain functional at the familial and marital level after they have diminished in relevance in other spheres (cf. Bailey 1960: 240). Cultural diversity seems to diminish in many modern, urban contexts, while structural distinctions between groups remain important, although the composition or boundaries of those groups are often redefined (e.g., caste associations in place of *jatis*). Thus, *jatis* may well disappear before caste does; caste boundaries are likely to be redefined, their identifying characteristics changed, and their functions altered or adapted, while the hierarchical, segmentary, group-interest-promoting, power-building principle persists.

At the other extreme we see avenues to individual mobility replacing traditional efforts at raising the status of the entire caste when assimilation is defined as possible. Individuals move from untouchability to high secular status, for example, entirely outside of the constraints of caste (cf. Isaacs 1964). People move out of villages into cities where traditional caste is less important in day-to-day social relations, employment, etc., where caste roles are less clearly defined and less relevant, and where the division of labor and economic and social interdependence are less closely tied to caste. In the United States, Negroes leave the South, become educated or join the army, and in this manner escape some of the more painful aspects of their caste status, by leaving the contexts in which it is most relevant.

People thus come to see traditional caste as irrelevant to new concerns. Those who benefited from it, of course, object to the changes and resist them. The confrontation of equalitarian and caste ideologies is a source of powerful conflict, for it threatens a basic change in social organization—an upsetting of heavy vested interests, a changed relationship among individuals and groups, a change from the articulation of diversity based on social separation and enforced by the free use of power to the replication of uniformity based on common experience, pervasive communication, and intensive interaction. This is the source of the explosive results wherever caste systems have been challenged by equalitarianism.

CONCLUSION

Caste organization has been viewed by many scholars as an integrative mechanism in society and as non-conflictive, based upon consensus and mutual respect. Thus, it has often been explicitly or implicitly adjudged individually and socially eufunctional, giving it as does to each individual a place in society and a sense of social worth. This tends toward the "conservative thesis" regarding social inequality described by Lenski (1966:5-17).

The view advanced here is that caste systems are held together by power, concentrated in certain groups, more than by consensus; that they work (and in that sense are functional) by facilitating the articulation of culturally diverse groups; that they are enabling devices for cultural pluralism and for the protection of privilege. They are threatened and they inevitably change when power relations change and also when consensus becomes the primary basis for social integration, for then pluralism —an essential ingredient of caste systems—is threatened or disappears. This approximates the view of social inequality which Lenski calls the "radical antithesis" (1966:5-17). That caste systems often succeed in articulating the activities of diverse groups does not mean that for individuals and groups such systems may not be starkly dysfunctional by limiting opportunities, thwarting aspirations, and precluding effective alternatives. Ultimately caste systems are likely to lead to overt conflict as mass media and other appurtenances of modernization afford opportunities for those who suffer denigration under caste organization to challenge it or throw it off, and as these opportunities are interpreted by other groups as threatening.

Caste is thus a means of ordering the relations among disparate groups. As a form of pluralism, it is an alternative to assimilation or eradication of groups in contact, as Toynbee has noted, although it is not the only alternative. Non-hierarchical pluralism is another possibility, but how often such pluralism in fact occurs is a moot point; perhaps hierarchy almost inevitably develops if pluralism persists, for power is never held equally, and group identity, loyalty, and self-interest may tend to cause it to be passed on within the group, i.e., frequently by birth. Caste organization can be effective in achieving ordered relations among groups for a time, but its ability to withstand universal education, mass media, equalitarian ideologies, and the elimination of monopolies on power which these engender is highly doubtful.

BIBLIOGRAPHY

BAILEY, F. G.
  1957 *Caste and the Economic Frontier,* Manchester University Press.

  1960 *Tribe, Caste and Nation.* Manchester: Manchester: Manchester University Press.

BENEDICT, BURTON
  1962 Stratification in Plural Societies. *American Anthropologist* 64:1235-1246.

BERREMAN, GERALD D.
  1960a Caste in India and the United States. *American Journal of Sociology* 66:120-127.

  1960b Cultural Variability and Drift in the Himalayan Hills. *American Anthropologist* 62:774-794.

  1962 Caste, Racism and Stratification. *Contributions to Indian Sociology* 6:122-125.

  1964a Aleut Reference Group Alienation, Mobility and Acculturation. *American Anthropologist* 66:231-250.

  1964b Fear Itself: An Anthropologist's View. *Bulletin of the Atomic Scientists* 20:9:8-11.

  1965 The Study of Caste Ranking in India. *Southwestern Journal of Anthropology* 21:115-129.

  1966 "Caste in Cross-Cultural Perspective," in *Japan's Invisible Race: Caste in Culture and Personality* (ed. by G. DeVos and H. Wagatsuma), pp. 275-324. Berkeley: University of California Press.

  1967a "Stratification, Pluralism and Interaction: A Comparative Analysis of Caste," in *Caste and Race: Comparative Approaches* (ed. by A. de Reuck and J. Knight), pp. 45-73. Boston: Little Brown and Co.

  1967b "The Concept of Caste," in *International Encyclopedia of the Social Sciences.* New York: Crowell, Collier and Macmillan Company (in press).

BUCKLEY, WALTER
  1958 Stratification and the Functional Theory of Social Differentiation. *American Sociological Review* 23:369-375.

  1959 A Rejoiner to Functionalists Dr. Davis and Dr. Levy. *American Sociological Review* 24:84-86.

COHN, B. S.
  1954 *The Camars of Senapur: A Study of the Changing Status of a Depressed Caste.* Unpublished Ph. D. dissertation, Cornell University, Ithaca, New York, (Also, microfilm, University of Michigan, Ann Arbor, Michigan.)

DAVIS, KINGSLEY
1949 *Human Society.* New York: The Macmillan Company.

1953 Reply. *American Sociological Review* 18:394-397.

1959 The Abominable Heresy: A Reply to Dr. Buckley. *American Sociological Review* 24:82-83.

DAVIS, KINGSLEY, and WILBERT E. MOORE
1945 Some Principles of Stratification. *American Sociological Review* 10:242-249.

DEVOS, GEORGE
1966 "Motivational Components of Caste," in *Japan's Invisible Race: Caste in Culture and Personality* (ed. by G. DeVos and H. Wagatsuma), pp. 325-384. Berkeley: University of California Press.

FESTINGER, LEON
1957 *A Theory of Cognitive Dissonance.* Evanston: Row, Peterson.

FIRTH, RAYMOND
1956 *Elements of Social Organization. 2nd ed.* London: Watts and Co.

GHURYE, G. S.
1952 *Caste and Class in India.* New York: Philosophical Library.

HYMAN, HERBERT
1942 *The Psychology of Status,* New York: Archives of Psychology no. 269.

ISAACS, HAROLD R.
1964 *India's Ex-Untouchables.* New York: The John Day Co.

KARVE, IRAWATI
1961 *Hindu Society: An Interpretation.* Poona: Deccan College Postgraduate and Research Institute.

LENSKI, GERHARD
1966 *Power and Privilege: A Theory of Social Stratification.* New York: McGraw Hill.

LEVI-STRAUSS, CLAUDE
1966 The Disappearance of Man, *New York Review of Books* 7:1:6-8.

LEVY, MARION J.
1959 Functionalism: A Reply to Dr. Buckley. *American Sociological Review* 24:83-84.

LEWIS, OSCAR
1959 *Five Families: Mexican Case Studies in the Culture of Poverty.* New York: Basic Books.

LYNCH, OWEN M.
1966 *The Politics of Untouchability: Social Structure and Social Change in a City of India.* Unpublished Ph. D. dissertation, Columbia University, New York, New York.

MARRIOTT, McKIM
1959 Interactional and Attributional Theories of Caste Ranking. *Man in India* 56: 171-222.

McLUHAN, MARSHALL
1965 *Understanding Media: The Extensions of Man.* New York: McGraw-Hill (paperback).

MILLS, C. WRIGHT
1963 "The Sociology of Stratification," in *Power, Politics and People: The Collected Essays of C. Wright Mills* (ed. by I. Horowitz), pp. 305-323. New York: Ballatine Books.

MOORE, WILBERT
1953 Comment. *American Sociological Review* 18:397.

NADEL, S. F.
1954 Caste and Government in Primitive Society. *Journal of the Anthropological Society of Bombay* 8:9-22.

ORANS, MARTIN
1959 A Tribe in Search of a Great Tradition: The Emulation-Solidarity Conflict. *Man in India* 39:108-114.

1965 *The Santal: A Tribe in Search of a Great Tradition.* Detroit: Wayne State University Press.

PIERIS, RALPH
1952 Caste, Ethos, and Social Equilibrium. *Social Forces* 30:409-415.

ROWE, WILLIAM L.
 1960 *Social and Economic Mobility in a Low-Caste North Indian Community.* Unpublished Ph. D. dissertation, Cornell University, Ithaca, New York. (Also, microfilm, University of Michigan, Ann Arbor, Michigan.)

 1963 *The New Chauhans: A Caste Mobility Movement in North India.* Center for South Asia Studies, Institute of International Studies, University of California, Berkeley (mimeographed).

RUDOLPH, LLOYD I. and SUSAN H.
 1960 The Political Role of India's Caste Associations. *Pacific Affairs* 33:5-22.

SINHA, SURAJIT
 1959 Bhumij-Kshatriya Social Movement in South Manbhum. *Bulletin of the Department of Anthropology* (Calcutta) 8:2: 9-32.

 1962 State Formation and Rajput Myth in Tribal Central India. *Man in India.* 42:35-80.

SMITH, M. G.
 1960 "Social and Cultural Pluralism," in *Social and Cultural Pluralism in the Caribbean,* pp. 763-785. Annals of the New York Academy of Sciences, vol. 83, art. 5.

SRINIVAS, M. N.
 1956 A Note on Sanskritization and Westernization. *Far Eastern Quarterly* 15:481-496.

 1966 *Social Change in Modern India.* Berkeley: University of California Press.

TOYNBEE, ARNOLD J.
 1934 *A Study of History,* vol. 2. London: Oxford University Press.

TUMIN, MELVIN M.
 1953 Some Principles of Stratification: A Critical Analysis. *American Sociological Review* 18:387-394.

WALLACE, A. F. C.
 1962 *Culture and Personality.* New York: Random House.

WATSON, JAMES B.
 1963 Caste as a Form of Acculturation. *Southwestern Journal of Anthropology* 19: 356-379.

WRONG, DENNIS H.
 1959 The Functional Theory of Stratification: Some Neglected Considerations. *American Sociological Review* 24:772-782.

---

4.   THEORIES OF REVOLUTION AND RACE RELATIONS*

Leo Kuper

This article, which uses African countries for support, discusses the relationship between race and class in African revolutions. By a thorough analysis of empirical data, Kuper concludes that racial rather than economic factors were crucial in these countries revolutionary patterns.

I

Most contemporary theories of revolution are derived from the analysis of conflict between social classes in racially homogeneous societies, and they may not be very illuminating when applied to situations of revolutionary struggle between racial groups. This is the problem I discuss in the present paper, and my purpose, in general, is to raise some questions concerning the applicability of theories of class revolution to racial revolution.

The main source of many of these theories is the Marxist theory of revolution as a product of a dialectical process of polarization between classes, defined in their rela-

tionship to the means of production, and I shall deal with it in the more general terms of the role of economic stratification in racial revolutions.

I shall define revolution as a form of "internal war"[1] in which there is a violent assumption of power and substantial change in the structure and values of the society.[2] I shall exclude from the concept of revolution used in this paper internal wars between sections which occupy roughly the same level in the hierarchy (as for example Ibo and Hausa), and struggles for liberation from colonial rule, save where the structure of the colonial society comprised also a settled racially distinct dominant section (as for example, a stratum of white settlers or of pastoral ruling aristocracies). Thus, the cases of racial revolution (or attempted revolution) I have in mind include the revolution of Hutu against Tutsi in Rwanda

SOURCE
From *Comparative Studies in Society and History,*
**Vol. 13, January, 1971. Reprinted by permission
of the author,** *Comparative Studies in Society and
History* **and Cambridge University Press.**

*The research on which this paper is based was supported by a grant from the National Science Foundation. I would like to acknowledge gratefully this support, help from my research assistant Sondra Hale, and criticism of an earlier draft by Sam Surace.

[1]Following Harry Eckstein's use of internal war, namely 'any resort to violence within a political order to change its constitution, rulers, or policies' (1965: 133).

[2]See Bienen (1968: Section 3) for critical comments concerning the emphasis on change in conceptions of revolution.

(where the Belgian tutelary power supported the domination of the pastoral Tutsi over the agricultural Hutu until almost the final stage of independence), the revolution of Africans against Arabs in Zanzibar (where the British supported the Sultan and the Arab oligarchy), and the revolutionary movement of Africans and Indians against white domination in South Africa in the period 1948-64. The Algerian revolution, though not a revolution involving racially different groups, is also relevant, since it has provided a model for racial revolutionary struggle.

II

If a major theme in revolutionary theory is the Marxist dialectic in the economic process, resulting in the polarization of classes, the variations on this theme appear to exhaust almost every logical possibility.[3] There are theories of a predisposing condition in immiserization of the masses, or in economic advance,[4] or in economic growth followed by recession, or in the disjunction between desire (or aspiration) and reality,

---

[3]See Harry Eckstein (1965: 136-40) for a discussion of the somewhat chaotic abundance of hypotheses about the etiology of revolutions, and his listing of different emphases on 'intellectual' factors, economic factors, social structure and social mobility, political factors, and such social processes as rapid or uneven social changes. See also the comments by Aron (1965: 250 ff.) on the different emphases in Marx and Tocqueville, both explaining political conflicts in terms of social conflicts, but Tocqueville maintaining 'the specificity, at least the relative autonomy, of the political order'.

[4]Olson (1963: 543) makes the interesting point that there is nothing inconsistent in saying that both rapid economic growth and rapid economic decline would tend toward political instability, and that it is economic stability that should be regarded as conducive to social and political tranquility.

or in the tension between the processes and relations of production (such as has characterized South African society for over a generation). What these situations have in common is that they involve disequilibrium, between classes as in the immiserization of the masses, or within a class, as in the disequilibrium resulting from economic progress followed by recession. The theories may then be reduced to the more basic theory that economic disequilibrium is a precondition, or precipitant, of revolutions between classes. Since classes are defined in economic terms, or largely in economic terms, the basic theory may be somewhat tautologous.

In regard to the relevance of these theories for racial revolutions, two extreme positions may be taken. The first position attaches overwhelming significance to economic relations, arguing that racial discrimination is only found in association with economic exploitation, and that racial conflict is simply a particular expression of class conflict. The causes of racial revolution are therefore the same as those of class revolution, for example, polarization of the races in their relationship to the means of production. The second extreme position emphasizes the absolute primacy of the racial structure. Racial revolutions are viewed as inherent or endemic in structures of racial domination, opportunity being the precondition or precipitant. From this perspective, economic change is somewhat marginally relevant to the preconditions or precipitants of revolution.

THEORIES OF REVOLUTION AND RACE RELATIONS

There is a long-standing and continuing controversy between advocates of these different perspectives. In the U.S.A., shortly after the Second World War, Cox (1948) sought to establish the origins of racial discrimination in the growth of capitalism, and to demonstrate that black and white workers shared common class interests. In the U.S.A. today, the failure of black and white proletariat to combine, and the clashes of interest between them, lend support to the contrary view of many black revolutionaries that the conflict is essentially racial.[5] There is a similar controversy in the interpretation of African revolutions, which take the manifest form of racial conflict. Marxists find in these a class basis. Thus, with reference to Zanzibar, Bochkaryov (1964: 13-15), writing in *New Times*, charged that the British colonial administration and the imperialist press sought to interpret as racialist, a revolution which arose out of class differences and was directed against the big landowners and the Sultan. Rey, in the *New Left Review* (1964:31), viewed the revolution in Zanzibar as a social, not an ethnic, revolution, carried out by groups representing, first and foremost, the Zanzibar City proletariat, but supported after the revolution by a general rallying of all the exploited against the Arab ruling class. In South Africa, these different perspectives of the society in terms of class or race were influential in the political division of Africans into two parties, the African National Congress being more Marxist in its ideological orientation, while the Pan-Africanist Congress emphasized the primacy of racial discrimination against Africans (Kuper, 1965: Chapter 23). Fanon (1966: 32-3, first publication in 1961), examined this problem of class and race, no doubt largely in the context of the Algerian revolution, and emphasized the racial aspect, but with a complex lyricism, which gives an elusive quality to his meaning. Standing Marxism somewhat on its head (the phrase used in

the translation is that Marxist analysis must be "slightly stretched"), he argued that:

"In the colonies the economic substructure is also a superstructure. The cause is the consequence; you are rich because you are white, you are white because you are rich. . . It is neither the act of owning factories, nor estates, nor a bank balance which distinguishes the governing classes. The governing race is first and foremost those who come from elsewhere, those who are unlike the original inhabitants, 'the others.' "

III

Both aspects of Fanon's paradox, "you are rich because you are white" and "you are white because you are rich," are in fact inaccurate. But they do bring out a basic problem in the controversy, namely the difficulty of clearly distinguishing racial divisions from class divisions, and hence the difficulty of assessing the relative significance of class and race in racial revolutions. In the abstract the terms are quite distinct: race refers to physical differences, whether measured by 'objective' criteria or by social definitions, and class refers to socio-economic differentiation, whether defined by "objective" measures such as the relationship to the means of production, or by social perception. In the concrete situation, however, it may be difficult to differentiate the two structures. Race and class divisions generally overlap. Race and class may be closely related genetically, since a system of stratification which is socially defined as a class system, may have originated in a system of racial stratification, the contemporary class differences coinciding appreciably with racial differences, as in many Latin-American and West Indian societies. And separation of the phenomena may be further complicated by the presence of

[5]See Timothy Ricks (1969: 21-6) and Cruse (1968: Chapter 10) for a discussion of some aspects of this controversy in the U.S.A.

socio-economic differentiation within each of the racial divisions. The problems raised by this merging of the phenomena can only be resolved partly. They are the empirical basis for the ideological controversy, whether racial stratification is epiphenomenal and simply a particular manifestation of class stratification, or whether racial differences provide an independent basis in the genesis and persistence of social stratification.

If racial divisions and class divisions coincided, so that, for example, the whites in a particular society were all members of the bourgeoisie, and the blacks were all members of the proletariat or peasants, some insight into the relative significance of race or class could no doubt be derived from a comparison of revolutions in such societies with revolutionary struggles between social classes in racially homogeneous societies. Where economic differentiation and racial stratification are in some measure divergent, as in the contemporary revolutions involving racial groups, interpretation becomes exceedingly complex.

The two recent revolutions, in Zanzibar and in Rwanda, may serve as an illustration of some of the complexities of the relationship between race and class, or race, class and caste.[6]

In the Protectorate of Zanzibar, comprising Zanzibar and Pemba Island, the main racial and ethnic sections were the Shirazis, Mainland Africans, Arabs and Asians; there were also small numbers of Comorians, Goans and Europeans. The total population, according to the 1958 Census, was some 299,000, comprising over 165,000 on Zanzibar Island, and almost 134,000 on Pemba Island. The Shirazis were the largest section, constituting in 1948 over half the population on both islands (see Table below). The Shirazis, who claimed that they had intermingled with Persians who migrated to Zanzibar in about the tenth century, most nearly correspond to indigenous African groups. The second largest section was Mainland African, comprising in 1948, almost one-fifth of the total population, that is 25.1 percent of the population on

[6]See Rene Lemarchand, 'Revolutionary Phenomena in Stratified Societies: Rwanda and Zanzibar' (1968), for an analysis of the problem of revolutionary change in racially or ethnically stratified societies.

Distribution of Population, Zanzibar Protectorate, 1948*

Section	Zanzibar Island NO.	%	Pemba Island NO.	%	Total Zanzibar Protectorate NO.	%
Arab	13,977	9.3	30,583	26.7	44,560	16.9
Indian and Goan	13,705	9.2	2,187	1.8	15,892	6.1
Mainland African	37,502	25.1	13,878	12.1	51,380	19.5
Shirazi	81,150	54.2	67,330	58.8	148,480	56.2
Other	3,241	2.2	609	0.6	3.850	1.3
Total	149,575	100.0	114,587	100.0	264,162	100.0

*Source: Notes on the Census of the Zanzibar Protectorate, 1948, Tables I and XV. A small number of persons who did not state their tribal origins, I have classified with Mainland Africans.

Zanzibar Island, and 12.1 percent on Pemba.[7] Figures are nor available for 1958, but in that census, 10.9 percent of the population on Zanzibar Island and 6.7 percent on Pemba were shown as born on the East African mainland: most of these would be Mainland African. The foreign born population in general was an older population. 81.4 percent being over twenty years of age as compared with 51.1 percent of the local born, and had a higher sex ratio, 215.9 males per 100 females as compared with 101.7 (Zanzibar, 1960: 32, 35). The indications therefore are of an appreciable adult male African migrant population. The Arab population which included a variety of Arab groups, was the third largest section: in 1948. Arabs comprised 16.9 percent of the total population, i.e. 9.3 percent on Zanzibar and 26.7 percent on Pemba (Zanzibar, 1953: 2, 4). Mainland Africans, that is to say, were almost three times as numerous as Arabs on Zanzibar Island, whereas on Pemba Island they were less than one-half the number of Arabs. Finally, Asians, mostly Indians and some Goans, comprised 6.1 percent of the total population in 1958, the great majority residing on Zanzibar Island, and indeed in Zanzibar City (Zanzibar, 1960: 18, 21).

Zanzibar economy rested largely on the marketing of cloves, and on subsistence agriculture and fishing. There was some employment by Government, some development of commerce, but little in industry, and that mainly in the processing of foods.[8] Cloves, the main export, were uncertain both as a crop and as a commodity. There was an appreciable seasonal immigration from the mainland for the picking of cloves, most of the plantations being located on Pemba Island. The dependence of the economy on cloves was such that decline in the world market for cloves created a serious economic crisis for the government, and resulted in a reduction of social services in the period immediately preceding the revolution.

It is difficult to give a clear picture of the distribution of resources and occupations among the different sections. The image of Arabs as senior bureaucrats and large plantation owners, of Indians as merchants, and of Africans, both Shirazi and Mainland, as fishermen, cultivators and laborers is of course, quite false. Most Arabs, Shirazis and Africans were poor, and there were many poor Indians. What can be said is that senior bureaucrats and many of the large plantation owners were Arab, that merchants tended to be Indian, that most of the cultivators and fishermen were Shirazi, and that most Mainland Africans were either employed as laborers in Zanzibar City, where many of them lived, or they were occupied as squatters or seasonally in clove-picking. There was, however, considerable overlapping of the occupations followed by members of different sections. Middleton and Campbell (1965: 39) comment on an intermingling of Arab and Shirazi plantation owners on Pemba Island, but not on Zanzibar Island. Lofchie (1969: 293-309) examines landownership (measured by number of clove trees), occupational distribution and access

---

[7]*Notes on the Census of the Zanzibar Protectorate 1948* (Zanzibar Protectorate, 1953: 11-12). There are difficulties in specifying the numbers of different sections in the 1958 Census, since the "racial grouping" is Afro-Arab, Asian other than Arab, European, Somali and other. Political agitation had preceded the Census, and some persons, at the instance of political parties, returned themselves as Zanzibaris (*Report on the Census of the Population of Zanzibar Protectorate, 1958.* Zanzibar Protectorate, 1960: 17). Composition of the population had probably not changed greatly since 1948.

[8]For figures of employment in Government, Commerce and Industry, see Zanzibar Protectorate, *Labour Report for the Years 1960 and 1961* (Zanzibar: Government Printer, 1963), 11-12.

to education in the year 1948, when a survey was conducted; the tables he presents show appreciable overlapping. Lofchie concludes "that Zanzibar's major communal groups were differentiated by economic and social status" and that "Zanzibaris of different races did not share sufficient common occupational or economic interests to create politically meaningful bonds of solidarity across racial lines" (306). But it is here

that difficulties begin to arise, since the figures show similarities between the different sections,[9] and there is need for a valid measure of similarities and differences in socio-economic situation (occupation, landownership and education) and for a valid

[9]Tables 3, 4 and 5 are here reproduced (Lofchie, 1969: 303-5).

Table 3. Landownership in Zanzibar by Racial Community, 1948

| NUMBER OF TREES | PERCENTAGE OF PARCELS | | | | TOTAL NUMBER OF OWNERS |
	ARAB	ASIAN	SHIRAZI	MAINLAND AFRICAN	
3,000 or more	68.8	31.2	—	—	240
1,000–2,999	56.1	6.1	20.2	17.7[a]	570
250–999	51.9	5.2	33.8	9.1	3,635
50–249	14.5	0.3	74.2	11.0	13,680
Less than 50	16.0	0.1	66.6	17.3	10,250

[a]This figure, which represents 100 Mainland African landowners, was recorded entirely in Pemba.

Table 4. Occupational Distribution in Zanzibar by Racial Community, 1948

| OCCUPATIONAL LEVEL | PERCENTAGE OF WORKERS | | | | TOTAL NUMBER OF WORKERS |
	ARAB	ASIAN	INDIGENOUS AFRICAN	MAINLAND AFRICAN	
Upper	4.2	95.8	—	—	120
Upper middle	26.0	59.2	6.3	8.5	710
Middle (non-manual)	26.1	33.3	27.3	13.3	5,400
Middle (manual)	6.0	34.9	12.1	47.0	1,735
Lower Middle	17.1	4.7	54.1	24.1	35,160
Lower	13.5	0.9	36.9	48.7	14,635

Table 5. Access to Higher Education in Zanzibar by Racial Community, 1948

| EDUCATIONAL LEVEL | PERCENTAGE OF STUDENTS | | | | TOTAL NUMBER OF STUDENTS |
	ARAB	ASIAN	INDIGENOUS AFRICAN	MAINLAND AFRICAN	
Standards I–VI	30.4	7.8	40.2	21.6	12,205
Standards VII–IX	29.9	41.3	12.8	16.0	1,440
Standards X–XII	31.4	46.8	3.2	18.6	620

The figures are for 1948, and though they are the best available, they relate to a period some fifteen to sixteen years before the revolution.

methodology for drawing conclusions as to their political significance.

The population of Rwanda at the time of the revolution was some 2.5 million, predominantly Hutu (about 85 percent), ruled by an aristocracy drawn from the Tutsi (totalling about 14 percent) and including small numbers of Twa. The sections varied somewhat in physical characteristics, perceiving their differences in terms of racial stereotypes.[10]

The country was, and continues to be, exceedingly poor and densely populated.[11] Its economy rested essentially on subsistence farming and herding.   Productivity was greatly limited by geographic environmental factors, by ignorance, by poor health consequent upon malaria, intestinal parasites, tuberculosis, dysentery and malnutrition, by the rudimentary techniques of hoe cultivation and by the social and political order (Leurquin, 1960: Part I).   With a narrow margin over bare subsistence, famine constantly threatened.   Coffee was the main cash crop and export.   There was little urbanization, the most important agglomeration having a population of about 20,000, and little industrialization, that being mainly in mining.   Foreigners largely controlled both industry and commerce. The different sectors of industry, commerce and agriculture provided some employment for, on the one hand, the "proletarized worker, torn from his tribal roots, living only from his work . . . and, on the other hand, the peasant laborer, the occasional plantation worker, the roadman's or foreman's often undependable day worker" *(Ruanda-Urundi, Economy I,* 1960: 16). About 54,000 were so employed in 1958.   In addition, there was a small professional stratum.

The nature of the distribution of resources between the sections is conveyed by the description usually applied to Rwanda, namely caste or feudal society.   Maquet compares the relationship between Tutsi and Hutu to that between nobles and peasants in the Ancien Regime, or, in certain respects, to the relation between industrial capitalists and proletarian workers in Europe in the nineteenth century (1964: 552). The two sections were distinguished by their hereditary occupations of agriculture for the Hutu and pastoralism for the Tutsi. In fact, many Hutu looked after cattle and many Tutsi were not engaged in pastoral activities, but, nevertheless, a Hutu was always a man of the hoe, and a Tutsi a man of the cow (Maquet, 1964: 553). Economic and political relations were organized in such a way that rights over cattle provided some exemption from manual labor for the Tutsi.

Maquet, drawing on an analogy to the concept of surplus profit in Marxist class analysis, argues that the system was possible by reason of an agricultural surplus: he was obliged to add, however, that agricultural production was very little above the subsistence level, and that both surplus and malnutrition often co-existed (1964: 554). The Tutsi appropriated the agricultural "surplus" by the effective monopoly of government, the imposition of the corvee and of heavier taxes on the Hutu, and the system of clientage through which the client, in exchange for protection and the use of

_____

[10]I am following Maquet here, but I do not know how adequate his evidence is.   Maquet (1964: 553) writes of the differences between Hutu and Tutsi that they were distinct, 'enfin par leur apparence physique: les Tutsi etaient grands, minces, au teint clair; les Hutu, de taille moyenne, trapus, de peau foncee. Tels etaient au moins les stereotypes acceptes par tous les Rwandais memes s'ils ne se verifiaent que chez certains individus'. The Twa are pygmoid.

[11]In *Rwanda Carrefour d'Afrique* (May-June 1967: 21), the caption to a photograph of a child beside a banana tree quotes the dictum: 'sous chaque feuille de bananier se cache un Rwandais'.

cattle, undertook to render services and produce to his patron.[12]

Given the low level of economic productivity, there could not have been a great difference in standard of living between many Tutsi and Hutu. The Tutsi however constituted the privileged section. They provided the ruling class, the aristocracy of wealth, the warriors; they appropriated the control over cattle, and they enjoyed a more favored position than the Hutu in the system of clientage, though Tutsi were also involved as clients in a hierarchical system which extended throughout the society. But the near monopoly by the Tutsi of power, privilege and wealth was an attribute of the Tutsi viewed as a collectivity. Seen as individuals or as family units, in their daily routine, there was considerable similarity between Tutsi and Hutu in material conditions of living.

Leurquin, in a careful study of the standard of living of the rural populations of Ruanda-Urundi during the period from September 1955 to August 1956, provides some measure of similarity between Tutsi and Hutu in terms of subsistence production, daily consumption of food, distribution of cattle, monetary revenue, and expenditure. His sample of six regions included four regions in Rwanda. Traditional authorities, from whom a measure of collaboration was necessary, traders with large establishments at the beginning of the inquiry, and persons living in indigenous towns and non-traditional centers ("centres extra-coutumiers"), were excluded from the study (132-3). Thus the sample excludes chiefs and subchiefs, almost entirely Tutsi, and the functionaries and bureaucrats living in the urbanized zones, also predominantly Tutsi (203,

250, 277-8). These were the categories of rich Tutsi (278).

The most important economic sector for the sample population was production for subsistence which contributed two-thirds in money value, while revenue from the money economy contributed one-third (179, 274). The table on the next page provides a comparison between Hutu and Tutsi in the sample population, in Rwanda-Urundi: where Leurquin gives separate comparative figures for Rwanda and Urundi, these are shown.

The figures given in the table are averages, but it is clear from the relatively small differences between Tutsi and Hutu in the annual value of subsistence production (4,439 francs as compared with 4,249 francs per family) and in the annual value of monetary revenue (2,795 francs as against 2,189 francs per family) that there must have been considerable continuity and overlapping of standards of living in the two sections. The main difference is in the annual production of milk (181 litres per family compared with 66 litres) and in the distribution of cattle (2.6, 1.2, 2.4 and 1.6 as compared with 1.7, 0.7, 1.2 and 0.5 in the Rwanda regions).

Leurquin (1960: 203-4), in summarizing the position, comments that the material superiority of Tutsi over Hutu is always established by reference to the holders of positions of authority, that is chiefs and subchiefs, and civil servants, categories virtually excluded from the sample. He points out that the cleavage: Tutsi = pastoralism = riches, Hutu = agriculture = poverty has ceased to be always true. In regions where an artisan category had developed, or where coffee plantations had multiplied, there were to be found rich Hutu, while Tutsi small-owners of cattle, deprived of their prerogatives and obliged to tend the soil, often proved to be mediocre cultivators: in a group of forty families studied at Karama,

---

[12]*Rwanda Carrefour d'Afrique* in a discussion of the animal resources of Rwanda quotes the Tutsi proverb, 'Toi, vache qui m'epargne la honte et la fatigue de la houe' (April 1965: 8).

Comparison of the Value of Subsistence Production and of Monetary Revenue, Quantity of Milk Consumed, and Distribution of Cattle per Family—for Tutsi and Hutu in Rwanda and Urundi in the Period September 1955–August 1956

CATEGORY	VALUE OF SUBSISTENCE PRODUCTION (FRANCS)[1]	VALUE OF MONETARY REVENUE (FRANCS)[2]	PRODUCTION OF MILK (LITRES)[3]	DISTRIBUTION OF CATTLE BY REGION[4]					
				RWANDA				URUNDI	
				VALLEE de l'AKANYARU	BWANA-MUKARE	NDUGA	KINYAGA	BUYENZI	MUGAMBA
Tutsi	4,439	2,795	181	2.6	1.2	2.4	1.6	1.9	0.5
Hutu	4,249	2,189	66	1.7	0.7	1.2	0.5	0.3	0.2

Sources: All figures are from Philippe Leurquin, *Le Niveau de Vie des Populations Rurales du Ruanda-Urundi* (Louvain: Editions Nauwelaerts, 1960).
[1] Table 26, p. 203.
[2] Table 50, p. 278.
[3] pp. 229–30.
[4] Table 45, p. 263.

eighteen Tutsi of thirty-four possessed no cattle and in Rukoma a Tutsi died of hunger, because he had no servants and had never learnt to cultivate.   Leurquin comments that the modest advantage enjoyed by Tutsi in the subsistence economy seemed to be concentrated in certain sectors, the most marked being in the production of milk. "Pour le reste, les differences de caste ne suffisent plus aujourd 'hui a expliquer les differences de revenue en milieu rural."

IV

Among the many difficulties of interpretation which flow from the lack of correspondence between racial and economic differentiation, there is first of all the problem of the differential impact of economic change on different strata within each of the racial sections. Then, in view of this diversity within each racial section, there is the problem whether it is meaningful to define the racial sections as entities.   What is the relationship between collective attributes and individual situation? In what sense were the Tutsi the dominant caste in Rwanda, or Arabs the ruling stratum in Zanzibar? Finally, there is the problem of the disjunction between the objective situation and the perception of it, facilitated precisely by the lack of coincidence between racial and economic differentiation.

First, in regard to economic change, it cannot be assumed that the consequences are the same for all members of a social class, and such general measures as economic growth and *per capita* income may be quite misleading in the analysis of class structures.[13]   The assumption of a uniform

[13]See Anthony Oberschall, 'Group Violence: Some Hypotheses and Empirical Uniformities'. paper presented at the meeting of the American Sociological Association, San Francisco, 1969, and Mancur Olson, 'Rapid Growth as a Destabilizing Force', *Journal of Economic History*, 23 (1963: 529-52).

impact of economic change on members of a racial category may be even more misleading in the analysis of racial structures. The economic position of professionals and businessmen of the subject race may continue to improve, while that of the workers remains constant or deteriorates: or the position of the urban proletariat may improve, and that of the peasantry deteriorate. Similarly, the economic changes may have quite varied consequences for different strata in the dominant group. It is possible that the crucial stimulus which serves as a catalyst of revolution is some particular combination of these consequences for different strata within the dominant and subordinate racial sections.

The second difficulty arises from the equating of collective attributes with individual attributes.   Thus, it is a very common practice among scholars, as well as laymen, to describe Indians in East Africa or South Africa as a trading class. The position varies in the different countries from situations in which most trade is (or was) in Indian hands, as in Zanzibar, to situations in which Indian trading is a negligible portion of the total trade, as in South Africa. In the case of Zanzibar, there is no published information regarding the distribution of occupations among Indians at about the time of the revolution, though there is earlier evidence, in a proposal for a survey conducted by Batson in 1946, that "among the Indians there are a great many petty traders who are as poverty-striken as the natives or even more so, and undernourishment exists, particularly among the Hindus" (1948: 26).   Most Indians at that time were engaged as uncertified professional workers, clerical personnel, skilled and semiskilled workers, vendors, itinerant peddlers and unskilled laborers (Lofchie, 1965: 88-9). Clearly the fact that the main traders and financiers in Zanzibar were Indian by no means constitutes Indians as a trading class.

In South Africa, the great majority of Indians are working class and poor. In what sense then can they be described as a trading class? If Indians, as a category, are legally entitled to acquire the means of production in some areas of South Africa, and if in fact a few Indians have started industrial enterprises and a larger number have entered into commerce, does this constitute a class of Indian bourgeoisie? If the criterion is the theoretical possibility of mobility into the ruling stratum, or the legal right to acquire productive property, then the Marxist distinction between bourgeoisie and proletariat would be quite meaningless outside of such countries as South Africa, where the laws largely deny Africans the right to acquire productive property.

Similar problems arise with reference to the Tutsi caste in Rwanda and the Arab oligarchy in Zanzibar. The fact that the rulers were Tutsi or Arab, and monopolized positions of power traditionally and under colonial administration, by no means implies that these qualities of power of the dominant caste or oligarchy inhered in the rank and file of impoverished Tutsi or Arabs. Nor do the attributes of Tutsi or Arabs viewed as a collectivity necessarily affect the class situation of commoners. And yet in certain circumstances, as for example in the type of society van den Berghe characterizes as "Herrenvolk Democracy" such as South Africa and U.S.A. (1969: 73), the attributes of the racial section clearly affect the situation of the individual members of that race. Thus the monopoly of political power by whites in South Africa so sharply differentiates the economic position or life chances of white and black workers that they can hardly be regarded as sharing a common class situation. The relationship between collective and individual attributes is clearly an empirical question, requiring systematic analysis and more refined categories than such descriptions as Tutsi dominant caste.

The perceptions of the structure of the society may be at least as significant in the revolutionary process as the "objective reality" and they may be quite varied in their relationship to that reality.[14] Indeed, part of the revolutionary struggle consists essentially in a conflict of ideologies, and the attempt to mobilize sections of the population behind particular perceptions of the structure of the society. The very complexity of the relations of race, class and caste in a society, and the diversity of positions within the structure of that society, would encourage these varied perceptions. If Mainland Africans in Zanzibar perceived Arabs collectively as racial oppressors, or if Hutu peasants perceived Tutsi collectively as a dominant caste, what significance is to be attached to the fact that the great majority of Arabs and Tutsi did not share in the enjoyment or in the exercise of wealth and power, and had no prospects of access to wealth and power?

V

Given the complex interrelations between racial and economic differentiation, and the consequent problems of interpretation, is it possible to test the relative significance of racial factors and of economic factors? Perhaps, the distinction used by Dumont (1966: 17-32) between the encompassing principle and that which is encompassed may be helpful. Thus, when Lofchie (1965: 10) writes that the Afro-Shirazi Party, which had attempted to unite Mainland Africans and Shirazi in Zanzibar, was motivated by a resentment of the Arab oligarchy, a resentment "which expressed itself in virulently anti-Arab propaganda and in the publicly

---

[14]See my paper, "Race Structure in the Social Consciousness," *Civilizations* (1970: 88-102).

expressed desire of ASP leadership to transform Zanzibar into an African-ruled nation," he would seem to be describing a situation in which the encompassing principle is that of race. It can only be by virtue of this encompassing principle that an antagonism against a section of the Arabs is expressed in antagonism against all Arabs. So too, when Africans and Whites in South Africa see Indians as wealthy traders, when most Indians are working class and poor, it can only be by reason of a transformation of perception in terms of a general encompassing principle of racial stratification: in an objective situation, where some Indians are traders, the subjective perception is that all Indians are traders. Similarly in Zanzibar, where most trade was in Indian hands, the categorization of Indians as traders involves the transformation of the attributes of individual Indians into the attributes of Indians as a collectivity. Again, the encompassing principle is race, and the description of Indians in Zanzibar, or East Africa generally, as traders, though seemingly a description in terms of class, is in fact a racial categorization.

There are obviously very great difficulties in attempting to determine which is the encompassing principle and which the encompassed. In the context of revolutionary change, two measures may be suggested. The first measure relates to the target group, the persons actually killed by the revolutionaries, whether persons of a particular class, or persons of a particular race and class, or members of a particular race, regardless of class. Presumably where revolutionary violence expresses itself in the indiscriminate slaughter of members of a racial group, then the encompassing principle is race. The second measure is that of the precipitating events, in terms of differences between impulses affecting racial differentiation and activating racial

conflict on the one hand, and impulses affecting economic differentiation and activating class conflicts on the other. This is a more dubious measure, since subjective factors enter into the interpretation of the precipitating events by the analyst, and into the perception by the participants themselves of exacerbating events in the prelude to revolution. The measure is certainly more ambiguous than a counting and racial identification of corpses.[15]

In the Zanzibar revolution, the encompassing principle appears to have been racial. The initial revolutionary assumption of power was effected by a force made up largely of Mainland Africans on Zanzibar Island. Thereafter, Mainland Africans on Zanzibar Island came out in violent support of the revolution, with the participation of Shirazi, more particularly the Hadimu Shirazi who had been most affected by Arab occupation. Arabs were slaughtered, regardless of class.

Economic change appears to have been of little significance. Prior to the revolution, there was extreme economic stagnation as a result of a decline in Zanzibar's market for cloves, and schools had been closed and welfare programs cut back (Lofchie, 1965: 273). But the market for cloves was always variable, and previous crises had not led to revolution. Moreover, about 85 percent of the cloves were produced on Pemba Island (Middleton and Campbell, 1965: 35), and the revolutionary activity was on Zanzibar Island. Middleton and Campbell (1965: 40 -2) refer to changing economic relationships among farmers on Zanzibar Island, expressed in competition between Africans, Shirazis and Arabs in the marketing of food crops; but this competition was between Africans

---

[15]However, counts of corpses in revolutionary contexts are exceedingly unreliable. Le Tourneau (1962: 350) comments in relation to the Algerian rising in 1945, that 'les discussions statistics autour des cadavres sont aussi vaines que derisoires'.

and Shirazis as well as with Arabs. There was, however, a common class situation for Shirazi and African squatters in their relations with Arab landlords.

In Rwanda, the complex interweaving of race, ethnic group, caste and economic differentiation served, like a Rorschach test, to stimulate the most varied interpretations as to the dominant or encompassing principle. There was, for example, the declaration by Hutu leaders in their manifesto of March 1957, that the question whether the conflict was a social or racial conflict was a literary question, and that it was in fact both one and the other (Nkundabagenzi, 1961: 22). Here the implication is that racial or economic differentiation could not be separated out as an encompassing principle. Tutsi students at Lovanium University, on the other hand, argued that the problem must be social because if it were racial, this would mean that all the Hutu were oppressed, and all the Tutsi oppressors, whereas, in fact, the great majority of Tutsi (99.9 percent) were entirely without political, social, cultural or other privilege (Nkundabagenzi, 1961: 107). The argument perhaps carries the implication that the encompassing structural principle is a division between a small Tutsi oligarchy and a mass of oppressed Tutsi and Hutu. But the fact that many Tutsi were as underprivileged as Hutu by no means necessarily implies that racial division was not perceived as the encompassing principle or that it could not become the encompassing principle in the unfolding of the revolution. Luc de Heusch (1964), in his analysis of the revolution, in fact asserts that it did become racial, in the sense of emphasizing physical differences, during the course of the struggle. It is possible to derive from this the suggestion that the racial hierarchy was the encompassing principle, because it is otherwise difficult to understand why the struggle should ultimately have taken a racial form.

There was certainly a process of economic change in Rwanda as a result of action by the Belgian administration for the suppression of the clientage system, the development of cash crops and wage employment. Lemarchand (1966: 602) argues that the entire political structure collapsed with the abolition of clientship, ushering in a bitter struggle for supremacy between Tutsi and Hutu. Economic change was clearly relevant for the role of the rural proletariat and intellectuals.   But the conflict was not between economically differentiated groups, but between the two collectivities of Tutsi and Hutu.   The actual empirical socio-economic differentiation which cut across the division between Tutsi and Hutu was encompassed within a more general principle, opposing Tutsi and Hutu as collectivities, whether by racial, ethnic and/or caste criteria. The targets of the revolutionary uprising were Tutsi, again apparently without discrimination in terms of economic position, and the precipitating events were such as to activate Hutu and Tutsi in a struggle for power, and not economically differentiated strata in Rwanda society.

In neither Zanzibar nor Rwanda, did the revolutions arise out of an economic polarization of classes, or increasing immiserization of the masses, or in economic growth followed by recession, nor are the revolutions to be explained by economic advance. The economy in Zanzibar was stagnating. In Rwanda, there was some economic growth, the development of new economically differentiated strata, and some modification of traditional patterns of economic relationship. But the struggle was not between sections defined by economic criteria; it was a struggle between racial or ethnic sections, stimulated by democratization and the movement toward independence.

VI

However fundamental racial differences may be in particular societies, it is clearly impossible to develop a general theory of society and history based on racial differentiation, as was possible with class differentiation. Nothing could be more absurd than the proposition that the history of all living societies is the history of racial struggle. Racial difference has no intrinsic significance. Even when it is present in a society, as an objective fact, it may not be relevant in social relationships; and where it is recognized as relevant, its significance is highly variable, depending entirely on the way in which it is socially elaborated.

Under certain circumstances however, race may come to have a primary significance in the social structure. Demands for civic rights by a racial section are accompanied by labor disturbances, school and trade boycotts. An accident involving people of different race sets off racial rioting. Race is so woven into the fabric of the society that conflict between races in one situation or structure immediately ramifies to a wide range of situations and structures, whether related or unrelated; and conversely, a conflict on non-racial issues is readily transformed into a racial conflict. Racial consciousness becomes acute, and racial identity becomes the basis for political organization.

These are societies, characterized by a high degree of racial pluralism,[16] in which there has been an elaboration of racial differentiation into an encompassing principle. The structural basis of this elaboration and pluralism would seem to be 'differential incorporation', a system of racial stratification in which the racial sections are incorporated into the society on a basis of inequality (Kuper and Smith, 1969: Chapters 4 and 13). This may be *de jure*, as in South Africa where the constitution denies Africans the franchise, or largely *de facto* as in the U.S.A. It is associated with segregation, with unequal access to power, status and material

resources, and often with cultural differences, resulting in sharp discontinuities between the racial sections. Issues of conflict are superimposed on each other, lines of cleavage tend to coincide, providing the social basis for the escalation of conflict from minor incidents.

For analysis of revolutions in this type of society, it may be useful to develop hypotheses on the assumption that change in racial status is the crucial variable, in much the same way as hypotheses have been developed regarding the crucial role of economic change in revolutions between social classes. Thus the propositions in Section II of this paper, dealing with theories of economic change as predisposing factors in revolution, would yield a range of propositions, one or other of which might be used to explain particular racial revolutions with some plausibility. The predisposing conditions might be found in increasing racial subordination and discrimination (corresponding to immiserization of the masses) or in the advancing status of the subordinates, or in the disjunction between aspiration and reality, or in the tension between *de facto* racial interaction and mobility, on the one hand, and *de jure* separation and rigidity on the other. No doubt, in some cases, several of these propositions might be applied with equal plausibility to the interpretation of a particular racial revolution.

But the emphasis on either race or class invites an ideological commitment. If class is seen as the major determinant, then racial differences are subordinated to the role of a dependent variable, as in the theory that they provide the bourgeoisie with the means for a more thoroughgoing exploitation of workers of the subordinate race, by a process of dehumanization. If the emphasis is on race, then Marxism may be declared irrelevant to the black experience, or the significance of class differences may be minimized.

The more promising perspective would be to assume that these racially plural societies

---

[16]See Kuper and Smith, 1969, Chapter 14.

are in certain respects somewhat *sui generis* and that theories of revolution derived from the analysis of revolutions in racially homogeneous societies cannot readily be applied to societies in which there is differential incorporation of racial sections. Rather, an approach should be developed which analyzes the revolutionary process in terms of the interrelations between class and race, between economic and racial differentiation.

This is an approach which is becoming well established in the analysis of ethnic conflicts in Africa. Thus Balandier (1965: 140) sees the crises in African states since 1960 as determined by two sets of facts, namely the resurgence of old antagonisms, notably tribal and religious, and the struggle for power between members of the directing class *(des dirigeants et des bureaucrates)*. Le Tourneau (1962) systematically analyzes the role of different classes (Muslim bourgeoisie, both traditional and modern, proletariat, peasants) in the conflict between the indigenous peoples of Algeria and the French. Sklar (1967:1-11) examines class factors in the ethnic conflict in Nigeria, arguing that the activating force was an intra-class conflict between sections of the bourgeoisie, who set the ethnic groups against each other in the interests of their own struggle for power. While Sklar is concerned to show the significance of the class factor, his argument may also be interpreted from the point of view that the social force which provided the raw power for the conflict and made it possible was the force of ethnic antagonism. The position would be similar to class conflict in Marxist theory, in which the raw power is the antithetical relationship of sections to the means of production, but in which leadership may be governed by a different principle.

If a general theory of racial revolutions is to be developed, it is not sufficient simply to demonstrate that a conflict of classes, or a process of class formation, was interwoven with the racial conflict. There is need to develop a set of propositions concerning the interrelations of economic and racial stratification in revolutionary change, as Fanon (1966) attempted in his controversial theory of the revolutionary role of peasants in the colonial situation. The two main variables would relate to economic development and stratification on the one hand, and to racial structure on the other. Presumably revolutionary potential and process will be affected by the nature of the economy, whether highly industrialized as in the U.S.A. or rapidly industrializing as in South Africa, or largely subsistence pastoralism and agriculture as in Rwanda, or combining dependence on a major marketable crop with subsistence agriculture and a stagnating economy, as in Zanzibar. Similarly, racial structure will affect revolutionary change, with extreme racial division being represented by the systematic development of differential racial incorporation, as in South Africa. If, in addition to consummated revolutions, revolutionary movements are included, such as those in South Africa and the U.S.A., then there is a sufficient range of cases available to cover wide variations in economic and racial structure.

VII

My initial assumption was that theories of revolution derived from the analysis of conflict between social classes in racially homogeneous societies might not be very illuminating when applied to situations of revolutionary struggle between racial groups. Indeed, I would argue more positively that the theories may be quite misleading in the context of racially structured societies. In the rapidly industrializing society of South Africa, working class movements across the racial boundaries between whites and Africans have been negligible, and white workers have strongly supported the government in its racially oppressive apartheid policies. In the U.S.A., under conditions of the most advanced industrialization, there are tensions between the races as white workers resist movements by black workers for equality of participation; white workers constitute a conservative stratum in race relations, and black and white workers have not come together in a significant working class movement. As for the Zanzibar and Rwanda revolutions, I have presented discussion in this paper to suggest that the encompassing principle was racial rather than economic, and that economic change was not the catalyst of revolution.

Of course, I do not question the very great significance of economic factors in racially structured societies. I would suppose that wherever there is racial stratification there is also economic stratification. The relations between them may be conceived as a continuum. At one extreme, racial and economic divisions tend to coincide, as in the initial stages of colonial domination. At the other extreme, perhaps purely hypothetical, there has ceased to be stratification by race, and racial differences though present, are no longer salient in a system of stratification based on differences in economic status. Between the two extremes fall those societies in which both racial and economic stratification are present, but do not fully coincide. This is the more general case in the contemporary world, and the one with which I deal in the present paper.

As a result of the intermingling of race and class, and of incongruities in racial and economic status, the situation is ambiguous and encourages different perspectives and ideologies. The consequences of this ambiguity may be seen in the vacillating policies of communist parties committed to a thoery of revolution which is non-racialist and obliged to come to terms with racially based nationalist movements. The ambiguity is often expressed in divergent political tendencies among racially subordinate groups, a dualism in political parties, committed either to accommodation and reform, or to radical opposition and revolution. At the level of the dominant racial group, the ambiguity may be expressed in conflicting theories of economic change, as for example, the theory that the creation of a bourgeoisie among the subordinate race would be counter-revolutionary, or conversely, that it would be the catalyst of revolution. In social theory, the ambiguity may be resolved by distillation into two extreme theories, either that the causes of racial revolution are the same as those of class revolution, namely polarization of the races in their relationship to the means of production, or alternatively that the racial structure is primary and economic change somewhat marginally relevant. And it is precisely because of the ambiguity in the intermingling of class and race, that ideologies assume an added significance as directions to perceive the society, and to act, in terms of racial or class perspectives.

If the problem of the relevance of theories of revolution between social classes for the interpretation of racial revolutions is not to be left at the level of ideological preference, or in the form of a projective test into which the analyst pours his own inclinations, there is a need for comparative studies. The main variables would be different forms of economic structure and stratification, and of racial structure and stratification. This paper stresses in various contexts the salience of subjective perceptions, and it is necessary to analyze these perceptions and the ideologies in which they are conveyed. The historical dimension is also an essential aspect for analysis of the changing salience of class and race in periods preceding the revolution and during the course of the revolution itself.

In this way, it may be possible, by the comparative study of revolutionary struggles between racial groups, to test the argument in this paper, that under certain conditions of racial pluralism, such as characterized Zanzibar and Rwanda, the racial divisions are the propelling force in the revolutions, the predisposing factors are those that affect racial status in any of its many social dimensions, and the dialectic of conflict is essentially racial.

BIBLIOGRAPHY

ARON, RAYMOND
    1965 *Main Currents in Sociological Thought.* New York and London: Basic Books.

BALANDIER, GEORGES
    1965 "Problematique des Classes Sociales en Afrique Noire." *Cahiers Internationaux de Sociologie,* XXXVIII, 131-42.

BATSON, EDWARD
    1948 *Report on Proposals for a Social Survey of Zanzibar, 1946.* Zanzibar: Government Printer.

BELGIAN CONGO AND RUANDA-URUNDI INFORMATION AND PUBLIC RELATIONS OFFICE
    1960 *Ruanda-Urundi, Economy I.* Brussels.

BIENEN, HENRY
    1968 *Violence and Social Change: A Review of Current Literature.* Chicago and London: The University of Chicago Press.

BOCHKARYOV, YURI
    1964 'Background to Zanzibar.' *New Times.* 5 (February 5), 13-15.

COX, OLIVER CROMWELL
    1948 *Caste, Class, and Race.* New York: Doubleday & Company.

CRUSE, HAROLD
    1968 *Rebellion or Revolution?* New York: William Morrow & Company.

de HEUSCH, LUC
    1964 'Massacres Collectifs au Rwanda?' *Syntheses,* 221 (October), 416-26.

DUMONT, LOUIS
    1966 'A Fundamental Problem in the Sociology of Caste.' *Contributions to Indian Sociology,* IX (December), 17-32.

ECKSTEIN, HARRY
    1965 'On the Etiology of Internal Wars.' *History and Theory,* IV, 2, 133-63.

FANON, FRANTZ
    1966 *The Wretched of the Earth.* (First publication 1961.) New York: Grove Press.

KUPER, LEO
    1965 *An African Bourgeoisie: Race, Class and Politics in South Africa.* New Haven: Yale University Press.

    1969a "Ethnic and Racial Pluralism: Some Aspects of Polarization and Depluralization," in Leo Kuper and M. G. Smith, eds., *Pluralism in Africa.* Berkeley and Los Angeles: University of California Press.

    1970 'Race Structure in the Social Consciousness.' *Civilisations,* XX, 1, 88-102.

KUPER, LEO and SMITH, M. G., eds.
    1969 *Pluralism in Africa.* Berkeley and Los Angeles: University of California Press.

LE TOURNEAU, ROGER
    1962 *Afrique Nord Musulmane.* Paris: Librairie Armand Colin.

LEMARCHAND, RENE
    1966 "Power and Stratification in Rwanda: A reconsideration." *Cahiers d'Etudes Africaines,* VI, 4, 592-610.

    1968 "Revolutionary Phenomena in Stratified Societies. Rwanda and Zanzibar." *Civilisations,* XVIII, 1, 16-51.

LEURQUIN, PHILIPPE
    1960 *LeNiveau de Vie des Populations Rurales du Ruanda-Urundi.* Louvain: Editions Nauwelaerts.

LOFCHIE, MICHAEL F.
  1965 *Zanzibar: Background to Revolution.*
       Princeton: Princeton University Press.

  1969 "The Plural Society in Zanzibar" in Leo
       Kuper and M. G. Smith, eds., *Pluralism
       in Africa.* Berkeley and Los Angeles:
       University of California Press.

MAQUET, JACQUES-J.
  1964 "La Participation de la Classe Paysanne
       au Mouvement d'Independance du
       Rwanda," *Cahiers d'Etudes Africaines,*
       IV, 4, 552-68.

MIDDLETON, JOHN and JANE CAMPBELL
  1965 *Zanzibar—Its Society and Politics.* Lon-
       don and New York: Oxford University
       Press.

NKUNDABAGENZI, F., ed.
  1961 *Rwanda Politique,* Brussels: Centre de
       Recherches et d'Information Socio-
       Politiques.

OBERSCHALL, ANTHONY
  1969 "Group Violence: Some Hypotheses
       and Empirical Uniformities," paper pre-
       sented at the meeting of the American
       Sociological Association, San Francisco.

OLSON, MANCUR
  1963 "Rapid Growth as a Destabilizing Force."
       Journal of Economic History, 23 (De-
       cember), 529-52.

REY, LUCIEN
  1964 "The Revolution in Zanzibar," *New
       Left Review,* 25 (May-June), 29-32.

RICKS, TIMOTHY
  1969 Black Revolution: A Matter of De-
       finition." *American Behavioral Scientist,*
       XII, 4 (March-April), 21-6.

RWANDA CARREFOUR d'AFRIQUE
  1965 April.

  1967 "L'Economic Rwandaise." 66-7 (May-
       June), 1-27.

SKLAR, RICHARD
  1967 "Political Science and National Inte-
       gration—A Radical Approach." *The
       Journal of Modern African Studies,* V,
       1, 1-11.

VAN DEN BERGHE, PIERRE L.
  1967 *Race and Racism.* New York: John
       Wiley.

  1969 "Pluralism and the Polity: A Theo-
       retical Exploration," in Leo Kuper and
       M. G. Smith, eds., *Pluralism in Africa.*
       Berkeley and Los Angeles: University
       California Press.

ZANZIBAR PROTECTORATE
  1953 *Notes on the Census of the Zanzibar
       Protectorate 1948.* Zanzibar: Govern-
       ment Printer.

  1960 *Report on the Census of the Population
       of Zanzibar Protectorate, 1958.* Zanzi-
       bar: Government Printer.

  1963 *Labour Report for the Years 1960 and
       1961.* Zanzibar: Government Printer.

5. THE CLASS STRUGGLE

W. E. B. Du Bois

This short excerpt from the work of one of the foremost black leaders and sociologists discusses the question of blacks as a social class. Originally published in 1921, it shows the direction of DuBois' thinking during the latter part of his life.

The NAACP has been accused of not being a "revolutionary" body. This is quite true. We do not believe in revolution. We expect revolutionary changes in many parts of this life and this world, but we expect these changes to come mainly through reason, human sympathy, and the education of children, and not by murder. We know that there have been times when organized murder seemed the only way out of wrong, but we believe those times have been very few, the cost of the remedy excessive, the results as terrible as beneficent, and we gravely doubt if, in the future, there will be any real recurrent necessity for such upheaval.

Whether this is true or not, the NAACP is organized to agitate, to investigate, to expose, to defend, to reason, to appeal. This is our program and this is the whole of our program. What human reform demands today is light—more light; clear thought, accurate knowledge, careful distinctions.

How far, for instance, does the dogma of the "class struggle" apply to black folk in

the United States today? Theoretically we are a part of the world proletariat in the sense that we are mainly an exploited class of cheap laborers; but practically we are not a part of the white proletariat and are not recognized by that proletariat to any great extent. We are the victims of their physical oppression, social ostracism, economic exclusion and personal hatred; and when in self-defense we seek sheer subsistence we are howled down as "scabs."

Then consider another thing: The colored group is not yet divided into capitalists and laborers. There are only the beginnings of such a division. In one hundred years, if we develop along conventional lines, we would have such fully separated classes, but today to a very large extent our laborers are our capitalists and our capitalists are our laborers; Our small class of well-to-do men have come to affluence largely through manual toil and have never been physically or mentally separated from the toilers. Our professional classes are sons and daughters of porters, washerwomen, and laborers.

Under these circumstances, how silly it would be for us to try to apply the doctrine of the class struggle without modification or thought. Let us take a particular instance. Ten years ago the Negroes of New York City

SOURCE
From W. E. B. Bu Bois: a Reader, edited by Meyer Weinberg. Copyright © 1970 by Meyer Weinberg. Reprinted by permission of Harper and Row, Publishers, Inc.

lived in hired tenement houses in Harlem, having gotten possession of them by paying higher rents than white tenants. If they had tried to escape these high rents and move into quarters where white laborers lived, the white laborers would have mobbed and murdered them. On the other hand, the white capitalists raised heaven and earth either to drive them out of Harlem or keep their rents high. Now between this devil and the deep sea, what ought the Negro socialist or the Negro radical or, for that matter, the Negro conservative do?

Manifestly, there was only one thing for him to do, and that was to buy Harlem; but the buying of real estate calls for capital and credit, and the institutions that deal in capital and credit are capitalistic institutions. If, now, the Negro had begun to fight capital in Harlem, what capital was he fighting? If he fought capital as represented by white big real estate interests, he was wise; but he was also just as wise when he fought labor, which insisted on segregating him in work and in residence.

If, on the other hand, he fought the accumulating capital in his own group, which was destined in the years 1915 to 1920 to pay down $5,000,000 for real estate in Harlem, then he was slapping himself in his own face. Because either he must furnish capital for the buying of his own home, or rest naked in the slums and swamps. It is for this reason that there is today a strong movement in Harlem for a Negro bank, and movement which is going soon to be successful. This Negro bank eventually is going to bring into co-operation and concentration the resources of fifty or sixty other Negro banks in the United States, and this aggregation of capital is going to be used to break the power of white capital in enslaving and exploiting the darker world.

Whether this is a program of socialism or capitalism does not concern us. It is the only program that means salvation to the Negro race. The main danger and the central question of the capitalistic development through which the Negro-American group is forced to go is the question of the ultimate control of the capital which they must raise and use. If this capital is going to be controlled by a few men for thier own benefit, then we are destined to suffer from our own captialists exactly what we are suffering from white capitalists today. And while this is not a pleasant prospect, it is certainly no worse than the present actuality. If, on the other hand, because of our more democratic organization and our widespread interclass sympathy, we can introduce a more democratic control, taking advantage of what the white world is itself doing to introduce industrial democracy, then we may not only escape our present economic slavery but even guide and lead a distrait economic world.

2. HOSTILITY, TENSIONS AND ETHNIC RELATIONS

Sociologists and psychologists have recognized for a long time the need for individuals and groups to release their tensions and hostilities. In large organizations, suggestion boxes and "gripe sessions" with management are often utilized to allow workers to express hostilities. Japanese companies are now beginning to construct special rooms in their factories where workers can release their pent-up agression on plaster dummies and other symbolic objects.

Simmel and Coser stress the importance of social conflicts as a means of releasing hostilities. As Gelfand (1973) points out in his article in Section I, hostilities often fail to develop into social conflicts. This failure may be dysfunctional for intergroup relationships. This is especially true in ethnic relationships. The inability of a group to release hostility toward other groups may lead later to the development of more intensive conflicts. Thus, the open expression of hostility through conflicts between ethnic groups may be crucial in the maintenance of contact between these groups. When these hostilities cannot be expressed, one of the groups may withdraw from the relationship.

Subordinate groups unable to express hostility openly may attempt to find covert ways of expressing their antagonism. This may include the development of humor that portrays the dominant groups either as stupid or crass, and the use of terms expressing hostility toward dominant groups that are known only to subordinate group members.

These patterns may be combined with attempts to displace hostility onto other groups who have less power to retaliate. The "scapegoat" mechanism discussed by psychologists is seen in many of the historical relationships between whites and blacks, and Protestants and Catholics in the United States. Instead of concentrating their anger upon employers, many whites in the United States focused their ire upon blacks during the early attempts at unionization. They saw blacks being brought in to occupy their jobs, while they were on strike. Blacks unable to refuse this rare offer of work from large corporations thus became caught in the crossfire between unions and employers. Older union members remembering this pattern have continued to portray blacks as strike breakers and have supported efforts to prevent their admission to industrial unions.

As Coser (1956) has correctly noted, the displacement of hostility onto substitute ethnic groups has served in many countries to retard the development of strong political forces focusing on large scale economic and social changes. Group occupying positions of high visibility because of their ethnic identity have thus found themselves burdened with the failures of other subordinate groups as well as the failures of the dominant groups. In turn, dominant groups have often utilized hostility towards ethnic groups to explain misfortunes that may have resulted from their inability to adjust to changing conditions. Reactions in Germany to the country's defeat in World War I concentrated much of its attention on those groups that supposedly had "stabbed the country in the back." These groups included gypsies and Jews. The hostility of ethnic groups toward each other thus reflects their relative position of domination and subordination.

The articles included in this section provide some illustration of the way in which the release of tensions and hostilities has been handled by ethnic groups in various societies. For blacks in the United States, as Johnson notes, the release of hostilities has had to be on a covert level because of the possibility of reprisals by whites. For whites, the release of tensions in the twentieth century has often meant the attacking and killing of blacks in large metropolitan areas. This history is documented by Meier and Rudwick.

Studying the sit-in movement and its phases, Oppenheimer shows the importance of recognizing hostility between groups. Without this recognition and the development of means to allieviate the basis of this hostility, the resulting conflict may be of high intensity. The ethnic conflicts between Chinese and Malays in Penang, discussed by Snider, are an important example of the physical violence that can erupt when hostilities and tensions are not overtly recognized and reconciled.

Finally, White's account of conflict between blacks and Pakistanis in Great Britain sheds some light on interethnic patterns in a country where this form of conflict has been relatively recent. In Britain the strong culture and in-group solidarity of the Pakistanis combined with Britain's economic problems have made the Pakistanis targets for white hostility. Recognition and resolution of the tensions and hostilities between ethnic groups thus remain a problem in many societies.

REFERENCES

COSER, LEWIS
1956 *The functions of social conflict.* New York: Free Press

GELFAND, DONALD E.
1973 "Ethnic relations and social research: A reevaluation."
      Section I of this volume.

---

1.   COVERT HOSTILITY AND DEFLECTED AGGRESSION

Charles S. Johnson

This excerpt, by another undervalued black sociologist, is taken from a
study originally conducted for Gunnar Myrdal's **American Dilemma**. Johnson
provides concrete examples of the way blacks use covert hostility to com-
pensate for their inability to be openly aggressive towards whites.

Covert Hostility and Deflected Aggression

The weapons employed by lower-class
Negroes in expressing hostility covertly may
take the form of petty sabotage, unexplained
quitting of jobs, gossip, pseudo-ignorant
malingering.   Middle-class Negroes are in
better position to use the economic weapon
of controlled purchasing power. Upper-
class Negroes may use this also, but in addition they find it effective to use the method
of indirect attack on the offending institutions by arousing outside public opinion.

One of the milder forms of indirect aggression is the use of one group of whites to

SOURCE
From *Patterns of Negro Segregation* by Charles
S. Johnson. Copyright © 1943, by Harper and
Row Publishers, Inc.

punish another. Connection with influential
whites may serve not only to protect lower-
and lower middle-class Negroes from lower-
class white annoyance and police interference,
but in the absence of Negro political participation it often provides the only means
of redress once an injury has been perpetrated.   A barber in one of the plantation
counties cited a case in which Negroes got
redress for certain indignities:

*"The police are pretty brutal in the way
they treat Negroes. Most of them whip you
when they arrest you.   One of the night
"laws" went to one of the colored churches
one night, got a colored woman, dragged
her out of the church and whipped her.
Some of the better class of white people
got behind it and he lost his job.   The*

woman worked for some good white folks and they had him arrested."

In the rural South covert hostility motivated by the desire to maintain or to achieve physical security is by no means limited to situations involving police officers. There are manifestations of Negro hostility in other areas of contact: on the highways, in personal encounters in business and in other personal relations.

Indirect aggression is generally resorted to by Negroes who for various reasons have found it expedient to conform to their caste role externally but who privately nurse intense hostility toward whites. Owing partly to external circumstances and partly to personality predispositions, the ways in which hostility is expressed are often indirect and subtle and in some cases so ingenious that discrimination itself is turned into a channel of aggression toward the oppressor. Instead of fighting wherever they are discriminated against, Negroes adopting this type of response choose their own battleground.

Those who can afford to own an automobile have a way of expressing their hostility toward whites in a more or less indirect manner. A furnace worker in Texas said of his own experience, "I drive in a way that makes it look like I'll run over them if they walk in front of me when I have the right. I act like I don't see them. I have had some of them curse at me for this, but I just laugh at them and keep on driving." In such cases the automobile not only gives the Negro a sense of power and prestige but shares the blame for any damage that occurs. Thus, there is little wonder that only a few years ago the possession of a car by a Negro was considered something of a criminal offense in the deep South.

One of the most interesting and in some instances quite effective ways of expressing hostility, used by Negroes in different walks of life, is that of being polite and courteous enough to guard oneself from being insulted and at the same time inflict pain on the white person. This is the "gentleman's way" of getting even with whites without incurring further aggression. An insurance agent, after relating how he asked a group of white men to come into his house when the latter came to inquire about his wife's pay and asked her to come out, said, "I spoke to them in a firm manner and I was courteous all of the time." As to his general policy, he added:

"I come in contact with some of the toughest of them, but I always try to be courteous with them and nothing ever happens to me. That is the best think that you can do to get the white man's nerves. If you can still be courteous and let him know where to get off and don't get all excited and scared when he blows up, you can handle him pretty well. They get all excited quick and if the Negroes do not get scared too, they think that they had better be careful."

This is a Negro's use of the "war of nerves" strategy, but it is adopted primarily for self-defense.

A schoolteacher in Arkansas has her way of using politeness as a weapon. Referring to white insurance men who, according to her, "are the talk of the town among colored people," she said:

Sometimes when they come here and act so smart—they always have some nasty joke to tell you—I make them stand out on the porch, and when it's cold it is not so comfortable. You know there is a way of being so polite to white people that it is almost impolite. I say polite things, but I look at them hard and I don't smile, and while what I am saying is polite the way in which I say it isn't."

A slight variation of the same technique is the private differentiation some Negroes make in using such terms of address as "Mr." and "Mrs." An elderly Negro school principal in South Carolina, whom white people used to call "professor" not because they had any special respect for him but because they did not want to address him as "Mr.," described his way of addressing whites:

"I address older white men as 'Mr.' and white woman as 'Miss' or 'Mrs.' when I know them and 'Ma'am' otherwise. Young white men I give 'Sir'; I reserve Mr. for settled men."

The differentiation made here is obviously not at all common to users of the English language or even to any large number of Negroes; it is private and is used to express and at the same time to hide hostility toward certain white persons.

An interesting expression of covert hostility is revealed in the experience of a rural Negro school principal who in most respects managed to remain acceptable to white people. This principal knew how to behave well enough to survive seven white superintendents. They all had about the same attitude in the matter of limiting the financial allocation to the Negro school program, although their methods of accomplishing it varied. On one occasion when he went to visit the new superintendent, the Negro principal was greeted as follows: 'Well, uncle, how many students you got in your school?" Some time later, when asked by a member of the school board how he liked his new boss, the principal said:

"It speaks bad for a man who's been to the highest schools in the state, and occupying the position he does, to call me 'uncle' at this late time. 'Uncle' belongs to a plantation time. When masters wanted their children to show some kind of respect they taught them to call them 'uncle,' but it's too late for that now. He went back and told him, just as I wanted him. The next time I went there he said, 'Good morning, Jenkins, come in and have a seat.' "

One method of defeating a situation that is resented is to be clever enough to take advantage of the competing self-interests of white officials and supervisors. In one county, for example, a member of the school board owned a paint store; and it was not difficult for him to be persuaded to look favorably upon the idea of painting the school. In another county, after completing his term of office, the ex-superintendent of schools opened a hardware store. When he approached the Negro principal about the need of oil for his school floors, the principal replied apologetically, but with sly intent to convey his real feeling:

"But, Mr. ——, you know how hard it is to get a little oil for our floors. Even you turned it down when you were superintendent."

In conversations between Negroes open hostility toward whites is frequently expressed, but it becomes covert in face-to-face situations between Negroes and whites. The white person is not always aware of the depth or character of this feeling. A Negro worker in a South Carolina soft drink plant went into a store to make a purchase and was followed by a white person. The clerk passed the Negro and waited on the white customer. When the Negro started to leave the store, the clerk shouted, "Wait and I'll wait on you"; but the Negro went on out. In commenting on this he said, "I'd die before I'd go back to them. But the clerk thought he had merely lost a sale.

Similarly, a construction laborer in Birmingham reported encounters on streetcars that kept him enraged, but he could only express his hostility in wishful thinking. His report of the following incident is illuminating:

"They have a conductor on the car that carries a gun sometimes. He tries to treat you in a pretty rough way sometimes.

It is because he has a gun that he is so rough. There is one Negro who burned for stopping him from being so rough one time. I reckon that there are more than that that let the conductor have a dose of his own medicine. One guy left one of them laying right there in the door, and I wish that more of them would do the same thing."

There is a type of covert hostility that takes the form of destructive gossip. A Mississippi Negro informant, commenting about a prominent white political figure in the state, said:

"This is the way old —— got rich working prisoners on a farm. He had all of his prison farm where you had to work. They did not do anything but raise cotton. They made plenty of cotton, too. Old —— was too slick to let anything happen to him like that stuff that happened down in Louisiana. He would do almost anything for money that you asked him to do, but he never would take any money directly. One time he was asked by a man to pardon his son. He offered him a thousand dollars. He got mad with the man, but told him to sit down.
"Then they went out and looked at some stock that he had. He told the man that he ought to buy one of his bulls. He offered the man the bull for a thousand dollars. The man was a long time catching the point, and said that he had no way of getting him home. B—— told him that his son could drive him home. He was a slicker, that ——."

Covert expressions of hostility among middle-class Negroes may be prompted by factors beyond purely personal considerations. Generalized hostility toward whites may be aroused by injustice in the local administration of federal programs. Interest in the schools of the community, for example, may make this class of Negroes sensitive to local policies of discrimination resulting in disparities in financial support. Referring to a Negro school, one such informant said:

"It has a mighty poor rating, and gets hardly any consideration. The colored teachers get very little money and they are greatly underpaid compared with white teachers. The superintendent, being white, looks after his race first. So the school building over there isn't fit to raise pigs in."

Sexual jealousy is also responsible for hostility that remains covert. "White men have their fun with colored women," said a Birmingham Negro. "It's against the law, but who says anything about it. Anything goes but the nigger, they say." The interest in the celebrated Scottsboro trials of Negro boys for alleged rape drew out some hostility, which was expressed in sympathy for those youths. One informant, in a burst of indignation, said:

"Look at those Scottsboro boys. They spent all that time in the jail and the penitentiary. What for? Those boys did not have any more to do with those women than I did, and I was not even there. How in the world could they take on all of those boys? Why in the world anybody would lie like that, I don't know. It seems like the white folks get to thinking about making the nigger suffer, and they lose all human nature. They don't think at all. Ain't no way that they can make me see any excuse for what they tried to do to all of those Negroes just because they happened to be on the train with some white whores who decided to turn a trick with some white fellows. I tell you, it makes a man feel pretty hot sometimes."

Some Negroes who are helpless and dependent on the dominating whites have a way of expressing hostility that is perhaps universal with any people in the same predicament. They deliberately play the role of parasites and often in the name of loyalty or submission live or prosper at the expense of their victims.

An unskilled laborer in Cleveland, Mississippi, has developed almost to perfection the art of submission for aggressive purposes. The superficial character of his accommodating behavior and the intensity of his inner resentment may be seen in the following statments:

"I have had it pretty easy with these white people here since I have been here. . . . I know just how to get along with them. I can make them think they own the world. It is nothing but a lot of jive that I hand them. If I was a little better off, I would get away from around here and all of the white folks could kiss where the sun don't shine. This place is all right in a way, but a man has to be less than a man to get along most of the time."

Commenting on the whites' entering Negroes' homes at will, he added:

"That is why I wish that I was where they didn't want to mob a fellow when he stands up for his rights. I would really bust some of them down. As the saying goes, I would make black look just like white. I would cut some of these red necks down my size."

His means of retaliation for discrimination is described in these words:

"They want all of the Negroes to jump and pull off their hats when they start talking to them. I know that is what they want, and since I am down here in it I can do it. When 'Mr. Charlie' has something that I want, there is nothing that I can't do to get it. That is because he has something, and if I don't get it from him where can I get it?"

In other words, surface observation of the racial etiquette in order to get things from whites is his way of aggression.

Perhaps the lowest type of passive aggression is exemplified by the pimp or the pimp-like character. The author of the statement just quoted made a keen observation on this point when he said, "Now in regard to a Negro marrying a white man's mistress, all that had happened was that the white man had another Negro to support." It should be noted in this connection that in some places in the South some Negro men are reduced to such low economic status that resort to this parasitic form of aggression is probably due more to external circumstances than to their own psychological inclinations. Others, however, deliberately set out to make "suckers" out of the white men, as one Negro put it, by enticing them to the lure of Negro women, and make this a regular business either in houses of prostitution or in private night clubs. The psychology of this sort of behavior may be complex, but the destructive motive behind it is self-evident.

Telling jokes is another indirect method of expressing hostile impulses. A factory hand in Cleveland, Mississippi, reported that at the place where he worked the white foreman and the Negro workers often exchanged jokes. One morning he told one of the boys, "Hurry up there, you son-of-a-bitch. Your mammy must not have given you any breakfast." The colored boy retorted, "You skinny bastard, look like your mammy never gives you anything to eat." Then they all laughed. In fact, he said that those colored boys played the "dozens" with that white fellow any time.[2] Games and jokes of this sort make life a little easier for all parties involved in a strained relationship, for they give a certain amount of sanction to the expression of impulses that are suppressed only with

---

[2]John Dollard, "The Dozens: Dialetic of Insult, "The American Imago, 1:1-25 (November 1939).

great difficulty. Even among Negroes themselves the proverbial laughter and light heartedness are not without aggressive import. James Weldon Johnson made a shrewd observation in this connection. After having studied the phenomenon for some time he concluded:

"But I did discover that a part of the laughter, when among themselves, was laughter at the white man. It seems to me that for the grime white man in the backwoods of the South the deep laughter of the Negro should be the most ominous sound that reaches his ears."[3]

In still another form of indirect aggression, hostility toward the dominant whites is deflected toward other peoples having less capacity for retaliation. Examples include the resentment toward upper-class Negroes felt by certain lower-class Negroes who can neither avoid contact with whites nor assert themselves in any adequate manner when they are the victims of discrimination; and the resentment of those who are economically better off but are so weak and helpless in expressing their hostility toward whites that they "take it out" on other racial groups such as the Jews, the Chinese, the Mexicans, the West Indians, and those whom they call "Dagos," "Polacks," and others.

It has been noted that there are Chinese merchants in several of the Delta towns in Mississippi and that Negroes patronize them because they "feel freer." This situation offers an opportunity for some deflected hostility, since the nonwhites provide a substitute for Negro counteraggression. A lower-class Negro reported this experience:

"A bunch of us went in one of them Chinese stores. I asked for a match, and he got mad because I didn't say 'Mr.' We was about to turn the joint out. He called me

a *son-of-a-bitch, and told me to call him 'Mr.' I don't 'low no man to call me a son-of-a-bitch. I called him a Chinese son-of-a-bitch, and started to get him. One of them other Chinese said for him to let it drop."*

In some cities this hostility is deflected toward the Jewish merchants in Negro neighborhoods who, for business and other racial reasons of their own, are less likely to use forceful measures in retaliation for Negro aggression.

At the other social extreme is the Negro college teacher whose reaction to discrimination is one of avoiding scenes. He refrains from expressing resentment toward the white man when he is discriminated against; but he confessed that he took a certain delight in embarrassing whites who visited the college as guests and who were not informed about the amenities of upper-class Negro life. Since whites who visit these schools are usually friendly ones, they are a safe outlet for aggression on the part of a Negro who avoids direct conflict in a potentially dangerous racial situation.

THE NORTH

The complexities of Negro status in the North are commensurate with the intracacies of the northern cities where Negroes live. The population of a large city not only has well-defined classes but many interest groups with characteristic reaction patterns. The large concentrations of Negro population in New York and Chicago offer a wide range of positions within the Negro status, from those who live in a world almost entirely Negro to those who "pass" and have only casual and infrequent contacts with the Negro world.

In the northern city there is preoccupation with class both within the Negro group and between race groups. In the former case concern for the upper classes of the Negro

---

[3]James W. Johnson, *Along This Way* (New York: Viking Press, 1933), p. 120.

population is a reflection of the basic opposition to the popular tendency to confuse Negro status with servant status. Acute consciousness of class is an oblique recognition of the existence of "the Negro status"; and the attitude of lower-class Negroes toward the Negro is one form of indirect expression of hostility. Preoccupation with class in interracial situations appears to. grow out of the need for a common defense of economic interests, strong enough at times to cut across race lines.

There is a considerable amount of racial discrimination in the North, but it is a common observation, that the Negroes who discuss these discriminatory practices most frankly are those who originally came from the South. The Negro pattern of behavior outside the Negro residence areas is carefully molded to permit maximum freedom within the vague margins of acceptability. Within the Negro areas there is more realization and sense of both security and possession. Buried racial antagonisms can easily be called to the surface, however, in a variety of overt expressions with or without strong provocation. Migrants from the South in particular, who have stored away memories of deep-cutting offenses discreetly tolerated in the South, may reveal undue aggressiveness in the areas of open competition.

Personal Racial Aggression

In the North the Negro escapes many of the more obvious forms of segregation and discrimination, and little of the racial etiquette is in force. When discrimination occurs it is more subtle, and hence most of the experiences recorded were reported by middle- and upper-class Negroes. Occasionally it happens that an institution or relationship may involve personnel with a southern background, and difficulties may develop; but usually some form of redress is possible through formal channels. Where such redress

is not possible, the situation may result in physical conflict.

The most common form of aggression in the North is vehement verbal assertion of rights. Some temperaments lend themselves to this more readily than others. The tendency to talk back to offending whites and to resort to every possible means of aggressive retaliation, short of physical violence, is illustrated in the case of an accomplished woman lawyer in Chicago. On one occasion she went to shop in a fashionable district. First, the elevator girl refused to take her upstairs, and then after she got upstairs nobody waited on her. When a man finally came to order her out, the lawyer attacked him verbally with great violence. She reported the story in part:

"I really shouted then. I was pointing my finger in his face and I said, 'If you touch me again [the man had touched her hand while she rang for the elevator], even my little finger, I'll have you arrested, and I've practiced in the courts long enough to have just enough influence to do it. Why,' I said, 'I kick your kind around every day in court. You've been used to Negroes who tuck their heads and run when you scowl. Well, let me tell you, this is a new kind of Negro and there are plenty more like me, so you'd better watch out. If I were a man I'd knock you down.'

A more formal, and sometimes quite effective, way of expressing aggression directly is to sue the white offenders. This type of response is consistently practiced by a real-estate man in Chicago. When he brought a charge against a white woman, the owner of a restaurant on the South Side, she was fined $25, and the story of the lawsuit was carried in the local newspapers. As a result he felt that some other restaurants in the city had changed their policy toward Negroes. One interesting aspect of this Negro's policy toward whites is his constant readiness to challenge any white establishment in which discrimination is practiced contrary to the law of the state,[4] and to bring suit whenever he can procure the necessary evidence. On one occasion he purposely went into an "exclusive" bar in the Loop. The very reluctant bartender gave him the glass of gin he ordered and charged him $1.25 instead of the usual price of 15 cents. He immediately took issue with the bartender and followed this up with legal proceedings against the owner. This Negro is an out-and-out fighter, but he uses means that are socially approved and relatively effective.

Some middle- and upper middle-class Negroes in northern areas make a point of seeking opportunities to assert their resentment of discrimination. An upper middle-class Negro woman said:

"I wish I had nothing to do but float around and let myself in for it because I like to fight. They don't put a lot over me. I don't care where I am or who is around. I know I am as good as anyone. I know I've got something most white people haven't got even if I belong to a minority group, and I know my rights. I'll fight for them with anybody or any time."

A contrasting case was that of a woman real-estate agent in Chicago. One of the main topics of her conversation was her disagreement with a Negro man in the same business with respect to his petty attitude toward discrimination. She said:

"Mr. ——, who is in the kitchenette business like I am, believes in fighting these old white people any time he gets a chance. Now he went up here on 60th Street and bought a building in the white section. They had to get cops to guard the place. The white people were going to try to run

them out. They threw rocks through his windows. . . . I can't understand why he wanted to do that. . . . He is always going to some place where he knows he isn't wanted. I don't believe in that."

Following her own policy of avoidance, she always goes to places where she knows she is welcome, does not eat out, and has never tried to eat in downtown drugstores although she believes that they would serve her.

Except in cases of southern Negroes who have recently migrated to the North, there is not the same frequency or variety of devices substituted for direct aggression. Cases are reported of southern Negroes who had restrained their impulses in the South out of consideration for personal safety, but in the North were prompt to resent violently any attempt at personal discrimination on racial grounds or any insult from a white person. Such encounters have been frequent in the thickly settled Negro sections of northern cities.

When a Negro redcap in Chicago was assisting a passenger who happened to be from the South and called him "darky," he had to be restrained from doing violence to him. A Negro passenger on a bus struck the white driver in a trivial argument over change and accused him of trying to import "crackerism" into New York.

Where racial segregation and formal discrimination do occur in the northern cities, they are so strongly supported that it is difficult for individual Negroes to make any effective protest. As a result they either tend to ignore the areas in which discrimination is known to occur and content themselves with thinking that they could receive the service or use the facility if they tried, or they use their collective strength to attack discrimination through formal channels. The ballot is perhaps the most effective means of combating discrimination in the North. This has been the weapon most used and most relied upon by Negroes of all classes who

---

[4]It should be noted that this legal weapon against discrimination is not effective in all states. For statutes on this matter see Chapter IX.

were interviewed on this question. In fact, it may be said that it was the voting power of the Negro populations in northern cities that brought about the new civil rights bills.

Race Riots

Several cities in the North may be listed in a description of a type of collective resistance to white aggression—race riots. Where these have occurred, the underlying problem has been that of racial segregation and discrimination in recreational areas, residence areas, and industry. In East St. Louis, Illinois, during the first stages of the northward migration of southern Negroes in 1917, there was a race riot which resulted in the death of 39 Negroes and 8 whites. The Chicago riot in 1919 started over an apparently trivial incident at a bathing beach. White bathers objected to a Negro boy's crossing an imaginary line dividing the two races in the water. They stoned the boy and he drowned. In the racial clashes that continued for several days 22 Negroes and 16 whites were killed, while 342 Negroes and 178 whites were injured. There have been riots in Springfield, Illinois, Washington, D.C., and New York City, although that in the last-named city was only partly racial in motivation. A race riot is differentiated from a lynching in that in the former there is direct, violent, and collective resistance on the part of the Negroes.

Organized Aggression

Direct action in opposition to racial discrimination has been attempted by several organizations with some measure of success. The more aggressive Negroes have directed their resentment of personal and group discrimination through these organizations which have more power to effect changes or to punish. One of the earlier efforts to combat racial discrimination was the so-called "Niagara Movement," organized in New York by W. E. B. Du Bois in 1905. Out of this, in 1910, grew the National Association for the Advancement of Colored People, which is the most effective of the present organizations combating discrimination. It is supported very largely by Negro membership throughout the country. It has an impressive record of successful court battles against racial discrimination in social, civil, legal, and political relations. It has won practically every case carried to the Supreme Court, and each of them has involved the protection of the fundamental citizenship rights of Negroes.

In 1931 the success of the boycotting and picketing movement against white merchants who discriminated against Negroes as employees was recognized; and the movement began to spread through northern and a few southern cities.

The National Urban League, using more pacific methods, has sought to combat racial discrimination in industry. It has been active since 1911 and has branches in many cities, chiefly in the northern industrial areas.

The most recent of the combative organizations is the National Negro Congress, which has attempted to unify local movements in protest against injustices, on a united front principle.[5]

The Negro press should be mentioned in this connection, notably those newspapers published in the North and having a national circulation. Racial discrimination is news of high value and appeal, which has kept Negroes alert and helped to solidify opposition to any and all forms of segregation and discrimination. In notable instances the Negro press has been effective in bringing about changes. It has served two

---

[5]"The Programs of Organizations Devoted to Improvement of the Status of the American Negro," *Journal of Negro Education*, 8:539 (July, 1939).

useful purposes: it has been a direct weapon of attack on segregation and discrimination; it has been a medium through which individual Negroes could relieve their aggressive feelings, both through reading it and through contributing to it.

One of the more recent forms of racial aggression in the North is the consolidation of racial issues with economic and political disaffections of non-Negro groups, usually to some punitive end. The case of the Scottsboro boys helped to arouse northern Negroes and Communists to action. The food riots in Harlem during 1933, although precipitated by economic frustration of both Negroes and whites, nevertheless revealed a residue of racial hostility in the bitter fury of the Negroes toward the objects attacked and the immunities.

In Chicago residence problems cause more friction and conflict situations than in New York. The battle for living quarters has called forth antagonism, violence, and court action. Refusals to sell or lease property to Negroes, reinforced by court action, are used to keep Negroes out of some residential areas. The wrecking of buildings and personal violence toward Negroes who get into a building in an area considered as restricted to white families are not as common as formerly.

The hostility of the Negro must be expressed through various intricate procedures which do not always dramatize the situation. The conflict in its indirect action is intense, often because of emotionally charged consideration of status. In general, it may be said that, although there is greater freedom for overt expression of racial hostility in the North, there is actually less of it than of covert hostility in the South.

2. BLACK VIOLENCE IN THE 20th CENTURY: A STUDY IN RHETORIC AND RETALIATION

August Meier and Elliott Rudwick

The assasinations of the Kennedys and Martin Luther King have resulted in numerous works examining violence in the United States. Originally writing for the "violence commission," Meier and Rudwick examine the development, changes, and rationale behind racial violence in the United States during the last 70 years.

For most Americans, the increasingly overt talk of retalitory violence among Negro

SOURCE

From *The History of Violence in America* **edited by Hugh Graham and Ted Gurr. New York: New York Times, 1969.**

militants, and the outbreaks in the urban ghettos over recent summers, signify something new and different in the history of Negro protest. Actually, retaliatory violence has never been entirely absent from Negro thinking. Moreover, advocacy of retaliatory violence, and actual instances of it, have tended to increase during periods of heightened Negro protest activity.

Thus the past decade of rising Negro militance has been no stranger to the advocacy of retaliatory violence.   For example, as far back as 1959, Robert F. Williams, at the time president of the Monroe, North Carolina, branch of the NAACP, came to public attention when the Union County Superior Court acquitted two white men of brutal assaults on two Negro women, but sentenced a mentally retarded Negro to imprisonment as a result of an argument he had with a white woman.   Williams angrily told a reporter, "We cannot take these people who do us injustice to the court, and it becomes necessary to punish them ourselves. If it's necessary to stop lynching with lynching, then we must be willing to resort to that method."   The NAACP dismissed Williams as branch president, but he remained a leader of Monroe's working-class Negroes, who for several years had been using guns to protect their homes from white Klansmen.   In 1961, falsely charged with kidnapping a white couple, he fled from the country. Williams became the most famous of that group of militants existing at the fringe of the civil-rights movement, who in their complete alienation from American society articulated a revolutionary synthesis of nationalism and Marxism.[1]   From his place of exile in Havana, Cuba, Williams undertook the publication of a monthly newsletter, *The Crusader*.   In a typical issue, he declared:

"Our only logical and successful answer is to meet organized and massive violence with massive and organized violence. . . . The weapons of defense employed by Afro-American freedom fighters must consist of a poor man's arsenal. . . . Molotov cocktails, lye, or acid bombs [made by injecting lye or acid in the metal end of light bulbs] can be used extensively. During the night hours such weapons, thrown from roof tops,

will make the streets impossible for racist cops to patrol. . . . Yes, a minority war of self-defense can succeed."[2]

Subsequently Williams was named chairman in exile of an organization known as the Revolutionary Action Movement (RAM),[3] a tiny group of college-educated people in a few major northern cities, some of whose members have been recently charged with plotting the murder of Roy Wilkins and Whitney Young.

Williams, RAM, and the better known Black Muslims[4] were on the fringes of the Negro protest of the early 1960's.   More recently violence and the propaganda for violence have moved closer to the center of the race relations stage.   Well over 200 riots have occurred since the summer of 1964.   The incendiary statements of the Rap Browns and the Stokeley Carmichaels became familiar TV and newspaper fare for millions of white Americans.   The Oakland, California, Black Panthers and other local groups espousing a nationalist and revolutionary rhetoric thrived and received national publicity.   As has been often pointed out, there is no evidence that the race riots of the 1960's have any direct relations to the preachings of Williams, of these various groups, even of the SNCC advocates of armed rebellion and guerrilla warfare.   Yet both the statements of these ideologists, and the spontaneous actions of the masses, have much in common.   For both are the product of the frustrations resulting from the growing disparity between the Negroes' status in American society and the rapidly rising expectations induced by the civil-rights revolution and its earlier successes.

Historically, this doctrine of retaliatory violence has taken various forms.   Some have advocated self-defense against a specific attack.   Others have called for revolutionary violence.   There are also those who hopefully predicted a general race war in which Negroes would emerge victorious.

Though seldom articulated for white ears, and only rarely appearing in print, thoughts of violent retaliation against whites have been quite common. For example, Ralph Bunche, in preparing a memorandum for Gunnar Myrdal's *American Dilemma* in 1940, noted that "there are Negroes, too, who, fed up with frustration of their life, here, see no hope and express an angry desire 'to shoot their way out of it.' I have on many occasions heard Negroes exclaim, 'Just give us machine guns and we'll blow the lid off the whole damn business.' "[5]

In surveying the history of race relations during the 20th century, it is evident that there have been two major periods of upsurge both in overt discussion by Negro intellectuals concerning the desirability of violent retaliation against white oppressors, and also in dramatic incidents of actual social violence committed by ordinary Negro citizens. One was the period during and immediately after the First World War. The second has been the period of the current civil rights revolution.

W. E. B. Du Bois, the noted protest leader and a founder of the NAACP, occasionally advocated retaliatory violence, and somewhat more often predicted intense racial warfare in which Negroes would be the victors. In 1916, inspired by the Irish Rebellion, in an editorial in the NAACP's official organ, *The Crisis*, he admonished Negro youth to stop spouting platitudes of accommodation and remember that no people ever achieved their liberation without an armed struggle. He said that "war is hell, but there are things worse than hell, as every Negro knows."[6] Amid the violence and repression that Negroes experienced in the postwar world, Du Bois declared that the holocaust of World War I was "nothing to compare with that fight for freedom which black and brown and yellow men must and will make unless their oppression and humiliation and insult at the hands of the White

World cease."[7]

Other intellectuals reflected this restless mood. The post-war years were the era of the militant, race-conscious New Negro of the urban North, an intellectual type who rejected the gradualism and conciliation of his ancestors. The tone of the New Negro was recorded by Claude McKay, who in 1921 wrote his well-known poem, "If We Must Die": "If we must die/let it not be like hogs; hunted and penned in an accursed spot!/ . . . . If we must die; oh, let us nobly die/dying but fighting back." A Phillip Randolph, editor of the militant socialist monthly, *The Messenger*, organizer of the Brotherhood of Sleeping Car Porters, and later leader of the March on Washington Movements of 1941 and 1963, also advocated physical resistance to white mobs. He observed that "Anglo-Saxon jurisprudence recognizes the law of self-defense . . . . The black man has no rights which will be respected unless the black man forces that respect. . . We are consequently urging Negroes and other oppressed groups concerned with lynching or mob violence to act upon the recognized and accepted law of self-defense."[8]

The legality of retaliatory violent self-defense was asserted not only by A. Philip Randolph, but also by the NAACP, which Randolph regarded as a moderate, if not futile organization, wedded to the interest of the Negro middle class. In 1925, half a dozen years after *The Messenger* article, the NAACP secured the acquittal of Dr. Ossian Sweet and his family. The Sweets were Detroit Negroes who had moved into a white neighborhood, and fired on a stone-throwing mob in front of their home, killing one white man and wounding another.[9] More than a quarter of a century later, at the time of the Robert Williams episode, the NAACP in clarifying its position, reiterated the stand that "The NAACP has never condoned mob violence but it firmly supports the right of Negroes individually and collectively to defend their person, their homes, and their property from attack. This position has always been the policy of the NAACP."[10] The view of intellectuals like Du Bois, McKay, and Randolph during World War I and the early postwar years paralleled instances of Negro retaliatory violence which actually triggered some of the major race riots of the period.

The East St. Louis riot of 1917, the bloodiest in the 20th century, was precipitated in July when Negroes, having been waylaid and beaten repeatedly by white gangs shot into a police car and killed two white detectives. On the darkened street a Negro mob of 50 to 100 evidently mistook the Ford squad car for the Ford automobile containing white "joyriders" who had shot up Negro homes earlier in the evening. The following morning the riot began.[11]

In Houston, several weeks later, about 100 Negro soldiers broke into an Army ammunition storage room and marched on the city's police station. The troops, mostly Northerners, were avenging an incident which occurred earlier in the day, when a white policeman used force in arresting a Negro woman and then beat up a Negro soldier attempting to intervene. A Negro provost guard was pistol whipped and shot at for asking the policeman about the wounded soldier. Even before these events, the Negro soldiers nursed a hatred for Houston policemen, who had attempted to enforce streetcar segregation, frequently used the term "nigger," and officiously patrolled the Negro ghetto. The Houston riot was not only, unusual because it involved Negro soldiers, but also because white persons constituted most of the fatalities.[12]

By 1919 there was evidence that the Negro masses were prepared to fight back in many parts of the country, even in the Deep South. In an unpublished report to the NAACP Board of Directors, a staff member, traveling in Tennessee and Mississippi during early 1919, noted that "bloody conflicts impended in a number of southern cities." Perry Howard, the leading colored attorney in Jackson, and R. R. Church, the wealthy Memphis politician, both reported that Negroes were armed and prepared to defend themselves from mob violence. Howard detailed an incident in which armed Negroes had prevented a white policeman from arresting a Negro who had become involved in a fight with two white soldiers after they had slapped a colored girl. In Memphis, R. R. Church, fearing armed conflict, privately advised the city's mayor that "the Negroes would not make trouble unless they were attacked, but in that event they were prepared to defend themselves."[13]

The Chicago race riot of 1919 grew out of Negro resentment of exclusion from a bathing beach dominated by whites. One Sunday, while Negroes and whites scuffled on the beach, a colored teenager drowned after being attacked in the swimming area. That attack was the most recent of a long series of assaults against Negroes. A white policeman not only refused to arrest a white man allegedly involved in the drowning, but actually attempted to arrest one of the complaining Negroes. The officer was mobbed and soon the rioting was underway.[14]

The Elaine, Arkansas riot of 1919 was precipitated when two white law officers shot into a Negro church, and the Negroes returned the fire, causing one death. The white planters in the area, already angered because Negro cottonpickers were seeking to unionize and obtain an increase in their share-cropping wages, embarked upon a massive Negro hunt to put the black peons "in their place."[15]

The Tulsa riot of 1921 originated when a crowd of armed Negroes assembled before the courthouse to protest the possible lynching of a Negro who had just been arrested for allegedly attacking a white girl. The Negroes shot at white police and civilians who attempted to disperse them.[16]

In each of these conflagrations, the typical pattern was initial Negro retaliation to white acts of persecution and violence, and white perception of this resistance as an organized, premeditated conspiracy to "take over," thus unleashing the massive armed power of white mobs and police. In the Southern communities, Negro resistance tended to collapse early in the riots. After the church incident in the rural Elaine area, most Negroes passively accepted the planters' armed attacks on their homes. At Tulsa, Negroes retreated from the courthouse to the ghetto, and throughout the night held off by gunfire the assaults of white mobs. But after daybreak, many Negroes fled or surrendered before the white onslaught burned down much of the ghetto.[17] One exception to this pattern was the Washington riot of 1919, where it appears that Negroes did not retaliate until the third and last day of the riot.[18]

Negro resistance generally lasted longer in Northern riots than in Southern ones, but even in East St. Louis and Chicago the death toll told the story: in East St. Louis, 9 whites and at least 39 Negroes were killed. In Chicago, 15 whites and 23 Negroes lost their lives. Negroes attacked a small number of whites found in the ghetto or on its fringes. Negro fatalities mainly occurred when victims were trapped in white-dominated downtown areas or residential sections. Negroes were also attacked on the edges of their neighborhood in a boundary zone separating a colored residential district from a lower class white area.[19] In the face of overwhelming white numerical superiority, many armed Negroes fled from their homes, leaving guns and ammunition behind. In East St. Louis, for example, there was a constant rattle of small explosions when fire enveloped a small colored residential district. Perhaps psychological factors contributed to the terrified inactivity of some Negroes. Despite the wish to meet fire with fire, over the years they had become so demoralized by white supremacy and race discrimination that effective armed defense could exist only in the realm of psychological fantasy.

During World War II, the most important race riot erupted in 1943 in Detroit, where nine whites and 25 Negroes were killed. In many respects the riot exhibited a pattern similar to East St. Louis and Chicago. The precipitating incident involved an attack on whites at the Belle Isle Amusement Park by several Negro teenagers who, a few days earlier, had been ejected from the white-controlled Eastwood Park. In the mounting tension at Belle Isle, many fights between Negroes and whites broke out, and the violence spread to the Negro ghetto where patrons at a night club were urged to "take care of a bunch of whites who killed a colored woman and her baby at Belle Isle." Although there had been no fatalities at the park, the night club emptied and revengeful Negroes stoned passing cars driven by whites. They began smashing windows on the ghetto's main business street, where the mob's major attention was directed to destroying and looting white-owned businesses.[20]

It was this symbolic destruction of "whitey" through his property that gave the Detroit holocaust the characteristic of what we may call the "new-style" race riot. It may be noted that in all the riots discussed above, there were direct clashes between Negroes and whites, and the major part of the violence was perpetrated by the white mobs. The riot pattern since the summer of 1964, however, has involved Negro aggression mainly against white-owned property, not white people. This "new style" riot first appeared in Harlem in 1935 and 1943.[21] The modern riot does not involve white mobs at all, and policemen or guardsmen constitute most of the relatively small number of casualties.

One can identify perhaps two major factors responsible for this contrast between the old-style and the new-style riot. One is the relatively marked shift in the climate of race relations in this country over the past generation. On the one hand, whites have become, on the whole, more sensitive to the Negro's plight, more receptive toward Negro demands, and less punitive in their response to Negro aggression. The black masses, on the other hand, have raised their expectations markedly and, disillusioned by the relatively slow pace of social change which has left the underprivileged urban Negro of the North scarcely, if at all, better off then he was 10 or 15 years ago, have become more restless and militant than before.

In the second place, there is an ecological factor. From South to North, the migration of the World War I period was a mere drop in the bucket compared to what it later became. The migration to the North in each of the decades since 1940 has been equal to or greater than the migration of the whole 30-year period, 1910 to 1940. At the same time, owing to the Supreme Court's outlawing of the restrictive covenant in 1948, and the tearing down of the older slums through urban renewal, the Negro population has been dispersed over a wider area, thus accentuating the trend toward the development of vast ghettos. Indeed, compared to the enormous ghettos of today, the Negro residential areas of the World War I period were mere enclaves. Today, of course, Negroes are close to becoming a majority in several of the major American cities.

The character of American race riots has been markedly affected by these demographic changes. Even if white mobs were to form, they would be unable to attack and burn down the Negro residential areas; even in the 19th- and early-20th-century riots, white mobs did not usually dare to invade the larger Negro sections, and destroyed only the smaller areas of Negro concentration. Nor, since the Negroes are such a large share of the population of the central city areas, would white mobs today be in a position to chase, beat, and kill isolated Negroes on downtown streets. More important, from the Negroes' point of view, the large-scale ghettos provide a relatively safe place for the destruction and looting of white-owned property; it is impossible for local police forces to guard business property in the farflung ghettos; even State police and federal troops find themselves in hostile territory where it is difficult to chase rioters beyond the principal thoroughfares.

It is notable that during the 20th century, both the overt discussion of the advisability of violent retaliation on the part of Negroes, and also actual incidents of violence were prominent in the years during and after World War I, and again during the 1960's. While there have been significant differences between the outbreaks characteristic of each era, there have been also important similarities. In both periods retaliatory violence accompanied a heightened militancy among American Negroes—a militancy described as the "New Negro" in the years after World War I, and described in the sixties, with the phrase, "the Negro Revolt." In neither case was retaliatory violence the major tactic, or the central thrust, but in both periods it was a significant subordinate theme. However, in both periods a major factor leading Negroes to advocate or adopt such a tactic was the gap between Negro aspiration and objective status. The rapid escalation of the aspirations of the Negro masses who shared Martin Luther King's "dream" and identify vicariously with the success of the civil-rights revolution, while their own economic, housing, and educational opportunities have not improved, is a phenomenon of such frequent comment that it requires no elaboration here.

A comparable situation occurred during and shortly after the First World War. The agitation of the recently founded NAACP, whose membership doubled in 1918-19, the propaganda of fighting a war to make the world safe for democracy, and especially the great Negro migration to the Northern cities which Southern peasants and workers viewed as a promised land, all created new hopes for the fulfillment of age-old dreams, while Negro soldiers who had served in France returned with new expectations. But the Negro's new hopes collided with increasing white hostility. Northern Negroes assigned to southern army camps met indignities unknown at home. They rioted at Houston and came so close to rioting in Spartanburg, South Carolina, that the army hastily shipped them overseas. In the northern cities like East St. Louis and Chicago, Negroes found not a promised land, but overcrowded ghettos and hostile white workers who feared Negro competition for their jobs. The *Ku Klux Klan* was revived beginning in 1915, and grew rapidly in the North and South after the war ended. By 1919 economic opportunities plummeted as factories converted to peacetime operations. For a while Negroes resisted, protested, fought back, in the South as well as the North; but the superior might of the whites proved overpowering and the Southern Negroes retreated into old paths of accommodation where they generally remained until the momentous events of the past decade.

There has been no systematic research on Negro advocacy of violence prior to the First World War, but the available evidence supports the thesis that increased overt expression of this tendency accompanies peaks in other kinds of protest activity. For example, it appears likely that Negro resistance to white rioters was minimal in the riots at the turn of the century—at Wilmington, North Carolina, in 1898, and at New Orleans, Akron, and New York in 1900[22]—which

took place in a period when the sentiment of accommodation to white supremacy, epitomized by Booker T. Washington, was in the ascendency.

Again, during the ante-bellum period, one can cite two noted cases of incendiary statements urging Negroes to revolt—*David Walker's Appeal* of 1829, and Rev. Henry Highland Garnet's suppressed *Address to the Slaves of the United States of America,* delivered at the national Negro convention of 1843.[23] Both coincided with periods of rising militant protest activity on the part of the northern free Negroes. *Walker's Appeal* appeared on the eve of the beginning of the Negro convention movement, and at the time of intensified Negro opposition to the expatriation plans of the American Colonization Society.[24] Garnet's speech was made at a time when free Negro leaders were disturbed at the prejudiced attitudes of white abolitionists who refused to concern themselves with obtaining rights for the free people of color, or to allow Negroes to participate in the inner circles of the leadership of the antislavery societies. Consequently they had revived the Negro national convention movement which had been inactive since 1836. (Garnet's speech was also in part a product of disillusionment with the lack of actual progress being made by the antislavery societies toward achieving abolition.)

We lack any careful analysis of race riots during the 19th century. Some certainly were pogrom-like affairs, in which the Negroes were so thoroughly terrorized from the beginning that they failed to fight back. (Perhaps the Draft Riots, and some of the Reconstruction riots as in Mississippi in 1876 were of this sort.) Yet other riots were characterized by some degree of Negro retaliatory violence, such as the Snow Hill riot in Providence, in 1831, and the Cincinnati riots of 1841. Both appear to have been, like the Chicago and East St. Louis riots, the climaxes to a series of interracial altercations. In the Providence riot, a mob of about 100 white sailors and citizens advanced on a small Negro section; a Negro shot a sailor dead, and within a half hour a large mob descended upon the neighborhood, damaging many houses.[25] In the Cincinnati riot, a pitched battle was fought on the streets; the blacks had enough guns and ammunition to fire into the mob such a volley that it was twice repulsed. Only when the mob secured an iron six-pounder and hauled it to the place of combat and fired on the Negroes were the latter forced to retreat, permitting the rioters to hold sway for 2 days without interference from the authorities.[26] A careful study of interracial violence during Reconstruction will undoubtedly produce evidence of comparable situations. These riots occurred at a time of high Negro expectations and self-assertiveness, and seem to have been characterized by a significant amount of fighting back on the part of Negroes.

One period of marked and rising Negro militance, however, was not accompanied by a significant increase in manifestations of Negro retaliatory violence. This was the one following the Second World War. Indeed, the Second World War itself witnessed far less Negro violence than did the First World War. The reason for this would appear to be that the 1940's and early 1950's were years of gradually improving Negro status, and a period in which the expectations of the masses did not greatly outrun the actual improvements being made. In fact, from 1941 until the mid-1950's the relative position of the Negro workers, as compared to the white wage earners, was generally improving and it was not until the recession of 1954-55, for example, that the Black Muslims, with their rhetoric of race hatred and retaliatory violence, began to expand rapidly.

It would appear that both in the World War I period, and today—and indeed during the ante-bellum era and at other times when manifestations of violence came to the fore— there has been a strong element of fantasy in Negro discussion and efforts concerning violent retaliation. Robert Williams talked of Molotov cocktails and snarling up traffic as devices for a largely poverty-stricken ethnic minority to engineer a revolution. The Black Muslims talk of violence, but the talk seems to function as a psychological safety valve; by preaching separation, they in effect accommodate to the American social order and place racial warfare off in the future when Allah in his time will destroy the whites and usher in an era of black domination. Similarly, in view of population statistics and power distribution in American society, Du Bois and others who have spoken of the inevitability of racial warfare and Negro victory in such a struggle were engaging in wishful prophesies. And Negroes have been nothing if not realistic. The patterns of Negro behavior in riots demonstrate this. In earlier times, as already indicated, those who bought guns in anticipation of the day when self-defense would be necessary usually did not retaliate. And Negro attacks on whites occurred mainly in the early stages of the riots before the full extent of anger and power and sadism of the white mobs became evident.

Negroes of the World War I era resisted white insults and attacks only as long as they had hopes of being successful in the resistance. It should be emphasized that one of the remarkable things about the riots since 1964, in spite of their having been marked by particular resentment at police brutality, is the fact that Negro destruction was aimed at white-owned property, not white lives, even after National Guardsmen and policemen killed scores of Negroes. And in those cases where retaliatory violence has been attempted, Negroes have retreated in the face of massive white armed force. Economically impoverished

Negroes press as far as they realistically can; and one reason for the explosions of recent years has been the awareness that whites are to some degree in retreat, that white mobs in the North no longer organize to attack, and that to a large degree the frustrated Negroes in slums like Watts, Detroit, Washington, or Newark, can get away with acts of destruction.

It is impossible of course to make any foolproof predictions for the future. Yet, judging by past experience and present conditions, it is our view that, despite all the rhetoric of engineering a social revolution through armed rebellion and guerrilla warfare, of planned invasions of downtown business districts and white suburbs, the kind of violence we are likely to witness will, at most, continue to be the sort of outbreaks against the property of white businessmen such as those we have witnessed in recent years. The advocacy and use of violence as a deliberate program for solving the problems of racial discrimination remains thus far, at least, in the realm of fantasy; and there it is likely to remain.

REFERENCES

1. For accounts, see Julian Mayfield, "Challenge to Negro Leadership," *Commentary* Vol. XXXI (Apr. 1961), pp. 297-305; "The Robert F. Williams Case," *Crisis,* Vol. LXVI (June-July-August-September, 1959), pp. 325-329; 409-410; Robert F. Williams, *Negroes With Guns* (New York: Marzani & Munsell, 1962).

2. *Crusader*, Vol. V (May-June, 1964), pp. 5-6.

3. See the RAM publication *Black America* (Summer-Fall, 1965); *Crusader*, (Mar. 1965).

4. C. Eric Lincoln, *The Black Muslims in America* (Boston: Beacon Press, 1961), p. 205.

5. Ralph Bunche, "Conceptions and Ideologies of the Negro Problem," memorandum prepared for the Carnegie-Myrdal Study of the Negro in America, 1940, p. 161.

6. *Crisis*, Vol. XII (Aug. 1916), pp. 166-167; Vol. XIII (Dec. 1916), p. 63.

7. W. E. B. Du Bois, *Darkwater* (New York, 1920), p. 49.

8. A Philip Randolph, "How To Stop Lynching," *Messenger*, Vol. III (Apr. 1919), pp. 8-9.

9. Walter White, "The Sweet Trial," *Crisis*, Vol. XXXI (Jan. 1926), pp. 125-129.

10. "The Robert F. Williams Case," *Crisis*, Vol. LXVI (June-July 1959), p. 327.

11. Elliott M. Rudwick, *Race Riot at East St. Louis* (Cleveland and New York: Meredian Books, 1968), pp. 38-39.

12. Edgar A. Schuler, "The Houston Race Riot, 1917," *Journal of Negro History*, Vol. XXIX (Oct. 1944), pp. 300-338.

13. *NAACP Board Minutes*, Secretary's Report for June 1919.

14. *The Negro in Chicago* (Chicago, 1922), pp. 4-5.

15. *Crisis*, Vol. XIX (Dec. 1919), pp. 56-62.

16. Allen Grimshaw, *A Study in Social Violence: Urban Race Riots in the U.S.*, University of Pennsylvania unpublished doctoral dissertation, 1959, pp. 42-47.

17. *Ibid.*

18. Constance M. Green, *Washington, Capital City, 1879–1950* (Princeton: Princeton University Press, 1962), pp. 266-267; John Hope Franklin, *From Slavery to Freedom* (New York: Alfred A. Knopf, 1947), p. 473; *New York Times*, July 20-22, 1919.

19. Rudwick, *op. cit.,* pp. 226-227; *Negro in Chicago, op. cit.*, pp. 5-10.

20. Alfred McClung Lee and Norman D. Humphrey, *Race Riot* (New York, 1943), pp. 26-30.

21. Roi Ottley, *New World A-Coming* (Boston: Beacon Press, 1943), pp. 151-152; Harold Orlansky, *The Harlem Riot: A Study in Mass Frustration* (New York, 1943), pp. 5-6,

14-15; New York Age, Mar. 30, 1935, and Aug. 7, 1943.

22. In the New York riot, however, the precipitating incident was a physical altercation between a white policeman and a Negro; see Gilbert Osofsky, *Harlem: The Making of a Ghetto* (New York: Harper & Row, 1966), pp. 46-52.

23. Herbert Aptheker, *A Documentary History of the Negro People in the United States* (New York: Citadel, 1951), pp. 93-97, 226-233.

24. Founded in 1817 by a group of prominent white Americans, the American Colonization Society officially encouraged colonization as a means of furthering the case of antislavery. Most Negroes, even most of those who themselves at one time or another advocated emigration to Africa or the Caribbean as the only solution for the Negro's hopeless situation in the United States, denounced the society as a cloak for those attempting to protect slavery by deporting free Negroes.

25. Irving H. Bartlett, "The Free Negro in Providence, Rhode Island," *Negro History Bulletin,* Vol. XIV (Dec. 1950), p. 54.

26. Carter G. Woodson, The Negroes of Cincinnati Prior to the Civil War," *Journal of Negro History,* Vol. I (Jan. 1916), pp. 13-15.

---

3.   THE SOUTHERN STUDENT SIT-INS: INTRA-GROUP RELATIONS AND COMMUNITY CONFLICT

Martin Oppenheimer

This article is a discussion of the southern sit-in movements of the 1960s. The author uses the sit-ins to illustrate how conflicts develop, and how these conflicts allowed tensions and hostilities to be expressed openly. Coser's work on conflict theory is used as the theoretical model for the analysis.

The sociology of conflict encompasses several traditions. There are those who have been interested primarily in intra-group conflict from the angle of control, or power;[1] others have put their emphasis on the field of community relations and inter-group conflict;[2] and overlapping both in the field of sociometry and the study of small groups.[3]

SOURCE
From *Phylon,* **The Atlanta University Reveiw of Race and Culture, Vol. 27, no. 1, (Spring, 1966). Reprinted by permission of the editor.**

[1]For example, the work of Pareto, Mosca, Michels, Selznick.

[2]Robin M. Williams, Jr., *The Reduction of Intergroup Tensions* (New York, 1947) and other studies in the field of prejudice analysis.

[3]K. Lewin, Bales, Borgatta, Hare, Homans, Moreno, Mayo and many others. See especially the recent work by Kenneth E. Boulding, *Conflict and Defense* (New York: 1962).

While much of the historical background in this field comes from the work of German sociologists such as Georg Simmel,[4] it was only recently that an American sociologist, Lewis Coser, managed to bring these emphases together. Coser, in *The Functions of Social Conflict*,[5] brought in also the work of psychologists, including Freud, and derived from this synthesis a series of propositions which analyze social conflict from a functional standpoint.

From the works of Coser and others, it would appear that there are some rules which enable groups following them, even though not consciously, to succeed in attaining their goals. In other words, some activities by groups engaged in community conflict are functional to the attainment of goals, while others are dysfunctional.

It should be possible, therefore, to identify these rules from the existing literature, and, in the light of a specific community conflict situation, see if they are pragmatically useful in making predictions and in working out solutions. The conflict situation which has been chosen as a test is the Southern Student Sit-In Movement of 1960.[6] The paper will be divided into a general discussion of the internal relationships of parties involved in conflict situations, and the interactive relationships of contending groups in conflict situations and the

---

[4]George Simmel, *Conflict* (Glenco, Illinois, 1955) and Theodore Abel, *Systematic Sociology in Germany*, (New York, 1929).

[5](Glenco, Illinois, 1956). Lewis Killian and Charles Grigg, *Racial Crisis in America* (Englewood Cliffs, New Jersey, 1964), closely follow this orientation.

[6]See Also Martin Oppenheimer, *The Genesis of the Southern Negro Student Movement (Sit-In Movement): A Study in Contemporary Negro Protest* (Doctoral dissertation, University of Pennsylvania, 1963). Data are based on study of some 70 communities involved in sit-in activity during 1960 and 1961.

conditions of conducting and settling a conflict.

INTERNAL RELATIONSHIPS

It has long been an axiom in the field of race and ethnic minority relations that the internal cohesion (or ingroup identification, or morale) of a group is heightened by hostility from the outside. Coser and other recent writers suggest, in addition, that for successful conduct of a conflict there must also be a consensus within the group as to how to carry out that conflict. In addition, the morale of participants can be heightened by conducting the conflict in terms of some super-individual goals, such as an appeal to religion or other values. But while on the one hand a consensus, a sense of group identification, and an ideology are needed, on the other hand the more totally an individual particpates in a group (in terms of involving his personality and dedicating himself to the purposes of the group) the more tensions tend to arise; hence mechanisms must be supplied to get rid of these tensions in a constructive rather than a destructive way if the group is to survive.

A sit-in protest group, and for that matter any group confronting great physical danger in a subordinate status in the society, in fact involves a good deal of an individual's personality. To be successful, the group must be cohesive and well-organized. The "self-image" of the participant is involved in everything the group does. Within the social context, which to begin with is one of frustration, a great deal of aggressive energy, or hostility, accumulates. This frustration is increased by the negative response of the dominant power structure—in the form of refusal of service at a lunch counter, etc., and is accompanied by great hostility by white persons in the area; the participant cannot give way to his pent-up frustrations, hostilities, and aggressions in physical or vocal acts of violence, because his tactics and strategy are based on nonviolence. The result is that hostility tends to turn inward, either upon the participant himself, and/or upon his group. Unless measures are taken to provide a channel for this aggression, the individual may be rendered useless rapidly by his feelings in the situation (a kind of battle-fatigue which has been observed in the race relations field) and the group broken up under the strain.

Three devices have been observed which to one degree or another appear to release just such tensions: singing, joking, and the workshop.   What cannot be said in words is said in music, not only to the white opponents, but to other persons within the group, or to institutions and ideas which must be criticized, but without creating the appearance of division. Song inspires morale and group identification by expressing the group's ideology as it is universally perceived by the participants. It unifies the group in a stressful situation and permits release of emotions which have been pent up in circumstances of conflict where emotions, particularly of the violent kind, cannot be permitted.   Thus the songs of the sit-in movement have become an integral part of the image of civil rights in this country.

Joking, or humor, has long been recognized as an indirect way of expressing hostility towards an object.   Political jokes in totalitarian countries are only one example of this, for jokes, like song, permit one to drain off hostilities without the danger of direct confrontation. There are now dozens of jokes which had their origin in the sit-in demonstrations, altogether aside from the more standard jokes of the Negro community. And a series of Negro comedians has risen to fame because of a certain brand of humor that pokes fun at Negroes and white liberals alike.   The sociological and psychological function of this kind of humor is not hard

to uncover if one has any close acquaintance with the Negro community and its behavior patterns.

The workshop is probably the most formal device associated with tension-releasing mechanisms.   This was initially associated with the Congress of Racial Equality, which has been experimenting with it since the early 1940's, and is now inseparable from nonviolent direct action campaigns.   The workshop is essentially a socio-drama in which the participants, Negro students planning an action, play a variety of roles, including white parts.   On the surface this merely serves to prepare the students emotionally for what to expect—and, in the case of violence, how to react. It is seen, in the main, as simply practice in the perfection of control of oneself in stress situations. One latent function of the workshop is as a morale-builder. The students who go into a conflict situation after the socio-drama are not only better prepared emotionally to deal with violence in nonviolent ways, but also know each other, hence trust each other, and know what the group's code of behavior is.   They tend to be loyal to the buddies with whom they have been trained, and to their values. As *The American Soldier* series pointed out, in a combat situation loyalty to one's buddies is often more important to success than hatred of the opponent or knowledge of the reason for the battle.[7]

In the workshop itself, intense feeling is invested in the roles being played, and much latent hostility is released.   Negro students play roles of white policemen, store managers, university administrators, etc., with quite a depth of understanding.   They imitate the actions of hoodlums with a vehemence which actually calls forth violent reaction from Negroes playing the roles of Negro students, even though the actors are

---

[7]S. A. Stouffer *et al, The American Soldier: Adjustment during Army Life* (Princeton, 1949).

their own peer-group associates. Words are thrown about as if the actor had been waiting all his life for a chance to use the words as others have used them in relation to himself. But, solidified by the exclusiveness of membership in a group which has undergone treatment somewhat akin, one supposes, to fraternity hazing, and having drained off latent hostility through play-acting, the group goes forth to function more positively in terms of its goals.

INTERACTIVE RELATIONSHIPS

Conflict between groups is frequently unrecognized. That is, the absence of conflict does not mean there is an absence of hostility. In fact, the longer hostility remains suppressed, the more violent it tends to be once it does break out into the open, as in the case of civil rights. But before hostility can come out, a channel of relationship between the conflicting groups must be present. In a sense, therefore, the act of conflict already presupposes progress towards communication between the contending groups, because, at the very minimum, a common field of action is created, underneath which there sometimes lie common values or goals.

Once conflict has broken out, new relationships are constantly being created between the groups involved. Conflict not only presupposes some agreement as to the rules, but is in addition often a necessary prerequisite to finding out, realistically, what the opponent's strength is, which in turn is a prerequisite to realistic negotiations. Hence conflict can perform a positive function on the road to settlement of a dispute.

A problem, however, is generated by the fact that as the group under attack becomes aware of itself as a group (self-identification) and takes countermeasures, the opposing group also enhances its self-image, takes countermeasures, and so on. Thus the organization of counteractive moves (specifically the founding of the Citizens Councils) on the part of segregationist elements immediately after the Supreme Court decision of 1954 served to make Negroes more aware of their identity, which in turn served to increase the resistance of some white groups, which in turn increased the militancy of Negro groups, etc.

These two elements in the conflict situation are of different weights, depending on circumstances, and play varying roles, which can be decisive in whether or not a settlement takes place. Obviously, "reconciliation will presumably be easier if reconciliation itself is highly valued as a process by the contending parties."[8] The key to an understanding of these two elements in the conflict situation is the degree of reality with which the contending forces approach each other. Realistic perception of the strength of the opposing party is difficult if that perception is clouded by preconceptions inherited from the past. In case after case, the white community leadership in the South has been unable to recognize the seriousness of civil rights movement efforts. Only when students demonstrated their staying power after the initial, and sometimes following rounds of negotiations had failed, did merchants and city officials begin to realize the real strength of the opposition, and, in the light of a new and realistic appraisal, come to terms.

A significant factor determining the degree of resistance to a realistic appraisal—one might say the reality-testing level—in any community seems to be the relative sizes of the dominant and subordinate groups.[9] Where the white group is dominant and the Negro group is large (say, 35 percent of the population or more) but subordinate,

---

[8] Boulding, *op. cit.,* p. 312.
[9] An exception to this rule is large urban centers. See Oppenheimer, *op. cit.*

the white group tends to regard the protest activity of Negroes as endangering the white status quo altogether and tends to resist despite risks to business and commercial activity. Where the Negro group is small, protests by Negroes are not a real threat to the total white status, power, and leadership structures. Since such communities historically also tend to be more commercially oriented, it becomes far more probable that a common acceptance of aims can be reached, aims which will stop trouble and which will give some measure of relief to the Negro group. In the former case, compromise is emotionally impossible; in the latter, it is acceptable. Willingness to create a normal situation, one in which business can be conducted as usual, or nearly so, is more likely when compromise is emotionally acceptable, and when some mechanism for negotiation such as a bi-racial committee is available in addition. As Boulding points out,

" . . . when there are no institutions for procedural conflict, violence is likely to result . . . violence in itself prevents the conflicts from being resolved and indeed perpetuates them. . . . [Violence] creates an atmosphere in which reconciliation is difficult. . . . It likewise makes compromise difficult."[10]

Once the hostility between groups on the community level has come to the surface and conflict has broken out, a series of unfolding stages can be identified, varying somewhat with some of the conditions described above. First, there is an incipient stage, characterized by a good deal of spontaneity and lack of formal mechanisms of control or organization on either side. Both the attacking and defending groups are unorganized and unfamiliar with the strengths and weaknesses of the other. Reactions tend

to be swift and uncontrolled, unplanned, and not thought through. This is the stage of the first demonstration, the early growth of the protest organization, and the relatively unplanned reaction to it by the police, by managers of stores and by other officials and vigilante groups.

Then comes a counteractive phase, which is characterized by the formation of a consensus by the white power structure on tactics of dealing with the demonstrations. Here patterns begin to develop for both sides, and the Negroes become formalized and structured in their organizations. Further training to cope with the counteraction of the whites takes place in the ranks of the Negroes. Store managers move to end the dispute without changing existing patterns of segregation. At the close of this phase, in part due to a failure of the contending forces to come to full-scale grips with each other, the dominant power structure offers to negotiate, or accepts student offers to negotiate, at the price of calling a halt to demonstrations.

Third is a stage of detente, stoppage of action, or "cooling-off period," during which there is no action but the opponents engage in negotiations and size up each other. The student movement gradually comes to the realization that it has misapprehended the purpose of the negotiation and underestimated the staying power of the local power structure. Some become impatient and call for immediate resumption of direct action; others advocate this also, but for a different reason—they realize that further delay will undermine the faith of the rank-and-file in themselves and in their leaders. The end of this phase is often marked by handing to the store managers a deadline or ultimatum naming a date for the resumption of action.

There are situations, however, where no detente ever takes place. Sometimes the dominant group is so prepared to use violence, despite its consequences to the community,

[10]Boulding, op. cit., p. 323.

that no common ground for negotiation can be reached. In fact, it appears that the greater the amount of violence utilized by the dominant group, the less likely it is that any subsequent stage will take place at all. Where, for various historical reasons, resistance to integration is small, the conflict will tend to follow through a normal series of stages until an agreement is achieved; where there is greater resistance (usually in areas with high proportions of Negro population) the movement for integration will bog down in earlier stages possibly even being totally suppressed during the incipient stage.

Assuming a normal development, a reorganizational stage follows the detente. Both sides retrench for a long struggle. Negro students enlist new numbers in their campaign, train them, obtain legal assistance, sit-in and picket, make liaison with the Negro community, whose aid is obtained for auxiliary action such as boycotts and selective buying campaigns. White merchants and city officials make arrests, obtain anti-picketing ordinances and injunctions and urge various compromises at the negotiating table. The economic boycott becomes a serious factor during this stage.

A show-down phase concludes the development. Basically, this is the final test of nerve for both sides in the controversy. If the white community is prepared to utilize violence on a large scale, it can still dominate the situation and crush the civil rights organizations at this point. Or, the white leadership may split, enabling the students to settle with some, who obtain a competitive advantage commercially. More commonly, merchants await the coming of summer in the hope that the departure of local college students will take the steam out of the campaign. Meanwhile, however, as a side effect of the detente stage, there now exists a mechanism for settlement: the negotiating group, or the interracial com-

mission. The merchants, weakened by a continuing boycott by the adult Negro community which does not stop during the summer, finally surrender to the interracial committee, which quietly and without publicity arranges a truce with Negro leaders and provides tests on a predetermined date for the newly integrated facilities.

These stages can be seen functionally as performing two tasks: (1) they create a changing and new set of relationships among the contending forces, including the centralization of command on both sides so that negotiation and mediation can take place if white resistance is not too severe; and (2) they enable the parties to gauge the strengths of each other as a prerequisite to realistic negotiations.

Thus a sociological and historical investigation of contemporary protest activities on the community level illustrates a host of concepts which have been in literature for some years. The positive functions of conflict, the functioning of a group for survival, how ecology affects social action, and the life cycles of local movements are only a few of the many phenomena illuminated by the events of the day. The civil rights movement is a veritable mine for sociological investigation, one which remains relatively unexplored some six years after the outbreak of the sit-ins in Greensboro, North Carolina.[11]

---

[11]A revised version of this paper was read at the meeting of the American Sociological Association, Chicago, August 31, 1965. For a more detailed discussion of the "Workshop" and of specific tactics used in conflict situations by both nonviolent civil rights groups and law enforcement agencies, see Martin Oppenheimer and George Lakey, a *Manual for Direct Action* (Chicago, 1965).

4.   WHAT HAPPENED IN PENANG?

Nancy L. Snider

Since its founding, Malaysia has faced both the external hostility of Indonesia
under Sukarno and the internal problems of a country with large Chinese and
Malay populations possessing conflicting values and economic patterns.
Violence between Chinese and Malays erupted in Penang in December, 1967.
The author reviews the ethnic composition of Malaysia, the political factors
that precipitated the violence, and the possibility of continued violence
between these two groups.

*"If the time should come when the British Empire had passed away . . . these
monuments to her virtute will endure when her triumphs have become an
empty name."*[1]

Thus spoke Sir Thomas Stamford Raffles, founder of Singapore, referring to his own far-sighted efforts to establish sound systems of administration, commerce and education on that island and in neighboring British colonial areas.

The time has indeed come; the Empire has passed away in both substance and name. The closing of British military bases in Singapore and Malaya, now scheduled for

SOURCE
© 1968 by the Regents of the University of
California. Reprinted from *Asian Survey,* Volume
8, Number 12, pp. 960-976, by permission of The
Regents.

[1]Quoted in Charles Robequain, *Malaya, Indonesia, Borneo, and The Philippines* (New York: Longmans, Green and Company, 1958), p. 383.

1971 instead of 1975 due to devaluation pressures, makes fact of Raffles' fancy. Many are willing to give the former colonial power credit for establishing foundations of a reasonably efficient and honest civil service in Malaysia and Singapore.   But British favoritism toward *bumiputera* (sons of the soil) Malays in the Malayan government establishment on the one hand, coupled with encouragement of Chinese and Indian entrepreneurship in the economic sphere on the other, tended to reinforce ethnic divisions already solidified by religious and linguistic divergencies. In addition, the colonial power's policies toward education were very flexible in allowing the immigrant groups to set up and run their own school systems.   This left Singapore and Malaysia with a patchwork legacy of racially and linguistically fragmented educational institutions. In trying to "nationalize" these schools and standardize curricula, the Malaysian government's difficulties during the ten years since Malayan independence have been legion. And it has been attempts by Malaysian government leaders to deal with this highly sensitive problem of education and the closely related one of language use that have frequently caused latent racial tensions to break through the superficial calm of postwar Malaysian society. In retrospect it becomes evident that during the colonial era, in almost all areas of Malaysian development, patterns of growth were encouraged which evolved along mutually reinforcing ethnic lines. This tended to minimize occasions for communal interaction among the distinct segments of the population.

Population estimates for Malaysia in 1966[2] showed penninsular Malaya's population of 8.5 million divided roughly into 50% Malay, 36% Chinese, and 14% other races (mostly Indians and Ceylonese). Malaya's history since World War II, in contrast to that of Singapore, shows little overt evidence of racial violence.[3] The 12-year Malayan Emergency (1948-1960) was consistently put into the framework of a Communist war of insurgency by both sides. It was true of course that the vast majority of the guerrillas

were Chinese, while counterinsurgency efforts were carried out mainly by British and Malay military and civil forces. But there were also supporters of the government forces at almost all levels of the Chinese community in Malaya. Thus, while racial factors played an important role in the Emergency, characterising the conflict simply as a race war would be ignoring other aspects as important or even more important than ethnic distinctions.

The fairly close numerical balance between Malays and Chinese in Malaya seems to have been an important factor in maintaining reasonably good relations for more than twenty years. Implicit in this balance is an almost visceral awareness among members of both communities that neither would gain through a resort to open struggle. The two groups have lived in a relationship of uneasy but tolerant symbiosis for the past two decades.

In rapidly urbanizing Singapore, on the other hand, total population was estimated in 1960 to be about 2 million, of which 80% are Chinese. There have been several racial disturbances in Singapore since 1945. In the mid-fifties Communist extremists playing upon ethnic feelings generated serious riots. In 1964, the year after Singapore became a part of the Malaysian Federation, Malay-Chinese antagonisms erupted into more rioting.[4] Communal tensions had been exacerbated by Singapore's special status in the new Federation as *imperium in imperio*, and by the dynamism of Singapore's Prime Minister, Leo Kuan Yew, who found himself hemmed in by the Malay-dominated central government in Kuala Lumpur. These were the roots of the difficulties which ultimately led to Singapore's expulsion from the Malaysian Federation one year later, in 1965.

---

[2]The last official census for Malaysia and Singapore was taken in 1957, and the next is scheduled to be held in 1970.

[3]However, there may have been quite a few unrecorded incidents, since publicity on such matters may be minimized or suppressed to lessen tensions. At least one major outbreak of Malay-Chinese rioting occurred on Pangkor Island (off Malaya's west coast) in May 1959, but it received little press coverage. About 2,000 of the 6,000 Chinese on the island (which has a total population of about 8,000) were evacuated. See Margaret F. Clark (Roff), "The Malayan Alliance and Its Accommodation of Communal Pressures, 1952-1962," (unpublished M.A. thesis. University of Malaya, Kuala Lumpur, 1964), p. 78.

[8]See Michael Leifer, "Communal Violence in Singapore," *Asian Survey,* Vol. IV. No. 10 (1964), p. 1115.

It was therefore with some sense of complacency and self-satisfaction that Malaya in August 1967 celebrated its own tenth anniversary of independence from Great Britain and, concurrently, the fourth anniversary of the formation of the Federation of Malaysia. Singapore's departure from the Federation in 1965, and the end of Indonesian *konfrontasi* in 1967, had stabilized relations between Malaysia and these neighboring areas. For the first time since World War II, serious discussions regarding Southeast Asian regional cooperation were being undertaken among these countries, with the Philippines and Thailand also actively participating.[5]

Internally, the Malaysian economy remained basically sound in spite of falling prices for Malaya's two main export items, rubber and tin. The ruling Malayan Alliance Party had been the majority party since before Malayan independence. Its position seemed stronger than ever on the basis of a large winning vote in the 1964 elections. The Alliance's troika-like substructure of three communally based parties—the United Malays National Organization (UMNO), the Malayan-Chinese Association (MCA), and the Malayan Indian Congress (MIC)—had produced cooperation among the elites of the three main racial groups in Malaya. Alliance leaders were hopeful that tolerance, if not cooperation, among the peoples of the various racial communities in the country was also increasing, paralleling their own structural and practical example of communal togetherness in acting to govern Malaysia. The party and the government (which have tended over the years to become more and more indistinguishable in the eyes of the voters) have long been embarked on a campaign to mitigate ethnic

antagonisms in a variety of ways. Through programs instituted in government departments, and especially through the Ministry of Information and all communications media, efforts are made to minimize communal differences. Beyond this, the government also tries to promote a sense of overarching Malaysian national identity, separate from and more meaningful than a purely communal sense of identity.

An example of such efforts which relates directly to the political sphere is the 1966 decision by Alliance chiefs to change the Alliance organizational structure to permit direct membership. Up until that time it had not been possible for individuals to join the Alliance Party *per se*. Membership had to be undertaken via one of the three communal sub-parties—UMNO, MCA or MIC. This arrangement laid the Alliance open to charges of furthering racial *apartheid* within its own organizational setup. It also made it difficult for a European Malaysian, aboriginal Malaysian, or indeed any Malaysian not of Malay, Chinese or Indian ethnic origin, to join the party. By spring 1968 the new procedure had brought in some 200 direct members, mostly Ceylonese and Eurasians. At a reception given for these new members, Malaysian Prime Minister (and head of UMNO) Tunku Abdul Rahman reiterated that at this stage of Malaysian political development it was not possible to dissolve the tripartite Alliance racial groupings because "the various races are still conscious of their identity and of the countries of their origin."[6] The "direct members"

---

[5]Since then, of course, the Philippine claim to Sabah has again become an issue of bitter dispute between Malaysia and the Philippines, and regional cooperation has suffered new blows as a result.

[6]*Straits Times* (Malaysia), March 28, 1968. The anomaly of a racially compartmentalized party trying to encourage racial mingling among the people of Malaysia is illustrated by a report of a speech given on the same day by a lesser figure in the Alliance Party. Articles reporting these two speeches appeared on the same page of March 28 *Eastern Sun* (Kuala Lumper). While the Tunku was reiterating the necessity of maintaining

arrangement, however, provides at least a token gesture toward implementing changes in accord with the oft-repeated Alliance view that its own ethnic subgroups will eventually submerge their racial distinctions and fade away, leaving the Alliance a truly *Malaysian* party in which communal differences play little or no part. In this way the Alliance organizational structure itself is meant to serve as a microcosmic paradigm to be imitated, hopefully, by the macrocosm of the Malaysian nation.

During the past decade the apparent success of the Malaysian government and the Alliance Party in dealing with Malaysian ethnic pluralism has been remarked upon by both Malaysians and foreigners. To some it seemed as though, by the very reiteration of the desire for racial cooperation, the fact of it was almost miraculously being brought about.[7] The Penang crisis in November and December 1967, and its aftermath, exposed the superficiality of Malaysian ethnic harmony in terms of its slight degree of penetration into Malaysian society as a whole. Events of the crisis revealed the thinness of the veneer that covers over deep communal cleavages in Malaysia.

THE PENANG CRISIS

In the wake of the British devaluation in mid-November 1967, the Malaysian govern-

---

communal divisions in the Alliance Party, Bernard Lu, political secretary to Finance Minister Tan Siew Sin, said (referring to the need for all segments of Malaysian society to work together to build up a sense of nationhood): "In a multi-racial nation there is no room for watertight compartments split on racial lines."

[7]See Clifford Geertz, *Old Societies and New States* (Glencoe, Illinois: Free Press of Glencoe, 1963), pp. 134-36, for a discussion of the successful functioning of the Alliance Party in multi-ethnic Malaysia.

ment had to decide whether or not it would devalue the Malaysian dollar also. At that time there were two types of currency in circulation in Malaysia and Singapore. Old currency based on sterling had originally been issued for use in Singapore, Malaysia and Brunei when these areas were still under British control. New national currency based on gold had first been issued by the Malaysian government in June 1967, at par value with the old. This new money was eventually expected to replace the old, but no time limit had been set for phasing out and terminating the validity of the old money. After the British devaluation, the Malaysian government suddenly acted to devalue old currency *only*, making it 15% less valuable than new money. The resulting confusion started a groundswell reaction of annoyance and anger among all races and economic groups in Malaysia. The move was especially hard on rural farmers (mostly Malays) and on the poorer urban groups (mainly Chinese and Indians). Many of these people had kept their savings tucked away somewhere in their homes, and the bulk of it was in old currency, not new. The Association of Banks of Malaysia estimated that in the process of converting old money to new the general public lost about $42 million (U.S. $14 million). The public was angry with the government for two reasons: First, it had reneged on its repeated promise that equal value would be maintained for both old and new currencies; and second, it had foisted the devaluation burden, which many thought it should rightly have borne itself, onto the people. Furthermore, this burden fell most heavily on those least able to afford it—the poor.[8]

[8]It has since been reported that the Malaysian government made a profit of M $43.1 million (US $14.5 million) on devaluation in terms of its external sterling holdings. It lost M $14.5 million on investments, but repayment of its predevaluation sterling loans was decreased by M $57.6 million. *Straits Times*, Agu. 21, 1968.

Prime Minister Tunku Abdul Rahman and Finance Minister Tan Siew Sin (who is also head of MCA) initially replied to criticisms by saying that they had had no choice but to devalue the old currency. There were many who questioned the validity of this stand, technically correct though it may have been. The widespread public outcry continued, and Alliance leaders began to reevaluate their attitude. They were rapidly finding themselves in the unusual position (for the Alliance) of facing a rising popular animosity which crosscut racial divisions in the Malaysian polity. Within a few days they decided to adopt one of the suggestions put forth by the opposition Labour Party, that is, to allow five and ten cent coins of both old and new currencies to circulate freely at the same value. This move, although undermining the Alliance leaders' original contention that they had been forced to devalue old currency by circumstances beyond their control, was seen as the lesser of two evils. Mounting public frustration was already being translated into a lack of confidence in the integrity of the government and of its alter ego, the Alliance Party. Malaysia's small and generally disorganized opposition parties were moving to take advantage of the situation. The Labour Party in particular saw an opportunity to cash in on the ineptitude of the Alliance's handling of the problem. This party, whose members were mainly Chinese, had provided weak but reasonably well organized opposition to the Alliance for some time. Its leaders on the island of Penang, where it had a major source of strength, called for a *hartal* (general strike) to protest the situation.[9]

Penang Island covers approximately 108 square miles and lies off the coast of Northwest Malaya. Its 1957 population of about 340,000 included 230,000 Chinese, 60,000 Malays and 40,000 Indians. Penang, like its neighboring island of Singapore, has a long history of direct British colonial rule, first as a Straits Settlement, then as a Crown Colony. Also like Singapore, the majority of Penang's population was and is Chinese. Commercial trade and a growing tourist industry constitute the main sources of income for these two entrepot islands. However, Penang's entrepot trade (much of it with Indonesia) had fallen off badly during *konfrontasi*. Recovery of this lost trade since the end of *konfrontasi* last year seemed to be coming about much more slowly in Penang than in Singapore. One of the reasons for this was a 2% surtax imposed by the Malaysian government on Indonesian goods reexported from Penang. This tax placed Penang in an uncompetitive position vis-a-vis the free port of Singapore. Unemployment on the island was and is high—the state government early this year estimated it at about 20% of the work force, with 10,000 young people leaving school each year, needing jobs.[10] Thus, in the closing months of 1967 Penang's economic situation was somewhat precarious at best. The devaluation of old currency added to Penang's economic problems, providing a unique chance for the Labour Party to exploit economic unrest on the island at the expense of the Alliance central government and the local Alliance organization.[11]

---

[9]*Ibid.*, Nov. 23, 24 and 25, 1967.

[10]*Straits Echo* (Penang), Feb. 13 and 14, 1968.

[11]It should also be noted here that during the months preceding devaluation, the Labour Party had been undergoing internal upheaval. The leftist, more militant, wing had taken control of the party. There is little doubt that this group was initially to blame for the destructive turn of events in Penang in late November, Malaysian government raids carried out then on Labour Party offices uncovered large stores of weapons. Viet Cong-Maoist literature, and even a banner calling for the hanging of the Tunku. Plans for carrying out violent demonstrations and strikes had apparently been drawn up by party leaders some time before the Penang riots. They were only awaiting the right moment to bring

The potential for violence in Penang was also linked to the fact that for some time the municipal government had been rent by factionalism and charges of corruption. Criminal elements and secret society thugs, taking advantage of the tension and confusion that followed the Labour Party strike call, terrorized the area. On November 24, the first day of the Penang *hartal*, 5 people were killed and 92 injured. The federal government immediately put the island under 24-hour curfew and sent in extra police and army troops from Kuala Lumpur to keep order. Communications media, including the government-controlled television station, carefully refrained from naming victims or terming the conflict racial. But it soon became evident that continuing outbreaks of violence had rapidly assumed communal overtones. This was not too surprising given the highly urbanized and racially tense atmosphere of Penang. However, Alliance officials as well as other more objective observers of the Malaysian scene were amazed when a few days later racial disturbances spread from Penang Island across to the relatively peaceful rural Malay areas of the nearby mainland.[12]

Meanwhile, Kuala Lumpur itself was being swept by persistent rumors and threats of a general strike—again organized and generated by the left-wing elements of the Labour

Party. The Prime Minister and his deputy, Tun Abdul Razak, along with other government officials, worked around the clock to prevent a *hartal* and to stem potential clashes in the capital. Through press, radio and television they urged that the public keep calm and refuse to cooperate with lawless elements. The Tunku personally pleaded with Malaysians of all races not to allow themselves to be provoked and to continue with their normal activities, assisting government forces in every way possible to maintain public order. Hawkers and small shopkeepers in particular were requested to carry on business as usual; the government promised them full protection if they refused to be intimidated and kept their shops open. Police and military units, including light armored vehicles, spread throughout the capital city from a staging area at the Stadium Negara. Soldiers with rifles at ready were stationed at ten-foot intervals along many of Kuala Lumpur's busy shopping streets. There is little doubt that it was these strict preventive measures which made intimidation ineffective. The city was very tense, but the shops stayed open. Groups of illegal demonstrators were quickly dispersed by the police. The initial and rather feeble attempt to call a general strike on November 27, and a second more forceful attempt four days later, were both failures. Although some of the suburbs of Kuala Lumpur were put under curfew it was not necessary to impose one in the capital. By early December the crisis in Kuala Lumpur had passed, and the Tunku gratefully praised those who had helped prevent violence.

Following the failure of the *hartal* in Kuala Lumpur, the situation throughout the rest of Malaya gradually began to improve. By the end of December curfews in all sections of the country had been lifted. It was later officially reported that 29 people had been killed, over 200 injured, and some 1300 arrested. Of those arrested, 113 were found

---

about a showdown with the government. That moment came with the devaluation issue. *Straits Times* (Malaysia) and *Eastern Sun* (Kuala Lumpur), Nov. 27 and 28, 1967.

[12] A month after the riots it was revealed that in the wake of the disturbances the police had discovered a Malay religious secret society operating in Kedah on the mainland near Penang. Fourteen leaders of the group, known as *Tentera Sabilullah* (Holy War Army), were arrested for their part in stirring up racial violence. Many of the members were also members of the Pan Malayan Islamic Party (PMIP), a legitimate right-wing extremist party. *Straits Times,* Dec. 27, 1967, and *Eastern Sun,* Dec. 28, 1967.

to be aliens, and the government instituted banishment proceedings against four of them.[13] Political leaders detained included members not only of the Labour Party but also of the right-wing Pan Malayan Islamic Party, and even a few members of the Alliance itself who were foolish enough to make public pronouncements of a racialist nature during the period of the disturbances. At the same time, insistent demands by some Alliance and opposition politicians that the Labour Party be banned were met with a firm "no" from the Tunku. In justifying this stand, he stressed the value of the Malaysian nation of having a loyal opposition. The Prime Minister said that he hoped the Labour Party would now clean house and eliminate the bad elements in the party so that it could become part of this healthy opposition.[14] As if to give substance to his words, late in December the government released Lim Kean Siew, Chairman of the Penang Division of the Labour Party and a member of Parliament, whose sister was then serving as a member of Malaysia's delegation to the United Nations General Assembly in New York. Lim had been arrested and detained at the height of the Penang disorders. Upon his release he stated that he condemned all forms of violence and wished to devote himself to reorganization of the Labour Party with emphasis on strict registration of members and obedience of members to party discipline.[15] It is possible

that the Tunku's refusal to ban the Labour Party is attributable to his realization of the bitter fact that while that party was initially to blame for advocating violence, once racial undercurrents had surfaced, members of other parties (even including the Tunku's own UMNO) were equally culpable in further aggravating communal strife. The cure for the Malaysian malaise obviously involves something more than simply banning a political party.

AFTERMATH OF THE RIOTS

The Penang riots and the events which followed seemed at the time to have a tramatic effect on both the Malaysian government and the people. The rapid and effective moves by the government to immobilize troublemakers and to establish and assure maintenance of order throughout the peninsula were timely and crucial in preventing more serious clashes from developing. These actions were taken in such a way as to restore and enhance public confidence in government efficiency and ability to impose authority—confidence which had been sadly eroded by the handling of the devaluation issue. The Alliance Party, confronted by Labour Party extremist tactics, was given an opportunity to convert its political gaff *re* devaluation into actions that refurbished its public image. Its claim to the allegiance of the electorate as the most pragmatic, efficient and truly multi-ethnic party in Malaysia was revalidated through its successful efforts in dealing with the crisis situation decisively and even-handedly (including the disciplining of its own party members as necessary).

Nevertheless, it has become increasingly clear since that time that the Alliance and

---

[13]*Eastern Sun*, Feb. 9, 1968.

[14]*Ibid.*, Dec. 6, 1967.

[15]*Straits Times* and *Eastern Sun*, Dec. 27, 1967. Shortly after this, Lim was reprimanded by higher-ranking party leaders who said he had no right to make such statements or initiate a reorganization. In March 1968, when many right-wing LP members defected to join the new *Gerakan Ra'ayat Malaysia* (Malaysian People's Movement), Lim denied that he was reorganizing the party to prevent more defections or that he himself was on the verge of defection to the MPM. He reiterated this stand

again in July. *Sing Pin Jih Pao* (Penang), March 26, and *Sin Chew Jit Poh* (Malaysia), July 3.

the Tunku are either unwilling or perhaps unable to take a careful introspective look at Malaysia's racial situation. This would be done for the purpose of proposing long-range constructive steps to prevent or lessen the possibilities of further violent outbreaks of the Penang type. In an historic context, it is perhaps legitimate to blame the racial *apartheid* of Malaysia's contemporary scene on British colonial processes and organizations which tended to encourage ethnic cleavages. However, the pressures of contemporary evolutionary forces in ethnic relations are very great. Past wrongs provide little excuse or comfort in the face of present ignorance or avoidance of the complexities of the current situation.

Since the Penang explosion various suggestions have been made by Alliance and opposition politicians, as well as by academicians, regarding practical moves to improve the country's racial climate. Shortly after the riots, Finance Minister Tan Siew Sin proposed the establishment of an all-races club to promote communication among the races. This suggestion was quickly vetoed by the Tunku, who said what most people were thinking—that he did not really believe that such a club would be of much use in promoting communal harmony.[16]   There were calls for the establishment of a Government Commission of Inquiry to produce a white paper on the riots. These came from opposition party leaders[17] and from the

100,000-member Congress of Unions of Employees in the Public and Civil Services.[18] At first this idea seemed to find favor in government circles. However, early in 1968 it was smothered by comments from the Tunku and other Alliance spokesmen that there was no need for such an investigation. It was obvious to everyone, they said, that the disturbances had been caused by Labour Party extremists and criminal elements ("bad hats" seems to be the preferred term). An editorial entitled "Back to Normal," appearing in the semi-official *Straits Times* on December 13, 1967, made it clear that the Penang riots had sparked no major changes in Alliance policies toward the question of communal harmony in Malaysia. It termed as "psychologically wrong" the suggestion that a Ministry of Race Relations should be established, and claimed that the solution to communal problems ". . . lies in a more deliberate attempt to foster the non-communal society." This would be done through the setting up of more citizens' good will committees and through efforts by civic and volunteer organizations working for the public good to create a sense of national identity beyond communal identity.[19]

a commission of inquiry composed of leading Negroes and white men. Americans have blundered all over the world, but at least they are not afraid to face up to their problems squarely." *Straits Times,* Apr. 8, 1968.

[18] *Eastern Sun,* Dec. 17, 1967.

[19] In a more practical vein, three steps were taken by the government early in 1968 specifically to improve the social and economic climate on Penang Island. In late February the Penang police force was completely overhauled and Malacca's former Chief Police Officer, who had broken the hold of Chinese secret societies on Malaccan businesses, was appointed Chief Police Officer in Penang. Concurrently, a new Superintendent of the West Malaysia Federal Reserve Unit (riot police) was appointed (*Straits Times,* Feb. 29 and Mar. 2, 1968). Finally, in mid-March the 2% surtax on

---

[16] *Straits Times* and *Malay Mail* (Malaysia), Dec. 17, 1967; *Eastern Sun,* Dec. 21, 1967.

[17] They came in particular from leaders of the moderate socialist Democratic Action Party; see for instance the article in the *Straits Times,* Dec. 14, 1967. See also comments by DAP Secretary-General Goh Hock Guan at a forum on problems of racial integration held at the University of Malaya in April 1968. Goh's strident plea for the establishment of such an inquiry commission included the following statement: "The Americans, after their riots six months ago, immediately set up

A sophisticated call for a change in the overall approach to race relations in Malaysia was sounded by Professor Ungku Abdul Aziz, Dean of the Faculty of Economics and Administration at the University of Malaya in Kuala Lumpur. Speaking in mid-December 1967 to the Annual Conference of the Malaysian Trade Union Congress, Aziz called for a commission of inquiry to examine Malaysian race relations in general, rather than just the specifics of the Penang riots. He suggested that this step be taken in order to get at the roots of what he termed

a "spiral of violence" that threatens to create chaos in Malaysia. He proposed that the latent potential for violence in Malaysian society should be carefully investigated in terms of the complex political, social, economic and cultural factors which bear upon it.[20]

There was no public response from the Malaysian government to Aziz's suggestions. The Alliance Party and the government apparently continue to hold to their pre-Penang assumptions regarding the best ways to minimize communal violence in Malaysia. Racial incidents are given as little publicity as possible. Concurrently, the government continues to conduct positive and intensive campaigns exhorting Malaysians to make every effort to get along with each other harmoniously and to refuse to be moved to rash actions by "disloyal elements." The speech made by the Tunku to the Malaysian Chinese community on the occasion of the Chinese New Year in February 1968 mirrors this positive but indirect approach toward racial unity. In what he termed a "heart to heart talk," the Tunku asked the Malaysian Chinese to resist destructive elements such as those calling for *hartals* in Penang and Kuala Lumpur. He requested that they work together with Malaysians of all races to create a peaceful and prosperous land—a land "fit for the gods." He continued:

"We cannot expect Malaysia, torn in the past by colonial administration into racial fragments, separate components, each with their own prejudices, all of a sudden to come together into one whole piece. . . . We have to work continuously and consistently on the principle of unity in diversity, aiming to make this very diversity the source of our strength . . ."[21]

imports into Penang was lifted, pending the completion of a bonded warehouse and free trade zone area at the port, from which goods could be reexported without duty or customs formalities *(Straits Times* and *Eastern Sun*, Mar. 16, 1968). Penang's economic difficulties are far from over, however. Trade has continued to drop during the balance of 1968. New US $20 million wharves at Butterworth (on the mainland near Penang) began operating in September, further reducing Penang's attractiveness as an entrepot. A report by the Chairman of the Penang branch of the States of Malaya Chambers of Commerce, published on August 13 in the *Straits Times,* stated that Penang was "at the crossroads of economic progress." This report posited future development and progress on an increase in industrial development and tourism on Penang Island, and on the enlargement of Penang's hinterland, mainly through completion of a proposed east-west highway to Kelantan on Malaya's East Coast. The latter project's feasibility and practicality, however, have long been in some doubt, and the central government has been dragging its feet on implementation of plans to carry it out. The *Straits Times* said the situation in Penang, as described by this report, is "grave and frightening" (editorial, August 15). Alliance handling of these problems, as well as other "Penang ' issues such as the building of a university branch there, settlement of a festering dispute between Penang's trawler (deep sea) and inshore fishermen, and solving a nagging water shortage which caused rationing in July, may well determine whether or not a further explosion of racial violence on the island can be avoided in the future.

[20]For the entire text of the speech, see *Eastern Sun,* Dec. 19, 1967.
[21]Quoted in *Straits Times,* Jan. 29, 1968. For the entire text, see *Eastern Sun,* Feb. 1, 1968.

Criticism of this appraoch is becoming more vocal. Opposition parties have led the way in attempts to capitalize on it this year, and they will continue to do so during the months of campaigning for the national elections scheduled for May 1969.

The Democratic Action Party (DAP).   Many of the critics are leaders of the DAP, which appeared on the Malaysian political scene in 1966 as a Malayanized resurrection of the skeletal remains of Lee Kuan Yew's (Singapore) People's Action Party (PAP). The PAP had been forced to dissolve its Malaysian branches in 1965 upon Singapore's expulsion from the Federation of Malaysia. The tenor of DAP criticism can be seen in a typical speech given at a DAP rally by the Organizing Secretary of the party, Lim Kit Siang. Accusing the Alliance of playing racial politics, Lim stated that after eleven years of *merdeka* (freedom) more and more people were feeling less and less Malaysian. To remedy this he called for the dissolution of UMNO, MCA and MIC, and their replacement by a "truly multi-racial party, both in character and composition." He also requested that the Alliance abandon all policies and projects which were openly or covertly racist in tone, citing the Malay Regiment of the Malaysian Army as an example. Finally, he called upon the Alliance to stop dividing the people into *bumiputeras* (sons of the soil, i.e., Malays) and non-*bumiputeras* and to take action to raise the living standards of all the rural people rather than encourage the creation of a new class of rich Malays in both urban and rural areas.[22]   The success of the DAP in changing Alliance policies or winning votes by campaigning along these lines is likely to be limited. Such appeals are seen by most observers as thinly veiled attacks on the privileged position of the polity's majority Malays and on the over-riding influence of UMNO as the "senior partner" in the Alliance organization. In practical terms, the DAP is attempting to win the non-Malay vote (especially the younger and more liberal Chinese vote), and to do so its leaders also play racial politics, albeit in a rather indirect manner. In this the DAP is no more blameworthy than most of the small but articulate opposition parties in Malaya. Despite frequent public obeisance made by all the parties to the god of multi-racialism, appeals to the voters are invariably couched in terms easily interpreted by the average Malaysian as pro or con within the framework of his own sense of racial identity.

The Malaysian People's Movement (MPM). It seemed possible in March of this year that a more promising basis for criticism and change in Alliance policies might be found in the formation of a new opposition party, the *Gerakan Ra'ayat Malaysia* (Malaysian People's Movement, or MPM). All evidence suggests that one of the main reasons for the founding of the party was the dissatisfaction and anxiety of certain Malaysian political and intellectual leaders over the Alliance handling of the Penang crisis, and especially the Alliance's refusal to take a more dynamic approach to communal disunity since Penang. The new party's declaration of purpose stated that its founders were firmly convinced that the Alliance had not been and never would be able to meet the challenge of the times, including the national integration of various Malaysian community interests; the achievement of a just and equitable distribution of wealth and opportunities; the tackling of crises and problems in a sober, rational, disciplined manner without panic; and the creation of an atmosphere of security and genuine concern for the existing communities in Malaysia with their specific problems.[23]

---

[22]*Eastern Sun*, Mar. 24, 1968.

[23]*Ibid.*, Mar. 26, 1968.

Some brief notes on the backgrounds of five of the founder-members of the MPM serve to illuminate the personal roots of this dissatisfaction in each case. Dr. Lim Chong Eu of Penang, who apparently was the chief moving force behind the formation of the party, is a former President of MCA. He left that Alliance sub-party in 1959 in a disagreement with Alliance leaders over the number of seats MCA would be allowed to contest in the 1959 elections. In 1961 he founded his own Penang-based party, the United Democratic Party. He was the only UDP candidate elected to the *Dewan Ra'ayat* (House of Representatives) in 1964. Most of Lim's highly personalized retinue of UDP followers in Penang and elsewhere have gone with him into the new party, the UDP itself having been officially dissolved and replaced by the MPM upon its registration in May.[24]

Two other founder-members are Dr. Tan Chee Khoon (former national Vice-President of the Labour Party) and Mr. V. Veerapan (defeated as a Labour candidate in 1964, and recently returned from obtaining a law degree in London). Tan, the MPM Secretary-General, is popularly known as "Mr. Opposition" in the *Dewan Ra'ayat*, to which he was elected as a Labour Party (Socialist Front[25]) candidate in 1964. He had long been the leader of the right-wing faction of the Labour Party, which lost control in the months preceding the November disturbances in Penang. He could do little but stand by and watch helplessly when the left-wing bloc urged strikes and violence. In his letter of resignation from the LP, Tan stated that he was submitting it because " . . . events in the last year or so have indicated that I can no longer play a useful role in the Party." He then cited the need for opposition parties in Malaysia to come together and form an effective opposition to the Alliance with a view to forming an alternative government. He stated that it was the purpose of the MPM to struggle *within constitutional limits* to establish a socialist state and to weld the various races of Malaysia together to form a nation.[26]

Two more of the founders of the MPM are university intellectuals—the MPM's Chairman, Professor Syed Hussein Alatas, head of the Department of Malay Studies at the University of Singapore, and Professor Wang Gung Wu, head of the History Department at the University of Malaya. Early in March, Alatas had spoken out along lines similar to those taken by Aziz in his December speech to the MTUC Conference. He urged the Malaysian government to set up a special committee to conduct research into communal tensions in Malaysia. Remarking that the roots of Malaysian racial conflict are not so much found in social discrimination between groups as in the distorted images the groups have of each other, he suggested that the time had come to evoke genuine public interest in this problem. In a sharply worded criticism of the Alliance *laissez-faire* approach to dealing with communal disharmony, he stated that if the government failed to initiate a research

---

[24] A report in the Chinese-language *Sing Pin Jih Pao* (Penang) of March 31, 1968, stated that the MPM had been particularly active in recruiting new members in Penang, and that ex-Labour or other party members with political experience were especially welcome in the new party.

[25] The Labour Party and the rural socialist Party Ra'ayat formed a Socialist Front in 1957 and campaigned on this basis, winning 8 seats in 1959 and 2 in 1964. The Front broke up late in 1965, probably over a disagreement between the two parties regarding the status of the Chinese language in Malaysia. During the latter half of this year, the two parties have again made herculean efforts to reestablish the Front to fight in the 1969 polls. These efforts have produced some fragmentation in

both parties, but will probably eventually produce a workable coalition for the election period at least.

[26] *Straits Times*, Mar. 25 and 31, 1968.

committee it might expose itself to the charge of not taking the matter seriously. He continued:

"It may also expose itself to the charge that it is unable to think properly on vital problems as a result of continuous preoccupation with festivals, solidarity weeks, operation exercises, entertaining foreign guests, and blissful relaxation."[27]

Wang's affiliation with the new party came as a complete surprise. His resignation from the University of Malaya to take up a research appointment at Australian National University in Canberra in the fall of 1968 had been announced in the papers only a few weeks before. However, his disagreement with certain Alliance policies had been made clear in an exclusive interview in the March issue of *Alliance* (the official organ of the party), wherein he stated that the biggest challenge to Malaysia was communalism. He said that although Alliance government policies were basically sound, their implementation had caused tension between Malays and non-Malays. It was essential, he asserted, for politicians in Malaysia to stop appealing to the racial sentiments of the different Malaysian communities. Chiding the Alliance for its approach to racial discord, he said:

"It is most important . . . for the government to tackle the problems of communalism which have become more obvious, rather than to play on the communist bogey. We may even deceive ourselves that our real problems lie elsewhere if we continue in this way."[28]

The possibilities of success for the new party in opposing the Alliance are difficult to judge at this juncture. The MPM has easily attracted intellectuals, but it is now just beginning to work at the much more difficult practical and organizational tasks

of politics in order to build mass support from the *ra'ayat*, especially labor and rural groups. Without such support it cannot hope to challenge the power of the Alliance. For some months prior to the formation of the MPM, the Malayan Trades Union Congress (representing some 300,000 workers) had been hinting that it might be interested in becoming more active politically. The new party therefore had high hopes that the MTUC might throw its support behind it. These hopes were dashed early in April when the MTUC president announced that his organization would not back the MPM, since it had always been the policy of the MTUC to not be aligned with any political party. The bitterness of this pill was sugar-coated, however, by the announcement a day or two later that four union leaders, including the president of MTUC, would support the new party on a personal and individual basis. At the same time, Dr. Tan Chee Khoon announced that a likely strategy for the new party for the time being would be to seek a national following without a large mass membership.[29]

The initial reaction to the MPM was generally a positive one on all sides. Leaders of the Alliance and of some opposition parties spoke out in favor of the new party as a welcome addition to those providing responsible opposition in the Malaysian political arena. Tun Tan Siew Sin (MCA Chairman) greeted the MPM with the comment "the more the merrier." In cautioning its leaders that they would have to work hard to win support from the voters, he quoted an old Chinese saying: "It is one thing to open a shop, it is another to keep it open."[30] The extreme right-wing PMIP also welcomed the MPM, but leaders of

---

[27]*Ibid.*, Mar. 4, 1968.
[28]*Alliance*, Vol. II, No. 9 (March 1968).

[29]*Straits Times*, Apr. 2 and 4, 1968; *Malay Mail*, Apr. 4, 1968.
[30]*Eastern Sun*, Mar. 27, 1968. See also editorial, "A New Party," in *Eastern Sun*, Mar. 27, 1968.

the extreme left-wing parties, the rural socialist Party Ra'ayat and those remaining in the Labour Party, were a bit less cordial. They accused the new party of toeing the line of right-wing opportunists, and hinted that after they held their annual congresses later in 1968, they would again amalgamate into a Socialist Front to wage a more effective battle in the 1969 elections.[31]

The greatest disappointment for the leaders of the embryonic MPM was the fact that their pre-announcement, behind-the-scenes efforts to come to some sort of agreement with the moderate Socialist Democratic Action Party (and one or two other opposition parties) came to naught. The DAP, whose aims and political stance parallel those of the MPM, refused to merge except in terms of welcoming individual MPM members into the DAP fold. D. V. Devan Nair, member of the DAP Central Executive Committee and the only DAP candidate elected to the *Dewan Ra'ayat* in 1964, explained the DAP's position as one of not wanting to gamble on a new party after having spent some time building up the name and reputation of the DAP as a political entity. Thus, Nair said that when feelers were put out from the new party " . . . we explained that we did not relish the idea of periodically reappearing before the public in new political garbs and disguises."

A more caustic critical comment on the MPM by the DAP, reflecting the deep bitterness of the secret struggle which had taken place, appeared in the Chinese-language press. Lim Kit Siang was quoted as saying that the DAP did not wish to admit communalists, opportunists or political adventurers to its ranks. Its present function, he continued, was limited to broadening and strengthing its political base, rather than trying to capture the government, and only political

fools and swindlers would shamelessly say that they were able to topple the Alliance in the next election.[32]   Acrimonious exchanges of this genre continued throughout most of May and June this year, each leader or opposition party spokesman avidly proclaiming the desire of his party to have a united opposition and blaming other parties and their leaders for blocking this *desideratum*. The effect was to hang out to public view a great deal of the opposition parties' internal dirty linen, consisting of internecine sniping and personal vituperative remarks about the various parties and their leaders.

The DAP's refusal to cooperate with the MPM may be a legitimate stance from the DAP leaders' point of view, given the fact of DAP prior establishment and independent efforts to build an organizational structure in Malaya, Nevertheless, it reflects the divisive adulation of personal and party images which in the past has blocked every attempt by the scattered opposition parties to form a united front against the strong tripartite Alliance establishment.[33]   It is possible,

---

[32]*Nanyang Siang Pau* (Kuala Lumpur), Apr. 1, 1968.

[33]The DAP did manage, during the pre-MPM struggle, to conclude an agreement with the Ipoh-based People's Progressive Party to divide up electoral districts in the state of Perak, so that the two parties would not be competing with each other against the Alliance there in 1969. The DAP had also tried to negotiate a similar agreement with Dr. Lim Chong Eu (then of UDP, now of MPM) in connection with the four Penang electoral districts. Lim refused to negotiate, and there were some nasty exchanges between him and the DAP (*Straits Times,* Apr. 3, 4 and 5, 1968). The DAP eventually announced that it would be strengthening its position in North Malaya, and especially in Penang, because "existing political parties are unable to organize themselves against the Alliance." The DAP said it would contest three of the four Penang constituencies, leaving Lim to his seat in the fourth one, "where he is doing a useful job in his personal

---

[31]*Ibid.,* Apr. 7, 1968. See n. 25 regarding formation of the old and new Socialist Fronts.

however, that the DAP's doubts regarding the MPM's ability are quite genuine—Devan Nair voiced a general question regarding an obvious and possibly crucial weakness of the new party when, referring to founder-members Wang and Alatas, he said: "With the best will in the world, one wonders how the good fight for a multi-racial Malaysia can be fought from the campuses of Canberra or Singapore."[34] The net effect of all the infighting among opposition parties, however, was to reinforce divisions and make any future attempts at unity or even cooperation much more difficult to negotiate.

The test of the MPM's initial ability to make its mark on the Malaysian political world will come in the next few months of political campaigning. It has already been roundly criticized for backing off from some of the more nettlesome "hard issues" of Malaysian politics—language, education, aid to the rural poor, etc. It is presently occupied in establishing an organizational infrastructure throughout Malaya and in preparing a "Worker's Charter" which should boost its appeal to the growing Malaysian working class. A more exact statement of its method of approach in coming to grips with communal disunity may also be forthcoming in the next few months. It is probable that this method will be much more

individual capacity." (Statement of DAP Secretary-General, Goh Hock Guan, at a meeting of DAP members and supporters in Penang, quoted in *Eastern Sun,* Apr. 3, 1968.)

[34] *Straits Times,* Mar. 29, 1968. Nair is on shaky ground himself here, however, since he was elected to the Malaysian Parliament in 1964 as a Singapore PAP candidate, and his wife, until a few months ago, was still serving as an elected member of the Singapore Legislative Assembly. He announced in June that because of his close ties with Singapore, which have made him a political liability to his party, he will not stand for reelection in the 1969 elections in Malaysia. (*Straits Times* and *Eastern Sun,* June 2, 1968; *Utusan Melayu* (Kuala Lumpur), June 3, 1968.

overt and direct than Alliance techniques have been.

It is difficult to say whether or not the Alliance strategy of underplaying ethnic tensions, so effective in controlling race violence during the first decade of Malayan-Malaysian independence, will continue to be an adequate response to the demands of multi-ethnic national development in the future. In spite of the inflammatory occurrences in late 1967, it is clear that the Alliance does not intend to make any major changes in its strategy unless forced to do so by the political exigencies of the coming election campaign. It may well be, of course, that this policy is the wisest and indeed the only viable one, in a society where minor incidents all too easily assume racial overtones and become major problems. The success of the Alliance Party thus far has been remarkable. It has maintained political power while balancing racial tensions within both the party and the polity.

Nevertheless, the Penang riots and the strife which followed have forcibly raised the question of whether or not the muted Alliance approach of the past ten years has really been effective in reducing ethnic antagonisms or has merely been a holding action. So far the Alliance seems to have taken the public position that the Penang disturbances were exceptional. It is certain, however, that Alliance Party leaders and many other thinking Malaysians were jolted by those events into taking a more searching look at communal relations in their poly-phyletic nation. The MPM seems to be one practical result of this introspection. Hopefully, the 1969 election campaign will shed more light on this problem. But it will be absolutely necessary for all parties involved to exercise extreme caution in dealing with the issue during the campaign, in order to prevent a recurrence of overt racial violence in Malaysia.

5.   BLACK v. PAK?

David White

The racial situation in Britain is often viewed as a conflict between whites
and two major immigrant groups: West Indians and Pakistanis. The author
distinguishes between the life styles of these two groups and suggests that
one of the major reasons Pakistanis are not respected is that they do not
engage in conflict or "fight back." Racial and ethnic conflict in Britain,
especially among youth, is thus viewed by White as not merely the result of
antagonisms against nonwhite immigrants, but is differentiated according to
interests, backgrounds, and the cohesion of the various groups.

The hurried writing on the wall at Stoke Newington was brief and to the point: "Up the blacks, down with Paks." "Skinheads' work," the youth worker explained. "The West Indians wouldn't have painted that."

It's a point worth making. For when the Paki-bashing epidemic began in the East End of London, it was generally misunderstood by outsiders. One group—the skinheads—was seen to be putting the boot in to another —the community of Pakistani and Indian immigrants. But youth workers in the area soon noticed that the aggressors were drawn from every other race and nationality in the area, including West Indians. Derek Cox, an experienced and respected field worker of

SOURCE
Reprinted from *New Society*, the weekly review of the social sciences, December 10, 1970, by permission of *New Society* 128 Long Acre, London W. C. 2.

Avenues-Unlimited, the Tower Hamlets Youth Project, believes that perhaps only the Turkish Cypriots, as fellow Muslims, stood aside from the Paki-baiting and rolling (robbing). The rest were as guilty as the publicised bovver-booted skinheads.

Trouble began because, by 1969, the very high concentration of Pakistani immigrants in Spitalfields, on the western boundary of Tower Hamlets, posed a numerical threat to the other nationalities. And the climate was right for violence.

West Indian attacked Pakistani, not because he believed black was better than Pak, but because the relatively integrated community as a whole had decided that anything was better than Pak. The violence was no less ugly for that.

But it was not a symptom of a significant and disruptive racial antagonism between coloured nationalities. Youth workers in the Tower Hamlets area are now worried about "stroppy" groups of West Indians, exclusive and very conscious of being so, who have split with the whites and swiped their girls. Pushed out of the Aldgate cafes and discotheques by the police, these appear to youth workers to have become increasingly inwardlooking, isolating themselves, so that a general prejudice builds up between them and all other nationalities. And where there is strong polarisation of West Indians with totally inadequate commercial or council provision, as at Stoke Newington, this situation will become dangerously commonplace.

Finally, the scapegoat for the 1969-70 resentment in the East End—the Asian community—is still bound to be sufficiently inward-looking and self-contained to create antagonism among outside observers. This, in turn, reinforces the need for self-protection, vigilante groups, and small but worrying gestures of solidarity with black power across the river in the shape of the Universal Coloured Peoples' Association.

The only effective links between the bulk of the Pakistani community and the other nationalities they live beside are forged energetically by detached youth workers. Ashok Basvder, for example, a Kenyan Asian who became accepted as a mediator, has done much to sort out Pakistani-skinhead trouble and gain the trust of both sides.

These contrasting situations—the traditional insularity of the Asian community in Spitalfields, the new exclusiveness of the West Indian group that has for the moment settled on Wapping's youth club, and the traditional integration that has come with 100 years of immigration and dockland settlement in the East End—are reflected in the different races' and nationalities' attitudes towards each other. I think it's important to look at them separately before drawing any broad conclusions.

In one sense, Tower Hamlets has a lot going for it in terms of racial integration. The area has a long history of immigrant acceptance—the Huguenots in the 16th century, a wave of Jews from Russia and Poland towards the end of the 19th century, and in the 1950s large numbers of immigrants from Malta, Cyprus, the West Indies, Africa, India and Pakistan. A good record, blotted by anti-semitism in the thirties, anti-blacks in the fifties, and recently skinhead trouble.

But the area is wretched enough to discourage any social initiative. As the police close down clubs and cafes suspected of being centres for drug trafficking, "commercial provision," for what it is worth, is disappearing rapidly. At night, the isolated pubs shine out like good deeds in a naughty world. The area intersected by Commercial Road, Cable Street and the broad and barren Highway, though cleared of many of the slum dwellings that disfigure Spitalfields, is bleak indeed. A scruffy, listless district, it breeds an habitual lawlessness among the young, from petty theft to grievous bodily harm.

Wednesday evening off Cable Street, once notorious for prostitution, now blank-faced, its shabby shopfronts boarded up. The local detached youth worker is holding his youth club discotheque evening at the St. Paul's Mission for Seamen. He expects about 30 of his regular group to turn up and they do. Not much dancing, though the barely-lit room pulsates to the din of amplified reggae. The girls, white and coloured, sit and watch the group leader dance. A good-looking, stocky West Indian, with cropped hair, slim high-hitched trousers and boots, his favourite trick is to fall forward onto his palms and pick a handkerchief from the floor as part of the dance.

The group is as varied in race and nationality as it can hope to get. Many are half-caste, "porridge," as their youth worker terms them. When the disco evening ends, four of them agree to talk to me: a good-looking Sierre Leone half-caste, a Greek cypriot, a Somali and an Irish boy. All aged 16-17.

All are quick and canny East Enders. Yes, they get on all right with Pakistanis, and to prove it, there are two Pakistanis in their group. There is a bit of disagreement about *how* well they get on with them. "They can play football, you know, so they're accepted." "Bloody Pak" is thrown around in the same comic/insulting manners as "Barbadian Yid" and "Road-digging Paddy"—no worse or better than Spaghetti-bender." But they are critical about Pakistanis in general. Mike the Sierra Leone boy, says: "If Pakis don't push, we tread on them, empty their pockets, or ask 'em for money. If they do push, stand up a bit, we think they're a bit flash, you know." Dave, the Greek Cypriot, isn't so sure: "They cringe. If they did stand up to people we'd respect them."

One of them mutters, "Roll a Paki," and the others play with the phrase, laughing. I learn afterwards that the angel-faced Irish boy had once attacked an old Pakistani, "Just showing off."

They say they're mates with the West Indians, though they don't see many. They know the Wapping group, though they don't go down there. "This black power thing's gone to their heads," says Dave. The parents of two of the boys are fairly strict, and have great hopes for their futures. "Yeah, you get parents saying, don't hang around with so-and-so, but it isn't a race thing. There's no racialism here. Would be if I lived in Sidcup, though.

What sort of person do they admire, I ask. What qualification would he need to have? "Play football." The answer comes in unison. "And tough." A bit of push and an aptitude for football. This, they say, qualifies any teenager of any colour. None of the group makes the "jungle-boy" distinction between African and West Indian and new immigrants and second generation immigrants. "They get into groups, through friends. They soon get accepted. One of the Pakistanis in our group thinks he is an African. He *wants* to be one."

They'll tell you what they think you want to hear, the youth worker warns me. "At first you get on well, or you seem to, and it looks like they've accepted you. But then they draw back and you start from the beginning until you can build something permanent. And a lot of this is nothing to do with colour, just East End."

The situation of immigrant Pakistanis and Indians is still so totally different from that of any other minority group that it seems only fair that a survey of their attitudes should be dealt with separately.

Estimates of the number of Pakistanis in East London vary from 4,000 to 7,000—mainly Bengali-speaking East Pakistanis from the poorer regions—the largest concentration being in Spitalfields. Many arrive in Britain without families, live in housing which Derek Cox's inquiry team described as "indescribably wretched and insanitary," and depend, because of language difficulties, on their fellow countrymen to arrange jobs for them. Their culture isolates them and their Muslim religion isolates them.

They have their own mosque in Commercial Road, their own cinemas showing their own films, and small cafes which act as social centres. They look inward, and create their own rudely organised community, first because they depend on some sort of protection (which may develop into exploitation) in the early days, and second because of their attitude to work. Their stay is usually transitory. They have come to Britain to get a job, earn money, perhaps to gain qualification. They do not, like the West Indians, expect to be treated as British while they are over here.

Integration is made doubly difficult by the lack of a family structure. There are twelve Pakistani men to every Pakistani woman in East London, and therefore the boys and men often lead somewhat lonely and frustrated home lives.

Derek Cox's inquiry into the Pakistani community concluded: "We doubt if enough of the right kind of indigenous leadership has emerged from the Pakistani community . . . The lack of meaningful links with the wider community is an indication that the Pakistani leaders do not know, or do not want to know, how they can halp Pakistanis to integrate." The hold of "old men with beards" over the insular Bengalis, youth workers believe, halts any move towards closer ties with whites, and with them, other nationalities. The progressive leaders, drawn from a professional elite, seem to lose touch with the led.

Youth workers don't see the situation as hopeless, but are worried about the slow rate of progress. And while the bulk of Pakistanis remain divided, insular and ignorant of their own community dynamics, so relations with groups outside will be insignificant.

The inquiry team also found that "there was evidence to suggest that people from East and West Pakistan are not necessarily friendly to each other." This may be because they speak different languages, but it seems also to be a matter of temperament. The West Pakistani teenagers I interviewed made a "Them" and "Us" distinction now and then. "They" never fought back when attacked by skinheads; "They" wanted nothing better than a factory or sweatshop job in Britain.

With the help of Ashok, I was able to talk to a group of six teenagers, all aged between 15 and 17. We met at the International Leisure Centre, which, ignoring its puffed-up title, is a gallant little project in ramshackle rooms off Toynbee Hall, to teach boys and men English. The group were helpful, occasionally to the point of saying "Yes sir" to questions they did not understand.

Questions are the same as those posed to the Cable Street group, yet I soon realise that the Pakistanis are not really interested (or don't appear to be interested), in relations with other immigrants. They *are* interested in relations with white boys. Nassar, an unusually able 17 year old, now studying for GCES, CSES and A levels for the same year, has been in Britain for five years: "if you are with the English, I find you have new ideas. It is good to get together." What I ask, about other races and nationalities. "Ah, they will tell you about their country. You will tell them about yours, and that is all. But perhaps if you mix three countries' peoples you get new ideas."

Nassar makes the point early on that his people come to England to work, and considers there is a basic difference in attitude between Pakistanis and other immigrants: "All the Pakistanis want to do is work. They know they are here to learn and they learn." Other immigrant did not: "If they want to come and work in a factory, why come to this country. They can work in a factory anywhere."

Nassar's ambition enables him to brush aside prejudice, but again, prejudice he anticipates from white boys. "If you want to get on with English boys, you must get your name on to something. Like designing scenery for a school play, so people respect you." It is not that he doesn't think West Indians might be prejudiced against him. Rather, he doesn't think their prejudice important.

The other five, most of whom have been no more than two years in Britain, draw a firm line at contacts made at school and contacts made outside. In every case, after school or work, the boys go straight home. What do you do when you don't want to go home and you've got some spare time, I ask? "We come here."

Shakil, a quiet boy with a persuasive manner, explains why many first and second generations of Pakistanis made no contact: "The second generation go out only with English friends. And they move to Plaistow and Upton Park. They do not live here."

Shafik, a 16 year old who says he gets on well enough with other immigrants at school says of the Turkish Cypriots: "They do not think they are coloured or even foreign. They think they are English." Shakil says most of the Pakistani boys don't play football well enough to join in with other nationalities, particularly English and West Indians. "We think it is a disgrace to lose and that they will be angry. So we do not join." Nassar agrees: "Pakistanis have got to be damned good whatever they choose to do."

The six boys I spoke to were out-going and quick-witted. How the slower more retiring Bengalis would have reacted to this kind of questioning is hard to guess. One could possibly expect the attitudes that would spring from a situation of extreme polarisation—almost no contact or desire for contact with other racial groups or nationalities.

The last group—the nomadic black group which has pitched its tents at Ian Grant's converted fire station at Wapping, seems to provide an example of just that. And from West Indians, this is new. The group is not local. At Easter, it effectively took over Ian's club from the whites. Until Easter, the whites had been in the majority. This group had been moved out of Aldgate when the police closed down the cafes and discotheques it used. The ostensible purpose was to stamp out drug trafficking, but the group were doubtless considered an untidy menace. They moved down to Wapping and manage to hold on to not only the club but also the white girls.

Derek Cox, who with other youth workers has watched developments with interest, explained: "It was a case where the whites tried to get their girls back, and the girls told them 'only if you change the colour of your skin.' "

Ian, a young, friendly, underpaid Scot has won the admiration of detached youth workers for the way he had handled a potentially dangerous situation. Of course, it is he rather than the group who controls the club, though the group are thought to control membership. He reckons the club runs more smoothly than it did when the white boys were in the majority. He backs up the young West Indians, and is probably the first person to give them somewhere settled to go. He is well aware that the odds are stacked against him. The residents, already on edge because of the borough's policy of re-housing single Pakistanis, object to the youngsters.

The group, 80 on normal nights, 180 on big nights, is exclusively black. "There is no contact with Pakistanis at all," says Ian. And the whites have gone. Reggae, the West Indian dance that linked West Indians with skinhead gangs for some time, now bores them. "I think the white kids will try to take the club back." Ian believes; "I hope things don't turn nasty, but it seems likely."

The "stroppiness" of one particular racial group is disconcerting. At Stoke Newington, a youth worker who runs a black-white play group, together with black militants, but is irritated and frightened enough by police interference not to want his name mentioned, sees the groups of bored, bitter black teenagers as the inevitable result of the appalling dearth of social and recreational facilities in his area. "Black power," still a fuzzy enough term in this country, could find some response as an idea of exclusiveness, the one really backward idea that throws youth workers' multi-racial work into reverse. Then it would be all too possible to attribute an "Up black, down Paks" scrawl to a new aggressive race conciousness.

3. CONFLICTS, BOUNDARY MAINTENANCE AND COHESION

Conflict has many results including the development of contact between groups formerly unaware of each other's life styles and antagonisms. For ethnic groups conflict may bring the needs and grievences into public awareness for the first time. This awareness may win concessions from dominant groups within the society. Overt conflict between groups also helps to articulate positions and different stances on important issues among ethnic groups. As subordinate ethnic groups attempt to change their position the barriers to their mobility may become clear through conflict.

Initial concessions from dominant groups may be relatively easy to obtain on an individual basis. More extended fundamental changes will become progressively more difficult to secure and require group support and the mobilization of extensive resources. Boundaries between ethnic groups are indicated in these attempts to secure changes and the rights and privileges of dominant and subordinate groups delineated through the resulting social conflict.

Research on "social distance" has made it clear that intermarriage between many ethnic groups is a clear-cut barrier arousing intense, hostile reaction. from dominant groups within the society (Williams, 1964, Gelfand, 1973). This had been especially true in relationships between blacks and whites in the United States. For many groups, the barriers and boundaries may occur at less intimate points. Eating in restaurants with subordinate groups and primary social contacts may be viewed by dominant groups as a breach of the boundaries they have attempted to develop between themselves and subordinate groups. These barriers may be especially crucial in "competitive" (Van den Berghe, 1967) societies where dominant and subordinate groups are not separated by well-defined physical boundaries.

The discovery of the exact boundaries and barriers to their attempts to attain social mobility and equality may feedback on the efforts of subordinate groups. According to Mack (1965), the frustrations subordinate groups encounter may provide the impetus necessary for the coalesence of the group and its transformation from a statistical "social category" into a "social group" with strongly felt common needs. As this cohesion develops and boundaries between subordinate and dominant groups become defined, subordinate group members may be able to plan strategies more effectively.

Ethnic group boundaries may thus force subordinate groups to develop an "institutional structure paralleling those of dominant groups. Jews in the United States quickly learned that obtaining admission for Jewish students to medical school was difficult. They thus developed their own superior medical schools. Rejected by Christain country clubs they formed exclusive Jewish country clubs.

The articles in this section illustrate the mechanisms that dominant groups have utilized in order to develop boundaries between themselves and unwanted ethnic groups. They also detail the effects these mechanisms have had in developing cohesion among subordinate ethnic groups. Higham explores the forms of "nativism" that arose in the early 1900s to meet the incoming waves of immigration. Friedmann's controversial article attempts to show that the strong group ties of Jews throughout their history have been largely due to the social conflicts and discrimination they have encountered.

Eitzen's and Donoghue's articles are studies of the patterns of conflict and discrimination towards ethnic groups in three societies. For the Jews, Chinese, and Japanese discussed in these articles, social conflict has resulted in the development of boundaries that have fostered internal cohesion. This cohesion has been crucial in the attempts of the Chinese in the Phillipines and Jews in Poland to achieve social mobility, or the attempts of the "eta" in Japan to survive.

Marris' short article illustrates how formerly colonized countries have witnessed the development of social conflicts between outside ethnic groups who formerly dominated the economy, and newly emerging nationalist ethnic groups. In countries such as Israel, ethnic conflict has been subdued because conflict with outside forces has mobilized strong internal cohesion. Elon delves into the emergence of ethnic conflicts as a period of relative stability in Israel continues.

Finally, Fleurant details the ethnic situation in Haiti, a country whose political and ethnic structure remains relatively unexplored. His analysis reveals a pattern of control and coercion that has helped to perpetuate a rigid social system with strict boundaries between groups. Ethnic conflicts in all of these situations have thus had comparable results for the groups involved despite the disparate historical circumstances of the conflicts.

REFERENCES

GELFAND, DONALD E.
   1973 "Ethnic relations and social research: A reevaluation." Section I
          of this volume.

MACK, RAYMOND
   1965 "The components of social conflict." *Social Problems,* 12 (Spring):
          388-97.

VAN den BERGHE, PIERRE
   1967 Race and racism. New York: John Wiley.

WILLIAMS, ROBIN M.
   1964 *Strangers next door: Ethnic relations in American communities.*
          Englewood Cliffs: Prentice-Hall.

---

1.   THE LOSS OF CONFIDENCE

John Higham

This discussion of "nativism" focuses on the Progressive period of United
States history. During this period anti-immigration sentiment developed
among eastern "patricians," labor unions and southerners. All of these
groups perceived the immigrants entering the United States from Eastern
Europe as a threat to their dominance and their attempts to maintain
boundaries between themselves and subordinate racial and ethnic groups.

*"Heredity will tell the story of our greatest woes. It is like inoculating a
whole nation of people with leprosy, that can be eradicated from the blood
only by a racial lapse, through decades of time, to rejuvenating savagery."*
                                                    Charles Major, 1910

SOURCE

From *Strangers in the Land: Patterns of American
Nativism* **1860-1925, by John Higham, Rutgers
University Press, New Brunswick, New Jersey, 1955.**

In the decade from 1905 to 1915, while
patrician nativists were building a systematic
ideology, popular nativism was struggling to
recover the vitality it had had in the

mid-nineties. From 1906, when the literacy test reappeared in Congress, to the beginning of American involvement in the First World War, the jaunty self-assurance with which America as a whole had greeted the twentieth century was slowly deteriorating. Xenophobia was steadily on the rise. Although we may take 1905 or 1906 as its starting point, resurgent nativism did not announce itself with the explosive force of a second Haymarket riot. Nor did it, in all probability, regain even at the end of the period the hysterical intensity of the 1890's. Yet the prewar revival of nativism has major significance. It prepared the way for the greater passions of the war years, and it also set in motion trends that reached fulfillment once the war was over.

This most obscure of all periods in the history of American nativism eludes any simple or easy analysis. It started during relatively happy, abundant years, when most people felt sure that reform was liquidating problems of the nineteenth century. Furthermore, anti-foreign feelings steadily gathered strength at a time when the dominant force of progressivism was also surging upward in potency and enthusiasm. To understand the growing vigor of nativist movements in the late years of the Progressive era one must take account of many things: of changes in the pattern of immigration; of ideas, inherited from earlier periods, that had little to do with a progressive spirit; and of certain alterations that occurred in that spirit itself.

THE ETHNOCENTRIC BACKGROUND

All through the Progressive era, through its years of confidence and through its returning doubts, the human tide rolled in from crowded Europe. From a low point in 1897 the current ascended to its zenith in 1907 and then fluctuated at a level about 650,000 per year until the outbreak of the World War.

At no time in the nineteenth century had such numbers crossed the Atlantic. On the other hand, the proportion of native- to foreign-born in the total population did not substantially vary, and the cityward movement of the native population more than kept pace with the increasing urbanization of the immigrants. Percentagewise, the immigrants were barely holding their own.

What was changing significantly was their destination and their composition. Like the major domestic migrations, the transatlantic current was moving more than ever toward the cities; despite the efforts of private agencies and of the federal Division of Information, established in 1907, Europeans no longer in any number found homes in the small towns or the countryside of America. Also, the new immigration from southern and eastern Europe now thoroughly overshadowed the dwindling stream from Germany, Scandinavia, the Low Countries, and the British Isles. In the period from the Spanish-American to the World War the new immigration was nearly three and a half times the size of the old.[1] Few nativists, except the anti-Catholic crusaders who could never forget the Irish, now failed to attribute great importance to the shift in nationalities. Around this distinction between old and new—not around the general anti-foreignism that had prevailed in the 1890's—the return of nativism clearly centered.

The collapse of widespread hatred at the turn of the century by no means dispensed the new immigrants from the distaste which older Americans had always felt for their culture and appearance. Since only a small segment of progressive opinion sought positive values in the foreigners' way of life, a traditional ethnocentric aversion spread with the growing numbers of the newcomers and their increasing prominence on the American scene.

Among the score or more of nationalities now funneling through Ellis Island, only

Italians and Jews were commonly distinguishable in American eyes from the nameless masses who accompanied them, and Italians and Jews continued to suffer the most resentment. The Italian still bore as vividly as ever the stigma of impassioned crime. During the ebb of nativism in the early years of the century, headlines in metropolitan newspapers trumpeted the tale of Italian blood lust incessantly: "Caro Stabs Piro . . . Cantania Murdered . . . Ear-Biting Crime . . . Rinaldo Kills Malvino . . . Gascani Assaulted . . . Vendetta Near Oak Street . . ."[2] Doubtless the reports inspired less terror than they had a decade earlier, partly because the public was learning that the violence was almost entirely intramural. Italian lawlessness ignited no further jingoist explosions and precipitated fewer lynchings. Nevertheless, it was universally believed that serious offenses were rapidly increasing—as they probably were. Lax American law enforcement was attracting to the United States a considerable number of Sicily's bandits; here, through blackmail and murder, they levied tribute on their intimidated countrymen more successfully than they had at home. By 1909, when a combined drive of American authorities and Italian community leaders began to reduce these activities, the image of a mysterious Black Hand Society, extending from Italy into every large American city, was fixed in the public imagination.[3]

Although the Jews were certainly not exempt from the new immigrants' general reputation for criminality,[4] on the whole the anti-Semitic stereotype pointed to private misbehavior rather than public misdemeanor. With the return of confidence, the nationalistic fears of the 1890's, that the Jews were wrecking the American economy and conspiring to rule the world, had vanished; no one now accused the Jews of subversive activity. Nor were they so liable to physical attacks, except in the foreign quarters.[5]

But what did persist, and indeed advance, was the older Shylock tradition, the notion of the Jews as an immoral, unmannerly people, given to greed and vulgarity. The general American materialism and social climbing that followed the Civil War had thrown this image into relief and had set in motion a corresponding pattern of social discrimination. Throughout the late nineteenth century, beneath the stormy surface of harsher sentiments, this tendency to judge Jews as acquisitive barbarians and to recoil from association with them affected ever larger segments of American society. In the Progressive era social anti-Semitism was still spreading.

Part of the explanation for the sharpening of discrimination at a time of relative tranquillity lay in the swift upward thrust of the new Jewish immigrants. Like the German Jews who preceded them and whose social ascent had occasioned the earliest prohibitions, the refugees from Czarist persecution had a dynamism rare among foreign groups. They quit the slums in conspicuous numbers, produced an affluent class of real estate speculators and clothing manufacturers, and alone among recent immigrants sent a good many of their children to college.[6] As they rose, native Americans threw new obstacles across their path. Already shut out of clubs, most summer resorts, and many private schools, Jews found it increasingly difficult in the early twentieth century to enter college fraternities and faculties. Restrictive covenants became common in urban residential areas.[7] More important, job opportunities were beginning to contract. Sons and daughters of eastern European Jews were edging into the white-collar world and finding office managers unwilling to employ them.[8]

Because of their exceptional mobility, the Jews met the most economic discrimination, but at the same time other new groups ran athwart middle-class proscriptions. Italian applicants for clerical jobs often felt obliged to call themselves French or Spanish or Turkish,[9] just as some Jews denied their national origin. As if to demonstrate that the pattern of discrimination did not apply exclusively to any single nationality, state legislatures enacted prohibitions on the entry of all aliens into certain specialized occupations. In the nineteenth century, discriminatory legislation had aimed largely to exclude the immigrant from the relatively unskilled occupations he first sought out. But at the turn of the century states began to outlaw the unnaturalized foreigner from various white-collar jobs. Some revised their codes to require American citizenship of all attorneys. New York in 1909 adopted the same stipulation for private detectives. Michigan prohibited the issuance of a barber's license to any alien. About 1909 a successful legislative campaign to deny nondeclarant aliens acceptance as certified public accountants got under way. Three eastern states went entirely beyond the vocational field to regulate avocations. New York in 1908 required aliens to pay $20 for a hunting license, as against $1 for citizens. A little later Pennsylvania flatly prohibited aliens from hunting and so from possessing shotguns, rifles, or dogs of any kind. In two counties of Massachusetts it became a crime for an alien to pick wild berries or flowers except on his own property.[10]

Yet none of this unfriendliness necessarily signified a rebirth of the nativist spirit. Conceivably the coldness, the repugnance, and the exclusions could have resulted simply from the growth of the new immigrant population. Nativism cut deeper than economic jealousy or social disapproval. It touched the springs of fear and hatred; it breathed a sense of crisis. Above all, it expressed a militantly defensive nationalism: an aroused conviction that an intrusive element menaced the unity, and therefore the integrity and survival, of the nation

itself. The coming of the new immigration had contributed to late nineteenth century xenophobia, and its presence played a more crucial role in the twentieth century, but at both times the intensity of the hostility reflected larger factors in the American situation.

For clues to the distinctive sources of the new nativism one must turn to its earliest significant symptom: the fresh and surprisingly vigorous effort to enact a literacy test in 1906. This fourth failure to secure what had been defeated in 1897, in 1898, and again more dismally in 1902, revealed the emerging influence of the newer immigrants in American politics; but the narrow margin and desperate measures by which Uncle Joe Cannon and his immigrant allies prevented passage of the literacy test also signaled a recrudescence of nativist power. Here several of the tangled threads of modern American xenophobia first intersected, some old, others just coming into view. The incident furnishes a starting point for unraveling them.

Early on the Congressional scene appeared pressure groups which had labored for similar legislation in previous years: the veterans of immigrant controversies. The patrician intellectuals of the Northeast, while busy modernizing their ideology, had not changed their legislative tactics. The Immigration Restriction League, still supported by old New England families, was carrying on in 1905 and 1906 as it had since the 1890's. Sensing a shift in public opinion, the league hired a new Washington lobbyist and prepared another campaign. Henry Cabot Lodge again cooperated with the league in the Senate, although with unwonted circumspection. Seemingly the multiplication of immigrant votes in Massachusetts (and perhaps the pressure of business opinion) lent a certain prudence to Lodge's activities. He never again exercised the initiative and leadership on restriction which he had taken during the nineties. In his impetuous son-in-law,

Congressman Augustus Gardner, the league had a more aggressive spokesman in the House of Representatives. It was Gardner who forced the immigration bill out of the standpat Rules Committee and who struggled vainly against Speaker Cannon's strategems.[11]

Organized labor too returned to the fray and returned with unprecedented vitality. The unions had played a rather limited role in nineteenth century movements for general restrictions on immigration. Even in the feeble, literacy test campaign of 1902 the American Federation of Labor had not acted with conspicuous vigor or resolution. By 1906, however, conditions had changed, and labor's heart was in restriction. In the years from 1897 to 1904, a period of relative harmony between capital and labor, the A.F.L. grew enormously, in no small measure by recruiting native American artisans. Because of this expansion and also because most A.F.L. unions ignored the masses of unskilled workers, the proportion of native-born in the organization was evidently increasing; it was losing touch with its own immigrant roots.[12] The decline of immigrant influence in the federation might alone account for the organization's heartier acceptance of restriction, but after 1904 another factor gave a positive impetus to the idea. A massive attack by organized business threw organized labor on the defensive. The unions stopped growing blocked by boycotts, open-shop campaigns, and in some measure by employers' handling of cheap immigrant labor (notably through the practice of "balancing nationalities"). This display of corporate power whetted resentment against men who seemed more than ever pliant tools of the corporations. Fearful, angry, and discouraged, the A.F.L. for the first time turned to immigration restriction with determination. The literacy test became one of its cardinal legislative objectives as it warned recalcitrant Congressmen of retaliation at the next election.[13]

The strange alliance of patricians with union labor, an alliance which linked A.F.L. President Samuel Gompers and Henry Cabot Lodge in the only common endeavor of their two careers, would not of itself have made much headway against the powerful forces arrayed in opposition. The gathering resistance to restriction by big business and by the new immigration was creating a coalition at least as strong as the Lodge-Gompers axis, and because both alignments cut across party divisions, neither the Republican nor the Democratic party could serve as a nativist vehicle. The traditionally restrictionist groups needed substantial outside support for any show of strength, and this meant a shift in at least some sectors of public opinion. The shift was occurring in 1905 and 1906, chiefly in two regions of the country.

The veteran restrictionists felt the new wind that was rising in one section. In fact, they set their sails to catch it. Gompers later recalled: "When the Japanese school issue originating in San Francisco focused attention on the Japanese phases of the immigration question . . . there developed an opportunity of getting action on immigration." Lodge had the same perception. "This intense feeling on the Pacific Slope," he wrote to Theodore Roosevelt in the summer of 1905, "may help us to get some good general legislation . . . on the anti-Japanese-Chinese agitation supported by the labor people we might win."[14]

Neither Gompers nor Lodge realized that another section was taking their cause just as much or more to heart. The South as well as the Far West was stirring with nativist ferment. In fact, two southerners seized the initiative in Congress. An Alabaman, Oscar W. Underwood, was the first to raise the immigration question when the legislators convened in December 1905. Breaking irrelevantly into another debate, Underwood instructed the House on the pure whiteness of the old immigration in contrast to the mixture of Asiatic and African blood coursing in the veins of southern Europeans. When the Senate took up the issue a few months later, the literacy test was not introduced by the more cautious Lodge but rather by Senator F. M. Simmons of North Carolina. Simmons appealed fervently for the preservation of Anglo-Saxon civilization against immigrants who "are nothing more than the degenerate progeny of the Asiatic hoards [sic] which, long centuries ago, overran the shores of the Mediterranean . . . the spawn of the Phoenician curse. . . ."[15]

GRASS ROOTS OF ANGLO-SAXON NATIVISM

With these words, a new phase in the history of American nativism inauspiciously began. Although beaten in the legislative fight of 1906-07, the southern and western opponents of immigration, together with the eastern restrictionists, pressed steadily forward in succeeding years. And just as steadily the importance of the West and South in the nativist coalition grew, until the preponderant strength of the movement came from those outlying regions, where the main object of attack, the new immigration, was least numerous.

Throughout that whole vast area one prevailing quality and character stamped the anti-foreign drive from the outset. It was racial; it rang with the shibboleths of the Anglo-Saxon tradition. Yet the southern and western nativists knew little or nothing about the racial science that was beginning to affect literate northern circles. For some time the crude bombast of cotton Senators and California statesmen owed hardly anything to the pretentious doctrines of race suicide, eugenics, and racist anthropology. South and West were sectional spearheads of a popular kind of racial nativism that arose parallel with but was not dependent upon the new racial ideology.

The taproot of the reaction was gnarled and massive, imbedded deeply in the common folkways of the two areas. The South and the Pacific Coast alike thought of themselves as a "white man's country." They had long struggled—in different degrees and in different ways—to maintain white supremacy, often without the aid of a systematic ideology. From Seattle to Savannah primitive race-feelings, wrought deeply in the American character, flourished as nowhere else in the United States. Projected on the new immigration, these ancient feelings gave southern and western nativism its peculiar energy.

On the West Coast, as Lodge and Gompers appreciated, the Japanese question precipitated the racial anxieties which infected attitudes toward Mediterranean and eastern European peoples. Anti-Japanese sentiment, gathering strength slowly after 1900 as immigration from Nippon increased, burst forth in a raging flood in 1905. Alive with hysteria, the California legislature unanimously called for Japanese exclusion, boycotts of Japanese businesses began, and the San Francisco School Board ordered the segregation of Asiatic pupils. The fires of anti-Oriental hatred cast at least a pale reflection on European outsiders. California newspaper editorials excoriating the Japanese had a way of broadening into appeals to preserve America for Americans. The Asiatic Exclusion League, an organization formed in 1905 which soon claimed over one hundred thousand members, resolved that *all aliens* should be disarmed in order to prevent insurrection. Other anti-Japanese agitators on the West Coast trembled at the dangerously inferior blood pouring across the Atlantic from Southern Europe as well as across the Pacific. Far Western Congressmen repeatedly tried to attach anti-Japanese provisions to general immigration measures, and in doing so they became one of the foremost blocs in the whole restrictionist movement.

Occasionally a representative of the West Coast might regret that the literacy test was not more directly a test of blood and race, but by 1912 not a single member of Congress from the eight westernmost states voted against the literacy proviso.[16]

The threat of the "Yellow Peril" to white America touched a responsive chord in the South, the only other section of the country which sympathized quickly and widely with California's war against the Japanese.[17] Southerners also sensed the general, nativist significance of the Japanese issue, as the comments of Underwood and Simmons on the semi-Asiatic ancestry of southeastern Europe suggested. Fundamentally, however, the South's hostility to the new immigration reflected its own long-standing "ethnophobia"; the Japanese were settling in a section of the country so remote from the South that their presence could not concern it vitally. At bottom it was the Negro issue that stirred southern anxieties about European and Asiatic immigrants alike. For decades the South, above all other regions, had cherished race-feelings in order to keep the white man irrevocably superior to the black. Now, Dixie spokesmen warned time and again that one race problem was bad enough without further endangering white supremacy through immigration. In 1912 southern Senators voted 16 to 1 for the literacy test; southern Representatives 68 to 5.[18] And in both houses they supplied the driving force behind the measure.

The extension of southern and western race-feelings to include European immigrants seems, therefore, a simple and "natural" development as long as one does not ask why it occurred when it did. Both sections had nourished a pride of race for a very long time; yet only in the twentieth century did these regional patterns of white supremacy breed a related attack on the European newcomers. If residents of the Pacific Coast discovered a Japanese menace only

after 1900, they had fought another Oriental people, the Chinese, ever since the 1850's. It is significant that the anti-Chinese movement in the Far West in the late nineteenth century had not contributed directly to other anti-foreign phobias. Although the basic Chinese exclusion law was enacted in 1882, the year of the first general immigration law, the Congress that passed the two measures sensed no connection between them. At no time in the nineteenth century did immigration restrictionists argue that Chinese exclusion set a logical precedent for their own proposals. The two issues seemed so different that foreign-born whites felt no embarrassment in leading the anti-Chinese crusade, while San Francisco's most bitterly anti-European nativists held entirely aloof from the war on the Oriental.[19]

The nativist eruption in the South presents a still more difficult puzzle, for the Negro—unlike the Japanese on the West Coast—had always been there, and his presence never ceased to prey on the southern mind. Yet southern views on immigration underwent an astonishing revolution in the early twentieth century. Like the West, the South had shared in the nation-wide nativism of the mid-nineties, but what panic it felt then took a largely anti-radical and jingoist form. Southern spokesmen in the late nineteenth century seldom attacked immigrants in terms of race, and some invoked the unity of "the great Caucasian race" in resisting immigration restriction. Moreover, economic interests kept every kind of nativism so well in check that in January 1898, southern Senators voted 15 to 3 against the literacy test, supplying more than half the opposition to it.[20] A decade later the South was becoming the nativist section par excellence, its spokesmen soon to be prominent in every anti-foreign movement.

Undoubtedly one reason for the blossoming of these long encysted race-feelings lay in the character of the Europeans who were now arriving. The predominance of new over old immigration—a trend which was clearly appreciated in the early 1890's only in the Northeast—was now becoming apparent to Americans in every part of the country. Everywhere the thought of European immigration now suggested strange images of Mediterranean, Slavic, and Jewish types, rather than the familiar German, Irishman, or Scandinavian. The new groups did, on the whole, have an exotic look about them for ethnological as well as cultural reasons, and in sections with a highly developed race consciousness their whiteness was easily open to question. "The color of thousands of them," warned Congressman Thomas Abercrombie of Alabama, "differs materially from that of the Anglo-Saxon."[21]

Along with a general realization that the whole stream of immigration was changing, southerners and westerners were beginning to see a substantial number of the newcomers with their own eyes. In the early twentieth century a good many southern and eastern Europeans worked their way westward to the Pacific Coast. By 1907 they formed, together with the Mexicans and Asiatics, the great majority of the general construction workers and railway section hands. They provided a very large part of the common labor in mills and fisheries, while the Italians and Portuguese aroused sharp jealousy by duplicating the success of the Japanese in intensive truck farming. During the decade the total number of new immigrants in the Far West more than tripled.[22] At the same time a relatively less important but not insignificant stream was seeping into the South. Outisde of New Orleans and a few adjacent parishes, the South had known hardly any new immigrants until the very end of the nineteenth century. Then they became somewhat more common: Italian farmhands and railraod workers, eastern European shopkeepers and miners, scattered widely enough to be noticeable. While the

South's small population of northern European birth declined between 1900 and 1910, the number of southern and eastern Europeans more than doubled.[23] Both the southward and westward movements were only trickles compared to the great tide pouring into the North; the whole area beyond the Rockies and below the Mason and Dixon Line had only half as many new immigrants as did New York City. But sections deeply sensitive to complexion and cast of features readily detected a swarthy face.

In the South, the newcomer's "in-betweenness" seemed a double threat. He might endanger not only the purity of the white race but also its solidarity. In other words, the foreigners, partly because of their low cultural and social status, more largely because they had no background of southern traditions and values, might relax the pattern of white supremacy. Particularly the Italians, who sometimes worked beside the blacks on large plantations, seemed to lack a properly inflexible spirit. In the little town of Tallulah, Louisiana, for example, the coming of five Sicilian storekeepers disturbed the native whites because the Italians dealt mainly with the Negroes and associated with them nearly on terms of equality. They violated the white man's code. In a few years a quarrel over a goat resulted in the lynching of all five. In another locality the whites tried to keep the color line sharp and clear by barring Italian children from the white schools.[24] Meanwhile the Negroes too distrusted the "Third Force" entering the southern racial world, for the newcomers did their work and sometimes came as their competitors. Booker T. Washington echoed the sentiments of white nativists by warning that southern European immigration might create "a racial problem in the South more difficult and more dangerous than that which is caused by the presence of the Negro."[25]

To explain the nativistic thrust of southern and western race-feelings solely in terms of a change in immigrant types is, however, to tell only half of the story. If we conclude that the penetration of the new immigration into the South and West automatically activated the color phobias of those areas, we do little justice to the distinctive essence of all nativisms. In every guise, the nativist stood always as a nationalist in a defensive posture. He chose a *foreign* adversary, and defined him, in terms of a conception of the nation's most precious and precarious attributes. Along with the social impact of the new immigration, the South and the Far West in the early twentieth century were also tingling with the ideological stimulus of a new nationalism. Perhaps the kind of nationalism that flourished in the wake of the Spanish-American War did as much as anything else to enable the guardians of white supremacy to discharge their feelings on the new foreign groups.

Ordinarily, the almost instinctive pride and arrogance with which white men met black and yellow and red men in North America bore little relation to a nationalist spirit. The pattern of white supremacy crystallized long before the birth of American nationalism, and in the nineteenth century the latter, despite its gradual assimilation of race-ideas, remained largely detached from primitive race-feelings. The exaltation of white supremacy in the antebellum South had actually served to weaken national loyalty; and California's anti-Chinese hysteria had presented itself largely as a defense of "white civilization," not as an explicitly nationalist movement.[25] At the turn of the century, however, the Anglo-Saxon idea of American nationality was so widely popularized that the racial egoisms of South and West could easily permeate a nationalism ideologically adapted to receive them. The expansion of the Anglo-Saxon tradition at the turn of the century, while preparing the way toward racism among northern intellectuals, also opened a wider field for the popular hatreds at the grass roots of the South and West.

Every section of the country shared in the jubilant Anglo-Saxonism touched off by the victories of 1808. The South, though somewhat less enthusiastic about a colonial policy that other parts of the United States, found the ideological by-products of the new departure deeply satisfying. The imperialist theory of the superiority of the Anglo-Saxons seemed to southerners to vindicate their own regional pattern. White supremacy was becoming, in Professor C. Vann Woodward's phrase, the American Way. It was perhaps not entirely coincidental that the period of overseas expansion coincided with a general tightening of race lines within the South through disfranchisement and sterner segregation laws.[27] Moreover, the Spanish-American War itself set the South firmly in the midstream of American nationalism. As long as the bitter heritage of disunion dominated southern thought—and much sectional hatred persisted through the 1870's and 1880's—nearly all of the animus against outsiders centered on the northern Yankee. The War of 1898 completed a stage in sectional reconciliation by turning the martial ardor of the Confederate tradition into a patriotic crusade, by linking all parts of the country in a common purpose, and by giving the South an opportunity to demonstrate a passionate national loyalty.[28] Relatively secure now in its own acceptance in the Union, the South could join wholeheartedly in other crusades for national homogeneity, especially when racial sentiment synchronized with nationalism. Southerners (like New Englanders) had been proud of their Anglo-Saxon ancestry since ante-bellum days; in the twentieth century they found it easy to boast that this inheritance, buttressed by the code of white supremacy, made the South the real bastion of true Americanism.

The testimony of Congressman Martin Dies, Sr., of Texas, before a House committee is a fair illustration of how the southern assault on the new immigration blended race-feelings with the ideas of Anglo-Saxon nationalism.

MR. DIES. *As the little turtle, when the egg hatches on the sea shore instinctively makes for the water, so these beaten races of earth instinctively turn to the head of the government as the great father . . . I would quarantine this Nation against people of any government in Europe incapable of self-government for any reason, as I would against the bubonic plague. . . . I will admit the old immigration of the English, Irish, Germans, Scandinavians, and Swedes, the light-haired, blue-eyed Anglo-Saxons, or Celts—I mean the nations I have enumerated—*

THE CHAIRMAN. *Pure Caucasians?*

MR. DIES. *Yes; they were great in their own country and great in our country.*[29]

Apparently a somewhat similar process took place on the Pacific Coast, local race-feelings blending with nationalism, though usually in a milder and less explicit way. In both sections imperialism created a congenial atmosphere for nationalizing the spirit of white supremacy. Moreover, there were special incentives in the Far West for the offensive spirit of imperialism to lapse into a defensive nativism. Due to its geographical location, this region undoubtedly felt more keenly than other parts of the country the frustrations and difficulties to which the expansionist policy of 1898 soon led. In the flush of confidence at the turn of the century many westerners looked forward to vistas of enterprise and adventure in the Orient. But instead of substantial benefits the "large policy" bore bitter fruit of international rivalry and insecurity. Japan's stunning victories over the ponderous Russian war machine in 1904-05 placed her in a position to threaten America's new stakes in the Far East. As a result the West Coast felt a double sense of crisis: added to an internal fear of Japanese blood was an external fear of Japanese power. One exacerbated the other. From 1905 on, war scares recurrently agitated the Pacific states, and California nativists commonly looked upon Japanese immigration as a quasi-military invasion of soldiers and spies.[30] Consequently western race-feelings gained a nationalistic dimension not only from the philosophy of imperialism but also from the international discord that expansion engendered.

Homer Lea, the leading theoretician of the Yellow Peril, summed up the nationalist aspects of western nativism in their most naked and pretentious form. Lea, a frail, wizened Californian who worshiped power and spent most of his life playing at war, argued that nations flourish only through expansion and conquest. He believed implicitly in the mission of the Anglo-Saxon to rule the world, but in Japan he feared that America had met a race-enemy which was its match in militancy. In 1909 his most influential book, *The Valor of Ignorance,* worked out in startling detail a prediction of Japanese military occupation of the West Coast. The widening stream of European immigration, Lea warned, is augmenting the Japanese danger by sapping America's racial strength and unity.[31]

It remained, however, for a novelist to translate this creed into a frontal assault on the new immigration and to disseminate it far and wide. Jack London, the West Coast's most popular writer, came gradually to a fully nativistic position via an ingrained sense of white supremacy and an extensive education in imperialistic race-thinking. As a roustabout on the San Francisco waterfront he learned the white man's arrogance in boyhood. By 1900 he was reveling in the Anglo-Saxons' destiny to seize the earth for themselves. As a correspondent in the Russo-Japanese War he felt less assurance, turning from racial braggadocio to warnings about the Yellow Peril.[32] Finally, around 1913, London wrote in rapid succession two novels which showed "the dark-pigmented things, the half-castes, the mongrel-bloods" of southern and eastern Europe swamping the blond, master race in America. In both books the protagonists saw visions of their ancestors roving westward in beaked ships and winged helmets. In one, the heroine's name was Saxon.[33]

Both Lea and London echoed the biological pessimism—the appeal to iron laws of heredity, the morbid speculations on racial defeat—which eastern nativist intellectuals were adding to the Anglo-Saxon tradition in the early twentieth century. Both wrote for a nationwide audience, and both indicate that by 1910 the sophisticated theories of the patrician East were beginning to intermingle with popular nativisms of the West and South. By no means was the exchange all in one direction. If new doctrines spread gradually beyond an eastern elite, the mass sentiments of the West and South found an increasingly sympathetic response in the rest of the country. No part of the United States was immune to the spirit of white supremacy; in all sections native-born and northern European laborers called themselves "white men" to distinguish themselves from the southern Europeans whom they worked beside.[34]   And everywhere Anglo-Saxon nationalism, bereft of the exhilarating prospect of continued overseas expansion, was reverting to the defensive.

To this nation-wide trend the primitive race-feelings emanating from the South and Far West gave a constant spur. The East and Midwest, although inclined to depreciate anti-Japanese hysteria, could not entirely escape the influence of the Yellow Peril agitation and its broad racial implications. After 1908, for example, the national Socialist party abandoned a cosmopolitan immigration policy under the racist urgings of

one of its western leaders.[35]   Anti-Negro feeling radiated northward more easily than anti-Oriental feeling spread eastward. In northern attitudes toward Negroes a derogatory trend, evident since Reconstruction, sharpened during the 1900's under the pressure of an increasing Negro influx; and a series of race riots bloodied the streets of the Midwest.[36]   All this affected the image of the new immigration. As early as 1905 the *Outlook* asked if immigration might "so add to the serious race problems we already have that it will endanger the success of America's task." In every section, the Negro, the Oriental, and the southern European appeared more and more in a common light.[37]

The best single index to the nation-wide growth of Anglo-Saxon nativism was the hardiest, most vigorous of the nativist fraternal orders, the Junior Order United American Mechanics. Its career mirrored the history of popular xenophobia. Largely anti-Catholic during its formative years before the Civil War, the Junior Order's emphasis shifted to anti-radicalism in the 1880's and 1890's. At the turn of the century the order declined in size and energy; then another successful period set in. Membership rose from 147,000 in 1914. Significantly, much of the growth seems to have come from expansion into the South and West.[38]   The order took a very active part in the restrictionist campaign of 1906 and continued to agitate throughout the period. While anti-Catholicism persisted as a distinctly subsidiary part of the order's program, its former concentration on foreign radicals yielded to a primary fear of foreign races. Indeed, the organization echoed almost every theme in the racial polyphony. Its national chairman worried lest southern European immigrants should intermarry with Negroes, as in Latin America. The order's California council affiliated with the Asiatic Exclusion League   and   announced   that   southern

Europeans were semi-Mongolian. The national chaplain told a House committee quite simply that he wanted "the kind to come from which we came . . . I glory in my kinship. My father, on one side, was a German, my father upon the other was an Englishman. . . . That is the kind we want and can absorb. . . . They belonged to that independent race . . . who . . . came with the idea already imbedded in their hearts and minds of the beauties of self-government.[39]

Yet one should not overemphasize the strength of this nation-wide trend. Although racial nativism tugged at men everywhere in the United States, during the prewar years it never established a really firm grip on public opinion outside of the South and the West Coast. Those were its strongholds; the aroused and pervasive race-feeling of those areas touched the East and Midwest only to a limited degree. A spirit of confidence, sustained by the triumphant march of progressive reform, remained widespread throughout the era, and in the Northeast the regnant values of progressivism tended to inhibit racial anxieties. As long as northeastern progressives took to heart their optimistic faith in environmental reform, they held the Anglo-Saxon tradition in check. But this was not true of the South or the Far West. There, without anguish and with no apparent sense of inconsistency, reform-thinking accommodated itself to race-thinking; progressivism was for white men only. No prominent easterner exhibited such wildly contradictory attitudes as Jack London, a radical champion of social justice for exploited and submerged classes who was forever glorifying the ruthlessness of supermen and master races.[40]

Meanwhile the southern brand of progressivism actually reinforced the racial reaction. Concerted opposition to immigration crystallized in the South about 1905, in the form of a counter-attack against the large landlords and business interests then engaged in

a promotional campaign for European manpower. To many the power of organized wealth seemed to be undoing the South's long struggle to maintain race purity.[41] Much of the leadership in fighting the immigration promoters came from the fast-growing Farmers' Union, the largest farmer organization in the South, which leveled a fierce propaganda barrage at the state immigration bureaus and at the whole influx from southeastern Europe and Asia.[42] In South Carolina, Cole Blease, idol of the cotton mill operatives, seized upon the issue in 1908. The next year the state abolished its immigration bureau and prohibited its officials from encouraging immigration in any way. Several other states reduced the activities of their agencies, and by 1910 the promotional drive was moribund, the victim of a progressivism charged with racial nativism.[43]

REFERENCES

1. *United States Census; 1910*, Vol. I: Population, 174-75; Roy L. Garis, *Immigration Restriction: A Study of the Opposition to and Regulation of Immigration into the United States* (New York, 1927), 205.

2. New York *Tribune Index*, 1902, pp. 178-79. Out of 74 entries for the year under the heading "Italians," 55 are obviously accounts of crime and violence.

3. Robert E. Park and Herbert A. Miller, *Old World Traits Transplanted* (New York, 1921), 241-58; Arthur I. Street, ed., *Street's Pandex of the News*, 1908, pp. 30-31; *Hearings* (House Committee on Immigration and Naturalization, 60 Cong., I Sess., Washington, 1908), 10.

4. Theodore A. Bingham, "Foreign Criminals in New York," *North American Review*,

CLXXXVIII (1908), 383-94; *American Jewish Year Book*, 1909-10, pp. 62-63.

5. The chief anti-Semitic incident of the period between 1896 and 1913 was a funeral riot on New York's East Side in 1902, an affair which apparently pitted Jews against Irish. Philip Cowen, *Memories of an American Jew* (New York, 1932), 289.

6. The best treatment is Abraham Cahan's novel, *The Rise of David Levinsky* (New York, 1917). For unfriendly comments see Burton J. Hendrick. "The Great Jewish Invasion," *McClure's Magazine*, XXVIII (1907), 307-21; and Ralph Philip Boas, "The Problem of American Judaism," *Atlantic Monthly*, CXIX (1917), 147-51.

7. Norman Hapgood, "Jews and College Life" and "Schools, Colleges and Jews," *Harper's Weekly*, LXII (1916), 53-55, 77-79; Charles S. Bernheimer, "prejudice Against Jews in the United States," *Independent*, LXV (1908), 1106-1107; Alexander Francis, *Americans: An Impression* (New York, 1909), 84-85, 187.

8. A. J. Severson, "Nationality and Religious Preferences as Reflected in Newspaper Advertisements," *American Journal of Sociology*, XLIV (1939), 541-43; Cyrus Adler, Jacob H. Schiff: *His Life and Letters* (New York, 1928), 1, 363.

9. Park and Miller, *Old World Traits*, 51, 255.

10. *Compiled Laws of Michigan*, 1897, p. 439; *Session Laws State of Wyoming*, 1899, p. 60, and 1911, p. 61; *Session Laws of Arizona*, 1907, p. 138; *Laws of the State of New York*, 1908, I, 337, and 1909, II, 1324; *Callaghan's Michigan Digest*, I, 244; *Revised Laws of Minnesota; Supplement*, 1909, p. 622, *General Laws of Nebraska*, 1909, p. 2919; *A Digest of the Statutes of Arkansas*, 1921, p. 2151; *Diggest of Pennsylvania Statute Law*, 1920, pp. 1117-118; *Acts and Resolves Passed by the General Court of Massachusetts*, 1910, p. 428.

11. "Records of the Executive Committee of the Immigration Restriction League," May 13, October 2, and November 16, 1905, and January 20, 1906, in Files of the Immigration Restriction League (Houghton Library, Harvard University); Boston *Herald*, December 18, 1905, and June 26, 1906.

12. This is frankly an impression of mine, rather than a statistical fact; but for suggestive data see William Z. Ripley, "Race Factors in Labor Unions," *Atlantic Monthly*, XCIII (1904), 306; Selig Perlman and Philip Taft, *A History of Labor in the United States, 1896-1932* (New York, 1935), 13-19.

13. *Report of Proceedings of the Twenty-fifth Annual Convention of the American Federation of Labor*, 1905, pp. 75-76, 101-102, 238; Philadelphia *Public Ledger*, June 4, 1906, p. 16; *Congressional Record*, 59 Cong., 1 Sess., 9171, 9189; *Selections from the Correspondence of Theodore Roosevelt and Henry Cabot Lodge, 1884-1918* (New York, 1925), II, 204. See also *The Carpenter*, January, 1906, pp. 9-10; *Machinists' Monthly Journal*, XVII (1905), 394, 1113; *Appeal to Reason* (Girard, Kansas), April 1, August 12, and September 2, 1905.

Of course the unions that did have a large number of new immigrants among their members were hesitant to join in the drive. The United Mine Workers, for example, clung to the old, equivocal distinction between voluntary and assisted immigration; *United Mine Workers' Journal*, August 23, 1906.

14. Samuel Gompers, *Seventy Years of Life and Labor* (New York, 1925), II, 167, 171; *Selections from Correspondence of Roosevelt and Lodge*, II, 158.

15. *Cong. Rec.*, 59 Cong., I Sess., 551-55, 7293-95. For a much later indication of Lodge's failure to realize how profoundly southern opinion on immigration was changing see Lodge to Theodore Roosevelt, May 10, 1912, in Theodore Roosevelt Papers, Box 286 (Division of Manuscripts, Library of Congress).

16. Asiatic Exclusion League, *Proceedings*, February, 1908, pp. 19, 71, and December, 1908, pp. 17, 19: James N. Davis to Robert DeCourcy Ward, January 10, 1914, in Files of the I.R.L., Box 7; *Cong. Rec.*, 59 Cong., 1 Sess., 9187, and 64 Cong., I Sess., 4782. For the vote in 1912 cast by Congressmen from Washington, Oregon, California, Nevada, Arizona, Utah, Idaho, and Montana, see *Cong. Rec.*, 62 Cong., 2 Sess., 5023, and 62 *Cong.*

3 Sess. 864. Anti-Japanese sentiment was, of course, very strong throughout the Rocky Mountain area.

17. Thomas A. Balley, *Theodore Roosevelt and the Japanese-American Crises* (Stanford, 1934), 67-72, 108-109; Eleanor Tupper and George E. McReynolds, *Japan in American Public Opinion* (New York, 1937), 62-63.

18. *Cong. Rec.,* 62 Cong., 2 Sess., 5023, and 62 Cong., 3 Sess. 864. This was the first recorded vote on the literacy test since 1898, Cannon's maneuvers having prevented a recorded vote in 1906. For typical southern thinking about European immigration see *Cong. Rec.,* 59 Cong., 1 Sess., 9192, and 63 Cong., 2 Sess., 2623; *Reports of the Immigration Commission: Statements and Recommendations Submitted by Societies* (61 Cong., 3 Sess., Senate Document No. 764, Washington, 1911), 124.

19. John Higham, "The American Party, 1886-1891," *Pacific Historical Reveiw,* XIX (1950), 38; San Francisco *Argonaut,* January 9 and April 3, 1886. For a typical example of how California's race-feeling dissociated the Chinese from European immigrants see C. T. Hopkins, *Common Sense Applied to the Immigrant Question* (San Francisco, 1869), esp. 20-22. In the twentieth century William Randolph Hearst perpetuated this old Californian combination of sympathy for European immigration and hatred for Oriental. See the platform of his Independence party in Kirk H. Porter, ed., *National Party Platforms* (New York, 1924), 292-93.

20. *Cong. Rec.,* 51 Cong., 2 Sess., 2948, and 55 Cong., 2 Sess., 583, and see the roll call vote, 55 Cong., 2 Sess., 689. The Anglo-Saxon nativism of a Knoxville lawyer, Joshua W. Caldwell, was exceptional. See his "The South Is American," *Arena,* VIII (1893), 610-15.

21. *Cong. Rec.,* 63 Cong., 2 Sess., 2624.

22. *Reports of the Immigration Commission: Abstracts* (61 Cong., 3 Sess., Senate Doc. 747), I, 645-53; *United States Census, 1910: Abstract,* 197. See also Jack London, *The Valley of the Moon* (New York, 1913).

23. Rowland T. Berthoff, "Southern Attitudes Toward Immigration, 1865-1914," *Journal of Southern History,* XVII (1951), 332-36; *United States Census, 1910: Abstract,* 197. In 1910 the new immigration constituted 1 per cent of the white population in the South and 5.6 per cent in the Pacific states.

24. Frank Tannenbaum, *Darker Phases of the South* (New York, 1924), 177-78; Ray Stannard Baker, *Following the Color Line* (New York, 1908), 295; Norman Walker, "Tallulah's Shame," *Harper's Weekly,* XLIII (1899), 779. Southern Congressmen repeatedly referred to the mixed blood of southern Europeans and pointed to the further mixing of Latins and Negroes occurring in South America as an object lesson for the United States; *Cong. Rec.,* 59 Cong., 1 Sess., 9155, 9174.

25. Booker T. Washington, "Races and Politics," *Outlook,* XCVIII (1911), 264; Berthoff, "Southern Attitudes," 348.

26. A cross section of anti-Chinese sentiment can be studied in Elmer C. Sandmeyer, *The Anti-Chinese Movement in California* (Urbana, 1939), and in *Report of the Joint Special Committee to Investigate Chinese Immigration* (Report No. 689, 44 Cong., 2 Sess., Washington, 1877), esp. 1044-51.

27. C. Vann Woodward, *Origins of the New South, 1877-1913* (Baton Rouge, 1951), 324-26, 350-55. On the sectional response to imperialism see Richard Hofstadter, "Manifest Destiny and the Philippines," in Daniel Aaron, ed., *America in Crisis* (New York, 1952), 181, 187-189.

28. Paul H. Buck, *The Road to Reunion, 1865-1900* (Boston, 1937), 306-307.

29. *Hearings Relative to the Further Restriction of Immigration* (House Committee on Immigration and Naturalization, 62 Cong., 2 Sess., Washington, 1912), 49-50. See also *Cong. Rec.,* 59 Cong., 1 Sess., 9174; 63 Cong., 2 Sess., 2623-27; 63 Cong., 3 Sess., 3040.

30. Carey McWilliams, *Prejudice: Japanese-Americans, Symbol of Racial Intolerance* (Boston, 1944), 19; Bailey, *Roosevelt and the Japanese-American Crises,* 9-11; Tupper and

McReynolds, *Japan in American Public Opinion*, 33. In this respect too the anti-Japanese movement contrasts with the older anti-Chinese movement. Neither China nor any other nation posed a direct, international threat to the secure and isolated America of the seventies and eighties.

31. Homer Lea, *The Valor of Ignorance* (New York, 1909), esp. 124-28. See also his *The Day of the Saxon* (New York, 1912). For all of his militarism and racial nationalism, Lea was no ordinary anti-Oriental bigot. He became a general in the Chinese army and showed no sympathy for the popular indignities inflicted on the Japanese in America.

32. Joan London, *Jack London and His Times: An Unconventional Biography* (New York, 1939), 212-13; Jack London, *Revolution and Other Essays* (New York, 1910), 267-89, and *South Sea Tales* (Cleveland, 1946), 235-39.

33. Jack London, *Valley of the Moon*, 102-103, and *The Mutiny of the Elsimore* (New York, 1914), 197-201. See the comments on these books in Charmian London, *The Book of Jack London* (New York, 1921), II, 258, 274.

34. Charles B. Barnes, *The Longshoremen* (New York, 1915), 8-9; William M. Leiserson, *Adjusting Immigrant and Industry* (New York, 1924), 71-72.

35. Ira Kipnis, *The American Socialist Movement, 1897-1912* (New York, 1952), 278-88. Ernest Untermann of Idaho was apparently the moving spirit. For another indication of the infectiousness of the anti-Oriental movement see an article by an eastern physician, Albert Allemann, "Immigration and the Future American Race," *Popular Science Monthly*, LXXV (1909, 586-96.

36. Philadelphia *Public Ledger*, June 27, 1906; *Harper's Weekly*, XLVIII (1904), 1980; Ernest Hamlin Abbott, "Sectional Misapprehension," Outlook, LXXX (1905), 237-41; John Hope Franklin, *From Slavery to Freedom* (New York, 1948), 435-36.

37. Outlook, LXXXI (1905), 956; John R. Commons, *Races and Immigrants in America* (New York, 1907), 3-17, 39-62; *Christian Science Monitor*, September 27, 1913.

38. National Council, Junior Order United American Mechanics, *Official Proceedings*, 1907, p. 57, and 1914, p. 168; *Cong. Rec.*, 62 Cong., 2 Sess., 3531. The Junior Order's nearest competitor, the Patriotic Order Sons of America, was still surviving in the East in 1912 but was much less active; *ibid.*, 3531, 3535.

39. *Cong. Rec.*, 59 Cong., 1 Sess., 9174; Asiatic Exclusion League, *Proceedings*, February, 1908, pp. 55, 57; *Hearings* (House Committee on Immigration, 62 Cong., 2 Sess.), 6, 16.

40. The most nativistic of progressive intellectuals, Edward A. Ross, may also be understood in part as a product of the Far West. His fascination with the immigration issue dates from his turbulent years at Stanford University, and his first polemic on the subject was an attack on the Oriental, Edward Alsworth Ross, *Seventy Years of It: An Autobiography* (New York, 1936), 69-70.

41. *The Tradesman* (Chattanooga), July 15, 1905; "Immigration Clippings Collected by Prescott F. Hall" (Widener Library, Harvard University), VI, 220.

42. *Cong. Rec.*, 61 Cong., 1 Sess., 1526; *Hearings* (House Committee on Immigration, 62 Cong., 2 Sess.), 3-23; *Mississippi Union Advocate*, June 15, 1910; *The National Field*, January 15, 1914.

2.   JEWS AS THE PRODUCT OF HISTORY

Georges Friedmann

In this excerpt from his well-known book, Friedmann views antisemitism as the motive force in the development of the Jewish people, a force that caused them to band together and develop a distinct identity. The author discusses the possibility of Jews disappearing as a distinct ethnic group as boundaries between themselves and non-Jews decline and antisemitism disappears.

Since the beginning of the Diaspora, the Jews progressively formed less and less of a "people," a reality based on ethnic and national characteristics and even (in our time) only on a common attachment to traditions, beliefs or religious practices.

Before the Diaspora, however, there was a Jewish people, whose origins and beginnings of sedentary life we can nowadays follow with a considerable degree of certainty, thanks to the progress of archaeology and biology and critical study of the Pentateuch (which was set in train with admirable clarity by Spinoza in his *Tractatus Theologico-Politicus*). It is possible to observe the development of its religious institutions and its legal code impregnated with health rules and moral principles.[1] In or about the

eithteenth or seventeenth centuries B.C. nomadic Semitic tribes, whose long migration corresponds to the mission of Abraham, traveled from the region of Ur of the Chaldees to that of Aram-Naharaim, or "Syria of the two rivers," to the northwest, between the Euphrates and the Balykh, the religious center of which was Harran, where the moon-god was worshiped. One or two centuries later another migration of these tribes occurred, this time to the west of the Euphrates and then to the south, to the land of Canaan, where they took the name of Hebrews (Ivrim, "those from beyond" the Euphrates). They seem to have settled peacefully among the indigenous populations, whose language they spoke and at whose shrines they worshiped. Some of the Hebrews settled and remained in the land of Canaan.

One of the tribes, called the "Children of Israel" after one of its ancestors, went down into Egypt in or about the fifteenth century, no doubt to seek pasture for its flocks. At first it enjoyed the favor of the Pharaohs (the story of Joseph) but then, under the nineteenth dynasty, was reduced

SOURCE
From *The End of the Jewish People?* by Georges Friedmann, translated by Eric Mosbacher. Copyright © 1967 by Doubleday and Company, Inc. Reprinted by permission of the publisher.

[1]We owe a great deal to the fine edition of the Old Testament published by Edouard Dhorme (Gallimard, Paris, 2 Vols., 1962) and to his introduction, Vol. I, pp. xv-cxxvi.

to slavery. In the thirteenth century, before the time of Rameses II, the tribe began its exodus toward Sinai under the leadership of Moses. Moses gave the people the Law and the worship of Jehovah. According to the evidence of the stele of Pharaoh Menephtah,[2] their arrival in Transjordania and Canaan took place in approximately 1232–1225. They conquered the land of Canaan by force of arms, aided by tribesmen of the same origin as themselves who had been living among the indigenous population for several centuries,[3] and settled there under the leadership of Joshua and the Judges. The unified kingdom of the Hebrews lasted for barely a century (from about 1020 to 932), from Saul to the death of Solomon. It split into the kingdoms of Israel and Judah, of which the former collapsed in 721 with the capture of Samaria by the Assyrians, and the latter in 597 with the sack of Jerusalem by Nebuchadnezzar. The twelve tribes were deported to the Caucasus, Armenia and in particular Babylonia, and disappeared;[4] and with them the Jewish people in the plenitude of its existence as a simultaneously ethnic, national and religious community also disappeared forever.

Henceforth, even during the ephemeral restoration of the Kingdom of Judah under the Asmonean dynasty (from 168 B.C. onward) most Jews were dispersed in more or less developed communities far from the Holy Land; and from this time onward the notion of a "Jewish people" is closely bound up with the reactions provoked by attachment to the Mosaic law of the communities of the Diaspora in Egypt, Alexandria and other big Greek cities, and later in the Roman Empire. The Jews practiced an essentially religious separatism deriving from the Torah and the observance of the commandments and their sacred ritual; hence the mistrust and hostility to which they gave rise. These lie at the roots of pre-Christian anti-Semitism. (In Egypt after the Hyksos tyranny it was nourished by a secular hatred of Asian invaders, who were generally Semites; in other words, by an "anti-Semitism" in the proper sense of the term, that is, far wider than merely anti-Jewish.) From the first century B.C. onward these reactions were reinforced by Jewish resistance to Hellenization at the religious level and by the success of Jewish proselytism. The manifestations of pagan anti-Semitism in Egypt, the Hellenist world and the Roman Empire appear at a date much later than that attributed to them by those who maintain that "anti-Semitism is eternal, as old as Judaism itself,"[5] and take a form that clearly marks them off from Christian anti-Semitism. "It was generally a spontaneous reaction, and was only exceptionally directed and organized," while the Christian variety kept alive by the Church was from the outset official, systematic, consistent and

---

[2]The reading of the hieroglyphic inscription "Israel" has, however, been disputed (cf. Andre Neher, *Moise et la vocation juive*, Editions du Seuil, Paris, 1956, p. 67).

[3]This coming together of various tribes of Hebrews in Canaan in or about the twelfth century is important. It explains in a rational and plausible manner how a united Jewish people arose out of human groups from very different cultural environments; some Jewish theologians regard this as an "enigma" or "miracle."

[4]Among the members of the second of these groups (descended from the tribes of Judah and Benjamin), were believers in Jehovah whom Cyrus permitted to return to Palestine, where they rebuilt the Temple of Jerusalem at the end of the sixth century.

---

[5]Christian and Jewish "extremists" join in maintaining theologically and often passionately the eternity of anti-Semitism; the former in order to exonerate Christianity more or less completely of its responsibilities, the latter to confirm their mystic belief in the "difference" of the Jewish people called on in spite of everything to await the fulfillment of the divine promises.

"pursued the very definite aim of making the Jews odious."[6]

I have no desire to underrate the importance that attachment to the Torah played for centuries in the Jewish communities of the Diaspora. As I have said, Jewish separatism was originally essentially religious. In historical reality actions and reactions intertwine, leading to a "spiraling" causality. The religious separatism of the Jews caused hostile reactions, which mingled with those spread by the "education in contempt," nourishing and aggravating them. The latter, in turn, by setting up a wall of discrimination around the Jews (which extended to imprisoning them physically and morally in the ghetto) implanted in many of them a traditional loyalty rooted in these constraints. From many points of view the ghetto explains the religious history of Judaism, particularly certain characteristics of Hassidic mysticism. It was anti-Semitism, viewed as a whole, that encouraged fierce attachment to the Law, assured the survival of the Jewish consciousness, Jewish "difference," Jewish solidarity, which are the essential content of the idea of the "Jewish people" in the Diaspora. Without the persecutions, without the ghetto and its various forms and surrogates, the Jews, dispersed through the nations but taking part in the evolution toward political liberties and "enlightenment," would have been assimilated more rapidly and completely, as they have tended to be in the West since the end of the eighteenth century. Their separatism, fading with the weakening of its religious roots, would have ceased to make them "different," "alien" and suspect. Anti-Semitism produces Jewish feeling and is responsible for Jewish survival,[7] but Jewish separatism has

helped it and (to the extent that it is prolonged by anti-Semitism) still helps it at the present day.[8]

Those of many schools of thought who, often from a theological viewpoint (whether Jewish or Christian), talk of the survival of the "Jewish people" in spite of its millenary trials and tribulations as a miracle have got things the wrong way about. It is not in spite of but because of anti-Semitism (or, from the point of view of Zionist mysticism or nationalism, thanks to it) that a Jewish specificity has to an extent survived in certain physical, cultural, psychological and even religious respects.[9] The non-existence of the phenomenon of anti-Semitism in Israel leads to the rapid ending of what was held to be an eternal Jewish specificity, To Jewish and Christian believers the idea of the "Jewish people" is a theological notion; to the leaders of Israel and the Zionist movement it is a political one, and to obdurate anti-Semites it is an emotional one.

---

intensity and duration on the one hand and on the other the feeling of Jewish solidarity and the rejection of assimilation (held to be impossible on the reality plane and objectionable on the moral plane). It is the Jews most directly affected by the catastrophe (by personal or family experience) who state: "Jews cannot live in the *galut*," or "Any self-respecting Jew must settle in Israel" (S. N. Herman, Y. Peres, E. Yuchtman, *op. cit.*, Table II.

[8]One of the principal points made by Sartre in his *Reflexions sur la question juive* (Callimard, "Idees," 1962, pp. 83-84) is: "The Jew is a man whom other men hold to be a Jew; that is the simple truth that must be taken as the starting-point" In the light of study of the relationship between Jewish separatism and anti-Semitism and of the content of the idea of Jewishness and of the feeling of interdependence, this generalization seems to be penetrating but too simple in relation to the complexity of the facts.

[9]*Cf.*the current behavior of rabbinical orthodoxy in Israel and its motivation (Chapter 8).

---

[6]Marcel Simon, *Verus Israel. Etude sur les relations entre chretiens et juifs dans l'Empire romain* (134-425), Paris, 1948, p. 263.

[7]A correlation has been observed among Jews between their experience of anti-Semitism, its

As for Jews considered as individuals in the countries of the Diaspora of which they are citizens, they are the products of history that is, of the conditions in which they and their forefathers lived; very varied products, since these conditions—economic, social and psychological—varied greatly, were more or less rigorous and formative in different countries and different times in different communities. Where anti-Semitism fades, Jewish specificity tends to disappear, as has been shown by studies.[10] Where it survives, it expresses itself and desires to express itself only in religious forms. The grandson of a Polish Jew who emigrated to the United States with the heavy, "specifically" Jewish, luggage inherited from the ghetto *may* become an American citizen professing the Jewish faith and practicing religion within the framework of the American way of life. In extreme cases one already meets in the democracies of Europe and America Jews, both men and women, who have no religious beliefs and are so thoroughly assimilated to their environment that the only relic of their Jewishness is their name.

ANTI-SEMITISM AND THE "JEWISH PERSONALITY"

The conditions in which Jews have lived since the distant times when they really

---

[10]In particular the studies of Jewish communities in the United States, Canada and Argentina commented on the Moshe Davis, *Jewish Journal of Sociology*, June 1963, pp. 14-19. The relaxation of ties with Judaism among Jewish students in Argentina is well analyzed in the report published by the "Primera Conferencia de Investigadores y Estudiosos Judeo-Argentinos en el campo de las Ciencias Sociales y la Historia," Buenos Aires, October 1961. This states (p. 6) that to the Argentinian student "anti-Semitism automatically becomes the mirror of his Judaism. Everything that diminishes or is likely to diminish anti-Semitism automatically affects his Judaism."

were a "people," the anti-Semitism of varying degrees of acuteness they faced depending on the country and the period, the amount of freedom they had to work in fields of their choice and the degree of political liberty they enjoyed determined the Jewish "basic personaltiy," its varieties and transformations. What is there in common between the fierce warriors going from battle to battle, capable of the most appalling cruelties, with which the Old Testament abounds, or the companions of the Maccabees, or the indomitable rebels against Rome who were slaughtered arms in hand by the legions of Titus, and the somber, busy, anxious throng in long black coats one saw in Pilsudski's Poland, keeping to the wall whenever they ventured outside the Jewish quarter? Even then their condition had greatly improved since the Middle Ages. The immense majority of European Jews are more or less closely descended from men who lived in the ghetto, the perfection in discrimination and polyvalent psycho-sociological molding of the individual. At this point, let us reread a passage in which Bernhard Blumenkranz summarizes his conclusions: "When we think of the appalling situation of the Jews in the Middle Ages, it is the ghetto that comes to mind, the distinctive badge, the exclusion from a long list of trades and occupations, accusations of violation of the Host, of ritual murder, poisoning wells, and the horrible series of bloodthirsty persecutions that accompanies those accusations; religious debates carefully organized with a verdict in favor of the Christian prepared in advance, autos-da-fe of the Talmud, Jews who were serfs of lords and princes, simple merchandise with no will or rights of their own, bartered as advantageously as possible or sold to the highest bidder, Jewish usurers forced into that form of activity by an economy that closed all other outlets to them and hated and despised for it by all men of good will. They were a type of man whom society had put beyond the pale, exercising pressure for the greater profit of their prince or pressurized themselves at the prince's whim or pleasure, a mere form of currency exchanged among the great, an easy prey to hand over to the base instincts of an overexcited mob overstimulated by pious and bloodthirsty imagery and edifying and terrifying literature."[11]

On the one hand anti-Semitism fashioned the personality of the Jew who is alien to the society in which he lives[12] and is also a strange and evil creature; on the other hand its millenary influence fashioned the mass mentality from which were recruited in the twentieth century the organizers of the massacres and their innumerable followers who perpetrated them or accepted them without demur. Suspect, scorned, segregated, hampered in their working life, the Jews were forced to emphasize their peculiarities in every way. The laws of this complex determinism explain (1) the exaggeration of certain physical features, a bio-social phenomenon observable in isolated communities characterized by inbreeding; the conformity in mimicry, gestures and bearing of Polish and Ukrainian Jews descended from Slavs converted to Judaism is a phenomenon as remarkable as it is indisputable;[13] (2) the exaggeration of certain psychological features well described in the literature of the ghetto, including overdevelopment of the critical sense and of destructive analysis, escapism in dreams, an active imagination (which is peculiar to all minorities in a hostile environment, but among the Jews assumed special features), a cruel sense of humor, self-denigration and denigration of the community to which they belong;[14] (3) an intensification of cultural autarky, in other words an attempt to find within the segregated community something with which to satisfy all needs, from the prescriptions of the dietary laws to food for the mind, the need for beauty, mataphysical truth, mystic communion with God.

The basic Jewish personality formed by the slow action of centuries does not totally vanish with a change in the environment in which it was born. As long as anti-Semitism and discrimination persist anywhere in the world the sense of interdependence prevents it from vanishing. But it survives most strongly among Jews who go on living "among themselves," prolonging their segregation by the force of inertia in countries in which they could rapidly disappear in the assimilating crucible. This phenomenon is observable in the United States, Canada, Britain and even in France among recent immigrants and the succeeding generation.[15]

If the "Jewish personaltiy" was formed by conditions that breed anti-Semitism, it is bound to be profoundly affected by the disappearance of those conditions. That, as we have seen, is what is happening in Israel. Many young *sabras* already have little resemblance to their parents, and still less to their grandparents. Combatants in the Haganah and Palmah, soldiers in the Israeli

---

[11]B. Blumenkranz, *op. cit.*, p. 380.

[12]I recently asked a distinguished philosopher, a Jew driven from Germany by the Nazis who emigrated to the United States, what his definition of a Jew was. "A man who feels a stranger everywhere," he replied.

[13]*Cf.* Chapter 8.

---

[14]Rejection of members of their own community and hostility to them are characteristic of the internal relations of groups that are the object of discrimination and prejudice (e.g. Negroes in the United States). The "anti-Semitism" of certain Jews, their attitude of exasperation about other Jews, has often been noted. The explanation is the internalization of prejudice and self-hatred subtly analyzed by G. H. Mead (*Mind, Self and Society*, Chicago, 1934).

[15]In the new "ghettos" of Canadian or American suburbia the physical togetherness of the Jews does not prevent cultural integration and the decline of Jewishness, as Moshe Davis had noted, *op. cit.*, p. 17.

army, victors in the Sinai campaign, they say that they feel very different from the Jews assembled in concentration camps by the Nazis and sent "like sheep" to the gas chamber. The phrase I quoted earlier—"they have lost the defects of their parents, but also their qualities"—is no doubt an over-simplification of a deep truth. The intellectual and affective traits that are the good side of Jewish anxiety (which is sometimes carried to the point of neurosis) are disappearing in Israel, together with Jewish separatism. The basic Jewish personality is a complex product of the history of the Jewish communities in the Diaspora. In a different "history," in a different complex, a new personality is emerging.

The observer is struck by the speed of this development, which confirms the artificial character of the Jewish personality. It does not, of course, affect all Jewish immigrants to Israel, particularly the old, and when it does, the physical and moral effects are much less noticeable. But on the whole the impact of the experience is tremendous. In the land of Palestine, in a sum-total of geographic, climatic, social, cultural, political conditions profoundly different from those that formed it, the Jewish personality is disintegrating. The "Jewish people" is disappearing and giving place to the Israeli nation.

What a paradox. Israel, which to many practicing Jews foreshadows the fulfillment of the promises made by God to the chosen people, today demonstrates the chosen people's non-unity, non-uniqueness, non-eternity. The Israeli experiment is undermining the foundations of the Mosaic religion.

"Throughout the most diverse manifestations, whether in the case of Moses or Jeremiah, the Pharaohs or the Hasidium, Auschwitz or Tel Aviv, the Jewish testimony is always unique," André Neher writes. André Chouraqui, recalling the work of the historian S. W. Baron,[16] considers that the reunification into a single nation in the Holy Land of "human groups coming from different countries at different periods constitutes one of the great enigmas of history." To Rabbi Zaoui religious faith and collective prayer are "the secret of the duration of Israel, the people of the Bible that has survived all the tribulations of the centuries because of the synagogue and thanks to its prayers."[17]

Belief in the uniqueness and eternal specificity of the Jewish people and its messianic vocation is an article of faith, the basis of a religious attitude. Seeing the Jewish people as a group progressively built up out of Semitic nomadic tribes that gradually became sedentary and settled in Palestine, originated monotheism and created the Bible, and then from the eighth century onward was dispersed and subjected to repeated deportations, persecutions, massacres and severe social and psychological conditioning; believing there was nothing "miraculous" in the group's reactions of stubborn resistance and accentuated separatism and nothing eternal in the resulting physical and moral characteristics, especially when these are compared with the results of successful assimilation in modern democratic societies and in the Israeli community—all this is a positivist, agnostic attitude, shocking, I fear, to men such as I have just quoted whose faith I respect and whose courage and noble-mindedness I admire.

But what remains today of the "unity" of the Jewish people? The Jews of the *gola* and those of Israel preserve a link to the extent that anti-Semitism survives, in other words to the extent that their destinies are

---

[16]*A Social and Religious History of the Jews,* French trans. Paris, 5 vols. 1956-64.

[17]André Neher, *Esprit,* February 1958, p. 116; André Chouraqui, *Tiers-Monde,* October-December 1962, *op. cit.,* p. 665; André Zaoui, *Revue de la Pensee Juive,* October 1950, p. 132.

interdependent, or may be interdependent. The interdependence between a shoemaker in Kiev, an Iraqi worker in the Timna mines, an Argentinian *kibbutznik* in Galilee, a banker in Paris and a doctor in Brooklyn may seem very slender. Nevertheless it exists, actually or potentially, and it was strongly felt at the time of the European catastrophe. Nazi anti-Semitism revived the hazards and the tragedy of Jewish life.

In the twentieth-century Diaspora Jewishness is buttressed mainly by the sense of interdependence. It is because of that sense and the name I bear that I, a citizen of France, who recognize no homeland but France, accept and will to the end of my days continue to accept my Jewishness as a fact of my life, without pride or provocation but also without the slightest embarrassment or shame. It is also because of that sense that in Israel I do not feel a total stranger to a Kurdish patriarch who entertains me at his *moshav* at Nes Harim or a Moroccan barber whose complaints I listen to in a *shikun* at Katamon. So it will be as long as Jews anywhere in the world are considered guilty members of the "deicide people," suspected and decried by some, feared by others, useful scapegoats to many. Changing one's name (which in Israel is done with a view to Hebraization and national unification over and above the different ethnic groups) can in the Diaspora be a powerful catalytic agent of assimilation. To him who chooses this as a final solution of his personal problems or those of his children, to him who has only a minimal sense of interdependence and can ignore it without anxiety or a bad conscience, a change of name is justified. The decision whether or not to have recourse to it depends on him alone.

The expression "Jewish people," when used in connection with the realities of the present day, refers, in an often confused way, to the Jewish community in Israel and the sum-total of all the Jews in the Diaspora. I have stated all the reservations I have about the term. Let us nevertheless use it, attributing to it the various meanings attached to it by religious Jews, Zionists and the leaders of the state of Israel, and ask what are the principal dangers that today and in the immediate future threaten the survival of this "Jewish people."

They are of two kinds, having causes either outside or inside Israel.

III

ARAB THREATS: THE PALESTINIAN PROBLEM

The most obvious of the former is the Arab threat. The Arab states consider themselves in a state of war with Israel, and since 1948 have not ceased to proclaim their desire to throw the Israeli into the sea and wipe their state from the map of the Near East. The agreement proclaimed in Cairo on April 17, 1963, between Egypt, Syria and Iraq on the constitutional basis of a future Arab federation was accompanied by renewed threats to "settle the Palestinian problem" by the destruction of Israel. But Arab unity is fragile, and is liable to frequent and brutal shocks in various countries. Revolutions and bloodthirsty *coups d'etat* have taken place, particularly in Iraq and Syria. Nevertheless, in spite of divergencies and mistrust, dissensions and even conflicts between political regimes (e.g. between Boumedienne's Algeria, Nasser's Egypt, Hassan's Morocco, Saud's Arabia and al-Salal's Yemen), Arab unity is making progress, its principal objective and cementing factor being the setting up of a hugh anti-Israel front. In this sense the "summit" conference of thirteen Arab heads of state in Cairo (January 13-17, 1964) reinforced it. Only Arab solidarity, the final communique declared, could serve "the just cause of the Palestinian Arab people aspiring to self-determination and liberation from the imperialist Zionist grip."

ISRAELI THREATS: ASSIMILATION AND AFFLUENCE

As for the dangers that threaten the Jewish people with extinction inside Israel itself, we have already met them and need only recapitulate them briefly.

In the first place, the Israeli crucible tends to bring about profound changes in immigrants' Jewishness, disintegrating the traditions of each ethnic group and fusing them into a new complex corresponding to a new nationality. It must be admitted that from their own viewpoint the criticisms of the orthodox are not unfounded. In the Diaspora, assimilation, mixed marriage and the decline of religious practices are the gravest dangers that threaten the "Jewish people" with extinction; and, parallel with this, economic and social development in Israel constitutes a new kind of assimilation liable to produce "generations of Hebrew-speaking Gentiles," Israelis who are Europeans in Asia, no more and no less.

These views, which I heard expressed a number of times in religious circles, call to mind another internal danger—adaptation to the typical attitudes and ways of behavior of a society on the way to affluence, tending toward hedonism on the western and more particularly the North American pattern, precipitating the decline and oblivion of *halutzic* values. There is no doubt that in the towns of Israel we are confronted with ever-increasing psychological and sociological traits characteristic of a technical civilization. Israel seems ready to accept this; many young men in responsible positions in administration and business actually regard the process as desirable without seeing its dangers. In their pleasures and entertainments

and style of life a substantial proportion of young people have already been won over by the "models" of the industrialized societies of the west.

In Israel I was often reminded of dangers to which we have been alerted by certain humanist critics of our technological societies. The greatest works of human genius, Homer, Dante, Shakespeare, which have come down to us after surviving centuries of wars, revolutions and dark periods of history might (these moralists say) not survive the transpositions, manipulations, "digests" to which they are liable at the hands of a triumphant and universal mass culture (*Cf.* Norman Jacobs [editor], *Culture for the Millions?* Van Nostrand, Princeton, 1961), Similarly, the people of the Bible, after three thousand years of tribulations and persecutions, may contribute to their own destruction in their recovered home by surrendering to an imperious and undiscriminating mass culture. This is a danger Israel shares with other young nations whose economic growth coincides with a wholesale and (let me add, to avoid any misunderstanding) *necessary* spread of mass communications.

In his address to the second World Congress of Jewish Youth in Jerusalem Nahum Goldmann made an urgent plea for nonconformism, directed in particular to the Jews of the Diaspora. The exhortation might with equal or perhaps even more reason have been addressed to the Jews of Israel, to put them on their guard against their conformism to western mass culture. If the younger generations become deeply impregnated with this during the decades ahead, where will they find the strength necessary for the social advancement of their country, the development and extension of its pioneering institutions, its spiritual influence, the dangerous adventure of its mere existence and survival?

In the eyes of the religious, Judaism has been undergoing a miraculous renascence since returning to its sources. But dangers threaten it. The tribulations of Israel are not yet over. A proportion of its children, putting an end to their exile, have by heroic efforts acquired and built up a place of refuge for themselves. Two million Jews have gathered in Palestine, exposing themselves to new trials and new dangers—not only Arab hatred, but also the new industrial environment that many of them ardently desire and help forward with their own hands, although this may be like pouring water on the fire of the needs of social justice and the prophetic spirit.

Most of the Israeli leaders, whether political or religious, veteran *halutzim* or young *sabras,* over and above all their differences unite in their harsh judgment of the Jews of the Diaspora, whose only future role, in their view, is to serve Israel as the center and spiritual home of Judaism. Perhaps, in view of the preceding observations, they should be more circumspect. The "Jewish people" and the "Jewish spirit" are exposed to grave perils in Israel. Let me quote, for what it is worth, this sally by a young Canaanite intellectual: "The Jewish Agency ought in future to help Jews, not to leave the Diaspora, but to remain in it"—a cruel remark which offers food for thought.

---

3. TWO MINORITIES: THE JEWS OF POLAND AND THE CHINESE OF THE PHILIPPINES

D. Stanley Eitzen

The two situations discussed in this article have similar historical antecedents. The responses of these two ethnic groups have also been similar. Each group banded together to fight their subordinate status. In each case, one result was the stereotyping of their characteristics. Eitzen claims that these stereotypes have reinforced the hostility that resulted when these two groups were perceived as "alien" in the culture. The author thus indicates that historical factors and traditions may result in similar patterns of prejudice and boundary formation in countries as disparate as the two discussed here.

The universal problem of majority-minority group relations has been the focus of much

SOURCE
Reprinted from *The Jewish Journal of Sociology* Vol. X, No. 2, December 1968, by permission of the Editor.

research. Most studies of this phenomenon have dealt with the groups within a particular society or with a particular group that faces prejudice and discrimination in many societies. The literature comparing different minorities cross-culturally is generally lacking.

Since, as Schermerhorn has pointed out, there are underlying features of the minority situation which can be universally found,[1] cross-cultural comparison of different minorities must be used to find them. The problem for this study is to compare two different minorities in two *diverse* cultural settings. Such a comparison is necessary if we are eventually to develop generalizations about majority-minority relations which hold up cross-culturally.

Several writers have pointed to the many parallels between the Jews in Europe and the Chinese in Southeast Asia.[2] Wertheim in his essay on the trading minorities of Southeast Asia, for example, finds similarities between these two minorities in their refusal to assimilate into the dominant culture, their similar occupational interests, their being objects of commercial jealousy, and the similarity in the stereotypes of each group held by members of the majority.[3] It would seem appropriate, then, to compare these two minorities to ascertain whether similarities in majority-minority relations can be found in diverse cultural settings. With this in mind, the countries selected for this study are Poland and the Philippines. These two countries have three basic things in common: (1) a history of outside domination; (2) a predominantly Catholic population; and (3) a minority "problem"—the Jews in Poland and the Chinese in the Philippines.[4]

The basic questions I seek to answer in this study are as follows. In what ways are the historical factors parallel? To what degree has each minority responded similarly to acts of cruelty and repression? Are there common reasons for the anti-minority phenomenon in these two countries?

It is *not* assumed that the two cases to be examined are alike in all respects. The prejudice and discrimination against any group can only be explained by the com-bination of social, cultural, historical, and economic factors unique to that group in its particular setting. There are, however, striking similarities betweeen the Jews of Poland and the Chinese of the Philippines. It is hoped that the examination of these parallel groups—their economic and social situation, the configuration of historical forces, their group reactions to the discrimination of the majority, and the common reasons for their being victims of discrimination—will have broader implications for the understanding of majority-minority group relations everywhere.

I. THE CHINESE IN THE PHILIPPINES

Archaeological research has produced evidence of 'Chinese' inhabiting the Philippines as early as 5,000 years ago, but little information is available about the early Chinese settlements even as late as 1200 C.E. It has been established that during the Ming Dynasty (1368-1644) a rather large trade was carried on between the Philippines and China. During this period the eastern route of the Chinese junk trading system was established; this meant that Chinese junks passed periodically through the western side of the Philippine Archipelago. Thus, several areas in the Philippines enjoyed regular commercial and cultural contact with the Chinese. In connexion with this trade some Chinese merchants and craftsmen settled in the Philippines. According to Edgar Wickberg, nothing is known about how these early Chinese settlers may have fitted into the economic and social life of their host culture.[5]

The Spanish era (1571-1898)
When the Spanish took control of the Philippines, the few Chinese residents were not considered a problem. The Spanish initially

welcomed Chinese immigration because of the skills, energy, and capital resources of the newcomers. Most importantly, the Chinese provided needed commercial enterprises and services; they became the country's commercial and skilled artisan classes, filling the void between the Spanish and the mass of Filipino natives.

The Spanish soon, however, became fearful and suspicious of the potential economic power and the increasing numbers of the Chinese. This distrust led them in 1581 to force the Chinese to live in a segregated settlement (Parian) outside the walls of Manila; a strict curfew was enforced to keep all Chinese out of Manila after 8 p.m.[6]

The Chinese posed a special dilemma to the Spanish which is faced even today by the Philippine Government. On the one hand, the Chinese were considered a menace because of their control of trade and credit, control of certain products and services, and the drain of Spanish gold. On the other hand, the Spanish desperately needed the many services provided by the immigrants and their trading ties with other Chinese throughout Asia. Consequently, their policy towards the Chinese vacillated between encouragement and repression, with the stress on the latter. Examples of repressive actions by the Spanish were:

1. the deportation of 12,000 Chinese in 1596;
2. the killing of 23,000 in the revolt of 1603;
3. the killing of another 23,000 in the revolt of 1639; this revolt happened when the Chinese were required to pay a special tribute to the King for the privilege of living in the Islands;
4. the killing of 20,000 in the revolt of 1662;
5. the expulsion of all non-Christian Chinese in 1755; this resulted in many Chinese being quickly baptized as Catholics.[7]

6. the killing of 6,000 Chinese in 1764 for siding with the English;
7. the levying of special taxes in 1823 which caused 800 Chinese to return to China, 1,083 to flee to the mountains, and the jailing of 453.

According to Edgar Wickberg, it is especially important to examine the later part of the Spanish era (1850-1898) for the economic and social origins of the present-day anti-Chinese policies.[8]   Wickberg argues that before 1850 the Chinese were a problem for the Spanish, not for the Filipinos. This is because there were few Chinese, and in the activities they engaged in they competed with the Spanish, not the Filipinos. Furthermore, the Chinese were segregated and few Filipinos had actual contact with them. After 1850, however, the Spanish liberalized immigration policies which resulted in the number of Chinese growing from 8,000 in 1850 to 100,000 in 1885. This period also found the Chinese scattering into all the provinces instead of concentrating in the large cities as before. During this period the Chinese

1. acted as wholesalers and retailers of imported goods in all the provinces;
2. became processors of Philippine agricultural products;
3. gained virtual control of hemp, tobacco, and rice;
4. established import-export firms with agents in all the provinces.

Thus, for the first time, the Chinese came into contact with virtually everyone in the Islands. Furthermore, they competed so successfully that great numbers of native Filipinos were driven out of business and into agriculture or other economic pursuits. This resulted in an anti-Chinese movement which was an expression not of Spanish fears alone but also of Filipino economic interest.

The American Era (1898-1946)

The Chinese exclusion policy of the United States was extended to the Philippines when that country came under American control. This policy did not deter Chinese immigration, however, since dependants of the local Chinese were allowed to enter the country. In addition, there were numbers of Chinese who entered illegally. The Chinese benefited during this period from lowered taxes and the privilege of being in business. By 1932 they conducted 70 to 80 per cent of all the retail trade and a large percentage of internal commerce. Furthermore, Chinese commercial and credit systems covered virtually every business and reached from Manila to all parts of the Philippines.

During this period there was a widespread feeling of hostility towards the Chinese. It was manifested in sporadic Filipino risings against them and in repressive measures taken by the Philippine legislature. An example of such a measure was the Book-keeping Act of 1921, which required every merchant in the country to keep accounts of his business in English, Spanish, and a local language. The Chinese community fought the measure and took its appeal to the United States Supreme Court, which declared the act unconstitutional. But the Philippine Legislature passed amended laws to a similar effect. The net effect of this and other repressive measures was an increase in the Filipino participation in retail trade from 20 to 37 per cent from 1935 to 1939.

By the end of the American era there was widespread hatred and hostility directed towards the Chinese. The Filipinos generally believed the Chinese to be guilty of unethical business practices, charging exorbitant interest rates, monopolizing trade, controlling politicians through bribery, drawing off capital from the country by contributing to Nationalist China or sending money to relatives elsewhere, and circumventing the law at every opportunity.

Repressive Measures Since Independence

Since Independence in 1946, the Philippine Government, with nationalistic fervour, has adopted a policy of legislating the Chinese out of the retail trade. Since 1946 many laws have been passed directed at aliens (Chinese). The following are examples of these legislative curbs.

1. It is now most difficult to become a citizen of the Philippines. Some of the requirements are 10 years' residence; clearance from the National Bureau of Investigation and police and health authorities, ability to read and write fluent English or Spanish and a native language; a favourable court hearing; and an additional waiting period of two years without leaving the country. The cost of the citizenship process is 5,000 pesos and additional money for bribes if the applicant is known to have wealth.[9]

2. There are special taxes on aliens.

3. Professional opportunities are closed off to aliens (except doctors and nurses).

4. Aliens are not allowed to acquire, except through inheritance, forest, mineral, and agricultural lands.

5. Filipinos in certain businesses are exempt from taxes.

6. The Nationalization of Retail Trade Act of 1954 provided that:[10]

a. All present alien proprietors may retain their holdings.

b. Businesses cannot be passed to heirs if they are also aliens, with a proviso that the property must be liquidated within six months of the original proprietor's death.

c. No new licences for retail establishments may be issued to aliens.

d. Any violation of any law governing trade, industry, and commerce will result in immediate revocation of the alien's licence to engage in retail trade.

e. Corporations will be allowed ten years from the bill's enactment to liquidate, unless they are 100 per cent Filipino-owned.

7. The Rice and Corn Nationalization Act of 1960 required that aliens in the cereal industry must pull out of that business within three years. This would place all parts of the industry (planting, milling, warehousing, marketing, etc.) in the hands of native-born Filipinos.

8. Other measures prevent Chinese from buying land, eliminate them from city-owned markets, and hamper import-export activity.

II. THE JEWS IN POLAND

Polish Jewry from the tenth century to 1795
In the tenth century Jews began residing in the area known as Poland. The stream of Jewish migration to this area increased following the persecutions of the First Crusade (1098). At first the Jews were welcomed in Poland, for there was a need for a commercial class. The population of Poland previously consisted of two classes—the nobles, who owned the soil, and the serfs, who tilled it. The Jews migrating to Poland brought their skills as craftsmen, middlemen, innkeepers, moneylenders, and merchants. Such enterprise was needed to develop the country and its natural resources, and the nobles therefore encouraged the coming of the Jews.

Before the fourteenth century the chief disseminator of antisemitism in Poland was the Catholic Church, which was fearful of the possible influence by Jews on Christians. The Church fought for segregation of the Jews and incited the faithful to hate and abuse them for desecration of holy objects. The following are instances of the overt persecution of the Jews by the Church.[11]

1. In 1399 the Rabbi and 13 elders of a Jewish community were roasted alive for allegedly desecrating three hosts from the Dominican Church.

2. "In 1407, at Easter time, a priest at Cracow made a public announcement of a rumor that the Jews had slain a Christian child. The Jewish quarter was immediately attacked, many Jews were killed and their children baptized, property was looted and dwellings were set on fire.[12]

3. In 1556 a rumour spread that Jews of Sochaczev had procured a sacred wafer and desecrated it by stabbing it until it bled. Three Jews were burned at the stake for this crime.

By 1350 the Polish merchant class became strong enough to struggle against their Jewish competitors, but the Polish merchants found it difficult to compete with the Jews. Jewish merchants were quick to seize economic opportunities and to find loopholes in the restrictive laws; they could practise usury which was forbidden to Catholics; they had contacts with Jewish merchants in other cities, they engaged in practices frowned upon by the other town business men (e.g., Jews went to the homes of customers to solicit orders); and in trades where there were no restrictions, such as the garment industry, the Jews developed virtual monopolies.

Another area in which Jewish competition caused resentment was that of handicrafts. The Jews were in direct competition with Christian tailors, furriers, hatmakers, and goldsmiths. Since the Jews were excluded from the craft guilds, they ". . . started the production of standard articles for sale and thus they became the promoters of the capitalistic commercialization process of industry in Poland."[13] The Polish artisans also had reason for their hostility to the Jewish merchants: they had monopoly control over the trade in raw materials needed by artisans (e.g., skins and furs) and they imported commodities from the outside which undersold the articles produced by Polish artisans.

Restrictive legislation against the Jews was encouraged by Polish merchants and artisans.

1. The Piotrkov Diet of 1521 passed a law confining the trade of the Jews in Lemberg

to wax, furs, cloth, and horned cattle.

2. In 1556 at Posen, "... the limits of the ghetto were strictly defined; only 49 houses were allowed to the Jews, so that it became necessary to raise the height of many dwellings by additional stories. The magistracy of Warsaw refused to admit Jewish settlers, and Jewish merchants, visiting the city on business, could only tarry not longer than two or three days."[14]

3. In 1643 the Diet fixed the rate of profit at 7 per cent for native Christian traders, 5 per cent for foreigners, and only 3 per cent for Jews.

4. Generally, the Jews were not allowed to own agricultural lands, were excluded from certain occupations and all guilds, were forced to live in segregated areas of the city, and were required to wear a distinctive headdress.

The Jews were further disliked because of the work they did for the nobles and princes. They served as financial agents for the princes, leased and administered crown domains and estates of the gentry, and often worked as tax collectors.

In summary, the Jews became the objects of discrimination by most elements of Polish society during this early period.

"The Church, of course, was always inimical to the presence of the Jews in the country; the burghers saw in them undesirable competitors; the overburdened peasantry had no love for the exploiting nobles or their Jewish agents. The kings and the gentry, in conflict with one another found the Jews useful as sources of revenue or as creators of their wealth.[15]

The extent of antisemitic feeling in Poland was evidenced when, following the Black Death, about 10,000 Jews were slain there for supposedly being connected with that disaster.[16]

The Period from Polish Partition (1795) to the First World War

When Poland was partitioned, Polish Jewry came under the rule of three separate powers—Russia, Austria, and Prussia. The policies towards the Jews were generally the same under these three different political systems and were a continuation of the earlier antisemitic policies in Poland. There were restrictions on marriage, special taxes for the Jews, some expulsion, curtailment of business, and attempts to limit the power and rights of Jewish self-government.

In 1817 the Czar's representative to Poland proposed that the Jews be granted civil rights if they became farmers, discontinued their communal separateness, and changed their system of education. The polish members of the Council answered: "Let them first become Poles."[17] This cry points to a frequent criticism of the Jews (which we shall explore later in this paper)—their refusal to assimilate.

Poland between the World Wars

Following the First World War, Poland became independent. By 1921 the Jewish population of Poland was 2,854,364 (10-5 per cent of the total population). Again, as in the past, there were pogroms, mob outrages, and restrictive legislation directed against the Jews. They were forbidden to acquire land and forced to pay special taxes; many Jews were refused citizenship; Jews were eliminated from the match, tobacco, and salt productives, and the Sunday Rest Law (1920) caused serious economic hardship to the Jews who closed their stores and workshops on Saturday. As a result, the ratio of Jews employed in trade fell from 61.8 per cent in 1921 to 52.7 per cent in 1937.[18] However, Jews continued to play an important role in the crafts: 'Eighty per cent of the tailors, 40 per cent of the shoemakers, 25 per cent of the butchers and bakers, and 75 per cent of the barbers in Poland were Jews.'[19]

As was customary with the Jews throughout their settlement in Poland, they insisted upon minority rights, and this was regarded by the Poles as proof of their lack of patriotism.[20]

The Second World War

The story of the German treatment of the Jews is infamous. Weinryb divides German policy towards the Jews into three stages:[21]

1. The early period of anti-Jewish decrees, looting, pogroms, etc. (1939-1940).
2. The ghetto period, ending with the outbreak of the German-RussianWar (1940-1941).
3. The period of planned extermination (1941-1945).

Most of the nearly three million Polish Jews and approximately one million other Jews brought to Poland from elsewhere were killed in the Polish death camps. At the time of liberation only 50,000 had survived.[22]

Communist Poland

The Jews returning from the concentration camps did not receive a pleasant welcome from their non-Jewish neighbours. In many places there was an immediate wave of terror. 'In March, 1945, alone, 150 Jews were killed.'[23] This was a consequence of the fear of competition in an already impoverished land as well as of the rise of Polish nationalism.

Despite their hardships the Jews made a remarkable recovery. Since they found it dangerous to compete with Polish pedlars and shopkeepers, and the Communist ideology scarcely favoured private enterprise, they formed Jewish co-operatives, particu-larly in the tailoring, shoemaking, and other traditional Jewish crafts. From 1946 to 1948 the number of Jewish co-operatives increased from 13 to 203.[24]

The Jewish population in Poland has fluctuated widely since the War. Many Jews migrated to Poland and many more left. "Between 1948 and 1958 approximately 140,500 Jews left Poland for Israel."[25] In 1945 the Jewish population was 50,000, by 1955 it had grown to 75,000, and now it has stabilized at about 35,000.

Currently, the formal policy of the government is to halt antisemitic practices,* but this has been ineffective for the most part. According to Lucjan Blit there are elements in the government that use antisemitism to their advantage. ". . . antisemitism is being deliberately exploited by the pro-Moscow minority in the Polish Party . . ."[26]

Leon Shapiro for the last several years has summarized the Jewish community activities and antisemitic practices in Poland in the *American Jewish Year Book.* He stated that in 1958 antisemitism manifested itself in many ways.

. . . in a number of instances Jews were eliminated from their jobs in government and industry, and there were many cases of physical attacks on individual Jews; Jewish children were abused and attacked in schools and on the streets.[27]

Again in 1963, Shapiro writes,

". . . there was no overt antisemitism, but widespread prejudices among all classes of the Polish population created considerable difficulties for Jews, particularly those residing, in small towns and looking for jobs or other economic opportunities."[28]

---

*This paper does not take account of recent developments in Poland.

THE MINORITY RESPONSE TO MAJORITY HOSTILITY

I. The Chinese in the Philippines

Various social distance scales have demonstrated the anti-Chinese attitudes held by most Filipinos.[29]   Antipathy towards the Chinese is based on the belief that this minority controls the economy, engages in illegal activities (e.g., bribery and circumventing the law), is clannish, and owes its allegiance elsewhere.   While these charges are true to a certain extent,[30] the characteristics of the Chinese in the Philippines can be attributed, at least in part, to the effects of discriminatory acts directed against them by the dominant group.

The Effects of Restrictive Legislation.   The Filipinos as a group resent the economic role of the Chinese.   Yet Philippine law has had the effect of actually forcing the Chinese into trade since the Chinese have been barred from owning land, controlling natural resources, and joining the professions. [31]

After forcing virtually all the Chinese into trade, the government has imposed heavy restrictions which will eventually wrest this means of livelihood from them. Hartendorp suggests that from 1948 to 1957 Chinese control of the import trade has decreased by 25 per cent and their participation in export trade has decreased by 4 per cent.[32]

Legislation against the Chinese compels them to resort to illegal measures. One common technique used to offset the Nationalization of Retail Trade Act was for Chinese men to marry Filipinos and put the business in their wife's name. Baterina suggests that different groups of Chinese financially support different political parties and candidates in order to ensure that their economic investments will be protected regardless of the election's outcome.[33]   Furthermore, in order to stay in business, the Chinese must bribe officials who issue licences, assess taxes, give citizenship, and make the laws. Bribery, of course, is a "two-way street"—an offer and an acceptance of favours; both parties must share the guilt. Several authors have suggested that legislators often introduce discriminatory bills only to get the bribes which the Chinese then offer for killing the measures.[34]

The Chinese, to survive, must be ingenious and devious. They must use illegal methods to bypass discriminatory legislation.

"In the Philippines, Christian Filipinos have made the Chinese what they are, the objects of Christian complaints, the object of Christian acts of repression.   If Chinese businessmen hurt Filipino businessmen, that is not right—but who hurt whom first? Who is the villain?   The reconciliation of the two peoples should be the aim of legislation, not their further alienation.[35]

Organization of the Chinese Community. Two common complaints against the Chinese are about their clannishness and lack of loyalty to the Philippine Government. The discriminatory actions of the government and individual Filipinos have forced segregation of the Chinese and caused them to seek stability and protection from their own group and institutions. Chinese business organizations are an especially good example.

Perhaps the most important single group to a Chinese business man is the local Chinese Chamber of Commerce, Each Chamber of Commerce provides a forum for discussion, collects and disseminates information about trade conditions, investigates and guarantees the credentials of Chinese business men, settles disputes, conducts research, provides machinery for group action, and acts as a lobby and pressure group to promote the interests of the Chinese in their dealings with the Philippine government officials. Money is collected through the local Chamber for charity work, hospitals, cemeteries, social clubs, and especially the financing of Chinese schools. Chinese business men also seek protection through such trade organizations as the Philippine Chinese Hardware Association, Chinese Groceries Association, and the Philippine Manila Chinese Sari Sari Store Association. At present the larger trade associations and 120 Chambers of Commerce are united in the Federation of Chinese Chambers of Commerce to present a single cohesive front and facilitate business contacts in all the provinces.

In order to perpetuate strong in-group ties, the Chinese have placed strong emphasis on educating their children in Chinese schools. At present there are in the country about 160 Chinese elementary and second-ary schools with 52,400 pupils. There are two curricula in these schools: one based on the standard course found in Philippine public schools and the second stressing Chinese language and culture. The real function of the Chinese school system is to keep the child Chinese and thus to reduce the assimilation process. "The admitted ideal of the schools maintained by the Chinese communities for its own children is to form good Chinese *citizens* and good Philippine *residents*."[36]

Through business organizations, family ties, fraternal associations, and the educational system, the Chinese remain a tightly knit group resistant to the pressures of assimilation into the dominant culture.[37]

"While he maintains relationships with these groups, the Chinese man is assured both comradeship and economic aid; if he separates from them, he is on his own in an area which is rather unfriendly to members of his ethnic group."[38]

We see a common phenomenon in inter-group relations where the minority group is the target of discriminatory acts. These acts have the effect of forcing the minority group to take defensive attitudes and mea-sures, which in turn draw increased criticism by reinforcing the stereotypes of that group. Thus, further discrimination appears justified.

II. The Jews in Poland

Generally, the Jews of Poland have ex-perienced the same type of discriminatory acts as the Chinese in the Philippines: they were prohibited from owning land, forced into urban ghettos, excluded from certain occupations, and restricted in their activities.

The response of the Jews to these acts was also similar to that of the Chinese. They gravitated to certain occupations left open to them (eventually gaining monopolies in many of them), found loopholes in restrictive laws, used bribery and other illegal acts, and bound themselves into a tightly knit community for defence and welfare.

Community Organization. From the begin-ning, Polish Jews were voluntarily organized into communities which centred on the synagogue and cemetery. In 1264 a charter was drawn up giving the Jews the right of local self-government. Although advanta-geous to the Jewish community, this served to separate them further from local citizens and foster more hostility.[39]

In time, a system of strong community or-ganization developed. By the sixteenth cen-tury each Jewish community in Poland was organized in an association called the *Kehilla*. This association of all Jews within the city limits maintained the local synagogue, set reg-ulations, provided for education, gave econ-omic assistance, and acted as judges in dis-putes. The underlying reason for a separate Jewish community organization was the ne-cessity of group solidarity for defence against aggression from without, as well as for the improvement of the moral and religious life of the community within.[40]

By 1600, the local *Kehillot* were joined into regional organizations and a national organization, The Council of Four Lands. This Council was the supreme legislative, judicial, and executive body of Polish Jewry. It defended Jews in court, watched over Jewish interests in the Polish Diet, provided rules and curricula for Jewish schools, and sought to prevent friction between the government and the Jewish population. In addition, the organization wanted to ensure proper conduct by Jews so as not to raise the ire of others.[41]

In 1764 the Council of Four Lands was dissolved by the Polish Diet. The Jewish communities under the local synagogue councils continued to fulfill the functions carried out earlier by the *Kehilla* system. By this time, more and more emphasis was placed on the welfare functions of the community organization (e.g., free loans, public health, and credit co-operatives).

After the First World War another type of organization was formed. Jewish economic associations for merchants and artisans and trade unions were organized to consolidate the power of the Jews in a particular occupation.

After the Second World War Polish Jews again found it essential to organize. The Central Committee for Polish Jews was formed to carry on relief and welfare work and to reconstruct the Jewish community councils. The central Jewish organization is the Union of Religious Communities which supervises the network of schools, children's homes, and welfare institutions. A third contemporary national organization is the Cultural and Social Union of Polish Jews which attempts to revitalize Jewish cultural activities. In 1965, for example, this organization had over 100 projects (choral groups, dance groups, dramatic groups, etc.), the purpose of which was to stress Jewish tradition.[42]

Thus, throughout the history of Polish Jewry, this minority has banded together for protection and welfare. To ensure the continued solidarity of the group, the young must be taught the importance and uniqueness of their heritage, religion, language, and way of life. Consequently, formal education in Jewish schools has always been stressed. The avowed purpose of these schools is to preserve the Jewish cultural and linguistic heritage, thereby preventing assimilation.

Traditionally, scholarship has been highly prized among the Jews. This emphasis has been a unique feature of Jewish reaction to prejudice and discrimination. The result has been a disproportionately large number of Jewish scholars, scientists, and academicians.

"The cultural traditions of Judaism, the community solidarity (in important measure a result of discrimination), a high invividual desire for achievement (again, in part a result of discrimination), the intellectual alertness which come from the marginal position of membership in two cultures—these and other factors have encouraged high achievement."[43]

In summary, throughout the history of Polish Jewry the typical reaction of the group to the unfriendly environment was to close ranks and become more conscious of internal ties. Hence, the criticism arises that the Jews are Jews first and Poles second. In one sense the Jews separated themselves from the dominant culture voluntarily—they desired to cling to their traditional ways. In another sense the Jews were physically separated by ecological, occupational, and social restrictions.

They separateness of the Jewish community, then, is a consequence of the actions of the majority and the response to these actions by the minority. ". . . the positive pull of Jewish culture and the negative push of discrimination (leading to group solidarity and strong efforts to overcome discrimination) are indissolubly linked."[44] The solidarity of the minority and the resulting distinctiveness of the group are, then, a cause for further discrimination by the dominant group.

SIMILARITIES BETWEEN POLISH JEWS AND PHILIPPINE CHINESE

Majority-minority relations in every society are a configuration of historical, social, and cultural forces unique to the particular setting. With this qualification in mind, we can still find striking similarities between the Jews of Poland and the Chinese of the Philippines. We find common historical forces at work, common patterns of discrimination by the majority, common minority group traits, and common responses to discrimination. Generally, the differences found are of degree rather than kind. It is reasonable to suppose then, that if such commonalities are to be found, there are common bases for these similarities.

Common Patterns of Discrimination. Discrimination takes many forms. Peter I. Rose lists the three distinctive modes as:[45]

1. Derogation
2. Denial (establishing and maintaining some measure of physical and social distance from minorities)
   a. Avoidance
   b. Restriction
   c. Segregation
3. Violence
   a. Mob aggression
   b. Genocide

In their respective countries the Jews and Chinese have been victims of *each* of these types of discrimination. The particular form used by the majority varied with the time and place.

Individual and Group Traits due to Victimization. Gordon Allport in *The Nature of Prejudice* discusses the various ego-defence mechanisms which victims of prejudice and discrimination characteristically employ to protect themselves and advance their interests. These mechanisms are grouped by Allport into two types. The first response is aggressiveness directed against others; this is the mechanism typical of individuals who are extropunitive (i.e., they blame the outer cause of their handicap rather than themselves). The second type of response is withdrawal; this is the mechanism of those who take some responsibility for adjusting to the situation. Examples of the intropunitive individual's response to prejudice and discrimination are self-hate, in-group aggression, symbolic status striving, and neuroticism.[46]

While Allport is concerned with the response of the individual, these traits are also characteristic responses of the minority group as a whole. Both the Chinese in the Philippines and the Jews in Poland are basically extropunitive. Both groups have particularly responded with strong in-group ties, competitiveness, slyness and cunning, and enhanced striving. It should be noted that individuals within the minorities as well as minority groups themselves differ in their responses to discrimination and in the exact way in which they compete, strengthen in-group ties, etc. The mode of enhanced striving is a good example. Characteristically, the Jews have stressed scholarship and intellectual pursuits, as well as being good business men, as ways to get ahead, while the Chinese in the Philippines have stressed the quality of hard work and self-denial (e.g., long hours, living under meagre conditions) to outdo their competitors from the dominant group.

Because of their common reactions to discrimination, the Jews of Poland and the Chinese of the Philippines are viewed in similar stereo-typical terms by the dominant groups in these countries. The stereo-types which these groups share are: clannishness, refusal to assimilate, disloyalty to the government, unethical business practices, cleverness, adaptability, ambition, industriousness and mercenariness.

The Common Bases for Anti-Chinese and Antisemitic Attitudes.   One factor alone is never sufficient to explain the cause of anti-minority feelings.   A particular group is singled out for a number of interacting reasons.

"It is especially important to keep in mind that these forces are interactive, mutually reinforcing, and to an important degree self-perpetuating. Once a group has been set apart as a target of hostility, it is chosen more readily for that role the next time because tradition suggests it, guilt feelings demand it, and perhaps the responses of the minority group, having differentiated the group more sharply, encourage it."[47]

In addition, as was pointed out earlier, each group singled out by the majority in a particular complex of historical, social, and cultural forces, is unique. Therefore, our comparison of the common factors leading to discrimination against the Jews and Chinese in different societies is to be regarded as incomplete.   Our concern is with the complex interaction of causes which are common to both situations.

Common Historical Factors.   An important element affecting the subsequent relations between two groups is the degree of congruency between their value systems prior to contact. Conflict between these groups will tend to be greater to the extent that the values of the two groups are incongruent.[48]

The Chinese before contact with the native Filipinos (and the Spanish) and the Jews before entering Poland had value systems quite different from those of their respective host cultures (e.g., they had a different religion, were tradition-oriented, and were 'capitalistic'). Thus, both groups entered an alien culture. This helps to explain in part, the separation of both minorities from the majority and the conflict between the dominant group and the minority in each instance.

The Jews and the Chinese came to their respective countries under similar circumstances. Both Poland and the Philippines needed and encouraged the skills and capital brought by the immigrants. Thus, members of both minorities came originally as business men, money-lenders, and skilled craftsmen. The principle of cumulative directionality applies here: since the Jews and Chinese were allowed in these positions originally, they have tended to persist throughout the centuries in these occupations.[49] The stratification pattern that has resulted in both countries is one in which "Cultural subordinates are accorded a special selective status which is an addendum or supplement to the wider societal stratification."[50] Although victims of discriminatory practices, both minorities have had an intermediary status in their respective countries by virtue of their specialized occupations.

It is important to note that the two confrontations differ radically in one respect. The Chinese in the Philippines held religious views very much different from the religion of the majority in that country. The Jews in Europe, on the other hand, have a religious link with Christianity (e.g., belief in and worship of the same God, acceptance of the Old Testament). The common descent of Judaism and Christianity helps to explain partially the anti-Jewish attitudes in Europe. Norman Cohn gives several of the reasons for this situation: (1) the refusal of the

Jews to accept the divinity of Christ; (2) the belief that the Jews were responsible for the murder of Christ; (3) the Jews' belief that they are God's chosen people; and (4) the Christian belief, dating from the second and third centuries, that the Antichrist would be a Jew and that his most faithful followers would be Jews.[51] Cohn summarizes the role of the Catholic Church in fostering anti-semitic prejudice by saying that the Church '. . . had always tended to regard the synagogue as a dangerous influence and even as a potential rival and had never ceased to carry on a vigorous polemic against Judaism.'[52]

Thus, while the tie between Christianity and Judaism has led to overt hostility between the two groups, the radical differences in the religious beliefs of the Chinese and the Filipinos led only indirectly to anti-Chinese feeling.

The following historical factors help to reveal the traditional sources of prejudice, and the force for its continuation, which are common to both the Jews and the Chinese.

1. The basic conflict between Christianity and non-Christian religions. The Catholic Chruch, historically, has restricted contact with other religions for fear that aliens' beliefs would weaken the faith of their members.

2. The long and continued history of persecution, violence, and discrimination directed towards the alien minority. Violence creates an even more intense need for anti-minority feeling to justify it. "It is very difficult not to hate someone whom you have harmed."[53] This does not explain the source of the prejudice—only its continuation.

3. Intense group cohesion on the part of each minority. This separateness was proof to the members of the dominant group of the minority's lack of loyalty to the adopted homeland.

4. Both groups have been very successful against business competitor from the dominant group. "It always hurts to be outclassed by foreigners in one's own land."[54] In addition, they were believed to use illegal or fringe methods which gave them unfair advantage.

5. Various groups have used anti-minority propaganda to consolidate their own positions in the power structure.

6. Both nations have at various times in their history undergone periods of nationalistic fervour. This led to a revulsion against anyone or anything thought to be alien.

7. Once a group has been selected as an object of prejudice, it continues to be so because the young are socialized to think of the minority in derogatory terms and to respond to them in a prejudicial manner. This is possible because these acts have the sanction of tradition.

8. The wide dispersion of Jews and Chinese helps to reinforce prejudice against them. Because each group is a minority throughout much of the world, ". . . the apprehensions regarding them as a minority are transferable, interchangeable, and even cumulative to a degree."[55]

The common accusations against Jews and Chinese (e.g., of clannishness, sharp business practices, and lack of patriotism) are in part true. Where does the blame lie? Gunnar Myrdal's "vicious circle hypothesis" helps to explain this. This hypothesis assumes a general interdependence between all the factors in the minority problem. Majority group prejudice and discrimination force the minority to segregate itself for defence and welfare. To survive, they must circumvent laws directed at eliminating them from their means of livelihood. This in turn gives support to the prejudice of the majority—it justifies further discrimination. Thus, dominant prejudice and the minority response to it mutually cause each other and the process is self-perpetuating.[56] However, the principle demonstrates how prejudice is maintained, not how it came into being.

CONCLUSION

The aim of this study has been to discover similarities and parallels between two minority groups. The table below lists these similarities.

Similarities between the Jews of Poland and the Chinese of the Philippines

	JEWS	CHINESE
Historical factors:		
Values different from majority	X	X
Common occupational patterns	X	X
Located in urban areas	X	X
Segregation (compulsory)	X	X
Victims of common patterns of discrimination	X	X
Minority reactions to discrimination:		
Internal solidarity	X	X
Formation of business and community		
organizations for defence and welfare	X	X
Schools to promote cultural identity	X	X
Emphasis on intellectual pursuits	X	little
Competitiveness	X	X
Circumvention of restrictive laws	X	X
Stereotypes of the minority:		
Clannish	X	X
Control of business	X	X
Lack of loyalty to the government	X	X
Refusal to assimilate	X	X
Unethical in business	X	X
Clever	X	X
Adaptable	X	X
Ambitious	X	X
Industrious	X	X
Mercenary	X	X
Reasons for persecution:		
Economic	X	X
Nationalistic	X	X
Religious	X	not overt
The sanction of tradition	X	X

One should not infer from this comparison that these groups are identical. The many ways in which they differ (e.g., religion, customs, and forms of organization) have not been the focus of our enquiry. Nor would one conclude that the similarities noted in the table are applicable to all minority groups. What we have demonstrated is the following.

"A" equals the dominant group in country A and "a" equals the minority in that country.

"B" equals the dominant group in country B and "b" equals the minority in that country.

If "a" and "b" enter A and B respectively, to fill similar needs of that society, then "a" will be similar to "b" in certain respects (e.g., occupations and place in the stratification system).

Then, if "A" and "B" persecute "a" and "b" for similar reasons, "a" and "b" will be similar in their response to this discrimination.

Once this has been set in motion, the principle of cumulative directionality applies—"A" and "B" will continue their harassment of "a" and "b" respectively, justified by the responses of "a" and "b" which continue to be somewhat similar.

The above scheme suffers from its simplicity. First, because the social conditions in which groups come in contact are so varied and the number of variables that affect their interaction is so great, our comparison of the Jews and Chinese in two different countries may either be atypical (in that there are so many parallels which would not be found in other cross-cultural comparisons) or these apparently similar characteristics may be only superficially so. Second, our sample is too small. It would be instructive to compare a number of minorities which had initial contact with majority groups under analogous social conditions to determine the extent of subsequent similarities. It would then be possible to make generalizations and to develop interrelated propositions which could be applied cross-culturally.

REFERENCES

1. R. A. Schermerhorn, "Toward a General Theory of Minority Groups," *Phylon*, XXV, Fall, 1964, p. 238.

2. Cf, W. F. Wertheim, "The Trading Minorities in Southeast Asia" in *East-West Parallels: Sociological Approaches to Modern Asia*, The Hague, 1964, pp. 39-82; Maurice Freedman, "Jews, Chinese, and Some Others," *The British Journal of Sociology*, X, March, 1959, pp. 61-70; Asavabahu (King Rama IV), "The Jews of the East," cited in Kenneth Perry Landon, *The Chinese in Thailand*, New York, 1941, pp. 34-43.

3. Wertheim, op. cit.

4. The Jews of Poland and the Chinese of the Philippines were selected as the focus of this study because they represent certain common features in antisemitism in Europe and anti-Chinese feeling in Southeast Asia. The cases selected, however, are not truly representative of the majority-minority problems in other European and Asian countries, because each nation and its minorities are unique in many ways. Some excellent sources on the Jews in other European countries are: Lucy S. Daividowicz, *The Golden Tradition: Jewish Life and Thought in Eastern Europe*, New York, 1967; Ilse R. Wolff, ed., *German Jewry: Its History, Life, and Culture*, London, 1958; Cecil Roth, *A History of the Jews in England*, 3rd edn., Oxford, 1964; Max L. Margolis and Alexander Marx, *A History of the Jewish People*, Philadelphia, 1945. Some representative sources on the Chinese in other Southeast Asian countries are: George William Skinner, *Chinese Society in Thailand: An Analytical History*, Ithaca, New York, 1957; George William Skinner, *Leadership and Power in the Chinese Community of Thailand*, Ithaca, New York, 1958; Victor Purcell, *The Chinese in Southeast Asia*, 2nd edn., London, 1965; Maurice Freedman, *The Chinese in South-East Asia: A Longer View*, London, 1965; Donald Earl Willmott, *The National Status of the Chinese in Indonesia, 1900-1958*, Ithaca, New York, 1961; Ju-k'ang T'ien, *The Chinese of Sarawak: A Study of Social Structure*, London, 1953; and Richard J. Coughlin, *Double Identity: The Chinese in Modern Thailand*, Hong Kong, 1960.

5. Edgar Wickberg, *The Chinese in Philippine Life: 1850-1898*, New Haven, 1965, p. 4.

6. Jose A. Quirino, "The Parian: Circa 1581," *Manila Times: Sunday Times Magazine,* 15 March 1964, p. 54.

7. T. M. Locsin, "The Chinese Problem," *Philippines Free Press,* 8 December 1956, p. 35.

8. Wickberg, op. cit., and Edgar Wickberg, "Early Chinese Economic Influence in the Philippines, 1850-1898," Pacific Affairs, XXXV, Fall, 1962, pp. 275-85.

9. Albert Ravenholt, *Chinese in the Philippines,* New York, American Universities Field Staff, 1955, pp. 13-14.

10. Robert S. Elegant, The Dragon's Seed, New York, 1959, p. 87.

11. Raphael Mahler, "Antisemitism in Poland," in Koppel D. Pinson, ed., Essays on Antisemitism, New York, 1946, p. 146; and Margolis and Marx, op. cit., pp. 529-41.

12. Margolis and Marx, op. cit., p. 529.

13. Mahler, op. cit., p. 149.

14. Margolis and Marx, op. cit., p. 541.

15. Ibid, p. 532.

16. Maurice H. Harris, History of the Medieval Jews, New York, 1916, p. 324.

17. Margolis and Marx, op. cit., p. 665.

18. Bernard D. Weinryb, "Poland," in Peter Meyer et al., eds., The Jews in the Soviet Satellites, Syracuse, New York, 1953, pp. 207-11.

19. Ibid., p. 213.

20. Solomon Grayzel, A History of the Jews, Philadelphia, 1947, p. 769.

21. Weinryb, op. cit., p. 229.

22. Ibid.

23. Ibid, p. 252.

24. Ibid, p. 272.

25. Poland"", in Cecil Roth, ed., The Standard Jewish Encyclopedia, Garden City, New York, 1959, p. 1524.

26. Lucjan Blit, "Poland and the Jewish Remnant," Commentary, XXIII, March, 1957 pp. 216-17.

27. Leon Shapiro, "Poland," in Morris Fine and Milton Himmelfarb, eds., American Jewish Year Book, Volume 59, New York, 1958, p. 326.

28. *American Jewish Year Book,* New York, 1963, pp. 359-60.

29. Cf. Chester L. Hunt, "Comments on Patterns of Social Relationships in the Philippines," *Philippine Social Science and Humanities Review,* XIX, March, 1954, p. 11; and Benicio T. Catapusan, "Social Distance in the Philippines," *Sociology and Social Research. XXX* VIII, May-June, 1954, pp. 309-12.

30. There is one instance where the stereotype is false: currently the Chinese control only a small proportion (although it is disproportionate to the size of the Chinese group) of trade and commerce. Interestingly enough, Americans, although much less numerous in the Philippines than the Chinese, control over twice as much foreign trade as do the Chinese, yet they are not objects of prejudice and discrimination. Cf. Socorro E. Espiritu and Chester L. Hunt, eds., *Social Foundations of Community Development, Manila,* 1964, p. 11.

31. Robert B. Fox and Frank Lynch, eds., *Area Handbook on the Philippines,* Volume I, Chicago, 1965, p. 311.

32. A. V. H. Hartendorp, *History of Industry and Trade of the Philippines,* Manila, 1961, pp. 207-71.

33. Virginia F. Baterina, "A Study of Money in Philippine Elections," *Philippine Social Science and Humanities Review,* XX, March, 1955, p. 74.

34. Ravenholt, op. cit., p. 15; and Elegant, op. cit., p. 86.

35. Locsin, op. cit., p. 147.

36. Fox and Lynch, op. cit., pp. 312-313.

37. Although this statement is true for the majority of Chinese in the Philippines, it should be noted that many Chinese have assimilated. Cf. Freedman (1965), op. cit.

39. Harris, op. cit., p. 322.

40. Israel Halpern, "The Jews in Eastern Europe," in Louis Finkelstein, ed., *The Jews*, Volume I, London, 1949, p. 309; and Margolis and Marx, op. cit., p. 534.

41. Margolis and Marx, op. cit., pp. 538-39.

42. Shapiro (1965), op. cit., p. 435.

43. George E. Simpson and J. Milton Yinger, *Racial and Cultural Minorities: An Analysis of Prejudice and Discrimination*, New York, 1965, p. 228.

44. Ibid., loc. cit.

45. Peter I. Rose, *They and We: Racial and Ethnic Relations in the United States*, New York, 1964, pp. 100-19.

46. Gordon W. Allport, *The Nature of Prejudice*, Garden City, New York, 1958, pp. 138-58.

47. Simpson and Yinger, op. cit., p. 233.

48. Schermerhorn, op. cit., p. 244.

49. Ibid., pp. 242-43.

50. Ibid., p. 243.

51. Norman Cohn, *The Pursuit of the Millennium*, London, 1957, pp. 61-62.

52. Ibid., p. 61.

53. Simpson and Yinger, op. cit., p. 200.

54. Fox and Lynch, op. cit., p. 315.

55. Simpson and Yinger, op. cit., p. 235.

56. Gunnar Myrdal, *An American Dilemma: The Negro Problem and Modern Democracy*, New York, 1944, pp. 75-78 and 1065-1970; cf. Robert M. MacIver, *The More Perfect Union: A Program for the Control of Intergroup Discrimination in the United States*, New York, 1948, pp. 61-81; Simpson and Yinger, op. cit., p. 122; and Schermerhorn, op. cit., p. 243.

---

4.   THE SOCIAL PERSISTENCE OF AN OUTCASTE GROUP

John Donoghue

In this discussion of a Japanese "untouchable" group, the *eta* or Burakumin, Donoghue outlines the factors that have maintained the solidarity of one outcaste community. This solidarity has prevented the *eta* from achieving significant social mobility. Donoghue carefully details the class conflicts within this Burakumin community and the prejudices, fears, and boundaries that divide the *eta* community from the rest of the population.

SOURCE
From *Japan's Invisible Race*, **edited by George DeVos and Hiroshi Wagatsuma. Originally published by the University of California Press. Reprinted by permission of the Regents of the University of California.**

This chapter summarizes field research in which the major objective was to determine some of the factors contributing to the social persistence of Shin-machi—an outcaste community located on the outskirts of Toyoda City[1] in the Tohoku District of northeast Japan. The following description and analysis is directed to the two questions: Why do the outcastes remain a distinct subgroup in Japanese society? Why do Burakumin remain in overpopulated substandard communities, rather than migrate to large cities where their pariah stigma may be lost?

Let us summarize some of the points made in earlier chapters. The outcastes are not racially distinct nor do they have major overt cultural characteristics that might differentiate them from the majority society. They are not required to live in segregated villages, and the hierarchical social structure of the feudal period no longer exists. Moreover, Buddhist religious taboos against the taking of life and Shinto conceptions of pollution associated with blood, dirt, and death, both of which contributed to the early formation and development of the Eta, have undergone essential modifications. Most Japanese people now eat meat, and majority butchers, tanners, and shoemakers, occupations formerly held only by Eta, are found throughout the nation. The primary distinguishing feature of the outcaste is residence in a socially segregated and isolated community. What follows focuses specifically upon the dynamics of intergroup and interpersonal relations, and upon the socioeconomic organization that influences the social persistence of this community.

At present, the special communities, traditionally located on river banks and other marginal lands, maintain a perceptible distinctness because of substandard, slum-like dwellings and serious overpopulation. Although many of the Burakumin are employed in the customary Eta occupations of butchering, leather and fur processing, begging, and other menial tasks, the largest percentage

[1] All place names in this chapter are pseudonyms. The nature of the community and its relationship to the majority society makes this necessary.

are farmers, fishermen, and unskilled laborers. They are further differentiated from the majority by an income far below the national average, and by their tendency toward local and caste endogamy.

ATTITUDES OF NON-BURAKUMIN IN TOYODA

A great deal of misunderstanding concerning the Eta exists in Toyoda in the Tohoku District of northeast Japan. Most citizens prefer to avoid the subject of the Burakumin even in conversation. Most informants, although unaware of the location of Shin-machi, are familiar with the term *Shin-machi-nin* (people of Shin-machi), which is applied to the outcastes of Toyoda. Few city residents have ever been to Shin-machi and most have never knowingly met an outcaste. Buraku dwellers do not affect the lives of the Toyoda people, and do not constitute a recognized social problem. This lack of concern, however, in no way diminishes the attitudes of prejudice and hostility; rather, it propagates ignorance, obscurity, and even mystery. Four of the most general attitudes held by Toyoda informants toward the pariah caste are offered below.

Disgust is the most widely held and commonly verbalized attitude. Individuals who are unwilling even to discuss the outcastes distort their faces and exclaim, *kitanai* (dirty). These feelings are sometimes manifested more directly. For example, after one of the customers in a small wine shop noticed blood on the hands and shirt sleeves of a young outcaste he shouted disparagingly at him and was joined by several others: "You are dirty, you animal killer! Look at the blood all over you! You are a filthy *yaban* (barbarian, savage)!"

Fear is another commonly found attitude of the Toyoda people. Outcastes are considered dangerous and capable of inflicting bodily harm. There are exaggerated stories of physical prowess and fighting skill and they are likened to the gangsters and hoodlums portrayed in American films. There is also the fear that surrounds the unknown. Burakumin are believed by some to be sinister characters with evil powers, and mothers sometimes frighten their children with gruesome tales of the "eta" bogey-man. It is said, too, that the outcastes are afflicted with such contagious diseases as syphilis, gonorrhea, tuberculosis, and leprosy.

Because the Burakumin and their village are forbidden, the attitude of *erotic curiosity* prompts such questions as: "Do the 'eta' look different? Are the women really beautiful? Are they rough, like gangsters? Do they actually speak a different language? What kind of food do they eat?" Many wonder if Buraku girls are "better" than ordinary women, some young males have erotic desires for outcaste women, and restaurant hostesses often joke about an imputed enlargement or distortion of the genitals of the male "eta."

The spread of the final attitude, which might be termed *objectivity,* seems to be increasing steadily among the younger generation, but it has the fewest adherents in Toyoda. This attitude is not widespread because it depends primarily on observation.[2] "Look at the 'eta' and their houses—they *are* dirty, they have dirty occupations and they are diseased." "The 'eta' always marry each other, so their strain is weak. They are an exclusive, intimate group that rejects outsiders and any form of aid." "I feel sorry for the 'eta' because of their lowly position, but I will have nothing to do with them until they learn to live like other

Japanese, that is, give up their occupations, marry outside their small community, clean up their villages, homes, and themselves, and drop their hostile clannish attitudes." Such beliefs are based less on legend than others but, as with dominant Negro-white relations in the United States, they operate as a self-fulfilling prophecy in maintaining the outcaste status.[3]

The beliefs and myths of the Toyoda citizenry preserve majority group exclusiveness by associating the Burakumin with violations of some of the most fundamental and sacred Japanese values—those centering around purity, lineage, and health. The following are two of many popular legends heard in the city.

A young man met a beautiful girl in a restaurant. After a short courtship they were married against the wishes of the boy's parents. They lived happily for awhile, but when their children were born idiots with spotted complexions, it was discovered that the girl was a Burakumin.

It was customary prior to the turn of the century for Burakumin to wash the bodies of deceased commoners in return for an offering of *sake* but after the outcastes began to realize their emancipation, they frequently requested money for their services. Sometimes the demands were exorbitant. When the sum was refused, the Burakumin would threaten the family by vowing to drink the water used in bathing the body. The people were usually frightened into relenting to the Burakumin demands.

The general theme of the first story is the unhappiness of anyone who marries an outcaste, and the physical and mental deformity of the offspring. This is probably the most widespread myth, as it is employed by parents to discourage children from affairs that might result in a "love marriage."

[2] Such viewpoints exist, as Merton states in another context, not as prejudice or prejudgment, "but as the irresistible product of observation. The facts of the case permit no other conclusion." Merton (1949), p. 182.

[3] Merton (1949); Myrdal (1944); MacIver (1948).

Even the most informed Japanese balk at the thought of marriage to an outcaste because of the popular notion of their "weak strain" from long intermarriage. The second legend illustrates the supposed barbaric quality of the Burakumin; not only were they mercenary, but they profaned the sacred, defiled the dead, and imbibed the impure and dirty.

SHIN-MACHI

Shin-machi's 347 inhabitants are housed in 43 dwellings, some including as many as ten households, located on a narrow dead-end road on the southeastern edge of Toyoda. Several relatively new houses dot the village, but the majority are old and dilapidated. Windows are covered with newspapers, and holes in the roofs are patched haphazardly with cardboard and paper held in place by large stones.

Family genealogies indicate only 18 surnames in Shin-machi, and seven of these account for the majority of the 78 households. Sixty-two percent of the marriages are between residents of the community, and 79 percent between individuals with Eta occupations and status. Thus, almost every individual is either consanguineously or affinally related to every other individual. Adoptions are frequent, especially between siblings, and illegitimacy is common; few families have no illegitimate births recorded in the city registration book (koseki).

The traditional outcaste occupations support 30 percent of the households. Another 35 percent are day laborers or claim no occupation. The remainder are dependent upon menial, low-income occupations such as begging, rag collecting, knife-grinding, peddling small confectioneries at festivals, and collecting food and clothing left at graves after certain religious festivals. Only four residents hold jobs that might be construed as ordinary occupations.

Analysis of the social and economic structure of Shin-machi reveals two clearly defined status groupings, with marked differences in prestige, power, attitudes toward outcaste status, and systems of inter-personal relations. Individuals generally identify themselves with the group to which they objectively belong (in terms of occupation, wealth, education, house type, and kinship orientation), and they are rated by others as belonging to one group or the other. The terms "upper class" and "lower class" are used here to differentiate them: (The Burakumin themselves make the distinction between "the people down there" and "the people up there," which are not altogether accurate references to the geographical location of lower and upper class dwellings.)

The upper class is composed of 13 households with a total of 75 members, 46 female and 29 male. The residences, many of which are clustered in one section of the village, are typical modern Japanese houses, each owned by its occupant. The heads of the households are usually literate, and several have reached high school. Upper class children have attended school regularly since the end of the war, and most will probably finish high school. Constituted authority in Shin-machi is vested in the upper class, with the headman and his assistant being members of this group.

There is a high degree of occupational stability in this class. All of the trades have been practiced in the households for at least three generations and, typically, a household has only a single occupation, such as drum-maker or shoemaker. In some instances, however, secondary income may be supplied by the employment of unmarried sons and daughters in wine factories and in offices outside the community.

The lower class has a total of 272 persons, 137 males and 135 females, residing in 65 households. The makeshift lower class dwellings, none of which is owned by the occupants, are overcrowded and poorly heated and lighted, thus sharply differentiating them from the upper class houses. Only two lower class individuals have completed the third grade. Though recent educational reforms have tended to increase the school attendance of lower class children, it still remains sporadic, primarily because of inadequate clothing, irregular diet, and prolonged illnesses. Also, ridicule by both teachers and students in the public schools reduces incentives for education; postwar hostility against Buraku children in schools is apparently directed at lower class students, who are distinguished by shabby clothing and dirty appearance.

In contrast to the upper class, the low-income occupations of the lower class are marked by diversity and irregularity. Of those interviewed, 43 of the families receive the major part of their incomes from fur cleaning and processing (12), day labor (17), begging (4), peddling (7), and relief (3). Another ten families claim no employment. Since these jobs are seasonal and part-time, lower class families are generally supported by more than one occupation.

The class division is a fairly recent phenomenon in Shin-machi. Prior to the depression of the 1930's, the Burakumin had been a rather homogeneous and economically prosperous group. Although overt discrimination had been more severe, the monopoly in the fur and leather crafts had assured them an adequate income. During the depression, however, many of the outcastes, especially the animal slaughterers and fur workers, suffered a marked decline in income. The demand for leather goods declined, the prices of traditional handicraft were depressed, and opportunities for outside employment were virtually eliminated. Few Burakumin starved during this crisis, partly because of their reliance upon the meat from slaughtered animals, but many were reduced to begging. Some sold all personal belongings, including houses, household equipment, and clothing.

The demand for fur goods never again reached a pre-depression level, so the majority of those engaged in the fur business have not been able to regain their former living standard. But all outcastes were not equally affected by the depression and many have since become prosperous, so that there are now two sharply differentiated groups, the relatively wealthy and the poor.

At the outset of the research in Shin-machi, it was believed that all the residents were forced to remain in the outcaste community because of the discrimination and prejudice of the larger society. But as our study progressed, it became increasingly apparent that the problem was not simply the relationship of the outcaste group to the larger society, but also relationships within the Buraku. Although the Burakumin are despised and discriminated against, the attitudes, beliefs, and fears of the outsiders do not fully explain the persistence of the community. In response to the external forces and outcaste subordination, Shin-machi has developed internally a distinct socio-religious identity and unity, and a strong set of social, economic, and psychological restraints upon individual mobility.

Community Organization and Social Solidarity

Although Shin-machi is a subdivision of Toyoda City, it is the only district that elects its own headman, holds town meetings, and maintains liaison with the municipal government. These are extra-legal functions, not provided for in the postwar city charter. However, they indicate that both the city officials and the Burakumin recognize the "special" (*tokushu*) character of Shin-machi. They also tend to stimulate community identity and cohesiveness by directly involving community members in local Buraku problems.

The village headman (*soncho*) and his assistants (secretary, treasurer, fire and health commissioners, and shrine attendant) handle disciplinary matters within the community, cases of discrimination by outsiders, and such issues as the raising of money for special purposes, collecting taxes, and arranging religious festivals. General meetings, held in the village shrine and attended by at least one member of each household, are called by the headman to discuss village problems and, if possible, to reach decisions by agreement among the villagers.

In addition to sounding out opinion and disseminating information, the town meetings reinforce community solidarity. Few issues are settled at any meeting, but individuals become involved in the problems of the whole community. The town meetings generate feelings of belonging primarily because the problems are unique to the community and, in most instances, directly related to outcaste status. Except for religious celebrations, these meetings are the only occasions when all members of the community assemble for business and entertainment. Large quantities of *sake* are consumed, and status differences and special interests are subordinated to the greater general interest.

The pattern of social control that has developed in Shin-machi is related to its system of self-government. The Burakumin, particularly those at the apex of the power structure, are intent upon concealing from outsiders every aspect of their mores, especially those believed to violate or differ from majority Japanese standards. Stringent controls are therefore exerted upon community members to restrict relationships with the majority society. Public disturbances, lawbreaking, or any behavior that might bring disrepute to the Buraku are discouraged by ostracism, ridicule, and criticism, and even by threats or acts of violence. A person who discusses community affairs with an outsider is treated as a "fink" with pressures comparable to those employed by criminal groups and juvenile gangs in America. These measures obviously stimulate ingroup exclusiveness and set the Burakumin off as a closed subgroup.

Religious affairs also function to integrate the community. These observances, like all public community activities, are held at the Shinto shrine in the center of the Shin-machi graveyard, and are presided over by the headman. Religious celebrations are of two kinds: Buddhist festivals to commemorate the dead, and Shinto or shrine festivals in honor of the local tutelary deities. While the themes differ, the rites are identical, and the overall unifying symbols are those of common ancestry, common territory, and common problems.

On Buddhist holidays the close kinship ties among the members of the community are made explicit by the homage rendered to common ancestors. These bonds are reinforced by community decoration of the graves, and prayers and speeches at the shrine make constant reference to relationships between the behavior of the living and expectations of the dead. Perhaps the most dramatic suggestion of kinship unity occurs during the spiritual interaction between the old men of the village and their common ancestors through a medium at the celebration of *Higan* (a Buddhist holiday commemorating the dead).

At the Shinto festivals, major emphasis is on cooperation and community welfare. The headman reviews past accomplishments and failures of the community, suggests ways to bring about greater realization of community goals, and asks the gods for their protection and good will. The principal concern is the continued well-being of the Buraku.

In every speech and in every prayer mention is made of the community in its relation to the world outside. Some are pleas for greater cleanliness in the village, or for curtailing the slaughter of dogs; other centers on the outcaste's low position in Japanese society, or on the cruelty of the world as signified by a particular instance of discrimination. Some orations invoke the intercession of the gods for the attainment of economic success, for the marriage of daughters, and for less discrimination by majority society members. Clearly, the shrine and its gods are the locus of community identification; the religious rites express a system of relationships that differentiate this group from those surrounding it, and give it a distinct socioreligious identity and unity.

During the drinking sprees accompanying the festivals, conversation invariably turns to the common enemy, the outsider. Occupations and poverty, family difficulties and poor living quarters, are all discussed in the context of relationships with the majority. All the fears and hopes expressed in the ceremonials are reiterated in conversation at the sake parties. Songs are often sung in a secret traditional Eta vocabulary (a kind of Japanese pig-Latin used frequently when outsiders are present) with an enthusiasm that reflects the intensity of the individual's identification with the community. The subordinate relationship of the community to the larger society, then, is an essential aspect of the social and religious life of Shin-machi, and it is an important mechanism for maintaining social solidarity.

Social Organization and Patterns of Stability and Mobility

Individual members of Shin-machi are torn between the desire to emigrate and so lose outcaste identity, and the desire to remain in the community, thereby assuring

a degree of social and economic security. Since the Eta emancipation in 1871, and probably before, individuals have passed into the larger society. However, the opportunities for leaving the Buraku have become greater since World War II, and this has intensified the ambivalence about remaining in the community. Remaining in the community has so far been the stronger sentiment, and the community has even increased in population from 310 in 1920 to 347 in 1954. A brief analysis of the socioeconomic organization of the two classes may reveal some of the factors underlying this situation.

Upper Class Burakumin

The household is the basic social and economic unit of the upper class. Each household is ideally composed of a man and wife, their eldest son and his wife, and unmarried children. The eldest son inherits the family property, debts, obligations, and occupation. He is also obligated to support his aged parents and to maintain the lineage, and at the death of the head of the household he is bound indefinitely to the residence and trade of his father.

Junior sons in the upper class are encouraged to migrate and seek employment in one of the larger cities. This accomplished, all obligations between the migrant and his family are terminated by mutual consent. When such emigration occurs, outcaste identity presumably is lost and the individual may be assimilated into the general population. Although the position of the younger sons appears advantageous insofar as it enables them to escape the outcaste stigma, considerable anxiety results from the situations into which they are thrust. Outside the community, migrants live in constant fear of discovery, and the consequences for those detected in their attempts to pass are usually disastrous. Several disillusioned persons have returned to Shin-machi after such failures; breakup of marriage, loss of family and job, and sometimes suicide, result from detection in an attempt to pass.

However, one of the greatest sources of frustration for the emigre stems from the still undeveloped wage-earning economy, combined with the pressure of overpopulation. Employment opportunity in Japan is still largely regulated by kinship affiliation and its extension—"The society is no more than an organization of families."[4]   The migrant outcaste has no family connections; he has no sponsor and no reference in the society outside his community.   Furthermore, in order to lose his stigma it is almost essential that he move to the urban centers, the major underemployment areas of the country into which a vast number of persons from rural areas flow daily.

The social and economic factors that arouse anxiety in the junior sons also tend to reduce mobility aspirations of the eldest sons, whose duty is to remain in the community. Those of upper class families are highly skilled craftsmen as a result of years of apprenticeship in the family trade. If they remain in the community, as they must in order to practice the inherited occupation, they are assured a degree of economic security.   The choice therefore lies between abandoning a means of livelihood in order to erase the degradation of caste, and remaining a low-status Burakumin with an assured means of subsistence.   The psychological dilemma is never solved.

The precarious economic balance in the upper class depends upon the regular out-migration of junior sons.   The household economy is unable to support an additional individual or family, and the overcrowded housing conditions in Shin-machi make it impossible to shelter new members. Moreover, the Buraku occupational monopolies

are so marginal that the addition of a single competitor would seriously depress individual incomes. Although mass production in the leather industries has reduced the market for handicrafts, the Shin-machi tradesmen still have a steady if limited outlet for their goods; if these conditions remain unaltered, the upper class Burakumin are assured a regular and relatively high income. The system of out-migration may therefore be viewed as a conscious attempt by the craftsmen to limit competition from junior sons who are potentially new members of the guild. Consequently, both the guild and the separate families have a vested interest in maintaining the continual flow of individuals from the community.

The upper class attitude toward the elevation of outcaste status also bears upon the emigration pattern. The intensity of their desire to erase all caste barriers cannot be overemphasized.   They believe that they have acquired the material symbols and social skills necessary for recognition as members of the Japanese middle class but that they remain in the community because of family obligations, because of the order of their birth.   Their interest and effort is focused upon raising the collective status of the Buraku. Members of this class believe that the outcaste stereotype held by the majority society will be modified by changes in the condition of the community. And as the deplorable physical environment of Shin-machi results in part from large population and low income, Buraku leaders feel that a stable population is a major factor in the status enhancement of the whole community. The notion of total caste mobility does not spring from a deep-rooted sympathy with the Burakumin and their problems, but has developed because the leaders feel that they will be able to enhance their own status only by elevation of the entire caste.

The fervor with which the upper class now seeks social and economic equality has coin-

---

[4]Stoetzel (1955), p. 57.

cided in general with the rising educational standard and the decrease in direct discrimination. Prior to World War II, the aspiration of community leaders of Shin-machi was predominantly for simple acceptance by the majority; the role the outcastes were destined to play in the society was conceived as immutable. With the return of the war veterans, the character of the upper class and the pattern of community leadership underwent significant changes. The young returnees were literate, optimistic, and experienced. They were unable to accept the inferior outcaste status based upon tradition, ignorance, and prejudice; rather, they felt that the majority society must eventually regard them as equals.

The recent decrease in the incidence of overt and direct hostility toward the Burakumin has tended to reinforce the new upper class beliefs, since it appears that majority attitudes are now shifting toward greater tolerance. This apparent trend has impressed upper class members with the proximity of their goal of equality, but psychological anxiety has been magnified because the actual status of the Burakumin has not changed significantly, and there are still sporadic cases of discrimination and outgroup hostility.

In order to facilitate changes in majority attitudes, upper class leaders have instituted an improvement program designed to eliminate conditions within Shin-machi believed to be at variance with the prevailing standards of the larger society. Specific improvement is sought in the dirty physical appearance of the community, and in the "barbarian" behavior of certain Shin-machi residents. The former is difficult to eradicate because it is largely a consequence of inadequate housing and overpopulation. However, periodic inspections are made by the health and sanitation officers, and suggestions offered for the improved use of existing facilities. Communitywide cleanup days are held several times a year; and such practices as killing animals within the community and littering the area with garbage are discouraged.

The upper class Burakumin are at least partially aware of the outsiders' conception of them as immoral, criminal, irresponsible, and alcoholic, and they are also aware that such accusations are sometimes justified. There is promotion of such Japanese virtues as maintenance of family obligations, honesty in business dealings, moderation in drinking, and interest in child welfare. Failure to conform evokes gossip, ridicule, and condemnation.

Obviously, the specific improvements desired by the upper class require alterations in the living conditions and behavior of the lower class. But by and large, this class does not act in accordance with the new rules, thereby evoking hatred and disgust from their "superiors," attitudes similar to those expressed by outsiders toward the outcaste. In fact, upper class Burakumin often refer to members of the lower class as "those barbarians," "those dirty people," "beggars," and "Hinin."

Lower Class Burakumin

The social and economic life of the lower class is dominated by the fur and leather processing industry and regulated by a system of fictive kinship relationships: nearly two-thirds of the lower class households receive a proportion of their income from this industry. One wealthy and powerful individual, himself an outcaste, has an absolute monopoly in it, including the allocation of employment and the ownership of all lower class houses—the homes of his employees.

In this Buraku one finds a type of social-occupation-power relationship between this man and his tenants which is in effect a traditional set of diffuse reciprocal obligations known as the *oyabun-kobun* system, long an essential feature of the socioeconomic life of the lower class. Knowledge of this sytem is crucial to the understanding of community persistence.

The oyabun-kobun (literally, father role—child role) is a system "in which persons not usually related by close ties of kinship enter into a compact to assume obligations of a diffuse nature similar to those ascribed to members of one's immediate family."[5] It is a ritual kinship generally established by a special rite of passage. Members address one another by familial terms. Although it satisfies many of its members' needs, its primary function is the ordering of economic relationships. It operates in many spheres and on various levels in Japanese society, and there are a number of variations in its form, duration, and specific functions.

In Shin-machi the oyabun-kobun institution regulates two interrelated aspects of economic organization: landlord-tenant and employer-employee relationships. During the depression, a representative of a large Tokyo fur company loaned money to a number of Shin-machi inhabitants, as well as to the Toyoda butcher shop proprietors. In time, the borrowers became hopelessly indebted and were forced to sell their homes and businesses to their creditor, and a group of Burakumin thus became dependents of the new landlord, who required them to work for him to pay the high rents he exacted. Through his financial control over the local butchers he demanded the hides of all animals slaughtered in the Toyoda area. He now owns the large leather and fur stores in Toyoda as retail outlets.

By incurring obligations (*on*) to the oyabun, the followers are pledged to his service: in return, he assumes responsibility for their support. Because of his control over

the supply of hides, his readily available labor force, and his system of distribution, the oyabun gradually forces the smaller independent furriers into the organization. At present, all but one of the furriers in the community are his employees, and he allocates the amount and kind of work done by each. Except for a few wealthy individuals, all are financially dependent upon him.

The oyabun is the most revered man in the community and there are innumerable stories of his kindness and generosity. He continues to aid the poor with favors and loans and thereby reinforces his dominant position. The patron is committed to aid impoverished families, to assign jobs to clients in proportion to need, and to assure a certain minimum income to the families under his protection. Because of his wealth and record of generosity, he has created a kind of economic security for the lower class.

The obligations that characterize the oyabun-kobun relationship are a powerful deterrent to mobility, especially when reinforced by financial indebtedness. The oyabun is outside the community class structure because he does not participate in community affairs, and because he is not considered a member of Shin-machi by other members of the community. However, he lives on the periphery of the Buraku, and is regarded by Burakumin and non-Burakumin alike as an outcaste.

The obligation of the patron to assure his followers subsistence is an incentive for individuals to remain in the community. Although several lower class families must resort to begging, and others may occasionally go hungry, it is believed that no one will starve in Shin-machi as long as the oyabun-kobun system exists. The people have faith that any crisis can be met by resort to the patron's benevolence and there is also the possibility that some may gain more than mere subsistence. In addition to the opportunity for at least limited mobility

---

[5]Ishino (1953), pp. 695-707.

within the occupational hierarchy, there are other possible advantages, such as loans for house repair, clothes, tools, and in one case, the initial investment in a confectionery and wine shop.

Although economic considerations are the major factors inhibiting lower class movement from Shin-machi, the same cultural and psychological conditions exist as those discussed in the preceding chapter. A large percentage of lower class Burakumin would be unable to pass into the larger society because they lack the ability properly to handle social relationships and speech forms outside the community.

Since the Japanese language is a highly respected art and an index of social class, people are most conscious of the variations in dialects and of the kinds of individuals who use them. Upper class urban dwellers, for example, use standard forms, while rural inhabitants speak local dialects, which immediately mark them as rustics. The lower class Burakumin in Shin-machi have a distinctive dialect similar to that spoken in isolated communities in the mountains nearby. They are also distinctive because they are illiterate in a society in which literacy and learning are valued skills. Additionally, their knowledge of correct Japanese behavior is insufficient. Since the way in which inter-personal relations are conducted indicates an individual's background, lower class outcastes are often branded as curious, different, or barbarous. The Burakumin are conscious of differences between themselves and outsiders and tend to withdraw from situations that might demand social interaction with majority people.[6]

Members of the lower class generally regard themselves as truly inferior, believing that their position in Japanese society is predetermined and immutable.[7]

Outcaste status for lower class Burakumin is a matter of indifference and acceptance, except when specific questions are asked about it. In general, they are willing to discuss Eta problems, and are even flattered that outsiders will deign to speak to them. Similar questions about the Buraku could never be asked of upper class members, who vigorously deny that there is any difference between themselves and the majority and resent insinuations that such distinctions exist.

---

[6]An example is afforded by the following experience told to me:

A young man left the community to look for employment in Hokkaido, where there is little discrimination against Burakumin. Upon his arrival, he became lonesome because he had no place to go and had no acquaintances in the city. In an

attempt to ward off solitude he stepped into a cabaret, but as he pushed open the doors, the hostesses began to laugh. Embarrassed, he immediately returned to Shin-machi. The young man claimed that "the girls laughed at me because they knew where I came from." (Obviously the girls would be unable to distinguish him from any other stranger.)

[7]The following excerpts from an interview with a lower class Burakumin convey this self-image clearly:

Q. Are you the same as common people (heimin)?
A. No. We kill animals. We are dirty, and some people think we are not human.
Q. Do you think you are not human?
A. (long pause, and then) I don't know.
Q. Are the common people better than you?
A. Oh, yes!
Q. Why?
A. They do not kill animals. They do not live here (in the Buraku). They are good people.
Q. Do you think you or your children will ever leave this district or change occupations?
A. No, we are new common people (shin-heimin).
Q. Do you think outsiders will ever come to this village and treat you as friends?
A. No, people on the outside don't like us. Things haven't changed for a hundred years.
Q. Do you believe this is right or fair?
A. (long pause) I don't know; we are bad people, and we are dirty.

Intra-Group Relations: A Summary

In part as a result of the differences among outcastes in their attitudes toward their own status, hostility developed between the classes; the net effect of this has been to increase community solidarity by intensifying intra-group interaction. It has been suggested that members of both groups are constrained to remain in Shin-machi. However, the upper class is mobility oriented while the lower class is characterized by status acceptance and indifference. The upper class is committed to improving conditions in Shin-machi in order to raise the collective status of the Buraku, a program that requires total community participation. Since they are not mobile, persons of the lower class either do not comprehend or are unable to respond to the upper class innovations. This refusal or inability to conform to the standards dictated by the community leaders has separated the two groups. Members of the upper class feel disgust, hatred, and embarrassment because of lower class indifference, while lower class members believe that upper class policies are unnecessarily restrictive and unwarranted. If this situation were to exist in a society where both groups were really readily mobile, the differing orientations would either stimulate serious conflict or be eliminated altogether. But since both segments of this community are predisposed toward spatial immobility, the latent conflict is partially channeled into solidarity behavior.

The mechanisms described earlier for maintaining Buraku secrets have been designed and implemented by the upper class, and are directed specifically at the lower class. Clean-up days, sanitary inspections, town meetings, and religious ceremonials are also intended to educate the lower class to upper class conventions. These events, sanctions, and regulations require a high degree of interest and participation by the upper class. Therefore, leadership which might otherwise be directed away from the community and toward tasks more directly relevant to individual or class mobility is oriented toward the internal affairs of the community. Although the motivations of the dominant group spring from a desire for individual status enhancement, the consequence of these drives is to solidify the community by focusing social action on problems of an intra-community nature. The integration thus achieved functions to maintain Burakumin as a distinct and unified subgroup of the larger Japanese society.

CONCLUSION

The social persistence of Shin-machi is determined by a variety of conditions governing both the internal and external social relationships maintained by Burakumin. A sanctioning system exists that is intended to conceal from outsiders many of the physical and social characteristics of the community. These controls engender exclusiveness and prohibit intercourse with members of the majority society.

The socioreligious organization, which is oriented toward the social problems of the underprivileged minority, stimulates ingroup unity and identity. The regular system of Japanese social relations, with its emphasis on obligation, loyalty, and duty, discourages migration.

True mobility aspirations have been inhibited by negative selfconcepts, poor education, and the maintenance of traditional occupations. Because of vested economic interests in Shin-machi, the community leaders are oriented toward caste mobility, and are therefore predisposed to remain in the community, and to emphasize stability and unity. Although tensions have developed between the two classes within the Buraku, mutual hostility actually serves to increase the intensity of social interaction among community members.

We conclude therefore that the persistence of the outcaste in contemporary Japan cannot be explained simply by the discriminatory attitudes and prejudices of the majority. Attitudes toward self, the traditional system of Japanese social and economic relations, and the internal structure and organization of the Buraku itself are all essential in maintaining this continuity.

Economically marginal groups in Japan, such as the outcastes of Shin-machi, are often bound internally by close-knit systems of social and economic relationships and characterized by the prevalence of protective, hierarchical, and kinship-oriented institutions such as the oyabun-kobun system and the extended family. These traditional Japanese tendencies, which may develop as adjustments to precarious social and economic conditions, foster ingroup solidarity, dependency, and socioeconomic rigidity. However, a decline has been noted in the importance of "feudal" socioeconomic institutions that has been caused by the recent prosperity.[8] It is possible that if the employment capacity of the economy is expanded, the outcastes may gradually disappear as a distinctive subgroup of the society. But if they continue to remain an economically underprivileged group, they may also remain dependent upon "feudal," protective institutions and continue to reside in Buraku despite possible changes for the better in the majority society's attitude toward them.

---

[8]Ishino and Bennett (1953)

REFERENCES

ISHINO IWAO
  1953 "The Oyabun-Kobun: A Japanese Ritual Kinship Institution," *American Anthropologist*, Vol. 55, pp. 695-707.

ISHINO IWAO, AND BENNETT, JOHN W.
  1953 *Types of the Japanese Rural Community*, Interim Technical Report No. 6, Research in Japanese Social Relations, Ohio State University.

MAC IVER, R. M.
  1948 *The More Perfect Union*, New York: Macmillan Co.

MERTON, ROBERT K.
  1949 *Social Theory and Social Structure*, Glencoe, Illinois; The Free Press.

MYRDAL, GUNNAR
  1944 *An American Dilemma*, New York: Harper and Bros.

STOETZEL, JEAN
  1955 *Without the Chrysanthemum and the Sword*, New York: Columbia University Press.

5.   NAIROBI DIVIDES

Peter Marris

Asians have played an important part in the development of modern
Kenya, especially in commerce. Their concentration in commercial fields
has made them extremely visible, especially in Nairobi. Conflicts with
Africans since independence have made Africans demand that the commercial
privileges of Asians be limited. Discussing attempts to maintain their
position, Marris notes the increasing recognition among Asians that their
dominant position in commercial fields must decline and that many of them
will have to leave Kenya.

In 1877, Allidina Visram, a young Isman boy from Kutch region of India, arrived in Zanzibar to serve his apprenticeship with an old established merchant. Within a few years, he had begun to pioneer trade on the mainland of East Africa, organising caravans far into the interior. In 1898 he established a branch of Kampala, and moved on to the western borders of Uganda. With the building of the East African railway, he opened a chain of trading stores in Kenya, stretching from Mombasa to Kisumu—buying ivory, hides and skins, groundnuts and cotton from the local people, selling goods imported from India and Europe.

By 1908 he had set up business in almost every township of Kenya and Uganda, and was employing over five hundred Indian storekeepers. He launched a steamboat on

Lake Victoria, built cotton ginneries, sawmills, furniture and soda factories, and at his dealth in 1916 had created a commercial network covering the greater part of East Africa. A "kindly and generous man," his importance was acknowledged by the colonial administration: and the King of Buganda attended his funeral.

Allidina Visram was followed by other Indian merchant entrepreneurs, who between them built up a structure of commerce and local manufacture which has endured to this day. But their personal empires$_o$did not survive them, breaking down characteristically into small family businesses, the commercial network sustained by strong ties of kinship, caste and religion. Throughout the colonial era, the local Indian shopkeeper was the mainstay of trade, his only competitors the European firms who found it profitable to establish business in Nairobi and the centres of white settlement.

The economic development of East Africa owes a great deal to the early enterprise and

SOURCE
Reprinted from *New Society*, the weekly review of the Social Sciences, March 7, 1968 by permission of *New Society*, 128 Long Acre, London W. C. 2.

doggedness of these Indian traders. But the commercial structure which developed was effective largely because it was also exclusive. Patel retailers dealt with Patel wholesalers. Shahs with Shahs; community loyalties sustained commercial relationships stretching from the Mombasa importer to the country store a thousand miles away.

The sanction of ostracism from the community made credit secure, so that retail businesses with little capital could still acquire substantial stock. As a means of mobilising finance, and a sensitive system of commercial intelligence, such a pattern of trade proved extremely efficient. But it rested on an inward-looking community-mindedness, and this has inhibited East African Asians from either coming together in defence of their interests, or of making any real gesture of integration with African society.

The racial segregation of colonial Kenya reinforced this exclusiveness. In the 1920s, Indian leaders protested successfully against white settlers' demands for political autonomy and saved Kenya from the fate of Rhodesia. But as African nationalism grew, the Asians retreated into neutrality, seeking to protect their investment against the hazards of politics by placating both white and black with vague protestations of goodwill. When the Emergency was declared in 1952, they were caught between administrative pressures to commit themselves against rebellion, and Mau Mau threats of reprisal: they skilfully evaded the issue, at the cost of never identifying themselves with the cause of African nationalism.

At Independence, there were about 180,000 Asians in Kenya. But though this amounted to no more than 2 per cent of the population their concentration in commerce made them conspicuous. The local Indian trader was familiar to every African farmer, and his apparent prosperity—the well-stocked shop, the Peugeot station wagon, his children

in their clean shirts and crisp dresses—could easily be interpreted as exploitation. An Indian shopkeeper generally bargains, and charges what the market will bear, in a way which Africans often interpret as trickery, even though his prices are generally lower than any European or African shop can offer. And the officiousness with which he greets an important customer (who may be white tends to contrast with the off-hand brusquences of his treatment of most Africans.

But although Indian shopkeepers have spread all over Kenya, half the Asian population is concentrated in Nairobi, and another quarter in Mombasa. In the capital city of an independent African nation, there is still scarcely an African shop to be seen on any of its main streets: and the faces in the cars which stream in and out of the city centre are mostly brown. The pressure of public opinion to redress the balance is naturally insistent.

In a society where unemployment grows alarmingly, as each year's school leavers flood a constricted labour market, the presence of a prosperous alien minority becomes an explosive trigger of resentment. The government is bound to show that it is following a vigorous policy of Africanisation, with visible results. If it did not, there would probably be outbreaks of spontaneous violence against Asians. Even at the risk of disrupting Kenya's economy, the Asian dominance of commerce had somehow to be dislodged.

Yet since Independence the Kenya government has consistently maintained that it would not practice racial discrimination, though it was entitled to discriminate in favour of citizens. It was up to the Asian community to commit itself to Kenya by taking citizenship, and cooperating in African development. The government repeatedly urged Asian businessmen to prove their sincerity by going into partnership with

Africans, training them in their skills, and conceding them the right to compete fairly.

But the nature of the commercial network which the Asians had established was very ill-placed to respond, since it depended essentially on family and community ties. African businessmen complain continually that Asian wholesalers discriminate against them in price and credit terms, Asian competitors resort to ruthless price-cutting to drive them out, and Asian employers will do their best to prevent African employees from learning their business. And since an African newcomer has to deal with Asian wholesalers, and (in the townships) to rent from an Asian landlord, he feels caught in a stranglehold. Some of the accusations may be unfair, or a misunderstanding of legitimate preference to established, more important customers. But the resentment is bitter, and demands for restriction on Asian freedom to trade become more and more insistent.

In these circumstances, how does the Asian community see its future? Would there, without any threatened constraint on entry to Britain, have been an overwhelming flood of immigrants seeking to escape from an untenable situation? Last August, Donald S. Rothchild of the University of California and I made a survey of Asian businessmen in and around Nairobi, to ask them how they saw the possibilities of social and economic integration, and reacted to the growing pressures against them.[1]

Our findings suggest that, in practice, Asian businesses cannot easily assimilate African participation as partners and shareholders. Two fifths of the Nairobi businesses in our sample were owned by a single proprietor, and about half were owned

[1]author's note: I have not had time to consult my colleague, Dr. Rothchild, in preparing this article, so the interpretation of our survey is my own. I owe the historical information to an unpublished paper by J. S. Mangat.

entirely by members of the same family. There were no public companies. None had any European partners or shareholders, and only three out of the 238 businesses an African. The majority of the businessmen said they preferred their own relatives as business associates.

Such a structure of ownership does not seem very adaptable. A man who is used to taking his own decisions, or in consultation with his brothers or his sons, cannot incorporate an outsider without a radical revision of his whole manner of conducting affairs. Understandably, then, although about half the businessmen considered that partnerships between Asians and Africans might have advantages from an Asian point of view, only ten had tried it—seven of them unsuccessfully—and less than a fifth had even considered it. Though they recognised, for instance that partnerships might gain them African customers and improve race relations, they doubted whether mutual trust and a compatible business outlook were possible, and whether many Africans had capital to put up, enough to make the deal attractive.

The businesses did, however, mostly employ Africans, nearly always in skilled or unskilled manual work. Only one business employed an African in a managerial position, and very few in clerical jobs. Since over half of them also employ relatives, it seems likely that responsible jobs, where a man might learn the running of a business, remain within the hands of the family or the proprietor himself. But over 60 per cent of the businesses had given practical on-the-job training in skills to their African employees—and on the whole, felt the training had been successful.

If the Asian business community cannot readily respond to demands for economic integration, can Asians protect their position by taking out citizenship, when discrimination against them in licences and distributing agencies would be much harder to justify? Even if the Kenya government were willing now to grant citizenship to many of them, which I doubt, the answers suggest that they do not have much faith that this would really improve their prospects.   Three quarters claimed British citizenship, and they generally believed that to surrender this for Kenyan would leave them only more vulnerable.

They might gain some advantage over non-citizens, but they pointed out that the Kenya government had deported Asians, even though they were Kenya citizens, and so citizenship provided no certain protection, while it sacrificed their right of entry elsewhere. (Under Kenya law, dual citizenship is not allowed, but in certain circumstances a person who has acquired citizenship can be deprived of it.)   Only about 12 per cent mentioned greater security as a potential advantage of citizenship.

In practice, naturally enough, discrimination is bound to rest on visible differences of race, rather than on abstract legal status. Nor will Asians have the same chance as African citizens in commercial opportunities. The Nairobi city council recently tried to rescind all licences to Asians in the city market, and only in response to pressure conceded that some account should be taken of whether the licensees were citizens or not.

On the whole, then, the Asian community is in a weak position to adapt to African demands. They are, in fact, not one community but several—Hindu, Moslem, Sikh, Goan, Ismaili—each with its own language, culture and leadership, who find it even more difficult to work together, than to integrate effectively with the African majority. Their businesses are characteristically family affairs, and the commercial network depends greatly on mutual trust within each group. It is a commercial pattern whose effectiveness rests on its parochial loyalties, and cannot at all readily adapt to include Africans.

But this does not mean that it will be impossible for any Asians to settle permanently in Kenya. It does mean that the Asian community must become much smaller, and increasingly turn from commerce.

The Asian businessmen interviewed in our survey recognised this. Asked what advice on his future they would give to a ten year old Asian boy, they recommended above all that he should train for a profession. Very few recommended commerce. About 40 per cent would encourage him to make his home in Kenya, if he could. As for themselves, only a quarter of those with British citizenship hoped to retire in Kenya— though another 15 per cent thought they might retire there if the political situation allowed.   As a whole, then, the Asian business group in Nairobi recognised that, though there are still opportunities in Kenya, over half will have to leave: and whether they leave or not, their future will lie in highly skilled employment and services, rather than commerce.

Without any restriction on entry to Britain, these pressures would result in a gradual dispersal and diversification. Though 70 per cent of the businessmen we interviewed believed that the Asian community was bound to decline, mostly because of discrimination and political insecurity, a third of them said they had no problems at present: and only a third, too, mentioned discrimination as an immediate difficulty. Had they remained secure that entry to Britain was always open, if the situation in Kenya became unmanageable, there would have been no rush to leave while commercial opportunities lasted. And in practice, at least in Nairobi, the opportunities will probably last longer than public statements on Africanisation might suggest, because African businessmen with the capital and confidence to take on sophisticated urban enterprises are still scarce.

Nor would the characteristics, which make the assimilation of many Asians into Kenya society doubtfully possible in the long run, tend to inhibit similarly their integration into British society. Their relative prosperity and urban sophistication, which arouse resentment in Nairobi, would be assets in Britain. Their higher level of skills and education (60 per cent of our sample had some secondary schooling), which seem to stand in the way of African employment, would make them easier to absorb here. And the introverted structure of East African trade, which has so uneasily outlasted the circumstances in which it was viable, could not, I think, ever be repeated in a much more advanced economy.

Was it, then, really necessary to restrict the entry of Kenya Asians into Britain?

Nothing in the findings of our survey suggests that there would have been any overwhelming inrush, if the fear of legislation had not intervened, and the British government had instead declared firmly that it would honour the promise of citizenship. The legislation seems rather to have disrupted a gradual dispersal, causing hardship and distress to thousands of people, damaging Kenya's economy, and starting the newcomers on their life in Britain in the worst of circumstances.

But the legislation also denies the evidence that most of the British citizens among Kenya's Asians cannot be assimilated there in the long run. If we refuse them the rights we promised, they will become refugees. So it was, I believe, a tragic mistake.

---

6.   THE BLACK PANTHERS OF ISRAEL

Amos Elon

Tensions between European and North African Jews have smoldered under the surface of Israeli society for 25 years. With the onset of a period of relative peace between Israel and the Arab countries, these problems have begun to manifest themselves more openly. Elon discusses the recent manifestations of these tensions and the growth, strategy, and concerns behind the development of a new militancy among North African Jews in Israel. This new militancy has resulted in the questioning of the social and economic boundaries that exist between these two ethnic groups.

SOURCE

o o o

From *The New York Times Magazine,* September 12, 1971. Reprinted by permission of Julian Bach Literary Agency, Inc. Copyright © 1971 by Amos Elon.

Most of the 300 demonstrators gathered at the Town Hall were slum dwellers under 30 and of Moroccan, Algerian or Iranian origin, the "Pantherim Shechorim," the Black

Panthers of Israel. They were joined by a handful of sympathetic students and a few members of the left-wing splinter group Matzpen to protest what they called discrimination against Oriental Jews in Israel by the politically, culturally and economically dominant minority of Western and East European Jews.

Their large, hand-painted placards demanded increased Government subsidies for slum clearance, an end to "black ghettos" (housing developments inhabited exclusively by poor North African and Asian Jews), increased welfare payments and free schooling from the age of 4 through college.

"Immigration from Russia, yes," the young protest leader screamed, "but not at the expense of the poor!" He was Saadia Marciano, a leader of the Panthers, a native of Morocco who had arrived in Israel in 1950 as a 2-month-old baby. His parents had settled in an abandoned ruin in the Musrara section of Jerusalem, a dismal slum close to the Jordanian frontier, which ran at that time through the center of downtown Jerusalem. At the age of 11 he had dropped out of school and had since lived on the margin of society, often in trouble with the law, at times sent to correctional institutions, finally rejected for service in the Israeli Army.

o o o

In that nationally televised scene most Israelis learned in April of the Pantherim Shechorim, a new militant protest movement whose highly disconcerting name Israelis largely associate with the resurgence of anti-Semitism in America.

The movement has spread to Tel Aviv, Haifa and some smaller towns, and now claims a national membership of 2,000. It is difficult at this stage to predict with any confidence the future of the Panthers, but among Sephardic, or Oriental, Israelis—

those of North African or Near Eastern extraction—there appears to be considerable support for the causes the Panthers espouse. Even Mordekhai Ben Porath, the Iraqi-born deputy secretary general of the ruling Labor party—the very heart of the Israeli establishment—has expressed his sympathy for the Panthers and has justified what he called their "rebellion."

The Panthers are not yet a political movement, although they have received some leftist support. A few local bigots have accused them of receiving financial assistance from Al Fatah or Moscow. Actually, many of the Panthers are rather right-wing nationalists; some claim to have supported the ultranationalist Herut party. Two are known to have participated in an ugly anti-Arab riot in 1967.

After their first violent eruption, the Panthers' public appearances were peaceful, a fact that caused some Israelis to hope that the movement was being "absorbed" by the system. But on Aug. 23 violence again broke out as the Panthers paralyzed downtown Jerusalem for more than three hours. Their demonstration, sparked by the devaluation of the Israeli pound, which caused an immediate rise in the price of food, produced injuries among both Panthers and policemen and considerable damage to property.

Now the movement is preparing to send a delegation to the United States "to explain our program to American Jewry." It was high time, Panther spokesmen said at a news conference in Tel Aviv, that U.S. Jews became aware of the dismal poverty still rampant in large sectors of Israeli society.

There is no apparent connection between the Israeli and the American Black Panthers, and little if any ideological affinity. Obviously, the Israeli Panthers chose their name for its shock value, and there is little doubt that much of the publicity they won in the local and foreign press would have been lost if they had called themselves the

"National Association for the Advancement of North African Youth." As it is, they helped to focus widespread attention on a festering sore in Israeli life which had not provoked sustained concern except in a small group of social workers, educators and anthropologists. On a visit to Israel in 1966, the late anthropologist Oscar Lewis warned that a dangerous subculture of poverty and crime might be perpetuating itself in Israel, but no one paid much attention.

Now the emergence of the Panthers has shed new light on the problem of poverty and ethnic tension. For in Israel, which was founded by European pioneers but settled in later years by a majority of immigrants from North Africa and Asia, the difference between poverty and wealth is still often ethnic. Says one Panther: "Almost all new immigrants came to this country as equals, completely penniless or quite poor. But within two decades the Government changed one people into two— one rich, one poor. The line dividing them is ethnic."

It is perhaps no accident that this new awareness has arisen now, during a cease-fire between Israel and the Arab states, when an eerie, perhaps misleading calm prevails along Israel's borders. Foreign Minister Abba Eban recently said that the dangers threatening Israel from within are far greater than those threatening her from without. There has been no war now for more than a year. The Palestine guerrilla movement has suffered a number of serious setbacks and may be declining. For the first time in memory, there is much public and private talk of a possible peace settlement with the Arabs. Little wonder, then, that grave social problems, which for a long time have been submerged by more pressing concerns of national survival, are suddenly surfacing.

Israel's social problems are twofold: There are the ethnic strains generated in a hybrid society of extreme diversity, comprising North African and Near Eastern—Sephardic, or Oriental—Jews and Ashkenazim, or Jews of Western or East European origin. And there are the growing social tensions created by an explosion of rising expectations, by more and more conspicuous consumption among the rich or privileged (many of whom are Ashkenazim) and by an increasingly visible gap between them and the poor (many of whom are Sephardim). The emergence of the Pantherim Shechorim has dramatized the issues of equality and prejudice, real or imagined. And in some intellectual circles and an influential segment of the Labor party, the issues have given birth to a crisis of conscience. Premier Golda Meir not long ago spent an evening in her home arguing with a half dozen young Panther leaders, and in the Finance Ministry and the Ministry of Housing a red warning light has suddenly been lit. It has not yet led to any significant changes in policies or spending priorities, but few people doubt that it will.

Such a reaction is not surprising because equality has always been a touchy issue in Israel. Though egalitarianism was deeply imbedded in the ideology of the early Zionist pioneers, the importation of enormous poverty and ignorance with the massive immigration from such areas as Morocco, Tunisia, Libya, Iraq, Iran and Kurdistan seriously jeopardized some of the more Utopian dreams. The Zionist mystique of a "return to the land," for instance, did not appeal to people who had lived on the land anyway and were anxious to move to the cities; the goal of a national economy owned by the workers through their trade unions had little effect upon Afro-Asian immigrants who were refugees, not ideologists.

But through the early nineteen-sixties Israel was still an extremely egalitarian society. The president of a large industrial corporation earned only six or seven times the lowest wage paid an unskilled laborer in his plant. Only within the last few years, with Israel's rapid transformation to an industrialized managerial society, has the visible or assumed image of things seriously changed.

The standard of living has risen steadily during the industrialization of recent years, and—though 20 per cent of the people still live below the "poverty line"—it has risen in every income group. Simultaneously, though, an ethnic split seemed to be appearing. Israel was becoming a managerial meritocracy; the Ashkenazim were the managers and Sephardim the managed. Dr. Jochanan Peres, a noted sociologist at Hebrew University in Jerusalem, says the average income of a Sephardic family in 1969 was only 69 per cent of the average income of an Ashkenazi family. And, Dr. Peres points out, the economic gap between ethnic groups is getting wider; in 1957, the average Oriental family's income was 74 per cent of the average Ashkenazi family's income. And since the average Sephardic family is considerably larger than its Ashkenazi counterpart, the per capita income of Sephardic Israelis is considerably less than these figures suggest. When the statistics are weighted to take family size into account, according to official estimates, average gross income for a Sephardic family is 54 per cent that of an Ashkenazi family.

Related to the economic gap is an educational disparity. On the elementary school level, where attendance is required, 59.3 per cent of the pupils in 1970 were Sephardim. On the secondary level, only 35.6 per cent of the students were Sephardim, although they outnumbered the Ashkenazim in that age group. At the university level only 14 per cent of the students were Sephardic, and at the graduate-school level the percentage dropped 8.

The undereducation of the Oriental Jews stems from diverse economic and cultural factors. Oriental families are large and often crowded into small apartments in which it is difficult for children to study. The tradition of the mother and father who slave day and night to assure their children a college education is widespread among Eastern European Jews, but rarer among North Africans. On the contrary, North African parents frequently expect their children to begin early to help support their large families. And despite a special program for Sephardic pupils under which they need achieve only 70 per cent of the minimum grade, a considerable number of educators and sociologists fear that the teaching program itself—devised largely by Ashkenazi teachers for Ashkenazi pupils may discriminate against students of North African or Asian background.

This may not be so, but the theory is given some credence by the fact that for years leading members of the Israeli establishment, which is largely Ashkenazi, have voiced warnings about what they called the "Levantinization of Israel"—the suffusion of her strictly East European Jewish heritage.

Some Oriental immigrant families have turned against newer arrivals from Russia and the United States, often because of the Government's housing policy. An immigrant arriving in Israel today need not live in the cramped, ugly, badly built apartments which were the rule as recently as 1958. In the fifties, families of five or six rarely received more than two rooms, sometimes less. But today's immigrant receives public housing in relatively spacious and well-built garden apartments of three or four rooms. And most of the immigrants of the last five years are Ashkenazim from Russia, Western Europe or America. Oriental immigrants who still inhabit the cramped, austere public-housing developments built for them 15 years ago are incensed by the almost luxurious quarters given new arrivals. Some are prone to see this as proof of prejudice.

Moreover, despite crushing taxation—almost all income over $400 monthly is taxed at 72 per cent—a new, relatively prosperous middle class has sprung up. Israeli tax laws are notoriously complicated, but there are few binding rules for the self-employed, much is open to negotiation with the authorities and there are loopholes galore—for recipients of Government development loans, importers of foreign, capital, developers and contractors in desert or border regions and defense contractors. Others have benefited enormously from the astronomic rise in real-estate prices. The Ashkenazi immigration preceded the Sephardic, so it is usually the Ashkenazi landowner who has owned his tract longest and profits most. And only Jews of European origin, naturally, receive German pensions and compensation payments for deprivations suffered under the Nazis. This has helped widen the ethnic gap.

The new middle class is quite frequently ostentatious and, rightly or wrongly, its image is Ashkenazi. Its visible prosperity compounds the frustrations of embittered young Sephardim. Such pockets of relatively great wealth as the predominantly Ashkenazi Tel Aviv suburbs of Savyon or Herzlia Pituah (where three-bedroom or four-bedroom homes on half an acre cost between $60,000 and $120,000) contrast more sharply than ever with the neighboring working-class sections and the dismal and predominantly Sephardic slum areas of Tel Aviv South.

Political power, too—membership in the Cabinet or the Knesset, high rank in the bureaucracy or the army—is largely Ashkenazi. Though half the population is of Afro-Asian background, only one Cabinet minister and 20 per cent of the Jewish Knesset members are Sephardim, and there are no Oriental generals in the army. "We are 1 per cent in Government," says a Panther leaflet, "and 96 per cent in jail." Yehuda Nini, an embittered second-generation Israeli of Yemenite ancestry, a graduate of Jerusalem University and once a top aide in the Ministry of Education, recently created a small furor by complaining that he and other Oriental Jews were "a cheated generation." Though the Sephardim had fought in three Israeli wars, he charged, the Ashkenazim had "divided between themselves the riches of the land." "Was it for this," he asked, "that we abolished Disaporas, fought wars, established a state? I don't know the 'state' in the abstract. What counts is the people who inhabit it."

o o o

That the problem between Sephardic and European Jews is above all social, not necessarily ethnic and certainly not racial, is borne out by the accelerating rate of intermarriage. In a recent public-opinion poll 81 per cent of the respondents were in favor of or not opposed to "mixed" marriages. More than 17 per cent of all Israeli marriages in 1970 were "mixed." The percentage has doubled over the last decade, and is now growing at a rate of about 1 per cent a year.

Yet only recently has it begun to dawn on many Israelis that real or "complete" integration is difficult, perhaps impossible, certainly much more complicated than the nation's founders expected. Much of the dismal poverty and *de facto* segregation have survived into the second and third generations. The Panthers are breaking out of the silent misery of their wretched slums, acting out their despair, registering a violent if inchoate protest and also, perhaps, serving a timely reminder.

7.   CASTE, CLASS CONFLICT AND STATUS QUO IN HAITI

Gerdes Fleurant

The analysis of caste and class conflicts in Haiti has been a relatively unexplored area in social science research. Examing Haitian history
Fleurant argues that color prejudice is an effect of class antagonisms. He
sees in the Haitian educational system, dominated by foreign ideas and
interests, the primary mechanism maintaining the boundaries between the
upper classes and subordinate groups. These class boundaries have been
crucial in the chronic underdevelopment of Haiti.

INTRODUCTION

Class and caste antagonisms have permeated
all segments of the Haitian social structure.[1]
Yet such antagonisms have been primarily
an urban phenomenon. In urban areas the
elites and the middle class have to deal with
all the pettiness and susceptibility that
surround the sensitive question of color. It
is also in the urban centers that the need for
social distance is most acute because of the
threat of social and residential mobility
during the last two decades. The peasant
class that comprises about 85 per cent of
the total population has for a long time
lived in the margin of the social conflicts
that have chronically shaken up the country.
Although in the past "revolutions" have
been made in the name of the peasant,
some of which he himself has taken part in,
the Haitian peasant is above all a marginal
person.

Haitian society is more complex than
some social scientists, both from Haiti and
other countries believe. Most analysts are
content to observe that Haiti is the poorest
country in the Western Hemisphere and
then cite statistics for support. What they
seem unable to understand is that Haiti, the
second oldest republic in the New World, has
acquired in the course of her history the
worst of both the developed and the under-
developed worlds. Her history consists
primarily of a series of conflicts and forces
that militate in favor of the status quo.

SOURCE
Original article prepared for this volume.

[1] I believe that caste and color antagonisms
are a latent function of class and economic exploitation, and as such must be seen in a proper
light. There are currently two opposite views
on this issue: one overemphasizes the question
of color and the other ignores it altogether or
accords it minimal importance. I do not subscribe to either view and welcome this opportunity
to treat this sensitive question of caste and class
conflict in Haiti, although I am well aware that
my comments may not satisfy all interested parties. My prime interest is to explore objectively
the Haitian social structure and attempt a socio-
historical analysis based on conflict theories. I
hope I will not be accused of reviving a dead
issue.

Caste and class conflicts, encouraged by the manipulations and instigation of other countries, appear to be largely responsible for the sorry state of present-day Haiti. To elucidate and reveal these forces is the purpose of this chapter.

This chapter makes use of Lewis A. Coser's theory of social conflict to delineate the main characteristics and the boundaries of the groups we are discussing. It will, illustrate the thesis that conflicts often function as a boundary maintenance device that works in the interest of the status quo. This chapter, however, will depart from tradition and present the components of the current social structure in its historical dimensions.

A basic assumption is that the Haitian social structure has not changed markedly in the last two centuries. The reasons for such a static situation have not been fully elucidated. In this analysis I will go beyond the usual categories used as indicators of the Haitian malaise.

Haiti is usually depicted and characterized by its "retard" or its degree of underdevelopment for which the only remedy is massive foreign intervention. Paul Moral (1961), the author of a book some consider the century's definitive study of the Haitian peasantry, does not escape from this view. To him, France has an important role to play in the development of Haiti. Moral observes accurately that after more than a century and a half of an independence heroically won, the Haitian nation is yet to be built. The leadership of the big powers, he contends, must play a *decisive* and *generous* role. France, in particular, could not forget the old Saint Domingue, for in the recess of the mountains of Haiti, her name has continued to command an incomparable prestige. Although Moral's analysis is largely factual and brilliant, it remains in essence an exercise in comparative ethnography, an approach highly detrimental since its ulti-

mate result is to impose as alien perspective on the Haitian situation. This tendency has been termed "the dictatorship of white (alien) definitions" (Watkins, 1971).

The vicissitudes of present-day Haiti can be understood only in historical perspective, and a sociological analysis should be careful not to project the impression that the Haitians alone are the cause of their shortcomings. This cannot be emphasized enough since both the new media and many scholarly works about Haiti have been purely descriptive. This chapter will, thus, make an effort to avoid this capital sin against the Haitian people.

CASTE AND CLASS CONFLICTS IN HISTORICAL PERSPECTIVE

The caste and class structure of Haiti contains certain elements that can largely mislead the modern analyst. To the Marxist, for example, the question of color is secondary, while to the nationalist it is of prime importance. Even Fanon (1967) approached this question vividly in his book, *Black Skin, White Mask*, a title that seems to grant to color a singular importance. If indeed the question of color is of secondary importance, the Haitian definition of the situation declares otherwise. Color has always been at the center of the conflicts among classes in the course of Haitian history.

My position is that color prejudice, as it is usually called in Haiti, is the effect of economic exploitation. However, when an effect has lasted for almost 200 years and has led to disastrous consequences, that effect ceases to function as such and acquires the characteristics of a cause. This paper takes issue with those who see Haitian society purely in terms of caste conflicts, just because 90 percent of the elites are mulattos, and the quasi totality of the peasantry, workers, middle and lower middle classes are black (Leyburn, 1966; Lobb, 1940). Color alone cannot be the determinant of a class structure. Such a point of view seems as unfounded as the one that minimizes its importance. A look at history may clarify my position, and reveal the dynamics of the forces that maintain the status quo.

Although the history of Haiti began before Columbus's landing in the Bahamas, for most people 1492 was the beginning of Haiti and, indeed, for the Indians it was the beginning of the end. The Spaniards exterminated the Awawak and Carib Indians and after cleaning out the gold mines in the western part of the island, entrenched themselves in the eastern section, which is now the Dominican Republic. In 1697 the French at the Treaty of Ryswick became the legitimate heirs of the western third of Haiti, the section that the Spaniards abandoned. Thus, the island of Haiti (the real Indian name means mountainous land) became divided into two sections, with the French in the west and the Spaniards in the east; both practiced African slavery.

The French section under the name of Saint Domingue flourished so well that by 1791, the date of the final slave revolt, the colony had a population of 700,000 slaves, about 40,000 whites and an equal number of mixed bloods (from the white master and the African woman) or *Affranchis*, meaning freedmen. According to James G. Leyburn (1966), in 1789 two thirds of the foreign commercial interests of France centered in Saint Domingue and the colony's combined export-import business was valued at more than $140,000,000. The importance of Saint Domingue in the economic life of France is further substantiated by the following: "its sugar, coffee, indigo and cotton supplied the home market and employed, in prosperous years, more than 700 ocean-going vessels, with as many as 80,000 seamen" (Leyburn, 1966: 15).

The result of such wealth produced in Saint Domingue one of the most rigid and destructive caste and class systems in the Caribbean, with the whites at the top, the Affranchis in the middle, and the slaves at the very bottom of the socioeconomic order. The whites (big planters, landowners, and government officials) had all the privileges, the Affranchis some, and the slaves none. The Affranchis were primarily concerned about equality with the whites, still within the framework of a slave society. It was ironic that after the slave revolt of 1791 and the war in the South (1799) of the island, a war in which Toussaint Louverture and Andre Rigaud were opposed, the freedman had to join the newly freed in the final struggle against the French colonialists.[2]

The roots of the caste and class antagonisms in Haitian society are in the colonial order. The first Africans that arrived in Hispanola around 1517 lived under a parternalistic regime, and the color difference did not have the importance it would have later—and has today. The high visibility of black or white made it easier to enforce a code of socioeconomic distance based on color, since the western part of the island that became French in 1697 had an increasing number of slaves from Africa that had to be controlled. By 1789 the colony of Saint Domingue was receiving an average of more than 1000 persons a month from Africa, and the slaves outnumbered the whites by 17 to 1. The necessity of controlling a growing and restless population of slaves and Affranchis, led to the elaboration, passage, and enforcement of some of the most rigorous *codes noirs* in the history of the Caribbean.

---

[2]It is beyond the scope of this chapter to give an extended treatment to any single period of Haitian history; the interested reader should consult among other books, C.L.R. James, *Black Jacobins,* and Leyburn, *The Haitian People,* two classics in the English language.

The point to be made clear is that a slave society is not only a socioeconomic order, but it carries also a psychology and a theology. In a word, it is a global system with an all-encompassing ideology that usually preserves the status quo. Physical difference becomes a criterium for entry in certain groups, professions, or functions, for example, Leyburn shows that the Affranchis owned over one third of the wealth of the colony, yet their economic prosperity did not lead to all social and political privileges.[3] The colonial order not only gave birth to color prejudice, but it nurtured, reinforced, and sold it on the world market as one of the most secure devices for the maintenance of the status quo. A good example was the skillfully staged war in the South in 1799 that opposed blacks to mulattos. Hedouville, the agent from France, seized every opportunity to blow out of proportion the rivalry between Toussaint (a black) and Rigaud (a mulatto).[4] For example, Hedouville, while conferring with Rigaud, made sure that Toussaint was listening in an adjacent room so the latter would hear the former's derogatory comments about him. Although the French were thrown out of the island in 1803, they succeeded in passing out to the newly emerging Haitian nation the superstructure of the colony. The French spirit was living without the French

_____

[3]A point the advocates of black capitalism should keep in mind, whether in the U.S. or abroad.   Haiti after 1946 is a case in point, as we will see later.

[4]*La Guerre du Sud* remains still one of the most sensitive areas in Haitian history, because few Haitian and foreign historians have applied to it a rigorously objective analysis. In fact, the smart student at the national examination for the baccalaureat, skillfully avoids any questions having to do with the Civil War of 1799, since the corrector might be a black or a mulatto with a different perspective on the events and their interpretation.

being physically present. Dr. Jean Price-Mars (1928) summarized it eloquently: "Haiti revetit la defroque de la civilization occidentale au lendemain de (l'independance) 1804."

The manifestations of the caste and class antagonisms have been present throughout Haitian history. Its first manifestation was the assassination of Dessalines, the founder of the nation, two years after Independence was proclaimed. Haiti was divided into two political entities, governed by Henri Christophe, a black in the North (he was later to become king, 1807-1820), and Alexandre Petion, a mulatto, in the west and south. The peasants in the south under the leadership of Goman revolted and forced Petion (1807-1818) to undertake an agrarian reform. According to Manigat (1962), the land issue was at the heart of the crisis that culminated in Dessalines' death. Yet Petion's Agrarian Reform was never intended to reach the lower strata of the society. In 1843 Accau and the Pickets, peasants armed with machettes and pics, were still asking for the land they were supposed to have obtained from the Petion government. Government by interposed person or "doublure," and the opposition of Solomon (1789-1888) to the mulatto elite continued this pattern. He was a blackman who served as Faustion the First's (1847-1859) minister of finance, and later spent twenty years in exile. Solomon was the crystalization of black nationalism. He eloquently eulogized Dessalines in 1841 when it was unpopular to do so. He also defended the cause of the peasants and supported Soulouque or Faustion I against the attacks of the mulatto elite. But this is also the period of the ideological struggle between the *Liberal Party* and the *National Party*, a struggle that culminated in the Civil War of 1883.[5]   The coup de grace was the

_____

[5]A majority of the Liberal Party was composed of the elites and their sons who studied the

American Occupation (1915-1934), which capitalized on the caste division of Haiti and secured the position of the elites until 1946, when the government of Elie Lescot (1941-1946) was overthrown by a coalition of the middle class, the working class and the liberal students—the volatile "Lyceens."

One feature of Haiti from 1804 to the present, is that the distribution of wealth, status, and power has hardly changed. This analysis attempts to elucidate the elements, mechanisms, or devices, and the enduring characteristics of the status quo. The unresolved caste and class conflicts in Haitian history have functioned as a boundary maintaining and braking mechanism. Such braking mechanisms have even resisted the test of the commotion of 1946.

1946, BENCHMARK OR SOCIAL RESOLUTION

Most social scientists who have looked at the Haitian scene before 1946 neglected the middle class. To them, conflicts in Haitian society have always been along the line of caste, that is, between blacks and mulattoes (Leyburn, 1966). Such analysts have failed to grasp the dynamics of the government of doublure or by interposed person. This device has at times sidetracked the oppressed rural masses and calmed down the aspirations of the urban middle class, a politically unconscious group that has often served the interest of the status quo. The Haitian social structure remains what it is because the

middle class betrayed its roots and often gave free rein to its regressive and repressive tendencies.[6]

Numerically, the middle class has always been small and at this writing it is no more than 4 percent of the total population (Wingfield and Parenton, 1965). To some analysts the birth of the Haitian middle class dates from the 1946 "revolution." Its sociological importance has been minimized by some while others tend to capitalize on its political visibility, since presidents, elected and appointed administrative officals have been chosen from the black bourgeoisie. The high visibility of middle class blacks since 1946 in all echelons of the administrative and political machinery has led many to term the movement that led to Elie Lescot's fall a *Social Revolution*. The objective realities of the Haitian social structure 25 years later tend to show an adverse result. In fact, a good look at the 1946 movement yields little in the way of evidence of socioeconomic progress that could be called a revolution. To attach the term revolution—a qualitative change in a social structure—to the fall of Lescot (1941-1946) and the advent of Estime (1946-1950) to the presidency is the supreme mockery of a concept.

In 1946 there was a bourgeois movement, the logical outcome of the literary movements of the previous generation—a generation morally and psychologically wounded by the American Occupation (1915-1934). The concept of *Negritude* emerged during that period more as a response to the white imperialist and colonialist, than as a revolutionary ideology capable of leading to qualitative social change. The glorification of mother Africa and blackness was never

humanities in France. They were primarily poets and idealists. They believed in parlimentarian rule and their slogan was "the power to the most capable." The National Party had in its ranks the Black Bourgeoisie and their sons who pledged their sympathy to the lower classes and the peasants. Their slogans were, "the power to the majority" and "the greatest good to the largest number."

[6]The fourteen years of the Duvalier regime (1957-1971) with its balance of crime, incompetence, and corruption is the crystalization of middle class opportunism and betrayal of the masses.

intended to reach the masses in a country where 90 percent of the population is illiterate, nor was it backed by an indepth analysis of the Haitian socioeconomic realities. The movement of 1946 was hardly different.

One organization, however, deserves special mention. It is the MOP or Movement Peasants and Worker. The movement emphasized jobs and the right for the Snydicated Unions to strike. Although the movement acknowledges the existence of the Haitian peasants, the MOP remained primarily an urban movement that claimed its strength among the slums inhabitants, colorfully renamed the *Rouleau Compresseur* (bulldozer). The strength and breath of the MOP is seen in the liquidation of its principal protagonist 10 years later, while he was a candidate to the presidency, during the 1957 campaign. The MOP was an urban movement with neither a leadership nor an ideology —a characteristic of many Haitian political organizations —gathering around a flamboyant personality that had tempted the lumpenproletariat with promises and images that he was in no position to fulfill nor materialize. Thus, it is no accident that such a movement, and others like it, have risen and withered away as their romantic leaders followed a similar fate.

The movement of 1946, while at best succeeding in maintaining and increasing the size of a buffer class, was quite insignificant in terms of real political and economic power. The psychological meaning of the event is, however, another matter and has often been confused with its socioeconomic and political aspects. This is a vital distinction since unless all the variables are considered, the full dimension of 1946, as a turning point for better or for worse, will not be grasped. The idea of a black middle class has fulfilled a psychological need for the Haitian masses; hence they

have been receptive to it. It is seen as something to strive for, an end in itself on the stratification ladder.

The concept of a new middle class has been used as a device for the maintenance of the status quo, since after 1946 the socioeconomic relations between classes remained almost the same. The gains were minimal and included: (1) two more secondary schools, (2) the opening of the medical school to the sons of the middle class, (3) the opening of the military academy to the lower and middle classes, and (4) a black president and black administrators.   The land tenure system remained unchanged, the ownership of the means of production foreign, the distribution of goods in the hands of the upper class, the hierarchy of the Roman Catholic Church was foreign, and department and retail stores were still controlled by foreign entrepreneurs and the money elites or bourgeoisie "d'affaire."

What occurred in 1946 was the emergence of and substitution of a new class of unconscious bureaucrats that have been opportunistic from the start and have remained so to this day.   They have never aspired to more than a piece of the pie. Rugged individualism has always been rampant among the middle class; so was its greed for power.   These easily contented individuals often lose their revolutionary zeal as soon as their basic needs are met.

Nevertheless, they were quite marketable in the process.   Because sociologists have a tendency to emphasize the social and cultural aspects of a society, instead of its infrastructure, they were often misled by the high visibility of blacks in the political-administrative apparatus.   But a serious analysis of Haitian society will reveal a country where the essential relations between classes have not changed for over a century. The characteristics and composition of the various classes are evidence to this point of view.

CLASS AND CLASS RELATIONSHIPS IN HAITI

Characteristics of the Middle Class

Numerically the Haitian middle class is small. About four percent of the total population, it is composed of government functionaries and clerks, some professionals, sales clerks, accountants, and so on (Wingfield and Parenton, 1965). They are literate and their education can be called good to fair. They have in most cases terminated their secondary education, that is, their baccalaureat I or II, and many have completed college. In the last two decades an increasing number of middle class sons have been attending college abroad, and it is from them that the most active and flamboyant politicians are recruited.

The middle class is largely miseducated because it has gone through an educational process designed for the sons of the elites, an educational process utterly oriented toward the outside world, particularly France. It is not surprising, until lately (1964), that a young person terminating his secondary studies knew more about France and the outside world than about Haiti. This explains why the Haitian middle class — in fact the Haitian in general — suffers from the complex of the "stranger." The term "a l'etranger" is the most convincing proof one can bring to support any argument or practice, in the eyes of the Haitian. Those who come back from abroad have acquired special status in the community. An old friend who himself has visited the outside world, put it this way: "If one dies without visiting even the Dominican Republic, that person dies in darkness." It is customary for

professionals who have studied and worked abroad to come back home with foreign license plates on their latest American model cars and show off around town for two or three months.

A large majority of the middle class attends the Roman Catholic church at the same time that they practice vodoun as a way of life. Vodoun is a practical philosophy that provides solutions to everyday problems. Many belong to the Catholic Church because it is the church of the state and is also the institution through which a worldly education is provided. Few members of the middle class admit their affiliation or their sympathy to vodoun, although, in their view, coupled with Catholicism it forms a coherent system of action. The relations between vodoun and Christianity seem well expressed in this laconic formula of a middle person: "In everything one must deal with God, the Virgin Mary, and the Vodoun mysteries." This formula suggests that vodoun is largely a syncretism and as such has permeated the very basis of the middle class. It is the general feeling however that "pure" vodoun is practiced only in the countryside.

Middle class people are upwardly mobile, and most of them, for example, aspire to live beyond the statute of Dessalines, a popularly accepted boundary between the inner city and the better "quartiers" like BoisVerna and Turgeau. Residence is quite important, and often among the middle class youth, a newcomer may be asked: "Where do you live, before or beyond Dessalines?" A large majority of the middle class lives in the city,[7] although the opening of the Cites (urban development projects) have triggered

---

[7]The city of Port-au-Prince is used as a model. I grew up there and I spent an average of five to six hours a week of my teenage years visiting the most remote areas of the city. This is how I became acquainted with the indescribable misery of the lower classes.

a movement out, either in the direction of St. Martin, northeast, or Martissant (Cite Beauboeuf) and Carrefour, southwest of Port-au-Prince.

The middle class family income range is considered modest; it goes from 500 to 2000 dollars a year (Wingfield and Parenton, 1965). Because the members of the middle class often try to live above their means, or have been unable to collect their paycheck from the government—the government often runs two to three months in arrears due to insufficient budget or misplaced priorities — they live in debt. The middle class father is more often than not a responsible citizen who uses all available means to provide for his family. Because he values education, the mastery of French, and non-manual labor, he will make sure that his children are in school and have the necessary tools to succeed. In some families all children go to school through section A., B., or C., allowing the father to make an investment in books only once. (Textbooks in Haiti are standard throughout the school system and may not change for as many as 20 years.)

Among the middle class color is a sensitive point. Members of the middle class in Haiti take the caste and class structure for granted. Although no one seems to like it, people avoid talking about it. They seem to suffer from an inferiority complex when facing the member of the elites, who are mainly mulattoes. The company of the sons of the elites seems quite valued in their eyes, and the middle class sons often brag about being the friend of "Ti Lou Lou" (Little Louis).[8] A point that the foreign analyst often misses is that a combination of money and color, family origin, etc., classifies a person as elite in the eyes of the middle class. For example, a light skinned middle class son

_____

[8]The prefix "Ti" is used by every class; however, the tonal inflection, either soft or harsh, indicates the class of the person it is applied to.

who would try to assert himself over his peers on the basis of his color alone would be frowned on by them in the following way: "Who do you think you are, your little color does not frighten us." And if a lighter skinned lower class person tries to get too familiar, he may be called not only, "Ti Rouge" (Little Red), but heard himself told: "Go away, I am not your class."

The importance of color becomes evident when one becomes aware of who is usually chosen as the godparent of the middle class baby. The same is also true for who is chosen as best man or maid of honor in the middle class marriage. In both of these cases, such persons are chosen from the mulatto caste, and if by mistake the chosen person refuses, then he will be vehemently accused of color prejudice, and such an incident will be long remembered.

The question of color has penetrated Haitian society to an unbelievable extent, and unwittingly has functioned as a boundary maintaining device. There have been charges and countercharges of color prejudice throughout the history of Haiti and no group or sector of the population has been immune from it. As a political device it has been used both by genuinely uninformed nationalist leaders and by demagogues courting the masses for their votes.

The Urban Proletariat

Below the middle class is what is usually known as the masses or _la masse_. This group technically forms the urban proletariat. It is about six percent of the total population and lives in the poorer section of town or in one of the many slums of Port-au-Prince. Students of the Haitian class system often fail to mention the urban proletariat, although together with the middle class and working class they form 10 percent of the total population.

The urban proletariat is illiterate, though many of them have at some time attended night school. Their illiteracy is no surprise, since night school is taught in French, a language the masses do not understand. There have been some efforts to teach them in Creole, but Creole, although spoken by all Haitians, is still waiting for the codification that would make it available to all in the same version and spelling.

The urban proletariat is made up of mostly peasants without land, hard pressed by the pitiful economic conditions of the countryside and the mountains. They are the many porters, domestics, unskilled laborers, factory workers, retail "Revandeuses" at the market place, and have some less honorable ways to make a living.

Two categories must be distinguished within the proletariat. (1) The unskilled laborers who do temporary work around market places and often have to resort to all sorts of expedients to make a living, and (2) the semipermanent job holders who work in factories (sugar factories, coffee, sisal, cotton, soap, etc.) and various small business enterprises. In the former category, one should notice the despised and yet famous "Bourrettier," a porter with a push cart, and the fierce "Boeufchaine," the loading men aboard commercial trucks. These porters and less prestigious others in their category are among the worst off of the group generally known among Haitians as the "malheureux" or unlucky. They believe in and practice vodoun and seldom have contact with the Catholic Church. They make up the core of the famous "Mardi Gras bands," such as the variety of "Orthophonics" and the "Rebordailles" of which "Ti Boute" (a one armed hungan or vodoun priest) is the most notable.[9]

[9]It must be made clear that the Mardi Gras is enjoyed by all in Haiti (except a few fundamentalist Protestants), and that on Sundays, after 10:00 P.M., when the middle and upper class bands retired, their followers often joined the Orthophonics and the Rebordailles for the rest of the night.

The semipermanent job holders differ from the others in the sense that they often have some contact with the Catholic Church and many of them belong to some of the fundamentalist Protestant churches. Those who belong to a Protestant church often severed all contact with vodoun and other worldly things such as Mardi Gras and Ra-Ra. They share some of the characteristics of the middle class, in the sense that they seem to be upwardly mobile and value education and savings that is not put in a bank but is kept around in the house at a safe location. They usually attend night school and often send their sons and daughters to primary and secondary schools. Many in the new middle class emerged from this group. However, they are not exempt from any of the calamities that befall the Haitian masses.

The Haitian proletariat is the hardest hit in a socioeconomic structure where 46 percent of the labor force is unemployed. No statistics are available for the proletariat, which makes it difficult to establish the extent of their poverty. The infant mortality rate is 17.5 percent in Haiti, and tuberculosis and other chronic diseases caused by poor nutrition or even starvation (a large number of poverty stricken people often eat one meal a day or every other day) contribute to a high death rate among the urban masses (Inter-American Bank, 1962). Infant death among the masses is often attributed to a curse, bad luck, or the action of the "loup-garou" or werewolf. Ironically, anthropologists both Haitian and foreign have described the proletariat as superstitious. This label may be inappropriate since these people have had to devise ways to cope with an untenable situation.

The masses are misled and baffled by unscrupulous politicians. They are despised by the upper and middle classes that often refer to them as the "Gros orteils," or big toes, "Malendrins," and "Sans Aveux," meaning badly off and disregarded. They are left to the goodwill of some of the most unscrupulous characters the Haitian society ever produced: the "caporal," or policemen. The caporal has right of life and death, so to speak, on these "malendrins." Three of these pitiful characters who patrolled the market place are worth mentioning for their cruelty to the Haitian masses. "Trois pas" or three steps, whose name means that he could catch anyone in three steps, reigned over the masses in the early 1940s. In the late forties he was succeeded by "Archange" or archangel, who in turn was replaced in the 1950s by "Seraphin." Notice that the last two are named after two powerful angels in the heavenly hierarchy. These individuals made for themselves a reputation of "Mechant" or tough guys, the prototype of the authoritarian personality, the precursors of the formidable "Tonton Macoutes" of the Duvalier regime.

Those who work in factories or public works are equally at the mercy of the foreman. In the same way women who sell their products around the market places, have to put up with the abuses and caprices of the tax collectors. Tax collectors, foremen, supervisors, and "gensdarmes" or police are often among the most powerful figures on the Haitian urban lower class scene. They make their living by preying on the defenseless masses. Foremen and supervisors can and often do dock a worker for as much as two days of an already meager pay, an amount that they do not report in the books but share among themselves.[10] Such practices have generated at times the worse conflicts among the masses and these middlemen.

The upper classes have little contact with the proletariat except through the "bonne a tout faire" or maid, who is usually paid from

$5.00 to $8.00 a month depending on her expertise and the employer's means, the unpaid "Domestique" also known as "reste avec," usually children from six to eighteen years old who do the house cleaning in return for room and board, and the "gerant la cou," or yardman, the male counterpart of the maid, who performs the heavy duties. Social distance is maintained between these groups and the elites through a set of well-defined and enforced rituals.

The bonne, the domestiques, and gerant, are not allowed in the living room; they usually share a shack in the backyard, where they eat after everyone else. If the man of the house gives a lift to the maid on her way to the market place (one shops every day in Haiti at the open market) she will not be allowed to sit in the front with him (though they often get closer at other places and other times), since societal "covenance" requires that the maid take the back seat. At this level of relationship paternalism seems most prevalent since the system of adopted "Parrain" and "Marraine" or godfather and godmother takes special meaning when "etrennes" or bonus are given out. These groups have been entangled in a long and unresolved conflict that functions as a boundary maintaining mechanism and that could be considered a system of tension management. Although the physical distance may be somewhat small, the social distance between the urban proletariat and the elites is extreme.

Characteristics of the elites

The elites seem to stand in a similar position, to a greater or lesser extent, vis-à-vis the other classes in the society. They are the principal enforcers of the caste and class system in Haiti and beneficiaries of the status quo. The elites differ from the rest of the society by their religion, education, income, residence, life style, leisure, their

---

[10] The minimum wage in Haiti is 70 cents a day. However, its purchasing power is much higher when comparing with the U.S. or other developed countries in the Western Hemisphere.

color and an inherent inferiority complex vis-a-vis the white foreigner, their occupation, professions, and a traditional aversion for manual labor. However, the elites and the middle class share at least two of the above characteristics and in certain ways it is difficult to draw rigid lines between these two classes. For example, the elites and the middle class share a common aversion of manual labor and a similar inferiority complex when faced with the white foreigner and his culture.

Numerically the elites (called bourgeoisie among the Haitians) are small. They are a mere 2 percent of the population, yet they control over 70 percent of the production and wealth of the country. They have always been the natural allies of foreign imperialists and a sub-group of the elites have earned the label of *bourgeoisie export-import.*

The bourgeoisie export-import analytically could be distinguished from the rest of the elites. They are a minute fraction of the group, yet their assets vary from several thousand to millions. In this group are people who hold dual nationality and often have business in other parts of the Caribbean.[11] According to Pierre-Charles, "The Reimbolt, Brandt, Wiener, Madsen, Dufort and Berne factories command an enormous part of the coffee transactions. In 1955–56 among the 26 authorized exporters, these five principals share 62 percent of the total exportation of coffee. In general, these enterprises and a few others control the import business" (Pierre-Charles, 1967). A characteristic of this group is that their wealth is not reinvested in Haiti. On the contrary, their dividends are safely placed in foreign banks. The bourgeoisie export-import's social concern for Haiti is nicely summarized in the following terms:

"These establishments . . . limit themselves exclusively to the exportations and speculations based on price variations. All that for the purpose of raising enormous fortunes and to build luxurious homes. To contribute to the economic development, to create new sources of employment, to ameliorate the commercial balance and a better distribution of the national income, is another matter. The houses of exportations dominated by Italians, Syrians or Americans, do not fare any better as to the way their dividends are used" (Pierre-Charles, 1967:122).

The larger segment of the elites is related to this subgroup at various levels of transactions and in values and interests they share a common definition of the situation. It may be appropriate to quote a striking remark made by two foreign observers,". . . this class has maintained its prestige position and lighter color by endogamy and interlocking family ties. In fact, they have intermarried to such an extent that they all seem related" (Wingfield and Parenton, 1965). These "interlocking family ties" are primarily economic and it can be argued that the color issue is a device to mitigate the economic exploitation of the Haitian people. Under the guise of protecting "its prestige position and lighter color" the elites are primarily protecting their economic interests.[12]

---

[11]Most studies of the Haitian caste and class structure neglect this group altogether, and even the radical newspapers published abroad failed to provide statistics, thus making it difficult to really assess the actual wealth of this group. Certain well-known Haitian industrialists, however, are reported to be millionaires.

---

[12]It is beyond the scope of the present study to investigate in greater detail the economic aspects of caste and class conflicts in Haiti; however, I must dissociate myself from those who enjoy describing the Haitian social structure without offering an explanation of it, thus according greater importance to secondary questions to the detriment of a more logical and substantial analysis.

Besides the high standard of living and substantial economic assets, there are other visible traits that distinguish the rest of the elites — other than the bourgeoisie export-import — from the other classes of Haitian society. These include the education, religious practices, residence, and life style of the bourgeoisie that are utterly different from those of the rest of the country.

The education and religious practices of the bourgeoisie are alien to Haiti. The educational system is based on the French model. It is primarily a classical education designed to enhance and perpetuate the love of France and the superiority of its culture. In Haitian society, education and religion are separable only analytically, for the establishments dispensing it to the children of the elites are primarily religious. Since the Concordat of 1860, the Roman Catholic Church has become the church of the state and as such has enjoyed a monopoly on the Haitian educational system. The caste structure is also maintained through such a combination. For example, it used to be the covert practice, and maybe still is, for the religious instructors in religious schools to favor mulatto students to the detriment of darker pupils, even when a darker skinned student may have scored higher than the others. There are many stories of darker skinned pupils in such institutions who have been flunked at final examinations — in Haiti they use the word dawn or "coule" — or pushed down to the bottom of the merit list in favor of mulatto pupils.

The elites or the bourgeoisie, in contrast to the rest of the country, attend the Catholic Church and some of them may even be fervent Catholics.[13] Since attendance at mass on Sunday and other obligatory days is compulsory for those who attend religious schools, parents of this class have no serious problem sending their children and also the women to church. Most men do not attend church, but insist on their children going, since in their view it is good for the children and considered a good habit to acquire. The members of the elites have developed a serious inferiority complex vis-à-vis the religious institutions. Although they will not go to church, they insist that women and children go. Although they sometimes criticize the Catholic schools, they continue to send their children to them. Such a state of contradictions has generated among the elites a taste and behavior that is alien to Haitian culture. This tendency is most visible in their place of residence and life style.

The elites live in the suburbs often located on a colline where the climate is less torrid. In Port-au-Prince, for example, the elites live in the "quartier" of Petionville; at the Cape in the northern part of the island, it is the "quartier" of Carenages. The houses are European in style, although in the last two decades the primitive paintings of "Ti Joseph" have reached the living rooms of this class. The elites followed these new patterns only after the white man, particularly the American tourist, pronounced the works of lower class Haitian painters worthy of appreciation.[14]

Their life style differs greatly from that of the rest of the country. For example, they have managed to keep open some highly exclusive clubs like the "Circle Bellevue," the "Circle Port-au-Princien," the "Club Militaire," (for commission officers only), etc. The elites speak French in public at all times and seem to practice a sort of

---

[13]Although a large majority of the elites attend the Roman Catholic Church, when under serious pressure many of them do pay a visit at night to the hougan or vodoun priest.

[14]A good example was the resistance of the elites in the 1940's to the ideas of an Episcopal Bishop to commission some biblical scenes with a peasant background to be painted on the wall of the Cathedral.

"noblesse oblige." They try to maintain their social distance from the rest of the population and manage to always "keep face" or not to "lose face" (Goffman, 1967).

The elites are turned toward the outside world; that is, Europe and the United States. They seem to be constantly entertaining and housing foreigners, who may not always be impressed. In the words of a European who visited Haiti and was a guest of an elite family that had gone out of its way to please her: "They are cute" ("Ils sont gentile"). Some members of this class are alarmed by the critical conditions in Haiti, and many feel threatened by the possibility of a grass-roots revolution. To many of them only American intervention could establish order in Haiti once and for all. As a member of this class, who was trying to convince me of the need for such an eventuality, put it: "Let me tell you young man, what we need to straighten up things for us is an American intervention. The Americans should have taken Haiti a long time ago. *Your* only problem would be that you would have to step aside on the sidewalk or lower your head and take off your hat when you speak to the white man."[15] This seems to be an opinion that a large majority of the elites subscribe to and is also popular among many members of the middle class. Apparently only one group of people, the largest and the worst off in the country, the peasant class, opposes foreign intervention and external domination. They should be called the "original Haitians." They are the only ones than can not go anywhere when conditions deteriorate to a critical point. As such, they are the only people who have a vital interest in the well-being of Haiti.[16]

[15]This was the feeling of many members of the elite in 1963-1964 when they lost hope of overthrowing Duvalier.

[16]This was particularly true during the Occupation (1915-1934) when only the peasants or "cacos" took arms to defend the national soil.

The peasantry: the backbone of Haiti

It is generally admitted that over 85 percent of the Haitian population lives in the countryside. This class constitutes the backbone of Haiti, for it is the general feeling that if it were to disappear, the country would collapse. Leyburn puts it in vivid terms: "The products of the peasant's labor, when marketed, have brought whatever prosperity the state and its ruling caste (class) have enjoyed" (Leyburn, 1966: 250). Yet, to a large extent, the Haitian peasant is among the worst off of the society.

Some of the characteristics of the peasantry are well known. They are illiterate and live in the margin of the political conflicts; they also live on a subsistence economy, although they contribute more than 50 percent of the GNP. Contrary to the beliefs held among Latin Americans, the Haitian peasant owns little land, and many own no land at all. The host of domestics and porters mentioned above bears witness to this fact. According to the Social *Progress Report* of the Inter-American Bank (1962), over 83 percent of all farms are smaller than six hectares (one hectare = 2.741 acres) and they represent a little more than 70 percent of the area under cultivation (Leyburn, 1966). Some 30 percent of the cultivated area is divided among a few big landowners, like the American controlled company Derae-Phaeton, which operates in the northeast of Haiti, one of the largest sisal plantations in the world (Dauphin Plantation) (Manigat, 1964). Many of these plantations employ large numbers of peasants at substandard wages.

The Haitian peasant, a descendant of the African slave of Saint Domingue, is primarily black and adheres to vodoun as his religion. A small minority of the countryside belongs to some fundamentalist Protestant cults. There is some interesting regional diversities in the Haitian countryside, although no conclusive studies have been made. For example, vodoun is practiced differently in the north, the central west, and the southwest of the country. However, vodoun, as a monotheistic religion and a practical philosophical system, is the heart of peasant life, the center pillar of the extended family system throughout the country (Metraux, 1959).

The attitudes of the upper and middle classes toward the peasant are summarized in a series of ready-made and preconceived ideas. To them, the peasant is everything non-worldly, which to these classes implies non-European. Creole, for example, is a bastard dialect and not to be spoken in public or the living room, French being "la langue de salon." Vodoun is also dismissed as a savage cult whose adepts are the personification of backwardness and superstitious behaviors. As late as 1957 the elites referred openly to the peasants as the "Ruraux," a pejorative epithet equivalent to "primitives," "rurals," or "natives." In the views of the upper and middle class, the peasants are stupid, uneducable, and thickheaded. They are the "negres sottes" or the "gros orteils" that will have to be broken in or "degrossir" in order to make them suitable to work in the houses of the elites or in the cities. Few remarks, in my view, are as accurate as the one made over 30 years ago by a foreign sociologist:

"Although persons of culture exist who are generally solicitous for the betterment of their (the peasants) life, there is really no comparison which will make clear to the . . . reader the ordinary attitude of mind of elite toward les noirs. The mildest expression of general opinion is that it would be a waste of time to try to educate the masses, for they are so nearly like animals that they could not absorb even the simplest education. Peasants eat when they are hungry, rise and go to sleep with light and darkness, are unable to count, like animals sense changes in weather; peasants are kindly

but stupid, like donkeys: this is the kind of summary one hears from the mouths of the elite. It is possible that the elites are merely imitating the attitude toward the Negro of many white people they have seen" (Leyburn, 1966: 287-88).

These shared and nourished attitudes toward the peasants function as boundary maintenance devices and they will take long to die out. The peasant in most cases accepts the definitions the upper classes have imposed on him and on the Haitian social order. Their only weapon is their mutism and the hope that things shall soon get better. Thus, the peasant continues to work day after day and the parasite classes live off his work. A well-known saying characterizes this situation, "Bourrique travail, cheval gallonin," meaning, "the donkeys work and the horse gets the benefits." This kind of situation keeps the country and its priviledged classes going. Should the peasant go on strike, the entire country could be paralyzed.

Special mention should be made of the social organization of the countryside or the peasant world. Of primary importance in the peasant world are vodoun and the family. The peasant family is primarily an extended family, and vodoun as a religion and a system of socialization is the cement of the family. Vodoun and family forms a unit that can be separated only analytically. For example, the vodoun ceremony is planned and carried on with substantial help from everyone in the "lakou" or compound, the area on which live the extended family. In such occasions, every man, woman, and child is given certain duties, for which each is held responsible. The same is true of the "coumbite," another occasion where everyone gathers to help a relative or a friend farm or harvest his "jardin" or garden — a miniature farm. The socioeconomic functions of vodoun cannot be overemphasized; (though at times, unscrupulous politicians have exploited its positive and attractive aspects). Its rejection would be equivalent to the rejection of the Haitian peasant — the people themselves, Vodoun is not only a family religion, it is a whole system of socialization. In the words of Mathilde Beauvoir, a *mambo* (a priestest), *"a humfor* (a temple) is not only a place to pray; it is also a hospital where people are cared for with the use of natural products such as leaves and flowers. It is a nursery, a day care center, where little ones are cared for free of charge while their mothers are away. It is also a school where young girls learn how to sew, to cook, to wash clothes, to iron, etc." (*Jeune Afrique,* 1971: 56-61). This social organization is the backbone of Haiti, and the irony is that it is this aspect of Haitian way of life that the middle and upper classes seem to despise most.

CONCLUSION

The caste and class structure of Haiti, a fact of life for all segments of the society, is the outcome of years of unresolved conflicts. Such conflicts have succeeded in solidifying both the physical and the socioeconomic distance among the various classes. Consequently, the chronic socioeconomic stagnation of Haiti is understandable only in these terms. In fact, recently socioeconomic conditions have declined. Caste and class antagonisms seem to have functioned not only as system maintenance devices, but actually have had a more far-reaching effect. They are the very basis for the deterioration of present-day Haiti.

It is misleading, however, to see these conflicts as the sole reason for the stagnation and decadence in Haiti. Foreign interests have often instigated these class conflicts and the caste antagonism has been used as a means to mitigate them. Color prejudice, a manifestation of class exploita-

tion, is too often seen as the actual cause of the conflicts. It is the result, however, of an educational system dominated by foreign ideas and interests. These interests found that a code of socioeconomic distance based on color was not difficult to enforce. The present structure of Haiti has its roots in the colonial period when color was used as a means of social control.

A tangible sign of foreign ideas and interests has been also the Christian churches, particularly the Roman Catholic Church. The "best schools," by European standards, are the ones owned and managed by the Catholic Church. These institutions, after 19th century European, models, not only dispense an antiquated education that paralyzes the country but succeed in instilling two contrasting values in the Haitian population: (1) the hate of everything *black, African,* or *Haitian* and (2) the love of everything *white, French,* or *étranger.* These values are also taught in nonchurch owned schools, that is, throughout the Haitian school system, which is modeled after these religious establishments.

The attitudes, values, and characteristics of the various classes of Haiti thus become understandable, and it would be surprising if they were otherwise. The middle and upper class aversion to manual labor, Vodoun, and other manifestations of Haitian culture both material and nonmaterial, and their love of French poetry, culture, and "produits de France" also should be seen in this light. These attitudes result in the "self-hate" that explains the inferiority complex, almost inherent in the middle and upper class Haitians when facing the white foreigner and his culture.

The proletariat and the peasantry, about 90 percent of the total population, bear the burden of upper class social inadequacies. Should this most populous and active lower strata disappear, the country would collapse. The activity of the peasant and the enterprising "Madame Sarah" (Proletarian woman retailer) keeps the country, with its parasitic class, going. They also are the only link to the Haitian culture. Without them, all vestiges of authentic culture would have disappeared long ago. One should remark, however, that the proletariat and the peasantry are not free either from the paralyzing forces of caste and class exploitation. They also suffer from the inferiority complex mentioned above.

The many uprisings, called "revolutions," in Haiti did little to change both the contour and the distribution of wealth, status, and power within the society, many of these being "palace revolutions" where one clique of the same class replaces another. What has not been so obvious was the fact that within the upper or the middle class are individuals of all colors, making it difficult to unmask potential oppressors or agents of foreign socioeconomic interests. Thus, in terms of caste and class conflicts and the ideologies that underlie them, it is appropriate to conclude that: "Class ideologies create three images of the class that is struggling for dominance: an image for itself; an image of itself for other classes, which exalts it; an image of itself for other classes, which devalues them in their own eyes, drags them down, tries to defeat them, so to speak, without a shot being fired" (Lefebvre, 1967: 76).

REFERENCES

COSER, LEWIS A.
1956 *The functions of social conflict.* New York: Free Press.

FANON, FRANTZ
1967 *Black skin, white masks.* New York: Grove Press.

GOFFMAN, ERVING
1967 *Interaction ritual: Essays on face to face behavior.* New York: Doubleday and Company.

INTER-AMERICAN BANK
1962 *Social Progress Trust Fund.* Haiti: 299-307.

JEUNE AFRIQUE
1971 May 11: 56-61

LEFEBVRE, HENRI
1969 *The Sociology of Marx.* New York: Random House.

LEYBURN, JAMES
1966 *The Haitian people.* New Haven: Yale University Press.

LOBB, JOHN
1940 "Caste and class in Haiti." *American Journal of Sociology,* (July): 23 - 24.

MANIGAT, LESLIE F.
1962 *La politique agraire du gouvernement d'Alexandre Petion, 1807-1818.* Port-au-Prince: Imp. La Phalange.

1964 *Haiti of the Sixties, object of international concern.* Washington, D.C.: Center for Foreign Policy Research.

METRAUX, ALFRED
1959 *Voodoo in Haiti,* New York: Oxford University Press.

MORAL, PAUL
1961 *Le Paysan Haitien: Etudes sur la vie rurale en Haiti,* Paris: Maisonneuve and Larose.

PIERRE-CHARLES, GERARD
1967 *L'economie Haitienne et sa voie de developpement.* Paris: Maisonneuve and Larose.

PRICE-MARS, JEAN
1928 *Ainsi parla l'onele.* New York: Parapsychology Foundation.

WATKINS, MEL
1971 "The last work: The black scholar," *New York Times,* (May 30).

WINGFIELD, ROLAND AND VERNON J. PARENTON
1965 "Class structure and class conflict in Haitian society." *Social Forces,* 13 (Spring): 338-47.

4. THE SHAPE OF INTERGROUP CONFLICT

In his analysis of class conflicts, Dahrendorf outlines the variables that shape conflicts. Conflicts may vary in their intensity and violence. Intensity refers to the amount of energy invested in the conflicts while violence refers to the weapons utilized. It is possible to apply Dahrendorf's analysis to ethnic conflicts.

Dahrendorf proposes four variables that he assents affect the intensity and violence of conflict. The first variable is what he terms pluralism versus superimposition. The theory underlying this analysis has become familiar in the attempts of political scientists to explain the failure of extreme political ideologies to gain support in the United States. According to this explanation the allegiances that individuals have in organizations with varied interests and somewhat conflicting political positions such as union, political parties, and churches tend to keep them anchored into a moderate political stance.

One of Dahrendorf's examples is explicitly related to ethnic relations. He argues that when Catholics occupy subordinate positions and Protestants are dominant in all aspects of the social structure, there will be a superimposition of conflict upon religious identity. This can be seen in the conflicts between Protestants and Catholics in Northern Ireland. Blacks and whites in South Africa and the United States, Indians in the United States, and Jews in Europe are concrete examples of subordinate groups whose relationships with other groups within their society has been totally based on their ethnic identity. The superimposition of all relationships upon ethnic identity increases the intensity of conflicts if not their violence. This is in contrast to pluralistic conflict situations where "every particular conflict remains confined to the individual in one of his many roles and absorbs only that part of the individual's personalities that went into this role" (Dahrendorf, 1959:215).

The relative openness or closedness of the societal structure has comparable effects to that of pluralism and superimposition. "There is an inverse relationship between the degree of openness of class and the intensity of class conflict. The more upward and downward mobility there is in a society, the less comprehensive and fundamental are class conflicts likely to be. As mobility increases, group solidarity is increasingly replaced by competition between individuals and the energies invested by individuals in class conflict decrease" (Dahrendorf, 1959:222).

In this instance patterns of ethnic group conflict and class conflict are not totally comparable. Unwilling to view themselves as objects of collective discrimination, ethnic groups may remain atomistic as individual members attempt to achieve mobility through their own efforts. As ethnic groups increasingly view their inability to achieve mobility as a result of discrimination and not of their own individual failings, conflict of a high intensity may result. Organization, however, may decrease this intensity. Coser (1956) notes that organized conflict may produce recognition of the legitimacy of claims that may mute the intensity of the conflicts between ethnic groups.

Sociologists have extensively researched the affects of status inconsistency. For Dahrendorf the degree of consistency underlying the distribution of authority in a society is a third variable affecting the shape of social conflict. The inability of an ethnic group to obtain any economic rewards coupled with their "exclusion from authority" (Dahrendorf, 1959:217) increases the intensity of the conflict and in cases of severe deprivation of an ethnic group, the violence of the conflict. This issue of authority is central to the demands for community control of police, education, and other institutions by segregated ethnic groups and radical whites in the United States. In Dahrendorf's terms we can expect these demands to be stronger among subordinate ethnic groups than among radical whites who still possess major opportunities for economic gains and social mobility.

Finally, the pattern of conflict regulation in society affects the intensity of the conflict. Where mechanisms such as conciliation, mediation, or arbitration are regularized and established, "group conflict loses its sting and become an institutionalized pattern of social life" (Dahrendorf, 1959: 230). Although the intensity of the conflict may remain great, it can then be channeled into models that lessen the violence.

The articles in this section illustrate the applicability of Dahrendorf's analysis to several societies. In most of the interethnic situations described, conflicts have been superimposed upon ethnic differences. Van den Berghe focuses on the basic value conflicts between blacks and whites in South Africa. Differences in values and social mobility also precipitated much of the conflicts between Gentiles and Mormons discussed by MacMurray and Cunningham.

Present-day barriers to black social mobility forms the basis of Gans' discussion of the relationship between blacks and Jews in New York City. Van der Kroef details the questions of social mobility, distribution of authority, and problems of conflict resolution that figured in the reactions of Chinese and Malays to Indonesian attempts to prevent the formation of Malaysia in the 1960s.

The maintenance of authority by whites is crucial to the colonial pattern in Mexico described by Casanova. For Indians in the United States, it has been the lack of authority over their own lifes that has shaped their continual conflict with the federal government. In French Canada, the lack of authority of the culturally distinct French Canadians and their subordinate economic position have resulted in an intense separatist movement that has been marked by outbreaks of bombings. The Chinese in the United States have developed a unique distribution of authority within present-day Chinatowns. This pattern strengthened by major blockages to social mobility that have faced people of Chinese descent within the larger American society. As Lee's article indicates, this distribution of authority has affected the shape of Chinese-white conflicts.

While none of the authors in this section explicitly utilizes Dahrendorf's variables in their analysis, we hope the application of this approach may help the reader to place these diverse ethnic conflicts in a larger theoretical perspective.

REFERENCES

COSER, LEWIS
   1956   *The functions of social conflict.* New York: Free Press.

DAHRENDORF, RALF
   1959   *Class and class conflict in industrial society.* Stanford: Stanford University Press.

1.

SOUTH AFRICA, A STUDY IN CONFLICT

Pierre Van den Berghe

Economic, social, and political conflicts in South Africa have been super-imposed upon the basic struggle between blacks and whites. This excerpt from Van den Berghe's book on South Africa examines cultural clashes that have contributed to the intense and violent conflicts that have characterized South Africa.

What are the main sources of value conflict and dissension in South Africa? Basically they are reducible to two. First, since South Africa is a culturally pluralistic society, each culture represented in that country has its own idiosyncratic value system. In this respect South Africa is far from unique. Indeed, almost all of the world has experienced, at one time or another, the co-existence of widely different cultural traditions within broader social structures. Secondly, the value system of the dominant White group contains within itself crucial contradictions. Here, also, South Africa is not unique, but it certainly represents an extreme case. Both of these sources of value conflict will now be examined in greater detail.[1]

The different value orientations represented in the various ethnic groups, while not always conflicting, have nevertheless entailed tensions, misunderstandings, and mutually unfavourable stereotypes. A complete account of this source of value conflicts would involve a depth study of the value systems of all the cultural groups represented in South Africa. This is obviously beyond the scope of this study. We shall therefore confine ourselves to a few salient aspects of the problem. Different notions of property, and more particularly of land ownership, have often led to conflict in European-African contacts. In South Africa, as elsewhere, the Europeans have introduced the alien notion that land could be individually owned and sold like any other

SOURCE

From *South Africa: A Study in Conflict* by **Pierre van den Berghe. Copyright © 1965 by Wesleyan University. Reprinted by permission of Wesleyan University Press.**

[1]While solid quantitative data on value differences between various groups in South Africa are still scanty, the few studies in this area have shown important group differences. Cf. S. Biesheuvel, "Further Studies on the Measurement of Attitudes Towards Western Ethical Concepts"; Leonard Bloom et al., "An Interdisciplinary Study of Social, Moral and Political Attitudes"; K. Danziger, "Value Differences among South African Students"; J. M. Gillespie and G. W. Allport, *Youth's Outlook on the Future;* J. W. Mann, "Race-Linked Values in South Africa"; Pierre L. van den Berghe. "Race Attitudes in Durban, South Africa."

commodity. On the other hand, the indigenous African groups shared a totally different conception of land, generally described as "communal tenure." In traditional African culture, land is a natural resource; land occupation by a certain group gives that group the right to exploit the land, but no individual may lay a property claim on any part of it. Within the group, land may be redistributed for use, according to the needs of the extended families which compose the larger group. As in many other parts of Africa, such widely different notions of property have led to misunderstandings and violent conflicts, especially in the period following the Great Trek, when landcession "treaties" were signed between the Boers and the African nations.

Incompatible attitudes concerning cattle still play an important role in cultural clashes. The Europeans view cattle as consumption goods, whereas the traditional African outlook is to consider cattle primarily as capital goods. Heads of cattle are accumulated mainly for prestige reasons, and because cattle is the main medium of exchange in payment of the bride-wealth (*lobola*). The consumption of meat, milk, and hides is only a secondary by-product of livestock ownership. As cattle is convertible into women (and, hence, even more importantly into children), the entire network of matrimonial exchanges, and, indeed, the whole kinship structure, and much of the legal system revolve around it. In terms of the role of cattle in traditional rural African society, it becomes perfectly rational to maximize the size of one's herd, irrespective of meat quality and milk production, and beyond the point of what Europeans consider economically sensible. To say that Africans are indifferent to stock quality is, however, completely untrue. One should rather say that the African sense of quality in cattle is more aesthetic than economic.

When the government, therefore, attempts to limit the size of herds, and to improve stock quality at the expense of quantity, it meets with stubborn (and understandable) opposition. Cattle culling not only means a destruction of capital (in much the same way as burning of banknotes would to a European), but also undermines the entire social structure of traditional African society. Not only do the Whites attempt to impose their view of cattle as the only valid and rational one, but they also disregard the fact that they have themselves contributed greatly to the economic vicious circle of overgrazing and erosion, by depriving Africans of most of their land. As a Zulu told a White official who inveighed against overgrazing, "It is not that we have too many cattle for our land, we have too little land for our cattle."[2]

A similar ethnocentrism and cultural misunderstanding characterize the entire government-imposed programme of "land betterment" which is so bitterly opposed by many rural Africans. There is increasing evidence that traditional African techniques of agriculture and animal husbandry were well adapted to soil and climatic conditions, and much less wasteful of natural resources than many of the European techniques of intensive exploitation. Yet, after having been confined to overpopulated Native Reserves which cannot possibly support their population, Africans are accused of being backward, conservative, and wasteful of land resources, and are expected to turn into intensive cash farmers without the capital necessary for such development, and without any consideration for the socially disruptive implications of technological innovations. For example, the introduction of the oxen-drawn plow has revolutionized the sexual division of labour in many African societies, where agriculture has traditionally been the task of women, and animal husbandry that of men.

---

[2] Quoted in Max Gluckman, *Analysis of a Social Situation in Modern Zululand*, p. 67.

In short, Europeans have uncritically assumed that economic rationality and materialism are universally valid concepts, and have more or less forcibly imposed these values on African populations in total disregard of indigenous values. In many cases, new techniques were introduced without any proof that they were adaptable to the African environment, and that they would, in the long run, be more productive than traditional methods. On the whole, it appears that Europeans are responsible for a much more wasteful exploitation of African resources than the Africans themselves. One needs only to think of wanton destruction of game; large-scale deforestation; and soil exhaustion through intensive planting of such crops as cotton, and through large-scale sheep grazing; not to mention the colossal waste of human resources, first through the slave trade (which cost Africa at least fifty million lives), and then through various forms of compulsory labour conscription and "contracting" on mines, plantations, railway and road construction projects, etc. These considerations apply not only to South Africa, but to the continent as a whole.

Other incompatible values have led to friction and conflict between Whites and non-Whites in South Africa. A classical example is the European (or, more generally, industrial) notion of time as a valuable and rigorously measurable commodity. While insistence on punctuality and speed is obviously functional in an urban, industrial society, it is much less important in a rural context, and, hence, alien to traditional African values. Also related to industrialization, and alien to African culture, is the "Protestant Ethic" concerning work and the accumulation of material goods as morally desirable ends in themselves. The absence of such values in indigenous cultures has led to the European stereotypes of the African as "lazy," "indolent," "improvident," "irre-

sponsible," etc.[3]   In terms of practical policy, the Western outlook on work has led to the introduction of such measures as "poll taxes," and more or less compulsory "recruitment" schemes to force Africans into the wage economy and "teach the Natives habits of industriousness."

These measures have been bitterly opposed by Africans, not so much at first because they were discriminatory and reduced them to industrial wage slavery, but rather because they were utterly senseless in terms of traditional values. Failing any incentive to accumulate wealth for its own sake (and, for that matter, any opportunity to do so to any significant extent), and viewing work as a necessary evil to sustain life, rather than as a rewarding and morally laudable end in itself, the traditional rural African has little motivation to participate in the wage economy, other than the sheer necessity of survival.[4]

---

[3]These stereotypes have a long history. See MacCrone, *op. cit.*, pp. 46-49. In 1653, one year after founding the Dutch settlement at the Cape, Van Riebeeck describes the Hottentots as "these stupid, lumpish, and lazy, stinking people." Quoted in H. Sonnabend and C. Sofer, *South Africa's Stepchildren*, p. 17. In 1831 Peter Kolben devotes an entire section of his *The Present State of the Cape of Good Hope* to "A Review of the Vices and Virtues of the Hottentots," in which he describes them as lazy and improvident. Cf. *op. cit.*, Vol. I, pp. 324-339. However, indignant as the Dutch were about the "laziness" of slaves and Hottentots, they were themselves unwilling to do any manual labour, which they regarded as degrading. Jan van Riebeeck already complains that the Whites "preferred like Seigneurs to spank about with the cane in the hand and leave everything to their slaves." Quoted in Victor de Kock, *Those in Bondage*, p. 65.

[4]For an eighteenth-century account of value conflict, see Sparrman, *op. cit.*, pp. 232-233. He writes: "The extreme indolence of the [Hottentot] lad . . . excited in me just at that time the greatest indignation, as well as the utmost contempt for the Hottentot nation . . . the lad, from his habits as well as nature, could very easily

This lack of motivation is interpreted by the Whites as "laziness," and used as a rationalization for low wages. Since rural Africans do not want to earn as much as possible, but rather earn enough in a few months of work to be able to live from the savings for the rest of the year, many Whites argue, a rise in wages leads to a decrease in the labour supply. Therefore, wages must be kept low. That this rationalization is based on less than a half-truth does not concern us here. Even when the African becomes Westernized enough to accept the "Protestant Ethic" on work, productivity, and wealth accumulation, he finds himself caught in an exploitative and grossly discriminatory system of production from which there is no escape, and which makes his newly acquired values a source of frustration and bitterness rather than an incentive to work. We shall return to that point later, as it belongs more to the second major source of value conflict.

African and Indian values regarding marriage, sex, and the family are also a common source of European stereotypes and misunderstandings. For example, the more permissive standards of premarital sexuality found in many African cultures, and the payment of fines in cases of adultery, lead to the European stereotypes of Africans as being "lascivious," "oversexed," and as prostituting their wives.[5] The custom of *lobola* is viewed by most Europeans as a degrading trade in women, whereas, in fact, the payment of *lobola* gives status and security to the wife in traditional African society. The African and Indian desire for a large number of children is interpreted as improvidence, irresponsibility, and animal-like behaviour. ("They multiply like rabbits.") In fact, traditional African techniques of birth control and prohibitions favouring the spacing of pregnancies (such as the postpartum sex taboo) have fallen into disuse largely because of disruptive Western influences.

Polygyny is also completely misunderstood, and accepted as evidence of African lasciviousness. Clear deviations from traditional standards of morality and behaviour, such as high rates of illegitimacy, delinquency, prostitution, alcoholism, and divorce in urban centres, are interpreted, not as the consequences of social disorganization brought about by industrialization and racial discrimination, but as reflecting the "aggressive," "violent," or "immoral" nature of Africans, for which the only cure is police repression.

Of course, misinterpretation of behaviour based on misunderstanding of underlying values is mutual. Many Africans and Indians regard White bathing costumes and heterosexual dancing as immoral, to cite only two examples. However, as many Africans and Indians have become largely Westernized, and have themselves internalized European values, the stereotypes and distorted views are stronger on the White side of the colour fence. This is particularly true of those Europeans who claim to "know the Native" because they have spent much time in close physical contact with Africans (e.g., farmers, administrators, plan-

---

make shift with a moderate quantity of food . . . . The principal reason of this disposition that prevails with most Hottentots is, perhaps, that their wants are extremely few; and consequently, being without care or employment of any kind, they are inactive and idle."

[5]Thus, as early as 1831, Peter Kolben writes: "The Negro-Women at the *Cape* are very lascivious Creatures. As they are excus'd there from Working, and indulg'd in an idle Life, for about Six Weeks before and Six Weeks after Travail, they are the most intemperate Wretches upon Earth in the Article, and greedily swallow, and enflame themselves with, all the Provocatives they can come at, till they are got with Child." *Op. Cit.,* Vol. II, p. 340.

tation and mine supervisors). In fact, as these whites have only had highly segmental and utilitarian relations with Africans, and as these relations have been defined by a rigorous strait jacket of master-servant etiquette, such Europeans generally exhibit in strongest form all the prevalent stereotypes about Africans.

In summary, South Africa, as a culturally pluralistic society, represents a wide variety of value systems. The racial situation, by discouraging contact between members of different ethnic groups, and indeed by making completely uninhibited relationships across the colour line virtually impossible, perpetuates cultural misunderstandings and reinforces stereotypes. If the consequences of value pluralism were to stop at misunderstandings, stereotypes, and invidious comparisons, such pluralism would simply lead to interpersonal frustration, annoyance, and tension, more than to an intensification of group conflict. Through its dominant position; however, the White group has been able to impose its value system, and to transpose value-judgments in the realm of discriminatory and coercive policies.

We have already given several examples of the practical implementation of European values, such as the capitation or poll tax, land-betterment schemes, and cattle culling. But we must examine more closely the mechanisms through which values have been translated into policy. The simplest and most direct one is ethnocentrism. Europeans have naturally assumed that their values had absolute validity and universal applicability, and that any other outlook was either immoral or irrational. They have consequently imposed their values on the non-Europeans, and framed policy accordingly. However, European ethnocentrism in South Africa has not entailed its logical corollary, namely a policy of cultural assimilation, as has been practiced, for example, by the Portuguese and Spaniards in America. Had the White

South Africans adopted assimilation as the consequence of their belief in their own cultural superiority, a short phase of acute cultural and social disorganization would have resulted (as in the period following the Spanish conquest of America), but the end result would have been considerable cultural homogeneity.[6]

White South Africans were, however, quick to perceive that cultural assimilation would be accompanied by social integration and "bastardization" of the *Herrenvolk*. Within a generation of the first Dutch settlement at the Cape in the seventeenth century, the baptism of slaves began to be resisted, and White South Africa launched on a deliberate anti-assimilationist policy. In this respect, as in many others, the Nationalist programme of apartheid represents a mere continuation and accentuation of a long-standing trend. The Nationalists not only endeavour to prevent Africans from becoming "imitation Englishmen," and to "keep the Bantu essentially Bantu"; they even want to reverse the process of "detribalization," to revive moribund traditional institutions, and to "re-Bantuize" the urban Africans.

The official position of the Dutch Reformed Churches (D. R. C.'s) is identical with that of the government. Though the D.R.C.'s engage in missionary activities and do not oppose the Christianization of Africans, they strongly assert the principle of "separate development," and defend it on Biblical grounds.[7]   A 1952 statement, for example, reads:

---

[6]For a treatment of important differences in the colonization of Africa and the Americas, see my article "Racialism and Assimilation in Africa and the Americas."

[7]For a long time the Dutch Reformed Churches have been much less active than English and foreign missionary societies, except, for historical reasons, among the Cape Coloured. Consequently, as of the 1951 population census, only 3.9 per cent of the Africans belonged to the three principal D.R.C.'s, compared to 12.2 per cent who were

"The Conference [of Dutch Reformed Churches] holds that our Church's acceptance of a policy which regards the separate development of the various races each according to its own nature, is in accordance with the teachings of Scripture. The fundamental principles of Diversity in Unity, of the recognition of the Divine Purpose, and of the urge for national self-expression must be borne in mind."[8]

How has this White-imposed nativism been implemented in practice? Clearly, traditional African societies have not been kept intact, even in the remotest rural areas. For one thing, no amount of government regulation could stop the process of acculturation. Secondly, while anti-assimilation was unambiguously aimed at the perpetuation of White political and economic supremacy, certain important aspects of traditional society obviously had to be modified in order to entrench. White domination. Notably the entire African political system was completely subjugated to the White authorities, and reduced to a shadow of its former self. Large nations were broken up (as were the Zulu after the war of 1879) to destroy their military power; chiefs were divested of most important powers; the White govern-

ment arrogated itself the power to install and dismiss chiefs; standing armies were dissolved, etc. In short, while the forms of traditional rule were retained, within well-defined limits, to facilitate administration, much of the substance of power and authority was removed from African political systems.

Thirdly, "Native Law and Custom" have been reinterpreted, consciously and unconsciously, in terms of Western values. Here we return to our earlier question, namely how European values have affected practical policy. Not only have these values influenced policy directly through the operation of ethnocentrism, but they have also been introduced indirectly, under the guise of preserving "Native institutions." "Native Law and Custom" were codified by Whites in the Province of Natal, and a special system of Native courts was instituted, wherein Africans are judged by low-ranking White commissioners; the latter often have neither a knowledge of African languages nor any formal legal training. Court proceedings are translated by White interpreters who themselves typically have only an imperfect and unnuanced command of Bantu languages.

It is easy to imagine what distortions and misunderstandings arise from the routine administration of "justice" in such courts, all the more so when cases are expedited at a rate of twenty to thirty an hour, the average for pass offences.[9] But even the codification and interpretation of African law are distorted. In the first place, "Native Law" was deliberately changed to make it congruent with the codifiers' conceptions of "civilization," "humaneness," and "justice," in such matters as penal sanctions, "sorcery," and the like. Furthermore, Eu-

----

Methodists; 6.8 per cent, Anglicans; 5.4 per cent, Roman Catholics; and 4.9 per cent, Lutherans (Table XIV). Even many of the Coloured have turned away from the D.R.C.'s. Although 89 per cent of the Coloureds speak Afrikaans as their home language, only 29.5 per cent belong to the D.R.C.'s. The respective percentages for Whites are 57 and 53.2. In other words, whereas for Whites, membership in the D.R.C.'s and speaking Afrikaans as a mother tongue are nearly synonymous, this is very far from true for the Coloureds. It is not unreasonable to attribute much of the disaffection of Coloureds from the D.R.C.'s to the latter's racial policies. Cf. Horrell, *A Survey of Race Relation in South Africa*, 1959-1960, pp. 25, 27.

[8]Anonymous, *The Racial Issue in South Africa*, p. 9.

----

[9]The record speed which I witnessed during a morning's observation in Durban was fifty seconds; the longest case took four and one-half minutes; the average was about two minutes and forty-five seconds.

European biases and insufficient ethnographic knowledge led to unconscious misunderstandings and distortions of traditional law. Finally, the application in an urban and industrial society of a code of law which evolved in a rural, non-literate society has paradoxically encouraged a complete transformation in the functions and significance of such institutions as the *lobola*.

The second broad source of value conflict in South African society is perhaps even more important than the first. The crux of the conflict is found in the internal contradictions within the value system of the dominant White group. Not only is the ascriptive and particularistic ideology of racialism in disharmony with other elements of the social structure, notably with principles of economic rationality in an industrial system of production; racism also conflicts with basic political, ethical, and religious values which are an integral part of the Western tradition. While South African racialism constitutes a major deviation from the dominant current of the modern Western ethos, this deviation coexists, within the White group, with the Christian ethic of love, brotherhood, and charity, and, to a lesser extent, with the Western political ideology of democracy, freedom, and equality. This deep conflict within the value system of the dominant White group is becoming increasingly acute, and can itself be decomposed into two primary aspects, namely its effect on the non-Whites, and on the Whites. We shall successively examine the complex ramifications of this second type of value conflict on the two sides of the colour-bar.

In spite of the anti-assimilationist policy of the successive South African governments, acculturation of the non-Whites to the Western way of life started in the seventeenth century, and continues at a rapid pace. The process can be roughly divided into two phases. The first phase of Westernization, which lasted until the third or fourth decade of the nineteenth century, gave rise, in combination with extensive miscegenation, to the Cape Coloureds.

The Coloureds find themselves in a typically marginal position. On the other hand, they have assimilated Western values (including, for the most part, the White outlook on colour), and have become culturally undistinguishable from the Europeans. On the other hand, the Coloureds are the object of racial discrimination, and find themselves rejected by White society, solely on grounds of colour. Their steadily deteriorating position makes any hope of eventual assimilation to the whites more unrealistic than ever.

The position of the Coloureds shows that acculturation does not lead to the elimination of value conflicts. In the presence of racial prejudice and discrimination, acculturation is likely to *accentuate* value conflicts. To the extent that the Coloureds share White values, they face, in a particularly acute form, all the contradictions inherent in the dominant value system of the Europeans. So far, the prevalent Coloured "solution" to these contradictions has been to use the egalitarian, Christian aspect of the White ideology to demand acceptance into European society, while, at the same time, adopting White colour attitudes to keep themselves separate from the Africans. Furthermore, the adoption of physical criteria of status among Coloureds has led to profoundly divisive tensions within the Coloured community, not to mention more latent attitudes of self-hatred and self-deprecation.[10]   In recent years, however, the

---

[10]Racialism among Coloureds goes back to the days of slavery, when women slaves were already trying to "improve the stock" by having affairs with White men. Cf. V. de Kock, *op. cit.*, p. 118. Sparrman gives evidence of self-deprecation among Westernized Hottentots in the eighteenth century. He writes: "Some Hottentots, who spoke the Dutch language readily, and with

Coloured leadership and intelligentsia have become clearly aware that racial prejudice among Coloureds undermines any legitimacy to claims of equality with the White group, and that the obvious solution to the value conflict lies in the total rejection of prejudice.

whom, both in company and separately, I conversed on this subject [i.e., the existence of God] always answered me to this effect: *We are poor stupid creatures and have never heard, neither are we able to understand, any thing of the matter."* Sparrman, *op. cit.,* p. 220 (author's italics).

---

2.   MORMONS AND GENTILES: A STUDY IN CONFLICT AND PERSISTENCE

Val Dan MacMurray and Perry H. Cunningham

This paper is an effort to describe some of the consequences of social conflict that increase rather than decrease the adaptation and development of particular social relationships or groups. These functional aspects of conflict are illustrated by an historical analysis of three periods of intense persecution experienced by the Mormon church: Jackson County, Far West, and Nauvoo. The authors discuss how specific episodes and incidents helped create the ethnic and religious boundaries of this American minority and strengthened the sense of identity and the unity of its members prior to their exodus to the Rockly Mountains.

INTRODUCTION

The history of the Church of Jesus Christ of Latter-day Saints, more commonly referred to as Mormons, illustrates a predominant pattern of persistence and growth in the midst of social conflict.[1] This chapter will analyze particular episodes of conflict that occurred during the three major periods of the Mormons' early development in nineteen-century America. We have not attempted to explain the complex set of social conditions that determine whether conflict will prove functional for a group, but rather our concern has been to present a general outline of the significant events that ultimately served to strengthen the identity and unity of the Mormon Church and its members (Figure 1).

"The history of Mormonism reaches back to the fervor of religious enthusiasm which engulfed western New York during the first

---

[1]For our purposes social conflict is a struggle over values or scarce resources in which the aims of the opponents are to neutralize, injure, or eliminate their rivals (Coser, 1965).

SOURCE
Original article prepared for this volume.
Acknowledgement: The authors wish to acknowledge the help of the following persons who criticized earlier drafts: Richard L. Bushman, Gene W. Dalten, Donald E. Gelfand, T. Allen Lambert, and Peter Johnston.

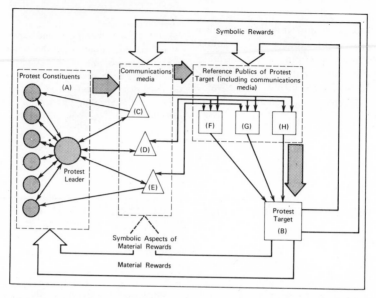

half of the nineteenth century. During the 1820's Joseph Smith, an uneducated but sensitive Vermont-born farm youth, purportedly received visitations from heavenly beings and translated from gold plates a six-hundred page record of the ancient inhabitants of the Americas called the Book of Mormon. His prophetic powers were accepted by a small group of relatives and friends and, on April 6, 1830, in Fayette, Seneca County, New York, the Church of Jesus Christ of Latter-day Saints was organized" (Arrington, 1958: 2). As a religion it contained several elements common to that time and place—a feeling that the millenium was imminent and a tendency to expect the intervention of heavenly forces to bring about the rapid, apolcalyptic triumph of the Kingdom of God on earth. One of the Church's earliest teachings called on the "pure in heart" to gather out of the world to "Zion" where "God's people" would build the kingdom and prepare for the millenium.

As new converts joined the Church they were instructed by their leaders to "gather" to the various sites where the Church was currently building its communities—Kirtland,

Ohio, Jackson County and Far West, Missouri, and Nauvoo, Illinois (Figure 2). Although the establishment of separate communities symbolized their withdrawal from the secular world, the Mormons at the same time attempted to remain within the political structure of the American federal system.

"The simultaneity of withdrawal from and participation in the larger secular community did not . . . prove workable. The presence of an exclusive body convinced of its own unique role in relation to the region—to wit, to make it a holy city for itself—with its own distinctive beliefs and ethic, resulted inevitably in intergroup conflict. The result was the Saints' expulsion from Jackson County, the Mormon War at Far West, and the second war at Nauvoo" (O'Dea, 1957: 113).

JACKSON COUNTY—AN EMERGING SOCIETY OF MORMONS

Shortly after the establishment of the Church, it was "revealed" to Joseph Smith that "Zion" was to be established in Western Missouri. In August, 1831, Joseph Smith

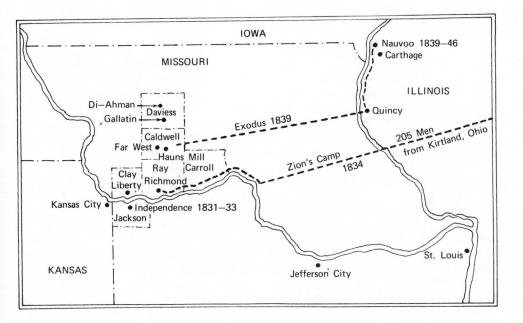

and several other leading members of the Church traveled from Kirtland, Ohio, to Jackson County, Missouri (near what is now Kansas City), where they designated the small frontier town of Independence as the site for the establishment of "Zion" or the "New Jerusalem." The members of the Church were instructed to begin purchasing land and settling in the area around Independence. Within a few months hundreds of converts, eager to establish themselves in the land of the New Jerusalem, were on the trail westward. So contagious was the movement to Zion, that within two years, twelve hundred Mormons would settle in Jackson County (Grant, 1955).

Jackson County, Missouri, was very sparsely settled in 1831 when the Latter-day Saints began pouring into that area. The established residents included slaveholders who had migrated from the mountainous parts of the southern states, a handful of trappers who used Independence as a rendezvous and outfitting post, a few itinerant ministers of various denominations, and refugees who had violated the laws elsewhere. B. H. Roberts (1930:Vol I, p. 260), a Mormon historian, describes the Mormons' reaction to their new surrounding in western Missouri.

"It was to them like some limitless paradise, these immense alternating stretches of open, rolling prairie and densely wooded water courses, as compared with the closed-in heavily wooded hill country from which they came. It would not be difficult to regard western Missouri in 1831 as a ·promised land ..."

Despite their positive expectations the

Mormons experienced the social conditions in western Missouri as a sharp contrast to their own New England cultural heritage. The profane, seemingly nonreligious life of the Missourians was forbidden to the Mormons who had been commanded to keep the Sabbath Day holy and to "keep themselves unspotted from the sins of the world." These divergent conceptions of moral and religious duty proved to be a source of irritation between the two groups. In addition the Missourians were seekers of office and the honors accompanying such positions and feared that the rapidly increasing Mormon population would soon take these offices away from them. All of these fears and irritations were further aggravated by the general suspicion and dislike that existed between people from slaveholding and free states during that period. The social relationship that developed between the Mormons and the Gentiles[2] in Missouri was characterized by a growing animosity and antagonism on matters of ideology and practice.

In July, 1833, the Missourians published their complaints and grievances in a document known as the "Manifesto" or "Secret Constitution." Four major points were outlined in the document: (1) the Missourians charged that the Mormons were trying to bring "free Negroes" into the state; (2) they feared that the Mormons were fast gaining the balance of power in elections; (3) the Missourians felt that the Mormons kept themselves too socially and religiously aloof from their neighbors; and (4) they accused the Mormons of teaching that they were the rightful owners of Jackson County. Furthermore, those who signed the document also pledged themselves to assist in removing the Mormons from Jack-

son County. "The signers believed an important crisis was at hand in their civil society, because a pretended religious sect— the 'Mormons' had settled in their midst" (Roberts, 1930: Vol. I, p. 324).

The publication of this document led to several specific episodes of conflict between the Mormons and Missourians in Jackson County that finally resulted in the Mormon minority being forced to leave their homes and move into an adjoining county. The first incident, as described by the Mormons, occurred in the spring of 1832 when ". . . in the deadly hours of the night, the houses of some of the saints were stoned, the windows broken, and the inmates disturbed" (Roberts, 1930: Vol. I, p. 323). This action against the Mormons was repeated again in the fall, when bands of horsemen rode through outlying districts, setting haystacks ablaze, smashing windows, shooting at homes, and threatening the owners.

The second instance of actual conflict between Mormons and Gentiles resulted from a series of misunderstandings concerning the status of "free Negroes" in the Church. The Missourians claimed that the newcomers, being nonslave holders, were deliberately attempting to free the slaves and make them equal to the whites. This dispute finally resulted in the destruction of the Mormon printing office and store on July 20, 1833. Roberts (1930:Vol I, pp. 332-333) dramatically describes the incident as follows:

". . . with demoniac yells the mob surrounded the printing office and home of W. W. Phelps. Mrs. Phelps, with a sick infant in her arms and the rest of the children, were forced out of their home, the furniture was thrown into the street and garden, the press was broken, the type pied; the revelations, book-work and papers were nearly all destroyed or kept by the mob; and the printing office and home of W. W. Phelps were both razed to the ground."

Moments afterwards, two church leaders

---

[2]For Mormons, the term "Gentile" is used in referring to all non-Mormons in much the same way that the term is used in general when referring to non-Jews.

were "stripped of their clothing, and be-daubed with tar, mixed with lime, or pearl-ash, or some other flesh-eating acid, and a quantity of feathers scattered over them."

Three days after the destruction of the printing press and the Phelps store, a band of five hundred men rode through town carrying a red flag denoting blood and death. At this time Mormon leaders were forced to enter into a treaty with mob leaders to leave Jackson County the following spring. Prior to this, the Mormon Saints had sent a written appeal to Governor Dunklin of Missouri. In his reply he had advised the Mormons to present their grievances to the courts of Independence and although this effort was made, it proved to be unsuccessful. In fact, according to Grant (1955:176), the Missourians did not even wait until spring but attacked the Mormons again on October 31.

"After the saints living on the Big Blue River had retired to bed, some fifty horsemen galloped furiously into the sleeping village, and with the aid of horses and ships, unroofed a dozen homes and seized the men and whipped them excessively. The lash of whips, the shouts of the mobbers, and the cry of the injured sent half-clad women and children scurrying into the darkness."

During the first two weeks of November, 1833, men, women, and children fled in confusion from their burning homes. "One company of one hundred and ninety—all women and children, except three decrepit old men—were driven thirty miles across a burnt prairie. The ground was thinly crusted with sleet, and the trails of these exiles were easily followed by blood which flowed from their lacerated feet" (Grant, 1955:177).

By the close of this third episode of conflict with the Gentiles, one man had been killed, several men had been wounded, 203 homes and one flour mill had been burned, and some twelve hundred Mormons had been driven northward to the bluffs of the Missouri River where they camped awaiting their turn to ferry across the river into Clay County.

When the Mormon Saints first arrived in Jackson County, they experienced considerable internal discord over religious ideology and economic practices among themselves. For example, during this period an attempt was made to implement the "law of consecration," a kind of frontier communal economic system. Initially, this caused a great deal of disagreement because of what many felt to be inequities in the way the system provided for the differing wants and needs of the members. But as their awareness of the social and cultural differences between them and the Missourians grew, they began to develop a conception of their own separateness and peculiar character. Their encounter with a hostile environment also served to strengthen the growing sense of collective identity among these individuals from diverse religious backgrounds who at that time had been members of the newly organized Mormon Church for less than two years.

Another direct consequence of the conflicts in Jackson County that turned out to be beneficial for the growth and development of the Mormon Church was the organization of the Zion's Camp. The camp, composed of 150-200 Mormon men, gathered at Kirtland, Ohio, in the spring of 1834 and marched as a group to assist the Mormon Saints gathered in Clay County, Missouri. After arriving, they reopened negotiations with Governor Dunklin asking him to fulfill his earlier promise to reinstate the exiled Mormons to their homes and properties in Jackson County. Although this proved to be a futile effort, the march of Zion's Camp did have a positive outcome for the Church. The difficulties and hardships encountered on the trip proved to be an invaluable source of experience and knowledge in organizing and sustaining the two great Mormon exoduses: first, the movement of twelve thousand people from Missouri to Illinois in 1839; and second, the journey of twenty thousand Mormons from Illinois to the Salt Lake Valley in 1846. In fact, the organization of the Church was expanded the following year and many of the men who had participated in Zion's camp were called to fill important leadership positions in the emerging Mormon society in Missouri.

FAR WEST–STRENGTHENING THE MORMON SOCIETY

In the spring of 1836, the residents of Clay County, where the Mormons had moved after leaving Jackson County, began to fear they were being engulfed and as a result called mass meetings and adopted resolutions demanding that the growing number of Mormons in their county move to another location.   To avoid any new conflicts with the Missourians, the Mormons secured and organized the northern half of Ray County into Caldwell County. Lands were purchased and the town of Far West, which was to become the principal settlement of the Mormons in upper Missouri, was established in the summer of 1836. In addition to the exiled Saints from Jackson County and new converts to the Church from Canada and the eastern states, many Church members from Kirtland began moving to Far West in 1837-38 when a banking endeavor sponsored by church leaders failed and left many of the Church members in that area in financial ruin.

Although it had been nearly a wilderness in 1836, by the fall of 1838 nearly five thousand Saints had settled in Caldwell County.

"At Far West, by that time there were one hundred and fifty houses, four dry goods stores, three family groceries, half a dozen blacksmith shops, a printing establishment and two hotels. A large and com-fortable school house had been built in 1836, and served also as church and court-house" (Grant, 1955:211).

As in the case of Jackson County, the increasing strength and unity of the Mormon community in Far West again aroused the suspicions and animosities of the older settlers in surrounding communities.   On July 4, 1838, in Far West, Sidney Rigdon, one of the two "counselors" to Joseph Smith, proclaimed what became known as the "Mormon Declaration of Independence."

"We are weary of being smitten, and tired of being trampled upon . . . from this day and this hour, we will suffer it no more. And that mob that comes on us to disturb us, it shall be between us and them a war of extermination; for we will follow them until the last drop of their blood is spilled; or else they will have to exterminate us, for we will carry the seat of war to their own houses and their own families, and one party or the other shall be utterly destroyed. Remember it then, all men. We will never be the aggressors, we will infringe on the rights of no people, but shall stand our own until death." *(Roberts, 1930: Vol. I, p. 441).*

Clearly, the Saints were assuming a strong defensive posture, one not previously characteristic of this group.   The Mormons now were prepared to organize troops and take up defensive positions against any outside contender.   Not long afterwards, the anticipations reflected in this declaration proved a reality.

A melee that broke out at an election held in Gallatin, Daviess County, on August 6, 1838, initiated a series of events leading up to what historians have referred to as the "Mormon War." W.P. Peniston, a candidate for the state legislature, had been active in removing the Saints from Clay County and fearing that the Mormons would not support him in the election, planned to prevent them from voting at all in Daviess County. Peniston was at the polls on election day, and warned that if the Mormons were allowed to vote the older settlers would soon lose their suffrage. In the midst of his harangue, a local resident assaulted one of the Mormons and in the fight that ensued, a number on both sides were bruised and injured, although no one was killed.

As a result of exaggerated reports about the Gallatin incident and other allegations concerning the subsequent activities of certain Mormon leaders, Governor Boggs issued an order on August 30 to raise and hold in readiness a militia force of 2,800 men. "...the recent civil disturbances in the counties of Caldwell, Daviess and Carroll are said to render the order necessary as a precautionary measure" (Roberts, 1930: Vol. I., p. 452). Once mobilized, groups from the militia began conducting raids against Mormon settlements in Daviess and Carroll Counties.

In the meantime most of the Saints had gathered into the towns of Di-Ahman and Far West and were preparing to defend themselves as best they could. A second incident occurred on October 25 at an encampment on the Crooked River outside Far West. After learning that a band of soldiers from the state militia had taken three Mormons prisoner, the Caldwell County judge in Far West ordered Colonel George Hinkle to raise a company of militia from among the Mormons to disperse the band of soldiers and rescue the prisoners. According to Roberts (1930: Vol. I., p. 475), a company of seventy-five men reached Crooked River at the break of day and dismounted some distance from the camp. They formed into three divisions and advanced.

"They encountered one of Bogart's picketmen who fired upon them, mortally wounding young Patrick O'Banion. Patten ordered a charge upon the enemy and the conflict was hand to hand. Bogart's forces broke and fled, leaving horses and camp equipment.

In the charge Captain Patten was mortally wounded, Gideon Carter instantly killed and nine others were wounded. Of the casualties in Bogart's forces the most reliable account fixes the number as one killed and six wounded."

When news of this skirmish reached Governor Boggs, he ordered the deployment of a large force of the state militia that had been mobilized earlier and on October 27 issued his so-called "Order of Extermination."

"The Mormons must be treated as enemies, and must be exterminated or driven from the state if necessary for the public peace—their outrages are beyond all description." (Roberts, 1930: Vol. I., p. 479).

The order was forwarded to General Lucas who as commander of the state militia began at once to coordinate the movement of the various militia companies in the surrounding counties into position around the main Mormon communities of Far West and Di-Ahman. Enroute several companies of the state militia attacked a small Mormon settlement at Haun's Mill killing 15 persons and wounding 17 others. The "Mormon War" had begun.

On the afternoon of October 30, large forces of militia were approaching Far West. During the evening the local Mormon militia of Caldwell County numbering between six and eight hundred formed into a line just south of the city to oppose the advance of much larger state militia. Both parties sent out a flag of truce, under which representatives of the respective sides met. In order to avoid a losing battle, the officer representing the Mormons agreed to deliver several church leaders to the state militia as hostages and to surrender the weapons of the militia in Far West. Although the so-called "Mormon War" ended without a major battle being fought, the Governor's order to remove the Mormons from the state remained to be executed. Under the pretext of searching for arms, the state militia then ransacked most of the houses in Far West and in the process destroyed a large amount of property and shot many cattle. About eight more men were taken as hostages, and the remaining Saints were ordered to leave the state as soon as possible.

Shortly afterwards, Joseph Smith and several other Church leaders were imprisoned at Liberty, Clay County, while the rest of the Saints prepared to leave Missouri. Once more these people were driven from their homes and forced to leave all they had created and developed. Between twelve and fifteen thousand Mormon Saints were involved in the exodus under the leadership of Brigham Young. Throughout the winter and spring of 1838-39, wagons carried whatever was moveable and the Mormons made their way eastward about 200 miles and crossed the Mississippi River into the State of Illinois. Crosby Johnson in his *History of Caldwell County*, depicts the adverse conditions of the expulsion:

". . . the old and young, the sick and feeble, delicate women and suckling children, almost without food and without clothing were compelled to abandon their homes. . . farms were sold for a yoke of oxen, an old wagon or anything that would furnish means of transportation. Many of the poorer classes were compelled to walk" (Grant, 1955:248).

In spite of their feelings of rage and bitterness at the injustice received at the hands of the state officials and the people of Missouri, the embattled Saints now possessed a mission and a social structure that would remain intact. "Stakes of Zion" had been established and laid out according to revelations received by the Prophet Joseph Smith. By April, 1838, a name had been given to the Church and the quorum of Twelve Apostles and the first quorum of Seventy had been established. The principles and ordinances of the Church had been published in what was known as the "Doctrine and Covenants" and the "Law of Tithing" had been instituted among the general church membership in July, 1838, to provide economic stability and replace the "frontier communial" system. What was once an "emerging society" of Mormons was now an established group with their own system of government and a determination to set up the Kingdom of God.

The struggles at Far West had confirmed the Saints' loyalty and solidarity that together with their shared beliefs and social organization gave them the strength and unity to overcome the overwhelming problems involved in relocating a community of fifteen thousand people.

"To themselves they were chosen in these last days in a new and everlasting covenant, while to nonmembers they appeared a misled, deluded little band" (O'Dea, 1957: 48).

Again, the Mormons persisted in the midst of conflict. As Johnson states: " . . . their trials and sufferings instead of dampening the ardor of the Saints, increased in ten fold. 'The blood of the martyrs became the seed of the church'" (Grant, 1955: 248). Exiled from Missouri, they fled east to Illinois and in a wilderness on the banks of the Mississippi began building a new city — Nauvoo.

NAUVOO—BECOMING A PEOPLE

A direct consequence of the conflicts in Missouri was the establishment of a semi-independent system of local government in Nauvoo. In December, 1840, the state of Illinois, with Stephen A. Douglas as Secretary of State and Abraham Lincoln as an influential member of the legislature, incorporated the city of Nauvoo and granted the most liberal charter ever given to an American City.

"The experiences of the Missouri persecutions . . . taught the Mormons that they needed

new means to guarantee the safety and integrity of the Kingdom. The Nauvoo Charter was the result" *(Flanders, 1965: 284).*

As Joseph Smith later commented, "I concocted it for the salvation of the church, and on principles so broad that every honest man might dwell secure under its protecting influence, without distinction of sect or party" (Smith, 1949: 249). The Nauvoo Charter not only provided for the establishment of the city government and municipal courts, but also for the establishment of a university within the city and the organization of an independent military body to be called the Nauvoo Legion.

"Joseph Smith and the Mormons realized that security lay in power and a peculiar group like this could not safely rely on tolerance. He recognized that their beliefs, ideals, as well as their activities and ambitions, were bound inevitably to arouse suspicion and hostility. Power meant politics and armed force, and the saints now went after both" *(O'Dea, 1957: 51).*

The period from 1841 to the early months of 1844 was one of rapid growth and prosperity for the Church in Nauvoo, Not only was the city the gathering place for the majority of exiles from Missouri, but it was also the destination of converts to the Church migrating from eastern states and foreign lands. By 1844, the population of Nauvoo alone was estimated to be approximately 14,000.

In spite of the strong unity and cohesion experienced by the majority of Saints in Nauvoo, internal strife and dissension were always a potential threat to the Mormons. In the spring, of 1844, disputes over the practice of plural marriage culminated in repudiation of several men who at one time had occupied high positions in the church organization. A few of these men who joined together in a conspiracy to overthrow Joseph Smith and the established church leadership

are reported to have taken the following oath:

"You solemnly swear, before God and all holy angels, and these your brethern by whom you are surrounded that you shall give your life, your liberty, your influence, your all, for the destruction of Joseph Smith and his party, so help me God." *(Smith, 1950: 364-365).*

In an effort to accomplish their purpose, they imported a press into the city and proposed publishing a newspaper to be called the *Nauvoo Expositer.* In its prospectus the following objectives were announced: (1) to persuade the State Legislature to repeal the Nauvoo Charter; (2) to break up the power of the Church at Nauvoo; (3) to prevent the Mormon leaders from holding civil offices; and (4) to expose the Mormons to the world. (Smith, 1950: 443-444). After its first issue was published on June 7, 1844, the city council, under authority of the Nauvoo Charter, determined that the press should be destroyed. As soon as the press had been dismantled, Sheriff Bettisworth from Carthage issued a warrant for the arrest of those persons who attacked and destroyed the press and *Expositor* office.

The destruction of the *Expositor* press stimulated and provoked renewed conflict between the Mormons and the surrounding Gentile community. By this time, the Mormons' strength in Nauvoo was becoming evident through their military independence and their strategic role in state politics. As a result, persecution and violence from without again threatened the Saints.

Several events preceded the actions that finally forced the Mormons to leave Illinois. On June 21, 1844, messengers arrived in Nauvoo with a letter from Governor Ford, addressed to General Joseph Smith, Mayor of Nauvoo City. In the letter was a demand from Governor Ford that "well informed and discrete persons" be sent to Carthage at once to explain fully the destruction of the *Nauvoo Expositor.* After an exchange of correspondence, the Prophet with his brother and several friends finally submitted themselves to stand trial at Carthage. Upon presenting themselves for arrest and trial, Joseph Smith and those with him were freed on bail. Learning that the Prophet was out on bail, the leaders of the hostile forces secured what the Mormons considered false papers and again arrested Joseph and Hyrum Smith.

While the Prophet was imprisoned in the jail at Carthage, several threats to destroy Nauvoo were made. In his *History of Illinois,* Governor Ford writes:

"The force assembled at Carthage amounted to about twelve or thirteen hundred men, and it was calculated that four or five hundred more were assembled at Warsaw. Nearly all that portion resident in Hancock County were anxious to be marched into Nauvoo, Occasional threats came to my ears of destroying the city and murdering or expelling the inhabitants" (Roberts, 1930: Vol. II, p. 274).

On the afternoon of June 27, 1844, a hostile band of about 150 men attacked the Carthage jail and killed Joseph Smith and his brother Hyrum. On that same day, Governor Ford and his staff were in Nauvoo publicly warning the Saints about the threats they had heard. Following the burial of Joseph and Hyrum Smith and after lengthly discussions and special meetings, Brigham Young was chosen to succeed Joseph Smith as the prophet and president of the Church.

The event that removed the Saints last hope of survival in Illinois came in January 1845, when the Illinois legislature repealed the Nauvoo Charter. This action forced the Mormon Saints to operate under their church in lieu of the city government. During this time, the residents of the city continued the construction of the Nauvoo Temple that was completed on May 24, 1845. Seeing what appeared to be the continued prosperity of

Nauvoo, anti-Mormon forces began attacking the homes and farms of the Saints all over the southwestern portion of the country around Nauvoo.

In early September, 1845, anti-Mormons met near "Morley Settlement" to make plans for getting rid of the Mormons living there. Governor Ford speaking of this occasion said:

"In the fall of 1845, the anti-Mormons of Lima and Green Plains, held a meeting to devise means for the expulsion of the Mormons from the neighborhood. They appointed some persons of their own number to fire a few shots at the house where they were associated; but to do it in such a way as to hurt none who attended the meeting. The meeting was held, the house was fired at, but so as to hurt no one; and the anti-Mormons suddenly breaking up their meeting, rode all over the county spreading the dire alarm, that the Mormons had commenced the work of massacre and death" (Roberts 1930; Vol. II, p. 474).

On the evening of September 11, 1845, these same anti-Mormons attacked the Morley Settlement. Twenty-nine houses were burned, and their occupants were driven into the fields where the men, women, and children lay drenched in the rain throughout the night.

Shortly afterwards, the *Quincy Whig* published the following warning:

"It is a settled thing that the public sentiment of the State is against the Mormons, and it will be vain for them to contend against it; and to prevent bloodshed and the sacrifice of many lives on both sides, it is their duty to obey the public will, and leave the state as speedily as possible. That they will do this we will have a confident hope—and that too, before the last extreme is resorted to— that of force" (Roberts, 1930: Vol. II, p. 504).

The Mormons agreed to leave, but in spite

of Brigham Young's promise that "we will leave this country next spring," Mormon men and boys were often attacked and whipped while gathering their crops, and many of the oxen and horses that the Saints had secured to aid them on their journey westward were stolen.

During the winter every available building in Nauvoo was turned into a workshop. Governor Ford describes the preparations:

"During the winter of 1845-46 the Mormons made the most prodigious preparations for removal. All the houses in Nauvoo ... were converted into workshops; and before spring more than twelve hundred wagons were in readiness. The people from all parts of the county flocked to Nauvoo to purchase houses and farms, which were sold extremely low, lower then the prices at a sheriff's sale, for money, wagons, horses, oxen, cattle and other articles of personal property, which might be needed by the Mormons in their exodus into the wilderness" (Roberts, 1930: Vol. II, p. 536.)

But the pressure continued. Armed mobs threatened the lives of the people, and finally, in February, 1846, while it was still winter, 16,000 Mormons evacuated the city of Nauvoo, crossing the Mississippi River on the ice and in ferries.

Although the Mormon Saints left their homes in Nuavoo with a knowledge of their ultimate destination and the magnitude of the task before them—a journey of 1200 miles on foot and the settlement of an unknown wilderness, they faced this prospect with a faith and confidence in their ability to deal with adversity and hardship. The years of suffering and persecution in Missouri and Illinois had not only strengthened their religious identity and social unity, but it had also resulted in the creation of a distinctive Mormon culture.

"They had a tradition—a legend preserving past heroism and nurturing future hopes—

that had been inscribed upon their hearts in letters of fire. Religious peculiarity had been confirmed, and what had at first been a scriptural idea and a convert's wish was now transformed into a fundamental world view permeating their consciousness and making them not just a church but a people (O'Dea, 1957: p. 75).

CONCLUSION

As Coser (1956) mentions, intergroup conflict can serve at least two positive functions: (1) the maintenance of group identity and boundaries; and (2) the strengthening of group unity and cohesion. It is argued that this kind of conflict makes members more conscious of group bonds, increases participation, leads to mobilization of group energies, group defenses, and a reaffirmation to their own social system. The extended conflict experienced by the Mormons in Missouri and Illinois from 1831-1846 accomplished both of these functions. They became a centralized corporate sect, a tightly knit cohesive society with strong central direction; they achieved a distinct political separation, and a consciousness whereby members were expected to contribute time, means, and loyalty to group enterprizes. Dissenters placed their fellowship in jeopardy and were often left behind as the Mormons moved throughout Missouri and Illinois. In Jackson County, a Mormon identity evolved as the Saints recognized differences between themselves and the Missouri settlers. As their awareness of these differences grew, they began to develop a feeling of separateness that was interpreted by the Missourians as aloofness and that became a source of hostility and persecution. As the Saints turned inward to defend themselves, group boundaries were delineated and a unique Mormon society began to emerge.

However, it was not until Far West that the

Mormons experienced a real sense of strength and unity as a separate collectivity. "Stakes of Zion" were established, beliefs and doctrines were published, an official name was given to the Church, priesthood quorums were organized, and the economic system of "tithing" was instituted. What was once an "emerging society" was now an established organization with its own unique social structure and system of government. The conflicts at Far West increaced the solidarity of the Saints and gave them the strength and unity to face the difficulties of building a new city.

In Nauvoo, the Mormons established a comprehensive system of local government with its own military establishment that was largely free from outside interference. However, the rapid growth of the Church in Nauvoo and its expanding influence in state politics were viewed as a threat by the surrounding communities that eventually led to the assassination of Joseph Smith and the Saints being forced to abandon their homes. By the time they left Nauvoo, the years of suffering and hardship had transformed the Mormons from a religious collectivity into a distinct people with a tradition and a culture.

LOOKING TO THE FUTURE

The Mormon Church has frequently been cited as being one of the most rapidly growing churches in the world. From its inception in upstate New York in 1830, the Mormons have maintained themselves as a separate and distinct religious community while at the same time remaining an integral part of American society. Today Mormons are perhaps the clearest example in our national history of a "native and ethnic" religious minority. However, their distinctiveness comes not from the fact that they have a unique socioeconomic system, not from the "Book of Mormon" that purports to contain

an historical account of the American Indian, not from their belief in powers of revelation, nor even from their claim of a restoration of primitive Christianity but most of all, their distinctiveness comes from the capacity to transform the crisis situations that all sects have known into an enduring program of social organization. In contrasting Mormons with other religious sects, De Pillis (1966: 93) has recently commented on this unique characteristic of Mormonism.

Consider the fate of its contemporaries, Campbellism and Shakerism, the one with practically nothing left of its original distinctiveness, the other with practically nothing left in membership. Christian Science has shown an ability to survive, but its distinctiveness is quite diluted because it did not, like Protestantism, Judaism, Catholicism—and Mormonism—create a distinctive culture.

Although its influence on American culture has been minor when compared with the impact of the three major religions, Mormonism is one of the largest religions in the United States associated with a particular socioeconomic community (although an ethnic group that comes close to it is the Black Muslims). In spite of its minority status, the Mormon Church in the past decade has continued to expand into a world wide organization.

As in the 1800s, the Mormon Church in the years ahead is again likely to confront disparities between its unique culture and system of government and the predominant culture and society in which its members reside. However, in contrast to that earlier period the prevailing conditions in the latter part of this century suggest new and different issues around which Mormon-Gentile conflicts may arise—population control, civil rights, increased church growth, decentralization, and the "Mormonization" of foreign cultures. Although the Mormon exoduses from Missouri and Illinois provided an effective mechanism for insulating the Church from conflict situations in the 1800s, such an alternative today is impossible as the global village "fills up" not only in India and China, but also here in the United States, which has heretofore considered itself as possessing a limitless frontier.[3] The question now for what some have described as the "Mormon Empire" is what new alternatives are available. Will these eventual conflicts serve to undermine and weaken the Mormon people, or as history illustrates, serve to strengthen and unite them even more?

BIBLIOGRAPHY

ANDERSON, N.
  1942 *Desert saints: the Mormon frontier in Utah.* Chicago, University of Chicago Press.

ARRINGTON, L. J.
  1958 *Great basin kingdom: an economic history of the Latter-day Saints 1830-1900.* Cambridge, Mass.: Harvard University Press.

BERNARD, JESSIE
  1965 Some current conceptualizations in the field of conflict. *American Journal of Sociology,* **60**, 442-454.

BERRETT, W. E. and A. P. BURTON
  1955 *Readings in L. D. S. church history.* Vol. II. Salt Lake City, Utah: Deseret Book Company.

BUSHMAN, R. L.
  1960 Mormon persecutions in Missouri, 1833. *Brigham Young University Studies,* **3,** 11-20.

CLEBSCH, W.A.
  1966 Each sect the sect to end all sects. *Dialogue: A Journal of Mormon Thought,* **1** (2), 84-89.

COOLEY, C. H.
  1909 *Social organization.* New York: Schocken.

COSER, L. A.
  1956 *The functions of social conflict.* New York: Free Press.

COSER, L. A.
  1962 *Continuities in the study of social conflict.* New York: The Free Press.

DAVIS, D. B.
  1960 Some themes of counter-subversion: an analysis of anti-Masonic, anti-Catholic, and anti-Mormon literature. *Mississippi Valley Historical Review,* **47,** 205-224.

DAVIS INEZ SMITH.
  1943 *The story of the church.* Independence, Mo.: Harold Publishing House.

DEPILLIS, M. S.
  1966 Mormonism and the American way. *Dialogue: A Journal of Mormon Thought,* **1** (2), 89-97.

The doctrine and covenants of the Church of Jesus Christ of Latter-day Saints.
  1962 Salt Lake City, Utah: The Church of Jesus Christ of Latter-day Saints.

EVANS, J. H.
  1946 *Joseph Smith: an American prophet.* New York: Macmillan.

FLANDERS, R. B.

---

[3]It should be noted, however, that the Mormons may still be considering a form of isolation in the sense that they claim during the second coming of Christ they will retreat again to Missouri and separate themselves, their social system, and their economic structure from outside governments. Once this is accomplished they hope to have influence in outside society not as an isolate but as a social order amidst general social disorganization.

1965 *Nauvoo: kingdom on the Mississippi* Urbana, Ill.: University of Illinois Press.

GOULDNER, A. W.
1970 *The coming crisis of Western sociology.* New York: Basic Books.

GRANT, C. E.
·1955 *The Kingdom of God restored.* Salt Lake City, Utah: Deseret Book Company.

LINN, W. A.
1923 *The story of the Mormons.* New York: Macmillan.

McGAVIN, C.
1946 *Nauvoo the beautiful.* Salt Lake City, Utah: Stevens and Wallis.

O'DEA, T. F.
1957 *The Mormons.* Chicago: The University of Chicago Press.

PARSONS, T.
1951 *The social system. New York: Free Press.*

ROBERTS, B. H.
1930 *A comprehensive history of the Church of Jesus Christ of Latter-day Saints.* Vol. I, II.   Salt Lake City, Utah: Deseret News Press.

SIMMEL, G.
1955 *Conflict.* New York: Free Press

SMITH, J.
1949 *History of the Church of Jesus Christ of Latter-day Saints.* Salt Lake City, Utah: Deseret News Press.

SMITH, J. F.
1950 *Essentials in church history.* Salt Lake City, Utah: Deseret News Press.

TAPPEN, P. W.
1945 The Mormons: legal constraints of a minority, *Journal of Legal and Political Sociology,* **4,** 77-91.

WEST, R. D.
1957 *Kingdom of the saints.* New York: Viking.

3   NEGRO-JEWISH CONFLICT IN NEW YORK CITY
A SOCIOLOGICAL EVALUATION

Herbert J. Gans

"Succession" has been a major concept in analysis of ethnic relations. Gans utilizes it to place recent conflicts between blacks and Jews in a sociological perspective. He argues that Jews, prominent in positions as teachers and white-collar workers, are seen by blacks as barriers in their attempts to achieve upward mobility. The inability of blacks to "succeed" Jews in these positions has exacerbated hostility and conflict between blacks and Jews.

I

The conflicts between black advocates of local control and Jewish teachers during the school strikes, the anti-Semitic outbursts of various black militants, and the

SOURCE

From *Midstream: A Monthly Jewish Review,* **Vol. 15, no. 3, March, 1969. Reprinted by permission of the author and** *Midstream.*

angry counter-reactions by Jewish leaders and citizens are generally thought to have ended the once seemingly peaceful relationship between Negroes and Jews in New York City. There is no doubt that new tensions have developed in recent months, of course, but instead of dwelling on these—or on further exegeses of public statements to determine whether the Ocean Hill-Brownsville Governing Board is anti-Semitic or the United Federation of Teachers racist—it is more useful to look at the Negro-Jewish relationship from a longer sociological perspective. From that perspective, the recent incidents are only more visible instances in a long series of primarily economic conflicts between blacks, Jews (and other ethnic groups) which are endemic to New York and to several other large American cities, and which can only be dealt with through economic solutions.

To a considerable extent, these conflicts have been about what sociologists call *succession,* the process by which members of one ethnic or racial group (the departing group) move up a notch on the socioeconomic ladder and are succeeded in their old position by a less affluent group (the successors). The history of professional boxing, an occupation of low status and uncertain reward, offers a typical example of the process. The initial American pugilists were mainly poor white Protestants, who were succeeded first by Central Europeans, then by a predominantly Irish contingent, then by Italians, and some Jews, and since World War II, by Negroes, Puerto Ricans and other Latins, as young men in each of the earlier groups found more secure and respectable jobs.

In this instance, the succession process has been tranquil, but conflict can develop, especially if the departing group is not leaving quickly enough to make room for the successors. When the economy is not expanding sufficiently or when the departing group lacks the skill or inclination to take better jobs, large remnants will stay put and block the upward move of the successors. Thus, the underworld went through the succession process from Protestant to Irish to Italian and Jewish, but while most Jews departed two generations ago, many Italians did not, preventing the entry of Negroes and others. Similarly, when the Jewish captains of the New York City Police Department thought the time had come for one of their men to head the department, the Irish portion of the force put its foot down, and Irish commissioner was brought in from Philadelphia.

It should be emphasized that succession is neither automatic, universal, nor inevitable. Sometimes a poor group will remain in an occupation because it is unable or unwilling to depart or because no successors are knocking at the door. As a result, the Chinese still dominate New York's hand laundries. Moreover, all departing groups try to hold on to the most profitable sources of income in the old occupation. Thus, New York's slums were originally owned and managed by WASPs, but while they eventually passed into ethnic hands, the mortgages are often still held by WASP-run institutions. And because of racial discrimination, Negroes have usually been excluded from succession until the courts have stepped in. In fact, the only jobs which blacks have been able to enter and to move up in relatively freely from the lowest-paid levels are in government, where civil service has, with some notable exceptions, allowed them to compete on the basis of skill.

II

In American cities, the succession process has generally reflected the order in which ethnic and racial groups have arrived in the city, and the succession from English Protestants to Northern European Protestants and

Catholics to Irish to Italians and Jews (and Greeks and Poles, etc.) to Negroes tions—except that Negroes have often been pushed out of jobs by new white immigrants. In New York, the succession relationship between Jews and Negroes, and more recently Puerto Ricans, has been particularly close, if only because the three groups constitute a major portion of the city's population. Although good data on ethnic succession is scarce, it seems clear that as Jews moved up the economic ladder, their places were often taken by blacks and Puerto Ricans with many Jews holding on to the more profitable sources of income in the occupations from which they departed. For example, Puerto Ricans and blacks now hold many of the low-wage jobs in the garment industry, while Jews have kept many ownership and managerial posts as well as union officerships. (Several generations earlier, German Jews had been the owners and managers of garment industry firms until they were succeeded by Eastern Europeans.)

Similarly, when the Jews moved out of the slum neighborhoods in which they began life in America, they were frequently succeeded by Negroes, but retained ownership of many tenements and stores in these areas. For example, a recent study by Hunter College Professor Naomi Levine showed that 37 per cent of the stores in a 20 block area of Central Harlem were owned by whites, and 80 per cent of these, by Jews.* Since the study limited itself to "neighborhood stores" and excluded the large shops on 125th Street and other major business streets, it underestimates the proportion of Jewish ownership however. This is suggested by the report of a 1968 Mayor's Task Force which showed that 47 percent of *all* stores in Central Harlem are owned by white.** (Negro ownership is concentrated in service establishments, particularly barbershops and beauty shops, dry cleaning stores and restaurants; whites, however, own 74 per cent of the food stores, 72 per cent of the apparel stores, 89 per cent of the hardware, furniture and appliance stores, and over 60 per cent of liquor and drug stores.) Assuming that clothing stores in Harlem are, as they are everywhere else, more likely to be owned by Jews than by other whites, the Task Force Report data would suggest that Jews own at least two-thirds of these stores. Consequently, if the results of the Levine study are extrapolated to all of Harlem, it seems likely that Jews own about 40 per cent of the stores—*as many as* 40 per cent, or *only* 40 per cent, depending on one's values. This figure is similar to a Kerner Commission study of 15 cities which found that 39 per cent of the ghetto storeowners were Jewish.*** Moreover, although most Harlem stores, white or black owned, are small, the Task Force study indicated that whites owned the larger stores, and concluded that "non-whites would be shown to own about 10 per cent of less of the capital invested in the community. A similar pattern would also be obtained if a comparison of gross sales were to be made."****

Beginning with the Depression, Negroes often became clients of Jewish professionals, for at that time Jews began to find jobs in the public schools and in the social work agencies. Today, it is estimated that about 60 per cent of New York City's school teachers are Jews. They came into "munici-

---

*Naomi Levine, "Who Owns the Stores in Harlem?" *Congress Bi-Weekly,* September 11, 1968, pp. 10-12.

**The Mayor's Task Force Report on the Economic Redevelopment of Harlem,* January 15, 1968, Table IV-3.

***Supplemental Studies for the National Advisory Commission on Civil Disorders,* July 1968, p. 126.

****Mayor's Task Force Report, p. IV-17.

pal professions" during the 1930's partly because of the workings of the succession process, the Jews replacing the Irish who had previously dominated the school system, and partly because jobs were now scarce in the private professions. For example, a number of Jewish men who had planned to become lawyers joined the Police Department in the Depression, and today they account for some of the high-ranking Jews on the force.

During the prosperous years after World War II, many—but not all—Jews continued to move up in the economic hierarchy, and today young Jews rarely replace their parents as slum storeowners, tenement managers or cabbies. Blacks (and Puerto Ricans) are succeeding to many of the jobs now being given up by Jews. For example, Levine found that among Harlem stores in business from 5 to 10 years, two-thirds were Negro owned. While the *number* of black owners, white collar workers and professionals is still far too low, the *rate of growth* of Negro white collar and professional employment in the country is now higher than among whites.

Jews continue to enter public school teaching, however, at least in New York. A generation ago, the city still had sizeable Jewish blue collar and poor white collar worker populations and their children presumably saw teaching as an attractive opportunity for upward mobility. Although the one available study showed that the proportion of Jews among teachers entering the city's public schools declined in 1960 after a peak in 1950, the percentage of Jews among the 1960 entrants was still 59 per cent.*

For many of New York's poor blacks, then, a large proportion of regular economic and professional contacts—as employees, tenants, customers and clients—are with whites, and although no conclusive figures are available, it seems likely that more of these contacts—but by no means all, as some black militants suggest—are with Jews than with other ethnics. Consequently, when blacks seek to obtain better jobs, the succession process frequently involves Jews, just as generations earlier, Jews competed with other ethnic groups for better jobs.

The reason for this Negro—Jewish relationship, and for the lesser economic involvement of blacks with the Irish, Italians, and other ethnics is a by-product of rapid Jewish upward mobility. Jews moved into white collar and professional jobs, and into ownership of factories and stores more quickly than other ethnics, so that they not only hired more employees, but were less likely to find fellow-Jews, at least for the low-wage jobs. In recent decades, they seem to have hired blacks and Puerto Ricans more often than Irish or Italian workers, partly because they were easier to hire, but perhaps also because Jews always discriminated less against them than did other whites. Moreover, Jews left the slums more quickly than the other ethnics, so that at the time when most Irish, Italians, Poles, Hungarians, etc., were still too poor to move to middle class neighborhoods, Negroes could often find housing only in a Jewish neighborhood in which an exodus was taking place. Thus, Negroes replaced the Jews in Central Harlem, and today they and Puerto Ricans are replacing them on the Upper West Side, in Washington Heights, the South Bronx, the

_____

*The study, based on judgments about religion from names on lists of entering teachers, showed that in 1920, Jews made up 26 per cent of entrants. The percentage rose to 44 in 1930; 56 in 1940; and 65 in 1950. (Stephen Cole, "The Unionization of Teachers," *Sociology of Education*, Vol. 41, Winter

1968, Table 13, p. 85.) Needless to say, findings gathered by judging names are not very reliable, but this method tends to underestimate the number of Jews because of the 2nd and 3rd generation tendency to Americanize Jewish sounding names.

Grand Concourse and elsewhere.

While the Negro—Jewish relationship may have appeared to be peaceful in the past, it has always been tense below the surface, at least in the slums. Owners of tenements and stores, whatever their race and religion, often exploit the slum dwellers, whatever *their* race and religion, if not always intentionally. The poor pay more, partly because insurance rates and other costs of doing business are higher in the slums, and partly because they are a captive market, particularly when they are segregated. Frequently, the poor also suffer in their contacts with professionals, for when ghetto schools are inadequate and welfare payments insufficient, the professionals cannot help their clients very much. Also, some professionals are trained only to work with middle class clients—or with poor people who have taken on middle class ways. When the poor do not behave in these ways, and professionals find that their techniques of teaching or counseling do not work, they may "put down" their poor clients, often without being aware of doing so.

The tension in Negro—Jewish relations is probably heightened because the majority of Jews whom blacks (and Puerto Ricans) deal with are of middle age, and many of the businessmen among them are engaged in small or declining enterprises. Thus, the Kerner Commission study cited previously reported that "our typical merchant was a man about fifty years old with a high school education, . . . most likely Jewish [and] if he belonged to any group or organizations, he belonged to only one." Such businessmen and perhaps even the professionals are the remaining lower-middle class members of an ethnic group which is rapidly becoming upper-middle class in its choice of occupations. Many Jews who work in the ghetto therefore are, or feel they are, being left behind in the mobility race, and such feelings do not foster tolerance or empathy with the problems of a poor population. The lack of empathy often develops into hostility as militants demand that blacks be allowed to move up in the succession process and to take over the ghetto properties and positions held by Jews and other whites.

III

Although the current tensions in the Negro-Jewish relationship are to some extent instances of the "normal" (historically speaking) conflict between the remnants of a departing groups and the upwardly mobile successors, some new elements have also changed the nature of the succession process, and are now overturning all kinds of historical precedents.

We have long known that the succession process has broken down at the bottom of the economic ladder, for the unskilled jobs by which European immigrants made their way into the main-stream are not as often available for the rural in-migrants, black and white, who have come to the city in the last two decades. The process seems to be breaking down at higher economic levels as well, however, for in these days of chain stores and corporate mergers, it is more difficult than ever to become a store owner or small entrepreneur. Some children of blue-collar workers cannot move out of the working class because they failed to obtain the schooling or diplomas now required for white collar jobs, and as automation proceeds, it is not at all clear whether the supply of technical and semi-professional jobs will be sufficient for the millions currently attending college. And now as in the past, the succession process is complicated by both blue and white collar workers who, satisfied with their jobs, do not want to move up to a higher status, thus blocking the way of their successors.

At the same time, many yound blacks —although not as many as fearful whites think—are less willing than their parents to repeat the traditionally slow, step-by-step climb up the economic ladder. Having been held back by discrimination for so long, they are now asking that they be allowed to succeed to the profitable or prestigious jobs which whites have not been willing to give up. For example, Negroes employed in the Italian-dominated numbers game of New York have demanded, without much success so far, that they be given their fair share of the better jobs, and black as well as Puerto Rican teachers are demanding principalships in the city school system. In cities all over the country, upwardly mobile elements in the black community are demanding more jobs as teachers (in New York City, only about 10 per cent of teachers are black or Latin), college professors—and students—policemen and firemen, anti-poverty officials, and in other municipal and public service positions.

To achieve these demands, the organized ghetto and its mobile young leaders are turning to political means for speeding up the succession process. As a result, this process is now being politicized, making it more visible than it was in the private economic sphere, and more important, transforming succession conflicts into public issues. When Negroes fought for better jobs in the numbers racket, no one, other than the underworld or the ghetto, paid much attention, but the struggle between the teachers and the decentralized ghetto schools in a public conflict between organized groups, with government firmly in the middle and ultimately required to find a solution. The conflict thus becomes raw material for newspaper headlines and TV leads, which in turn draws in previously uninvolved citizens who then side with their own ethnic or racial group.

As a result, both sides in the school strikes employed the politically potent weapons of ethnic and racial loyalty to influence public opinion. Blacks who resent the Jewish role in the ghetto economy and the U.F.T.'s attacks on local control occasionally resorted to widely publicized outbursts against the Jews, Jewish teachers occasionally made less publicized anti-black remarks, and the U.F.T. appealed to New York Jewry for support by intimating that the anti-Jewish rhetoric of black militants constituted the re-emergence of organized anti-Semitism.

In the heat of political battle, each side saw its opponent as more cohesive and unified than it actually is. Thus, despite the union's efforts, many Jews and other whites began to believe that the entire ghetto was in favor of local control, whereas in reality, many blacks still believe strongly in the desirability of integration. Some black advocates of local control argued that all Jews were against them, when in fact the city's Jewish population is not homogeneous, and on this issue, as on others, was divided along class lines. Lower-middle class Jews seemed to be solidly behind the U.F.T., for while they had supported the civil rights movement in the past, they became edgy when Negroes began to ask for local control, and thus for some of their jobs, and properties as well. The latest phase of the succession process is threatening their income and status, making them react with the same "backlash" previously expressed by other ethnics of the same socio-economic level.

The smaller but influential upper-middle class Jewish population, the highly educated professionals, managers and intellectuals of Manhattan and the expensive suburbs who provided a significant proportion of the funds for the national civil rights movement seem to be more sympathetic to local control.* Since this population has little to

*An earlier and similar split between lower middle class and upper-middle class Jews over a New York City school issue, the attempt to pair schools in Queens, is described by Kurt Lang and Gladys Engel Lang, "Resistance to School Desegregation: A Case Study of Backlash among Jews," *Sociological Inquiry*, Vol. 35, Winter 1965, pp. 94-106.

fear—or to lose—from school decentralization, it has not responded to the U.F.T.'s appeals to fear of anti-Semitism, and this is presumably why major Jewish organizations dominated by upper-middle class Jews did not take a stand on the union cause.

Yet another change has taken place to increase the visibility and bitterness of succession conflict: the breakup of the traditional ethnic-Negro alliance in the Democratic party. Before the black community began to demand its rights of succession, the ethnics in the Democratic party were usually able to maintain their power by granting a few concessions to the ghetto or buying off its leaders. Today, however, as Negroes are seeking their fair share of public jobs and political power from the ethnics, the party has become a warring camp. Although it was bareable to preserve the traditional coalition in the last national election, at the local level, the party is split in almost every city. A Democratic mayor cannot continue to favor the ethnics without angering the ghetto, and he cannot often grant the demands of the blacks without enraging the ethnics.

In New York City, where the Democratic split and the availability of a liberal Republican candidate led to the election of John Lindsay, the black-ethnic conflict has moved beyond the confines of the Democratic party and thus into the public arena. Indeed, one of the major reasons for Lindsay's failure to settle the school strikes was his inability to use party loyalty as a tool in negotiating with the U.F.T. or with the ethnic labor unions in the Central Labor Board who stood behind the teacher's union.

IV

While anti-Semitism and anti-Negro prejudice were very visible in the school strikes, neither played a major causal role in the strikes, however. The strikes were, I believe,

largely an economic and political struggle over the succession process, and a class conflict, primarily over jobs, between the upwardly mobile black poor and a coalition of unions and other organizations representing white working class and lower-middle class New Yorkers, people who might be described as sub-affluent."

The U.F.T., which has always worked for the improvement of ghetto schools and even supports some form of decentralization, turned against local control the moment when Ocean Hill-Brownsville demanded the right to transfer or fire teachers, and to hire its own. The union seems to have reacted less against this demand than against an assumption about the future, that in a totally decentralized school system and with the proportion of Negroes in the city and in the public schools rising, many white teachers might someday find themselves rejected by black (or Puerto Rican) school districts. Indeed, the union membership perceived the strike as being concerned first and foremost with job security, and implicitly with the succession process, for as one much quoted union member put it, "We don't deny their equality but they shouldn't get it by pulling down others who have just come up."* The U.F.T.'s feelings about the future were shared by other predominantly white ethnic unions, for example, the electricians and plumbers who feared that under local control, their members would lose their jobs, not only in decentralized schools but also in the Model Cities programs and whatever other ghetto municipal programs might be decentralized in the years to come.

---

*The succession process was also alluded to in the recently controversial statement of the Metropolitan Museum's "Harlem on my Mind" catalogue. that "behind every hurdle that the Afro-American has yet to jump stands the Jew who has already cleared it." Needless to say, neither all Jews nor *the* Jew stand behind every hurdle, and if some Jews stand behind some hurdles, Jews also have some hurdles yet to clear.

Nevertheless, the contested issues are over the economic positions of the participants, not their ethnic characteristics. When Negroes express their anger in anti-Semitic terms, it is only because many of the whites who affect their lives are Jewish; if the ghetto storeowners, landlords and teachers were Chinese, Negro hostility would surely be anti-Chinese, Similarly, when Jews resort to overt racism, they do so primarily because they feel their economic and social position is threatened by blacks, just as they sometimes make racist remarks about "the goyim" when their economic progress is held back by non-Jews.

Still, ethnic and racial considerations have been raised, and therefore become part of the issue and even of the succession conflict. The fact is that the school strike was perceived as setting Jewish teachers against blacks, whereas neither the struggle of the Welfare Rights movement against the Department of Welfare, nor that of the ghetto against the Police Department has involved ethnic hostility. Of course, these municipal agencies are ethnically more heterogeneous; policemen these days are no longer just Irish and the department includes a sizeable proportion of Italians and even white Protestants. Moreover, it is entirely possible that if and when ghetto demands for decentralization extend to police and fire protection and garbage removal, and jobs will be at issue, the political rhetoric of the succession conflict will include anti-Irish and anti-Italian outbursts.

Why black leaders have so far resorted to public expressions of anti-Semitism while not deprecating the ethnic origins of policemen or social workers, at least in public, is probably a result of the greater ethnic homogeneity in the city's public schools. When this is combined with the large number of Jewish landlords and storeowners in the ghetto, racially hyper-conscious blacks may easily if inaccurately conclude that they are being held back by *the* Jews. Undoubted-

ly, some militant leaders believe this to be the case, while others are reflecting sentiments among their followers, making statements they do not believe but must make— or be replaced by other leaders. But then, leaders of every race, religion on political affiliation sometimes make statements they do not believe but which express the sentiments of their followers.

Some black leaders may also be reacting against the reduction of Jewish support that took place after the civil rights movement turned toward Black Power, for people are always angrier at rejections from old friends than from traditional enemies. It is unlikely, however, that the rank-and-file ghetto resident was disappointed; he has had little contact, after all, with the liberalism of organized Jewry, and the Jews he sees regularly often call him "the schwarze" behind his back. And finally, one cannot ignore the habitual anti-Semitism that exists within the Christian culture shared by Negroes.

Nevertheless, when all is said and done, the crucial issues are more economic than ethnic, and if these issues which are polarizing New York and much of American society generally are to be dealt with, it is high time to find appropriate solutions—and to refrain from the politics of ethnic and racial labeling.

The black militants who have resorted to anti-Semitic attacks should realize that they are criticizing practices which have nothing to do with ethnicity. However much some Jewish businessmen or professionals have exploited black customers and client Negroes in the same occupational position have done exactly the same—or worse, because usually their insurance rates and other costs of doing business are even higher. Moreover, black businessmen are often no more a part of the ghetto than whites; Levine found that only a little more than half of the black storeowners her students interviewed lived in Harlem. The militants must also understand that Jews, more than other whites, have supported not only integration but Black Power. But most important, the militants must realize that they are pursuing an immoral as well as dangerous tactics they fan the flames of anti-Semitism either in anger or to please their constituents, they will encourage the fascist and other anti-Semitic groups that still exist in America, who, if they obtain power, will deal as ruthlessly with blacks as with Jews.

Conversely, Jews should refrain from anti-black attacks, especially when they are really objecting to the militancy rather than the racial characteristics of their target. They should also beware of what Roy Innis has called "the double standard that characterizes much of the dialogue on black anti-Semitism." As he points out, and rightly so, Jews can and have criticized black leaders, especially those considered to be militant or nationalistic, with impunity. If a Jewish organization issues a statement tomorrow harshly criticizing a black leader, it will not be accused of anti-black sentiments. But let a black leader criticize Israel or a Jewish group, and he automatically becomes anti-Semitic."

At the same time, Jews should be careful not to over-react, and to interpret all attacks on them as instances of one undifferentiated entity called anti-Semitism. There is a difference of degree between attacks on Jewish individuals and on the Jews as a group, and a difference in quality between attacks on Jews who behave unethically as businessmen, professionals or politicians, and attacks on Jews as persons. There are also differences in the content of the attacks; describing Jews as greedy is a calumny; calling them clannish is closer to the truth—and a truth that is celebrated by Jews themselves when the word cohesive is substituted.

Attacks on the Jews as a group, on behavior that is attributed to Jews as persons, and on personal qualities that are attributed to

being Jewish are clearly instances of anti-Semitism; attacks on individual Jews or on the unethical behavior of individuals and quasi-accurate statements about Jews as a group are no more justifiable, but they are not quite the same. Of course, ascribing any behavior or attitude to a person because he is Jewish—or because he is black—is racist, but as long as television entertainers can tell "Polish" or "Italian" jokes without blinking, Jewish leaders should not rush to the mimeograph machine every time a black militant points out that most school teachers in New York are Jewish.

Obviously there are many—and tragic—justifications for the Jewish sensitivity to any attack that bears even the slight resemblance to anti-Semitism, and as Earl Raab pointed out in the January 1969 *Commentary*, enough anti-Semitism is still buried in the American psyche to put Jews perpetually on their guard. But in responding to the outbursts of black militants, Jews should also realize that the use of demagogic rhetoric is frequent among political organizations of the poor, black or white, just as pentecostal preaching is in their churches. There is a danger that Jews will develop the same over-reaction to the black rhetoric and the black demands for equal rights that has emerged among poor and sub-affluent whites in recent years: for example, the panicky demands for law and order after the ghetto rebellions even though these rebellions did not touch white areas; and the exaggerated fears that the federal government and the Lindsay administration are favoring the blacks and ignoring white demands, when in fact precious little money or power has flowed into the ghetto since the federal civil rights efforts and the War on Poverty began.

The U.F.T.'s reprinting of anti-Semitic literature spawned by the school strikes surely encouraged white over-reaction to ghetto demands and rhetoric, as did the union's too-easy assumption that the Ocean Hill-Brownsville Governing Baord was responsible both

---

*Manhattan Tribune, November 30, 1968.

for initiating and not repressing the anti-Semitic outbursts in the school district. The union not only exaggerated the power of the Board over its community, but forgot that Rhody McCoy was hiring mainly white teachers, many of them Jewish, to replace the union teachers who had walked out.

Since the end of the last strike, both sides have been over-reacting dangerously. Jews are justified in attacking radio poetry that preaches Jewish extermination, but they should not make a fuss over every streetcorner slur about the Jewish role in the ghetto. Blacks are justified in objecting to exploitation, but they have no right to describe it as a Jewish practice, and not even the most intense black anger can justify comparisons of Jews with Nazis. In the present political climate, in which every over-reaction by one side leads to an over-reaction from the other, the resultant spiral can only increase racial polizaration. Jews and other whites will feel that their anti-Negro prejudices are now more reasonable, and the many ghetto residents who still retain deep faith in racial integration will begin to think that maybe the militants are right after all.

Clearly, both Jews and blacks should think about the consequences before they attack each other. Blacks must understand that any program of Black Power or local control that does not involve some cooperation with whites is bound to fail, for whites are the political majority in the city, and they control the purse-strings here and in Washington. Jews and other whites must understand that traditional integration policies have helped the middle class Negro but not the rank-and-file ghetto resident, and that the Black Power movement emerged precisely because of this reason. Whites need to realize that the movement is a serious striving for dignity and self-respect, seeking to exercise the unconscious rejection and depersonalization of the poor, black or white, which more affluent people and their institutions, black or white, often express in dealing with groups they consider inferior. Thus, for ghetto residents, at least, the demand for local control of the schools is principally an attempt to find teachers, curricula and school infra-structures which do not put down their children as culturally disadvantaged or "hard-core."

Moreover, while Black Capitalism cannot upgrade ghetto incomes by itself, and local control may not improve the educational performance of poor black children significantly, Black Power is a social movement, and social movements are militant, quasi-religious (and somewhat paranoid) bodies which are not deterred by logical critiques of their fundamental beliefs or their political irrationalities. They lose their supporters' allegiance only if society as a whole does something about the deprivations that give rise to social movements in the first place.

Unfortunately, political organizations rarely think about the consequences before they attack each other. Such groups think first and foremost about their own survival; how to retain their members and followers and to prevent their departure to a more militant competitor. If the constituents of Jewish defense organizations and black militant groups urge their organizations to attack and counterattack, a skirmish of speeches and press releases can easily escalate into a full-scale war of words and political acts. Of course, no one knows how much pressure black and Jewish constituencies are putting on their organizations, and it might therefore well be worth calling a summit meeting of leaders of all Jewish defense organizations and black groups to see if a joint moratorium on attacks and counter-attacks can be declared in order to prevent further escalation of the war.

V

Above all, Jews, other whites and Negroes must start to deal with the fundamental economic issue which underlies all of the recent conflicts: that technological change and other economic and social trends are creating a post-industrial society in which the policies of both private enterprise and government tend to favor first and foremost the college-educated professional and technical population. These days, the best jobs, public and private, the highest government subsidies go to the middle and upper-middle classes, leaving the sub-affluent population and the poor to divide the economic left-overs. When automation comes to the factory or a computer is installed in the office, they eliminate jobs among sub-affluent and poor workers while increasing the need for educated technical and professional workers. Indeed, that portion of the economy in which the sub-affluents and the poor play a major role is constantly decreasing in size and importance, so that the two groups are fighting each other for an even-smaller share of the economic pie. Similarly, with suburbanities having a clear majority of the votes in the nation—or in metropolitan government if it ever comes to be—if they choose to vote in unison, the urban sub-affluents and the poor are also fighting over their share of a constantly decreasing amount of political power.

In short, national economic and political changes have so altered the urban succession process, in New York and elsewhere, that many sub-affluent and poor cannot move up, or make sure that their children will be able to improve their position. As a result, the sub-affluents are opposing the poor in order to maintain their present status and to prevent succession from taking place. And since education is one of the basic ingredients to success in the post-industrial society, it is no coincidence that a major locus of the current conflict, in New York and other cities, is in the schools.

My description of the baisc class-conflict in the post-industrial society might suggest that the sub-affluent population should join with the poor to fight the common enemy,

but such a coalition is highly unlikely Given the heterogeneity and conflicting interests within each of these aggregates, there can probably be no organized union of the poor, or of the sub-affluent, or of both, and there is not even a united affluent enemy. Indeed, radical and liberal segments among the affluent often side with the poor against the sub-affluent, if only because the latter are a numerical majority in the country and can out-vote radicals, liberals and the poor. Also, in the short-run world of politics, sub-affluent people find it easier and more effective to attack those below them in income and status than to fight the affluent sector which they are themselves trying to enter.

The competition between the sub-affluents and the poor is of course interlaced with ethnic and racial considerations, and some observers are already fearful that Jews and blacks will be fighting each other on many fronts—or will be urged to do battle by affluent WASPs. Although evidence for a WASP conspiracy is hard to find, there is no doubt that sub-affluent Jews will continue to fight with poor blacks over succession, and that affluent Americans will not do much to ameliorate the conflict unless it begins to hurt them. Affluent Jews (and blacks) will probably also remain on the sidelines, making it unlikely that the conflict will ever involve *all* Jews and *all* blacks. Indeed, economic interests may instead create a wider split within the Jewish population between affluents and sub-affluents, just as these interests have split the affluent and the poor in the black community.

Nevertheless, even if the conflict between sub-affluents and the poor—and its ethnic and racial spinoffs—increases, it is unlikely that the kind of class-consciousness postulated by Marx or ethnic and racial consciousness based on economic considerations will ever develop to the point that Americans, rich or poor, act only on their so-called class-interest. The modern economy is just too diverse for lower-middle class employers of a national corporation to feel much communality of interest with lower-middle class shopkeepers. Nor are ethnic and racial allegiances strong enough for all members of an ethnic or racial group to unite politically when their economic and status interests diverge.

The solution, then, is not to be found in a 20th century doctrine of the class struggle, and it may even be too late for the coalition of the poor, the working class and the democratic radicals which Bayard Rustin, Michael Harrington and their associates have been urging. The working class it not only shrinking in size but is finding that it often has more in common with the lower-middle class than with the poor, and it is entirely possible that the organizations of the sub-affluents might try to build an alliance against both the poor and the affluent. Still, there is something to be said for the Rustin-Harrington coalition model, particularly if it can overcome its animus against all forms of Black Power and New Left thought, and admit the democratic and programmatically oriented among these two movements, and if it can attract the disaffected among the lower middle class as well.

Planning or predicting coalitions is always risky, however, and it is probably more realistic to think in terms of programs and policies that will attract various sectors of the total population than to begin with hypothetical conditions and then find programs on which they can agree.

Such programs can be described only briefly here, but in addition to anti-poverty efforts, the elimination of unemployment and underemployment, and the establishment of a guaranteed income policy and a higher minimum wage, the time has come also to reinvigorate the succession process. This reinvigoration should use public funds and public power to create jobs in the professional, semi-professional, and technical occupations that would allow both the sub-

affluent and the poor to move up in the economic hierarchy. What I have in mind is a massive federally-aided job development scheme in those occupations which are most likely to grow anyway in the post-industrial economy: teachers and teachers aides, and a variety of other professionals, semi-professionals and para-professionals in the public services. For example, the expansion and improvement of educational institutions—from nursery schools to post-graduate university departments—would create the kinds of jobs to which both the poor and the sub-affluent are aspiring, and would at the same time provide citizens with the schooling they need to enjoy life in post-industrial modernity. Such a program would enable many people to move up to new occupational slots, and others to succeed to the vacancies so created. If federal funds could be used to make public school teaching a less strenuous and better-paid profession, it would attract people now working in or preparing themselves for various blue and white collar jobs, and these jobs could then be taken by less skilled workers who are not yet ready, for one reason or another, to enter the professions. Their jobs could be upgraded by yet other means, for example, by increasing the worker's autonomy and providing for the application of his craftsmanship in mass production, and by the automation of "dirty" elements of work.

A publicly stimulated succession process would not eliminate all conflict over succession, but it would go far to reduce the insoluble elements of the conflict by providing new resources. Suppose the federal government had been able to provide funds to New York City last fall to create a few hundred new teaching positions. These funds could have produced additional slots in Ocean Hill-Brownsville, or offered new job possibilities to the union members who were removed from or who wanted to leave the Brooklyn school district, thus reading the job security fears of the U.F.T. membership. The two strikes might have been avoided and the current Negro-Jewish animosity might not have become so heated. Ethnic and racial conflicts are part of American life, but there is nothing like an infusion of new economic opportunities to erode the sharp edges of these conflicts.

---

4   THE SOCIOLOGY OF "CONFRONTATION"

Justus M. Van Der Kroef

After the founding of Malaysia, antagonisms between Chinese and Malays in Malaya were heightened by the opposition of Indonesia. Many Chinese viewed the Malays as attempting to maintain the conservative traditional social system as a barrier to their upward social mobility and thus looked with favor upon the Indonesian opposition. Although Indonesian attitudes toward Malaysia changed after the downfall of Sukarno, this article is still a valuable examination of the factors contributing to the ethnic conflict in Malaysia.

Beyond the political moves and countermoves of the Indonesian-Malaysian "confrontation" crisis there would seem to lie a deeper social conflict which, paradoxically, is experienced all the more acutely because of the broad spectrum of similarities between the two countries. Malaysia and Indonesia share a common racial background, language roots, and a host of cultural and social institutions ranging from the influence of Islam to various indigenous kinship patterns. Yet from this common base the development of the two nations in the past few decades, and in particular since World War II, has significantly diverged. Today Indonesia can see in Malaysia's social and economic structure all that which, in the opinion of currently dominant Indonesian political leaders and ideologues, needs total repudiation. By the same token, Malaysia veiws the course of her neighbor's national development as something to be avoided at all costs if it is to realize its professed aims of "happiness and prosperity" in the Tunku's words ("Hungerland," headlined *The Straits*

Times of Singapore recently, referring to Indonesia). From this vantage point the Indonesian-Malaysian dispute, part from its origins in the pattern of domestic Indonesian politics described elsewhere,[1] at bottom involves two contrasting social systems which Indonesia, as the originator of the "confrontation" policy, believes to be irreconcilable with each other.

Both in Indonesia and Malaysia the colonial system tended to augment indigenous feudal tradition and aristocratic political and social dominance, although not to the same degree. The Dutch, in pursuing a policy of "indirect rule" in Indonesia, absorbed and

SOURCE
Reprinted from The (Southwestern) *Social Science Quarterly* December, 1964.
Vol. 45, No. 3 by permission of the author and *Social Science Quarterly.*

---

[1]See my "Indonesia and the Confrontation," The Bulletin (Sydney), December 14, 1963, pp. 23-26.

identified with existing patterns of aristo-cratic power, although their later policies encouraged non-aristocratic elements in society to rise to prominence. In Malaysia—particularly in the Malay Peninsula—the Sultanates were protected by the British; indigenous royal prerogatives and jurisdiction over custom, and religion were preserved, and with it the traditional feudal structure of society.   But while in Indonesia the growth of revolutionary nationalism, and subsequently the war of independence against the Dutch (1945-1949), irreparably undermined the feudal system as the modern Rousseauist egalitarianism of mass democracy made ever further inroads, in Malaysia little or no such sweeping development took place. This was due in part to the relative lateness of the nationalist emergence in Malaysia. In Indonesia the birth of major indigenous nationalist parties antedates World War I; in Malaya, with few exceptions, they do not appear until after World War II, and in the Borneo territories not even until 1959. Then, too, Malaysia, unlike Indonesia, was not required to liberate itself from colonial rule: by 1954 the question was not *when* Malaya would become independent but *how,* and espceially after 1960 this *how* increasingly involved consideration also of the future status of Singapore, Sarawak and Sabah.   Finally, and perhaps most importantly, the political left in Malaysia, unlike that of Indonesia, has not thus fare had a significant impact on indigenous social processes, ideologies, and values.   The Communist guerilla uprising in Malaya (1948-1955) and its failure not only discredited the left, including many of its non-Communist elements, but as Britain mobilized available Malayan social groupings to combat the insurgents also tended to strengthen the Malayan feudal establishment and its leaders in the new political movements after the war.   The result was, as will be more fully indicated shortly, that the conflict between the indigenously Malayan aris-tocratic pattern of life and its political organizational expressions, on the one hand, and the left wing radical and egalitarian elements on the other, came to assume eventually almost entirely a communal or racial character, with the left being drawn largely from Chinese and some Indian quarters.   In contrast, in Indonesia since independence, communalism was progressively de-emphasized by various (including government-sponsored) processes of enforced political and social assimilation, or—as, for example, in the case of the Chinese—occasionally by outright expulsion from the country.

Much of Malaysia's social structure today seems to represent a determined effort at retaining indigenous traditions, many of which, inevitably, are feudalistic in character. It is not just a matter of an "upsurge of Malay nationalism" which "has brought with it a new pride in all that is symbolic of ancient Malay greatness" so that even among the common folk "it is unthinkable now for the bridegroom at a Malay wedding to wear anything but the Malay national costume."[2]   The issue goes deeper than that. Next to Britain Malaysia today is probably the only country in the world where new patents of nobility with their appropriate traditional titles (for example, *Dato, Tun,* or *Panglima*) continue to be granted frequently, both by the paramount ruler and by the Sultans of the Malayan states.   The indigenous nobility still constitutes what might be called the Malaysian "establishment," and the present premier of Malaysia is himself of the royal house of Kedah.

The new Malaysian constitution continues to preserve the traditional authority of the rulers in matters of custom and religion, thus again safe-guarding the traditional feudal pattern of society.   Continued, too, is the old land reservation system under which

---

[2]Mahathir bin Mohamad, "Interaction, Integration," Intisari (Malaysian Sociological Research Institute), vol. 1 (1962), no. 3. p. 44.

Western, Chinese, or Indian planters or entrepreneurs are barred in many areas from exercising proprietary rights over native land, thus preventing not only alienation of the economically weaker Malay's most valuable possession, but also placing it outside the modern plantation economy. In the state of Kelantan 87% of the land is under such reservation, in the state of Kedah about 66%. The reservation system along with the preservation of traditional royal authority in custom and religion, and, subsequently, the inclusion in the constitution of special protection of and priveleges for Malays in such matters as the granting of scholarships, public appointments, and certain business licenses, all have had the effect of creating a wall around traditional Malay life. These measures, originally enacted as part of colonial policy and perpetuated under the present Malaysian constitution, were and are deemed necessary in order to protect the Malay from the business acumen and drive of the Chinese and from the onslaught of the Western plantation or mining economy. But they also tended to shelter the Malay so completely from the winds of change that, in the words of one Malayan official: [3]

"It is often said that these concessions, instead of helping the Malays makes them weaker; protected and spoonfed, they are not encouraged to stand on their own feet and learn to compete with the other ethnic groups in the economic as well as other fields."

One finds this protective pattern, with some modification, also in the Borneo territories of Malaysia, where it particularly applies to the indigenous Dayak, who being economically weak, are also surrounded by Chinese.

---

[3]Raja Mohar Bin Raja Badiozaman, "Malay Land Reservation and Alienation," Intisari, vol. 1 (1962), nol 2, p. 25.

The social effects of the "wall of protection" in Malayan society were probably even more important than the economic ones. For the wall perpetuated the hothouse climate of Malayan feudal tradition, in which processes of economic modernization flourished as poorly as more democratic and egalitarian notions of the social order. These stirred not the indigenous Malay but the Chinese immigrant community and, in time, they provided the principal dynamic for the emergence of racial-occupational stereotypes today, in which the Malay is typically either a tradition-bound agriculturist, or else a white-collar conscious bureaucrat, equally tied in habits of thought to the predominant position of the royal courts, while the Chinese occupies the whole spectrum of dynamic economic activity, from export agriculture to market gardening, and from unskilled labor to multi-million dollar commerce, and, while lacking virtually all identification with the traditional Malayan royal order, at the same time is far more susceptible than the Malay to all the pressures and appeals of modern political ideology and international affairs. Given the extent of continuing British economic interests in Malaysia, it needs little elaboration that British capital has much more to fear from the economic and political dynamics of the volatile Chinese community than from the tradition-bound Malayan establishment.

It is also not difficult to see in the very constitutional structure of Malaysia today an attempt to curtail the power of the burgeoning Chinese community, and hence of the anti-feudal, political and social dynamics within it. There are, for example, the rigid restrictions on citizenship and the special electoral qualifications prevailing exclusively in the state of Singapore (where the Chinese account for more than 80% of the population), and barriers on free movement of citizens from Singapore to the Malayan and Borneo states. There is also the absence of the principle of proportional representation in the Malaysian parliament, as a result of which Singapore is entitled to send only 15 deputies to the lower house of parliament, although its population (1.8 million) is more than twice that of Sarawak (760,000) which sends 24 deputies, and almost four times that of Sabah (455,000) which is entitled to 16 deputies. Above all, there is the continuing preferred status given to Malays by constitutional directive in respect to positions in the public service, in granting of scholarships, and so on. Moreover, the headship of the Malaysian state is exclusively reserved for a Malay of royal blood, and even in those component states of the Malaysian federation which do not have a hereditary Malay ruler Malay headship is regarded as essential, though a particular state constitution may not demand it. For example, even in the predominantly Chinese state of Singapore the head of state today is a Malay, recently ennobled by the Malaysian king. While some Chinese are quite prepared to accept this, others are not, and Malay attempts to secure Malay headships in states other than those of the Malayan peninsula proper have already created deep resentment in non-Malay circles.

For example, shortly before the official proclamation of Malaysia on September 16, 1963, a political crisis developed between Sarawak and the federal Malaysian government over the headship of the state of Sarawak. The Malaysian premier, Tunku Abdul Rahman, insisted on a Malay head although Sarawak's population is distributed as follows: 32% Chinese, 18% Malay, and 50% various indigenous Dayak and related tribes. Rahman claimed that since the present Sarawak premier is an Iban Dayak and his vice-premier a Chinese, a Malay needed to be appointed head of state in order to preserve "racial balance." But the dominant Sarawak Alliance party wished the paramount chief of the Iban Dayak, who is also Alliance chairman, to be Sarawak's

chief of state. The ensuing impasse was finally broken when the Sarawak Alliance gave in to Rahman and a Malay was appointed head of state. But the aftermath of the affair left angry rumors among both Sarawak Chinese and Dayak leaders over Kuala Lumpur's alleged attempts to "Malaycize" the state leadership even further. In Sabah, leaders of the Sabah National Party, which is almost entirely Chinese, in November 1963, expressed to this writer their concern, not just over the appointment of a Malay (and leader of Sabah's principal Malayan party) as head of state of Sabah, but particularly over the entrenchment and expected future spread of Malay communal interests from the Malay peninsula proper to the Borneo states of Malaysia via the conduit of the office of the head of state and its powers and influence.[4] Nearly 30% of Sabah's population is Chinese, with various Malay elements amounting to less than 10%, while the remainder is distributed among indigenous Dayak groups. But, it is well to note that the current fear of an accelerating "Malaycization" process is not just a reflection of ancient communal rivalries augmented further today by the conflict between newly emergent political parties. It is a sociological question also, involving the future structure and character of Malaysian society and the clash between a traditional feudal temper and a more modern, radical, and socially levelling spirit.

As in Indonesia so in Malaysia conservatism is further buttressed by Islamic ortho-

---

[4]In an attempt to broaden their base a number of Sabah national parties, early in 1964, made determined efforts to bring members of different population groups into their ranks. This heightened racial-political rivalries, and in the middle of June, 1964, major Sabah parties agreed to "freeze" the racial composition of their parties, e.g. the predominantly Chinese Sabah National Party promised not to recruit new non-Chinese members. *Sabah Times* (Jesselton), June 16, 1964.

doxy.   Just as Indonesia has its Muslim irreconcilables of the Darul Islam ("House of Islam") who seek the establishment of the Islamic state in Indonesia by violent means, so Malaysia (particularly Malaya) has its Pan Malayan Islamic Party (PMIP) which urges a "truly indigenous" Malaya with Islam as state religion.   As an ultra-conservative Malayan party the PMIP is, at least by implication, anti-Chinese, and some of its leaders only recently provoked heated reactions by proclaiming that any relationship, political or otherwise, between Muslim and non-Muslim is unlawful for the former. But compared to Indonesia modern Islamic reform movements have touched the Malaysian area but lightly, and it would seem that this is due again to the continuing power of those traditional elite elements in Malayan society that also had paramount authority in Islamic legal matters (that is, the Sultans). The communal issue also obtrudes in this area: for, as is the case with most Indonesians, Islam is also inseparable from the Malayan's sense of personal identity, and the political and economic pressures from the Chinese community which is proportionally so much larger in Malaysia than in Indonesia, have tended to make the Malayan more uncompromisingly orthodox than his co-religionist across the Straits of Malacca.

If one travels through the cities of Malaysia today, including those in the Borneo territories, one is—with the exception of Singapore—reminded of the involuted placidity of the Indonesian towns of several decades ago.   Indeed, much of the Malaysian social structure today reminds one of Indonesia before the onset of nationalistic movements in the latter area just before the First World War.   For example, Malaysian aristocratic prominence in political life had its counterpart in the various movements of national awakening in Indonesia, whose early leaders also tended to come from the Javanese nobility.   In fact the first Indonesian na-

tionalist organization, Budi Utomo ("Noble Endeavor"), founded in 1908, was almost entirely composed of younger and progressive Javanese aristocrats.   But in Indonesia there soon took place what in Malaysia today has occurred only to a limited extent and then primarily among the Chinese element. And that was the development of a genuine mass political consciousness, often inchoate and inarticulate to be sure, but nevertheless capable of being mobilized by the nationalist elite.   Soon political leadership in Indonesia passed out of the hands of the aristocracy to leaders who openly championed the cause of proletarian action and saw the future in terms of the age of the common man.   In 1933, for example, Sukarno urged the Indonesian *marhaen* (common man) to be on guard against both feudalism and against the "bourgeoisization" of Indonesia and warned that great care had to be taken lest "the victory chariot" that would be driven cross "the golden bridge" of national independence should be driven by anyone other than the *marhaen*.[5]

The Indonesian aristocracy did not altogether disappear as a polticial force, however, for one thing because its experience in the colonial government services proved too valuable to be wholly disregarded by the newly independent Indonesian   republic. Moreover, the aristocratic traditions were incontestably an important dimension of the "Indonesian identity," to the rediscovery of which so many Indonesian leaders seemed to be dedicating themselves.   Indeed, more than

---

[5]See Sukarno's essay "Mentjapai Indonesia Merdeka,"   in the collection of his writings Dibawah Bendera Revolusi (Djakarta: 1959), vol. 1, pp. 315-316. Sukarno's egalitarianism in relation to the anti-Malaysia campaign is well illustrated by such recent accusations that much of the national income of the "Common Malayan People" is being   "devoured by Malayan princes and Kuomintang capitalists."   Antara Daily News Bulletin, August 27, 1964.

a decade after the Revolution, the Indonesian government found itself complaining that many Indonesians were even arrogating to themselves traditional noble titles without having the right to do so. As in Malays, in Indonesia too the appeal to ancient grandeur provided a new importance to the aristocracy and its traditions. But unlike Malaya, Indonesia in the past century had not been sealed off in large measure from unsettling economic influences emanating from Western enterprise. Agrarian legislation in Indonesia in 1875 had accelerated the opening up of the country to estate export agriculture on leased native lands and financed by foreign capital, and had given a new impetus also to mining and industrial development. No "reservation" policy, such as that in Malaya, impeded the disruption of the traditional order. In their colonial jurisprudence the Dutch attempted to preserve the local *adat* (custom law), but they did not acknowledge the indigenous Indonesian rulers as primary sources of authority in the regulation of that custom. Though they relied on the aristocracy in their civil administration, the Dutch allowed a pattern of Western influences to work its transformation of the native social structure far more incisively than occurred in Malaysia. By the end of the First World War Indonesian society exhibited marked differentiations of social elites and social strata, in which new elements of potential political power—for instance, the trade unions, the landless rural proletariat, and the new intelligentsia of the commoners—rapidly began to assert themselves and soon over-shadowed the indigenous aristocracy in importance. A profusion of indigenous political parties—from conservative to radical nationalist and Communist, and representing native ethnic (for example, Sundanese or Ambonese), as well as foreign communal (for instance, Dutch or Chinese) interests—accentuated the appearance of heterogeneity and flux in the Indonesian social structure and its many competing interest and elite groupings. Kindred developments in Malaysia existed at best in embryo form only, or not at all.

But the speed and variety of social changes in Indonesia in the last few decades before the Second World War was not balanced by a solidification of the institutions of government. In Malaya and the British Borneo territories a disinclination toward constitutional experimentation, and a continued recognition of anciently established power structures tended to be the rule. In Indonesia, on the other hand, the Dutch never seemed to weary of administrative reform, including the establishment of local, and even of nationwide, representative government. The Second World War disrupted this experimental process and left no established and commonly understood and accepted practices for decision-making or for the solution of governmental conflict. Moreover, to a far greater degree than in Malaya the Japanese authorities during their occupation of Indonesia in World War II promoted the creation of emotion charged, political mass movements, and acquainted Indonesian leaders with the techniques of mobilizing such movements for desired political ends. After the war the Indonesian Revolution not only amplified these tendencies but provided them with a new patriotic justification. The result, simply, was that the competing elite groups in the heterogenous Indonesian society were never habituated to a settlement of their problems through the formal processes of constitutional government, while the decorum of such government never passed (as it was to do so noticeably in Malaya after World War II) into the political temper of the country. Indeed, there was no single acknowledged Indonesian elite, no established pivot of authority like the Sultans and their courts in the Malay states, or even the hereditary tribal chiefs in the Broneo areas. There was instead—when freedom from colonial rule finally came (1949)—an ill-defined revolutionary leadership, experiencing widely divergent pressures from the various social movements and interest groups in their environment, and agreeing at best only upon some general symbols of national unity and aspiration.

The momentum of Indonesia's social revolution carried it far beyond the ability of the feeble political institutions to contain it, and, in a few short years after independence was formally won, attempts to contain it were in fact abandoned. In the context of Sukarno's authoritarian "guided democracy" the momentum of the social revolution in Indonesia became itself the basis of the new political order, and an ideology of perpetual *Sturm and Drang,* of an "unfinished revolution," or of *vivere pericoloso* ("live dangerously"), as Sukarno with an openly acknowledged debt to Mussolini put it, became its rationale. The levelling radicalism of a new mass society which these processes called forth was eagerly espoused by Indonesia's growing Communist Party, whose chairman, D.N. Aidit, paraphrased Sukarno along Dantonesque lines, also calling on the nation for increased audacity in a "year of daring" and of risking danger.[6] The sheer magnitude of the numbers involved (by the end of 1963 the Indonesian population numbered about 100 million) in this social upheaval could not but have serious consequences for the surrounding area, particularly for Malaysia, and by comparison to the Indonesian scene the social systems of virtually all other Southeast Asian nations seemed anachronisms, with equally outmoded institutions of power.   To refer specifically to Malaysia for the moment: the Sultanates, the persisting feudal prerogatives, the entrenched Islamic orthodoxy, the protective reservation of Malayan land tenure—all these seemed and continue to

be but so many features of a social and cultural lag from the standpoint of the Indonesian development and its protagonists.

The channel through which the ideological dimensions of Indonesia's social revolution are increasingly beginning to pass today into Malaysian reflection and experience is made up out of Chinese, particularly the younger generation.   Apart from the obvious and ready identification of many young Malaysian Chinese with Peking and its achievements, a corollary of traditional Chinese chauvinism, the present writer has been struck again and again also by the sympathies of young Malaysian Chinese not just for Sukarno's anti-Malaysia confrontation policies, but also for what they sense to be the social and ideological forces behind this confrontation.[7] Unquestionably some of this sympathy is motivated by practical political considerations: the opposition to Malaysia in many Malaysian Chinese quarters, stemming from a combination of long-felt discrimination and frustrated cultural and political ambitions in the Chinese community in Malaysia, coincides at the moment with the current Indonesian strategy to "crush" Malaysia, and a sense of *rapport* is understandable considering, for example, that young Chinese in Sarawak, many of them belonging to the Communist infiltrated Sarawak United Peoples Party, have joined Indonesian and other volunteer groups based in Indonesian Borneo in guerilla attacks in Malaysian Borneo.[8] Yet

[7]These sympathies were particularly apparent among a large segment of the students at Nanyang University, Singapore, which is virtually entirely Chinese and where the author served as visiting professor of Southeast Asian studies during the latter half of 1963.

[8]On the presence of young Chinese among the anti-Malaysia Indonesian guerillas see *Malayan Times,* September 8, 1963, and The *Straits Times,* October 19, 1963, and generally, Justus M. van der Kroef, "Communism and the Guerilla War in Sarawak," *The World Today* (February, 1964), pp. 50-60.

[6]D.N. Aidit, *Berani, Berani, Sekali Lagi Berani!* (Djakarta: 1963), p. 4.

it is remarkable that such sympathies exist despite the widespread knowledge of government instigated anti-Chinese pogroms in Indonesia in recent years.

The answer is that apart from their unassuaged feelings of cultural chauvinism many young Chinese, whether in Malaya, Singapore, or the Borneo territories of Malaysia, perceive in the dynamics of Indonesian social development a model of what they consider to be Malaysia's own inevitable future course, once the modernization of its society has begun to acquire momentum. For this restless Chinese segment of Malaysian society today the oft repeated Indonesian (and Communist Chinese) accusation that Malaysia is a "neocolonial" creation has not just a *political,* but more particularly also a *social* meaning, referring not just to Britain's continuing influence in the military and economic establishment of the new federation, but especially to the extent to which that influence perpetuates the traditional Malaysian social system and its strata rigidities, also insofar as it preserves the special problems of the Chinese community. Just as Indonesian leaders, particularly after the outbreak of an anti-Chinese incident, are wont to urge the million and a half or so Chinese in Indonesia to "assimilate totally," including an "Indonesiazation" of their names and habits,[9] so the author has heard

younger Chinese in Singapore and Malaya today urge a breakdown of communal barriers and greater social "unity." Malays fear that this call for a more "homogeneous" existence actually means that the Chinese, given their greater and more rapidly increasing numbers and economic assets would in effect quickly swallow up the Malay community, and that preservation of Malay tradition and its political concomitants is, under the circumstances, an indispensable barrier of self protection against an assimilation process that would in effect make Malaysia eventually into a Chinese state.

It is, moreover, not only the fear of being submerged by the Chinese community as such that motivates many Malaysians in desiring the maintenance of the aristocratic and conservative features of the present government and social system. As was mentioned earlier, the fact that Peking by skillfully playing on traditional Chinese cultural pride, especially among the younger politically highly conscious Chinese generation, has managed to exercise great appeal is an added disturbing factor. Quite clearly many younger Chinese, graduates of the frequently intensely chauvinistic Chinese Middle Schools in Malaya, see their future preferably in terms of a general "massification" of Malaysian society, in which new social differentiations will occur on the basis of functional or economic special interest groups and in which, naturally, the Chinese element, with its intelligence, energy, and leadership capacities, is likely to emerge in decisively commanding positions. From this point of view the political orientation of this new Malaysia would be, to say the least, quite sympathetic to Peking. Such a "massification" of Malaysian society with its sweeping social levelling, its breakdown of special protective reservations for the Malay, its

---

[9]The pressures on the Chinese in Indonesia wholly to assimilate have been varied and complex. Perhaps the most effective, in the long run, have been the discriminatory provisions in public law against those Chinese who, though opting for Indonesian citizenship, still retained sufficiently distinct Sinic identity to be considered as warga negara asing (or "non-indigenous citizens") as opposed to warga negara asli citizens of "non-indigenous descent" (see, for example, Gouw Giok Siong, Warga Negara dan Orang Asing. Berikut Peraturan dan Tjontoh-Tjontoh [Djakarta: 1960]. "Total assimilation," that is, name changing and obliteration as far as possible of Sinic

traces in one's background, all in keeping with the levelling rationale of Indonesian political ideology, has been given an added impetus.

virtual disappearance of royal and feudal authority, and its emphasis on social and cultural homogenization and assimilation into a single national identity, would, for Malaysia of course be but the counterpart of similar developments in Indonesia, and to younger Malaysian Chinese in particular, also of the social evolution that has taken place in People's China.

Indonesia's attempt, through her confrontation campaign, not only to remake the political structure of Malaysia, but in effect, also the social system that lies in back of it, is unquestionably also inspired by notions of historic and racial affinity with the Malaysian population. In line with official emphasis on the rediscovery of the "Indonesian identity" there has come renewed interest in the ancient Indonesian empires like Criwijaya and Modjopahit which extended their spheres of influence far beyond the Indonesian islands into the Malayan peninsula, and periodically even to the rest of the Southeast Asian mainland. A vision of a "Greater Indonesia" (*Indonesia Raya*) that would include the inhabitants of the present Malaysian Borneo territories has quite clearly animated some official Indonesian spokesmen in the current anti-Malaysian confrontation campaign, and this vision clearly reflects the concept of a Malay racial unity as well. For example, on August 22, 1963, the Indonesian Information Minister Ruslan Abdulgani declared in an address in Pematang Siantar, Sumatra, that the people of North Borneo wished to unite with Indonesia, and that Indonesia was in a position to help them. He said that "The people there want to be free and join the country of our grandfathers and grandmothers." Subsequently, after his remarks caused a furore also among Chinese supporters of Indonesia's confrontation campaign in Sarawak, Abdulgani denied that he had said this, and had only remarked that authorities in North Borneo should not arrest those opposed to Malaysia, "especially those who are pro-Indonesia and who want to

reunite with our fatherland." Most observers agreed that the thought of Abdulgani's second statement, particularly the idea of a "reuniting" of the North Borneans with their Indonesian "fatherland," differed in no substantial way from the first one attributed to him.[10]

Another recent manifestation of the same concept was the idea of *Mapilindo,* a term in the form of an acrostic, referring to the unity of the three principal Malay Republics: Malaysia, Phipinas (the Philippines), and Indonesia. The idea of *Mapilindo*, apparently first mooted early in 1963 by Philippine President Diosdado Macapagal, acquired greater solidity at the Manila Conference on Malaysia in July, 1963, when machinery for increased cooperation among the three powers was agreed to on paper. The continuing conflict between the Philippines and Indonesia on the one hand and Malaysia on the other, over the position of Northwest Borneo in the Malaysian Federation, soon seemed to render any *Mapilindo* machinery inoperative before it even had had an opportunity to commence functioning. It was noteworthy, however, that Indonesia continued to voice enthusiastic support for the *Mapilindo* idea, even at a time when Malaysian and Philippino officials seemed all but ready to declare the whole concept as having been still-born. Indonesian *Mapilindo* strategy is clear: supported by a vision of historic unity and racial identity Indonesia conceives of herself as the natural leader of the entire Malay community: of a Malay society possibly embracing a number of separate political entities but under federated Indonesian hegemony and exhibiting generally uniform social characteristics. The appeal to a Malay historic grandeur is thus matched by a vision of a new and single Malay society and state.

During the first years of Indonesia's independence the country was tied to the

[10]*Malayan Times,* August 24, 1963, and *The Straits Times*, September 4, 1963.

Netherlands in a Constitutional Union headed by the Dutch Crown. The provisions of this Union, as well as other regulations governing the special position of Dutch capital in Indonesia, and various cultural and military relations, had been laid down by the Dutch-Indonesian Round Table Conference (or RTC) in the Hague, in December, 1949. Also because of the then unresolved West New Guinea issue the RTC accords increasingly aroused bitter opposition in Indonesian circles. Radical nationalists and Communists took the lead in denouncing what was called Indonesia's "RTC culture" and "RTC pseudo-independence," terms which conveyed the same political temper as the word "neo-colonialism" does today when applied to the opposition to Malaysia. By 1955 the last vestiges of the RTC had been dissolved by unilateral action on Indonesia's part, and it is clear that the opponents of "neo-colonialist" Malaysia, whether in Malaysia or out, desire the same processes of a resolute break with the influence of the former colonial power, a radicalization of public policy and a restructuring of society. Just as prior to 1955 the cry was heard that Indonesia was only a "pseudo-independent" country, so in Malaysia today the radical Chinese opposition, such as Singapore's *Barisan Sosialis* party, and left-wing native Malay parties like the People's Party (*Partai Rakyat*), continue to call for "true independence for the motherland," free from Malaysia, the "liberation of the races," and a "socialist" future.[11] Some currents in this opposition desire a complete break-up of the component states of the present Malaysian Federation into separate and independent republics, other appear to have no objection to the continuation of a greatly weakened Malaysian Federation out of the Commonwealth, but are all agreed that Britain's influence and that of the social groups dependent upon that influence must end. Given the strong attraction for Peking in these anti-Malaysia Chinese circles, as well as their current sympathy for Sukarno which they share with the small group of native Malaysian Marxist radicals, it is clear that the new Malaysia that is envisaged by these circles—whatever its ultimate form—would be readily acceptable to both Djakarta and Peking. How long and how well Malaysia's present leaders can withstand the pressures of an "Indonesian style" political and social revolution in their country only the future can tell.

---

[11]See for example, Kaw Mao, "What is the Nature of Our Struggle Now? *Labour News* (Low Kong Pau), (Johore Bahru), August 15, 1963, p. 2; "Malaysia Bereti Penindasan oleh Tantara British," Banteng (Kuala Lumpur) (July, 1963), p. 2; "Expose of Malaysia Agreement," *Plebeian Express* (Singapore), August 19, 1963, no. 9, pp. 4-8.

5   PLURAL SOCIETY AND INTERNAL COLONIALISM

Pablo Gonzallez Casanova *

There is little equality in the distribution of authority in a colonial society.
nternal colonialism of whites toward Indians is seen by Casanova as a strong
pattern in Mexico. This pattern, which involves both prejudice and discrimination, results in distinctive patterns of dealing with authority on the part of
Indians and distinctive patterns of conflict.

The ideology of liberalism, which considers all men to be equal before the law, is a great advance from the racism prevailing in colonial times. Similarly, the ideology of the Revolution is a no less important advance over the social Darwinist and racist ideas of *porfirismo*. Today the Indian problem is approached as a cultural problem. No Mexican scholar or ruler believes that this is an inborn, racial problem. Social and political mobility in Mexico has allowed Indians to occupy the highest positions and to achieve the highest social status in Mexican society since Independence, and particularly since the Revolution. Even national history and its pantheon of heroes have viewed Cuauhtémoc, the leader of the resistance against the Spaniards, and Juárez, the Indian President and builder of modern Mexico, with highest regard.

The same equality has been recorded at national and local levels by anthropologists. Indians who participate in the national culture are able to achieve the same status as mestizos or whites in economic, political, and interpersonal and family relationships. An Indian particpating in the national culture is in no way an object of racial discrimination.

SOURCE

From *Democracy in Mexico* by **Pablo Gonzalez Casanova, translated by Danielle Salti. Copyright ©
1970 by Oxford University Press, Inc. Reprinted by Permission**

*Translated by Danielle Salti.

He may feel the consequences of discrimination because of his economic status, his occupational role, or his political role. But that is all. For these reasons, Mexican anthropology views the Indian problem as a cultural problem. This affirmation represents an ideological advance over the racism prevailing in the social sciences of the Porfirian period. From a scientific point of view, the statement corresponds to reality. Yet it does not explain all the basic characteristics of this reality.

The Indian problem is essentially one of internal colonialism. The Indian communities are Mexico's internal colonies. The Indian community is a colony within the national territory, and it has the characteristics of a colonized society. This fact has not been recognized by the nation. Resistance has been multiple and will be powerful. The habit of thinking of colonialism as an international phenomenon has caused people to overlook internal colonialism. The habit of viewing Mexico as an ex-colony or a semi-colony of foreign powers, and of seeing Mexicans generally as subjected to foreign colonization, has blocked the development of the view that Mexicans are colonizers and colonized. The past and present national struggle for independence is a factor in this problem, and it has made the men involved in this struggle national heroes. Another fact which has contributed to obscuring the situation is that both internal and international colonialism manifest their more extreme characteristics in typically colonial regions far from the metropolis. Although in the city there are no colonialist prejudices or struggles, but rather democratic and egalitarian styles of life, quite the opposite obtains in the outlying areas. Here we find prejudice, discrimination, colonial types of exploitation, dictatorial forms, and the separation of a dominant population, with a specific race and culture, from a dominated population, with a different race and culture. This is what occurs in Mexico. In the conflict areas, in those regions in which both Indians and Ladinos live, we find prejudice, discrimination, colonial types of exploitation, dictatorial forms, and the racial cultural alignment of dominant and dominated populations. From a social point of view, the most striking difference from international colonialism is the fact that a few members of the Indian communities can physically and culturally escape from these internal colonies. They can go to the cities and find a job, and they have the same chances of mobility as the members of the lower classes who have no Indian cultural background. Yet this mobility has limitations and does not end internal colonialism. Internal colonialism exists wherever Indian communities are found. Research done by Mexican anthropologists reveals the existence of a way of life that corresponds to that of the historical definition of colonialism. This is true among the Amuzgos, Coras, Cuicatecos, Chatinos, Chinantecos, Choles, Hauxtecos, Hauves, Huicholes, Mayas, Mayos, Mazahuas, Mazatecos, Nahoas, Mixes, Mixtecos, Otomíes, Popolocas, Tarahumaras, Tarascos, Tepehuanos, Tlapanecos, Tojolabales, Totonacas, Tzeltales, Tzotziles, Yaquis, and Zapotecos—that is, among several million Mexicans.

One form assumed by internal colonialism is when what anthropologists call the "ruling center" or "metropolis" (San Cristóbal, Tlaxiaco, Huauchinango, Sochiapan, Mitla, Ojitlán, Zacapoaxtla) exercises a monopoly over Indian commerce and credit, with relationships of exchange unfavorable to the Indian communities. This is manifest in a permanent decapitalization of the Indians at the lowest levels. The commerical monopoly isolates the Indian community from any other center or market, promoting monoculture and dependence.

Another form of internal colonialism is the exploitation of the Indian population by the different social classes of the Ladino population. This exploitation, as is the case of all colonies of modern history, is a combination of feudalism, capitalism, slavery, forced and salaried labor, share farming and peonage, and demand for free services. The despoliation of Indian lands performed the same two functions it fulfilled in the colonies: it deprived the Indians of their land, and it transformed them into peons or salaried workers. The exploitation of one population by another manifested itself in different salaries for the same jobs (in mines, sugare refineries, coffee plantations); in the over-all exploitation of Indian craftsmen (workers with wool, ixtle, palm, willow, ceramics); social, verbal, and dress discriminations; and, as we shall see, juridical, political, and trade-union discriminations. Such discrimination demonstrated colonialist attitudes on the part of local and even of federal functionaries, and of course on the part of the Ladino leaders of political organizations.

Still another form of internal colonialism is shown by cultural differences and differences in standards of living according to whether the population is Ladino or Indian. Observable differences, however, are not sharply divided between people speaking Indian languages and those who do not, because a large sector of the nearby non-Indian peasant population has standards of living as low as those of the Indian populations.[1]

Indian communities have the following characteristics: a predominantly subsistence economy, with minimal money and capitalization; lands unsuitable for crops or of low quality, unfit for agriculture becasue of hilly terrain, or of good quality but in isolated locations; deficient crop-growing and cattle-breeding because of low quality seeds and inferior animals smaller than the average of their kind and pre-Hispanic or colonial techniques of land exploitation; a low level of productivity; standards of living lower than those of peasants in non-Indian areas, exemplified by poor health, high rates of mortality, including infant mortality, illiteracy and the presence of rickets; lack of facilities and resources, such as schools, hospitals, water, and electricity; promotion of alcoholism and promotion of prostitution by hookers and Ladinos; aggressiveness among communities, which may be overt, or expressed through games or dreams; magic-religious culture; economic manipulation through the imposition of taxes and a status-bound economy; and, as we shall see, political manipulation.

All these conditions are basic to colonial structure and are found in the definitions and explanations of colonialism from Montesquieu to Myrdal and Fanon. They are also mentioned in the works of foreign writers and the antrhopologists of Mexico. Together they demonstrate the existence of internal colonialism, which is characteristic of those regions where Indians and Ladinos coexist. Internal colonialism is *also* characteristic of the national society, in which there is a continuum of colonialism from groups exhibiting the entire range of colonial characteristics to regions and groups in which only traces are visible. Internal colonialism affects an estimated 3 million Indians using the criterion of language, 7 million using the criterion of culture, and almost 12 million according to the index of Contemporary Indocolonial Culture created by Whetten.[2] In fact, internal colonialism encompasses the whole marginal population and penetrates the entire culture, society, and polity of Mexico in different ways and intensities, depending on the groups and regions.

The Indian problem is one of national scope; it defines the nation itself. It is the problem not of a small sector, but of many millions of Mexicans who do not share in the national culture and also of those who do participate in the national culture. The concept of internal colonialism explains the national structure as a whole better than the concept of social classes in a pre-industrial society, in terms of ideology, political affiliation, and class consciousness.

[1]Cf. Julio de la Fuente, "Población Indigena" (unpublished); Alejandro D. Marroquin, "Problemas Económicos de las Comunidades Indigenas de Mexico" (mimeographed course program), Mexico, 1956; Milguel O. de Mendizábal, "Los problemas indígenas y su más urgente tratamiento." *Obras Completas IV* (Mexico, 1946); Moisés T. de la Peña. "Panaorama de la Economía Indigena de México." *Primer Congreso Indigena Interamericano* (Pátzcuaro, 1946); Jorge A. Vivó, "Aspectos Económicos Fundamentales del Problema Indigena." *Revista América Indegena*, Vol. III. No. 1. January 1947; Gonzalo Agurire Beltrán and Ricardo Pozas, *Instituciones Indígenas en el México Actual* (Mexico: Instituto Nacional Intelligenista, 1954).

[2]Cf. Nathan I. Whetten, "Mexico Rural," *Problemas Agrícolas e Industriales de México,* Vol. V, No. 2 (Mexico, 1953),pp. 245 ff.

5. CONFLICTS AND ALLIANCES

The historical exclusion of most racial and ethnic "minority" groups from access to economic, political, and social rewards underscores the structural difficulties in initiating and promoting social change. Various social institutions that have traditionally served to enforce the unequal distribution of wealth and power do not alter their policies easily. A broadening of the base of support for the upward mobility of oppressed ethnic groups may be essential for dissolving the rigid boundaries of a purely ethnic stratification. According to Simmel (1955: 98–99), conflict

> "may not only heighten the concentration of an existing unit, radically eliminating all elements which might blur the distinctness of its boundaries against the enemy; it may also bring persons and groups together which have otherwise nothing to do with each other."

These alliances, even if they are only tenuous, may occur at crucial moments in the history or future of intergroup relations.

Daniel Katz (1969:127) in a provocative essay on grass-roots movements pointed out the limitations of a "minority" group in the United States acting alone to create forces for social change"

> "The majority group still has the power of superior number, superior resources, and an entrenched position in the social hierarchy. Morever, if the struggle is confined to mobilization of black power rather than generalized to embrace broad values, it produces repercussions in certain sectors of the white population.

The article by Leslie Pinckney Hill, origianlly published in the 1940's supports Katz's conclusion. According to Hill, blacks must demonstrate cooperativeness and nonviolence to attract members of the white majority to their cause.

Two articles discuss the values and consequences of protest and confrontation politics in implementing political change. The article by Ralph Conant examines the long-term limitations of confrontation politics in effecting sustained institutional changes. Blacks must develop and channel a social consciousness toward black control of vital social, economic and political institutions within the ghetto and the central cities. Alliances with third parties should not inhibit black political power. Michael Lipsky analyzes various forms of political protest. Essentially, he points out the numerous problems involved in trying to gain third party support for a protest movement.

Finally, the article by Donald Gelfand explores the consequences of a tenuous alliance between blacks, whites, and neighborhood organizations in preventing larger scale social change. The article indicates not only that alliances between members of different ethnic groups can influence integration of a neighborhood, but that the vested interests of certain members of a subordinate group may supersede their ethnic affiliations. Thus, alliances may be a force for promoting or impeding social change.

REFERENCES

SIMMEL, GEORGE
   1955 *Conflict and the web of group affiliations.* New York: Free Press.
KATZ, DANIEL
   1969 "Group process and social integration: A system analysis of two movements of social protest." Pp. 116–140 in H. P., Dreitzel (ed.), *Recent sociology, No. 1.* New York: Macmillan.

---

1.   WHAT THE NEGRO WANTS AND HOW TO GET IT:
            THE INWARD POWER OF THE MASSES

Leslie Pinckney Hill

Originally published in the early 1940s, this article by a black educator presented the dominant strategy of integrationists of that period. Hill argues that in order to attract a majority of whites towards an alliance with black Americans, blacks must demonstrate cooperativeness and nonviolence.

There is little doubt now as to what the American Negro wants. Never, perhaps, has the Negro himself been more vocal or emphatic in his appeal, and never have so many helpfully approving, influential voices been raised in the surrounding white world. We have heard Mrs. Roosevelt, Sumner Wells, Pearl Buck and Wendell Willkie sounding forth the warning that all the legitimate aims of the war and of the peace may be lost if America fails to accord to its Negro minority freedom, justice and fundamental equality. Negroes want to be accepted by our American society as citizens who in reality belong, who have the respect of their fellow man and equality of opportunity for life, liberty and the pursuit of happiness. Negroes want what good men want in every democratic society. If they wanted less they would not deserve the status of citizens.

These desires, harmonized with those four great freedoms which the Allied Nations have proclaimed as universal war objectives, are widely published by press and radio. They are now carefully documented. Negro and white leaders in many parts of the nation, and inter-racial committees North and South have been at pains to set out, in language which Negroes themselves have formulated, most of the specifics of the social, political and economic aims of Negro striving. When Negroes meet in Durham, North Carolina, to develop a platform of agreements, it is significant that white leaders in Atlanta, Georgia, are sitting down very soon afterwards to make known to the world the attitude of the white South. Both groups, fortunately, are at last making the attempt to find acceptable bases for agreement.

The National Broadcasting System made

SOURCE:

From *What the Negro Wants*, **Rayford W. Logan (ed.).   New York: Agathon Press, 1969. Reprinted by permission of the publisher.**

history recently by presenting for the first time its own attitude on the highly controversial race question.   Then it was that Wendell Willkie announced, and emphatically endorsed, at least six of the immediate aims of Negro effort:

1. Protection under the law and no discrimination in the administration of the law
2. Equality of education
3. Equality of expenditure for health and hospitalization
4. Elimination of all inhibiting restrictions in voting—through taxes or otherwise
5. Equal work opportunity and equal pay
6. The right to fight in any branch of the services

He might have included freedom from a generalizing press and from the usual moving picture presentation of the Negro as a scaramouch. These are minimum specifics. They are all, however, only items in the total urge of Negro life, under the impact of vast world forces, towards that status, precious now and consciously desired by all the peoples of the earth, in which equal recognition and full freedom will be accorded to the dignity and sanctity of all human personality in all human relations. The question is: How can the Negro achieve that status?

HOW CAN THE NEGRO GET WHAT HE WANTS—LEADERSHIP?

In attempting any answer to that question we have no lamp for our footing but the lamp of experience. Our light must shine from history, from the findings of all the sciences, and from the deathless words and example of those illumined spirits of every age and race in whom mankind has found inspiration and guidance. These all speak together of effort rooted in vision and long-enduring patience. No race or nation mushrooms up *en masse* into full-blown social accomplishment. No Rome was ever built in a day. There is no such thing as getting anywhere without going there. Time and the content we give it are always the final determinants.

And inasmuch as every people of whom we have record has been obliged to look to leaders through whose heart and mind they could express their hopes and define their directives—there is nowhere in history a single record to the contrary—it is clear that Negroes, whether in the disordered perspective-warping present time of tension and crisis, or in the outwardly calmer days of peace, will move forward only as the leaders whom they follow can effectively point the way. Of all the forces operating now toward the reaching of our aims and the molding of our future none is more potent for good or for evil than the force of this leadership.

Therefore I submit this fundamental thesis: The Negro will get the things he legitimately wants and strives for only if during the world crisis, and after it, he will follow leaders who have a known, articulate and unifying philosophy of life adequate to the exactions both of the crisis and to the still more difficult peace-time of reconstruction and rehabilitation. "The hungry sheep look up and are not fed." That was Milton's indictment of leaders whom he described as "blind mouths." But of another Leader it is written that the people heard Him gladly, that He spoke as one having authority because He brought the bread of life, the truth and a way. Who now will feed the discontented, disillusioned but waking masses of Negro people, and show them a path? What kind of leader must we magnify for a hindered but potentially great race?

We do not single out today any one all-dominating personality. There was a kind of social economy in the general uses made of the leadership of Frederick Douglass and Booker T. Washington. We have never had their equal in the responsibility these two men carried as referees in all the vexed issues

confronting their people. They dispensed a vast patronage, made nominations to the government for all kinds of services available to Negroes, were called into conference in all parts of the nation where dangers threatened, spoke with authority to both races and by both were gladly heard. Neither was a university man, and the scholars often raised the old question of the source of their authority. But they possessed high elemental powers which they wielded unwearyingly and unselfishly for the common good. Negro aspiration in America for generations was to be typified by the vigor and achievement of these two spokesmen.

Today the scene has changed. Not even in George Washington Carver were Negroes generally aware of a consciously accepted influence. He was for long years rather a self-effacing prophet representative of new interracial values which only the future of our culture will explore. Today there are many leaders, and their development in Negro life is deeply significant and heartening. These are men and women who have strong influence and loyal following in all those areas of action and interest in which Negroes struggle. They are teachers and preachers, business men and women, journalists, authors and artists, social workers, labor organizers, politicians, parents, farmers and soldiers. They are spread over the land, North, South, East and West. Each, in his community, has some positive effect upon the social, moral, political and economic life of both races. Their compounded power is immeasurable. A thousand men and women with self-possession, informed outlook and active energy must, in the nature of things, promise more than is desirable in a democratic society than one compelling figure, however gifted or potent.

The most impressive single fact in this wide dispersion of leaders is the unanimity of their convictions. What can be said or attempted or done differs, of course, with the geographical locus. Atlanta and New Orleans cannot duplicate the precise procedures of Philadelphia or New York. Nevertheless, Negro leaders in all these places want the same thing. They want in Georgia and Pennsylvania, here at home, the same freedom for which the democracies say they are fighting on the other side of the Pacific in Burma or Munda. They want that sense of being acceptable and belonging which can be realized only when there is ungrudging respect for all human personality, whatever the accident of color. And the legitimacy and the necessity of those aspirations are now progressively acknowledged not only by our comparatively liberal North but even by brave and democratic spirits emerging in our South.

Now this manifold leadership can be wrought into effective power if it can be inspired and harmonized by a conscious philosphy that will constitute an unfailing frame of reference for leaders in every field. Not always can that philosophy be translated easily into the language of the masses, but to those masses it will invariably be consecrated. Gradually the people will feel its power. The leader's philosophy must look before and after. It must be the sanctuary of his spirit, the repository of his social and moral values, must keep him calm and resourceful under every challenge or provocation, and strengthen him to survive the strain of mental and physical exertion. It must be the power of that grace which in the old world, as Plutarch reports, kept the face of Phocion serene and unperturbed, and in our century, made Gandhi a figure of world concern.

Long ago I formulated for myself as a teacher, and thus perilously and inescapably a leader of youth, a brief but comprehensive personal philosophy of human relations, which time and experience have seemed to confirm. When I think or speak in detail of the racial scene here at home it is always against this universal background. I submit this philosophy to my responsible brethren in the United States or elsewhere who find themselves swept by the sudden but tem-porary alarms of tension and conflict or challenged by the perduring blind pressures of prejudice.

A PERSONAL PHILOSOPHY OF HUMAN RELATIONS

The human family is one. The geographical or social factors that bind human beings together serve chiefly as conditioning settings from which proceed all those widely varying contributions, racial or national, that make up the culture of the world. Science continually proves the interdependency of all the races of man. Religion, education, politics and all the arts reinforce that proof. Race and nation are only terms by which we distinguish in this one human family vast aggragates of its members who have similar or identical characteristics.

. . .

No race or nation—as long as we think and behave under these concepts—can depend upon any other race or nation for its own advancement. Interdependency—now acknowledged everywhere—means fundamentally that each of the races must bear its own peculiar burden and, by working out its own salvation, help all the others.

. . .

Every race worthy of survival must make some definite and continuous contribution to the general welfare. Each, in good faith, must give as well as take. Rights must be balanced by obligations. Education must search out and develop every creative potentiality, large or small, and the whole group must magnify all the manifestations of genius.

• • •

No race can long survive or advance in full freedom if it fails to utilize its available resources and opportunities. These, left undeveloped, will be taken over and utilized, soon or late, by some other race.

• • •

Mandatory social objectives for the American Negro in his multi-racial environment must be adaptation and adjustment by co-operation. That indispensable cooperation will be powerfully assisted by strong personal self-control, good manners, intelligent tolerance, faith in the proved leaders and spokesmen of both races, and a reverent regard for the meaning and power of words. These are control factors directly related to the opening of opportunity for all kinds of participation and upgrading in the national service and elsewhere.

• • •

The greatest positive contribution the race can make to a deranged and demoralized civilization will be disciplined parents in upright, democratic homes wherein children are wanted and secure, and wherein they shall be taught respect for the laws of God and man, obedience to rightful authority, the universal need of self-sacrifice, responsibility for some worthy service to the family group, and the value of all work well done. Second only to the parent in all of this is the Negro teacher. Close to the school is the church. If these fail, the street will thwart home, school and church alike.

• • •

The race must keep all the friends it has in the dominant white world and work unceasingly to multiply them. Potent will be that discriminating intelligence by which Negroes will acknowledge the blessings they enjoy, as well as the wrongs they suffer. Praise must not be sacrificed to protest, nor protest to praise. No philosophy or procedure that produces racial hatred and antagonism can advance the common good.

• • •

World experience teaches that Negroes will make headway best by taking thought of one another and of their white friends in working out their common problems. Isolated individualism is impotent in an age whose genius is organization. By collective thinking every good mind, every skilled hand, every gift or grace of the spirit, every agency and every office is strengthened. In it there is room for all. Is is the only guarantee of that effective group action required by the ordeal of war or the exigencies of peace.

• • •

The common foe of the whole human race is war, because war is a heinous and blasphemous negation of all right human relations. Nevertheless, a nation is often drawn into this disaster, and then every citizen becomes a guardian, of his country's life. Then loyalty demands every sacrifice save that of honor.

• • •

In every emergency, the Negro race in America must give to the nation its unreserved allegiance. Wrongs will remain, but increasing opportunities and obligations will surpass them. Our democracy is not yet a satisfying reality, but Negroes are still free to live, strive, and die to make it come in God's unhurried time. All else by comparison is trivial.

---

2.   BLACK POWER: RHETORIC AND REALITY

Ralph W. Conant

"What is the fastest and most direct route to full social citizenship?" Conant
points out the long-term limitations of confrontation politics. If blacks are to
attain social equality, he argues, they must enlist the aid of influential whites
who could provide the resources necessary for blacks to attain control of the
economic and political institutions of ghetto communities.

The American nation is at least on the verge of coming to terms with the grossly inconsistent fact of an oppressed, excluded people in the midst of a body politic founded on principles of individual freedom and equality of opportunity. The founders knew the structure they designed could not survive in a system where slavery was tolerated, so they took the first step toward ending slavery by placing a limit of twenty years on the slave trade. The institution itself was abolished in a bloody confrontation between the North and the South more than eighty years after the founding of the nation.

In the century following that tragic and cleansing event, the Negro people have struggled to secure the full benefits of legal, political, and social citizenship[1] which are the requisites of equality of opportunity. The Negro gained legal citizenship a hundred years ago in President Lincoln's Emancipation Proclamation. Political citizenship, particularly the right to vote and to participate in political activities, has come to the Negroes

SOURCE
**"Black Power: Rhetoric and Reality" by Ralph
W. Conant is reprinted from** *Urban Affairs
Quarterly*, **Volume 4, Number 1 (September 1968)
pp. 15–25 by permission of the Publisher, Sage
Publications, Inc.**

recently and grudgingly, and in some sections of the country is still beyond their grasp, although vigorous registration activity by the Southern Regional Council's Voter Education Project has made remarkable progress throughout the South in the past few years. The rapid rise of Negroes holding public elective office in the South and throughout the nation is evidence that the new voting power of Negroes is being translated into effective political power. Social citizenship, the equal and unobstructed access to the institutions and instruments of social mobility and social welfare (in the broad sense), remains the central issue of oppression and exclusion today, and is the issue to which black power is rightfully addressed.

The question is, What is the fastest and most direct route to full social citizenship? Social citizenship does not require individual or group assimilation into the "mainstream," although that option must be retained. Social citizenship facilitates integration into the larger society without a necessary loss of ethnic or group identity, and therefore makes it possible for an ethnic group to integrate *as a group*, to enter and participate in the larger community without corresponding loss of ethnic identity. As Stokely Carmichael has pointed out, you can integrate communities, but you assimilate individuals.[2] Assimilation, a goal that is sought by many individual members of ethnic groups, including Negroes, follows the melting-pot theory, wherein ethnic groups disappear into the larger society. White Americans who promote integration on behalf of Negroes often seem to want black Americans to fade into the larger society, while whites who oppose integration seem to want to keep Negroes out of the white community. Most Negroes do not want to be forced in either of these directions, but want the freedom of choice that full social citizenship in our system provides.

Black Americans will eventually achieve full social citizenship; the question is how and when. There have always been a very few individual Negroes who have been able to make the grade as individuals, because in fact the barriers of discrimination are by no means impermeable. The routes to social citizenship open to the exceptional or exceptionally lucky individual are extremely narrow and tortuous. Achievement of full citizenship and mobility for the whole Negro community requires several broad strategies that have not heretofore been available in black communities. These strategies include: (1) black government of cities in which Negroes are the dominant voting block; and (2) black control of key social, economic, and political institutions of ghetto communities in cities where Negroes are not likely to become a majority in the near future. Both strategies require the emergence of effective leadership which can overcome the enormous problems of social and political disorganization that now typify black ghetto communities everywhere in the nation. At the present time, few Negro communities in the United States can be mobilized for anything short of spontaneous violence.

Unlike other ethnic groups that have passed through the familiar process of immigration, poverty, and the long climb to economic, political, and social well-being, black communities have never had or developed the institutional systems which are required to convert ethnic solidarity into economic and political power. Recently, Cleveland Negroes turned out in unprecedented numbers (close to 80% of these registered) to give almost unanimous support to Carl Stokes for Mayor, who as a result became America's first Negro big-city chief executive.[3] But because he had to have 30,000 white votes to win (out of 130,000)—and even then by the slimmest of margins (1,500 votes)—and because he could not count on as full a black vote again, Mayor Stokes has had to make conciliatory moves to strengthen his position in the white community, not all of which are seen by the black community as beneficial.

James Q. Wilson has documented some of the fundamental problems of organization and leadership in urban Negro communities in his 1960 study of *Negro Politics*.[4] Most of his analysis still applies to the situation in ghetto communities in 1968, although the added element of severe and widespread riots has given substance to the voice of militant leaders who until recently had little or no influence in the majority Negro community.

Now as Negroes are filling the old areas of our largest cities, are increasingly restive about conditions, and are less and less reluctant to press for effective action, and as resources, especially from the federal government, are becoming available in meaningful amounts, the problem of Negro leadership is approaching crisis proportions. Because Negro communities are tightly segregated (by white policy as well as by black choice), it is imperative that black leaders emerge to provide a decision-making apparatus for the management and distribution of the new resources. The current scene in ghetto communities all across the country is one of fierce (and sometimes destructive) competition among potential leaders. Old organizations are being challenged by new groups who often affect an abrasive stance in their relations with whites to prove "where they're at," especially to the youngsters who are ready to riot at almost any provocation. Indeed, the riot has become the chief threat weapon of the new militants. Not that they can call a riot into being or stop one once it has started; but they can and do involve the *preconditions* of riot as bargaining items, both in their approaches to whites with resources to distribute and in their competitive relations with older Negro leaders.

The riot as a threat weapon must be regarded by responsible militants as a temporary expedient of political organizational development in the black community, for riots are traumatic and destructive events. Up to a point, they will jolt the white community into constructive response. Beyond that elusive point, the white society will respond to the demands of hard-core bigots and other repressive forces to put down and further alienate the black community. The reality of a ten-to-one white majority must be taken into account by black leaders who aspire to constructive solution to their dilemma.

It seems to me that the most profitable course for black leaders to take, in cities that now have a 35% or more Negro population, is to try for a Negro mayor as soon as plausible candidates can be mustered. Twenty-two cities have already reached that level of black population; two of these have elected Negro Mayors (Gary, Indiana, and Cleveland, Ohio). Washington, D.C., whose population is 66% black, got a Negro mayor last year by the grace of a Presidential appointment. Several middle-sized cities whose Negro populations are under 20% have produced Negro mayors, including Flint and Saginaw, both in Michigan, and Springfield, Ohio.

The next large cities that elect Negro mayors are likely to be those whose black populations exceed 50%; Newark (now 52% black), Atlanta, Baltimore, and Detroit by 1975; Chicago, New Orleans, Oakland, and St. Louis by 1980; Camden and Trenton (both in New Jersey) by 1985. A number of other cities, including Cleveland and Gary, whose Negro populations go beyond 40%, will elect Negro mayors off and on until the Negro political base consolidates to the point of predominance.

By 1985, I estimate that there will be thirty-five million Negroes in the United States, nearly twice as many as there were in 1960. The vast majority (up to 80%) of this population will probably be living in cities. It seems reasonable to prognosticate that those cities which develop a majority black population, elect Negro mayors, and convert to black-dominated bureaucracies will become the strong magnets for migrating Negroes, and the opposite for whites. The all-black or mostly black central cities will, of course, number less than a dozen by the end of the century, but these cities will provide Negroes with opportunities to achieve a secure and powerful place in national as well as local politics.

The trend toward black government in cities will be deeply disturbing to whites, especially to those whose professional careers are spent in the heart of these cities and whose economic and cultural investments remain there. What the white community must understand and face up to is that black self-government must occur in substantial proportions in this country before blacks can integrate with the larger society on a truly equal basis. Whites must realize that a black takeover in some cities will have no more grim consequences for the white society than did the Irish takeover of Boston three generations ago. Out of that political evolution, the Irish integrated, on their own terms; they have grown to political maturity, as the blacks can; and they have produced a brilliant group of leaders, as the blacks can.

The prognostications offered here about which cities in the United States may have

Negro mayors within the next decade or two are based on observable trends in the growth rates of Negro populations in the cities (and corresponding white out-migration) and developments in Negro political activity, such as registration increases, voting, and the rapid upswing in the numbers of Negro office-holders.

From the standpoint of the black community these are hopeful trends, in that they represent actual opportunities to exploit traditional political avenues to real power and influence at all levels in the federal system. These trends also represent a challenge to aspiring leaders in the black communities of the cities I have named, to build the political base necessary to win out over the old established organizations (e.g., the political parties, the economic interest groups) which know only too well how to hold on to what they have got. No black leader, however skillful in the rhetoric of black power and "hate whitey," can bank on the existence of black pluralities or majorities to take over the reins of government in any city. There is and always has been a deeply rooted conservatism in black communities everywhere, not just in the South. Our surveys last year at the Lemberg Center for the Study of Violence of Brandeis University revealed overwhelming support of the "old line" civil rights organizations and the established national leaders such as the late Martin Luther King, Jr., Whitney Young, and Roy Wilkins.

Black government will indeed come to several large cities in the next few years, but it will come first in those cities whose black populations are overwhelmingly large, well organized, and led by energetic, responsible men who know the practical art of creating a constituency out of a pluralistic community. LeRoi Jones, the black poet and playwright, has announced a black convention in Newark to select black candidates for every city office in the next election. It will be an event of great significance to local Negro leadership in other cities if Jones achieves his aim, for his

political style is the hard-line militancy which most Negroes have shunned in the past.

Even if Negro communities begin to produce local political leaders who can appeal to and organize the broad spectrum of social and economic groups that inhabit the typical urban ghetto, it remains to be seen whether this leadership will develop rapidly enough to head off counter-actions by the white establishment. Temporary moves to dilute and circumvent potential Negro influence have been common in the South. These have included discouraging Negroes from registering or voting, electing city councils at large, and systematic annexations of white suburbs. These tactics are still commonly practiced in the South as ways of keeping Negroes off city councils and out of other political offices.

The North went through a period, in early decades of this century, of municipal consolidations, annexation programs, and other reform measures such as at-large elections and the short ballot (which decreased elective offices and increased appointive ones), all in the name of stamping out corruption and promoting efficiency and good management in local government. Annexations and consolidations as routes to large-scale metropolitan government (also for the sake of efficiency and economy) were pushed hard in the North and West all through the fifties and into the sixties, but most of these efforts failed because of intense opposition in suburban communities, where residents wanted to have direct local control of schools, zoning, and police. It has seldom occurred to political leaders or ordinary white citizens, either in the cities or the suburbs in the North, that metropolitan government might be a strategy for heading off black-dominated central cities. Only Newark, Baltimore, or Detroit might have thought of it as a significant issue, but the fact is that most northerners, until the recent crescendo of central city riots, had not thought about the matter at all. They will in the years ahead, though, and those who live or have significant investments in the central city will be thinking hard about ways to head off or dilute black political domination of the central city. The northern cities will never go to metropolitan government on this issue, however, except possibly a few of the smaller ones.

The most likely strategies in the largest cities will be to utilize massive urban development projects in the central cities, coupled with low-income and middle-income housing projects scattered in the near-in suburbs where old neighborhoods seem logical sites for residential redevelopment. Such a strategy will serve the desire of low- and middle-income Negroes to get out of the central city; the requirements of the central city to upgrade its tax base; and the needs of certain types of commercial activities to be located at the core of the city. Federal and local redevelopment programs will not again repeat the colossal blunders of the fifties in failing to provide adequate and attractive relocation programs. This new strategy will work, in the cities which whites control long enough to put it into execution. If it works, whites may retain indefinite control of some of the cities which otherwise would have shifted to black control in the next two decades.

The second major strategy whites will pursue to retain effective control of cities is through federally-sponsored metropolitan planning. Since the early 1960's, there have been a series of concerted efforts in Washington, spearheaded by the White House, the Bureau of the Budget, the Commission on Intergovernmental Relations, Senator Edmund Muskie's staff of the Senate Subcommittee on Intergovernmental Relations (Governement Operations Committee), and officials in the Department of Housing and Urban Development, to bring into being a comprehensive planning agency in every metropolitan area in the United States as a means of forcing a modicum of planning and

coordination among federally funded projects at the local level. The geographical purview of these metropolitan planning agencies usually extends to the boundaries of the standard metropolitan statistical areas as defined by the Bureau of the Census, although the boundaries vary according to the state laws which establish them. The program review jurisdiction established by Title II of the Demonstration Cities and Metropolitan Development Act of 1966 extends to open-space land projects, hospitals, airports, libraries, water supply and distribution facilities, sewerage facilities and waste treatment works, highways,, transportation facilities, and conservation projects.

The federal government had to move to mandatory planning at the metropolitan level because local jurisdictions within the metropolitan areas would not or could not develop the capacity to cooperate effectively in projects that require a metropolitan scale for planning and administration. The federal government has also recognized that local jurisdictions do not effectively represent the interests of its newer constituents, the Negroes and other new minority groups. Cities and suburbs alike have taken advantage of federal programs that benefit their middle-class white constituencies and have often ignored or passed up programs aimed at the urban poor, because of resistance from other adversely affected politically potent groups. Public housing, urban renewal, model cities, and education programs designed for the poor have been blocked in Congress or in the local communities. To circumvent local resistance, the federal government is developing a metropolitan administrative and planning apparatus empowered to see that localities comply with a comprehensive plan drawn up in accordance with federal guidelines. As Piven and Cloward point out,[5] such an apparatus will eventually be redefining political issues as matters for experts to decide. The metropolitan agencies will in effect, become metropolitan governments, and in the process may leave little of importance for local government—even the big-city governments—except to execute programs that have been formulated at the federal and metropolitan levels.

What difference will metropolitanism make to the new black mayors? Maybe not very much. As Piven and Cloward indicate, there will be some housing rehabilitation, expanded education programs, and social services of the human renewal variety—"programs which appease, guide, and control the recipients of service and which exact no visible toll from dominant groups. Local resistance, which until now has stymied even these programs, will be overcome, and that is what Negroes can expect to gain as a minority constituency in metropolitan consolidation."

In this strategy of metropolitan control, the Negroes in most of the cities I have listed will get their mayor and even their black bureaucracy, but will they have local self-government in the traditional sense? The answer is that it depends on the resourcefulness of black political leadership in initiating programs of social and economic development for the local community and in exercising vigorous leadership in seeing to it that metropolitan-wide programs also serve the local constituency.

Aspiring leaders in the black communities of America may require a period of separatism in order to develop viable political, economic, and social institutions that will put the Negro community on a truly equal psychological footing with the white community. But Negro leaders who do not look beyond separatism toward the political realities of an integrated society cannot survive or help their people to survive in a nation where consolidation and centralization are the inevitable responses to the technical demands of a society whose unparalleled resources are the driving incentive.

Black government in most American cities

is to far off to be an effective short-term solution to the crisis of confrontation which has come to the foreground in nearly every city where there is a significant black population. So far Phoenix (5% nonwhite), Seattle (7%), and San Diego (7%) have not had a riot in the current series of race-related civil disturbances which have been occurring continuously since 1964. But Minneapolis (4%), Milwaukee (10%), San Francisco, and Boston (about 12% each) have experienced very serious eruptions. The number or proportion of Negroes in a community is not the most significant factor in riot potential. For one thing, the percentages of blacks will continue to grow in every Northern city in the population range of 200,000 and above. For another thing, the grievances underlying the current wave of ghetto violence are commonly shared by all Negroes in the United States who find themselves blocked from access to housing, employment, and other avenues of full participation in the larger society.

White political and civic leaders boggle at the demands of black power militants who are now insisting on black control of the economic, political, governmental, and social institutions of the ghetto and suggesting that white proprietors and agents of the white power structure withdraw or be withdrawn from the ghetto. White leaders are appalled at the bold demands of the black militants for unconditional grants to ghetto leaders for ghetto development projects. One such group in Pittsburgh recently asked a group of corporation and foundation leaders in that city for a $2,200,000 grant for unspecified use in the ghetto community. The response was puzzled shock mixed with disbelief and indignation.

In short run, the direction and shape of the current urban crisis in America will be largely determined by the nature of the response of white influentials, both at the national and local levels, to the search for leadership in the ghetto communities. Should the whites take symbolic demands (and symbolic rhetoric) as literal demands—and, because they sound absurd, reject them? If so, the conflict will polarize and the crisis will deepen. When black militants make demands, these demands are absurd-sounding in inverse proportion to their perception of the confidence they feel the white influentials have in them: the less confidence they believe the white influentials have in them, the more absurd-sounding the demand. As positive relationships develop between white leaders and aspiring black leaders, the demands will become less symbolic and more realistic. If past relations between white leaders and black spokesmen have been poor, the white influentials may have to accede to the original symbolic demand before realistic next steps can be taken. In any event, some proof of confidence must precede entry into a relationship of mutual respect.

White influentials who find themselves confronted with "black power" demands ordinarily reject them as unrealistic. What they mean by unrealistic is that the blacks who present them have no bargaining power. The demands themselves are, in the main, forms of control and influence which whites are quite used to having and exercising. What appears to be a demand for separation is really a demand for local self-government, which is a cherished tradition in white America. When ghetto leaders in Harlem, Roxbury, Watts, and Hough call for locally controlled (and separate) school districts, they are demanding what whites already have and pay for in suburban communities. To put it another way, whites want to run their own schools, have their own police departments, determine land uses, and all the rest. So does the black community. The white man wants the freedom to move about in the larger community and be a part of it on his own terms. So does the black man. The white man wants to be influential in decisions that directly affect him. So does the black man. The white man wants privacy, separatism, identity, and self-government. So does the

black man. The white, however, must carry his own burden economically. The black can't, and this is an issue with which we must come to terms.

The white already has these things because he is in possession of his community and his government. Not so the black. What white influentials must understand is that the black must possess his own neighborhood, his own community, and eventually his own government before he can possess himself; and he must possess himself before he can embrace the larger community. The Negro will in time get a chance at self-government if the traditional processes of local political evolution continue to operate in his favor. In the meantime, the Negro must be encouraged and supported in his efforts to gain effective influence over the institutions of social mobility and control in his own community.

How can this aim be achieved, short of walling off the ghetto as a separate political entity? I recently suggested the following solution to black and white leaders in Pittsburgh: White leaders should raise a several-million-dollar endowment fund to support the creation of a nonprofit ghetto community corporation, which would use the income to build a staff of program and fund-raising experts to sort out and develop projects of all kinds—physical, social, and political—as needed in the ghetto community. The corporation would be run entirely by ghetto leaders selected in a community caucus in which all residents of the Negro community would be eligible to participate. The only hand the white community would have in the establishment of the ghetto corporation would be to provide the capital funding; and the only conditions attached to the funding would be that the corporation be created by an exclusively black but otherwise open community caucus, and that it be in accordance with the nonprofit corporation laws of the state and federal governments.

One of the toughest dilemmas white influentials face in relating to the black community is the confusing diversity of established and aspiring leaders. Even when white influentials want to aid in the development of ghetto leadership (as they seem to in Pittsburgh), they cannot be sure of the who's who; and indeed the who's who of most ghetto communities is a changing, fluid, highly competitive spectrum of able and not-so-able people. The white community has a fairly stable set of political, eocnomic, and social institutions which sort out and label white leadership along lines that are reasonably well-known and accepted. Most such institutions have not yet developed in black communities, and the white ones are not sufficiently open to Negroes to perform the sorting out and labeling process in lieu of black ones.

Given a high enough stake (in Pittsburgh it would probably take at least five million dollars), black communities could be induced to caucus and, in the process of organizing a ghetto corporation board of directors, actually sort out and float to the top a viable leadership. The moment the corporation came into being, the endowment—which must be available in escrow as a necessary incentive to a successful caucus—would become its funding base.

The Pittsburgh plan is a bold solution to the short-run problems of the black-white confrontation. It has the potential for resolving the crisis of confidence between black and white leadership. It provides a formula for identifying and bringing into play a spectrum of ghetto leadership, and for encouraging compromise and cooperation within the ghetto in developing solutions to ghetto problems. It avoids paternalistic overseeing of ghetto programs by white influentials, and indeed relieves the latter of responsibility for *direct* problem-solving. What may be the most important advantage of the plan, it provides a corporate mechanism for matching private and public resources to ghetto requirements. In time such a corporation might become the base for the development of political leadership in the ghetto, the source and training ground of Negro political leaders for citywide, state, and national positions. In the long run, the ghetto corporation could become the main instrument for repairing the schism that has tragically come between the black and white communities of America.

NOTES

1. See T. M. Marshal, *Class, Citizenship, and Social Development* (N. Y.: Doubleday, 1964), chap. 4; cited by Talcott Parsons in "Full Citizenship for the Negro American?" in *Daedalus,* issue on "The Negro American," Fall, 1965.

2. Stokely Carmichael in an interview in *The Militant,* May 23, 1966; cited by Christopher Lasch in "A Special Supplement: The Trouble with Black Power," *New York Review of Books,* X No. 4 (Feb. 29, 1968).

3. Jeffrey K. Hadden, Louis H. Masotti, and Victor Thiessen, "The Making of Negro Mayors, 1967," Trans-action, Jan.-Feb., 1968.

4. James Q. Wilson, *Negro Politics: The Search for Leadership* (N. Y.: Free Press, 1960).

5. Francis Piven and Richard Cloward, "Black Control of Cities," *The New Republic,* Oct. 27, 1967.

3   # INFLUX-EXODUS; AN EXPLORATORY STUDY OF RACIAL INTEGRATION*

Donald E. Gelfand

Racial integration of suburban communities has continually produced major conflicts and a seemingly inexorable "invasion-succession" pattern. Gelfand details the history of one suburban community facing racial integration and shows how suspicion and hostility prevented the development of alliances between blacks and whites that might have resulted in a different development of the situation. The author also examines other research in this area and suggests a theoretical approach toward studies in this area.

The occurrence of racially integrated housing has often provoked hostility and conflict, but the dynamics of these conflicts remains unclear. Attitudinal studies have failed to produce an explanatory or predictive model of this process. The fears whites have of lower property values resulting from the movement of blacks into an area has been well documented (Bressler, 1960; Fulton, 1959; McEntire, 1960). According to the "equal-status contact" hypothesis, these fears will be counteracted if whites and blacks intermingle in a neighborhood on an equalitarian basis rather than in a master-servant relationship. Early studies of public housing projects indicated that whites and blacks living together on this equalitarian basis had more positive attitudes toward racial integration than residents of a segregated housing development (Duetsch and Collins, 1951; Wilner, Walkley, and Cook, 1955). Despite these indications and the growing percentage of middle income black families, the number of integrated housing areas remains minimal.

The effectiveness of housing integration is related not only to the patterns of contact between whites and blacks but to the maintenance of institutionalized beliefs about various ethnic groups, the pressures exerted by significant "others" on residents of integrated areas, and the presence or absence of vital community organizations in these areas. The research discussed here is a preliminary attempt to develop a theoretical approach to the study of housing integration based on the factors noted above.

The focus of the discussion will be on the patterns that developed as a result of racial integration in four socio-economically distinct areas. After examining briefly the setting and historical development of housing in these areas, attention will be concentrated on the major forces in this situation and the mechanisms and patterns of reasoning that were crucial in the reaction of residents to the integration of the area.

* I am greatly indebted to Kent D. Rice for his advice and encouragement during the course of this research.

SOURCE
Original article prepared for this volume.

Setting

University City is the seventh largest city in the state of Missouri. Bordering St. Louis, it was the first muncipality to be founded outside the central city. Having developed over an extended period it now possesses a variety of homes ranging from the apartment houses which dominate its eastern end to a wide range of single family homes ranging in price from $5,000 to over $40,000. During the late 1960s all of these areas were subjected to an influx of black families, anxious to take advantage of the good housing available in University City. The support of fair housing resolutions in this city provided the opportunity for black families to purchase homes that were not available to them in other restricted communities.

Study Design

Intent on studying the conflicts that were developing over integration, four research areas were selected. The selected areas differed considerably in the price of the average home. Table 1 outlines the price ranges of the homes in the four areas and the predominant occupational characteristics of the residents.

by the changing population of the community. New black residents living at selected distances from whites were surveyed. Since there were already large numbers of black families living in the study areas, strict maintenance of this "epidemiological" model was difficult (Northwood and Barth, 1964). Every attempt was made to interview whites living next to black families. The major share of the interviewing was concentrated on those blocks with large numbers of black residents. In all, 62 whites and 22 blacks were interviewed during a period of two months.

PATTERNS OF INTERACTION

Black families moving into University City were solidly middle class in economic status and social orientation. White residents, carefully scrutinized their new neighbors and quickly recognized their middle-class orientations. A large proportion of them were teachers. In many cases both spouses were employed at full-time jobs and earning substantial incomes. Their standards of dress and behavior, the types of cars driven, the behavior of the children, and the maintenance of the homes indicated to white resi-

Table 1. Occupational Status of Residents and Price of Homes in Study Areas

Area	Occupational Status	Price of Homes
1	Professional	$25,000+
2	Professional and semiprofessional	$17,000–23,000
3	Semiprofessional, clerical and sales	$10,000–15,000
4	Semiskilled and unskilled	$ 5,000–12,000

As is apparent from this table, there was a strong relationship between the price of the homes and occupational status. There was also a strong relationship between the price of the home and the age of the residents, areas 1 and 4 having the highest concentration of older and retired residents.

A small sample was chosen from these areas. Not a random sample, interviewers attempted to question families most affected

dents that their new black neighbors did not fit any common stereotypic images. Despite this recognition, the fears of whites did not diminish.

Primary interracial contact may have promoted frank discussion and alliances to meet these fears of community change, but these personal relationships failed to extensively develop in any of the areas. Although secondary contacts in shopping areas naturally became more common as the number of blacks in the city increased, socializing on any personal level remained intermittent and relatively infrequent. The teas and parties that were held in an attempt to extend interracial contacts failed to promote lasting interracial friendships. As Brown and Alers (1956) noted in the 1950s whites in integrated areas are often unwilling to associate with blacks if they have to initiate the interaction. Black residents of University City waited for this initiative rather than risking rejection. Not receiving it, they accepted the chilly but passive attitude of whites in the areas as a satisfactory alternative.

A great deal of the hesitation by whites must be attributed to their general racial attitudes and specific fears of interracial dating and marriage. One resident in area 3, a semiprofessional area, prepared to live in an integrated neighborhood when she purchased her home in 1964, openly expressed these concerns. Her fears centered around allowing her children to play with blacks in the area while they were young and then having to forbid them at a later time to date black friends. This anxiety reduced her willingness to have any personal contact with neighbors. The results of an administered social distance scale (Williams, 1964) indicate that this attitude was common among respondents in all four areas (Table 2).

It is also probable that liberal sociologists have overstressed the importance of interaction with whites for middle-class blacks. The majority of black families implied that they regarded interracial socializing as definitely secondary to the acquisition of good housing for their families. Adequate housing, either in white or black neighborhoods, was, and would remain, their major objective. Though they all preferred integrated areas, none of the black respondents indicated that they would move if the neighborhood lost its integrated character.

Many of these residents were able to fulfill their social need by interaction with other black families in the community. This was relatively easy since many of these families moved not as isolated units, but in groups with friends and relatives. Most importantly, friends of these black families living in other areas supported their movement into formerly all white neighborhoods. As will be shown later, this situation was reversed for whites, with friends and relatives attempting to draw residents away from the integrating communities.

NEIGHBORHOOD ASSOCIATIONS

Initial attempts to implement primary interaction between whites and blacks in the four areas were supported by the neighborhood

Table 2. Social Distance Scale Scores—% Negative Responses

Questions: How do you feel about: (1) Eating at the same table with a Negro?
(2) Dancing with a Negro?
(3) Going to a party where the majority of guests are Negro?
(4) Having someone in your family marry a Negro?

Area	Question 1	Question 2	Question 3	Question 4
1	12	67	67	83
2	20	47	60	90
3	14	43	86	93
4	26	86	93	93

associations. These associations existed in three of the four areas when black families started purchasing homes in University City. However, aside from sporadic activities, these associations had made few effective attempts to become vital forces in the community. Given the dormitory nature of most suburban communities their lack of vitality is not surprising. As Keller (1968) has noted, the "neighborhood" concept appears to have lessening applicability to the realities of American residential patterns. Given the centering of work, and social networks outside suburban areas, it is not surprising that neighborhood associations find it difficult to foster neighborhood solidarity. The problems created by the influx of blacks into the four areas stirred the associations into action.

In areas 2, a professional and semiprofessional area, the association mobilized to meet what residents perceived as a crisis situation. It brought the first black resident into the organization soon after he moved into the area and other black families quickly became active in its ranks. The association also made an intensive effort to quiet the fears of white homeowners by means of newsletters, meetings, and speeches. These efforts aroused a negative reaction among many residents, who resented any questioning of their motives for selling their homes.

When the number of black families in the area had substantially increased, a group of new black homeowners attempted to slow the influx of blacks into the area. They stood on the street corners on a Sunday, assured prospective black homebuyers that they were welcome in the area, but at the same time handed them a listing of homes that were available in other areas. This strategy backfired. Blacks looking for homes in the area viewed it as an attempt to keep them out of the neighborhood, and white homeowners saw it as unwarranted attempt to prevent them from selling. Ventures of this

kind began to meet stiffening resistance from whites, and the neighborhood association lost its momentum as it failed to stem the influx of blacks into the area.

The associations in the other three areas did not have to face as intensive a crisis and, therefore, had a more stable existence. In area 4, the blue-collar area, the main overt function of the organization was to protect a deteriorating neighborhood from urban renewal. There was little discussion at the meetings about the effects of black families on the area. No effort was made to bring black residents in as members. While there was no open discussion of the integration of the community, city officials felt that private conversations among members helped to solidify negative attitudes of residents towards integration.

Isaacs (1948) and Sussman (1957) cite instances in which neighborhood associations have provided solidarity for an area and served as a means of thwarting integration, but this trend was evident only in the blue collar area. In the other three neighborhoods, the pattern that Sussman (1957) details, —initial enthusiasm over the formation of the organization, gradual disillusionment as the educational programs of the association fails to stem the influx of new residents, and the dissolution of the organization as the neighborhood becomes predominantly black—appeared to prevail.

Real estate agents

The neighborhood associations were neither the only or by any means the most important group active during the initial stages of the integration process. The most important influences were undoubtedly those of real estate agents, friends, and relatives of the residents. The exact role agents played in developing or allaying fears in the neighborhoods remains a subject of controversy, but there is no doubt that residents in all four areas received numerous calls from agents offering to list and sell their homes. The large number of calls accentuated negative attitudes toward the influx of blacks. Upon direct examination, few respondents were willing to recognize this influence. One knowledgeable informant in area 2 suggested that residents could be divided into two groups: those thinking about selling their homes at the time of the interview and those determined to stay in the area. Receiving the largest number of new black residents, area 2 also received a great amount of publicity from the local press during the early period of integration. It was also the focus of a long debate in the City Council over the need for a fair housing law. As residents influenced by publicity and pressure from real estate agents, left the area and black families replaced them the efforts of real estate agents subsided. It appeared that the movement of whites out of the area had already received an impetus not requiring any outside assistance.

Friends and relatives

White real estate agents were predominantly influential in questions of property values, friends and relatives were relied on by respondents for a definition of the desirability of an integrated neighborhood. As was expected, close friends and relatives of many of the respondents lived outside the immediate area. As greater numbers of blacks began to move into University City, residents became concerned about the judgments of their peers. Friends and relatives, viewing the influx of blacks from white suburban areas, made it clear that they had negative feelings about the situation. Property value declines, a takeover of the area by poor blacks and a decline in status were seen by friends and relatives as the probable consequence of the changes taking place in the areas.

Although there was little admission of this influence by respondents there was a good deal of informal evidence to support Hamblin's (1962) contention that friends and relatives are the most crucial influence in the tendency of individuals to discriminate. In one case, an interview was interrupted by the appearance of the respondent's sister-in-law, a former resident of the area. It was obvious from her conversation that she had been extremely influential in the decision of her brother and his wife to sell their home and move from the area.

The unwillingness of residents to recognize the influence of their peers or to discuss its effects is consistent with the need to maintain satisfying self-conceptions. Although group dynamics experiments (Asch, 1956) have demonstrated that individuals often remain unaware of the importance of group influences upon their decisions, dissonance theory may offer a more adequate explanation of the reaction observed in this research. A review of this literature (Deutsch and Krauss, 1964) suggests that dissonances arise not only during the course of decision making, but also when an activity is at odds with the individuals' self-image. Recognition of influential exterior forces is therefore viewed as an admission of a lack of control over a situation, i.e., of "not being able to think for yourself." Influences that interfere with independent action are seen as dissonant with the individual's valued self-conceptions. Respondents in the study areas repeatedly and emphatically asserted their ability to "think for themselves" and not be influenced by pressures exerted by their peers although there were numerous contrary indicators.

City government

Unfortunately, the negative impact of relatives, friends, and real estate agents could not be counteracted by the city. City officials entered the situation at a late date, attempting at first to bolster the efforts of the neighborhood associations. At a later point, a local minister was hired to dispel rumors about growing numbers of blacks and the lowering of property values. His primary tactic was to address meetings of P.T.A. and other neighborhood organizations. The inability of the neighborhood associations to counter the situation that was developing and the lack of neighborhood solidarity in any of the four areas doomed these tactics to failure. The negative opinions of other groups were too strong and well established and in the case of friends and relatives granted higher legitimacy than the views of city officials.

The actors and the influences they exerted did not vary greatly from area to area. Area 2 attracted the greatest publicity and the greatest number of black families because of the prices of the houses in this neighborhood. The pressures exerted on this area, however, were comparable to those that developed in the other three neighborhoods, varying only in their intensity.

THE MECHANISMS OF CHANGE IN INTEGRATING COMMUNITIES

The examination of the major actors in this situation leads to an analysis of the mechanisms and factors that produced the "invasion-succession" that developed in the four areas. Three mechanisms were crucial in this process: (a) the concentrated influx of black families that pushed these areas past the "tipping point"; (b) the concern of residents with "community identity"; and (c) the "exemption mechanism" by which residents explained the discrepancy between their stereotyped impression of blacks and their appraisal of new black residents.

Tipping and visibility

The "tipping point" has been a major construct of ethnic relations in recent years. When a new group moves into an area where they are unwanted, they are tolerated at first. When the proportion of residents in the area belonging to this group increases to the "tipping point" the population of the neighborhood begins to change drastically as residents feel they are about to be displaced. This "tipping point" is usually considered to occur when 30 to 40 percent of the area's residents are from the new group.

In the four study areas, the withdrawal of whites from the area could not be attributed solely to the numbers of new black families. An important factor was the heavy concentration of black families in segments of those four areas. This concentration was especially evident in area 2, a semiprofessional and professional area. Rose (1953) has noted the ability of an area to absorb a small number of blacks without undergoing a rapid withdrawal of whites. It is also likely that a neighborhood will be able to absorb a larger number of black families without panic on the part of the whites if these new families are spread throughout the area. A large number of black families moving into an area during a short period of time, especially if concentrated in one segment of the community makes the absorption process more difficult.

Community identity

This visibility and concentration added to the fears that black residents posed to many of the white homeowners' community identity. "Community identity" is an important component of status crystalization and presentation of self. It is characteristically a fundamental concern of upwardly mobile individuals such as the young professionals and semiprofessionals who were predominant in area 2. The type of house and car, the general layout of the area, and the ethnic, racial, and social characteristics of the population are all important aspects of "community identity." An individual's "community identity" is based on his position in the areas. Individuals at the extremes of the age pyramid are often anchored to a neighborhood. This may be due to a lack of income or lack of the stamina required to move. Young families concerned with maintaining their upward social mobility and at the peak of their earning power are prepared to move if their community identity is threatened.

The semiprofessionals in the two middle-priced areas were prepared to give the most consideration to moving. Although they admitted that the movement of black families into the area was not an automatic correlative of deterioration, their concern about the status of their "community identity" overrode these perceptions. Less secure in their social identity than older professional, they were attentive to safeguarding all external signs of successful mobility. They regarded their present homes as only temporary residences. Their eventual goal was the type of home predominant in the most expensive area. In contrast, residents who had reached this goal were content and more attached to their homes than homeowners in any of the other three areas.

Residents in the blue collar neighborhood had limited geographical mobility due to their generally advanced age, a lack of adequate financial resources for moving, and the small number of homes available in other areas for a comparable price. It was thus the residents in the middle-price neighborhoods who were first to move. They were interested in remaining in their area until their house became too small for their needs or they could afford a mortgage on a more lavish home. The influx of blacks into these areas was seen as posing a threat to their community identity and thus accelerated their movement. A segment of this population attempted to stabilize the neighborhood by becoming active in the efforts of the neighborhood association to preserve an integrated neighborhood. As these efforts floundered and other white families continued to move away their concerns about community identity became intensified and they also began to consider moving to other areas.

Exemption Mechanism

Given their realistic appraisal of black families moving into the area, it was difficult at first to understand why white homeowners still viewed the movement of middle class blacks into University City as a threat to their community identity. Black families moving into these neighborhoods did not fit the expectations of white residents in either their status attributes or their behavior. White residents in the four study areas developed a complex pattern of reasoning and analysis to resolve the discrepancy between their impressions and expectations.

There was widespread application of what Dean (1955) has referred to as the "exemption mechanism." This term refers to a tendency to view high status or "cultured" individuals in an ethnic group as exempt from that groups' general characteristics. The first black families moving into the four areas were not viewed as a threat. Residents observed that they were solidly middle class and above what they regarded as the characteristics of the "ordinary" black person. Concern centered around the second wave of black families who would follow the initial influx. It was assumed that these families would be of a lower socioeconomic class and transform the neighborhood into something resembling an inner city ghetto such as the west end of St. Louis.

A major factor in the transformation of the west end of St. Louis into a slum area was the overcrowding of single family residences by three families. Although officials insisted that the housing code in University City would prevent such a pattern from recurring, many residents remained unconvinced and awaited the occurrence of these conditions as soon as the first black families bought a home in the neighborhood. As more black families moved in, these fears were heightened.

As a result of the application of the "exemption mechanism" and the rapid influx of blacks into the area, residents developed a fear of being the last white family in this area. The events already described prevented frank communication and discussion of the issues among residents. This lack of communication facilitated the development of suspicions among white residents that their neighbors were secretly planning to move. On a block already containing black families, several white residents would express this fear during the course of an evening. As blacks continued to move into the area, the application of the "exemption mechanism" and the development of the fear of withdrawal by white families succeeded in actually producing a self-fulfilling prophecy and the changeover of the area from one that was totally white to one that promised to be totally black.

Finally some attention should be paid to education, a factor sociologists have often stressed as crucial in determining reactions to racial integration. It did not prove vital in this situation. The differences in the educational level of the respondents in the four areas did not prove a satisfactory explanation of differences in attitudes and behavior. More educated respondents expressed less negative attitudes towards the black families moving into the area, but had the same desire to move as their more poorly educated neighbors. Education may help to define a situation except when fundamental concerns such as community identity are threatened. In this case, residents, despite their educational background, will fall back on more basic protective motives to provide themselves with guidelines for the evaluation of alternative modes of action.

CONCLUSION

This study was a beginning exploratory effort but the elements that would provide a valid theory of racial integration in the urban community can be seen. As this research has attempted to indicate, this theory must go beyond continued reliance on the simplistic model of the "tipping point." Other variables such as visibility and concentration may confound or intensify the effect produced by large numbers of ethnic group members moving into an area.

Perhaps the best way to approach the topic of neighborhood integration is to start from the premise that racism is a strong motivating force in American society. Having become institutionalized, racism and ethnic hatred has forced groups such as blacks, Puerto Ricans, Chicanos, and Indians to occupy positions at the lowest level of American life. The life styles and behavior of groups struggling for survival at this level reinforces beliefs about their "innate characteristics." The strength of these beliefs is indicated by the inability of whites to believe that there exists a large core of middle class black families whose life styles and income are comparable to their own. Firm in their images, residents in University City developed a complex pattern of reasoning to explain satisfactorily their behavior and the attributes of their new black neighbors.

The uneasiness of whites about the movement of black families into the area stemmed not only from the usual concern about declining property values but the threats to their "community identity" that blacks posed. Convincing homeowners that this threat was based on mistaken conceptions was an impossible task. The negative attitudes of friends, relatives, and business colleagues were too strong a sanction for most residents to bear. For them to understand that black families in the area did not lower the status of the neighborhood did not mean that this understanding would be shared by outsiders. To them, the mere presence of blacks would be a symbol of the area's decline. Upwardly mobile residents who were sensitive to these pressures began to move from the area at an early date.

Real estate agents encouraged the movement by aggressive tactics, urging residents to list their property for sale. Neighborhood associations and the city did not have the solid support that would have enabled them to be strong counterforces. Alliances between whites and blacks through the neighborhood associations were unstable because the only strategy that the association could view as feasible was one that attempted to quell the desire of blacks to purchase homes in the area. This would stabilize the number of new black residents and convince whites that the "invasion" they feared was not forthcoming.   As already noted, blacks attempting to implement this policy found themselves receiving hostile reactions from whites in the area and from blacks inspecting homes in the neighborhoods. The fears of changes in community identity and the inability of neighborhood groups and city government to counter pressure from real estate agents, friends, and relatives in support of the withdrawal of whites from the area combined to produce a situation that precluded the possibility of a racially integrated neighborhood.

It was clear from this research that the "private" (Slater, 1970) atomistic existence that Slater noted pervades American life contributed to the development of this situation. Unattached to their respective communities, and unused to dealing with issues on a neighborhood basis, individual fears became heightened into suspicions about other residents' attitudes and behavior.   Efforts made by neighborhood associations and city agencies were thus sporadic, poorly coordinated, and ultimately ineffective.

The patterns witnessed in this community may develop differently in communities characterized by higher degrees of solidarity. This solidarity may result not in a greater receptivity to integration, but in a greater outpouring of coordinated opposition to the migration of ethnic group members into an area. The degree of community organization is a crucial variable that sociologists will also have to deal with as they move beyond a simplistic model and attempt to develop a theory adequate to understanding this pattern for social change.

REFERENCES

ASCH, SOLOMON
   1956 "Studies of independence and conformity: A minority of one against a unanimous majority." *Psychological Monographs,* **70**: no. 9.

BRESSLER, MARVIN
   1960 "The Myer's case: An instance of successful racial invasion." *Social Problems,* 8 (Fall: 216–242).

BROWN, WARREN and M. OSCAR ALERS
   1956 "Attitudes of whites and non-whites." *Sociology and Social Research,* **40** (May–June): 312–319.

DEAN, JOHN P.
   1955 "Patterns of Socialization and association between Jews and non-Jews." *Jewish Social Studies* (July): 247–284.

DEUTSCH, MORTON AND MARY COLLINS
   1951 *Interracial housing: A psychological evaluation of a social experiment.* Minneapolis: University of Minnesota Press.

DEUTSCH, MORTON AND ROBERT M. KRAUSS
   1964 *Theories in social psychology.* New York: Basic Books.

FULTON, ROBERT
   1959 Russel Woods: A study of a neighborhood's initial response to Negro invasion. Unpublished Ph.D. dissertation: Wayne State University.

HAMBLIN, ROBERT
   1962 "The dynamics of racial discrimination." *Social Problems,* (Fall): 103–121.

ISSACS, REGINALD R.
1948 "The 'neighborhood' unit as an instrument for segregation." *Journal of Housing,* 5 (August): 215–219.

KELLER, SUZANNE
1968 *The urban neighborhood.* New York: Random House.

McENTIRE, DAVIS
1960 *Residence and race.* Berkeley: University of California.

NORTHWOOD, I. K. and ERNEST BARTH
1965 *Urban desegregation: Negro pioneers and their white neighbors.* Seattle: University of Washington Press.

ROSE, ARNOLD et al
1953 "Neighborhood reactions to isolated Negro invasion: An alternative to invasion-succession." *American Sociological Review,* 18 (October): 497–507.

SLATER, PHILLIP
1970 *The pursuit of loneliness: American culture at the breaking point.* Boston: Beacon Press.

SUSSMAN, MARTIN B.
1957 "The role of neighborhood associations in private housing for racial minorities." *Journal of Social Issues,* 13 (4): 31–37.

WILLIAMS, ROBIN M.
1964 *Strangers next door: Ethnic relations in American communities.* Englewood Cliffs: Prentice-Hall.

WILNER, DANIEL M., ROSABELLE P. WALKLEY and STUART L. COOK
1955 *Human Relations in interracial housing.* Minneapolis: University of Minnesota Press.

---

4.   PROTEST AS A POLITICAL RESOURCE*

Michael Lipsky

This article is a complex detailed discussion of all types of political protest, the resources and types of organizations used in these protests, and the problem of gaining support from third parties in a protest movement. Many of Lipsky's examples are taken from recent ethnic and racial conflicts in the United States.

*This article is an attempt to develop and explore the implications of a conceptual scheme for analyzing protest activity. It is based upon my studies of protest organizations in New York City, Washington, D.C., Chicago, San Francisco, and Mississippi, as well as extensive examination of written accounts of protest among low-income and Negro civil rights groups. I am grateful to Kenneth Dolbeare, Murray Edelman, and Rodney Stiefbold for their insightful comments on an earlier draft. This paper was developed while the author was a Staff Associate of the Institute for Research on Poverty at the University of Wisconsin. I appreciate the assistance obtained during various phases of my research from the Rabinowitz Foundation, the New York State Legislative Internship Program, and the Brookings Institution.

SOURCE

From the *American Political Science Review,* vol. LXII, no. 4, Dec. 1968. Reprinted by permission of the author and the American Political Science Association.

The frequent resort to protest activity by relatively powerless groups in recent American politics suggests that protest represents an important aspect of minority group and low income group politics.[1] At the same time that Negro civil rights strategists have recognized the problem of using protest as a meaningful political instrument,[2] groups associated with the "war on poverty" have increasingly received publicity for protest activity. Saul Alinsky's Industrial Areas Foundation, for example, continues to receive in-

vitations to help organize low income communities because of its ability to mobilize poor people around the tactic of protest.[3] The riots which dominated urban affairs in the summer of 1967 appear not to have diminished the dependence of some groups on protest as a mode of political activity.

This article provides a theoretical perspective on protest activity as a political resource. The discussion is concentrated on the limitations inherent in protest which occur because of the need of protest leaders to appeal to four constituencies at the same time. As the concept of protest is developed here, it will be argued that protest leaders must nurture and sustain an organization comprised of people with whom they may or may not share common values. They must articulate goals and choose strategies so as to maximize their public exposure through communications media. They must maximize the impact of third parties in the political conflict. Finally, they must try to maximize chances of success among those capable of granting goals. The tensions inherent in manipulating these four constituencies at the same time form the basis of this discussion of protest as a political process. It is intended to place aspects of the civil rights movement in a framework which suggests links between protest organizations and the general political processes in which such organizations operate.

I. "PROTEST" CONCEPTUALIZED

Protest activity as it has been adopted by elements of the civil rights movement and others has not been studied extensively by social scientists. Some of the most suggestive writings have been done as case studies of

---

[1] "Relatively powerless groups" may be defined as those groups which, relatively speaking, are lacking in conventional political resources. For the purposes of community studies, Robert Dahl has compiled a useful comprehensive list. See Dahl, "The Analysis of Influence in Local Communities," *Social Science and Community Action*, Charles R. Adrian, ed. (East Lansing, Michigan, 1960), p. 32. The difficulty in studying such groups is that relative powerlessness only becomes apparent under certain conditions. Extremely powerless groups not only lack political resources, but are also characterized by a minimal sense of political efficacy, upon which in part successful political organization depends. For reviews of the literature linking orientations of political efficacy to socioeconomic status, see Robert Lane, *Political Life* (New York, 1959), ch. 16; and Lester Milbrath, *Political Participation* (Chicago, 1965), ch. 5. Further, to the extent that group cohesion is recognized as a necessary requisite for organized political action, then extremely powerless groups, lacking cohesion, will not even appear for observation. Hence the necessity of selecting for intensive study a protest movement where there can be some confidence that observable processes and results can be analyzed. Thus, if one conceives of a continuum on which political groups are placed according to their relative command of resources, the focus of this essay is on those groups which are near, but not at, the pole of powerlessness.

[2] See, e.g., Bayard Rustin, "From Protest to Politics: The Future of the Civil Rights Movement," *Commentary* (February, 1965), 25–31; and Stokely Carmichael, "Toward Black Liberation," *The Massachusetts Review* (Autumn, 1966).

---

[3] On Alinsky's philosophy of community organization, see his *Reveille for Radicals* (Chicago, 1945); and Charles Silberman, *Crisis in Black and White* (New York, 1964), ch. 10.

protest movements in single southern cities.[4] These works generally lack a framework or theoretical focus which would encourage generalization from the cases. More systematic efforts have been attempted in approaching the dynamics of biracial committees in the South,[5] and comprehensively assessing the efficacy of Negro political involvement in Durham, N.C. and Philadelphia, Pa.[6] In their excellent assessment of Negro politics in the South, Matthews and Prothro have presented a thorough profile of Southern Negro students and their participation in civil rights activities.[7] Protest is also discussed in passing in recent explorations of the social-psychological dimensions of Negro ghetto politics[8] and the still highly suggestive, although pre-1960's, work on Negro political leadership by James Q. Wilson.[9] These and other less systematic works on contemporary Negro politics,[10] for all of their intuitive insights and valuable documentation, offer no theoretical formulations which encourage conceptualization about the interaction between recent Negro political activity and the political process.

Heretofore the best attempt to place Negro protest activity in a framework which would generate additional insights has been that of James Q. Wilson.[11] Wilson has suggested that protest activity be conceived as a problem of bargaining in which the basic problem is that Negro groups lack political resources to exchange. Wilson called this "the problem of the powerless."[12]

While many of Wilson's insights remain valid, his approach is limited in applicability because it defines protest in terms of mass action or response and as utilizing exclusively negative inducements in the bargaining process. Negative inducements are defined as inducements which are not absolutely preferred but are preferred over alternative possibilities.[13] Yet it might be argued that protest designed to appeal to groups which oppose suffering and exploitation, for example, might be offering positive inducements in bargaining. A few Negro students sitting at a lunch counter might be engaged in what would be called protest, and by their actions

---

[4] See, e.g., Jack L. Walker, "Protest and Negotiations: A Case Study of Negro Leadership in Atlanta, Georgia," *Midwest Journal of Political Science,* 7 (May, 1963), 99–124; Jack L. Walker, *Sit-ins in Atlanta: A Study in the Negro Protest,* Eagleton Institute Case Studies, No. 34 (New York, 1964); John Ehle, *The Free Men* (New York, 1965) [Chapel Hill]; Daniel C. Thompson, *The Negro Leadership Class* (Englewood Cliffs, N.J., 1963) [New Orleans]; M. Elaine Burgess, *Negro Leadership in a Southern City* (Chapel Hill, N.C., 1962) [Durham].

[5] Lewis Killian and Charles Grigg, *Racial Crisis in America: Leadership in Conflict* (Englewood Cliffs, N.J., 1964).

[6] William Keech, "The Negro Vote as a Political Resource: The Case of Durham," (unpublished Ph.D. Dissertation, University of Wisconsin, 1966); John H. Strange, "The Negro in Philadelphia Politics 1963–65," (unpublished Ph.D. Dissertation, Princeton University, 1966).

[7] Donald Matthews and James Prothro, *Negroes and the New Southern Politics* (New York, 1966). Considerable insight on these data is provided in John Orbell, "Protest Participation among Southern Negro College Students," this Review, 61 (June, 1967), 446–456.

[8] Kenneth Clark, *Dark Ghetto* (New York, 1965).

[9] *Negro Politics* (New York, 1960).

[10] A complete list would be voluminous. See, e.g., Nat Hentoff, *The New Equality* (New York, 1964); Arthur Waskow, *From Race Riot to Sit-in* (New York, 1966).

[11] "The Strategy of Protest: Problems of Negro Civic Action," *Journal of Conflict Resolution,* 3 (September, 1961), 291–303. The reader will recognize the author's debt to this highly suggestive article, not least Wilson's recognition of the utility of the bargaining framework for examining protest activity.

[12] *Ibid.,* p. 291.

[13] *Ibid.,* p. 291–292.

might be trying to appeal to other groups in the system with positive inducements. Additionally, Wilson's concentration on Negro civic action, and his exclusive interest in exploring the protest process to explain Negro civic action, tend to obscure comparison with protest activity which does not necessarily arise within the Negro community.

Assuming a somewhat different focus, protest activity is defined as a mode of political action oriented toward objection to one or more policies or conditions, characterized by showmanship or display of an unconventional nature, and undertaken to obtain rewards from political or economic systems while working within the systems. The "problem of the powerless" in protest activity is to activate "third parties" to enter the implicit or explicit bargaining arena in ways favorable to the protesters. This is one of the few ways in which they can "create" bargaining resources. It is intuitively unconvincing to suggest that fifteen people sitting uninvited in the Mayor's office have the power to move City Hall. A better formulation would suggest that the people sitting in may be able to appeal to a wider public to which the city administration is sensitive. Thus in successful protest activity the *reference publics* of protest *targets* may be conceived as explicitly or implicitly reacting to protest in such a way that target groups or individuals respond in ways favorable to the protesters.[14]

_____

[14] See E. E. Schattschneider's discussion of expanding the scope of the conflict, *The Semisovereigh People* (New York, 1960). Another way in which bargaining resources may be "created" is to increase the relative cohesion of groups, or to increase the perception of group solidarity as a precondition to greater cohesion. This appears to be the primary goal of political activity which is generally designated "community organization." Negro activists appear to recognize the utility of this strategy in their advocacy of "black power." In some instances protest activity may be designed in part to accomplish this goal in addition to activating reference publics.

It should be emphasized that the focus here is on protest by relatively powerless groups. Illustrations can be summoned, for example, of activity designated as "protest" involving high status pressure groups or hundreds of thousands of people. While such instances may share some of the characteristics of protest activity, they may not represent examples of developing political resources by relatively powerless groups because the protesting groups may already command political resources by virtue of status, numbers or cohesion.

It is appropriate also to distinguish between the relatively restricted use of the concept of protest adopted here and closely related political strategies which are often designated as "protest" in popular usage. Where groups already possess sufficient resources with which to bargain, as in the case of some economic boycotts and labor strikes, they may be said to engage in "direct confrontation."[15] Similarly, protest which represents efforts to "activate reference publics" should be distinguished from "alliance formation," where third parties are induced to join the conflict, but where the value orientations of third parties are sufficiently similar to those of the protesting group that concerted or coordinated action is possible. Alliance formation is particularly desirable for relatively powerless groups if they seek to join the decision-making process as participants.

The distinction between activating reference publics and alliance formation is made on the assumption that where goal orientations among protest groups and the reference publics of target groups are similar, the political dynamics of petitioning target groups are different than when such goal orienta-

_____

[15] For an example of "direct confrontation," one might study the three-month Negro boycott of white merchants in Natchez, Miss., which resulted in capitulation to boycott demands by city government leaders. See *The New York Times*, December 4, 1965, p. 1.

tions are relatively divergent. Clearly the more similar the goal orientations, the greater the likelihood of protest success, other things being equal. This discussion is intended to highlight, however, those instances where goal orientations of reference publics depart significantly, in direction or intensity, from the goals of protest groups.

Say that to protest some situation, A would like to enter a bargaining situation with B. But A has nothing B wants, and thus cannot bargain. A then attempts to create political resources by activating other groups to enter the conflict. A then organizes to take action against B with respect to certain goals. *Information concerning these goals must be conveyed through communications media* (C, D, and E) *to F, G, and H, which are B's reference publics.* In response to the reactions of F, G, and H, or in anticipation of their reactions, B responds, *in some way,* to the protesters' demands. This formulation requires the conceptualization of protest activity when undertaken to create bargaining resources as a political process which requires communication and is characterized by a multiplicity of constituencies for protest leadership.

A schematic representation of the process of protest as utilized by relatively powerless groups is presented in Figure 1. In contrast to a simplistic pressure group model which would posit a direct relationship between pressure group and pressured, the following discussion is guided by the assumption (derived from observation) that protest is a highly indirect process in which communications media and the reference publics of protest targets play critical roles. It is also a process characterized by reciprocal relations, in which protest leaders frame strategies according to their perception of the needs of (many) other actors.

In this view protest constituents limit the options of protest leaders at the same time that the protest leader influences their perception of the strategies and rhetoric which

they will support. Protest activity is filtered through the communications media in influencing the perceptions of the reference publics of protest targets. To the extent that the influence of reference publics is supportive of protest goals, target groups will dispense symbolic or material rewards. Material rewards are communicated directly to protest constituents. Symbolic rewards are communicated in part to protest constituents, but primarily are communicated to the reference publics of target groups, who provide the major stimuli for public policy pronouncements.

The study of protest as adopted by relatively powerless groups should provide insights into the structure and behavior of groups involved in civil rights politics and associated with the "war on poverty." It should direct attention toward the ways in which administrative agencies respond to "crises." Additionally, the study of protest as a political resource should influence some general conceptualizations of American political pluralism. Robert Dahl, for example, describes the "normal American political process" as

"one in which there is a high probability that an active and legitimate group in the population can make itself heard effectively at some crucial stage in the process of decision."[16]

Although he agrees that control over decisions is unevenly divided in the population, Dahl writes:

"When I say that a group is heard 'effectively' I mean more than the simple fact that it makes a noise; I mean that one or more officials are not only ready to listen to the noise, but expect to suffer in some significant way if they do not placate the group, its leaders, or its most vociferous members. To satisfy the group may require one or

---

[16] *A Preface to Democratic Theory* (Chicago, 1956), pp. 145–146.

more of a great variety of actions by the responsive leader: pressure for substantive policies, appointments, graft, respect, expression of the appropriate emotions, or the right combination of reciprocal noises."[17]

These statements, which in some ways resemble David Truman's discussion of the power of "potential groups,"[18] can be illuminated by the study of protest activity in three ways. First, what are the probabilities that relatively powerless groups can make themselves heard effectively? In what ways will such groups be heard or "steadily appeased"?[19] Concentration on the process of protest activity may reveal the extent to which, and the conditions under which, relatively powerless groups are likely to prove effective. Protest undertaken to obstruct policy decision, for example, may enjoy greater success probabilities than protest undertaken in an effort to evoke constructive policy innovations.[20]

Second, does it make sense to suggest that all groups which make noises will receive responses from public officials? Perhaps the groups which make noises do not have to be satisfied at all, but it is other groups which receive assurances or recognition. Third, what are the probabilities that groups which make noises will receive tangible rewards, rather than symbolic assurances?[21] Dahl lumps these rewards together in the same paragraph, but dispensation of tangible rewards clearly has a different impact upon groups than the dispensation of symbolic rewards. Dahl is undoubtedly correct when he suggests that the relative fluidity of American politics is a critical characteristic of the American political system.[22] But he is less precise and less convincing when it comes to analyzing the extent to which the system is indeed responsive to the relatively powerless groups of the "average citizen."[23]

The following sections are an attempt to demonstrate the utility of the conceptualization of the protest process presented above. This will be done by exploring the problems encountered and the strains generated by protest leaders in interacting with four constituencies. It will be useful to concentrate attention on the maintenance and enhancement needs not only of the large formal organizations which dominate city politics,[24] but also of the ad hoc protest groups which engage them in civic controversy. It will also prove rewarding to examine the role requirements of individuals in leadership positions

---

[17] *Ibid.*

[18] *The Governmental Process* (New York, 1951), p. 104.

[19] See Dahl, *A Preface to Democratic Theory*, p. 146.

[20] Observations that all groups can influence public policy at some stage of the political process are frequently made about the role of "veto groups" in American politics. See *Ibid.,* pp. 104 ff. See also David Reisman, *The Lonely Crowd* (New Haven, 1950), pp. 211 ff., for an earlier discussion of veto-group politics. Yet protest should be evaluated when it is adopted to obtain assertive as well as defensive goals.

[21] See Murray Edelman, The *Symbolic Uses of Politics* (Urbana, Ill., 1964), ch. 2.

[22] See Dahl, *Who Governs?* (New Haven, 1961), pp. 305 ff.

[23] In a recent formulation, Dahl reiterates the theme of wide dispersion of influence. "More than other systems, [democracies] . . . try to disperse influence widely to their citizens by means of the suffrage, elections, freedom of speech, press, and assembly, the right of opponents to criticize the conduct of government, the right to organize political parties, and in other ways." *Pluralist Democracy in the United States* (Chicago, 1967), p. 373. Here, however, he concentrates more on the availability of options to all groups in the system, rather than on the relative probabilities that all groups in fact have access to the political process. See pp. 372 ff.

[24] See Edward Banfield, *Political Influence* (New York, 1961), p. 263. The analysis of organizational incentive structure which heavily influences Banfield's formulation is Chester Barnard, *The Functions of the Executive* (Cambridge, Mass., 1938).

as they perceive the problems of constituency manipulation. In concluding remarks some implications of the study of protest for the pluralist description of American politics will be suggested.[25]

II. PROTEST LEADERSHIP AND ORGANIZATIONAL BASE

The organizational maintenance needs of relatively powerless, low income, ad hoc protest groups center around the tension generated by the need for leadership to offer symbolic and intangible inducements to protest participation when immediate, material rewards cannot be anticipated, and the need to provide at least the promise of material rewards. Protest leaders must try to evoke responses from other actors in the political process, at the same time that they pay attention to participant organizational needs. Thus relatively deprived groups in the political system not only receive symbolic reassurance while material rewards from the system are withheld,[26] but protest leaders have a stake in perpetuating the notion that relatively powerless groups retain political efficacy despite what in many cases is obvious evidence to the contrary.

The tension embraced by protest leaders over the nature of inducements toward protest participation accounts in part for the style adopted and goals selected by protest leaders. Groups which seek psychological gratification from politics, but cannot or do not anticipate material political rewards, may

be attracted to militant protest leaders. To these groups, angry rhetoric may prove a desirable quality in the short run. Where groups depend upon the political system for tangible benefits, or where participation in the system provides intangible benefits, moderate leadership is likely to prevail. Wilson has observed similar tendencies among Negro leaders of large, formal organizations.[27] It is no less true for leadership of protest groups. Groups whose members derive tangible satisfactions from political participation will not condone leaders who are stubborn in compromise or appear to question the foundations of the system. This coincides with Truman's observation:

"Violation of the rule of the game normally will weaken a group's cohesion, reduce its status in the community, and expose it to the claims of other groups."[28]

On the other hand, the cohesion of relatively powerless groups may be strengthened by militant, ideological leadership which questions the rules of the game and challenges their legitimacy.

Cohesion is particularly important when protest leaders bargain directly with target groups. In that situation, leaders' ability to control protest constituents and guarantee their behavior represents a bargaining strength.[29] For this reason Wilson stressed the bargaining difficulties of Negro leaders who cannot guarantee constituent behavior, and pointed out the significance of the strategy of projecting the image of group solidarity when the reality of cohesion is a fiction.[30] Cohesion is less significant at other times. Divided leadership may prove productive by

---

[25] In the following attempt to develop the implications of this conceptualization of protest activity, I have drawn upon extensive field observations and bibliographical research. Undoubtedly, however, individual assertions, while representing my best judgment concerning the available evidence, in the future may require modification as the result of further empirical research.

[26] As Edelman suggests, cited previously.

[27] *Negro Politics*, p. 290.

[28] *The Governmental Process*, p. 513.

[29] But cf. Thomas Schelling's discussion of "binding oneself," *The Strategy of Conflict* (Cambridge, Mass., 1960), pp. 22 ff.

[30] "The Strategy of Protest," p. 297.

bargaining in tandem,[31] or by minimizing strain among groups in the protest process. Further, community divisions may prove less detrimental to protest aims when strong third parties have entered the dispute originally generated by protest organizations.

The intangible rewards of assuming certain postures toward the political system may not be sufficient to sustain an organizational base. It may be necessary to renew constantly the intangible rewards of participation. And to the extent that people participate in order to achieve tangible benefits, their interest in a protest organization may depend upon the organization's relative material success. Protest leaders may have to tailor their style to present participants with tangible successes, or with the appearance of success. Leaders may have to define the issues with concern for increasing their ability to sustain organizations. The potential for protest among protest group members may have to be manipulated by leadership if the group is to be sustained.[32]

The participants in protest organizations limit the flexibility of protest leadership. This obtains for two reasons. They restrict public actions by leaders who must continue to solicit active participant support, and they place restraints on the kinds of activities which can be considered appropriate for protest purposes. Poor participants cannot commonly be asked to engage in protest requiring air transportation. Participants may have anxieties related to their environment or his-

torical situation which discourages engagement in some activities. They may be afraid of job losses, beatings by the police, or summary evictions. Negro protest in the Deep South has been inhibited by realistic expectations of retribution.[33] Protests over slum housing conditions are undermined by tenants who expect landlord retaliation for engaging in tenant organizing activity.[34] Political or ethical mores may conflict with a proposed course of action, diminishing participation.[35]

On the other hand, to the extent that fears are real, or that the larger community perceives protest participants as subject to these fears, protest may actually be strengthened. Communications media and potential allies will consider more soberly the complaints of people who are understood to be placing themselves in jeopardy. When young children and their parents made the arduous bus trip from Mississippi to Washington, D.C. to protest the jeopardizing of Head Start funds,

---

[31]This is suggested by Wilson, "The Strategy of Protest," p. 298; St. Clair Drake and Horace Cayton, *Black Metropolis* (New York, 1962, rev. ed.), p. 731; Walker, "Protest and Negotiation," p. 122. Authors who argue that divided leadership is dysfunctional have been Clark, p. 156; and Tilman Cothran, "The Negro Protest Against Segregation in the South," *The Annals,* 357 (January, 1965), p. 72.

[32]This observation is confirmed by a student of the Southern civil rights movement:

[33]Significantly, southern Negro students who actively participated in the early phases of the sit-in movement "tended to be unusually optimistic about race relations and tolerant of whites [when compared with inactive Negro students]. They not only *were* better off, objectively speaking, than other Negroes but *felt* better off." Matthews and Prothro, *op. cit.,* p. 424.

[34]This is particularly the case in cities such as Washington, D.C., where landlord-tenant laws offer little protection against retaliatory eviction. See, e.g., Robert Schoshinski, "Remedies of the Indigent Tenant: Proposal for Change," *Georgetown Law Journal,* 54 (Winter, 1966), 541 ff.

[35]Wilson regarded this as a chief reason for lack of protest activity in 1961. He wrote: ". . .some of the goals now being sought by Negroes are least applicable to those groups of Negroes most suited to protest action. Protest action involving such tactics as mass meetings, picketing, boycotts, and strikes rarely find enthusiastic participants among upper-income and higher status individuals": "The Strategy of Protest," p. 296.

the courage and expense represented by their effort created a respect and visibility for their position which might not have been achieved by local protest efforts.[36]

Protest activity may be undertaken by organizations with established relationship patterns, behavior norms, and role expectations. These organizations are likely to have greater access to other groups in the political system, and a demonstrated capacity to maintain themselves. Other protest groups, however, may be ad hoc arrangements without demonstrated internal or external relationship patterns. These groups will have different organizational problems, in response to which it is necessary to engage in different kinds of protest activity.

The scarcity of organizational resources also places limits upon the ability of relatively powerless groups to maintain the foundations upon which protest organizations develop. Relatively powerless groups, to engage in political activity of any kind, must command at least some resources. This is not tautological. Referring again to a continuum on which political groups are placed according to their relative command of resources, one may draw a line somewhere along the continuum representing a "threshold of civic group political participation." Clearly some groups along the continuum will possess some political resources (enough, say, to emerge for inspection) but not enough to exercise influence in civic affairs. Relatively powerless groups, to be influential, must cross the "threshold" to engage in politics. Although the availability of group resources is a critical consideration at all stages of the protest process, it is particularly important in explaining why some groups seem to "surface" with sufficient strength to command attention. The following discussion of some critical organizational resources should illu-

minate this point.

Skilled professionals frequently must be available to protest organizations. Lawyers, for example, play extremely important roles in enabling protest groups to utilize the judicial process and avail themselves of adequate preparation of court cases. Organizational reputation may depend upon a combination of ability to threaten the conventional political system and of exercising statutory rights in court. Availability of lawyers depends upon ability to pay fees and/or the attractiveness to lawyers of participation in protest group activity. Volunteer professional assistance may not prove adequate. One night a week volunteered by an aspiring politician in a housing clinic cannot satisfy the needs of a chaotic political movement.[37] The need for skilled professionals is not restricted to lawyers. For example, a group seeking to protest an urban renewal policy might require the services of architects and city planners in order to present a viable alternative to a city proposal.

Financial resources not only purchase legal assistance, but enable relatively powerless groups to conduct minimum programs of political activities. To the extent that constituents are unable or unwilling to pay even small membership dues, then financing the cost of mimeographing flyers, purchasing supplies, maintaining telephone service, paying rent, and meeting a modest payroll become major organizational problems. And to the extent that group finances are supplied by outside

---

[36]See *The New York Times*, February 12, 1966, p. 56.

[37]On housing clinic services provided by political clubs, see James Q. Wilson, *The Amateur Democrat: Club Politics in Three Cities* (Chicago, 1962), pp. 63–64, 176.   On the need for lawyers among low income people, see e.g., *The Extension of Legal Services to the Poor*, Conference Proceedings (Washington, D.C., n.d.), esp. pp. 51–60; and "Neighborhood Law Offices: The New Wave in Legal Services for the Poor," *Harvard Law Review*, (February, 1967, 805–850).

individual contributions or government or foundation grants, the long-term options of the group are sharply constrained by the necessity of orienting group goals and tactics to anticipate the potential objections of financial supporters.

Some dependence upon even minimal financial resources can be waived if organizations evoke passionate support from constituents. Secretarial help and block organizers will come forward to work without compensation if they support the cause of neighborhood organizations or gain intangible benefits based upon association with the group. Protest organizations may also depend upon skilled non-professionals, such as college students, whose access to people and political and economic institutions often assist protest groups in cutting across income lines to seek support. Experience with ad hoc political groups, however, suggests that this assistance is sporadic and undependable. Transient assistance is particularly typical of skilled, educated, and employable volunteers whose abilities can be applied widely. The die-hards of ad hoc political groups are often those people who have no place else to go, nothing else to do.

Constituent support will be affected by the nature of the protest target and whether protest activity is directed toward defensive or assertive goals. Obstructing specific public policies may be easier than successfully recommending constructive policy changes. Orientations toward defensive goals may require less constituent energy, and less command over resources of money, expertise and status.[38]

III. PROTEST LEADERSHIP AND COMMUNICATIONS MEDIA

The communications media are extremely

powerful in city politics. In granting or withholding publicity, in determining what information most people will have on most issues, and what alternatives they will consider in response to issues, the media truly, as Norton Long has put it, "set . . . the civic agenda."[39] To the extent that successful, protest activity depends upon appealing to, and/or threatening, other groups in the community, the communications media set the limits of protest action. If protest tactics are not considered significant by the media, or if newspapers and television reporters or editors decide to overlook protest tactics, protest organizations will not succeed. Like the tree falling unheard in the forest, there is no protest unless protest is perceived and projected.

A number of writers have noticed that the success of protest activity seems directly related to the amount of publicity it receives outside the immediate arena in which protest takes place. This view has not been stated systematically, but hints can be found in many sources. In the literature on civil rights politics, the relevance of publicity represents one of the few hypotheses available concerning the dynamics of successful protest activity.[40]

---

[38]An illustration of low income group protest organization mobilized for veto purposes is provided by Dahl in "The Case of the Metal Houses." See *Who Governs?*. pp. 192 ff.

[39]Norton Long, "The Local Community as an Ecology of Games," in Long, *The Polity,* Charles Press, ed. (Chicago, 1962), p. 153. See pp. 152–154. See also Roscoe C. Martin, Frank J. Munger, *et al., Decisions in Syracuse: A Metropolitan Action Study* (Garden City, N.Y., 1965) (originally published: 1961), pp. 326–327.

[40]See, e.g., Thompson, *op. cit.,* p. 134, and *passim;* Martin Oppenheimer, "The Southern Student Movement: Year I," *Journal of Negro Education,* 33 (Fall, 1964), p. 397; Cothran, *op. cit.,* p. 72; Pauli Murray, "Protest Against the Legal Status of the Negro," *The Annals,* 357 (January, 1965), p. 63; Allan P. Sindler, "Protest Against the Political Status of the Negroes," *The Annals,* 357 (January, 1965), p. 50.

When protest tactics do receive coverage in the communications media, the way in which they are presented will influence all other actors in the system, including the protesters themselves. Conformity to standards of newsworthiness in political style, and knowledge of the prejudices and desires of the individuals who determine media coverage in political skills, represent crucial determinants of leadership effectiveness.

The organizational behavior of newspapers can partly be understood by examining the maintenance and enhancement needs which direct them toward projects of civic betterment and impressions of accomplishment.[41] But insight may also be gained by analyzing the role requirements of reporters, editors, and others who determine newspaper policy. Reporters, for example, are frequently motivated by the desire to contribute to civic affairs by their "objective" reporting of significant events; by the premium they place on accuracy; and by the credit which they receive for sensationalism and "scoops."

These requirements may be difficult to accommodate at the same time. Reporters demand newsworthiness of their subjects in the short run, but also require reliability and verifiability in the longer run. Factual accuracy may dampen newsworthiness. Sensationalism, attractive to some newspaper editors, may be inconsistent with reliable, verifiable narration of events. Newspapers at first may be attracted to sensationalism, and later demand verifiability in the interests of community harmony (and adherence to professional journalistic standards).

Most big city newspapers have reporters whose assignments permit them to cover aspects of city politics with some regularity. These reporters, whose "beats" may consist of "civil rights" or "poverty," sometimes develop close relationships with their news subjects. These relationships may develop symbiotic overtones because of the mutuality of

interest between the reporter and the news subject. Reporters require fresh information on protest developments, while protest leaders have a vital interest in obtaining as much press coverage as possible.

Inflated reports of protest success may be understood in part by examining this relationship between reporter and protest leader. Both have role-oriented interests in projecting images of protest strength and threat. In circumstances of great excitement, when competition from other news media representatives is high, a reporter may find that he is less governed by the role requirement of verification and reliability than he is by his editor's demand for "scoops" and news with high audience appeal.[42]

On the other hand, the demands of the media may conflict with the needs of protest group maintenance. Consider the leader whose constitutents are attracted solely by pragmatic statements not exceeding what they consider political "good taste." He is constrained from making militant demands which would isolate him from constituents. This constraint may cost him appeal in the press.[43] However, the leader whose organizing appeal requires militant rhetoric may obtain eager press coverage only to find that his inflamatory statements lead to alienation

---

[41]See Banfield, *op cit.*, p. 275.

[42]For a case study of the interaction between protest leaders and newspaper reporters, see Michael Lipsky, "Rent Strikes in New York City: Protest Politics and the Power of the Poor," (unpublished Ph.D. dissertation, Princeton University, 1967), pp. 139–49. Bernard Cohen has analyzed the impact of the press on foreign policy from the perspective of reporters' role requirements: see his *The Press and Foreign Policy* (Princeton, N.J., 1963), esp. chs. 2–3.

[43]An example of a protest conducted by middle-class women engaged in pragmatic protest over salvaging park space is provided in John B. Keeley, *Moses on the Green*, Inter-University Case Program, No. 45 (University, Ala. 1959).

of potential allies and exclusion from the explicit bargaining process.[44]

News media do not report events in the same way. Television may select for broadcast only thirty seconds of a half-hour news conference. This coverage will probably focus on immediate events, without background or explanatory material. Newspapers may give more complete accounts of the same event. The most complete account may appear in the weekly edition of a neighborhood or ethnic newspaper. Differential coverage by news media, and differential news media habits in the general population,[45] are significant factors in permitting protest leaders to juggle conflicting demands of groups in the protest process.

Similar tensions exist in the leader's relationships with protest targets. Ideological postures may gain press coverage and constituency approval, but may alienate target groups with whom it would be desirable to

---

[44]This was the complaint of Floyd McKissick, National Director of the Congress of Racial Equality, when he charged that ". . . there are only two kinds of statements a black man can make and expect that the white press will report. . . .First . . . is an attack on another black man. . . .The second is a statement that sounds radical, violent, extreme —the verbal equivalent of a riot. . . .[T]he Negro is being rewarded by the public media only if he turns on another Negro and uses his tongue as a switchblade, or only if he sounds outlandish, extremist or psychotic." Statement at the Convention of the American Society of Newspaper Editors, April 20, 1967, Washington, D.C., as reported in *The New York Times,* April 21, 1967, p. 22. See also the remarks of journalist Ted Poston, *ibid.,* April 26, 1965, p. 26.

[45]Matthews and Prothro found, for example, that in their south-wide Negro population sample, 38 percent read Negro-oriented magazines and 17 percent read newspapers written for Negroes. These media treat news of interest to Negroes more completely and sympathetically than do the general media. See pp. 248 ff.

bargain explicitly. Exclusion from the councils of decision-making may have important consequences, since the results of target group deliberations may satisfy activated reference publics without responding to protest goals. If activated reference publics are required to increase the bargaining position of the protest group, protest efforts thereafter will have diminished chances of success.

IV. PROTEST LEADERSHIP AND "THIRD PARTIES"

I have argued that the essence of political protest consists of activating third parties to participate in controversy in ways favorable to protest goals. In previous sections I have attempted to analyze some of the tensions which result from protest leaders' attempts to activate reference publics of protest targets at the same time that they must retain the interest and support of protest organization participants. This phenomenon is in evidence when Negro leaders, recognized as such by public officials, find their support eroded in the Negro community because they have engaged in explicit bargaining situations with politicians. Negro leaders are thus faced with the dilemma that when they behave like other ethnic group representatives they are faced with loss of support from those whose intense activism has been aroused in the Negro community, yet whose support is vital if they are to remain credible as leaders to public officials.

The tensions resulting from conflicting maintenance needs of protest organizations and activated third parties present difficulties for protest leaders. One way in which these tensions can be minimized is by dividing leadership responsibilities. If more than one group is engaged in protest activity, protest leaders can, in effect, divide up public roles so as to reduce as much as possible the gap between the implicit demands of different groups for appropriate rhetoric, and what in fact is said. Thus divided leadership may perform the latent function of minimizing tensions among elements in the protest process by permitting different groups to listen selectively to protest spokesmen.[46]

Another way in which strain among different groups can be minimized is through successful public relations. Minimization of strain may depend upon ambiguity of action or statement, deception, or upon effective inter-group communication. Failure to clarify meaning, or falsification, may increase protest effectiveness. Effective intragroup communication may increase the likelihood that protest constituents will "understand" that ambiguous or false public statements have "special meaning" and need not be taken seriously. The Machiavellian circle is complete when we observe that although lying may be prudent, the appearance of integrity and forthrightness is desirable for public relations, since these values are widely shared.

It has been observed that "[t] he militant displays an unwillingness to perform those administrative tasks which are necessary to operate an organization. Probably the skills of the agitator and the skills of the administrator . . .are not incompatible, but few men can do both well."[47] These skills may or may not be incompatible as personality traits, but they indeed represent conflicting role demands on protest leadership. When a protest leader exhausts time and energy conducting frequent press conferences, arranging for politicians and celebrities to appear at rallies, delivering speeches to sympathetic local groups, college symposia and other forums, constantly picketing for publicity and generally making "contacts," he is unable to pursue the direction of office routine, clerical

tasks, research and analysis, and other chores.

The difficulties of delegating routine tasks are probably directly related to the skill levels and previous administrative experiences of group members. In addition, to the extent that involvement in protest organization is a function of rewards received or expected by individuals because of the excitement or entertainment value of participation, then the difficulties of delegating routine, relatively uninteresting chores to group members will be increased. Yet attention to such details affects the perception of protest groups by organizations whose support or assistance may be desired in the future. These considerations add to the protest leader's problem of risking alienation of protest participants because of potentially unpopular cooperation with the "power structure."

In the protest paradigm developed here, "third parties" refers both to the reference publics of target groups and, more narrowly, to the interest groups whose regular interaction with protest targets tends to develop into patterns of influence.[48] We have already discussed some of the problems associated with activating the reference publics of target groups. In discussing the constraints placed upon protest, attention may be focused upon the likelihood that groups seeking to create political resources through protest will be included in the explicit bargaining process with other pressure groups. For protest groups, these constraints are those which occur because of class and political style, status and organizational resources.

The established civic groups most likely to be concerned with the problems raised by relatively powerless groups are those devoted to service in the public welfare and those "liberally" oriented groups whose potential

---

[46]See footnote 31 above.

[47]Wilson, *Negro Politics*, p. 225.

[48]See Wallace Sayre and Herbert Kaufman, *Governing New York City* (New York, 1960), pp. 257 ff. Also see Banfield, *op. cit.*, p. 267.

constituents are either drawn from the same class as the protest groups (such as some trade unions), or whose potential constituents are attracted to policies which appear to serve the interest of the lower class or minority groups (such as some reform political clubs).[49] These civic groups have frequently cultivated clientele relationships with city agencies over long periods. Their efforts have been reciprocated by agency officials anxious to develop constituencies to support and defend agency administrative and budgetary policies. In addition, clientele groups are expected to endorse and legitimize agency aggrandizement. These relationships have been developed by agency officials and civic groups for mutual benefit, and cannot be destroyed, abridged or avoided without cost.

Protest groups may well be able to raise the saliency of issues on the civic agenda through utilization of communications media and successful appeals or threats to wider publics, but admission to policy-making councils is frequently barred because of the angry, militant rhetorical style adopted by protest leaders. People in power do not like to sit down with rogues. Protest leaders are likely to have phrased demands in ways unacceptable to lawyers and other civic activists whose cautious attitude toward public policy may reflect not only their good intentions but their concern for property rights, due process, pragmatic legislating or judicial precedent.

Relatively powerless groups lack participation of individuals with high status whose endorsement of specific proposals lend them increased legitimacy. Good causes may always attract the support of high status individuals. But such individuals' willingness to devote time to the promotion of specific proposals is less likely than the one-shot endorsements which these people distribute more readily.

Similarly, protest organizations often lack the resources on which entry into the policy-making process depends. These resources include maintenance of a staff with expertise and experience in the policy area. This expertise may be in the areas of the law, planning and architecture, proposal writing, accounting, educational policy, federal grantsmanship or publicity. Combining experience with expertise is one way to create status in issue areas. The dispensing of information by interest groups has been widely noted as a major source of influence. Over time the experts develop status in their areas of competence somewhat independent of the influence which adheres to them as information-providers. Groups which cannot or do not engage lawyers to assist in proposing legislation, and do not engage in collecting reliable data, cannot participate in policy deliberations or consult in these matters. Protest oriented groups, whose primary talents are in dramatizing issues, cannot credibly attempt to present data considered "objective" or suggestions considered "responsible" by public officials. Few can be convincing as both advocate and arbiter at the same time.

V. PROTEST LEADERSHIP AND TARGET GROUPS

The probability of protest success may be approached by examining the maintenance needs of organizations likely to be designated

---

[49]See Wilson, *The Amateur Democrats,* previously cited. These groups are most likely to be characterized by broad scope of political interest and frequent intervention in politics. See Sayre and Kaufman, *op. cit.,* p. 79.

as target groups.[50] For the sake of clarity, and because protest activity increasingly is directed toward government, I shall refer in the following paragraphs exclusively to government agencies at the municipal level. The assumption is retained, however, that the following generalizations are applicable to other potential target groups.

Some of the constraints placed on protest leadership in influencing target groups have already been mentioned in preceding sections. The lack of status and resources that inhibit protest groups from participating in policy-making conferences, for example, also helps prevent explicit bargaining between protest leaders and city officials. The strain between rhetoric which appeals to protest participants and public statements to which communications media and "third parties" respond favorably also exists with reference to target groups.

Yet there is a distinguishing feature of the maintenance needs and strategies of city agencies which specifically constrains protest organizations. This is the agency director's need to protect "the jurisdiction and income of his organization [by] . . . [m]anipulation

of the external environment."[51] In so doing he may satisfy his reference groups without responding to protest group demands. At least six tactics are available to protest targets who are motivated to respond in some way to protest activity but seek primarily to satisfy their reference publics. These tactics may be employed whether or not target groups are "sincere" in responding to protest demands.

1. Target groups may dispense symbolic satisfactions. Appearances of activity and commitment to problems substitute for, or supplement, resource allocation and policy innovations which would constitute tangible responses to protest activity. If symbolic responses supplement tangible pay-offs, they are frequently coincidental, rather than intimately linked, to projection of response by protest targets. Typical in city politics of the symbolic response is the ribbon cutting, street corner ceremony or the walking tour press conference. These occasions are utilized not only to build agency constituencies,[52] but to satisfy agency reference publics that attention is being directed to problems of civic concern. In this sense publicist tactics may be seen as defensive maneuvers. Symbolic aspects of the actions of public officials can also be recognized in the commissioning of expensive studies and the rhetorical flourishes with which "massive attacks," "comprehensive programs," and "coordinated planning" are frequently promoted.

City agencies establish distinct apparatus and procedures for dealing with crises which may be provoked by protest groups. Housing-related departments in New York City may be cited for illustration. It is usually the case in these agencies that the Commissioner or a chief deputy, a press secretary and one or two other officials devote whatever time is necessary to collect information,

---

[50]Another approach, persuasively presented by Wilson, concentrates on protest success as a function of the relative unity and vulnerability of targets. See "The Strategy of Protest," pp. 293 ff. This insight helps explain, for example, why protest against housing segregation commonly takes the form of action directed against government (a unified target) rather than against individual homeowners (who present a dispersed target). One problem with this approach is that it tends to obscure the possibility that targets, as collections of individuals, may be divided in evaluation of and sympathy for protest demands. Indeed, city agency administrators under some circumstances act as partisans in protest conflicts. As such, they frequently appear ambivalent toward protest goals: sympathetic to the ends while concerned that the means employed in protest reflect negatively on their agencies.

[51]Sayre and Kaufman, op. cit., p. 253.
[52]See ibid., pp. 253 ff.

determine policy and respond quickly to reports of "crises." This is functional for tenants, who, if they can generate enough concern, may be able to obtain shortcuts through lengthy agency procedures. It is also functional for officials who want to project images of action rather than merely receiving complaints. Concentrating attention on the maintenance needs of city politicians during protest crises suggests that pronouncements of public officials serve purposes independent of their dedication to alleviation of slum conditions.[53]

Independent of dispensation of tangible benefits to protest groups, public officials continue to respond primarily to their own reference publics. Murray Edelman has suggested that:

"Tangible resources and benefits are frequently not distributed to unorganized political group interests as promised in regulatory statutes and the propaganda attending their enactment."[54]

His analysis may be supplemented by suggesting that symbolic dispensations may not only serve to reassure unorganized political group interests, but may also contribute to reducing the anxiety level of organized interests and wider publics which are only tangentially involved in the issues.

2. Target groups may dispense token material satisfactions. When city agencies respond, with much publicity, to cases brought to their attention representing examples of the needs dramatized by protest organizations, they may appear to respond to protest

demands while in fact only responding on a case basis, instead of a general basis. For the protesters served by agencies in this fashion it is of considerable advantage that agencies can be influenced by protest action. Yet it should not be ignored that in handling the "crisis" cases, public officials give the appearance of response to their reference publics, while mitigating demands for an expensive, complex *general* assault on problems represented by the cases to which responses are given. Token responses, whether or not accompanied by more general responses, are particularly attractive to reporters and television news directors, who are able to dramatize individual cases convincingly, but who may be unable to "capture" the essence of general deprivation or of general efforts to alleviate conditions of deprivation.

3. Target groups may organize and innovate internally in order to blunt the impetus of protest efforts. This tactic is closely related to No. 2 (above). If target groups can act constructively in the worst cases, they will then be able to pre-empt protest efforts by responding to the cases which best dramatize protest demands. Alternatively, they may designate all efforts which jeopardize agency reputations as "worst" cases, and devote extensive resources to these cases. In some ways extraordinary city efforts are precisely consistent with protest goals. At the same time extraordinary efforts in the most heavily dramatized cases or the most extreme cases effectively wear down the "cutting-edges" of protest efforts.

Many New York City agencies develop informal "crisis" arrangements not only to project publicity, as previously indicated, but to mobilize energies toward solving "crisis" cases. They may also develop policy innovations which allow them to respond more quickly to "crises" situations. These innovations may be important to some city residents, for whom the problems of dealing with city bureaucracies can prove insurmountable. It might be said, indeed, that the goals

---

[53]See Lipsky, *op. cit.,* chs. 5–6. The appearance of responsiveness may be given by city officials *in anticipation* of protest activity. This seems to have been the strategy of Mayor Richard Daley in his reaction to the announcement of Martin Luther King's plans to focus civil rights efforts on Chicago. See *The New York Times,* February 1, 1966, p. 11.

[54]See Edelman, *op. cit.,* p. 23.

of protest are to influence city agencies to handle every case with the same resources that characterize their dispatch of "crisis" cases.[55]

But such policies would demand major revenue inputs. The kind of qualitative policy change is difficult to achieve. Meanwhile, internal reallocation of resources only means that routine services must be neglected so that the "crisis" programs can be enhanced. If all cases are expedited, as in a typical "crisis" response, then none can be. Thus for purposes of general solutions, "crisis" resolving can be self-defeating unless accompanied by significantly greater resource allocation. It is not self-defeating, however, to the extent that the organizational goals of city agencies are to serve a clientele while minimizing negative publicity concerning agency vigilance and responsiveness.

4. Target groups may appear to be constrained in their ability to grant protest goals.[56] This may be directed toward making the protesters appear to be unreasonable in their demands, or to be well-meaning individuals who "just don't understand how complex running a city really is." Target groups may extend sympathy but claim that they lack resources, a mandate from constituents, and/or authority to respond to protest demands. Target groups may also evade protest demands by arguing that "If-I-give-it-to-you-I-have-to-give-it-to-everyone."

The tactic of appearing constrained is particularly effective with established civic. groups because there is an undeniable element of truth to it. Everyone knows that cities are financially undernourished. Established civic groups expend great energies lobbying for higher levels of funding for their pet city agencies. Thus they recognize the

validity of this constraint when posed by city officials. But it is not inconsistent to point out that funds for specific, relatively inexpensive programs, or for the expansion of existing programs, can often be found if pressure is increased. While constraints on city government flexibility may be extensive, they are not absolute. Protest targets nonetheless attempt to diminish the impact of protest demands by claiming relative impotence.

5. Target groups may use their extensive resources to discredit protest leaders and organizations. Utilizing their excellent access to the press, public officials may state or imply that leaders are unreliable, ineffective as leaders ("they don't really have the people behind them"), guilty of criminal behavior, potentially guilty of such behavior, or are some shade of "left-wing." Any of these allegations may serve to diminish the appeal of protest groups to potentially sympathetic third parties. City officials, in their frequent social and informal business interaction with leaders of established civic groups, may also communicate derogatory information concerning protest groups. Discrediting of protest groups may be undertaken by some city officials while others appear (perhaps authentically) to remain sympathetic to protest demands. These tactics amy be engaged in by public officials whether or not there is any validity to the allegations.

6. Target groups may postpone action. The effect of postponement, if accompanied by symbolic assurances, is to remove immediate pressure and delay specific commitments to a future date. This familiar tactic is particularly effective in dealing with protest groups because of their inherent instability. Portest groups are usually comprised of individuals whose intense political activity cannot be sustained except in rare circumstances. Further, to the extent that protest depends upon activating reference publics through strategies which have some "shock" value, it becomes increasingly difficult to activate these groups. Additionally, protest activity

---

[55]See Lipsky, op. cit., pp. 156, 249 ff.

[56]On the strategy of appearing constrained, see Schelling, op. cit., pp. 22 ff.

is inherently unstable because of the strains placed upon protest leaders who must attempt to manage four constituencies (as described herein).

The most frequent method of postponing action is to commit a subject to "study." For the many reasons elaborated in these paragraphs, it is not likely that ad hoc protest groups will be around to review the recommendations which emerge from study. The greater the expertise and the greater the status of the group making the study, the less will protest groups be able to influence whatever policy emerges. Protest groups lack the skills and resource personnel to challenge expert recommendations effectively.

Sometimes surveys and special research are undertaken in part to evade immediate pressures. Sometimes not. Research efforts are particularly necessary to secure the support of established civic groups, which place high priority on orderly procedure and policy emerging from independent analysis. Yet it must be recognized that postponing policy commitments has a distinct impact on the nature of the pressures focused on policymakers.

IV. CONCLUSION

In this analysis I have agreed with James Q. Wilson that protest is correctly conceived as a strategy utilized by relatively powerless groups in order to increase their bargaining ability. As such, I have argued, it is successful to the extent that the reference publics of protest targets can be activated to enter the conflict in ways favorable to protest goals. I have suggested a model of the protest process which may assist in ordering data and indicating the salience for research of a number of aspects of protest. These include the critical role of communications media, the differential impact of material and symbolic rewards on "feedback" in protest activity,

and the reciprocal relationships of actors in the protest process.

An estimation of the limits to protest efficacy, I have argued further, can be gained by recognizing the problems encountered by protest leaders who somehow must balance the conflicting maintenance needs of four groups in the protest process. This approach transcends a focus devoted primarily to characterization of group goals and targets, by suggesting that even in an environment which is relatively favorable to specific protest goals, the tensions which must be embraced by protest leadership may ultimately overwhelm protest activity.

At the outset of this essay, it was held that conceptualizing the American political system as "slack" or "fluid," in the manner of Robert Dahl, appears inadequate because of (1) a vagueness centering on the likelihood that any group can make itself heard; (2) a possible confusion as to which groups tend to receive satisfaction from the rewards dispensed by public officials; and (3) a lumping together as equally relevant rewards which are tangible and those which are symbolic. To the extent that protest is engaged in by relatively powerless groups which must create resources with which to bargain, the analysis here suggests a number of reservations concerning the pluralist conceptualization of the "fluidity" of the American political system.

Relatively powerless groups cannot use protest with a high probability of success. They lack organizational resources, by definition. But even to create bargaining resources through activating third parties, some resources are necessary to sustain organization. More importantly, relatively powerless protest groups are constrained by the unresolvable conflicts which are forced upon protest leaders who must appeal simultaneously to four constituencies which place upon them antithetical demands.

When public officials recognize the legitimacy of protest activity, they may not direct public policy toward protest groups at all. Rather, public officials are likely to aim responses at the reference publics from which they originally take their cues. Edelman has suggested that regulatory policy in practice often consists of reassuring mass publics while at the same time dispensing specific, tangible values to narrow interest groups. It is suggested here that symbolic reassurances are dispensed as much to wide, potentially concerned publics which are not directly affected by regulatory policy, as they are to wide publics comprised of the downtrodden and the deprived, in whose name policy is often written.

Complementing Edelman, it is proposed here that in the process of protest symbolic reassurances are dispensed in large measure because these are the public policy outcomes and actions desired by the constituencies to which public officials are most responsive. Satisfying these wider publics, city officials can avoid pressures toward other policies placed upon them by protest organizations.

Not only should there be some doubt as to which groups receive the symbolic recognitions which Dahl describes, but in failing to distinguish between the kinds of rewards dispensed to groups in the political system, Dahl avoids a fundamental question. It is literally fundamental because the kinds of rewards which can be obtained from politics, one might hypothesize, will have an impact upon the realistic appraisal of the efficacy of political activity. If among the groups least capable of organizing for political activity there is a history of organizing for protest, and if that activity, once engaged in, is rewarded primarily by the dispensation of symbolic gestures without perceptible changes in material conditions, then rational behavior might lead to expressions of apathy and lack of interest in politics or a rejection of conventional political channels as a meaningful arena of activity. In this sense this discussion of protest politics is consistent with Kenneth

Clark's observations that the image of power, unaccompanied by material and observable rewards, leads to impressions of helplessness and reinforces political apathy in the ghetto.[57]

Recent commentary by political scientsits and others regarding riots in American cities seems to focus in part on the extent to which relatively deprived groups may seek redress of legitimate grievances. Future research should continue assessment of the relationship between riots and the conditions under which access to the political system has been limited. In such research assessment of the ways in which access to public officials is obtained by relatively powerless groups through the protest process might be one important research focus.

The instability of protest activity outlined in this article also should inform contemporary political strategies. If the arguments presented here are persuasive, civil rights leaders who insist that protest activity is a shallow foundation on which to seek long-term, concrete gains may be judged essentially correct. But the arguments concerning the fickleness of the white liberal, or the ease of changing discriminatory laws relative to changing discriminatory institutions, only in part explain the instability of protest movements. An explanation which derives its strength from analysis of the political process suggests concentration of the problems of managing protest constituencies. Accordingly, Alinsky is probably on the soundest ground when he prescribes protest for the purpose of building organization. Ultimately, relatively powerless groups in most instances cannot depend upon activating other actors in the political process. Long-run success will depend upon the acquisition of stable political resources which do not rely for their use on third parties.

---

[57]Clark, *op. cit.*, pp. 154 ff.

A major thesis of this book is that conflict is a productive social force that can induce social change. As Piven and Cloward (1968:23) argue in the last article of this section, divisive tactics have already produced benefits for the subordinate ethnic groups in the United States. Although such protest activities as school boycotts or demonstrations have

> failed to achieve desegregation, the resulting dissensus was probably an important factor in the Administration's decision to press for enactment of the Primary and Secondary Education Act—a measure which can be understood as an effort to blunt the attack against de facto segregation by raising the level of ghetto education.

Thus, in spite of the mobilized reaction of many whites to the perceived threat of black upward mobility, disruptive tactics resulted in certain social reforms.

The first article of this section by Alden Miller utilizes a structural-functional paradigm of society to locate crucial institutions for bringing about social change. This partial shifting of the emphasis of Talcott Parson's model of society effectively serves as an introduction to conflict-oriented stategies for social change. The articles by Maldonado-Denis and Moore describe attempts by some members of Puerto Rican and Mexican-American groups to redefine their status in American society. The analogy of their plight to that of colonized peoples implies movement toward revolutionary independence.

Although conflict may lead to many important social reforms, the effects of a direct confrontation do not always lead to lasting benefits for the rebelling or revolting ethnic groups. The article by Joseph Boskin is a close look at the consequences of the Watts riots for the development of this particular ethnic ghetto. The conclusion that most of the social programs instituted after the riots were essentially failures leaves room for much discussion concerning the channeling of community and institutional support for viable social changes.

REFERENCES

PIVEN, FRANCES F. and RICHARD CLOWARD
1968 "Dissensus politics: A strategy for winning economic rights. *New Republic,* **158** (April 20): 20-25.

---

1   RADICALLY CHANGING THE SYSTEM BY TAMPERING WITH ITS FUNCTIONAL REQUISITES OR BASIC CHANGE BY ATTENTION TO BASICS

Alden Dykstra Miller

In this article the author shows how the theoretical work of Parsons, a conservative, can be used effectively to talk about radical change. The same ideas that Parsons uses to explain how society regulates itself, and thus should be left alone for the most part, can be used to identify a particular system's jugular vein—the points at which pressure for change can most effectively be applied. The argument of the conservative can thus become the tool of the radical—or of anyone else. The author uses ethnic relations as illustrations for his theoretical argument.

SOURCE

Original   article   prepared   for   this   volume.

Our problem is to develop a general theory of how to produce change. Mainstream sociology has been accused of being conservative and unable to deal with change. Yet one leading critic of mainstream sociology, and specifically Parsonian sociology, has suggested that in spite of its conservatism, Parsonian sociology is more widely "relevant" than anything that has risen to take its place (Gouldner, 1970: 138-163). That critic does not propose to harness that relevance and use it for the analysis of change and conflict. We do.

FOUR FUNCTIONAL PROBLEMS

We are concerned with open systems—systems that must deal with an environment. Open systems must incorporate solutions to certain generic problems, called functional problems or functional requisites in Parsonian theory (Parsons, 1951:131-142). Taking some liberties with terminology we present the Parsonian set of four problems.

1. Goal Commitment (G). The system must pursue some course in relation to its environment. We might say that it must have a goal in its relations with the environment. But the "goal" to which the system is "committed" may be emergent rather than declared, may be the resultant of conflicting forces rather than a consensus, and does not necessarily involve "will" or "intention." It is simply the direction or directions in which the system moves with respect to its environment.

2. Adaptation (A). The system must adapt to the environment in order to pursue its goal. That is, the system must employ some means of coping with the environment in order to move toward the goal or goals specified in G. or goal commitment. Again, no consensus, intent, or will is implied.

3. Internal Allocation (I). The system must pursue some course in allocating among its elements whatever properties those elements may possess differentially. It amounts to the questions, what element gets what, and why? Again, no consensus or intention is ascribed to the system. Allocation may

be based on a free-for-all as easily as some neatly made decision.

4. Lot Pattern Maintenance (L). The system must have some means of maintaining the pattern of allotments involved in I, or internal allocation. The process by which the lot of an element relative to the lot of another is maintained, like the processes for G, A, and I, may be emergent, as well as declared, the resultant of conflicting forces as well as a consensus, and does not necessarily involve intent or will.

These functional problems are crucial to our argument. A working, though not necessarily consistent, stable, or optimal set of solutions for these problems, A, G, I, and L, is a necessary and sufficient condition for an open system, whether a social system, a personality system, or a biological system such as a tomato plant. Change in such a set of solutions is a necessary and sufficient condition for change in an open system. Our problem is to explore the relevance of these facts for social change. We will focus on social systems and personality systems.

The idea of the four functional problems can be used to describe a social system. G, goal commitment, is how people in the social system, or those who control the system, orient the system toward goals concerning the environment, deliberately or otherwise. A, adaption, is the technical means by which the system seeks to implement these goals. I, internal allocation, is the pattern of relationships and the distribution of rewards, resources, duties, and obligations among people in the system. L, lot pattern maintenance, is the means by which these relations and distributions are effected and maintained, whether the means be peaceful culture-making and persuasion, force, or whatever. Again, it is not necessary to anthropomorphize the system and ascribe will or intent to it.

The idea of the four functional problems can also be used to describe a personality system. The social system is then part of the environment, and the functional problems in it, problems about how people act, are decisions about how a person adapts to his environment—or how he solves A, the adaptation problem, in the personality system. G, goal commitment, is set of reinforcers, with priorities, that people obtain by acting in certain ways. I, internal allocation, is the priorities among the needs of a person that underlie the effectiveness of the specific reinforcers. L, lot pattern maintenance, is the set of psychic processes, including, for example, defense mechanisms, by which needs are made to give way and adjust to each other following the pattern of priorities in I.

As with solutions to the social system problems, solutions to personality system problems can be either deliberate or emergent. There is no assumption of orderliness.

Parsons adopted a largely evolutionary posture emphasizing differentiation of function over time, where increased specialization results in the four functional problems being more and more obviously solved as separate and distinct questions (Parsons, 1961. Etzioni has, within the Parsonian framework, added and emphasized a counterpattern, epigenesis. In epigenesis, instead of having a social unit start homogeneous and become more complex and differentiated with specialized, separable parts, we see separate social units join together and gradually build a united social system (Etzioni, 1963). Both patterns of development emphasize a sequential attention to the four functional problems. Both are gradual, relatively "safe" change processes.

Because we are concerned in this article with *how to produce* change, we will abandon the whole idea of differentiation and epigenesis as inexorable, impersonal processes and instead speak of intentions of persons and, hence, of conflict. We will attend to sequential patterns in the four functional problems, however, as do Parsons and Etzioni.

SUPPOSE WE WANTED TO . . . STRATEGIC CONSIDERATIONS

Suppose we were a minority group. We would find ourselves subject, as members of a category, "to disabilities in the form of prejudice, discrimination, segregation, or persecution at the hands of another kind of social group" (Wagley, 1958: 4). All this would take place within a social or political group to which both we and our persecutors belonged. That is, we are not talking of war between independent states. We, as a minority group, would find our disabilities somehow related to "special characteristics which the minority shares and of which the majority (and often even the minority itself) disapproves in some degree" (Wagley, 1958: 5). We might be a self-conscious social unit, and our self-consciousness might help to keep us together as a group. There would probably be some way of identifying our minority membership on the basis of descent or some analogue, and we would associate and marry primarily within the group (Wagley, 1958: 4-11).

If we were such a group, we might find that we were being left out of our society's university educational system. We would find that we were being left out in two ways. First, we might find that we were being left out by being confronted with an educational system that provided only irrelevant education in ways that emphasized only its irrelevance. We might wish, therefore, that the university would come out to our communities—to meet us on our own ground, and to confront with us the problems we need education to confront. Second, we might find that within the university we were allowed no voice in decision making. We might wish that the university would let us into meet with its other members on the university's own ground, with equal voice.

Our twofold aim would then be to make the university an organization devoted to promoting and certifying learning experiences for all of its students wherever such learning occurs, and an organization committed to equality in internal decision making.

Our problem, since the university is composed of people, is to get people to do different things than they are used to doing. That means we must change A, adaptation to environment, in the personality system. We might do it by getting people to see that by doing different things they can get the reinforcers they want as effectively or more effectively than before. Or we might find that it simply and obviously was not true that people could get their same reinforcers by doing what we want. Then we would have to change either the reinforcers or the basic situation. Behavior modification and stimulus-response therapy in general might help change reinforcers. Or we might want to tinker with the I, internal allocation among needs, or L, the lot pattern maintenance in the personality system. That would probably by psychotherapy. It would be much cheaper and more practical, usually, to rely on changing the A, or adaptation, decision in the personality.

That brings us back to the functional decisions of the social system, the university itself, because in that system there are many things we would like people to do, and many of these things have implications for getting people to do other things. Let us conceptualize substantively.

We want the university to commit itself to providing and certifying learning experiences throughout society. That is a goal

commitment, or G. We also want, let us say, the university to be egalitarian in its decision makings. We want *all* students to have as much say as faculty and administration. This is an internal allocation, or I. Adaptation, or A, is then the means the university will use to promote and certify learning experiences throughout the society, perhaps a fantastically expanded directed study program instead of classes. Lot pattern maintenance, or L, is the means the university will use to develop and maintain egalitarian decision making—perhaps a series of representative groups charged with making decisions and with sanctioning those who depart from the egalitarian model.

Let us consider the promotion and certification of learning experiences, our proposed answer to the goal commitment problem, G. Suppose we got the highest university official, a person with great power, to say, "Yes, the goal of the university is to promote and certify learning experiences." What would happen? If that is all we did, probably nothing. So that is not the place to start. To get that proclamation to mean anything, we need some kind of support for it. That support could be of two kinds. First, the goal more likely will mean something if there is a means, A, immediately available for carrying it out. If such a means is not forthcoming, the goal may fade, or may never be adopted at all. Or even in the absence of a means, if enough people in powerful positions were determined to keep that goal, it might well survive until a means was fashioned for it. That means that we would want to get the distribution of resources, I, so that the people who support our proposed goal, G, would be able to do it some good. Or the I solution could be relevant in another way. In addition to an I that puts our supporters in power, an I that logically or otherwise implies G may help. Having a businessman for a president of a college implies business goals, quite aside from any power politics, and tends to lead to sound business management in the college, simply because that is the capability of the president and what is expected of him. Similarly, *our* Proposed G or goal commitment could benefit from an I or internal allocation solution that gave high position and visibility to academics, or equal positions for all members of the college community, since most members are actually involved in education. This would be particularly true for our G if we had a lot of people in the university who were trained in and active in, academic applications outside the university, both among the faculty and among students.

Support for G can be either A or I, then, or both. Without support, G probably will not survive. We need to work on A or I before we talk to officials or others about G.

Consider the other goal, egalitarian decision making, an answer to the internal allocation problem, I. Suppose we get a high official, perhaps the same one, to proclaim egalitarianism in decision making. Again, nothing will happen if that is all we have done. Again, the goal will fade if there is neither means nor mandate for it. We can provide the means first, by solving the L or lot pattern maintenance problem, or we could get the mandate first, by establishing an appropriate G or goal commitment.

A mandate for I from G, goal commitment, might be a clear relationship of egalitarian decision making to an already established goal of promotion and certification of learning experiences throughout society—a goal that implies negotiation and expertise in fitting a goal to specific situations, rather than a uniform following of authoritative directives decided upon by a top-level office. This is in clear contrast, for example, to the ways in which a goal of competition with other universities, or a goal of promoting patriotism, might imply an oligarchic and authoritarian internal allocation solution of I.

All this means that we do not start with I, but rather with L or G. But we already said we do not start with G, but rather A or I. That adds up to either starting with A, adaptation, or L, lot pattern maintenance, or if we are really moving, with both.

If we start with A, that will help us set up G, goal commitment, which will help us set up I, internal allocation, which will provide a reason for L. This is the order of development in Bales' task-oriented experimental groups, and perhaps in the development of international organizations in industrial society. If we start with L, lot pattern maintenance, then that will make it easier to set up I, which, if, for example, the majority is with us, will mandate G, which will be a reason for proceeding with A, adaptation. This is the order followed in social systems for socialization and resocialization, according to the Parsonian formulation, and perhaps in the development of international organizations in preindustrial society. Or, if we start with A and L simultaneously, they will respectively make G and I changes easier, and if we plan it well, G and I changes will reinforce each other.

A and L, the two means, adaptation and lot pattern maintenance, are relatively easy to start first because they are continuing actions, rather than intentions that die quickly without support. In fact, means can frequently be fully instituted in a social system, not just made clearly available, before goals are established. It is commonplace that if we get people doing a means without a goal, they will invent a goal, frequently, or make the means itself a goal, rather than abandon the means. Our problem is in steering the system, thus partially changed, toward the goals we are interested in, more than in sustaining the means.

In the university, then, we have to convince people to take one step at a time. We talk people into trying model programs consisting of directed studies on a broader scale, our proposed A or adaptation, and show them that they are rewarding to both students and faculty. Before this we figure out a form of directed study that will in fact work on a massive scale. And we talk people into trying in some model situations our proposed technique of representation in egalitarian decision making—our proposed L, or lot pattern maintenance, and show them that they can get reinforcement from them. Before we try it we figure out a way in which it can be done that *will* be reinforcing—not too cumbersome, and rich in the feeling that the right way, one's own, has prevailed most of the time. With this base of known and acceptable techniques of A and L we must move on and then suggest to the university that these same techniques can be used to completely reorient the university. We should also suggest that the reorientation, certifying learning experiences wherever they occur in society, our proposed G or goal commitment, and providing equal voice in decision making in general, our proposed I or internal allocation, would be positively reinforcing in the same way that A and L experiments were, and for the same reasons only more so, as well as because it better fits the needs of society, and all the advantages that may bring.

Of course we could also seize control of people's reinforcers and *change the situation* so that cooperation with our reforms would be more rewarding than noncooperation. We would have to persuade only key persons, who could then use financial or other control to influence others. Even with such potentially coercive tactics, we would still begin with A and L, and then move to G and I, both in persuading the key persons and in instituting the reforms with their help.

What about the whole issue of opposition? What can we expect to happen when both opponents use good strategy? They will both start in A and L, the two means problems, either both trying to change A and L in different ways, or one trying for change and the other merely opposing change. Then the conflict moves on to the G and I issues. But if the A and L issues make the two groups actually interfere with each other at the A and L stage, then the first group to succeed may be almost the winner already. The other side is stuck trying to undo the first side's work in A and L, and establish its own, while the first group is simply holding the line on its A and L solutions and going ahead with G and I. Thus the establishment in the university, seeing the handwriting on the wall, might oppose our trying to set up expanded directed study and model governing units on the egalitarian plan. However, if we succeed at that stage, we have already shifted the balance of power considerably, although not necessarily enough, if the balance was very much in favor of the establishment to begin with, and if the establishment is very opposed to our ideas. In the nature of the business, there is no sure formula for success—only formulae for exerting the strongest, most effective force possible. There is no new magic to being on the side of the right.

It is especially important to understand that there is within the AGIL model no assumption of lack of basic conflict. Even a strategy of destroying a society totally, in preparation for a new one, would be governed by the principle that A and L come first, before G and I. The tearing down of the old society would be accomplished by destroying the old society's A and L solutions, perhaps literally, with dynamite, and replacing them with new ones designed for the new society. The new solutions for A and L would be chosen to support the new G and I solutions that would be established after the A and L solutions were available. The new G and I solutions themselves would be chosen to be mutually reinforcing, just as in the less violent example of university reform to serve the interests of our hypothetical minority group. It is in fact an awareness of this very interconnectedness of G and I that probably brings about a strategy of preliminary destruction in the first place. When people say that we must destroy the military industrial complex before we can satisfactorily deal with discrimination, they are saying that there is a relationship between the goal commitments, G, of a society, and the internal allocations, I, of a society, and that effective efforts at change must take account of the interconnectedness of system properties. Such movements are also keenly aware of the importance of means, A and L, both for the maintenance of the current system and for its proposed destruction. It is perhaps unfortunate that many such movements are less sophisticated about what they hope to build anew—particularly since the abstraction of what they see in existing society would provide them with a much better theoretical starting point than might be available to most less radical members of society. Less radical members of society are perhaps less inclined to note possible connections between what they see as wrong in society and other fundamental structures in their own lives.

We should note here that this entire development of the interrelationships among the four problems in the social system also applies to the personality system. Thus, regardless of what we wish to change in the personality system, the two logical entry points are A and L, adaptation and lot pattern maintenance. Since we are, when considering social change most interested in changing A in the personality system, it is simplest to start there and go on further than necessary. That is basically what we concluded before.

To summarize to this point, we have a theory that says:

1.   Change in the working set of solutions to the A, G, I, and L problems of an open system is a necessary and sufficient condition for system change.

2.   Changes in G or I require support from

A or L, respectively, or support from each other.

We have a rule of practice that tells us to change a social or personality system by beginning with changes in A or L or both.

SOME TACTICAL CONSIDERATIONS— A LESSON FROM THE BLACKS

In talking of general strategy we have been dealing with four functional problems that must be solved in the process of change. It is important to realize that the functional problems are abstract, and that the concrete solutions to them are not necessarily mutually exclusive or separate acts. This is in fact one of the major lessons we can learn from the recent history of the Black Movement, as it changed character in the 1960s. Let us go back and take a look.

There was a time within most of our memories when the Black Movement was a very polite affair. This phase culminated in the Supreme Court Decision in 1954 on school desegregation. The court declared a change in the I, or internal allocation solution of the social system. All races were to have access to the same schools.

Nothing happened. There was no development before this to speak of in L, lot pattern maintenance. The G, goal commitment, of the social system contained little that would impell changes in I toward desegregation. The Court seemingly deciding, was actually only certifying that there was an issue. The movement then had to provide a means, L, for real change, desegregation, in I.

First there was a lot of discussion—sensitizing, negotiation, in some cases gradual consolidation of effective political organizations. These things persuade people and also are means, L, for the goal of internal allocation, I, because they

1.   Provide a language, a rhetoric if you will, which includes a body of standards

that resonate with known cultural values or cultural facts of life and can be used to evaluate and attack failures to desegregate.

2. Provide for what one might call watchdog committees, even at times promotion committees, with some few teeth with which to work.

Then, all of a sudden in the early 1960s, the movement began to move more swiftly with a whole new set of tactics. These new tactics were remarkable in that they were designed to have multiple functions. They were designed as answers to more than one of our four functional questions at a time.

The tactics (Anderson, 1969; Foner, 1970; Waskow, 1967; Daedalus, 1966; King, 1958) included organized sitins backed up with electronic communication and extensive training, the development of civil rights law with procedures and sanctions, that is, built-in means, and finally Black Power movements. These tactics were designed to do at least three things at once. First they were intended to move men. They were persuasive, in some cases applying considerable pressure. They either persuaded a person pure and simply that it was to his advantage to change his behavior, his answer to the A question in his personality, or if it really was not to a person's advantage to change, they changed things so that it would be. For instance possible loss of federal funds because of segregation made it to many people's advantage to change. Second and third, they provided a channel for the newly changed behavior, and that channel was directed simultaneously at the L, lot pattern maintenance, and I, internal allocation questions in the social system. Furthermore, the heaviest brunt of the direction was toward the L, so that while the I was constantly being worked on, it never got ahead of the L, and was thus not wasted. There were always means for changes made in I.

Consider, for example, a sit-in at a lunch counter. It applies pressure on an establishment to change its behavior. It encourages blacks to change theirs. It shows that people survive eating together. All of that is change in A, adaptation, in personality systems. It provides an organized force for maintaining desegregation. That is L, lot pattern maintenance, in the social system. It also announces that blacks are now equal with whites in being able to sit at the lunch counter and in having a certain influence. That is I, internal allocation, in the social system. It goes no further in I than it has gone in L. It does not claim equality in general, or even in all lunch counters. But where the means for maintaining desegregation have been provided, it announces desegregation, a change in the distribution of chances, a change in society's not necessarily voluntary or unanimous, or even majoritarian answer to the I question of the social system.

Similarly, the civil rights law proclaimed what it proposed to enforce, and Black Power movements proclaimed what *they* could enforce. The movement was very realistic about "the revolution."

From these aspects of the Black Movement we learn some very tangible things about what to do in trying to change the university. First, of course, we have a reiteration that there is an order, for sensibly attacking functional problems, namely to start with A and L, and move on the G and I. But beyond that, we might say that to seize the time means, among other things, to design multipurpose tactics.

In our program to change the university we might use confrontation tactics similar to those used by the blacks in the 1960s. The idea has a certain attractiveness because it involves a straightforward representation of the conflicts of interest between the two sides of the confrontation, and it seems elegant to have the proposed solution reflect so straightforwardly the problem for which it is proposed as a solution. But then again we might prefer more devious tactics, as blacks have themselves proposed at other times. We must be prepared, as the blacks have been, to recognize that the lessons of an experience are more abstract than the formula, "confrontation equals success," or, "sit-in equals desegregation." As times and situations change, so does the appropriateness of various tactics. The more abstract lesson is simply that what we do to deal with one of the four problems may have an effect on other problems as well. It may either hinder or help in solving another problem. In designing our tactics for changing the university, we need to be sure that what we do in attacking one problem does not worsen another problem and, if possible, we would like what we do to attack one problem actually to help in solving another.

Thus, when we consider setting up demonstration learning programs and demonstration governance programs, we want to be careful. We want to make the goals for which these programs could serve as means as attractive as possible to those we ultimately wish to convince or convert. Setting up the demonstration learning programs as we suggested, then, so as to provide both students and faculty with a sense of reward, is very important. We have to suggest, in our demonstration of the means, that the goal the means would lead to is a happy one. Similarly, it is important in our demonstration governance projects that we show not only that our organizations can produce egalitarianly made decisions, but also that they can provide to many participants rich feelings of satisfaction that the right way, usually one's own, has prevailed much of the time. Again, we have to shape what we do in demonstrating a means so that we, at the very least, avoid setting back acceptance of the goal, and hopefully move it ahead. Similarly, what we do to solve the A problem must not interfere with what we do to solve the L problem, and so on. *The four functional problems, so important as distinct problems that must be dealt with in sequence, must be attacked with a master plan that lays out nonconflict-*

ing solutions to all four, with the greatest possible economy.

REFLECTIONS IN ENDING

We have been concerned with the kind of theoretical apparatus that can not only account for but also direct social change. We have found such an apparatus in Parsonian theory.

What we have done is related to and may make more fully exploitable the work of conflict and change-oriented theorists such as Dahrendorf, conflict-oriented writers such as Coser, and dialectically oriented scholar-revolutionaries such as Marx. Much could be done in developing further and in greater detail our general scheme by taking account of such particulars of the Marxian model of revolution as the place of class consciousness in the casual chain leading from an unsatisfactory L solution in society to, ultimately, a new I. From Dahrendorf and others before him, on the other hand, comes, for example, the more abstract proposition that a conflict situation that is suppressed rather than regulated and resolved may blow up—*with specific, predictable factors determining the intensity and violence of the blowup.* Some radical movements try to play on these principles as a tactic in changing the A or adaptation answer in personality systems. We might profitably investigate such ideas closely, probably incorporating them in some form along with many other specific ideas from Dahrendorf. And many of Coser's ideas, such as the effectiveness of conflict with outsiders as a way of holding the internal system together, and the use of regulated conflict as a means of resolving differences and thus maintaining alliances, are crucial to mounting a social movement or maintaining an interest group, both of which are open social systems in their own rights. The first of these two ideas, the effect of external conflict, tells us a way to make G, goal commitment, support I, internal allocation. The second is a way to set up L, lot pattern maintenance, to support I by providing an escape valve for tensions and really resolving or managing problems of conflict. We can see in looking at black power movements that the value of such ideas has not been entirely missed. These and other ideas from Coser and other theorists can be explored and incorporated more systematically into a more detailed version of our model of "how to do a social change."

All of this is closely related to the problems of living in modern society. We have more to lose than our chains, for we must consider not only the present but also the future. Therefore we need to know what we are doing when we consider radical action. If change must come quickly, as many believe, we must learn quickly, frequently in the heat of action. A theory of change, including intentional change, may help.

REFERENCES

ANDERSON, W. (ed.)
    1970 *The Black Panthers Speak.* New York: Lippincott.

DAEDALUS
    1966 The Negro American, 1 & 2. *Daedalus.* (Fall and Winter).

ETZIONI, A.
    1963 "The Epigenesis of Political Communities at the International Level." *American Journal of Sociology* 68 (January): 407-421.

FONER, P. S. (ed.)
    1970 The Black Panthers Speak. New York: Lippincott.

GOULDNER, A.

    1970 *The Coming Crisis of Western Sociology.* New York: Basic Books.

KING, M. L., JR.
    1958 *Stride Toward Freedom.* New York: Harper and Row.

PARSONS, T., SHILLS, E. A. (eds.)
    1951 *Toward a General Theory of Action.* New York: Harper and Row.

PARSONS, T.
    1961 "Some Considerations on the Theory of Social Change." *Rural Sociology* 26 (September): 219-239.

WAGLEY, C., HARRIS, M.
    1958 *Minorities in the New World.* New York: Columbia University Press.

WASKOW, A.
  1967 *From Race Riot to Sit-In, 1919 and the*

1960's. Garden City, New York:
Anchor.

---

2   THE PUERTO RICANS: PROTEST OR SUBMISSION?

Manuel Maldonado-Denis

Utilizing the analogy of colonialism, the author argues that the situation of
Puerto Ricans, whether in Puerto Rico or in the "barrio" of New York City
is one of a colonized people. He fears that the failure of Puerto Ricans to
assert their autonomy and to oppose the imposition of a white American
culture on them can only lead to assimilation.

ABSTRACT: The situation of Puerto Ricans in the United States cannot be
seen as abstracted from that of those living in Puerto Rico. Puerto Rico has
been a colony of the United States since 1898, and the most pervasive characteristic of its population—both in the Island and in the Mainland—is its
colonialist mentality or world view: hence, the attitude of submissions and
acquiescene characteristic of the Puerto Ricans. The only forces in Puerto
Rico that represent Puerto Rican protest against the perpetuation of colonialism in Puerto Rico are the proindependence groups. In this respect, their goal
is similar to that of the Black Power advocates in the United States, because
both groups are faced with a similar situation. Only when Puerto Ricans have
achieved decolonization, both psychologically and politically, will they be
able to come of age as a true protest movement. Otherwise, they run the risk
of a total destruction of Puerto Rican nationality, and cultural assimilation
by the United States.

SOURCE

Reprinted from The Annals of The Amer. Acad. of
Political and Social Science
Vol. 382, Mar. 1969 by permission of the author
and *The Annals*

Among the minority groups in the United States, Puerto Ricans are latecomers. In what constitutes an impressive mass exodus after World War II, nearly a half-million Puerto Ricans emigrated to the United States between 1945 and 1959. As a noted demographer has indicated, from 1940 to 1960 the Island lost nearly a million persons as a result of this mass migration.[1] The majority of these Puerto Rican emigrants have settled in New York City, where an estimated three-quarters of a million live at present. They are concentrated mainly in East Harlem or Spanish Harlem—"El Barrio," as Puerto Ricans are fond of calling it. A recent study has pointed out that since the mid-1950's there has been a reverse flow of migrants to Puerto Rico, estimated to number at least 145,000.[2] Ease of communication with the Mainland, the absence of immigration requirements (Puerto Ricans have been American citizens since 1917), and the spur of economic necessity help to explain the reason why "at least one out of every three persons born in Puerto Rico has experienced living in the United States at some time in his life."[3]

Furthermore, it is the declared policy of the Commonwealth's government to foster this mass migration as an "escape valve" that will help to ease the pressures of a population growing at an annual rate of 2.1 per cent (as of 1966). This migration tends to be among those age groups whose economic productivity is greatest. According to Dr. Vázquez Calzada, in the decade from 1950 to 1960, 70 per cent of the migrants were persons ranging from 15 to 39 years of age. The Island's labor force faces an acute unemployment problem. Government economist Hubert C. Barton has estimated it at 30 per cent, while other economists estimate it at around 14 per cent. But the situation facing the Puerto Rican migrants in the United States is hardly any better. An Associated Press dispatch, quoted in *The San Juan Star*, May 22, 1968, points out that Labor Department official Herbert Beinstok indicated that a 1966 survey had shown that the subemployment rate for Puerto Ricans in slum areas in New York is 33.1 per cent, while the unemployment rate is 10 per cent. In this respect, one need only read Patricia Cayo Sexton's *Spanish Harlem: Anatomy of Poverty* or Helena Padilla's *Up from Puerto Rico* to understand that the lot of the Puerto Rican ghetto-dweller in New York is hardly any better than that facing the "lumpenproletariat" in the slums of San Juan, so vividly described by Oscar Lewis in his controversial book *La Vida*. But, notwithstanding Puerto Rican participation in the Poor People's March on Washington, and some sporadic outbursts of rebellion, it can hardly be said that Puerto Ricans in the United States—as a group that faces the prejudices and hardships of a nonwhite group in a racist society—have achieved in their struggle for liberation, a level of consciousness and of militancy similar to that of Afro-Americans.

ISLAND AND MAINLAND PUERTO RICANS: SIMILARITY OF PROBLEMS

It would be a grievous mistake, however, if the problems facing the Puerto Ricans in the United States were to be seen as abstracted from the situation of the Puerto Ricans who live in Puerto Rico. The essence of the matter really lies in the relationship that exists between Puerto Rico and the United States.

[1] José Luis Vázquez Calzada, "La emigración puertorriqueña:" ¿solución o problema?," *Revista de Ciencias Sociales*, Vol. VII, Núm. 4 (Diciembre 1963).

[2] José Hernández Alvares, *Return Migration to Puerto Rico* (Berkeley: University of California, 1967), p. 40.

[3] *Ibid.*, p. 40.

Puerto Rican nationality and United States colonialism

It is my contention that Puerto Ricans are a colonial people with a colonial outlook, and that, as such, they have not been able, so far—as the Afro-Americans groups are increasingly doing—to achieve a true "decolonization," either in the political or in the psychological sense of the word. This holds true for Puerto Ricans both in Puerto Rico and in the United States. All the problems faced by Puerto Rico as a colony of the United States are found—and magnified—in the American metropolis: the question of identity, the problem of language, and the achievement of political power commensurate with numerical strength. And, yet, an attitude of acquiescence, of passive submission, seems to characterize the Puerto Ricans both here and in New York City, with the exception of those groups within the Puerto Rican population which have mounted a persistant protest against the perpetuation of colonialism in our country ever since 1898. I refer in this instance to those sectors of our population which have carried on the struggle for independence from American domination.

Puerto Rico exhibits a distinct nationality. And Puerto Ricans—including those who live in the Mainland—are a people with a culture, a language, a tradition, a history. Nevertheless, the colonization of Puerto Rico under the American flag has meant the gradual erosion of our culture and the slow but persistant destruction of the Puerto Rican's sense of identity. This means, in effect, that, as the late nationalist leader Pedro Albizu Campos stated on one occasion, the essential goal of any colonial regime is the cultural assimilation of the colonized people. The process is not yet complete because Puerto Rican culture has shown a certain resilience, a certain capacity for survival and resistance, that has forced the colonial legislators and administrators to pause before continuing in their course.

As Frantz Fanon—the most perceptive and articulate writer speaking for the colonized, not the colonialists—has pointed out, colonialism creates in the minds of colonial peoples a sense of inferiority, a feeling of impotence and self-destruction, a desire to negate themselves by becoming more like the colonialists. Thus, aggressiveness tends to take the form of internal aggressiveness, an aggressiveness against one's own group. The situation is very similar to that of the black people living in a white man's world. They are faced squarely with the problem of either asserting their own "négritude" or assimilating to the ways of the whites. Accordingly, one of the responses to colonialism may be, not liberation, but submission to the colonizer: assimilation, not the struggle for identity. This, I submit, has been the case of the Puerto Ricans. It is only because there are groups within our society which fight for the survival of our nationality that it has survived to the present day. Otherwise, Puerto Rico would have disappeared as a nationality, to become another ingredient within the American melting pot.

Proindependence movements

American occupation of the Island in 1898 dealt a grave blow to those Puerto Ricans who believed that the United States would not impose upon the Puerto Rican people a colonial regime similar to that which had governed the Island during the four centuries of Spanish rule. And, in 1904, independence was adopted—together with statehood and autonomy—as one of the definitive solutions to Puerto Rico's political status by the Partido Unión de Puerto Rico, the most powerful political party at that time. However, the struggle for Puerto Rican independence reached its highest peak in this century during the decade of the 1930's, spearheaded by the Puerto Rican Nationalist party under the leadership of Pedro Albizu

Campos. Proindependence sentiment was strong in Puerto Rico at the time, and both Albizu Campos and Luis Muñoz Marin (who later was to reject the ideals of his youth) were outspoken in the defense of independence. After several violent encounters with the police, and the killing of the chief of police (an American) by members of the Nationalist party, all of its top leaders were jailed under a "conspiracy" statute of the federal government (1936). On Palm Sunday of 1937, the police carried out—under orders from Governor Blanton Winship—what is known as the "Ponce Massacre," in which the police shot unarmed demonstrators of the Nationalist party in the City of Ponce. With their leaders jailed, the Nationalist movement entered into a state of disarray, and official repression gained momentum.

Repression reached its peak in 1950 and 1954, as a consequence of the Nationalist uprising of October 30, 1950, the attempt to kill President Truman, and the shooting of several congressmen by four Puerto Rican Nationalists in 1954. As a result, Albizu Campos spent the rest of his life in prison, or under police detention in the hospital where he was interned following a stroke, until he was released by Executive order shortly before his death. Many of his followers were jailed or killed as a result of these acts, and there are, at present, seventeen political prisoners in Puerto Rican and American jails, some of them serving sentences of up to 460 years. It is fair to say that police persecution of Nationalist party members and the jailing of the leaders of the party were successful enough to blunt the effectiveness of the Nationalist party as a political force in Puerto Rico.

It was also in the 1930's that the Popular Democratic party (PDP) was founded by Luis Muñoz Marin. Although originally committed to independence, social justice, and the liquidation of colonialism, the PDP, once it achieved power in 1940; veered its course in

such a way that it is, at the present moment, the archenemy of independence. As a result, a group of the disenchanted founded the Puerto Rican Independence party in 1946, a party devoted to the search for independence through the ballot box. This party reached its greatest strength in the 1952 elections and then started to decline to its present all-time low. Dissidence within its ranks led to the creation, in 1956, of the Pro-Independence Movement (PIM), at present the most militant and radical of all proindependence groups in Puerto Rico. Although there are at least three other proindependence groups—the Puerto Rican Independence party, the Nationalist party, and the Socialist League—the PIM is undoubtedly the one which, by its policy of confrontation, exhibited through resistance to the military draft, alliance with United States New Left groups, and attendance at the Organization for Latin-American Solidarity (OLAS) Conference, as well as through political activism guided by a radical idology has been able to carry on the protest movement in Puerto Rico most successfully at the present time.

Contemporary conflicts

Puerto Rican youths are compulsorily drafted into the United States Army, as a result of the fact that, in 1917, Congress imposed American citizenship on the Puerto Rican people. A movement has emerged, particularly among university youth for the purpose of refusing to serve in the United States Armed Forces. About a year ago, more than a thousand Puerto Rican youths signed a public statement declaring that they would refuse to enter the United States Army under any circumstances. The United States District Attorney in San Juan has already indicted about fifty youngsters, but the number of opponents to the draft keeps increasing. So far, the policy of the United States government seems to be one of intimidation, but none of the cases have come up before a court. The matter is generally disposed of by means of technicality.

University students have also expressed their protest by battling the police on the campus at the University of Puerto Rico on October 28, 1964 and, more recently, on September 27, 1967. In May of 1967, more than a thousand students successfully disrupted a parade of the Reserve Officers Training Corps (ROTC) at the University of Puerto Rico, as a means of demonstrating their protest against militarism. The leaders were suspended as a result. Many of them now face indictments for the events of September 27, 1967, when the police shot at the students on two occasions, killing a man who happened to be on campus at the time as an innocent bystander.

"Repressive tolerance" and the colonialist syndrome

As an American colony, Puerto Rico illustrates very clearly what Professor Marcuse has called "repressive tolerance." The Puerto Rican is allowed to express his views about "the System," insofar as he does not endanger it. Indeed, "the System" itself fosters the kind of dissent that can be shown as a confirmation of its members' own "generosity" and sense of "fair play." In this respect, the colonial elite that rules Puerto Rico on behalf of the American power elite has been successful, so far, in muting Puerto Rican discontent or in suppressing it altogether by incorporating or assimilating it within the existing structures. The same holds true—with rare exceptions—with Puerto Rican leaders in New York. The Puerto Rican youngster is taught an official interpretation of our history that denigrates or ignores the independence movement and its tradition. Private schools in Puerto Rico—out of which come the future numbers of the colonial elite—indulge in the anti-pedagogic practice of teaching everything in

English. The mass media are almost totally controlled by Americans. Indoctrination to imitation of American middle-class values is constant in the mass media. Add to these factors the influence of absentee ownership of most of our industry (78 per cent is owned by Americans), commerce, and financial institutions; the occupation of more than 13 per cent of our tillable land by American Armed Forces; and the drafting of our youth into the United States Armed Forces, and the picture will emerge more clearly. Puerto Rico is a country that is threatened as its very roots by the American presence here, the rhetoric of "a bridge between two cultures" and "bilingualism" notwithstanding. After seven decades of American colonial rule, what is really surprising is that there is still a hard core of Puerto Rican culture and identity that holds out against the American cultures' penetration.

And yet, the most pervasive, the most significant, tendency that one finds among the Puerto Rican population, both in the Island and in the United States is what one might call the "colonialist syndrome": that aggregation of attitudes, orientations, and perceptions which magnifies the power, wisdom, and achievements of the colonizer while minimizing the power, wisdom, and achievements of the colonized. No one illustrates this attitude better than the completely "Americanized" Puerto Rican, who, in his quest to be more "American," seeks to identify as closely as possible with the patterns of culture of the metropolis. The grotesque aspect of this syndrome may be found in the "men" (as he is called), or cultural hybrid, resembling the Mexican "pachuco," whose sense of identity is so blurred that he—like his Mexican counterpart described so brilliantly by Octavio Paz in *The Labyrinth of Solitude*—has no roots and no bearings: a cultural schizophrenic who does not know what he is.

The colonialist "syndrome" is, of course, played down by the elite that helps it on its way, but it is nurtured by an almost complete dependence on the United States Congress as the main source of legislation for Puerto Rico, as well as by other federal aid programs extended to Puerto Rico and administered directly by the federal bureaucracy. As long as Puerto Ricans themselves do not control the decision-makers who determine their fate on a day-to-day basis, the the attitudes and orientations characteristic of colonial subservience to the wielder of power will continue to prevail in Puerto Rico and among Puerto Ricans in the Mainland. Today, the Puerto Rican protest is limited to a minority of the population, while the majority remains acquiescent, perhaps more out of a sense of impotence than out of approval of the present situation.

A Puerto Rican protest will only be effective when Puerto Ricans free themselves from the mental bonds that, more than anything else, hold them in submission. The real problem now is how to crystallize the Puerto Rican protest effectively, so that more and more groups within the population, here and in the Mainland, will come to understand, at the conscious level, that their true interest lies, not in assimilation and dissolution, but in assertion and identity. "Puerto Rican power" should be a welcome complement to Black Power, to the extent that it sees Puerto Ricans—as the Afro-Americans are increasingly seeing themselves—as a nationality that is faced with the threat of extinction within the framework of a colonial situation. This can only mean—as the one fruitful way of achieving "Puerto Rican

Power" —that charity begins at home, that is to say, that Puerto Ricans must achieve total power in Puerto Rico.

Independence versus assimilation

The definitive triumph of colonialism would be the total assimilation of our population into the American union. Insofar as the Puerto Rican protest movement is an anti-colonialist one—and so it has traditionally been—it will have to be attuned to the currents that are at present shaking the world with the demands of "the wretched of the earth." This means no more, and no less, than that the only way in which a protest movement can be successful in Puerto Rico is through the espousal of independence as a first step towards the achievement of economic independence. This struggle is at present being carried out by the Pro-Independence Movement of Puerto Rico, but also by other pro-independence groups in the Island. The message is being carried to the ghettos of New York and elsewhere. Colonialism as an institution is dead the world over. Puerto Rico cannot—will not—be the exception to this rule. Otherwise, we may be faced with a situation similar to that of New Mexico: cultural hybridization and eventual assimilation to American culture. This prospect—insofar as Puerto Ricans achieve consciousness of its real implications—should be enough to deter them from committing cultural suicide by becoming the fifty-first state of the American union.

3   COLONIALISM: THE CASE OF THE
                                MEXICAN AMERICANS*

Joan W. Moore

"Colonialism' has been increasingly used by minority ideologues to account for their situation in the United States. Adapting the concept for social sciences involves serious conceptual analysis. This is an attempt to specify the concept in the case of Mexican Americans, with political participation on the elite and on the mass level illustrating the varieties of internal colonialism to which this population has been subjected. Three "culture areas" are delineated: New Mexico, with 'classic colonialism'; Texas, with "conflict colonialism"; and California, with 'economic colonialism'. Ecology of settlement; historical discontinuities; and proportions of voluntary-immigrant as compared with charter-member descendants in the minority are among the factors distinguishing the three types. The chicano militant ideology incorporates symbols which attempt to transcend these regional differences."

American social scientists should have realized long ago that American minorities are far from being passive objects of study. They are, on the contrary, quite capable of defining themselves. A clear demonstration of this rather embarrassing lag in conceptualization is the current reassessment of sociological thought. It is now plain that the concepts of "acculturation," of "assimilation," and similar paradigms are inappropriate for groups who entered American society not as volunteer immigrants but through some form of involuntary relationship.[1]

The change in thinking has not come because of changes within sociology itself. Quite the contrary. It has come because the minorities have begun to reject certain academic concepts. The new conceptual structure is not given by any academic establishment but comes within a conceptual structure derived from the situation of the African countries. In the colonial situation, rather than either the conquest of the slave situation, the new generation of black intellectuals is finding parallels to their own reactions to American society.

This exploration of colonialism by minority intellectuals has met a varied reaction, to say the least, but there have been some interesting attempts to translate these new and socially meaningful categories into proper academic sociologese. Blauner's (1969) article in this journal is one of the more ambitious attempts to relate the concept of "colonialism" as developed by Kenneth Clark, Stokely Carmichael and Elridge Cleaver to sociological analysis. In the process, one

---

[1] Oddly enough it now appears that the nature of the introduction into American society matters even more than race, though the two interact. I think this statement can be defended empirically, notwithstanding the emergence of, for example, Japanese-American *sansei* militancy, with its strong race consciousness (see Kitano, 1968).

SOURCE

From *Social Problems,* **Vol. 17, May, Spring 1970**
Reprinted by permission of the author and *The Society for the Study of Social Problems*

*I would like to thank Carlos Cortes for his very helpful comments on an earlier draft of this paper.

kind of blurring is obvious even if not explicit: that is, that "colonialism" was far from uniform in the 19th Century, even in Africa.[2] In addition, Blauner (1969) makes explicit the adaptations he feels are necessary before the concept of colonialism can be meaningfully applied to the American scene. Common to both American internal colonialism of the blacks and European imperial expansion, Blauner argues, were the involuntary nature of the relationship between the two groups, the transformation or destruction of indigenous values, and, finally, racism. But Blauner warns that the situations are really different: "the . . . culture . . . of the (American black) colonized . . . is less developed; it is also less autonomous. In addition, the colonized are a numerical minority, and furthermore, they are ghettoized more totally and are more dispersed than people under classic colonialism."

But such adaptations are not needed in order to apply the concept fruitfully to America's second largest minority—the Mexican Americans.[3] Here the colonial concept need not be analogized and, in fact, it describes and categorizes so accurately that one suspects that earlier "discovery" by sociologists of the Mexican Americans, particularly in New Mexico, might have discouraged uncritical application of the classic paradigms to all minorities. The initial Mexican contact with American society came by conquest, not by choice. Mexican American culture *was* well developed; it *was* autonomous; the the colonized *were* a numerical majority. Further, they were—and are—less ghettoized and more dispersed than the American blacks. In fact, their patterns of residence

(especially those existing at the turn of the century) are exactly those of "classic colonialism." And they were indigenous to the region and not "imported."[4]

In at least the one state of New Mexico, there was a situation of comparatively "pure" colonialism. Outside of New Mexico, the original conquest colonialism was overlaid, particularly in the 20th century, with a grossly manipulated voluntary immigration. But throughout the American Southwest where the approximately five million Mexican Americans are now concentrated, understanding the Mexican minority requires understanding both conquest colonialism and "voluntary" immigration. It also requires understanding the interaction between colonialism and voluntarism.

In this paper I shall discuss a "culture trait" that is attributed to Mexican Americans both by popular stereotype and by social scientists—that is, a comparatively low degree of formal voluntary organization and hence of organized participation in political life. This is the academic form of the popular question: "What's wrong with the Mexicans?   Why can't they organize for political activity?"   In fact, as commonly asked both by social scientist and popular stereotype, the question begs the question. There is a great deal of variation in three widely different culture areas in the Southwest.   And these culture areas differ most importantly in the particular variety of colonialism to which they were subjected.   In the "classically" colonial situation, New Mexico, there has been in fact a relatively high order of political participation, especially by comparison with Texas, which we shall term "conflict colonialism," and California, which we shall term "economic colo-

---

[2]For a good analysis of the variation, and of today's consequences, see the collection of papers in Kuper and Smith, 1969.

[3]Mexican American intellectuals themselves have persistently analyzed the group in the conquest frame of reference. For a significant example, see Sánchez (1940).

[4]"Indigenous" by comparison with the American blacks. Spanish America itself was a colonial system, in which Indians were exploited. See Olguín (1967), for an angry statement to this effect.

nialism."[5]

NEW MEXICO

An area that is now northern New Mexico and parts of southern Colorado was the most successful of the original Spanish colonies. At the beginning of the war between the United States and Mexico, there were more than 50,000 settlers, scattered in villages and cities with a strong upper class as well as a peasantry. There were frontier versions of Spanish colonial institutions that had been developing since 1600. The conquest of New Mexico by the United States was nearly bloodless and thus allowed, as a consequence, and extraordinary continuity between the Mexican period and the United States period.[6] The area became a territory of the United States and statehood was granted in 1912.

Throughout these changes political participation can be followed among the elite and among the masses of people. It can be analyzed in both its traditional manifestations and in contemporary patterns, In all respects it differs greatly in both level and quality from political participation outside this area. The heritage of colonialism helps explain these differences.

---

[5] Of course, we are not arguing that colonialist domination—or for that matter the peculiar pattern of voluntary immigration—offers a full explanation of this complex population, or even of the three culture areas which are the focus of this paper. Mexican Americans and the history of the region are far too complexly interwoven to pretend that any analytic thread can unravel the full tapestry. For other theses, see the analyses developed in Grebler *et al.* (1970).

[6] This account draws on González (1967); Lamar (1966); Holmes (1964); and Donnelly (1947). Paul Fisher prepared a valuable analytic abstract of all but the first of these sources while a research assistant. I have used this document extensively here.

On the elite level, Spanish or Mexican leadership remained largely intact through the conquest and was shared with Anglo leadership after the termination of military rule in 1851. The indigenous elite retained considerable strength both in the dominant Republican party and in the state legislature. They were strong enough to ensure a bilingual provision in the 1912 Constitution (the only provision in the region that guarantees Spanish speakers the right to vote and hold office). Sessions of the legislature were—by law—conducted in both languages. Again, this is an extraordinary feature in any part of the continental United States. Just as in many Asian nations controlled by the British in the 19th century, the elite suffered little-either economically or politically.

On the lower-class level, in the villages, there was comparatively little articulation of New Mexican villages with the developing urban centers. What there was, however, was usually channeled through a recognized local authority, a *patrón*. Like the class structure, the patron and the network of relations that sustained him were a normal part of the established local social system and not an ad hoc or temporary recognition of an individual's power. Thus political participation on both the elite and the lower-class levels were outgrowths of the existing social system.

Political participation of the elite and the *patrón* system was clearly a colonial phenomenon. An intact society, rather than a structureless mass of individuals, was taken into a territory of the United States with almost no violence. This truly colonial situation involves a totally different process of relationship between subordinate and superordinate from either the voluntary or the forced immigration of the subordinate—that is, totally different from either the "typical" American immigrant on the eastern seaboard or the slave imported from Africa.

A final point remains to be made not about political participation but about proto-political organization in the past. The villages of New Mexico had strong internal organizations not only of the informal, kinship variety but of the formal variety. These were the *penitente* sects and also the cooperative associations, such as those controlling the use of water and the grazing of livestock.[7] That such organizations were mobilized by New Mexican villagers is evidenced by the existence of terriorist groups operating against both Anglo and Spanish landowners. Gonzáles (1967) mentions two: one functioning in the 1890's and one in the 1920's. Such groups could also act as local police forces.

Let us turn to the present. Political participation of the conventional variety is very high compared to that of Mexican Americans in other states of the Southwest. Presently there is a Spanish American in the United States Senate (Montoya, and "old" name), following the tradition of Dennis Chavez (another "old" name). The state legislature in 1967 was almost one third Mexican American. (There were no Mexican American legislators in California and no more than six percent in the legislature of any other Southwest state.) This, of course, reflects the fact that it is only in very recent years that Mexican Americans have become a numerical minority in New Mexico, but it also reflects the fact that organized political participation has remained high.

Finally, New Mexico is the locus of the only mass movement among Mexican Americans—the *Alianza Federal de Mercedes,* headed by Reies Tijerina. In theme, the *Alianza,* which attracted tens of thousands of members, relates specifically to the colonial past, protesting the loss of land and its usurpation by Anglo interests (including,

most insultingly those of the United States Forest Service). It is this loss of land which has ultimately been responsible for the destruction of village (Spanish) culture and the large-scale migration to the cities.[8]   In the light of the importance of the traditional village as a base for political mobilization, it is not really surprising that the *Alianza* should have appeared where it did.   In content the movement continues local terrorism (haystack-burning) but has now extended beyond the local protest as its members have moved to the cities. Rather than being directed against specific Anglo or Spanish land-grabbers, it has lately been challenging the legality of the Treaty of Guadalupe Hidalgo. The broadening of the *Alianza's* base beyond specific local areas probably required the pooled discontent of those immigrants from many villages, many original land grants. It is an ironic feature of the *Alianza* that the generalization of its objectives and of its appeal should be possible only long after most of the alleged landgrabbing had been accomplished.

Texas—Mexican Americans in Texas had a sharply contrasting historical experience. The Mexican government in Texas was replaced by a revolution of the American settlers.   Violence between Anglo-American settlers and Mexican residents continued in south Texas for generations after the annexation of Texas by the United States and the consequent full-scale war.   Violence continued in organized fashion well into the 20th Century with armed clashes involving the northern Mexican *guerilleros* and the U.S. Army.

This violence meant a total destruction of Mexican elite political participation by conquest, while such forces as the Texas Rangers

---

[7]Gonzáles (1967:64) concludes that *moradas or penitente* organizations, "were found in most, if not all, of the northern Spanish settlements during the last half of the 19th Century and the first part of the 20th."

[8]Gonzáles (1967: 75) analyses the *Alianza* as a "nativist" movement, and suggests that its source is partly in the fact that "*for the first time* many elements of Spanish-American culture are in danger of disappearing" (emphasis added).

were used to suppress Mexican American participation on the lower status or village levels. The ecology of settlement in south Texas remains somewhat reminiscent of that in northern New Mexico: there are many areas that are predominantly Mexican, and even some towns that are still controlled by Mexicans. But there is far more complete Anglo economic and political dominance on the local level. Perhaps most important, Anglo-Americans outnumbered Mexicans by five to one even before the American conquest. By contrast, Mexicans in New Mexico remained the numerical majority for more than 100 years after conquest.

Texas state politics reflect the past just as in New Mexico. Mexican Americans hold some slight representation in the U.S. Congress. There are two Mexican American Congressmen, one from San Antonio and one from Brownsville (at the mouth of the Rio Grande river), one of whom is a political conservative. A minor representation far below the numerical proportion of Mexican Americans is maintained in the Texas legislature.

It is on the local level that the continued suppression is most apparent. As long ago as 1965 Mexican Americans in the small town of Crystal City won political control in a municipal election that electrified all Mexican Americans in Texas and stirred national attention. But this victory was possible only with statewide help from Mexican American organizations and some powerful union groups. Shortly afterward (after some intimidation from the Texas Rangers) the town returned to Anglo control. Some other small towns (Del Rio, Kingsville, Alice) have recently had demonstrations in protest against local suppressions. Small and insignificant as they were, the demonstrations once again would not have been possible without outside support, primarily from San Antonio. (The most significant of these San Antonio groups have been aided by the Ford Foundation. The repercussions in Congress were

considerable and may threaten the future of the Ford Foundation as well as the Mexican Americans in Texas).

More general Mexican American political organizations in Texas have a history that is strikingly reminiscent of Negro political organization. (There is one continuous difference: whites participated in most Negro organizations at the outset. It is only very recently that Anglos have been involved with Mexicans in such a fashion. In the past, Mexicans were almost entirely on their own). Political organization has been middle class, highly oriented toward traditional expressions of "Americanism," and accommodationist. In fact, the first Mexican American political association refused to call itself a political association for fear that it might be too provocative to the Anglo power structure; it was known as a "civic" organization when it was formed in Texas in the late 1920's. Even the name of this group (LULAC or the League of United Latin American Citizens) evokes an atmosphere of middle-class gentility. The second major group, the American G.I. Forum, was formed in an atmosphere of greater protest, after a Texas town had refused burial to a Mexican American soldier. In recent years, increasing politicization has been manifested by the formation of such a group as PASSO (Political Association of Spanish Speaking Organizations). But in Texas, throughout the modern period the very act of *ethnic* politics has been controversial, even among Mexican Americans.[9]

California

The California transition between Mexican and American settlement falls midway between the Texas pattern of violence and the relatively smooth change in New Mexico. In northern California the discovery of gold

[9]This discussion draws on Guzmán (1967) and Cuéllar (forthcoming).

in 1849 almost immediately swamped a sparse Mexican population in a flood of Anglo-American settlers. Prior to this time an orderly transition was in progress. Thus the effect was very much that of violence in Texas: the indigenous Mexican elite was almost totally excluded from political participation. A generation later when the opening of the railroads repeated this demographic discontinuity in southern California the Mexicans suffered the same effect. They again were almost totally excluded from political participation. The New Mexico pattern of social organization on a village level had almost no counterpart in California. Here the Mexican settlements and the economy were built around very large land holdings rather than around villages. This meant, in essence, that even the settlements that survived the American takeover relatively intact needed to lack internal social organization. Villages (as in the Bandini rancho which became the modern city of Riverside) were more likely to be clusters of ranch employees than an independent, internally coherent community.

In more recent times the peculiar organization of California politics has tended to work against Mexican American participation from the middle and upper status levels. California was quick to adopt the ideas of "direct democracy" of the Progressive era. These tend somewhat to work against ethnic minorities.[10] But this effect is accidental and can hardly be called "internal colonialism," coupled as it was with the anti-establishment ideals of the Progressive era.

---

[10]Fogelson (1967) gives a good picture of political practices which had the latent consequence of excluding Mexicans from Los Angeles politics—a fact of great importance given the very large concentrations of Mexican Americans in that city. Political impotence in Los Angeles has effected a very significant fraction of California's Mexican Americans. Harvey (1966) gives a broader picture of California politics.

The concept of "colonialism," in fact, appears most useful with reference to the extreme manipulation of Mexican immigration in the 20th Century. Attracted to the United States by the hundreds of thousands in the 1920's, Mexicans and many of their U.S. born children were deported ("repatriated") by welfare agencies during the Depression, most notably from California. (Texas had almost no welfare provisions; hence no repatriation.) The economic expansion in World War II required so much labor that Mexican immigration was supplemented by a contract labor arrangement. But, as in the Depression, "too many" were attracted and came to work in the United States without legal status. Again, in 1954, massive sweeps of deportations got rid of Mexicans by the hundreds of thousands in "Operation Wetback." New Mexico was largely spared both waves of deportation; Texas was involved primarily in Operation Wetback rather than in the welfare repatriations. California was deeply involved in both.

This economic manipulation of the nearly bottomless pool of Mexican labor has been quite conscious and enormously useful to the development of California extractive and agricultural enterprises. Only in recent years with increasing—and now overwhelming—proportions of native-born Mexican Americans in the population has the United States been "stuck" with the Mexicans. As one consequence, the naturalization rate of Mexican immigrants has been very low. After all, why relinquish even the partial protection of Mexican citizenship? Futhermore the treatment of Mexicans as economic commodities has greatly reduced both their motivation and their effectiveness as political participants. The motivations that sent Mexican Americans to the United States appear to have been similar to those that sent immigrants from Europe. But the conscious dehumanization of Mexicans in the service of the railroad and citrus industries in California and elsewhere meant an assymmetry in relationship between "host" and immigrant that is less apparent in the European patterns of immigration. Whatever resentment that might have found political voice in the past had no middle class organizational patterns. California was structurally unreceptive and attitudinally hostile.

Thus in California the degree of Mexican political participation remains low. The electoral consequences are even more glaringly below proportional representation than in Texas. There is only one national representative (Congressman Roybal from Los Angeles) and only one in the state legislature. Los Angeles County (with nearly a million Mexican Americans) has no Supervisor of Mexican descent and the city has not Councilman of Mexican descent. Otherwise, the development of political associations has followed the Texas pattern, although later, with meaningful political organization a post-World War II phenomenon. The G.I. Forum has formed chapters in California. In addition, the Community Service Organization, oriented to local community political mobilization, and the Mexican American Political Association, oriented to state-wide political targets, have repeated the themes of Texas' voluntary association on the level of the growing middle class.

How useful, then is the concept of colonialism when it is applied to these three culture areas? We argue here that both the nature and extent of political participation in the state of New Mexico can be understood with reference to the "classical" colonial past. We noted that a continuity of elite participation in New Mexico from the period of Mexican rule to the period of American rule paved the way for a high level of conventional political participation. The fact that village social structure remained largely intact is in some measure responsible for the appearance of the only mass movement of Mexicans in the Southwest today—the *Alianza*. But even this movement is an outcome of colonialism; the expropriation of

the land by large-scale developers and by federal conservation interests led utlimately to the destruction of the village economic base—and to the movement of the dispossessed into the cities. Once living in the cities in a much closer environment than that of the scattered small villages, they could "get together" and respond to the anti-colonialist protests of a charismatic leader.

Again following this idea, we might categorize the Texas experience as "conflict colonialism." This would reflect the violent discontinuity between the Mexican and the American periods of elite participation and current struggle for the legitimation of ethnic politics on all levels. In this latter aspect, the "conflict colonialism" of Texas is reminiscent of black politics in the Deep South, although it comes from different origins.

To apply the colonial concept to Mexicans in California, we might usefully use the idea of "economic colonialism." The destruction of elite political strength by massive immigration and the comparative absence of local political organization meant a political vacuum for Mexican Americans. Extreme economic manipulation inhibited any attachment to the reality or the ideals of American society and indirectly allowed as much intimidation as was accomplished by the overt repression of such groups as the Texas Rangers.

To return to Blauner's use of the concept of "internal colonialism:" in the case of the Mexicans in the United States, a major segment of this group who live in New Mexico require no significant conceptual adaptation of the classic analyses of European overseas colonialism. Less adaptation is required in fact than in applying the concepts to such countries as Kenya, Burma, Algeria, and Indonesia. Not only was the relationship between the Mexican and the Anglo-American "involuntary," involving "racism" and the "transformation . . . of indigenous values," but the culture of the Spanish American was well developed, autonomous, a majority numerically, and contained a full social system with an upper and middle as well as lower class. The comparatively non-violent conquest was really almost a postscript to nearly a decade of violence between the United States and Mexico which began in Texas.

The Texas pattern, although markedly different, can still be fitted under a colonialist rubric, with a continuous thread of violence, suppression, and adaptations to both in recent political affairs.

The Mexican experience in California is much more complicated. Mexicans lost nearly all trace of participation in California politics. Hence, there was no political tradition of any kind, even the purely negative experience in Texas. Then, too, the relationship between imported labor and employer was "voluntary," at least on the immigrants' side. The relationships were much more assymmetrical than in the "classic colonial" case.

If any further proof of the applicability of the idea of "colonialism" were needed, we have the developing ideology of the new *chicano* militants themselves. Like the black ideologies, *chicanismo* emphasizes colonialism, but in a manner to transcend the enormous disparities in Mexican American experience. Thus one of the latest versions of the

ideology reaches out to a time *before* even Spanish colonialism to describe the Southwestern United States as "Aztlán"—an Aztec term. "Aztlán" is a generality so sweeping that it can include all Mexican Americans. Mexican Americans are the products of layer upon layer of colonialism and the overlay of American influence is only the most recent. That the young ideologues or the "culture nationalists" (as they call themselves) should utilize the symbols of the first of these colonists, the Aztecs (along with Emiliano Zapata, the most "Indian" of Mexican revolutionaries from the past), is unquestionably of great symbolic significance to the participants themselves. But perhaps of more sociological significance (and far more controversial among the participants) is the attempt to legitimate *chicano* culture. This culture comes from the habits, ideas, and speech of the most despised lower-class Mexican American as he has been forced to live in a quasi-legal ghetto culture in large Southwestern cities. These symbols are all indigenous to the United States and are neither Mexican, nor Spanish, nor even Aztec. But they *do* offer symbols to all Mexican Americans, after a widely varying experience with Americans in which, perhaps, the ideologues can agree only that it was "colonialist."

REFERENCES

Blauner, Robert
  1969 "Internal colonialism and ghetto revolt." Social Problems 16 (Spring, 1969): 393–408.

Cuéllar, Alfredo
  forthcoming "Perspective on politics." In Joan W. Moore with Alfredo Cuéllar, Mexican Americans. Englewood Cliffs, N.J.: Prentice–Hall, Inc.

Donnellys, Thomas C.
  1947 The Government of New Mexico Albuquerque: The University of New Mexico Press.

Fogelson, Robert M.
  1967 The Fragmented Metropolis: Los Angeles, 1850-1960. Cambridge, Mass.: Harvard University Press.

González, Nancie L.
1967 The Spanish Americans of New Mexico: A Distinctive Heritage. Advance Report 9. Los Angeles: University of California, Mexican American Study Project.

Grebler, Leo *et al.*
1970 The Mexican American People. New York: Free Press.

Guzmán, Ralph
1967 "Political socialization." Unpublished manuscript.

Harvey, Richard B.
1966 "California politics: Historical profile." In R. B. Dvorin and D. Misner (eds.), California Politics and Policies. Reading, Mass.: Addison-Wesley, Inc.

Holmes, Jack E.
1964 Party, Legislature and Governor in the Politics of New Mexico 1911-1963.

Ph.D. Dissertation, Chicago: University of Chicago.

Kitano, Harry H.L.
1968 The Japanese Americans. Englewood Cliffs, N.J.: Prentice-Hall, Inc.

Kuper, Leo and M. G. Smith (eds.)
1969 Pluralism in Africa. Berkeley and Los Angeles: University of California Press.

Lamar, Howard Roberts
1966 The Far Southwest, 1845-1912: A Territorial History. New Haven: Yale University Press.

Olguín, John Phillip
1967 "Where does the "justified" resentment begin?" New Mexico Business offprint, July 1967.

Sánchez, George I.
1940 Forgotten People. Alburquerque: The University of New Mexico Press.

---

4   AFTERMATH OF AN URBAN REVOLT:
THE VIEW FROM WATTS,
1965-1971

Joseph Boskin

The riots in the Watts area of Los Angeles in 1964 produced investigations and major examinations of living conditions of blacks in the United States. The author, an urban historian, examines the effects of the Watts riots in producing concrete changes for the people living in the area.

SOURCE

The substance of this paper was delivered before the Western Historical Association conference, October, 1970.

"As we left the Mess Hall Sunday morning and milled around in the prison yard, after four days of abortive uprising in Watts, a group of low riders[1] from Watts assembled on the basketball court. They were wearing jubilant, triumphant smiles, animated by a vicarious spirit by which they, too, were in the thick of the uprising taking place hundreds of miles away to the south in the Watts ghetto."

"Man, 'said one, 'what they doing out there? Break it down for me, Baby.'

"They slapped each other's outstretched palms in a cool salute and burst out laughing with joy.

"Home boy, them Brothers is taking care of Business! shrieked another ecstatically.

"Then one low rider, stepping into the center of the circle formed by the others, rared back on his legs and swaggered, hunching his belt up with his forearms as he's seen James Cagney and George Raft do in too many gangster movies. I joined the circle. Sensing a creative moment in the offing, we all got very quiet, very still and others passing by joined the circle and did likewise.

"Baby" he said, 'They walking in fours and kicking in doors; dropping Reds[2] and busting heads; drinking wine and committing crime, shooting and looting; high-siding[3] and low-riding, setting fires and slashing tires; turning over cars and burning down bars; making Parker mad and making me glad; putting an end to that 'go slow' crap and putting sweet Watts on the map—my black ass is in Folsom this morning but my black heart is in Watts! 'Tears of joy were rolling from his eyes.

"It was a cleansing, revolutionary laugh we all shared, something we have not often had occasion for.

"Watts was a place of shame. We used to use Watts as an epithet in much the same way as city boys used 'country' as a term of derision. To deride one as a 'lame,' who did not know what was happening (a rustic bumpkin), the 'in crowd' of the time for L.A. would bring a cat down by saying that he had just left Watts, that he ought to go back to Watts until he had learned what was happening, or that he had just stolen enough money to move out of Watts and was already trying to play a cool part. But now, blacks are seen in Folsom saying, 'I'm from Watts, Baby!'—whether true or no, but I think their meaning is clear. Confession: I, too, have participated in this game, saying, I'm from Watts. In fact, I did live there for a time, and I'm proud of it, the tired lamentations of Whitney Young, Roy Wilkins, and The Preacher notwithstanding."

Eldridge Cleaver's jubilation—felt hundreds of miles from the event—reflected the euphoric mood of the community in south-central Los Angeles. More than that, the description of the prisoners' *together* feelings accurately summed up the emotions of blacks throughout the country. Watts became a symbolic outcry against an oppressive society, a triumphant signal of community consciousness.

---

[1]*Low Rider.* A Los Angeles nickname for ghetto youth. Originally the term was coined to describe the youth who had lowered the bodies of their cars so that they rode low, close to the ground; also implied was the style of driving that these youngsters perfected. Sitting behind the steering wheel and slumped low down in the seat, all that could be seen of them was from their eyes up, which used to be the cool way of driving. When these youthful hipsters alighted from their vehicles, the term *low rider* stuck with them, evolving to the point where all black ghetto youth— but *never* the soft offspring of the black bourgeoisie—are referred to as low riders.

[2]*Reds.* A barbiturate, called Red Devils; so called because of the color of the capsule and because they are reputed to possess a vicious kick.

[3]*High-siding.* Cutting up. Having fun at the expense of another.

*Eldridge Cleaver, Soul on Ice (New York: Delta Books, 1968). pp. 26-27.

It would take two massive strikes by blacks in Newark and Detroit two years later to overshadow the event in Los Angeles. Yet, in a curious way, Watts has remained a significant episode in the Black Revolution of the 1960's, if only because it was not supposed to happen in America's garden city. Only a year prior to the occurrence, Mayor Sam Yorty—hardly known for his simpatico feelings towards non-whites or as one of the nation's outstanding thinkers—stated that a riot could not happen because conditions for blacks were better in Los Angeles.

But there is another reason for considering Watts as a separate event in the sweep of urban revolts across the country in the years from 1964 to 1967. If Watts was an example of the past attacked, it was also an illustration of future hope. The act of rebellion in Los Angeles was clearly the cry of a frustrated community; similarly, it was clearly the attack of a people committed to change. In sum, the actions of blacks in Los Angeles in August, 1965, represented the dual feelings of hate and hope. Because so much attention has been riveted on research and analysis into the causes of the event, it is the overall purpose of this study to explore its consequences, particularly in terms of its relationship to community attitudes and social change.

In the immediate aftermath, Watts signified a breakthrough. The term "Watts"—a misnomer in terms of the physical parameter of the violence in that it did not begin in nor was it confined to that area—became synonymous with a successful assault upon white society. "We put Watts on the map, baby," exulted a teenager.[1] It could be regarded as the urban counterpart to Mrs. Rosa Parks' refusal to relinquish her seat to a white man which occurred in Montgomery precisely a decade earlier. Jimmie Sherman, a late teenager at the time who became part of Budd Shulberg's Watts Writer's Workshop, expressed it best in a poem:

"The dead has finally awakened
A soul has found its way
And I'm a writer now!
Born through flames of August chaos
Into an era of self-help and progress . . .
From the ashes, I came,
And with me, many others. . .[2] "

In the same connection, two years later the entire urban conflagration was regarded as being "the heat people create when left to themselves."[3] Don Lee, a black poet, carried Jimmie Sherman's deliverance further when he wrote:

"after detroit, newark, chicago & c,
we had to hip
cool-cool/super-cool/real cool
to be black
is
to be
very-hot

The explosion in Los Angeles and other cities throughout the country in the mid-sixties generally reflected and contributed to the development of an urban-ethnic group consciousness. Although the rock-pelting and store-looting appeared to whites to be meaningless acts of tandem recklessness—if not madness—it is clear that blacks viewed their actions in quite different terms. More than one participant and supporter who was interviewed during or after the affair spoke directly to their expectations of change in majority attitude and behavior. Such statements can be found in testimony given before the Commission investigating the melee, known as the McCone Commission after its chairman, John J. McCone, as well as in interviews by novelists, journalists, and in other studies. The research report conducted by the Institute of Government and Public Affairs at the University of California, Los Angeles (the *Los Angeles Riot Study*) supported findings by the non-social scientists. "Looking back on the riot, Los Angeles Negroes were largely agreed that it had been a purposeful. directed protest."[4]   What was this purpose or direction? Overall, the dominant goal was to call attention to past and present conditions. Further, it was intended to create a high state of visibility: so high, in fact, that whitey would be unable to escape from his responsibilities regarding the deplorable state of racial affairs. The LARS study concluded that the "riot was expected to have important effects on white people, and these effects were generally expected to be favorable."[5]

For blacks in Los Angeles the collective action in Watts made for a fierce pride. Many persons—for the first time—"gained a momentary feeling of control over their own destinies."[6]   A sense of possession over an event which was *their* doing undercut decades of powerlessness and heightened a feeling of direction. Suddenly, many became, as in e.e. cummings' powerful poem, *1 X 1*. An immediate result was a change in black attitudes towards the oppressor.   In this connection, Jim Woods, initiator of the Watts Studio Workshop, reflected an attitude which could be found in black artists and others in the halycon days following the uprising: "Come, how much money do you have to study me—I'm worth something."[7] The remark also emanated from a cynicism involving white motives and long-standing voyeurism *vis-a-vis* the black, but it also reflected the possession of destiny. As Warren Hewitt expressed it, "the revolt was a mass sensitivity session for blacks."[8]

The collective action did have the significant effect of further alienating the middle class blacks and the civil rights leadership from the lower classes. Antagonisms between the classes had existed in the community long before the outburst and only a luke-warm feeling for the civil rights leadership could be discerned. The violence directed against the establishment was occasionally turned against these groups during the ac-

tions of the five days. When humorist Dick Gregory attempted to interfere, he was superficially wounded in the leg by a bullet. The Reverend Dr. Martin Luther King was not attacked when he visited the area, but neither was he heeded. Indigenous persons fared little better in turning the community around.

As the weeks passed and the euphoric, festive air faded, many individuals struggled with the problem of evaluating the event and reassessing their personal involvement. For some persons, like Jimmie Sherman, the violence led to a change in ambition and direction.   For others, the affair solidified into a moment, a curious break from the daily cycle of boredom and passivity. Others were puzzled by the sudden sweep of events. For most, however, a perspective developed as the episode receded. In place of the buoyant enthusiasm of the early days, an attitude of "wait and see whether the white man will really do something" prevailed at many levels of the community.[9]

Particularly important was the relationship between the community and the Los Angeles Police Department. The overall power of the event had produced a general lessening of fear of law enforcement authority and a concommitant expectation of change within law enforcement agencies.   In this connection the community was relieved to note the subdued attitude of the police in the weeks following the termination of hostilities. There appeared to be an attempt of outreach within the department characterized by the establishment of community relations programs.   Yet here, too, there was a wary acceptance of such programs. It was felt that the police would have to substantiate any shift in change of attitude by a profound change within police institutions and a pronounced shift in outward tactics.

This cautious mood regarding the effects of the violence was stated before the McCone Commission hearing by Opal Jones, a powerful community organizer who became head of the Neighborhood Adult Participation Project:

CHAIRMAN McCONE:

Do you feel the situation in your area is as tense now as it was prior to August 11th and as dangerous?

THE WITNESS:

I think there is a different kind of tenseness. I think there is a kind of wonderment, really, as to what is going on, and what difference did it make, what difference would it make to make people aware of the problems. This is reflected in the conversations that I have had with people representing some of the areas . . . I have heard people have a different kind of tenseness, really questioning whether or not anything is ever going to happen, or that things will ever be any different . . . they wonder, Why bother? Will it do any good? That's really the question.[10]

The collective thrust generated by the violence resulted in the creation of a myriad of organizations in the black community. Between 1965 and 1970 approximately twenty-five to thirty organizations were begun. They represented the affirmative intent to eradicate the ills which had caused the Watts revolt. They can be categorized into areas which in turn illustrate the specific problem areas of disfunction.

The first grouping includes independent self-help programs. Operation Bootstrap and Self-leadership for All Nationalities were formed to provide job training and job development. To offset the cry heard often during the violence, "Burn, Baby, Burn," Operation Bootstrap made its motto, "Learn, Baby, Learn." The Watts Labor Community Action Committee addressed itself to economic development. Cultural enrichment and black awareness groups flourished, foremost among these being US. Police harass-

ment was countered by the early Community Alert Patrol whose responsibility it was to follow police calls and provide community surveillance of their actions. To gather data and affadavits regarding police behavior for the American Civil Liberties Union, the Watts Malpractice Police Center was established. An organization which sought to direct the energies of young men toward self and community improvement was the Sons of Watts. Cultural and art development was encompassed by the Watts Happening Coffee Shop, Watts Writer's Workshop and Studio Watts Workshop, although the latter was actually formed by Jim Woods eight months prior to the outburst. Various associations were quickly established in schools. At Markham Junior High School, located in south-central Los Angeles, students set up the Student Committee for Improvement in Watts. Among its various goals was the improvement and betterment of the environment in Watts. To celebrate the surge of community control, the Watts Summer Festival Pageant emerged. Each year, for three days in August, a festival is held commemorating the community's identity which solidified during the revolt. The occasion is an Afro-American affair in its most valid sense. Marching bands, political and civic groups, local mass media celebrities all make their appearance. During the event, a queen is selected, local black art is displayed and a junior olympics is held. Although some whites attend the affair, the mood is militant. In 1970, a boarded-up liquor store contained a paint-sprayed message: GET OFF YOUR KNEES PRAYING TO BE WHITE.[11]

Not all of these organizations were exclusive of white support and efforts. The Community Alert Patrol expanded to include individuals in the middle and upper white classes. Similarly, among the organizers of the Watts Writer's Workshop was novelist-screen writer Budd Schulberg who, together with other writers, provided considerable direction and criticism.

A second large group of organizations also associated with community action received its impetus and/or support from federal poverty programs. Substantial amounts of monies were channeled into projects which paralelled those action programs initiated by the local communities. For example, Manpower and Training programs were created by the federal government and directed by local persons. The National Federation of Settlements was granted federal monies which enabled the formation of the Neighborhood Adult Participation Project. NAPP programming spans the areas of major community emphasis: education, consumer action, job development and new careers, neighborhood improvement and social welfare. To provide multiple community services, such as teen programs, consumer, tenant, welfare information and education programs and centers for working mothers, the Avalon-Carver Community Center and Westminster Neighborhood House were established.

In the immediate years following, other organizations were started as a consequence of the fusing of the Watts revolt with the evolving Black Power movement. They reflected a continuing attempt on the part of community persons to affect social change in relevant areas, such as social services, jobs, environmental upgrading and so on. The Black Congress, Inner City Cultural Center, Brotherhood Crusade, Black Student Unions, Black Panthers and others were examples of these strenuous organizing efforts.

Several years after the sudden revolt of 1965, then there could be discerned a reinforcing cycle of pride and community development efforts in the black community. A white writer for a popular magazine visited Watts a year after the event and assessed the mood:

"It is impossible to understand Watts without understanding the deep pride that the ghetto still takes in the riots. There is no sense of shame, no feeling that far more was lost than gained in the explosion that killed 34 persons burned and gutted nearly 1,000 buildings and caused property damage of $400 million. It is as if the riots were a mass bar mitzvah in which the entire black population of Los Angeles gained its manhood."[12]

Despite the continuity of community direction, however, important changes had occurred during the crucial months of watchful waiting. It is difficult to determine when patience with whites dissipated, but by the winter of 1966 blacks had serious reservations about any profound change. Many black community workers continued to work with Caucasians in an attempt to develop viable programs involving job training, economic development, education, communication and many others. But there was clearly a downbeat accent. Johnnie Scott, the budding poet who was associated with Budd Schulberg's Watts Writers Workshop, recalled that in the latter months of 1966 when he was trying to interest a number of youths gathered in a coffee shop in a new project, one exclaimed: "I'm tired of you pushing hope, man. There ain't none."[13]

Hope for change in white attitudes had begun to disintegrate for the young street workers and the south-central residents less than a year after the revolt. By the end of the second year the only group who attempted communication with whites were the committed black community workers. What accounted for the souring of the uprising? In the first instance, the physical remnants of the violence were virtually untouched. Although debris had been removed, the charred scars of the burned out stores and the empty lots where businesses once flourished were starkly visible. Moreover, because of the geographical factors in Los Angeles, urban blight is often unprotected. It soon became clear to blacks that neither the city nor the federal government was going to expend much energy beautifying Watts. Beautifying began with individual and cooperative blackness.

More serious was a series of clashes between the police and blacks. As all studies indicate, one of the primary causes of the urban revolts between 1964 and 1967 was the attitudes and behavior of law enforcement officials. "Police brutality" was a cry of urban blacks across the country long before it reached the mass media. It had been hoped that the revolt would bring the urgency of the problem into sharp focus and thereby initiate some means of providing a check on police misbehavior. In the absence of any white supported measure—such as a police review board—blacks formed a Community Alert Patrol. In cars equipped with two-way radios, blacks cruised the ghetto every night from 7:00 p.m. until 2:00 a.m., travelling to the scene of any incident reported in order to act as witnesses. The patrols angered the police, who already were hyper-sensitive to community charges and suspicions. Moves by the police to placate the moderate black spokesmen by conducting a Civilian Police Commission ended in a dismal failure. Several of the thirty black leaders invited by the Commission refused to speak because two groups, the Black Nationalist Movement and the W.E.B. Du-Bois Club had been excluded, an exclusion which angered others at the meeting.[14]

But the worst incidents between the two groups involved acts of violence on the part of the police. Nine months after the uprising the police were again involved in an ugly situation. On May 7, 1966, Leonard Deadweyler drove his pregnant wife swiftly down a main boulevard towards the County General Hospital. She was having labor pains. To ensure quick passage to the hospital, Deadweyler tied a handkerchief to the radio aerial as a distress signal. Within a short time three patrol cars were after him; and, after a wild chase, they finally brought his car to a lurching halt. A young police officer jumped from his cruiser, ran over to the car and for some unexplained reason reached into the passenger window with a revolver. What happened next is a matter of dispute. The car either lurched or the officer slipped. Whatever, the gun went off and Deadweyler fell dead across his wife's lap. In the ghetto the reaction was swift. Handbills were printed with a picture of officer Gerald M. Bova, and the words: WANTED FOR MURDER—BOVA. Cars were pelted with rocks, several molotov cocktails were thrown and the community seethed with tension. For their part, the police responded in this tense period by increasing their armaments and riot control techniques and heralded pacifying community relations programs. The community was generally suspicious.[15]

Two years later, at the Watts Summer Festival, the police further estranged the black community. Police forces at the festival arrested a woman at a park and then directed a massive force to festival headquarters in the belief that some shots had been fired from there. Area residents quickly met and issued seven demands through the Crisis Coalition, a spokesman organization representing the Black Congress, United Mexican-American Students Association, Southern California Council of Churches and Interdenominational Ministerial Alliance. The demands reflected the deep-seated antagonism for the police:

"Stop illegal killing by police in minority areas.
"Stop wholesale arrests of minority citizens.
"Stop intimidation, illegal detention and search of Negroes and Mexican-Americans.
"Reduce the concentration of police in Black and Brown neighborhoods.
"Change the total policy of the police department.
"Investigate criminal conspiracy of the police department to disrupt and destroy Black and Brown communities.
"Remove the white Gestapo police from the areas in question."[16]

Police-Black clashes reinforced other events in the late 'sixties' which lead to further disillusionments. Election results in 1966 and 1968 brought acrimony. In the first instance, Proposition # 14, one of many propositions which appear regularly in California election ballots, was voted down by more than a two-to-one vote. This particular issue dealt with fair housing and, although it was confusingly written, non-whites correctly assumed that it represented the racist feelings of the majority. In the second instance, a black politician, Thomas Bradley of the Los Angeles City Council, ran for office of mayor in Los Angeles and was beaten by incumbent Sam Yorty. The Mayor cleverly utilized fears in the white community and the blacks again assayed the result as another manifestation of racism. The assassinations of Dr. Martin Luther King and Senator Robert F. Kennedy in the same time period capped these feelings.

Finally, the south-central area had experienced a period of years in which some well-intentioned, but relatively poorly supported, programs effected minimal change. The attempts to alter institutional arrangements in the city were regarded as failures. By the end of the decade, local organization such as Operation Bootstrap, which had developed training programs and jobs, operated a Mattel-offered toy factory and other enterprises, were in serious financial straits. Other organizations faded from the scene or were hurting from lack of white support and community lethargy. With the election of Richard Nixon to the Presidency and the actions of Governor Ronald Reagan in the areas of welfare and education, blacks began to pull out.

Many continued their efforts in community development with minimum support and consent from the white community, thus indicating their continued desire to hack it by learning the techniques of bureaucratic survival. Out of the architectually condemned Watts Happening Coffee Shop emerged the Watts Neighborhood Center, a harbor for creative projects such as dance and drama classes as well as for grass-roots groups. Included in its broad reaches was space for film making and broadcast training and a studio layout for a proposed Watts Communications Bureau, an ambitious experiment in "interaction television" and FM radio broadcasting for Watts. Its refurbishment was the result of black initiative and support from the city of Los Angeles and the Office of Housing and Urban Development. Its significance was the education of alienated youth coping with administrative heaviness. "It demonstrates how alienated youth can work with government at all levels to get the things they identify as their needs," exclaimed Emma McFarland, regional HUD administrator and special representative. "To my knowledge, it's the first time outside the poverty programs that this has been successful."[17]

But the accent was clearly upon withdrawal from a white-black exchange. At a meeting of the Los Angeles County Human Relations Commission in September, 1970, whatever expectation the revolt of 1965 had generated was dissipated. Herbert Carter, Human Relations executive director, stated: "We used to have room to maneuver; in the last year room is becoming scarce. We can't even get people together to talk anymore—and talk is our business."[18] James Taylor, director of the Watts Neighborhood Center, concurred: "Time is running out on us."[19]

Frustration of a community—an emotion which pervaded the black community in the early 'sixties and which led to the uprising in 1965—was again wide-spread. To the blacks, whitey had not taken care of business and the attack against the white-dominated system had thus proved to be fruitless. In the final analysis, then, the revolt fused a powerful identity among many various age groups and factions in the black community; but its failure to produce meaningful institutional changes was a committment source of frustration.

NOTES

[1] *Los Angeles Times,* August 25, 1965, p. 3:3.

[2] Jimmie Sherman, "From the Ashes: A Personal Reaction to the Revolt of Watts" (*Antioch Review,* 27, Fall, 1967), p. 293.

[3] MSS, Michele G. Russell, "Reminiscences on a a Trip to Algeria," p. 3.

[4] T.M. Tomilnson and David O. Sears, "Negro Attitudes Toward the Riot," *Los Angeles Riot Study* (Los Angeles: Institute on Government and Public Affairs, 1967), p. 14.

[5] *Ibid.,* p. 18.

[6] *Interview,* Warren Hewitt, Greater Los Angeles Urban Coalition, 8/16/70.

[7] *Interview,* Jim Woods, President, Watts Studio Workshop, 8/3/70.

[8] *Interview*

[9] *Interviews,* Hewitt, Woods, *et al.*

[10] *Governor's Commission on the Los Angeles Riots, Volume* 9, pp: 26–27.

[11] *Los Angeles Times,* August 10, 1970, IV, p. 1:1.

[12] John Gregory Dunne, "The Ugly Mood of Watts," *Saturday Evening Post,* 239 (July 16, 1966), p. 84.

[13] *New York Times,* I December 10, 1966, p. 27:1.

[14] *New York Times,* I, June 12, 1966, p. 84:1.

[15] Dunne, p. 84.

[16] *Los Angeles Times,* I, August 13, 1968, p. 1:3.

[17] *Los Angeles Times,* January 4, 1971, pp. 1:3, 4, 5, 6 and 8:1, 2, 3.

[18] *Los Angeles Times,* II, September 21, 1970, p. 1:1.

[19] *Los Angeles Times,* January 4, 1971, p. 83.

5

DISSENSUS POLITICS
A STRATEGY FOR WINNING ECONOMIC RIGHTS

Frances Fox Piven and Richard A. Cloward

Contrary to the belief that gains in social equality have come about through majority consensus, the authors of the next selection argue that it was the "divisive impact of protest tactics that produced legislative gains" for blacks in the United States. Expanding on this premise they suggest patterns of conflict that may continue to produce social change.

SOURCE

Reprinted by Permission of *The New Republic,* © *1968,* Harrison-Blaine of New Jersey, Inc.

In the week after his death, Martin Luther King was memorialized as both leader and symbol of the Southern black confrontation with white America, a confrontation of such moral clarity and intensity that it moved a majority of Americans to unite in support of the civil rights legislation of 1964 and 65. This interpretation confirms the widely held belief that Negroes cannot obtain justice unless they coalesce with other groups in a majority alliance which means, of course, the national Democratic coalition. According to this view, it is the wishes of a majority that finally impel political leaders to act. The task, therefore, is to identify the issues and exchanges by which a unified majority can be culled from a people divided by class and region, by race and religion.

But the political dynamics of the Southern phase of the civil rights movement may have been quite the reverse of what is commonly supposed. We would argue that its legislative victories were not the product of a majority consensus, but of cleavage in the North-South Democratic coalition. The political impact of non-violent protests, of "moral confrontations," was to widen that cleavage. The legislative concessions of 1964 and '65 owed less to the numbers of people committed to the civil-rights movement—whether blacks or their white allies—than to the sharply divisive impact the movement had upon an already strained North-South Democratic partnership. And if this theory is correct, it may be that blacks and other minorities can also compel future gains from the majority coalition by threatening to disrupt it.

Negroes have been part of the Democratic coalition for almost four decades—that is, beginning with the reorganization of the Democratic Party during the elections of 1928 and 1932, when an alliance was struck between urban ethnic groups in the North and the traditionally Democratic South. In 1936, a majority of blacks voted Democratic for the first time. As members of that coalition, blacks have obtained minor concessions.

In 1940, for example, a Roosevelt-oriented Supreme Court declared the white primary unconstitutional and in 1941 FDR established the Fair Employment Practices Commission Each concession to Negroes was fiercely resisted by Southern Democrats who succeeded in warding off civil rights legislation of any significance for nearly three decades.

The first overt signs that the North-South partnership was in danger of dissolving appeared during the presidential campaign of 1948. Early in February, Truman, responding to the swelling numbers of blacks in the North, urged Congress to act on the recommendations of the President's Committee on Civil Rights, which had reported the previous year. He went on to press for a strong civil-rights plank in the party platform. Incensed, delegates from the Southern states convened in July to get a States' Rights Party on the ballot. An irate Georgia congressman summed up Southern sentiment with the declaration that "Harlem is wielding more influence . . . than the entire white South." In the subsequent election, four Deep South states—Louisiana, South Carolina, Alabama, and Mississippi—actually delivered their electoral votes to the States' Rights presidential candidate. The South has not been "solid" since.

At the convention of 1952 and again in 1956, Democratic leaders backed off, trying to placate the Dixiecrat delegates by adopting a watered-down "compromise" civil-rights plank and, after long drawn-out intraparty struggles, seating them without a "loyalty" pledge. The Dixiecrat states duly returned to the Democratic columns in 1952, but South Carolina and Louisiana by very slim majorities. Elsewhere in the South the Republicans made big gains: Florida, Virginia, Tennessee, and Texas went for Eisenhower in 1952, to be joined by Louisiana and and Kentucky in 1956. Missouri also voted Republican in 1952, although it returned to the Democratic fold in 1956. The party's hold on the South was slipping rapidly.

The South was, of course, provoked by the civil-rights challenges made by the Northern wing of the party, however ineffectual those challenges had so far been. Southern opinion was especially aroused by the Supreme Court's landmark decision against segregated education, won by NAACP attorneys in 1954, and which marked the emergence of desegregation as a national issue. But if that issue aroused fury in the South, it evoked considerable sympathy in the North, especially among the growing black electorate of the cities. Nevertheless, conciliation of the South was still the order of the day. Campaigning in 1956, Stevenson called for "slow but deliberate" efforts to desegregate.

It was not until 1955, when Martin Luther King led the Montgomery bus boycott, that organized civil-rights protests seized the attention of the nation. With each wave of protest, Northern black voters grew increasingly restive, and the Democratic Party could not ignore it. Appeasement of Southern racism was becoming a political liability, for Negroes who had been staunchly loyal to the party of the New Deal were beginning to defect. In 1952, Eisenhower won 21 percent of the black vote; in 1956 he won 39 percent. And in 1957 and 1960, a Democratic Congress passed the first civil-rights measures of the 20th Century.

By 1960, when John Kennedy campaigned on a strong civil-rights platform, the collapse of the Southern wing of the party was plainly visible: in the three previous presidential elections only Georgia, Arkansas, and North Carolina consistently gave their electoral votes to the Democratic candidate. Convinced that he could not resurrect Southern allegiance, Kennedy appealed to black voters in the industrial states. The choice was correct. While the Democratic showing in the South was poor, it was no worse than during the conciliatory Stevenson campaigns. The States' Rights Party won Mississippi and Alabama; Florida, Tennes-

see, Kentucky and Virginia voted Republican. And although Negro skepticism toward Democratic pledges on civil rights persisted, costing Kennedy 30 percent of the national black vote, the ghettos in a number of strategic Northern cities turned in extraordinary Democratic percentages, swinging several critical states in very close races to assure his election.

Nevertheless, Kennedy did virtually nothing on civil rights during his first two years. He had won office, but narrowly. Moreover, his overall legislative program was being throttled by the conservative coalition of Republicans and Southern Democrats, and the midterm elections of 1962 threatened to further deplete his congressional strength. It was not only that he wished to avoid fanning the fires of white resistance in the South; the racism of the white working class was also beginning to become an unmanageably divisive factor in the Democratic urban coalition. Accordingly, he signed an Executive Order barring discrimination in federally subsidized housing, but did nothing to implement it; he backed a bill to ease voter literacy requirements, but sent no substantial civil-rights legislation to Congress. And he waited apprehensively for the midterm election.

However, the Democrats in 1962 won an unprecedented mid-term victory, gaining four seats in the Senate and suffering only minimal losses in the House. Significantly, the small Republican advances were in the South, where they added five House seats (and very nearly won a Senate seat in Alabama); thus, Southern support was still eroding, despite continuing Democratic efforts at conciliation.

Meanwhile, civil-rights agitation reached its crescendo, with sit-ins, demonstrations, and boycotts which Southerners repaid with killings, jailings, burnings, and bombings. As the drama played itself out, North-South sentiments on civil-rights issues became sharply polarized, creating the political tension that would finally force legislative action. In February 1963, the President informed Congress of new civil rights proposals, dealing primarily with public accommodations, voting rights and equal employment. He submitted a bill in June.

But the proposed legislation was moderate, and even so it seemed likely to fall prey to the conservative coalition in Congress. Demonstrations escalated. In August, several hundred thousand people assembled for the March on Washington, and throughout the fall demonstrations were mounted in hundreds of cities and towns. In November, a much-strengthened bill was reported out of the House Judiciary Committee, a bill which Lyndon Johnson, following Kennedy's death, pushed through the Congress, using all the political resources of his office to obtain the necessary Republican support, including votes to shut off a filibuster in the Senate. The 1964 Civil Rights Act became law.

The reasoning underlying Johnson's extraordinary commitment to civil rights is not difficult to deduce. He was bidding for heavy Negro support in the upcoming presidential election. Like Kennedy before him, he judged that the Deep South would defect to the Republican Party, as five states subsequently did. But the Negro vote turned out to be decisive in a number of Southern states which hung in the balance, such as Arkansas, Florida, Tennessee, and Virginia. More important, Johnson received an astonishing 94 percent of the national black vote, which helped to give him the largest percent of the popular vote in history.

A year later, with a voting rights bill before Congress, Martin Luther King led thousands of supporters in the Selma marches. Congress enacted the bill. That phase of the civil-rights struggle was over.

We review this history so as to underline the fact that legislative victories were not a simple response to majority sentiments. Left to themselves, labor and liberal and minority groups in the North would not have taken the initiative. Nor was it the sheer numbers involved in the Southern movement that yielded those victories; the protesters were too few to compel the Administration to champion measures that would fracture the North-South coalition alliance. Rather, it was the divisive impact of protest tactics that produced legislative gains by accelerating defections among Southern white voters and threatening to produce defections in the urban ghettos as well.

Legislative concessions were made to mollify pro-civil-rights groups in the North. Notice, however, that the Civil Rights Act of 1965 also laid the groundwork for renewed Democratic strength in the South through provisions to enfranchise Southern Negroes. In time, Democratic constituencies may be rebuilt by drawing together white moderates and newly enfranchised Negores. So far, Negro resitration has increased from 856,000 to 1,493,000 in the six states covered by the Voting Rights Act. A few states in the Deep South may remain in doubt (Alabama, Mississippi, South Carolina, Louisiana, and Georgia went Republican in '64), but Negro voter registration (up from 8 to 47 percent in Mississippi, for example) may eventually restore even these states to the Democratic columns.

Although the civil-rights movement aggravated tensions in the regional coalition of the Democratic Party, it did not create them. These tensions were produced by the steady movement of blacks to the North and into the big-city Democratic folds, a process which has slowly shifted the balance of political forces in the North-South Democratic partnership. Disruptive protests made it impossible for majority politicians to persist in placating the South. Thus, although the party platform proposed desegregation of interstate transportation in 1948, it was the freedom riders and the brutality and public attention they provoked that produced an ICC order desegregating interstate transportation facilities more than a decade later.

The civil-rights movement is therefore an example of what might be called "dissensus politics": a cadre, acting on behalf of a minority within a coalition, engages in actions which are designed to dislodge (or which threaten to dislodge) not only that minority, but more important, *other significant constituents groups in that same alliance.* Through the cadre's ability to generate defections among other groups in a coalition, its impact becomes far greater than the voting power of the minority. If the strategist of consensus looks for issues and actions to bring groups together, then the strategist of dissensus looks for issues and actions which will drive groups apart.

Tactics to provoke dissensus are probably most effective at times when widespread social or economic change has already undermined a majority coalition, making it vulnerable to attack. Since the leaders of the coalition will tend to resist realignments of power and policy as long as possible, the disrupters must expose the underlying political tensions being produced by changing conditions. Then, confronted with actual or threatened electoral realignments, majority leaders will make concessions in an attempt to restore a weakening coalition or reorganize a shattered one.

Nevertheless, most leaders of the civil-rights movement remain committed to a strategy of influence through consensus politics, as advanced by Bayard Rustin in his article, "From Protest to Politics" *(Commentary,* February 1965). With the passage of the Voting Rights Act, Rustin called for blacks to move from the streets to the polls, especially in alliance with other voting blocs in the traditional liberal-labor-minorities coalition. He pointed to the potential power of newly enfranchised Southern blacks and to the growth of Negro electoral power in Northern cities. But Mr. Rustin does not see that mass action in the streets *did* produce

mass action at the polls—*not merely by blacks, but also and primarily, by whites.* If this interpretation has merit, then Rustin was not recommending a shift "from protest to politics" so much as a shift from one political strategy to another—in effect, from dissensus politics to consensus politics.

In the interim between Selma and King's assassination, the central concern of civil-rights forces shifted from legal rights to poverty. King himself began to work in the urban ghettos and to prepare plans for a poor people's campaign for jobs and income. Implicit in this shift is the belief that the tactics which produced legal victories in the South can produce economic gains in Northern cities, and for the same underlying political reasons.

In the past, the Democratic coalition was based on the state parties of the rural South and the big-city parties in the urbanized North. And while Southern defections have greater weight to the big-city organizations, the cities have become more important in their own right. Two-thirds of our population now live in metropolitan areas. The regional configurations which formerly dominated national politics are rapidly giving way to urban configurations.

The migration of blacks to the North which undermined the regional coalition has also undermined the Democratic coalition in the cities. As their incomes have risen, many traditional Democrats—Irish, Italians, Poles—have moved to the suburbs. Those remaining in the central cities confront growing numbers of newcomers, who are feared at the outset for being both poor and black. *That* fear deepens as the swelling masses of poor blacks threaten white residential enclaves and neighborhood institutions, compete for scarce jobs, and now for control of city government itself.

The urban parties are less capable of containing group conflicts than they once were, chiefly because of the passing of the political machine. In the earlier day, political support was built from among the diverse groups in cities by the conversion of public goods into private favors. With greater affluence and a changing class structure, however, the better-off majorities in the cities no longer require the personal services of machine politicians but demand instead public services to improve their environment and entrench their newly won class position. These services—whether in education, housing, law enforcement, or urban renewal—have become the grist of urban politics. And with the vast increases in migration during the '50's, it is these services which are the focus of political conflict, for they serve older groups in direct proportion as they victimize newcomers.

Divisive strains are already taking their toll. Besieged by internal conflict, the urban party machinery can no longer mobilize resources and voters in support of national candidates as vigorously as before—a circumstance from which Stevenson suffered badly in the campaigns of '52 and '56. As the racial crisis worsens, the spectre of massive electoral defections looms larger, especially in local contests. The white working classes deserted the Democratic Party in extraordinary numbers in the recent mayorality elections in Cleveland and Gary, and the same pattern will be repeated in other cities where blacks are sufficiently numerous to challenge white hegemony. These conflicts are debilitating the local organizations needed to carry national elections, and may weaken the allegiance of Democratic voters in national contests as well.

Federal programs initiated for the cities in the last few years were an effort to ease strains among competing groups and to solidify the urban coalition. But they have run aground as a result of the rising costs of the war in Vietnam. Eventually, however, the national party must move more vigorously to rehabilitate the cities. The black poor can hasten that day by exploiting class and racial divisiveness in the cities. For as these divi-

sions are widened, the Democratic coalition is endangered, and national leaders will proffer concessions to shore up their urban base. In sum, what urban blacks cannot get by playing consensus politics within the Democratic coalition they may win by dissensus politics.

Divisive tactics have already paid off. The school boycotts and demonstrations in various Northern cities which mobilized blacks around the cause of integrated education, produced violent hostility among whites. But although they failed to achieve desegration, the resulting dissensus was probably in important factor in the national Administration's decision to press for enactment of the Primary and Secondary Education Act—a measure which can be understood as an effort to blunt the attack against *de facto* segregation by raising the level of ghetto education. Similarly, although urban renewal stirred bitter protests among the dislocated poor, while drives for open occupancy engendered profound anger among whites, the resulting turmoil was a key force behind the Model Cities legislation—a measure to ease the conditions of blacks within the boundaries of the ghetto, and so avoid arousing the hostility of whites. Those of the middle class who place a high priority on heterogeneous communities may regard programs to improve the ghetto as Pyrrhic victories, at best; among the black poor, however, the proportions are somewhat different.

Race and class conflict in the cities, we have said, is being played out in the arena of public services. But because blacks are newcomers, and not well organized, policies have not generally been much modified in response to them. When existing policies blatantly ignore changing constituencies, disruptive tactics can expose them as anachronisms and force new accommodations. Public welfare practices are a prime example of such outmoded adaptations, and a national movement of welfare recipients is now growing whose strategy is to disrupt and expose them. In response to older constituent groups—the white working class which is concerned about taxes, and many in the middle class who suppose that poverty is better solved by "rehabilitating" the poor than by redistributing income—the administrators of pubic-welfare agencies keep the rolls low and budgets down. They refuse to inform the poor of their eligibility for assistance, erect a tangle of bureaucratic barriers against those who do apply, and simply reject many eligible applicants illegally. The public-welfare system distributes it meager benefits to but half of those who are legally eligible.

The welfare receipients movement is disrupting this pattern by mobilizing many of the poor to claim their entitlements under the law. Mounting claims mean higher costs and higher taxes. Predictably, spokesmen for the working classes are already showing alarm and indignation, liberals are troubled; but the masses of the black poor are also becoming aroused. Welfare reforms are to a major demand of the "poor people's campaign" this summer.

In the short run, the result will be chaos in the welfare program. But that chaos will expose the ways in which the poor have been sacrificed to more powerful groups in the Democratic coalition. To cope with the resulting dissensus, the national Democratic Party will try to lessen welfare costs to localities, while also liberalizing the entire program. Relieving localities of the financial burden would placate the working class and others in the urban coalition, and a more liberal income maintenance system (a federally guaranteed income perhaps) would be a major concession to the black poor.

Similar dissensual strategies can be employed to force concessions in other areas—for example, in housing which, for the black poor in the cities is substandard, overcrowded and overpriced. Small-time landlords grub a profit from slum housing by short-cutting on repairs and services, buying "political in-surance" against code enforcement with active support of local Democratic clubs. Liberals and "good government" groups, for their part, are satisfied with perennial reforms of the housing codes, to which political leaders acquiesce, knowing that cumbersome procedures of legal redress will do little except to satisfy the reformers. And even when legislation for new construction of rehabilitation is passed, only token funds are appropriated out of deference to other groups.

Housing agencies are thus the managers of a system of collusion; they do not enforce codes because to do so would bankrupt the slumlords and compel government to house the minority poor—a circumstance that would entail either diverting funds from programs serving other groups or raising local taxes. To avoid the ire which such actions would evoke, municipal government uses its enforcement powers gingerly and selectively, content to let the slumlord reap the fury of the ghetto.

These arrangements could be disrupted through massive withholding of rent, with tenants advised to spend the money instead for food and clothing. City governments would then be under great pressure to forestall evictions for fear of provoking widespread violence in the ghetto. Considering the marginal character of the slum market, many owners of deteriorated buildings, unable or unwilling to make the required repairs, would be forced out of business propelling government into taking over slum housing. The consequent drain on municipal revenues and the conflicts endangered among urban groups would intensify local political conflict. But local conflicts reverberate in the national Democratic Party, generating pressure for federal subsidies for low-income housing in large US cities.

As the foregoing examples suggest, to effectively disrupt the coalition in the cities, something more than the marches, demonstrations and sit-ins of the Southern movement will be required. Segregation in the

South was an entrenched symbolic system, and tactics of moral confrontation were sufficient to provoke pervasive electoral discord, particularly since it cost the North little to support the extension of constitutional rights to Southern Negroes. But in the era which Martin Luther King foresaw, blacks will be making economic rather than legal demands, and so challenging major class interests in the city. These interests will not be overcome by protests alone. They will be overcome, for example, by enrolling the poor to bankrupt the welfare system or inciting rent revolts to close down the slum society.

It will be said that dissensual politics may so aggravate the working class that it moves further to the right, or even out of the Democratic coalition altogether. While this danger exists, it must be said that the working class is now being held securely in coalition by policies which work against the black poor. It has opted only for specific and limited economic reforms, and has now become a major impediment to economic advances by the Negro.

It will also be said that disruptive tactics may spur greater violence in the cities, arousing so strong a backlash that politicians can no longer ease conflict by making concessions to different groups in a coalition. Violence *is* a danger, but since the conditions which breed violence already exist, the occasions which provoke it are manifold. To assume the burden for keeping the peace by refraining from disruptive tactics may be to forego the major reforms upon wnich a more enduring, less volatile peace depends.

A dissensual political strategy is risky for another reason. The poor who generate disruption have little control over the responses to it. Still, the only resource of an impoverished minority is to create the kind crises to which political leaders must respond, hoping that reforms will follow. In Martin Luther Kings' words, "We are aware that we ride the forces of history and do not totally shape them."

---

6   THE WAR BETWEEN THE REDSKINS AND THE FEDS

Vine Deloria Jr.

The situation of Indians in the United States is comparable to that of Indians in Mexico according to Deloria. Taking off from Walter Hickel's remark in 1969 that the United States government had been "over protective" of Indians. Deloria, a prominent Indian leader, reviews the history of the American Indian. His analysis reveals how the Indians lack of authority over their own lives, and their lack of united intertribal organization hampered their efforts to engage in productive conflicts with the federal government.

SOURCE
From *The New York Times Magazine,* December 7, 1969. Copyright © 1969 by *The New York Times Company.* Reprinted by permission.

If Secretary of the Interior Walter Hickel has any sense of history, he must have been impressed with his situation at the convention of the National Congress of American Indians held earlier this fall in Albuquerque, N.M. Not since George Armstrong Custer's sensitivity-training session on the banks of the Little Big Horn had so many angry Indians surrounded a representative of the United States Government with blood in their eyes. Of the estimated million Indians in the United States, the N.C.A.I. represents the reservation population of some 400,000. With spokesman for the remaining urban and other Indian communities of the East (500,000 urban Indians and 100,000 scattered Eastern bands) attending the convention, Hickel was greeted by representatives of the entire Indian community, including Eskimos, Indians and Aleuts from his home state of Alaska.

All summer, tension had been building within the Indian community as the tribes fearfully awaited the pronouncement of Indian policy by the new Nixon Administration. During the 1968 Presidential campaign Nixon had promised that, if elected, he would not unilaterally sever Federal relations with the tribes, nor would he allow the tribes to be pressured to alter the relationship themselves. Indian leadership recalling that Nixon had been Vice President during the Eisenhower Administration, when the hated policy of termination of Federal responsibilities for Indians had been forced on the unwary tribes, was alerted for any signs of change, and skeptical of the "New Federalism."

Hickel's performance in 1969 appeared to have justified Indian suspicions. In late July at a Western Governors' Conference in Seattle, he characterized the relationship of the Federal Government as "over-protective" of Indian rights. With a foot-in-mouth aplomb so characteristic of some of Nixon's interchangeable Cabinet members, Hickel compounded this error by labelling the reserva-

tions as "crutches" by which Indians avoided their full responsibilities as citizens. By later summer the moccasin telegraph was buzzing with rumors that the new Secretary of the Interior was a "terminationist," and that a great battle over the very existence of the reservations was imminent. Indian reservations have a total land base of more than 52 million acres, scattered in 26 states and providing a home for people of 315 different tribal groups. The life expectancy of a reservation Indian is 46 years, rising nearly a year each year under current programs. Although the average income is slightly over $1,500 per family annually, and the housing is generally substandard, the reservations are all that remain of the continent the Indians once owned, and they are determined to fight for every handful of dust that remains.

The National Traditionalist Movement, spearheaded by the Iroquois League, called for Hickel's removal from office. The Iroquois (the only Indian tribe to declare war on Germany in 1917) set a strong nationalistic tone to the resistance, which quickly sprang up in Indian country.

From the urban Indian centers on the West Coast, the third-world-oriented United Native Americans took up the battle cry. "IMPEACH HICKEL" bumper stickers blossomed beside' "Red Power" and the multitude of "Custer" slogans on Indian cares. Petitions calling for Hickel's removal began to circulate on the Coast.

As the N.C.A.I. convention opened, there was considerable discussion by the delegates as to the length at which Indians should *stabilize* Hickel's hairline. This remark was an obvious reference to Hickel's conception of his role as trustee in defining the water rights of the Pyramid Lake Paiutes of Nevada. The Pyramid Lake tribe has a beautiful lake, the largest fresh-water lake in the state. For the major part of this century it has tried to insure that sufficient water is delivered to the lake to maintain its excellent cutthroat trout fishery and its flock of pelicans. But the Federal Government has continually refused to defend the tribe's water rights by allowing other users to take water which is rightfully owned by the Paiutes. Consequently, the lake has had a declining shoreline for most of the century, a condition that precludes development of the reservation for recreation purposes.

Hickel's solution, proposed after a meeting with Governors Reagan of California and Laxalt of Nevada, was to reduce the water level 152 feet, creating a mud flat of 40,000 acres and thus "stabilizing" the water level. It was the same logic used by the Army to destroy a Vietnamese village—"We had to destroy the village to save it." It naturally followed that the only way to save Pyramid Lake was to drain it.

With these remarks to his credit, it is a wonder that Hickel was the recipient of only sporadic boos and catcalls when he attempted to address the Indian convention. No one even speculated on the possibility of a canine ancestor in Hickel's immediate family tree. "Terminationist" is a much dirtier word in the Indian vocabulary.

Wally Hickel is not that bad a guy. He was genuinely puzzled by the reactions which his remarks had created in the Indian community. In his own mind he was simply searching for a new approach to a problem that he, as Secretary of the Interior, has a responsibility to resolve. But he had unexpectedly hit the one nerve which had been frayed raw by century of abuse and betrayal: the treaty trust relationship between Indians and the Federal Government.

Hickel's remarks at Seattle and on the water problems in Nevada prior to the meeting of the National Congress of American Indians fitted exactly into prior speeches and problems of other times and places which had resulted in policies and programs destructive of the reservation communities. He could not have said anything more inflammatory than that the Federal Government had been "over-protective" of Indian rights,

implying that the Government would be less zealous in fulfilling its responsibilities during his tenure as Secretary of the Interior.

Had Hickel been thoroughly briefed on the sterling record his predecessors had achieved, it is doubtful that he would have made the "over-protective" statement. The Government has been over-protective of Indian rights only in the sense the John Dillinger "over-protected" banks by robbing them before other criminals showed up.

In 1908 the Supreme Court decided the case of Winter v. United States in which Indian water rights were given priority over any other rights on streams running through Indian reservations. It has been clear, therefore, for most of this century, that the Pyramid Lake Paiutes have first priority for sufficient water in the Truckee-Carson river system to stabilize their lake *at the level at which it stood when the reservation was established.* Yet Interior had watched as the Indian water went elsewhere and the lake declined precipitously each year.

In 1924 the Secretary of the Interior was authorized to construct the Coolidge Dam in Arizona. In the authorizing legislation it clearly stated that the project was "for the purpose, first, of providing water for the irrigation of lands allotted to Pima Indians on the Gila River Reservation, Arizona." The Federal Government delivered just about enough water for Ira Hayes, Pima Indian and Marine hero of Iwo Jima, to drown in. Never was there any good faith by the Government to help the Indians irrigate their lands. Consequently, the water made available by the project went to non-Indians residing off the reservation.

With water the crucial element in the development of Indian reservations, the concept of "overpopulation" appears nonsensical in view of the fact that, attached to every major Interior Department appropriation bill is a little rider stating that no Federal funds can go to develop the water rights of the tribes in California, Oregon and Nevada.

Indian reservations thus lie dormant and undeveloped in those states, while non-Indians have sufficient water to develop their own lands.

To add to the irony of the "overprotection" which Indian people supposedly receive is the fact that, when the United States has to deal with Foreign nations, it presents a clean and pious front. In 1913 the case of the Cayuga Nation, member of the Iroquois League, came before the American-British Claims Arbitration. The British Government wanted just compensation from the United States under the provisions of the Peace of Utrecht for lands which the state of New York took from the Cayugas after the War of 1812.

In the appendix to the answer filed by the United States to the British complaint, the Government declared:

"Under that system the Indians residing within the United States are so far independent that they live under their own customs and not under the laws of the United States; that their rights upon the lands which they inhabit or hunt are secured to them by boundaries defined in amicable treaties between the United States and themselves; and that whenever those boundaries are varied, it is also by amicable and voluntary treaties, by which they receive from the United States ample compensation for every right they have to the lands ceded by them."

Traditionally, Indian tribes had been treated in this manner. They were early regarded as distinct and sovereign nations fully capable of entering into compacts, agreements and contracts with the United States. The Delaware Treaty of 1778, the earliest published treaty, spoke of "peace and friendship" which was necessary between the peoples of the United States and the tribe. It described the Delawares as being "dependent upon the (United States) for all articles of clothing, utensils and implements of war."

It was fundamentally a trade agreement.

Until 1871 the tribes were treated as sovereign yet dependent domestic nations with whom the Federal Government was bound to treat for land cessions. In the treaties, the Government accepted the responsibility to protect the lands reserved by the tribes for their own use against encroachments by its own citizens. In that year, however, Congress decided that it would sign no more treaties with tribes. Instead, a policy emerged aimed at breaking up the tribal structure, even though the United States had promised in good faith that it would not interfere with traditional tribal customs and laws.

The shift in policy placed major emphasis on enticing, threatening, or deceiving individual Indians into forsaking their tribal relations. A comparable situation would exist if the Government refused to recognize General Motors as a corporation and insisted that it would become concerned with the individual stockholders, enticing them to sell their stock and liquidating the assets of the corporation, all the while wondering why General Motors was declining as an economic entity.

The tribes fought back. Asserting that the treaties were contracts between two parties, the tribe and the Federal Government, they often punished with death any leaders who signed away tribal rights. While fundamental logic supported the tribal position, overwhelming power and deceit by Government officials were able to carry the day. The treaties had been signed by nations, not an arbitrary conglomerate of individuals. Yet the official Federal policy was to assimilate individual Indians even if their rights as members of the tribes had to be breached.

A major influence against the tribes was the ideology of the missionaries who were attempting to force their own ideas of culture on the captive audiences on the reservations. The missionaries believed that only by inculcating selfishness and the concept of private property into tribal society would individual Indians be able to become Christians and be saved.

Church pressure to individualize the tribes and dispose of the tribal land estate resulted in the passage of the Dawes Act in 1887. This act divided the reservation up into allotments of 160 acres, and each Indian was given a piece of land for farming. The remainder of the tribal holdings was declared "surplus" and opened to settlement by non-Indians.

Before allotment was forced on the tribes there was no poverty on the reservations. The minority report issued against the policy mentioned the complete absence of pauperism among the Five Civilized Tribes of Oklahoma. It suggested that the Indian method of holding land for an entire community might be superior to the idea of non-Indian society, in that this method precluded a class of people that was perennially poor, while non-Indian society was plagued with poverty in its lower economic class.

The effect of individualizing the tribal estate was the creation of extreme poverty on many of the reservations. Individual Indians, unaccustomed to viewing land as a commodity, were easily swindled out of their allotments. Good farm land often went for a bottle of liquor, white trustees of individual Indian estates often mysteriously inherited their wards' property, and dying Indians were known to have mysteriously given their lands to churches before expiring. One Indian commissioner trod on eggshells during his term because a half-million-dollar Indian estate passed on to a missionary society instead of to the Indian heirs. Between 1887 and 1934 some 90 million acres of land left Indian ownership in a variety of ways. The actual circumstances in some cases have never seen the light of day.

Indians who sold their lands did not merge into white society and disappear. They simply moved onto their relatives' lands and remained within the tribal society. Thus, the land base was rapidly diminishing while the population continued to remain constant and, in some cases, grew spectacularly.

The situation had become so bad by 1926 that a massive study was authorized. It was called the Meriam Survey, and it pointed out that if the allotment process was not solved, the United States would soon have on its hands a landless, pauperized Indian population totally incapable of succeeding in American society.

In 1933, the New Deal Administration appointed John Collier as Indian Affairs Commissioner. He helped to write into law the basic charter of Indian rights called the Indian Reorganization Act. Indian tribes were given status as Federal corporations under this act, allotment was stopped and efforts were made to rebuild a land base for the Indian communities.

Tribal governments allocated a substantial portion of tribal income to purchase the allotments of individual Indians, thus holding in Indian hands the land that would have been lost forever. Tribes began their gradual revival of traditional ways, and were making excellent progress when World War II caused a dreadful reduction in domestic spending. Programs could not be funded until after the war.

In 1954 the chairmanship of the Indian Subcommittee of the Senate Interior Committee was taken over by Senator Arthur Watkins of Utah. Watkins was an archconservative who understood nothing of Indian treaties, was contemptuous of Indian people, and was determined to solve the "Indian problem" in his short tenure as chairman of the committee. He began a unilateral war against Indian communities that was known as "termination."

Watkins visualized himself as the Abraham Lincoln of the 20th century. Characterizing the reservations as havens of irresponsibility, and accepting the thesis that the Federal Government had been too protective of Indian rights, the Senator was determined to break the long-standing commitments of the

United States to its Indian tribes—whether it was just or not.

"With the aim of 'equality before the law' in mind, our course should rightly be no other," Watkins announced. "Firm and constant consideration for those of Indian ancestry should lead us all to work diligently with all other Americans. Following in the footsteps of the Emancipation Proclamation of 94 years ago, I see the following words emblazoned in letters of fire above the heads of the Indians—THESE PEOPLE SHALL BE FREE."

If Watkins was determined to *free* the Indians, he was a generation too late. In 1924 the Indian Citizens Act was passed making all non-citizen Indians American citizens with full rights and privileges. The act further declared that the "granting of such citizenship shall not in any manner impair or otherwise affect the right of any Indians to tribal or other property."

The Indian Citizens Act thus gave full constitutional rights to individual Indians insofar as they were individuals. It specifically exempted any rights that individual Indians may have had in tribal property from its operation. The dual citizenship of Indian people was thus recognized.

But Watkins was convinced that holding an interest in tribal property in addition to holding citizenship was a handicap. Under this theory, everyone who benefited from a trust fund was automatically a second-class citizen.

A number of tribes fell victim to Watkins's crusade. The Menoninees owned a forest in Wisconsin. They had a tribal sawmill and operated it to provide employment for tribal members, rather than to make a profit—although with their exemption from corporate taxation they often showed a profit. The tribe spent most of its income on social services, supporting its own hospital and providing its own law enforcement on the reservation. It was more genuinely a self-supporting community than many non-Indian communities near it.

Termination of Federal supervision meant an immediate tax bill of 55 per cent on the sawmill. To meet this, the saw mill had to be automated, thus throwing a substantial number of Indians out of work and onto the unemployment rolls. To meet the rising unemployment situation the only industry, the sawmill, had to be taxed by the county. There was an immediate spiral downward in the capital structure of the tribe so that, in the years since the termination bill was passed, it has had to receive some $10-million in special state and Federal aid. The end is not yet in sight.

When the smoke had cleared, some 8,000 Indians had been deprived of rights their grandfathers had dearly purchased through land cessions. The Paiutes of Utah and Klamaths of Oregon were caught in a private trusteeship more restrictive than their original Federal trust relationship, from which they were to have been "freed." Fortunately, Texas made a tourist attraction out of the Alabama-Coushatta reservation in that state, thus preserving most of the tribal assets. The mixed-blood Utes of Utah formed their own organization and tried to remain together as a community. The Siletz and Grande Ronde Indians of Oregon, the California Indians, and the Catawbas of South Carolina simply vanished. Menominee County became the most depressed county in the nation.

In Watkins' mind, and in the mind of his successors on the Senate Interior Committee, the opportunity to remake American Indians into small businessmen was too much of a temptation. The termination policy continued to roll in spite of its catastrophic effects on the Indian communities.

Tribes refused to consider any programs, feeling that it was no use to build good houses when the reservation might be sold out from under them at any time. Development schemes to upgrade reservation resources were turned down by people with no apparent future. The progress which had been made by the tribes under the Indian Reorganization Act ground to a halt. Indian people spent a decade in limbo, hesitant to make any plans for fear they would come under attack the irrational policy.

Watkins's rationale at the beginning had been that he was making the individual Indians first-class citizens, where they previously had been handicapped by maintaining their tribal relationships. It was the same reasoning that has led policy-makers in the last century to force allotment on the tribes and create the original poverty conditions drawn for the Menominees, the concluding phrase in section 10 of the bill was illuminating: "Nothing in this act shall affect the status of the members of the tribe as citizens of the United States."

The argument of "freeing" the Indians was as phony as could be. The act did nothing but dissipate tribal capital and destroy the rights of Indian tribes to have their own communities. But termination fitted exactly into the integrationist-thought world of the period, and the expanding Civil Rights movement of the black community, which had been given impetus by the decision of Brown v. Topeka Board of Education, the famous school desegregation case of 1954. So it seemed the right thing to do.

Society has come a long way in its understanding of itself since 1954. The ensuing civil rights movement, which had shaken the foundations of society during the nineteen-fifties changed abruptly into the black power movements of the late sixties. For half a decade we have been struggling to define the place of a group of people in American society and, as numerous reports have indicated, the divisions in the society have become more pronounced, the hatreds more violent and lasting.

Termination slowed down during the Kennedy-Johnson Administration, but the basic Congressional directive has never been changed. Policy-makers in Congress and in the Interior Depratment continue to regard decisions made in haste in 1954 as imperative which they must follow today. Only by a vigilant National Congress of American Indians watching the Washington scene day and night have Indian people been able to stop further implementation of this policy.

Walter Hickel, in his casual remarks, stirred up a hornet' nest of Indian concern. It did not seem possible to tribal leaders that the new Administration would return to a policy proven bankrupt when it was applied to their land holdings in 1887, again proven bankrupt in 1954 with the further dissipation of their remaining lands and resources, and completely out of tune with the social movements of today.

Indian tribes have been able, in spite of all pressures exerted against them, and the failure of the Federal Government to defend their rights, to maintain a capital in land and resources by which they can maintain their own communities. They have been able to keep tribal governments alive and functioning. In the War on Poverty, tribes provided services for all people within reservation boundaries, red or white, and many children received services that they would not have otherwise received because their counties did not want to sponsor programs under the Offfice of Economic Opportunity.

The record of Indian people as a recognized self-governing community is enlightening. The progress of the last decade is spectacular and sophisticated for a people with a national average of eight years of education. Indian people are now demanding control of education programs through the creation of Indian reservation school boards. They are certain they can do better than either the state or Federal education they have been given in the past. The variety of projects undertaken by Indian communities is staggering and encompasses everything from sawmills to ocean-going fishing vessels, motels to carpet factories.

American society has much to learn from Indian tribes. It may all be lost if another era of struggle over reservation existence is initiated. The black community, spearheaded by the demands for reparations by James Forman, is desperately seeking capital funds. Indian tribes already have capital in land and resources and have demonstrated how well it can be used.

Blacks and Mexicans are developing rural cooperatives in an effort to solve the poverty of their people in the rural areas. Indian tribes have already proven that rural corporations and cooperatives can and do work when undertaken by a united community.

Conservationists are pointing out not rapidly dwindling natural resources of the nation, the danger of total extinction of life unless strong conservation practices are begun at once. The Quinault and Lummi Indian tribes have already zoned their beaches to conserve their natural state, while the White Mountain Apaches have developed nearly 30 artificial lakes and maintain the best fishing and recreation areas in Arizona.

The power movements, the Amish situation in the Midwest, the desire of the Acadians in Louisiana to have French taught in schools, the conflict between the ethnic groups in the urban areas, all point toward new social concepts revolving around a number of ethnic and racial communities desiring to conduct their own affairs. Even the rising conservative trend in politics seeks power at the local level rather than continued direction from long distance.

Tribes have overcome enmities of the past. They were once far deeper and more bitter than in the current impasses between black and white. Unemployment is declining as tribal programs are committed to creating jobs, not simply making profits. Land is being renewed, beaches and rivers are being cleared and the reservations are becoming models of proper land use. Indian society is stabilizing itself to face the instantaneous electric world of today far better than are other segments of American society.

The Indian outrage at Hickel was a cry to society at large. "If you destroy us," it really said, "you will destroy your last chance to understand who you are, where you have been, and where you have to go next in order to survive as a people." One hopes Secretary Hickel and the Senators and Congressmen will hear this cry and understand.

---

7   THE NEW NATIONALISM

Edward M. Corbett.

Examining the development of nationalism among French Canadians, Corbett focuses on the retarded development of upward social mobility among this ethnic group. He details the relationship between this variable and the growth of conflict and nationalism in French Canada.

SOURCE
From *Quebec Confronts Canada* by Edward M. Corbett. Copyright © 1967 by The Johns Hopkins Press. Reprinted by permission.

After two centuries of daily contact and frequent discord, the two major national elements in Canada have left unexploited few areas of possible mutual recrimination. From the late 1700s, there is a continual record of French Canadian complaints a- gainst discrimination in the civil service, economic preference for *les Anglais,* or lack of regard for the French language. A pair of French-Canadian university professors ad- vance the hypothesis that a cyclical relation- ship can be established between the most extreme manifestations of Quebec nation- alism and various socioeconomic phenomena which breed similar responses among English- Canadians. Periodic rigidities in institutional structures, they say, choke off normal ave- nues of occupational mobility. Frustrated middle class elements react by attacking what they perceive as barriers to their social, economic, and political advancement.[1]

The predominance of the middle class in the development of French-Canadian nation- alism is beyond dispute; the expansion of that sector in the modern industrial society has accounted for much of the recent wave of nationalist sentiment in Quebec. Another professor, from Montreal, relates the ex- tremist drive to the end of the Duplessis regime and the implicit promise of a share in the exercise of power for the newly emerging social segments. These latter find the clergy dominant in education, English Canadians in finance, Americans in culture; only the Quebec state belongs to the entirety of French Canadians. Therefore, they rea- son, the totality of powers should be in the hands of the state, which will make accessible the various positions now monopolized by a limited group or by "foreigners."[2]

Whether because of socioeconomic factors or not, striking new facets have been unfold- ing in the most recent manifestation of

nationalism in Quebec. In the past, the key word was "survivance," and the primacy was given to defense. The French language was to be cherished and protected because it was the bulwark of the Catholic faith. Civil law and traditional practices were to be shielded from change, because the secret of survival was immutability. Though French Canada seems more deeply committed now than ever before to the defense of its cultural heritage, it is no longer on the defensive. It is press- ing the attack. Its new confident, aggressive attitude denotes a reversal of mind that was never evident before. It is true that the messianic nationalism propounded by Canon Groulx was optimistic in scope, but its overtones were otherworldly; it held out the promise of eventual reward for the practice of the simple virtues most readily applied in a rural environment. Groulx himself preach- ed the need to strive for economic power, but until the postwar period, the effect of such advice was minimal.

Formerly, French-Canadian nationalism was evoked by overt outside pressures, usually an eruption of English Canadianism, as in the school and conscription issues, or by economic depression. No such excitant is apparent in the current instance. The rapid postwar industrialization might be adduced as sufficient reason, but this is an intensification rather than a new phenome- non. Moreover, the reaction seems more far-reaching than the threat implicit in fur- ther industrialization would warrant. For want of more obvious external stimuli, the cause must be sought within French-Canadian society itself. The tenor of pertinent changes there is apparent from the evolution of some of Groulx's disciples.

Michel Brunet, professor of American his- tory at the University of Montreal, has made an avocation of Canadian history since the Conquest. A strong supporter of the

---

[1]Raymond Breton and André Breton, "Le séparatisme ou le respect du statu quo," *Cité libre* (April, 1962), pp. 17-28.

[2]P. E. Trudeau, "La nouvelle trahison des clercs," *Cité libre* (April, 1962), pp. 3-16.

majority-minority theory, Brunet argues that Quebec must maximize the number of situations in which provincial autonomy is effective. Thus the French-Canadian majority in the province will be independent of the English-Canadian majority in the rest of Canada in all decisions taken in fields where provincial autonomy is admitted. Quebec, moreover, can devote adequate attention to economic development, he maintains, by concentrating the energies formerly dissipated in endless struggles to safeguard traditions, language, and religion. Brunet's views on the economic handicaps French Canadians labored under since the Conquest have had wide dissemination, and their influence on Quebec youth should not be discounted. As with Groulx, for earlier generations, Brunet and his colleague Maurice Seguin have been extremely effective propagandists; unlike Groulx, however, they seem to be having considerable influence in orienting youth toward positive endeavors rather than toward squandering their energies in recrimination.

The neohistorians have been expounding their theories since the mid-1940s, but it is only since the end of the Duplessis regime that a broader segment of intellectuals has taken an active role in propagating nationalist dogma. Many leftist intellectuals who, under Duplessis, rejected all forms of nationalism as contrary to the dignity of the individual, changed their minds in the early 1960s; they began to see a national aspect in the dilemma of the French Canadian who feels completely foreign to the only concept of pan-Canadiansim available to him. They reason that respect for the individual implies respect for his language; by defending the language group, then, they are defending the rights of the individual.[3]

One incident a short time before Duplessis's demise was primarily responsible for the sharp rise in nationalism among intellectuals. For the first two months of 1959, the French network of the Canadian Broadcasting Corporation was silenced by a strike sparked by its program producers. René Lévesque, subsequently one of the most dynamic ministers in the provincial government, was a key figure among the strikers. He had been one of the most popular TV personalities in Quebec because of an outstanding news commentary program in which he had been featured. Lévesque made no secret of his conviction that the government would have taken immediate steps to settle a similar walkout on the English-language network. He drew the conclusion that Ottawa had little understanding of French Canada and even less concern about developments which affect only French-speaking citizens.

Lévesque's views help explain the commitment of a sizable proportion of educated young Quebeckers to a nationalist philosophy oriented toward their province rather than toward Canada. Lévesque is a symbol of French-Canadian aspirations; he says he wants to remain a Canadian, but not at any price: "I know Quebec is my country. I'm not quite convinced Canada is," he told one English Canadian in 1963, when he was Quebec's minister of natural resources."[4] Those who talk about that legal entity, the Canadian nation, he told an editorialist of Le Devoir, usually forget that a more basic and profound reality lies in the human, cultural, and social entity embodied in the French-Canadian nation.[5] He believes that no nation can get along without nationalism, which he defines as basically man's desire for the self-respect that comes from having control over his own destiny. He dismisses as a caricature of individualism the concern for human values expressed by some French

[3]Jean Blain, "La voie de la souveraineté," Liberté (March, 1962), pp. 113-21.

[4]H. B. Myers, The Quebec Revolution (Montreal: Harvest House, 1964), p. 16.
[5]Le Devoir (July 5, 1963), p. 4.

Canadians who question Quebec's ability to respect the individual. Such concern, he feels, would dehumanize the individual by cutting him off from the national community which supplies much of his strength. This consciousness of collective strength and particularly confidence in its use is something new in French Canada. It denotes a dynamic outward interest replacing the introspective defence mentality which characterized French-Canadian nationalism in the past.

Of signal importance to an assessment of the new face of French-Canadian nationalism is the changing role of the Church in Quebec. Traditional nationalist doctrine was in large part formulated by the clergy, and lay champions of nationalism stressed the role the language played in maintaining fidelity to the religious heritage. The Quebec Church no longer equates loyality to the French language with religious orthodoxy; well over one-third of Canada's Catholic population is not French-speaking, and adherence to French has not provided an absolute guarantee of religious practice in Quebec. Moreover, the new generations of young clerics are more interested in social action than in strictly French-Canadian national problems. Finally, many of the most fervent exponents of the new nationalism are frankly anticlerical; some of them are avowed agnostics. Most of the new nationalist leaders view the Church as only one aspect of a politico-socio-economic complex. The state and the economy are their major interests; they refuse to identify their national cause with religious belief.

Every French Canadian is a nationalist at heart; there are few who do not harbor some measure of resentment against their English-speaking fellows. There are wide variations, however, in what the concept of nationalism holds for individual *Canadiens* and in what each would consider desirable to achieve nationalist goals. The spectrum runs from acceptance of the status quo,

through several fairly definite democratic programs for change, and some less readily identifiable postures, to the totalitarian—and rare—commitment of the terrorists. Even for the majority, which has not found it too difficult, to date, to acquiesce in the limitations set by past political decisions, there is a deep conviction that an injustice has been perpetrated and that it should be righted. Most French Canadians remain hopeful that eventually their language rights will be respected across Canada.

It is not always clear where the line between confederation and independence would fall for many acknowledged nationalists. Jean-Marc Léger of *Le Devoir* has frequently expressed his separatist sentiments, yet he professes to see a future for Quebec within the Confederation. He warns against the "dangerous illusion" that "national emancipation" is really under way and lists his requirements for a "normal nation": its state, economy, and institutions at every level attuned to the national genius, "a certain measure of participation in international life."[6] The programs of the pro-independence groups demand little more. Many who stop short of Léger's position hold up the aim of commanding recognition by the sheer superiority of the French Canadian contribution to national life. This is the position of the moderates who insist that the Confederation assures Quebec all necessary safeguards for a separate cultural existence.

Practically all nationalists see the most obvious route toward greater autonomy in full use of the Quebec state. This is a novel idea for most French Canadians, for whom the state has always been the enemy. Such an attitude was encouraged by the clergy, whose influence had grown enormously after the Conquest because the state no longer competed with the Church for the loyalty of the French-Canadian people. The progressive

---

[6]*Le Devoir* (February 17, 1964), p. 4.

laicization of key posts has begun to restore an equilibrium that was long absent.

This is not without danger for the future of the Canadian Confederation, however. The old nationalism was clerical; it responded to clerical pressure for moderation. The Church has thrown its weight in favor of the government against the American colonists in 1775 and against the rebels in 1837; the pattern persisted through the several crises which threatened the Confederation in the past century. With more open dissension in Church ranks, and much of the new nationalist wave beyond clerical influence, there is less chance that the clergy's ability to restrain extremism will be effective in any future confrontation between the two language groups.

FRENCH-CANADIAN NATIONALISM IN PERSPECTIVE

Is French Canada a nation? This question continues to elicit considerable semantic juggling among those Canadians who do not reject the idea out of hand. The word "nation" is as ambiguous in French as it is in English. French Canadians are inclined to use it more readily than their English-speaking neighbors to cover the idea of common origin, traditions, and language—all of which may also differentiate a nationality. English Canadians are suspicious that there is at least an unconscious purpose in the choice of language; they charge that proponents are deliberately encouraging confusion in order to accustom their fellows to the idea that French Canada lacks only the formal institution of a sovereign state to complete its existence as a nation.

The fundamental psychological factor underlying the relationship between French-speaking and English-speaking Canadians is their own view of their kinship. Despite much emphasis, particularly since World War II, on unhyphenated Canadianism, the two major ethnic groups continue to describe each other in terms of nationality. The English Canadian, who traditionally identified his French-speaking compatriot as "French," more frequently refers to him today as "French Canadian." For generations French Canadians used "Canadiens" to refer to themselves; the other inhabitants of Canada were always "les Anglais." In recent years, however, French Canadians have increasingly come to refer to themselves as "Canadiens francais." This can be interpreted as a growing recognition that "the others" may be Canadians rather than English. It continues the implication of a distinction between the two elements of the population, however, and adds a restrictive connotation. The group loyalty is unaffected, but there is a suggestion of a more circumscribed concept. It may be a more or less conscious limitation, a withdrawal from a national Canadian context to the narrower provincial confines wherein French Canada is synonymous with Quebec.

Eugene Forsey, an English-Canadian political scientist who has exhibited considerable understanding of French-Canadian frustrations with the way confederation has evolved, is willing to admit the two-nation concept if Canada itself is accepted as a nation. Canada is two nations, he says, in the ethnic, cultural, sociological sense, but one nation in the political, legal, constitutional sense.[7]

Such an opinion admits too much and does not promise enough for many French Canadians, who are not themselves consciously separatist. They reject what they characterize as the folklore type of existence that would give French Canada a status comparable to Scotland or Wales. They charge that such a distinction amounts to proposing a divorce between their cultural

[7]"Canada: two nations or one?", *Canadian Journal of Economics* (November, 1962), pp. 485-501.

heritage and the practical demands of their daily existence. They insist that a middle ground be sought if Canada is to continue to exist.

The semantic distinctions between nation and nationality are largely irrelevant in this context. The champions of French-Canadian nationalism are indifferent to the views of the fathers of confederation or to the choice of words which made confederation acceptable. D. M. Potter points out that nationalism rests on two psychological bases rather than one. In addition to a feeling of common culture, there is also present a feeling of common interests.[8] In the current instance, the ideas behind the words are clear; nationalist aspirations relate the socioeconomic status of a dynamic segment of the Quebec population to the potential embodied or envisaged by the elements which make up that segment. Self-interest makes the *Québécois* impatient with linguistic niceties, which they see as legalistic fetters to block their access to power. Forsey strikes them as accepting the existence of a nationality as long as it is merely a community without a formal political organization. He would stall at granting the national trappings which make a society—that is a nation in the political sense.

Karl Mannheim traces the growth of national aggressiveness to social disintegration.[9] Disintegration is probably too strong a term to apply to the transformations Quebec society is undergoing today, but no one attempts to deny that wide-ranging change is in progress. Assessment is complicated by the ethnic factor and by the impulsion to make up for economic lag. The degree to which an accelerated social evolution gives impetus to political revolution is probably more closely related to self-interest than to cultural differences. If the forces pushing for influence today opt for a narrowly nationalistic program to achieve their objective, they have many of the prerequisites at hand.

The role of national consciousness in activating group distinctiveness is brought out by Karl W. Deutsch, whose application of communication theory to nationalism has established the basis for a quantitative study of its objective aspects. His work is particularly apt in relation to the Quebec situation: he stresses the role of national consciousness in making individual members of a given people explicitly aware of their membership in the national group at a time when other, non-national changes in society, economics, and culture make the group characteristics and group membership increasingly important to the individuals concerned.[10]   The careful methodology Deutsch has developed to analyze even such subjective aspects of nationalism as the national will and national consciousness stems from what he calls a "functional" definition of nationality. Membership in a people, he says, consists essentially in wide complementarity of social communication. He equates membership with the ability to communicate more effectively and over a wider range of subjects with members of one large group than with outsiders. Rather than specify nationality in terms of particular ingredients he looks to a detailed analysis of the functions performed.[11]   The range and effectiveness of social communication within a given people may tell us, he believes, how effectively it has become integrated and how far it has advanced, in this respect, toward becoming a nation.[12]

---

[8]"Historians' use of nationalism and vice versa," *American Historical Review* (July, 1962), pp. 937-38.

[9]*Man and Society in an age of Reconstruction*, trans. Edwards Shils (New York: Harcourt, 1940), pp. 126ff.

[10]*Nationalism and Social Communication* (New York: John Wiley & Sons, 1953), p. 152.

[11]*Ibid.*, pp. 71-72.

[12]*Ibid.*, p. 73.

For a retrospective appreciation of the basis of French-Canadian nationalism, however, it is probably more useful to recognize characteristics than to analyze their origin. To that end, reference to the categories associated with classical historical analysis should suffice. Boyd Shafer, a disciple of the pioneer U.S. student of nationalism, Carlton Hayes, has enumerated the conditions he considers essential before nationalism fully materializes. Among those that practically all French Canadians would consider applicable to their situation are common cultural characteristics, including language, customs, manners, and literature; a belief in a common history and in a common origin; a common pride in the achievements of their nation and a common sorrow in its tragedies; a devotion to the entity called the nation, which is more than the sum of the fellow nationals; a love or esteem for fellow nationals (not necessarily as individuals).[13]

The histories of Garneau and Groulx have done much to implant a solid emotional foundation for all of these; there would be some hesitation, however, on the part of a large number of French Canadians, to give full assent to the last two of them on an ethnic rather than on a pan-Canadian level, and even more would have reservations about a second group of Shafer's requirements: a certain unit of territory; common dominant social and economic institutions; and a disregard for or hostility to other like groups, especially if these seem to threaten the national existence. The territorial question is a major deterrent to adherence to the separatist dogma, because of the problem of the French-Canadian "Diaspora" outside Quebec if an independent "Laurentia" were established. As to the second point, there is little question that a Christian social philosophy has at least been given lip service in Quebec; there are serious misgivings, however, about how the absence of French Canadians from control of the "dominant economic institutions" would bear on an independence move. Many proponents often enlightened humanism would take violent exception to the last of these as vindictive and self-defeating. For the majority, however, the memory of English-Canadian nationalism in successive confrontations on the school question and on conscription enhances a sense of French-Canadian solidarity independent of any pan-Canadian sentiment. This is a particularly touchy aspect of the Canadian relationship. The emotions it arouses are evident in the reaction of a strong nationalist to a recommendation of the Provincial Commission on Education in Quebec.

The Parent Report cited "the air-tight separation" between the versions of history taught in Quebec and recommended that both French and English-speaking groups be given a good knowledge of both French and English regimes in a program with the same general lines for all. Michel Brunet, of the University of Montreal's History Institute, believes this recommendation is naive. There are two different presentations of history in Quebec, he says, because the Quebec population is made up of two distinct collectivities, each with its own historical evolution. Their experience is not identical because they did not always face the same problems; even when they did their response was not at all the same.[14] Brunet is not a separatist; he is a debunker of the legends for which his master, Canon Groulx, is largely responsible; he believes the French element must continue to support confederation, but he favors a revision to safeguard the rights of the linguistic minority.

---

[13]*Nationalism: Myth and Reality* (New York: Harcourt, Brace, 1955), pp. 7-8.

[14]"Extraits d'une causerie prononcée le 18 décember devant l'association des professeurs d' histoire du Québec," *Le Devoir* (December 29, 1965), p. 4.

On Shafer's two remaining points, the picture is much less clear, because they are the essential questions insofar as a separate national existence is concerned. The first is a common independent or sovereign government, or the desire for one, and the second is a hope that the nation will have a great future. Brunet's analysis of French-Canadian history centers on the dilemma embraced by these two concepts. He saw three dominant ideas in Quebec history: agriculturalism, antistatism, and messianism.[15] The first of these is no longer pertinent; the others are essential to an understanding of French Canada's future. Brunet holds that fear of the state prevented French Canadians from making adequate use of the provincial government the Confederation put in their hands. Today, when state intervention is essential in so many socioeconomic spheres, they are finally beginning to utilize this instrument. Will they be content to use it within the confines of the Confederation? The answer will depend on a reinterpretation of the messianic function. French Canada is reassessing the missionary role it has traditionally seen as its peculiar charge. If a majority of French Canadians become convinced that their cultural interests can be advanced without hindrance only by concentrating efforts on the territory where French-Canadian political control is beyond doubt, the outlook for confederation is dim.

For the pro-independence elements, Shafer's ten requirements are satisfied only within the confines of a sovereign state. For many others, they are satisfied in the context of confederation. For a still indeterminate number of French Canadians, the question is yet to be answered.

If the classic sequence of nationalist sentiment as it evolved in Europe as extrapolated to modern Quebec, some unsettling parallels appear. Particulary if the English-speaking middle class in Quebec is considered as an element foreign to the current evolution of Quebec society, the developments described by Hans Kohn in *Idea of Nationalism* require little transposition to fit the French-Canadian pattern. The biggest hurdle would be to assume that the ideas of popular sovereignty must first be accepted—that is, that the traditional concepts of authority must give way to a secularized view of society.[16] The patterns of economic life must be ruptured by the rise of a middle class ready to break with the past. Quebec could be compared to the Central European states where nationalism, at the beginning of the nineteenth century, found its expression largely in the cultural field. In France, Great Britain, and the United States, the more powerful middle class was able to assert itself at that time in the economic and political spheres. The Central European states eventually followed the same path. The pressure of an aggressive middle class is the cardinal factor in the quiet revolution.

The central theme of French-Canadian nationalism, in what might be considered the period of cultural predominance, was the service of nationality to religious belief. That is no longer true. Kohn lays great stress on the transfer of basic loyalty from religion to nation. "The fixation of man's supreme loyalty upon his nationality marks the beginning of the age of nationalism."[17] This state of mind, he says, is a driving force intent on the highest form of organized activity, a sovereign state. Some form of autonomy or pre-state organization is acceptable only as a stopgap. "Nationalism demands the nation-state."[18]

---

[15]*La Présence anglaise et les Canadiens*, pp. 113-66.

[16]*Idea of Nationalism: A Study in Its Origins and Backgrounds* (New York: Macmillan, 1944), p. 3.

[17]*Ibid.*, p. 18.

[18]*Ibid.*, p. 19.

It is enlightening in that regard to consider a statement made by Henri Bourassa at the beginning of the century. Bourassa's life was devoted to the flowering of a pan-Canadianism where French-language rights would be unequivocal. Nevertheless, he could look on the possibility of a free French state in North America, where there would be no need to share with another "race," as a legitimate and attractive dream which might be realized sooner than indications suggest.[19] Bourassa was a champion of Canadian autonomy vis-à-vis London. That step has been taken; Canada is now independent. In the minds of many French Canadians today, however, that was not the ultimate step.

CONCLUSION

The possibility of applying Deutsch's quantitative analysis to the Canadian problem is much more complicated today than it might have been in the 1950s. Deutsch proceeds on the assumption that the evolution of a confrontation between two cultural groups can be predicted by quantifying all aspects of nationalism which lend themselves to measurement. The limiting factor is whether major efforts are made to foresee and control the forces at work.[20] On the basis of the Central European examples Deutsch cites,[21] the Quebec hinterland could have been expected to supply indefinetly sufficient replacements to maintain the linguistic equilibrium Montreal has experienced in recent generations. The influx of non-French-speaking immigrants threatened that equilibrium, however, and helped generate

a reaction from French Canadians.

Despite the long history of nationalist sentiment in Quebec, economic determinism was largely untrammeled until the quiet revolution got up steam. This development injects a major subjective element that will strain the validity of Deutsch's equations. It also raises questions on the geographic confines of the problem. Should the confrontation of the two language groups be studied on a Canadian basis or be confined to the Province of Quebec? Or should it be limited to the island of Montreal? French-Canadian nationalists insist that the future of their cultural identity will be determined by the trend in the metropolis. Their ability to counterbalance the numerical weight of an accelerated socioeconomic evolution will probably be the preponderant factor.

How effective they may be is suggested by both Deutsch and Hayes in somewhat parallel terms. Deutsch stresses national consciousness arising from the assertion of unalienable rights, first in the language of religion, then in the language of politics, and finally in terms involving economics and all society.[22] Hayes saw three important factors in the propagation of nationalism, the first being the elaboration of a doctrine by various intellectuals.[23] Despite the flood of propaganda more or less directly aimed at developing an ideology for French Canada, there is still no clear delineation of a theory that can lay claim to wide acceptance. As Philippe Garigue points out, neither the Church nor the Confederation proved to be satisfactory foundations for the erection of such a theory, and the sense of alienation at the base of most separatist dogma is essentially negative.[24]

This has not prevented separatists from acting on the assumption they have some-

---

[19]Cited by Philippe Garigue, *L'option politique du Canada francais* (Montreal: Éditions du Lévrier, 1963), pp. 86-87.

[20]Deutsch, *pp. cit.,* p. 183.

[21]*Ibid.,* p. 137.

[22]*Ibid.,* p. 153.

[23]*Essays on Nationalism* (New York: Macmillan, 1926), p. 62.

[24]Garigue, *op. cit.,* pp. 123-42.

thing positive to propose. Hayes's second factor was the championing of the nationalist doctrine by a group of citizens who find it satisfying and perhaps remunerative. There is little evidence that the various proponents of Quebec's independence have yet found substantial monetary return for their efforts. There seems little doubt, however, than an increasing number of individuals, who have identified themselves with the separatist movement have derived considerable personal satisfaction from their endeavors. They are convinced they have made an impact on the popular mind—which is the third element in Hayes's scheme. They are satisfied that they have had some success in conveying the impression of a valid solution, which has elicited a partial expression of the popular will. This is the determining factor, in the opinion of Pierre Elliott Trudeau, who believes that neither language nor geography nor history is sufficient to delimit a nation.[25]

A creed of a nationalism and the will to implement it are probably more powerful than the economic arguments against it, at least if the promise of independence entails only a limited period of privation. The Rassemblement pour l'Independance Nationale (RIN) has stressed the economic problem, but holds out the hope of a brighter future. Though some Quebec commentators have used the economic argument to depreciate the appeal of separatism to the relatively well-off Quebeckers, some English Canadians have cautioned against counting too heavily on the economic deterrent. Prudence is warranted because the economic consequences of independence cannot be predicted with any degree of certainty, and particularly because the political imponderables are even more elusive.

Rupert Emerson believes that when a nationalist movement gets into full swing, the people at large are likely to follow the lead of the active nationalist elite, although they may have given little evidence earlier of political interest.[26] Although Quebec seems far from such a state of affairs at present, this warning may have more validity than surface indications suggest. The surprising support the RIN president received in 1966 in an eastern Quebec county raises questions in that regard. The RIN seems to have exploited skillfully an especially flagrant example of insensitivity to the language issue on the part of the major industrial employer in the county. The special circumstances in that instance made a nationalist appeal effective. It is significant, nevertheless, that one-third of the electorate in a single district could be swayed by this issue. Though nationalist dissatisfaction has been largely associated with the growing urban middle class, the rural unrest which put a Créditiste bloc in the national parliament can probably be readily exploited for nationalistic purposes.

Pierre Elliott Trudeau echoes Kohn in citing the threat of fascism inherent in nationalism. Trudeau bolsters his warning insofar as Quebec is concerned by citing the shakey commitment to democracy implicit in both the historical developments which culminated in the arbitrary attitude identified with the Duplessis regime, and in the poor examples in the practice of democracy English Canada has provided.[27] Emerson questions, however, whether nationalism has a clear tendency to produce one or another type of political institution.[28] It has been associated with almost every kind of regime.

[25]"Federalism, Nationalism, and Reason," in P. A. Crépeau and C. B. Macpherson (eds.), *Future of Canadian Federalism/L'Avenir du Fédéralisme canadien* (Toronto: University of Toronto Press, 1965), p. 20.

[26]"Nationalism and Political Development," *Journal of Politics* (February, 1960), p. 8.
[27]"Some Obstacles to Democracy in Quebec," in Mason Wade (ed.), *op. cit.,* pp. 241-59.
[28]Emerson, *op. cit.,* p. 18.

From the point of view that nationalism was initially a liberating force in France and Germany, and because it takes off from a wider recognition of democratic participation in government, an autocratic administration is not inevitable. What will eventuate in Quebec depends on too many variables for clear indications to emerge before a sharper confrontation of the two language groups takes place.

Separatism has still only minority support. A broader participation of French Canada in the direction of the Confederation is at least as likely an outcome as an independent Quebec. Economic and social factors may be preponderant in the long run, but, in the meantime, cultural questions provide a sounding board with a wide audience.

---

8.   PATTERNS OF COMMUNITY POWER: TRADITION AND SOCIAL CHANGE IN AMERICAN CHINATOWNS

Russell D. Lee

The persistence of ethnic ghettos in the United States often has led to the conclusion that the ghetto exists because an ethnic group voluntarily seeks to maintain the social institutions and culture of the old country. For the Chinese in America, this myth continues to persist. This article explores the historical background of the development of political institutions within American Chinatowns and some of the recent strains toward social change.

INTRODUCTION

In the United States and Canada, the existence of Chinatowns as cultural, social, and economic centers for over a half million people of Chinese descent is under question. Slight fissures in these once highly insulated ethnic communities reveal numerous social problems endemic to many other ethnic ghettos. Although the incidence of unemployment, inadequate health care, substandard housing, and juvenile delinquency in the larger Chinatowns has remained virtually hidden from outsiders, the traditional social institutions apparently are unable to cope with or hide the stresses that resulted from the increased immigration of Chinese from Hong Kong and Taiwan. Recent figures from the 1970 census indicate that the number of people of Chinese descent in the United States increased 83.3 percent, from 237,292 in 1960 to 435,062 in 1970. According to the United States immigration statistics, over 100,000 Chinese were admitted over the last decade. Although as much as one third of the new admissions were simply reclassifications of Chinese already residing in the United States, a considerable number of recent immigrants account for the 83.3 percent increase.

Since the initial liberalization in 1965 and 1968 of immigration restrictions, most

SOURCE:
Original article prepared for this volume.

of the new Chinese immigrants have found homes in the four largest Chinatowns. The attraction of these four Chinatowns—in San Francisco, New York City, Los Angeles, and Boston—is due to the location of many friends and relatives, the existence of a cultural community that absorbs some of the initial shock of American society, and the urban origin of most Chinese immigrants. With the greatest influx of Chinese coming from highly urbanized Hong Kong, the larger Chinatowns located in major metropolitan areas have become more familiar to the new immigrants than rural communities or the smaller Chinatowns scattered across the United States.

Besides the apparent inability of traditional social institutions and the residents of the larger Chinatowns to organize effectively in the face of internal strains, the threat of urban "removal" is rapidly affecting the very physical existence of Chinese communities in various cities. The strategic location of many Chinatowns next to the financial districts of large cities—especially in San Francisco, New York City, and Boston—and the generally substandard housing conditions encourage competition for redevelopment of these areas. While many of the smaller Chinatowns prior to 1960 declined and were razed as the economies of the surrounding "host" cities and towns declined (Kung, 1962), the recent threats to the remaining Chinatowns tend to originate from various private and governmental interest groups seeking to restore the inner city to white middle class businessmen and residents.

This article will explore the reasons for the inability of Chinatowns to organize effectively to deal with both internal and external threats to the community. In effect, this article will focus on the changing political organization of the larger Chinatowns in the United States. Although many observations and interpretations of contemporary Chinatowns will be drawn from the author's recent experiences in Boston and San Francisco, I

shall construct a more or less generic model of the primary social and political institutions that can be found in any of the larger Chinatowns. While each Chinatown certainly has a unique history of development, the similarities of social organization and customs stemming from a common heritage outweigh the differences.

PRELUDE TO EMIGRATION

A brief historical account of the events leading to the initial development of Chinatowns in the United States is essential for understanding the present social organization of these ethnic ghettos. As Stuart C. Miller (1969) argues, the American image of the Chinese prior to the California Gold Rush in 1848 was tinged with both curiosity and mild contempt. Reports from missionaries and American traders fostered an unfavorable image of the Chinese long before unrestricted Chinese immigration became a California, then a national issue. Only a handful of Chinese ever visited the United States between 1790 and 1848, hardly enough to arouse fears of unfair competition in the labor market. In fact, in California where anti-Chinese agitation was later to reach a feverish pitch, only seven Chinese were officially registered as residents by the end of 1848 (Jacobs, Landau, and Pell, 1971). This number increased to 700 a year later. By the time of the Chinese Exclusion Act of 1882, there were over 75,000 Chinese in California.

The rather sudden and increasing immigration up to 1882 can be traced to a number of simultaneous events in China and North America. The encroachment of the Western powers upon the territorial integrity of China in the eighteenth and nineteenth centuries had a profound effect on the stability of southern China. Canton, an early trading port between the Europeans and the Chinese, received the brunt of Western challenges to the traditional social and economic order. The attempts at forcing the Manchu government to end its policy of insulation from foreign contacts began in earnest after the "resolution" of the Opium War in 1842 (Waley, 1968). The defeat of the Chinese military and naval forces opened the path to unchecked European economic and territorial imperialism. The exposure of the political and military ineptitude of the Manchu government, and the impact of Western technology and Western economic practices on a basically agrarian economy served to disrupt the traditional society of Southern China.

Natural calamities also increased social disorders. Students at the University of Nanking were reported to have documented 1828 famines between the years 108 *B.C.* and 1911 *A. D.* (Mallory, 1967). In 1849, a devastating flood struck southeastern China, killing thousands of people and nearly destroying the annual crops (Lyman, 1971a). A major natural disaster in a region already suffering from overpopulation set the stage for popular opposition to the Manchu dynasty.

Throughout the 1840s there were numerous accounts of sporadic local revolts in the southern provinces of Kwangtung, Kwangsi, Kweichow, and Hunan (Yang, 1961). Religious sects and local bandits have played significant roles in the long history of Southern Chinese opposition to any centralized authority from the North. Indeed, secret societies—the so-called *tongs*—organized sustained social "protest" against local authorities as early as the tenth century *A.D.* The tongs will play an integral role in the social history of American Chinatowns.

This area in Southern China was the seedground for a fourteen year revolution that nearly brought the Manchu dynasty to an end. By the time of its conclusion in 1864, the Taiping Rebellion (1840–1864), as this unsuccessful revolution was called, resulted in an estimated loss of 30,000,000 lives. The Taiping Rebellion was essentially a political-religious-social movement (Franke, 1967). Socialistic in outlook the movement derived its ideological basis from an interpretation of Christian tenets. Basic land reforms, equality of women, abstinence from drugs, moderation in sexual attitudes—were all essential to the ideology of the Taipings and preceded the Communist Revolution in the twentieth century. The widespread support of the Taiping Revolution was a political coalition of anti-Manchu religious sects, secret societies, and landless peasants. The primary leaders of the Taipings were Hakkas, an ethnic minority in southern China. The Hakkas migrated originally from northern to southern China in the fourth century *A.D.* and have been struggling continually against discrimination from the dominant Han Chinese. With the initial organized opposition of the Hakkas to the Manchu government in 1850, various anti-Manchu (though not particularly pro-Taiping) groups cooperated to challenge the Manchu dynasty for 14 years.

Although the socialistic reforms espoused by the Taipings in contrast to the traditional Confucian ethics are interesting in themselves, the major consequences of this unsuccessful revolution were the extensive disruption of the agricultural and urban economies of southern China. With most of the violence having occurred in the rural areas, thousands of refugees fled to the major cities for protection. Canton, the largest of the Southern cities, provided the major source of surplus labor for emigration to North America from about 1850 through 1882.

THE UNWELCOME IMMIGRANT

The emigration of thousands of Chinese from Canton during the Taiping Rebellion was stimulated by the discovery of gold in California. With an economic depression rapidly paralyzing southern China, reports of the Gold Rush were enough to stir families and villages into financing some of the younger men for passage to California. The impact of social disorders in China and the potential fortunes in California on Chinese immigration can be seen by census data over two decades. Between 1841–1850, only 35 Chinese were listed by immigration authorities as being admitted officially into the United States. Between 1851–1860, over 60,000 Chinese were admitted, although over half of them returned to China (Lee, 1960). Even so, large scale emigration from China did not occur until after 1860 when the "coolie" trade was implemented to contract cheap labor for railway construction in both Canada and the United States.

Changes in the responses of Californians toward the Chinese immigrants essentially paralleled changes in the economic conditions in California and, to an extent, the national economy. From the discovery of gold in 1848 through 1849, the population of California increased from around 20,000 to nearly 100,000. By 1852, or two years after California became a state, the population had more than doubled to 225,000 (Fehrenbacher, 1964), With thousands of "Forty-Niners" heading to the mining fields, numerous occupational opportunities opened for those willing to cook and launder for the white miners. The combination of the miners' aversion to so-called "women's" work and the scarcity of women in the mining camps provided many Chinese with a special niche in the economic system. Indeed, during the early stages of the Gold Rush Chinese were even welcomed, though grudgingly, as much needed manual laborers. By 1852, approximately seven-eighths of all the Chinese in California were in the mining camps as cooks, launderers, and miners.

The gradual exhaustion of the mining fields brought the Chinese miners into more visible competition with the dwindling number of white miners. Whereas the Chinese comprised only 20 percent of the mining complement in 1855, by 1873 they contributed 60 percent of all miners (Farmer, 1969). Legal and extralegal sanctions were imposed on the Chinese to prevent any extensive economic competition in the mining areas. In 1852, with yearly increments throughout the decade, a Foreign Miner's Tax was instituted originally to force certain racial and ethnic groups out of the mining fields. As the percentage of Chinese miners increased, the law was applied specifically against the Chinese. In 1855, the California State Supreme Court ruled that Chinese were, in effect, Indians; since Indians were denied the right to testify against whites in the courts, Chinese were excluded from the legal system. Until this ruling was overturned by the United States Supreme Court a number of years later, there was no legal recourse for the many Chinese who became victims of vigilante attacks, murders, robberies, embezzlements, and frauds (Jacobs et al, 1971). With this framework of sustained anti-Chinese sentiments, Chinatowns originally developed as refuges from a hostile white society.

SAN FRANCISCO CHINATOWN: THE FORMATION OF AN ETHNIC GHETTO

Unlike the earlier frontier social movements, the California Gold Rush produced a society that was essentially urban. San Francisco became a major city within two years after the discovery of gold. In 1848, it had a population of only 1000. By 1850, the relatively small town had grown to a crudely constructed city of 30,000. As the major point of transfer between ocean and inland traffic, San Francisco became the primary seaport and financial center of the West Coast.

A common argument for the causes of the ethnic ghetto is that members of an ethnic group "voluntarily" segregate themselves from the larger society. For example, it is often argued that the development of Chinatowns in the United States is the result of language difficulties and a cultural dissimilarity with the larger white society. In part, this argument is valid, but the creation and development of Chinatowns were mostly necessities in the face of a mounting anti-Chinese movement spreading across the Western United States. As early as 1850, a very small Chinese quarter existed within the present day boundaries of San Francisco Chinatown. At this time, however, economic competition between the Chinese and whites was virtually nonexistent. Thus, many of the Chinese voluntarily lived, more or less, within the same block or so, but found employment in other areas of the city. As the numbers of Chinese immigrants increased over the next three decades and economic competition with whites also increased, various interest groups within the city pressured the Chinese to maintain a segregated community. As early as 1853, nearly the entire Chinese population of San Francisco was crowded along two blocks between Kearney and Stockton Streets, and between Jackson and Sacramento Streets (Kung, 1962). By the time of the 1906 earthquake when Chinatown was completely razed by fire, the boundaries of the ghetto had expanded to include fifteen blocks.

The early establishment of a segregated Chinatown in San Francisco unfortunately provided a model for future Chinese-white relations in the United States. Not only did both whites and Chinese expect the creation of segregated ghettos as the Chinese moved to other areas of the United States throughout the 1870s, but other European immigrant groups were being forced to establish distinct ethnic ghettos in many major American cities. By the late nineteenth century, the beginning of the black migration to the North set the stage for the formation of black ghettos around the time of World War I.[1]

The creation of Chinatowns outside of California can be traced to a changing period of American economic development. The acute demand for cheap labor to build railroads in the Far West ended with the completion of the Central Pacific Railroad in 1869. The release of several thousand Chinese railway construction workers in 1869 exacerbated the mounting economic competition of the Chinese with working class whites. Sustained immigration brought large numbers of Irish into direct competition with Chinese for a limited number of jobs as manual laborers. This resulted in further inflamation of anti-Chinese agitation in California. Thus, the demise of the Chinese in California can be seen as a confluence of interethnic and interclass conflict.

As can be expected, the increasing legal restrictions and violence against the Chinese not only in California but also Washington, Idaho, Wyoming, Colorado, and Alaska, motivated many Chinese to migrate to several of the larger cities in the eastern United States. S.W. Kung (1692), for example, estimated that the real beginning of New York City's Chinatown to be somewhere between 1872 and 1882. By 1887, the population of New York Chinatown was about 1000. Sullivan and Hatch (1970), in a recent report on the social problems of a major American Chinatown, place the beginning of Boston Chinatown around 1890.

In the midst of the growing American "nativist" movement in the late nineteenth century, the Chinese migrants found it necessary to cluster together into small Chinatowns. Reports of anti-Chinese agitation in the Far West encouraged fears of Asian labor competing with white labor on the East

---

[1] Stanford Lyman has suggested that the development of black ghettos in the early 1900s can be traced to the white experiences with the Chinese in California. The various analyses of the legal and extralegal forces creating segregated Black Harlem and Black Chicago (Osofsky, 1971; Drake and Cayton, 1962; and Spear, 1967) seem very similar to the social forces creating San Francisco Chinatown. The evidence for this hypothesis is still sketchy, however, and must be explored by further research.

Coast of the United States. To an extent, these fears were given some credence by the attempts of a few factory owners to hire Chinese as strike breakers. In fact, the earliest significant contingent of Chinese to arrive in Boston was a hundred scabs en route to a shoe factory in North Adams, Massachusetts, in 1875. Nevertheless, the actual migration of Chinese to the East Coast was virtually minischle compared to the masses of European immigrants flooding into New York City and Boston. John Higham (1971:167), in fact, dismissed the significance of the Chinese immigration on the total American nativist movement.

"It is significant that the anti-Chinese movement in the Far West in the late nineteenth century had not contributed directly to other anti-foreign phobias. Although the basic Chinese exclusion law was enacted in 1882, the year of the first general immigration law, the Congress that passed the two measures sensed no connection between them. At no time in the nineteenth century did immigration restrictionists argue that Chinese exclusion set a logical precedent for their own proposals."

What is significant, however, was the creation of a half dozen or so Chinatowns in the eastern United States, all of which maintained at least nominal relationships with the leadership of San Francisco Chinatown.

As mentioned earlier in the introduction, knowledgeable observers of the larger Chinatowns in the United States and Canada discover the marked similarities in social organization of these ethnic communities. The creation of the various Chinatowns during the 1880s and 1890s followed the relative "success" of San Francisco Chinatown in protecting the Chinese from the numerous mob activities of working class whites. Furthermore, the organization of the Chinese into ethnic communities with recognized leaders, both by the Chinese and the white authorities, provided at least an outward show of

unity. The few successes of the Chinese in challenging legalized discrimination in the American courts were often supported by the district and clan associations in Chinatown.

THE POLITICAL ORGANIZATION OF CHINATOWNS: A GENERIC MODEL

A major theses of this article is that the origin and development of Chinatowns were in response to the economic and political activities of outside interest groups. The formation of Chinatowns, in other words, was less a "voluntary segregation"[2] as some writers might argue, than a forced insulation from participation in the white society. Discrimination in housing and the racial "job ceiling" initiated and continue to maintain the ghetto boundaries. The so-called "voluntary" separation of Chinese into ethnic ghettos has historically been nurtured by the unwillingness of a white society to allow the assimilation of an ethnic minority.

Some historians (e.g. Barth, 1964) have argued that the need for an extralegal control over the system of indentured servitude of Chinese laborers resulted in the transplantation of Chinese social institutions to the United States. It has been argued that since

"the traditional Chinese system of indentured emigration lack the support of American courts and customs, its adaptation to California depended upon the development of extralegal controls as substitutes. Social organizations furnished the framework which guaranteed the operation of Chinese debt bondage on American soil. Through a set of associations the merchant-creditors main-

---

[2]Although the major proponents of this view recognize the role of active discrimination in maintaining the boundaries of the ghetto, then tend to avoid the economic and political underpinnings of the process of ghettoization. See D.Y. Yuan, 1963.

tained their hold over the indentured emigrants. The Chinese quarters of American cities were symbols of that control" (Barth, 1964; 77).

Thus, the early development of Chinatowns in the United States was supposed to be linked with a Chinese system of contract labor.

Unfortunately, this argument overlooks the actual role of the American legal system in maintaining the American economy. Although the Chinese institution of indentured servitude never had the official sanction of the American legal system, the failure of the courts and the police to enforce the laws prohibiting contract labor unofficially legitimated this source of cheap labor. Intragroup exploitation by a few Chinese merchant-creditors does not justify the contention that Chinese social institutions developed without outside encouragement. Indeed, the benign acceptance, or at least passivity, of the American legal authorities regarding an illegal traffic of indentured servants promoted the formation of a *coercive* set of ghetto institutions. In effect, the Chinese merchant-creditors of immigrant labor were agents or mediators for the American economic system.

It should not be surprising, at least for those familiar with the traditional village structure in China, that the anti-Chinese agitation in the 1850s also encouraged the Chinese to form district and clan associations for mutual aid and self-defense. As the tempo of white racism increased, the institutional leadership of the ghetto coalesced out of necessity. The refusal of the police and courts to protect the residents of the ghetto from white discrimination and violence or to interfere in the internal affairs of the ghetto forced the creation of some sort of internal political organization. The local and state agencies even encouraged the Chinese to create one representative voice for the community. Rather than acknowledge the right of Chinese to protection under American laws, the government agencies found it more desirable to negotiate with a small group of leaders supposedly responsible for all Chinese in the ghetto. Thus, a bargaining model was established in which white authorities would not interfere with the ghetto, so long as the activities of the residents remained within the ghetto.

Likewise, the Chinese agreed to remain separated from white society provided the white authorities allowed Chinese social, economic, and political institutions to exist without outside interference. The bargaining model has persisted for over a century in San Francisco with only a few exceptions. Most notably, the so-called "Tong Wars" at the turn of the century were tolerated by the police in both San Francisco and New York City until the violence spread outside of the ghetto and received public notoriety. Police action was extremely swift and efficient when the public order was threatened.

Chinatowns, like other ethnic ghettos, created a number of social institutions and associations to provide basic services for their residents. Unlike the social organization of other ghettos, however, Chinatowns have had a traditional institutional cohesiveness. Community leadership has tended to be drawn from a small group of wealthy merchants and businessmen who generally act as the heads of the various district and clan associations.

A community or ghetto is usually defined by the social institutions whose functions reflect the essential needs of its members. Thus, social institutions are relatively stable forms of human organization. Within the context of social organization in Chinatowns, the various district and clan associations present a conceptual difficulty. An association is usually considered to be less stable than a social institution (e.g. the family) as its membership is more or less voluntary. Rose Hum Lee (1960; 142) remarked that

"the compulsory nature of Chinese associational membership converts many associa-

tions into pseudo-institutions. Their means of social control are more extensive than those of the family or church; therefore they function more like institutions than associations.

Thus, an understanding of the political organization of Chinatowns must begin with a description of the associations that have traditionally controlled the ghetto. To most Americans, the complexity of the numerous associations in San Francisco Chinatown and elsewhere reinforces the "inscrutableness" and insulation of the Chinese ghettos from the white society. Furthermore, a distortion of the actual political organization of the ghetto can lead to a misperception of what groups actually represent the interests of the Chinatown residents.

Stanford Lyman (1971a) made a commendable effort to unravel the relationships of various types of associations to the community. He writes that there are "three basic types of association established in Chinatown, and in addition there are subsidiary and ancillary groupings, and, at the apex of the organizational pyramid, a confederation of associations which tends to govern the community" (1971a; 166). First, there are the clan associations based upon the idea of blood relationships of male members to a common ancestor. Overseas Chinese extended the membership to include all Chinese with the same surname. The function of the clan mainly involved the provision of social welfare services for its members. Sometimes, a clan was able to monopolize a certain occupation or enterprise, especially in the smaller Chinatowns. This would insure the employment of new clan members. At least ideally, the clan was supposed to form the basis of social control in the ghetto because kinship loyalty superseded all other associational loyalties. As will become apparent, however, the economic control of the ghetto fell to larger associations not based upon kinship.

The second basic type of association was the district association or *hui kuan.* Each district association was composed of persons emigrating from a particular area of the Kwangtung province in Southern China, speaking the same dialect, or belonging to the same ethnic group. By the time of the Chinese Exclusion Act of 1882, nearly all Chinese immigrants in the United States were from seven of ninety districts in the Kwangtung province: Toi Shan, Hoi Ping, Yan Ping, Sun Wui, Shun Tak, Nam Hoi, and Pun Yui. Then, according to Rose Hum Lee (1960), the seven district associations combined into two larger district associations, also based upon geographic and dialect divisions in China. The Sze Yup Association was formed from the Toi Shan, Hoi Ping, Yan Ping, and Sun Wui District Associations. The Sam Yup Association was formed from the Shun Tak, Nam Hoi, and Pun Yui District Associations. Other district associations were formed by Chinese emigrating later from other districts (e.g., the Chung Shan Association) or dissident splinter groups from the Sze Yup and Sam Yup Associations (e.g., the Hop Wo Association).

The various district associations originally provided social welfare services for new immigrants arriving from their respective districts in southern China. For example, representatives from a district association would arrange to meet the newcomer at the docks, provide living quarters, find him a job, etc. Often these services did not simply arise from the benevolence of the associations. Many associations actively sponsored the notorious "coolie" trade in which Chinese bonded themselves to work for several years at cheap wages to pay for the costs of transportation from China to the United States. The associations also maintained a special fund and food supply for indigent members, established a credit union to provide seed money for a member's business venture, sent money back to China for members unable to work, and guaranteed funeral expenses. The traditional Chinese reluctance to accept state charity in the United States was due in part to the mistrust of American social institutions and the ability of district and clan associations to provide social welfare services for their members. The increased immigration of Chinese since 1965 is overtaxing the resources of the various associations. With the inability of many Chinese to receive adequate aid from within the ghetto, the "phenomenon" of Chinese on welfare rolls is becoming much more frequent.

Perhaps the most important function of the district association, however, was the protection of the economic interests of its members. Each association attempted to control certain occupations and enterprises, as well as mediate intra- and intergroup disputes over territory. For example, the Sam Yup people at one time were the wealthy merchants in San Francisco Chinatown controlling the large import-export trade, the tailoring businesses, and traditional medicine. The Sze Yup people tended to control the small launderies and restaurants. When economic competition among rival district and clan associations could not be negotiated, an association often hired the third basic type of association in Chinatowns, the *tongs,* to conduct warfare against its competitors. Thus, the notorious Tong wars with their "hatchet men" at the turn of the century in San Francisco and New York essentially concerned an economic and political struggle for control of the communities.

The tongs were secret societies, and like the district and clan associations, originated in China. The tongs were originally secret societies in China organized for the purpose of challenging the authority of whatever government was in power. These secret societies were composed of rebels and bandits, the *lumpenproletariat* of Chinese society. Many Chinese immigrants were members of the Triad Society, probably the most famous and powerful tong in Southern China. Very early in the development of San Francisco Chinatown, the tongs were created to control certain illegal activities (e.g., prostitution, narcotics, and gambling) that the district and clan associations were reluctant to organize overtly. By the 1880s and 1890s, the tongs became the predominant political power in San Francisco Chinatown. Besides the control of the ghetto "vice," the tongs also maintained some financial support of the factions vying for control of mainland China. But for the most part, the political activities of the tongs were confined to the ghettos and occasionally to financing groups supporting a Republican China.

In the last several decades, the tongs have declined in power and influence. Their main sources of revenue—gambling and prostitution—required a population of isolated males. The stabilization of the family life of many Chinese after World War II and the rapid dying off of the older bachelors are reducing the historical role of the tongs in Chinatown affairs. Furthermore, most third generation Chinese-Americans and the recent immigrants from Hong Kong and Taiwan find the tongs to be an anachronism of the traditional Chinese society. Perhaps Stanford Lyman's prediction of their eventual disappearance will prove true. Nevertheless, many outsiders often walk by a tong headquarters, unaware that the association has been renamed the Chinese Merchants Association.

The Chinese Consolidated Benevolent Association (CCBA), traditionally the apex of power in the institutional hierarchy of the larger Chinatowns, can be considered a fourth major political unit. The larger Chinatowns in Canada and the United States each have a local CCBA, but generally recognize the symbolic leadership of the CCBA in San Francisco. The San Francisco CCBA—or the Chinese Six Companies, as it is often called—was formed originally from a confederation of six district association (hence, the name Six Companies): Ning Yung, Kong Chow, Young Wo, Shiu Hing, Hop Wo, and

Yan Wo. Later a seventh district association, the Sam Yup Association, joined the confederation, but the name remained the same.

A major purpose of the Chinese Six Companies was to provide the ghetto with a unified government, rather than a conglomeration of district associations *overtly* competing for power. As should be expected, covert struggles did occur since the resources of the member district associations varied. Nevertheless, this coalition not only provided the community with a quasijudicial and executive institution, but also presented a unified front to the outside governmental authorities. As the white officials were reluctant to interfere in ghetto affairs, the Six Companies were given the unofficial recognition by the outsiders as the representative voice of all Chinese. The consequences of gaining both internal and external legitmacy were both positive and negative. Although the Six Companies rallied community resources to oppose discriminatory laws and often settled intracommunity disputes peacefully, the maintenance of its status in the ghetto encouraged repressive measures to stifle any challenge to the supremacy of the association.

The resource base of the main and local CCBA's mainly involves a coalition of wealthy merchants, business and property owners in the various Chinatowns. The sustained urbanization of Chinese in the United States from the 1860s through World War II created a group of wealthy middle class merchants and business owners. The leadership of the district associations and the CCBA has tended to be drawn from these ranks. With the historical discrimination against Chinese in housing and jobs, the reliance of the residents in Chinatowns on the ghetto merchants and businessmen has inhibited direct challenges to the Chinese middle class leaders of the associations. Stanford Lyman (1971a; 167) writes that the CCBA

"commanded at least the grudging allegiance and obedience of the toiling Chinese laborers

and the respect of many well-meaning whites; however, in more recent times the association's alleged involvement in illegal immigration, its failure to meet the needs of San Francisco's new Chinese immigrant youth, its conservative and traditional orientation toward welfare, and its anachronistic appearance in acculterated American-born Chinese have led to a certain decline in its community power and a slight dampening of its popularity with white America.

Nevertheless, with its still considerable authority and economic resources, the CCBA can still apply considerable sanctions against dissidents.

CHALLENGES TO THE TRADITIONAL ORDER

The acculteration of second, and especially third generation, Chinese-Americans has brought about changes in the nature and types of voluntary groups within contemporary Chinatowns. Second generation Chinese-Americans often organize service associations concerned with the social life of Chinese-Americans with a white society. Such groups as the Chinese-American Citizens Alliance in San Francisco, the Wah Sung Service Association in Oakland, American Legion Posts in various Chinatowns, Young Republicans chapters reflect a more "Americanized" second generation. Indeed, although many of these groups maintain close alliances with the affairs of their respective Chinatowns, a considerable percentage is drawn from a Chinese-American middle class in the suburbs. For example, the Chinese-American Civic Association of Boston, a second generation service group, draws approximately 70 percent of its membership from the Boston suburbs.

With a decline in power and influence of the traditional district and clan associations, the second generation voluntary organizations often assume a more active role in the contemporary Chinatown affairs. The need for local, state, and federal funds to alleviate unemployment, substandard housing, and juvenile delinquency in the larger Chinatowns will encourage these service groups to assist in the planning and implementation of government-sponsored programs. Since the members of the traditional associations generally speak very little English and have limited familiarity with government bureaucracies, community leadership will probably shift às the first generation Chinese retire or die off. At least in Boston Chinatown, the Chinese-American Civic Association has been receiving the investiture of "legitimated" authority from the local CCBA.

The success of this transfer of authority from the first to second generation Chinese-Americans, however, is being challenged by a number of third generation Chinese-American groups and recent young immigrants from Hong Kong and Taiwan. The relatively limited success of the traditional associations and the second generation voluntary groups in coping with extensive community problems of unemployment and poor educational facilities in the ghetto have undermined the credibility of the official Chinatown leadership among the youth. To an even greater extent than in white society, the "generation gap" is a reflection of the rigidly defined hierarchy of power within the Chinese ghetto. The failure to include dissident groups in the decision-making process, especially when the various government programs directly, or indirectly affect Chinatowns' youth, is fostering the proliferation of young militants.

This is not to say that all the Chinese youth are unified in interests. Native-born Chinese-Americans and recent immigrants from Hong Kong and Taiwan are from different cultures. Gang conflicts are frequent occurrences between Chinese-American groups and immigrant groups in San Francisco and New York. Nevertheless, the increasing occurrence of militant slogans and ideology from both native-born and foreign-born Chinese groups indicates the stirrings of ethnic and class consciousness. Stanford Lyman (1971b) characterizes the changes in origin and function of Chinese gangs as a transformation of nonideological to ideological "primitive rebel"[3] groups. Perhaps the most important impetus for this changeover from social "banditry" to social protest was the Black Power movement of the 1960s. Prior to the advent of recent black militancy, the more publicized Chinatown "rebels" were members of petty criminal gangs, often supported by a tong.

Probably the first major gang to undergo an ideological transformation was "Leway, Inc.," whose name is a contraction of "legitimate way." As expected in a conservative community, the espousal of self-help by delinquents for delinquents met with active opposition by authorities within and outside of the ghetto. The refusal of official recognition by the San Francisco Chinese Chamber of Commerce and other Chinese institutions opened the way for harrassment of the Leways. The Leways found it difficult to obtain an office within Chinatown. Their members found difficulty in obtaining employment within the ghetto. Police surveillance and searches were encouraged by the attitudes of the Chinatown leaders. By mid-1969, the Leways were forced to disband.[4]

---

[3]The concept of "primitive rebels" is taken from an essay of the same name by E. J. Hobsbawm (1959); in a sense, the "primitive rebel" within Chinatown is the social bandit who acts more in protest against oppression and poverty than for simply personal gain.

[4]The reader who is interested in an account of the recent political activities of San Francisco Chinatown gangs is encouraged to read Stanford Lyman's account of the Hwa Ching and Red Guard movements (1971b). Gang activities in New York's Chinatown are frequently reported in the major news media.

CONFLICTS AND SOCIAL CHANGE   **353**

THE DISUNITED FRONT

Any attempt to mobilize the Chinese community in any major American city underscores the changing political organization of Chinatowns. Government agencies, sometimes interested in aiding the Chinese to cope with problems of unemployment, housing, education, and health care, frequently discover the limitations of the traditional associations in organizing and implementing reforms. For example, a recent "Conference for the Future of Chinatown" was held in Boston, concerning the social problems of the ghetto. Action for Boston Community Development (ABCD), supported the local CCBA and the Chinese-American Civic Association (the major second generation voluntary service organization of the community). Besides the failure of the conference even to tap a small proportion of the actual residents of Chinatown, the planning of the conference stimulated numerous protests by various groups (especially third generation youth groups (concerning the misrepresentation of Chinatown to outsiders.

In effect, the major result of the Boston conference was not especially a communitywide discussion of Chinatown's social problems, but rather the mobilization of ignored interest groups to challenge openly the traditional political organization of the Chinatown. Stanford Lyman (1971b: 124–125) again aptly described the plight of the larger American Chinatowns:

"The crust of Chinatown's cake of customary control may be beginning to crumble. The old order must contend not only with the mounting opposition of the community's respectable, professional and American-born younger and middle-aged adults, but also with the militant organization of Chinatown's disaffected youth. In addition, one cannot count on the new immigrants to bow to Chinatown's traditional power elite in the future as they have in the past. It is by no means clear, however, what the outcome of this continuing power struggle will be."

Whatever the outcome of this power struggle, the reluctance of the traditional associations to broaden the base of groups, especially dissident ones, participating in the governance of the community will probably forestall any viable programs to change the situations of the ghetto's poor. The failure to mobilize the community around a coalition of interest groups, furthermore, will continue to expose the ghetto to the "federal bulldozer," as the inner city of major metropolitan areas are redeveloped for the American middle class.

BARTH, G.
  1964 *A history of the Chinese in the United States, 1850–1870.* Cambridge: Harvard University Press.

DRAKE, ST. C. and H. CAYTON
  1962 *Black metropolis: a study of Negro life in a northern city.* Revised edition. New York: Harcourt, Brace, and World.

FARMER, G.
  1969 *Education: the dilemma of the Oriental-American.* Los Angeles: School of Education, University of Southern California.

FEHRENBACHER, D.

1964 *A basic history of California.* Princeton, N.J.: Van Nostrand.

FRANKE, W.
1967 "The Taiping rebellion." pp. 180–192 in F. Schurmann and O. Schell, editors. *The China reader: imperial China.* New York: Vintage

HIGHAM, J.
1971 *Strangers in the land: patterns of American nativism, 1860-1925.* New York: Atheneum

HOBSBAWM, E.
1959 Primitive rebels. *New York:* Norton.

JACOBS, P. and S. LANDAU with E. PELL
1971 *To serve the devil.* Volume II. New York: Vintage Books.

KUNG, S.
1962 *Chinese in American life.* Seattle: University of Washington Press.

LEE, R.
1960 *Chinese in the United States of America.* Hong Kong: Hong Kong University Press.

LYMAN, S.
1971a "Strangers in the city: the Chinese in the urban frontier." pp. 159–187 in *Roots: an Asian-American reader.* Los Angeles: UCLA, Asian American Studies Center.
1971b "Red guard on Grant Avenue." pp. 113–126 in I. Horowitz and M. Strong (eds.) *Sociological realities: a guide to the study of society.* New York: Harper

and Row.

MALLORY, W.
1967 "From China, land of famine." pp. 262–268 in F. Schurmann and O. Schell (eds.) *The China reader: imperial China.* New York: Vintage

MILLER, S.
1969 *The unwelcome immigrant: the American image of the Chinese, 1785-1882.* Berkeley and Los Angeles: University of California Press.

OSOFSKY, G.
1971 *Harlem: the making of a ghetto.* Second edition. New York: Harper and Row.

SPEAR, A.
1967 *Black Chicago: the making of a Negro ghetto, 1890-1920.* Chicago: University Chicago Press.

SULLIVAN, C. and K. HATCH
1970 *The Chinese in Boston, 1970.* Boston: Action for Boston Community Development, Inc.

WALEY, A.
1968 *The opium war through Chinese eyes.* Stanford: Stanford University Press.

YANG, C.
1961 *Religion in Chinese society.* Berkeley and Los Angeles: University of California Press.

YUAN, D.
1963 "Voluntary segregation: a study of New York Chinatown." *Phylon,* (Fall): 255–265.